Little Lulu ®

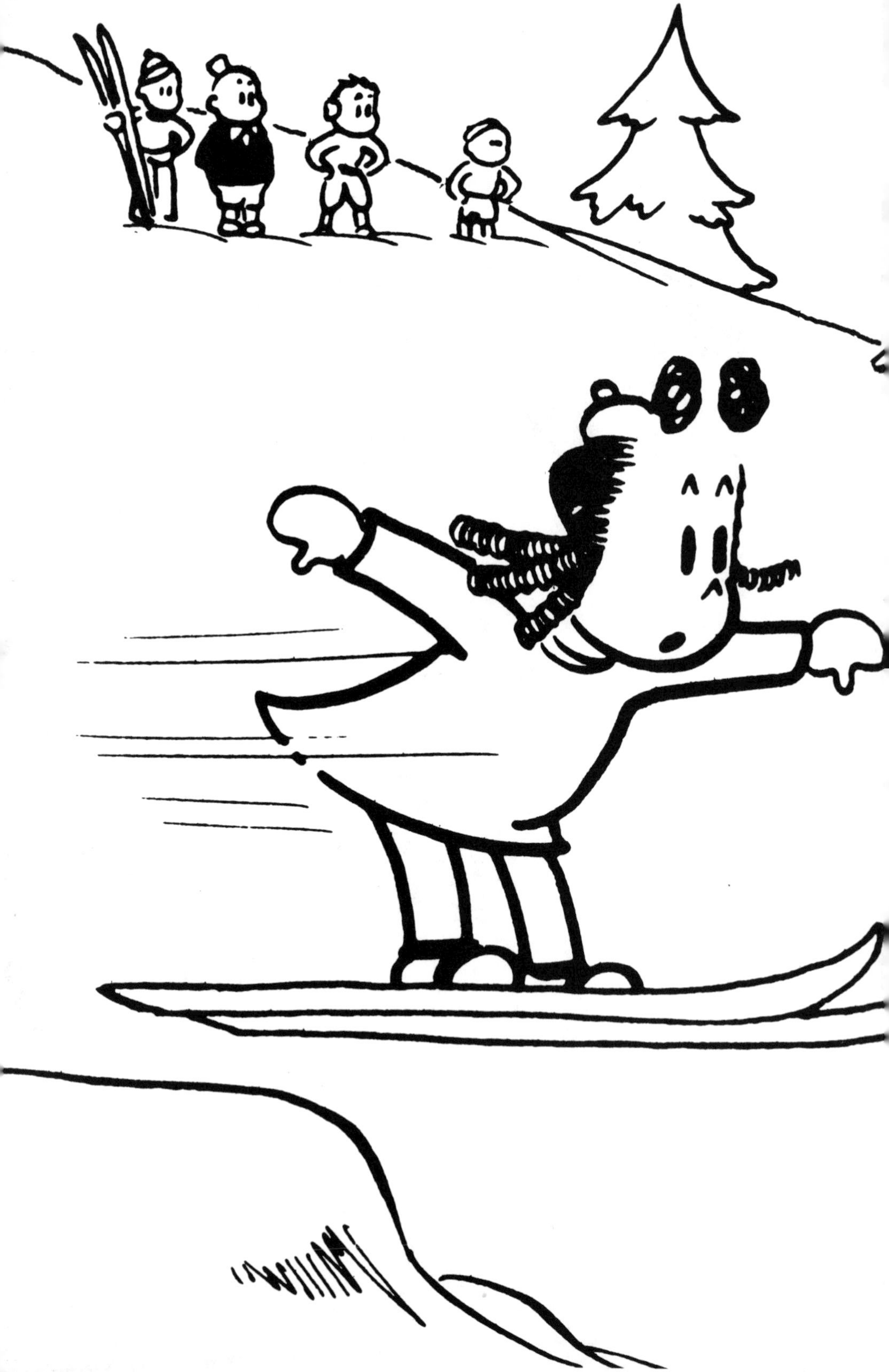

Little Lulu®

Letters to Santa

Story and Art
John Stanley
and
Irving Tripp

Based on the character
created by

Marge Buell

DARK HORSE BOOKS™

Publisher
Mike Richardson

Editor
Shawna Gore

Editorial Assistants
Rachel Miller
Gina Gagliano

Collection Designer
Debra Bailey

Art Director
Lia Ribacchi

Published by
Dark Horse Books
A division of Dark Horse Comics, Inc.
10956 SE Main Street
Milwaukie, OR 97222

darkhorse.com

First edition: October 2005
ISBN: 1-59307-386-0

1 3 5 7 9 10 8 6 4 2
Printed in U.S.A.

A note about Lulu

Little Lulu came into the world through the pen of cartoonist Marjorie "Marge" Henderson Buell in 1935. Originally commissioned as a series of single-panel cartoons by *The Saturday Evening Post*, Lulu took the world by storm with her charm, smarts, and sass. Within ten years, she not only was the star of her own cartoon series, but a celebrity spokesgirl for a variety of high-profile commercial products.

Little Lulu truly hit her stride as America's sweetheart in the comic books published by Dell Comics starting in 1945. While Buell was solely responsible for Lulu's original single-panel shenanigans, the comic-book stories were put into the able hands of comics legend John Stanley. Stanley wrote and laid out the comics while artist Irving Tripp provided the finished drawings. After a number of trial appearances in Dell Comics, Lulu's appeal was undeniable, and she was granted her very own comic-book series, called *Marge's Little Lulu*, which was published regularly through 1984.

This volume contains every comic from issues eighteen through twenty-two of *Marge's Little Lulu*.

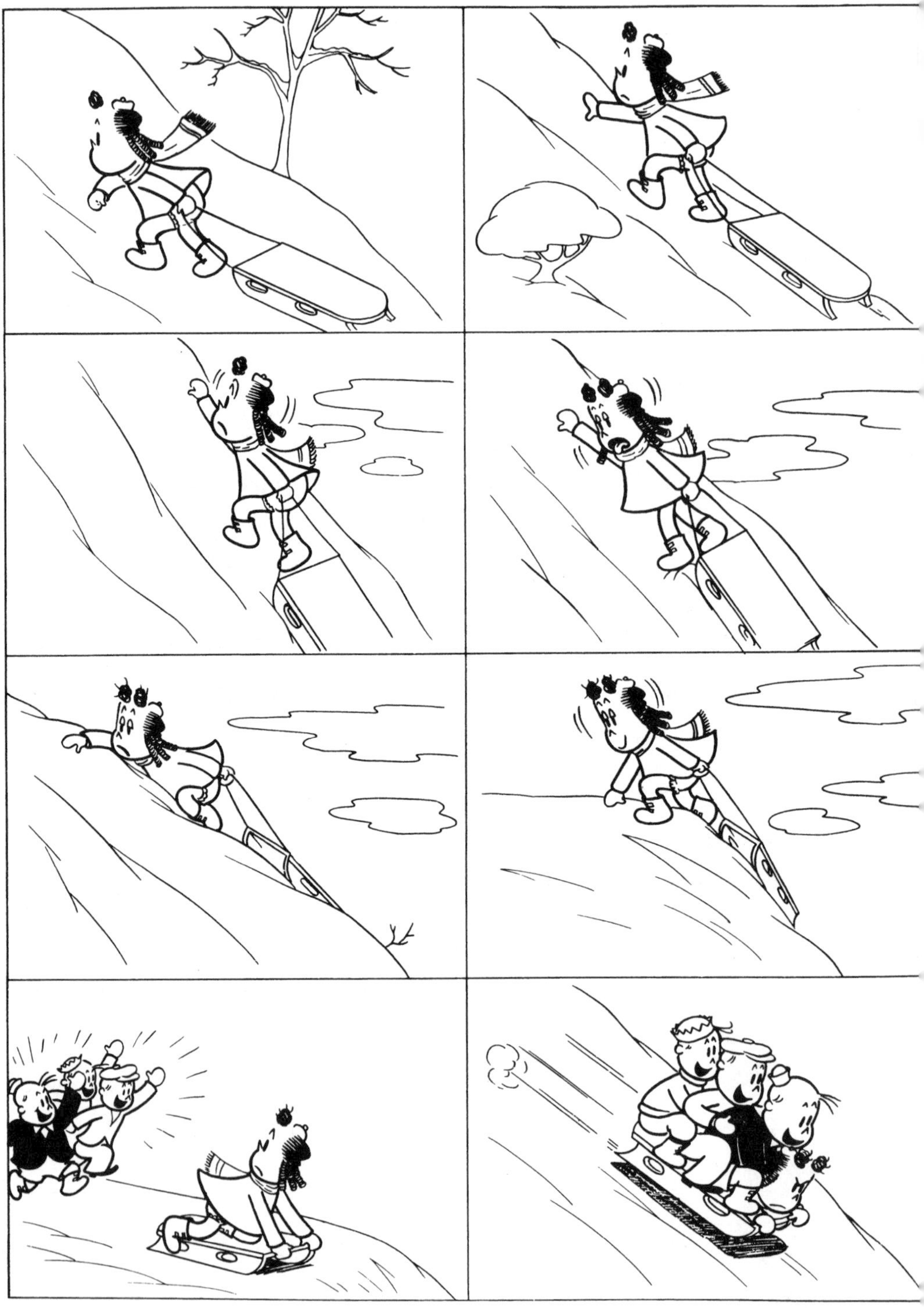

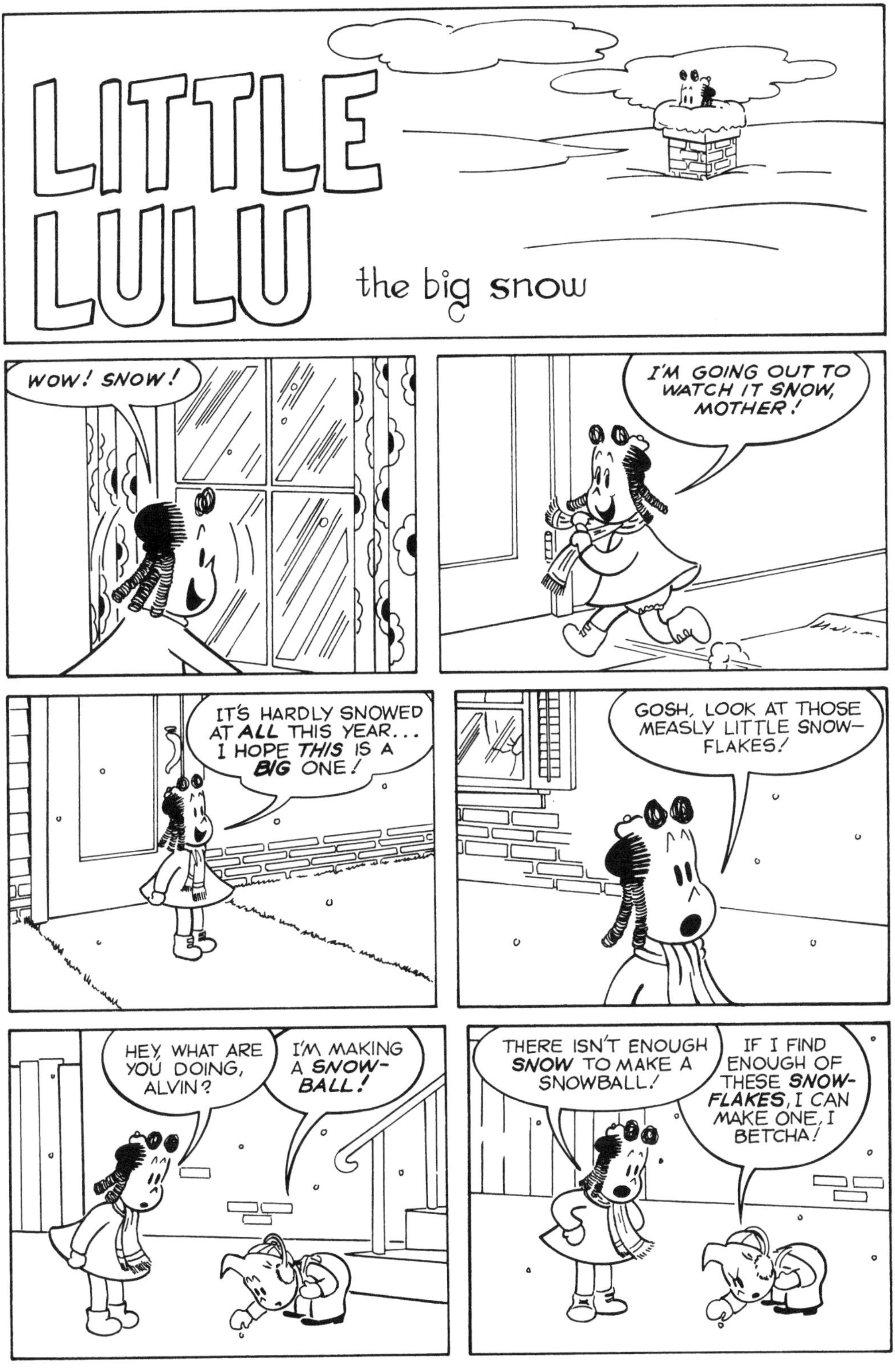
LITTLE LULU
the big snow
WOW! SNOW!
I'M GOING OUT TO WATCH IT SNOW, MOTHER!
IT'S HARDLY SNOWED AT ALL THIS YEAR... I HOPE THIS IS A BIG ONE!
GOSH, LOOK AT THOSE MEASLY LITTLE SNOW-FLAKES!
HEY, WHAT ARE YOU DOING, ALVIN?
I'M MAKING A SNOW-BALL!
THERE ISN'T ENOUGH SNOW TO MAKE A SNOWBALL!
IF I FIND ENOUGH OF THESE SNOW-FLAKES, I CAN MAKE ONE, I BETCHA!

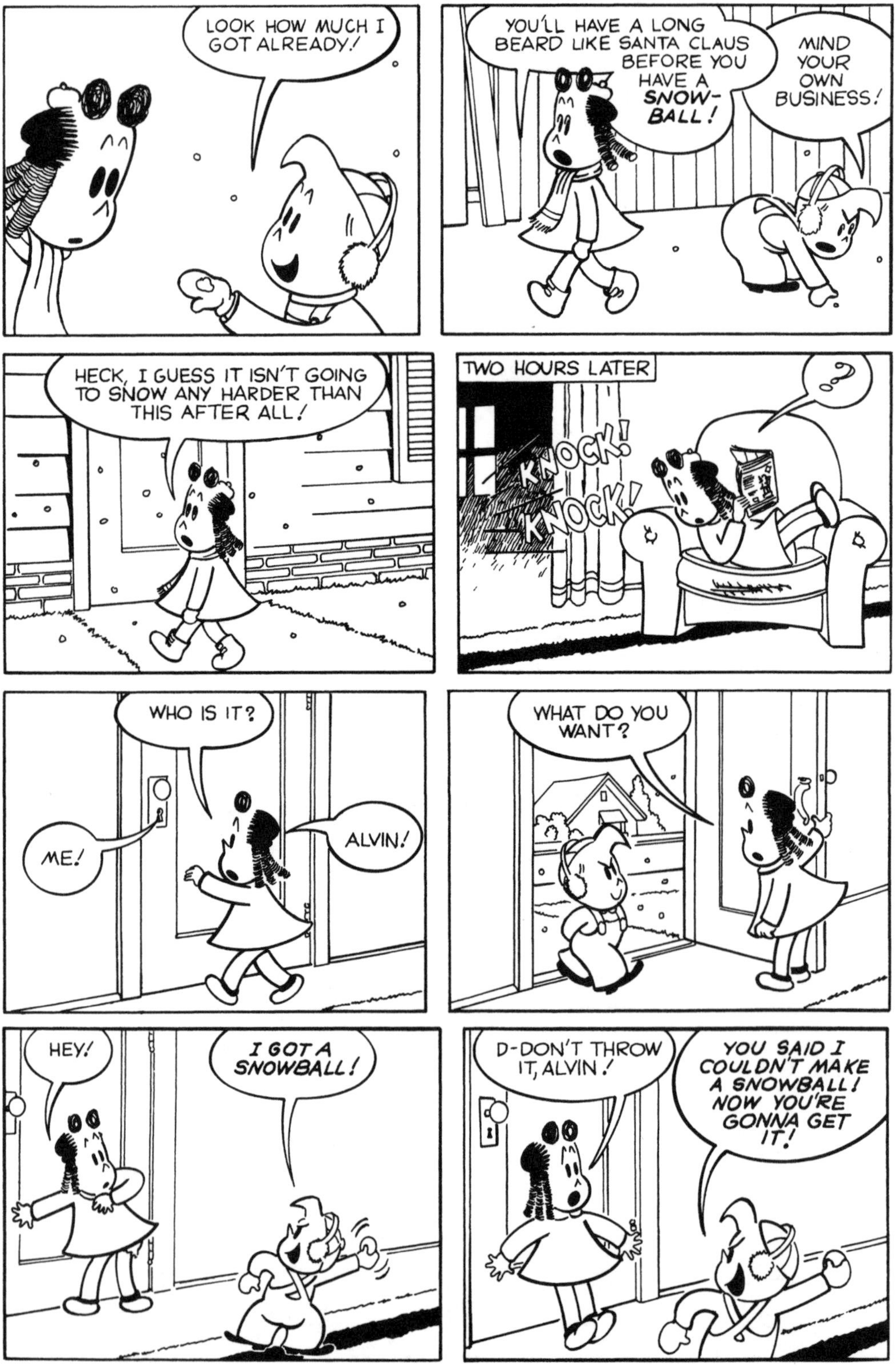
LOOK HOW MUCH I GOT ALREADY!
YOU'LL HAVE A LONG BEARD LIKE SANTA CLAUS BEFORE YOU HAVE A SNOW-BALL!
MIND YOUR OWN BUSINESS!
HECK, I GUESS IT ISN'T GOING TO SNOW ANY HARDER THAN THIS AFTER ALL!
TWO HOURS LATER
KNOCK! KNOCK!
?
WHO IS IT?
ME!
ALVIN!
WHAT DO YOU WANT?
HEY!
I GOT A SNOWBALL!
D-DON'T THROW IT, ALVIN!
YOU SAID I COULDN'T MAKE A SNOWBALL! NOW YOU'RE GONNA GET IT!

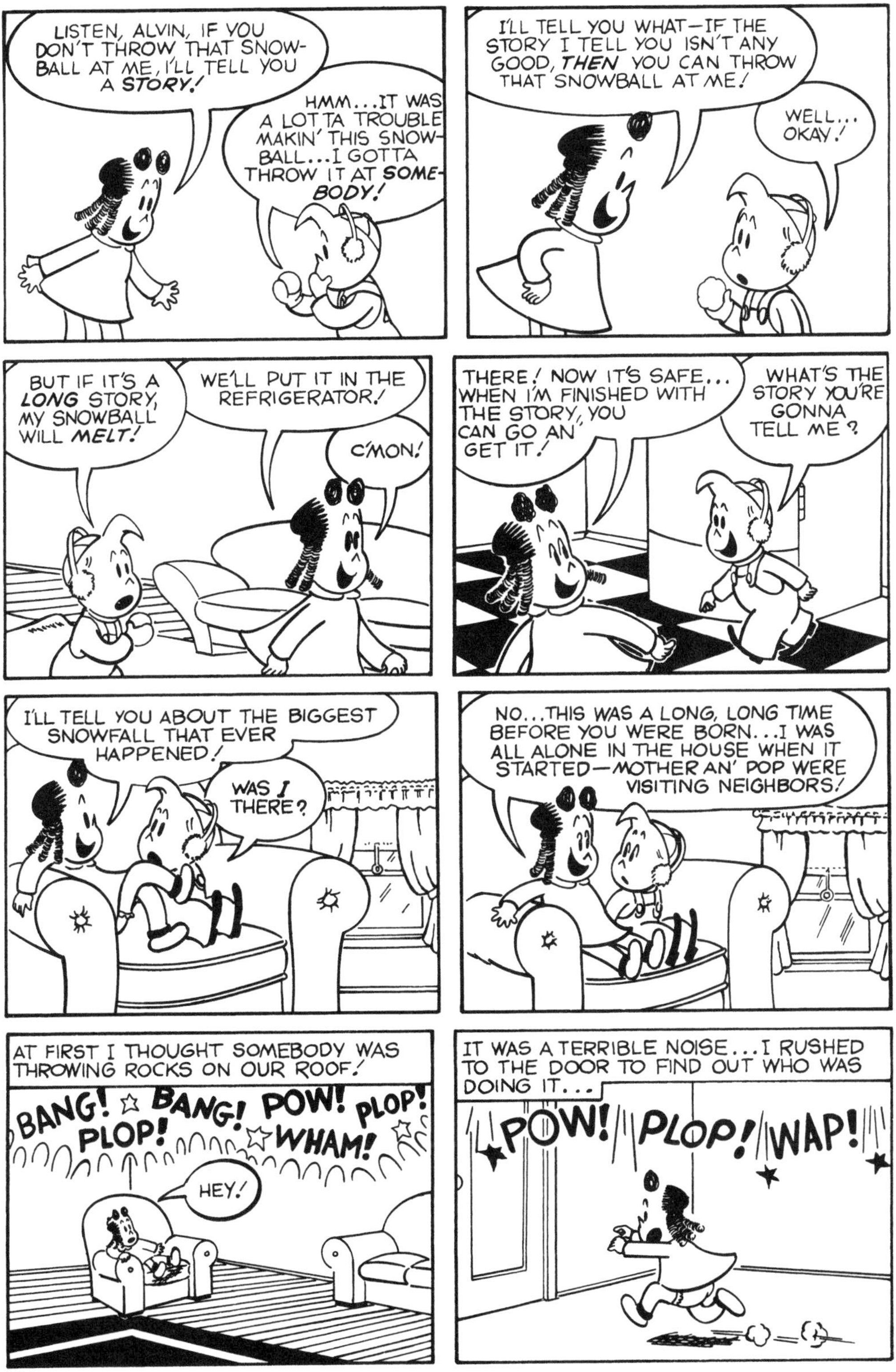
LISTEN, ALVIN, IF YOU DON'T THROW THAT SNOW-BALL AT ME, I'LL TELL YOU A **STORY!**
HMM...IT WAS A LOTTA TROUBLE MAKIN' THIS SNOW-BALL...I GOTTA THROW IT AT **SOME-BODY!**
I'LL TELL YOU WHAT—IF THE STORY I TELL YOU ISN'T ANY GOOD, **THEN** YOU CAN THROW THAT SNOWBALL AT ME!
WELL... OKAY!
BUT IF IT'S A **LONG** STORY, MY SNOWBALL WILL **MELT!**
WE'LL PUT IT IN THE REFRIGERATOR!
C'MON!
THERE! NOW IT'S SAFE... WHEN I'M FINISHED WITH THE STORY, YOU CAN GO AN' GET IT!
WHAT'S THE STORY YOU'RE GONNA TELL ME?
I'LL TELL YOU ABOUT THE BIGGEST SNOWFALL THAT EVER HAPPENED!
WAS *I* THERE?
NO...THIS WAS A LONG, LONG TIME BEFORE YOU WERE BORN...I WAS ALL ALONE IN THE HOUSE WHEN IT STARTED—*MOTHER AN' POP WERE* VISITING NEIGHBORS!
AT FIRST I THOUGHT SOMEBODY WAS THROWING ROCKS ON OUR ROOF!
BANG! BANG! POW! PLOP! PLOP! WHAM!
HEY!
IT WAS A TERRIBLE NOISE...I RUSHED TO THE DOOR TO FIND OUT WHO WAS DOING IT...
POW! PLOP! WAP!

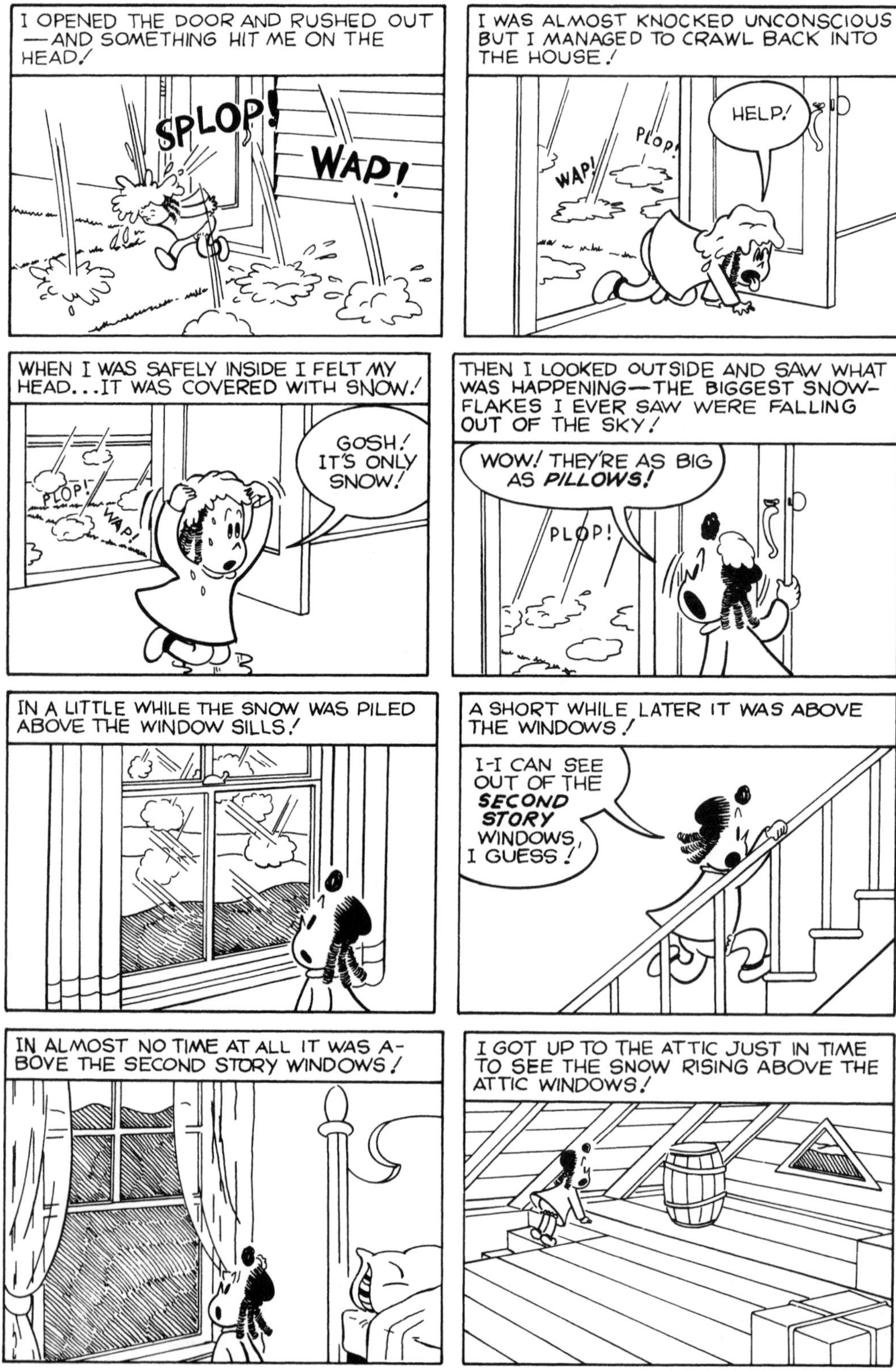
I OPENED THE DOOR AND RUSHED OUT —AND SOMETHING HIT ME ON THE HEAD!
SPLOP!
WAP!
I WAS ALMOST KNOCKED UNCONSCIOUS BUT I MANAGED TO CRAWL BACK INTO THE HOUSE!
WAP!
PLOP!
HELP!
WHEN I WAS SAFELY INSIDE I FELT MY HEAD...IT WAS COVERED WITH SNOW!
PLOP!
WAP!
GOSH! IT'S ONLY SNOW!
THEN I LOOKED OUTSIDE AND SAW WHAT WAS HAPPENING—THE BIGGEST SNOW-FLAKES I EVER SAW WERE FALLING OUT OF THE SKY!
WOW! THEY'RE AS BIG AS PILLOWS!
PLOP!
IN A LITTLE WHILE THE SNOW WAS PILED ABOVE THE WINDOW SILLS!
A SHORT WHILE LATER IT WAS ABOVE THE WINDOWS!
I-I CAN SEE OUT OF THE SECOND STORY WINDOWS, I GUESS!
IN ALMOST NO TIME AT ALL IT WAS A-BOVE THE SECOND STORY WINDOWS!
I GOT UP TO THE ATTIC JUST IN TIME TO SEE THE SNOW RISING ABOVE THE ATTIC WINDOWS!

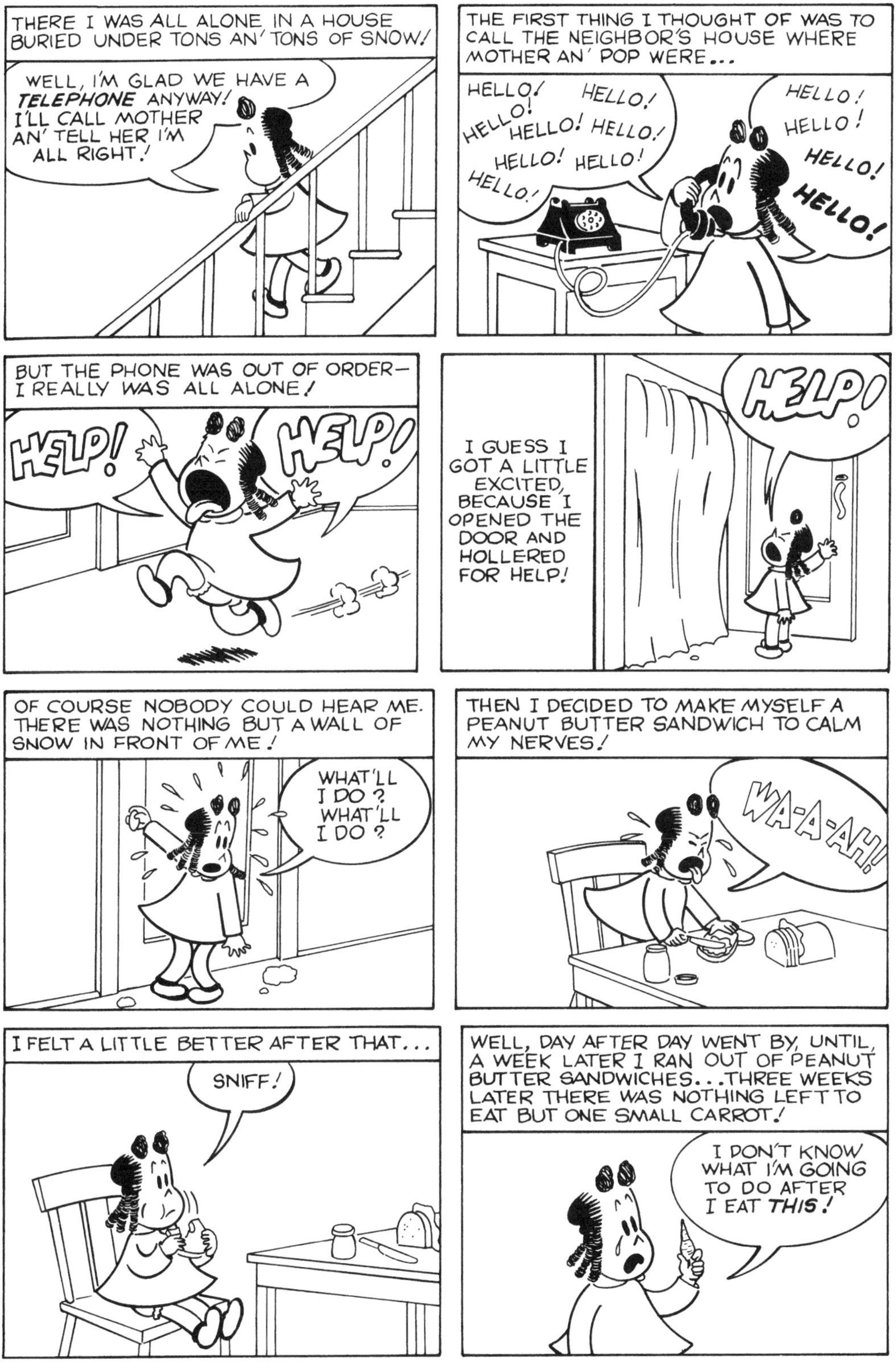
THERE I WAS ALL ALONE IN A HOUSE BURIED UNDER TONS AN' TONS OF SNOW!
WELL, I'M GLAD WE HAVE A TELEPHONE ANYWAY! I'LL CALL MOTHER AN' TELL HER I'M ALL RIGHT!
THE FIRST THING I THOUGHT OF WAS TO CALL THE NEIGHBOR'S HOUSE WHERE MOTHER AN' POP WERE...
HELLO! HELLO! HELLO! HELLO! HELLO! HELLO! HELLO! HELLO!
HELLO! HELLO! HELLO! HELLO!
BUT THE PHONE WAS OUT OF ORDER— I REALLY WAS ALL ALONE!
HELP!
HELP!
I GUESS I GOT A LITTLE EXCITED, BECAUSE I OPENED THE DOOR AND HOLLERED FOR HELP!
HELP!
OF COURSE NOBODY COULD HEAR ME. THERE WAS NOTHING BUT A WALL OF SNOW IN FRONT OF ME!
WHAT'LL I DO? WHAT'LL I DO?
THEN I DECIDED TO MAKE MYSELF A PEANUT BUTTER SANDWICH TO CALM MY NERVES!
WA-A-AH!
I FELT A LITTLE BETTER AFTER THAT...
SNIFF!
WELL, DAY AFTER DAY WENT BY, UNTIL, A WEEK LATER I RAN OUT OF PEANUT BUTTER SANDWICHES...THREE WEEKS LATER THERE WAS NOTHING LEFT TO EAT BUT ONE SMALL CARROT!
I DON'T KNOW WHAT I'M GOING TO DO AFTER I EAT THIS!

I DIVIDED THE CARROT INTO SEVEN PIECES AND HAD ENOUGH TO EAT FOR ANOTHER WHOLE WEEK!

THE WEEK DRAGGED BY SLOWLY AND STILL NOBODY CAME TO RESCUE ME... FINALLY, I ATE THE LAST PIECE OF CARROT.

GULP!

I WONDER IF THERE'S *ANYTHING* ELSE IN THE HOUSE I CAN EAT?

I THOUGHT MAYBE IF I BOILED OUR CHINESE RUG LONG ENOUGH IT MIGHT TASTE SOMETHING LIKE CHOP SUEY...

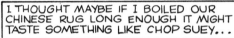

IT OUGHT TO BE DONE NOW!

BUT IT DIDN'T—IT TASTED JUST LIKE A BOILED CHINESE RUG!

UGH!

THEN, DECIDING I WOULD HAVE TO RESCUE MYSELF, I GOT THE BIGGEST SPOON I COULD FIND IN THE KITCHEN!

THIS ISN'T FUNNY ANY MORE!

...AND STARTED TO DIG MY WAY OUT THROUGH THE FRONT DOOR!

GOSH, IT WAS HARD WORK!

BUT I WOULDN'T GIVE UP!

I MUST BE SOMEWHERE NEAR THE SIDEWALK NOW!

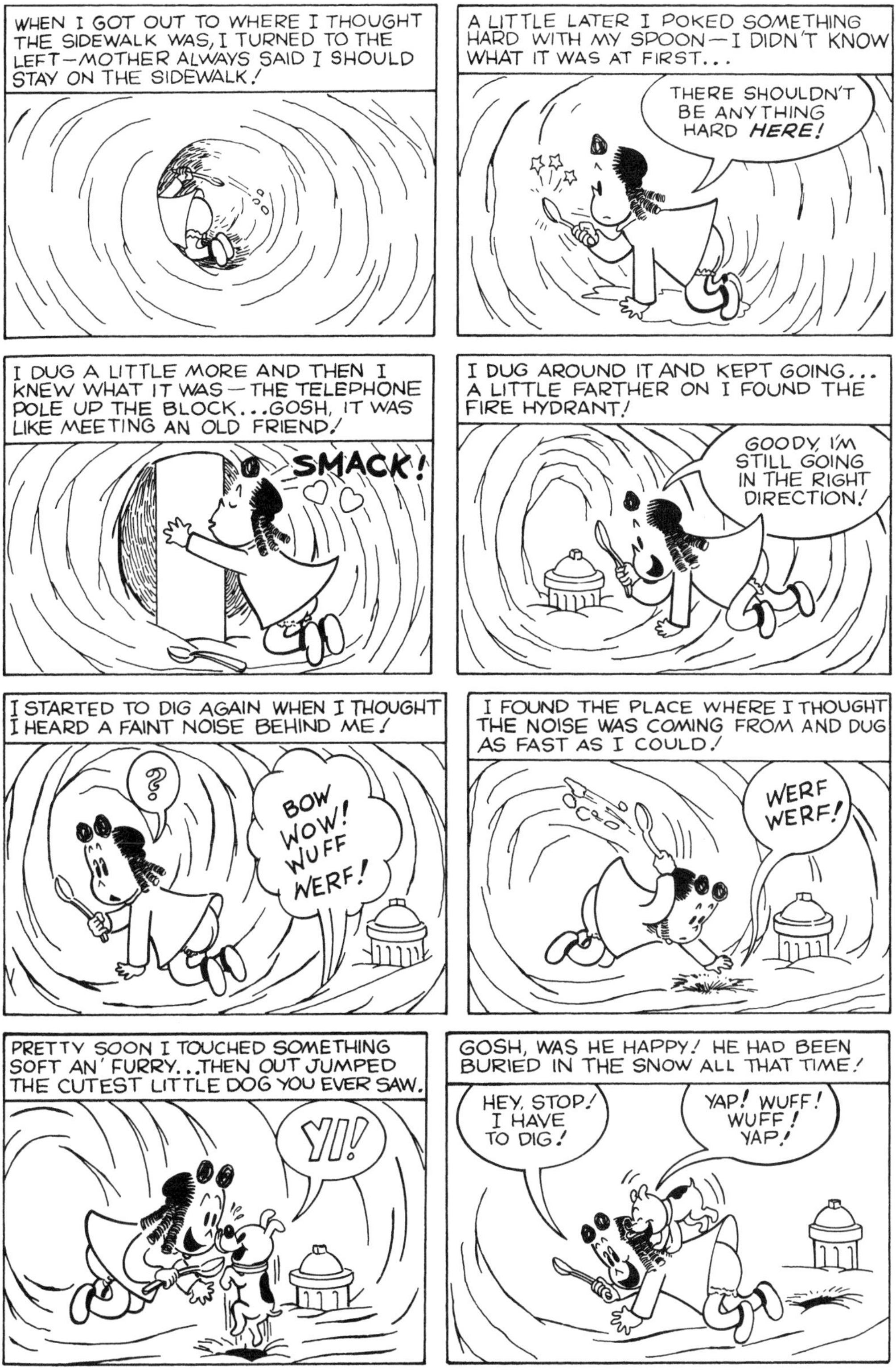
WHEN I GOT OUT TO WHERE I THOUGHT THE SIDEWALK WAS, I TURNED TO THE LEFT—MOTHER ALWAYS SAID I SHOULD STAY ON THE SIDEWALK!
A LITTLE LATER I POKED SOMETHING HARD WITH MY SPOON—I DIDN'T KNOW WHAT IT WAS AT FIRST...
THERE SHOULDN'T BE ANYTHING HARD *HERE!*
I DUG A LITTLE MORE AND THEN I KNEW WHAT IT WAS—THE TELEPHONE POLE UP THE BLOCK...GOSH, IT WAS LIKE MEETING AN OLD FRIEND!
SMACK!
I DUG AROUND IT AND KEPT GOING... A LITTLE FARTHER ON I FOUND THE FIRE HYDRANT!
GOODY, I'M STILL GOING IN THE RIGHT DIRECTION!
I STARTED TO DIG AGAIN WHEN I THOUGHT I HEARD A FAINT NOISE BEHIND ME!
?
BOW WOW! WUFF WERF!
I FOUND THE PLACE WHERE I THOUGHT THE NOISE WAS COMING FROM AND DUG AS FAST AS I COULD!
WERF WERF!
PRETTY SOON I TOUCHED SOMETHING SOFT AN' FURRY...THEN OUT JUMPED THE CUTEST LITTLE DOG YOU EVER SAW.
YI!
GOSH, WAS HE HAPPY! HE HAD BEEN BURIED IN THE SNOW ALL THAT TIME!
HEY, STOP! I HAVE TO DIG!
YAP! WUFF! WUFF! YAP!

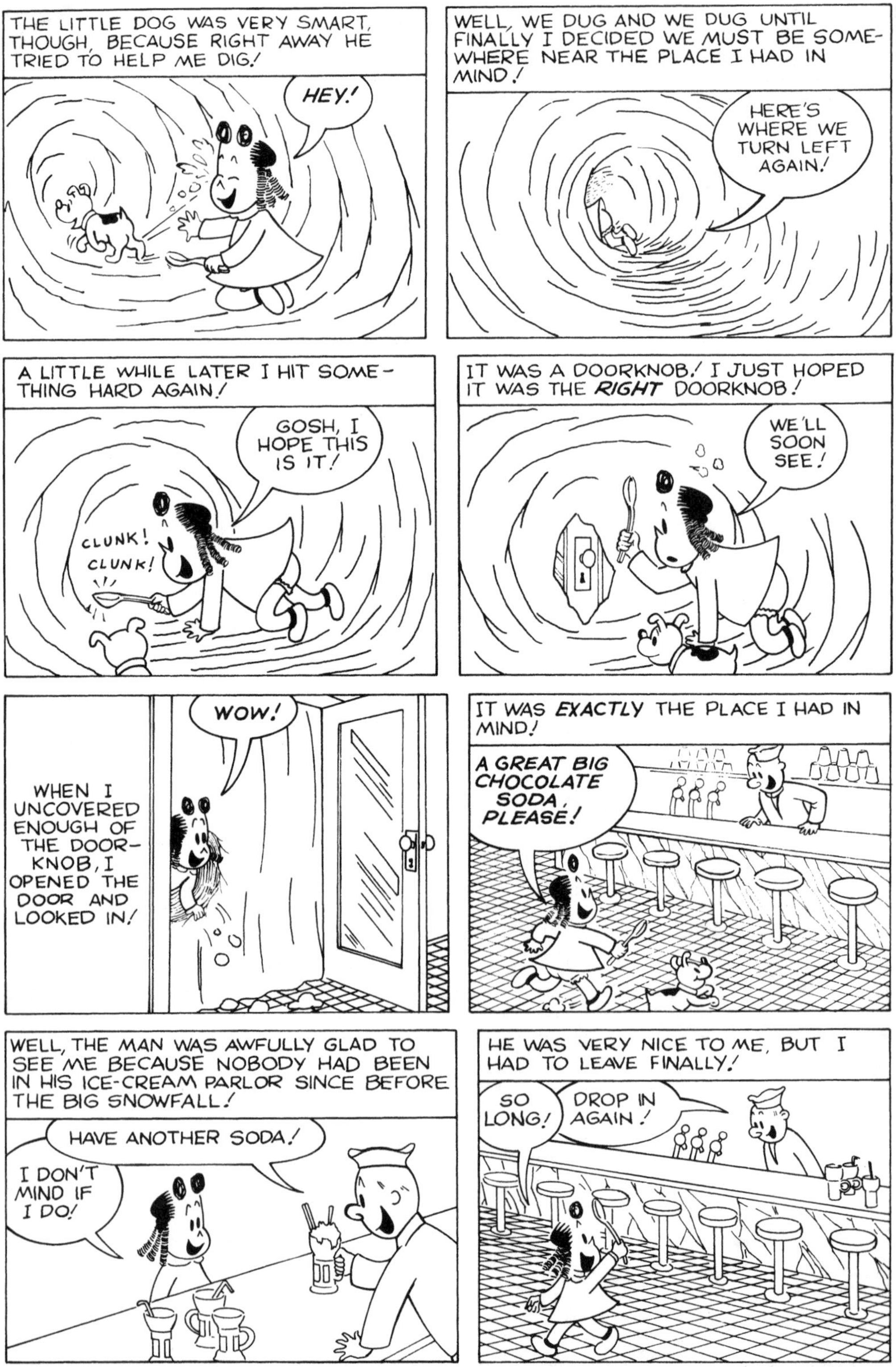
THE LITTLE DOG WAS VERY SMART, THOUGH, BECAUSE RIGHT AWAY HE TRIED TO HELP ME DIG!
HEY!
WELL, WE DUG AND WE DUG UNTIL FINALLY I DECIDED WE MUST BE SOMEWHERE NEAR THE PLACE I HAD IN MIND!
HERE'S WHERE WE TURN LEFT AGAIN!
A LITTLE WHILE LATER I HIT SOMETHING HARD AGAIN!
GOSH, I HOPE THIS IS IT!
CLUNK! CLUNK!
IT WAS A DOORKNOB! I JUST HOPED IT WAS THE *RIGHT* DOORKNOB!
WE'LL SOON SEE!
WHEN I UNCOVERED ENOUGH OF THE DOORKNOB, I OPENED THE DOOR AND LOOKED IN!
WOW!
IT WAS *EXACTLY* THE PLACE I HAD IN MIND!
A GREAT BIG CHOCOLATE SODA, PLEASE!
WELL, THE MAN WAS AWFULLY GLAD TO SEE ME BECAUSE NOBODY HAD BEEN IN HIS ICE-CREAM PARLOR SINCE BEFORE THE BIG SNOWFALL!
HAVE ANOTHER SODA!
I DON'T MIND IF I DO!
HE WAS VERY NICE TO ME, BUT I HAD TO LEAVE FINALLY!
SO LONG!
DROP IN AGAIN!

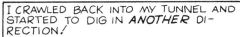
I CRAWLED BACK INTO MY TUNNEL AND STARTED TO DIG IN *ANOTHER* DIRECTION!

MOTHER WILL BE SO GLAD TO SEE ME!

...AN' POP TOO!

I WAS HOPING I COULD DIG MY WAY TO THE HOUSE WHERE MOTHER AND POP WERE VISITING!

DRIP!

BUT SOMETHING I DIDN'T EXPECT HAPPENED —

GOSH, *THE* SNOW IS *MELTING!*

BERF!

SPRING CAME VERY EARLY AND VERY SUDDENLY THAT YEAR!

WHAT'LL I DO?

THE SNOW MELTED SO FAST THAT BEFORE I KNEW IT, THE TUNNEL WAS FILLED WITH WATER!

C'MON, DOGGIE, MAYBE WE CAN GET BACK TO MY HOUSE!

AS FAST AS WE COULD THE LITTLE DOG AND I SWAM THROUGH THE TUNNEL TO MY HOUSE!

IT WASN'T VERY EASY TO SHUT THE DOOR, BUT WE DID IT!

PUSH!

THEN I SAW THE WATER COMING DOWN THE STAIRS!

OH! OH! OH!

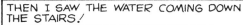

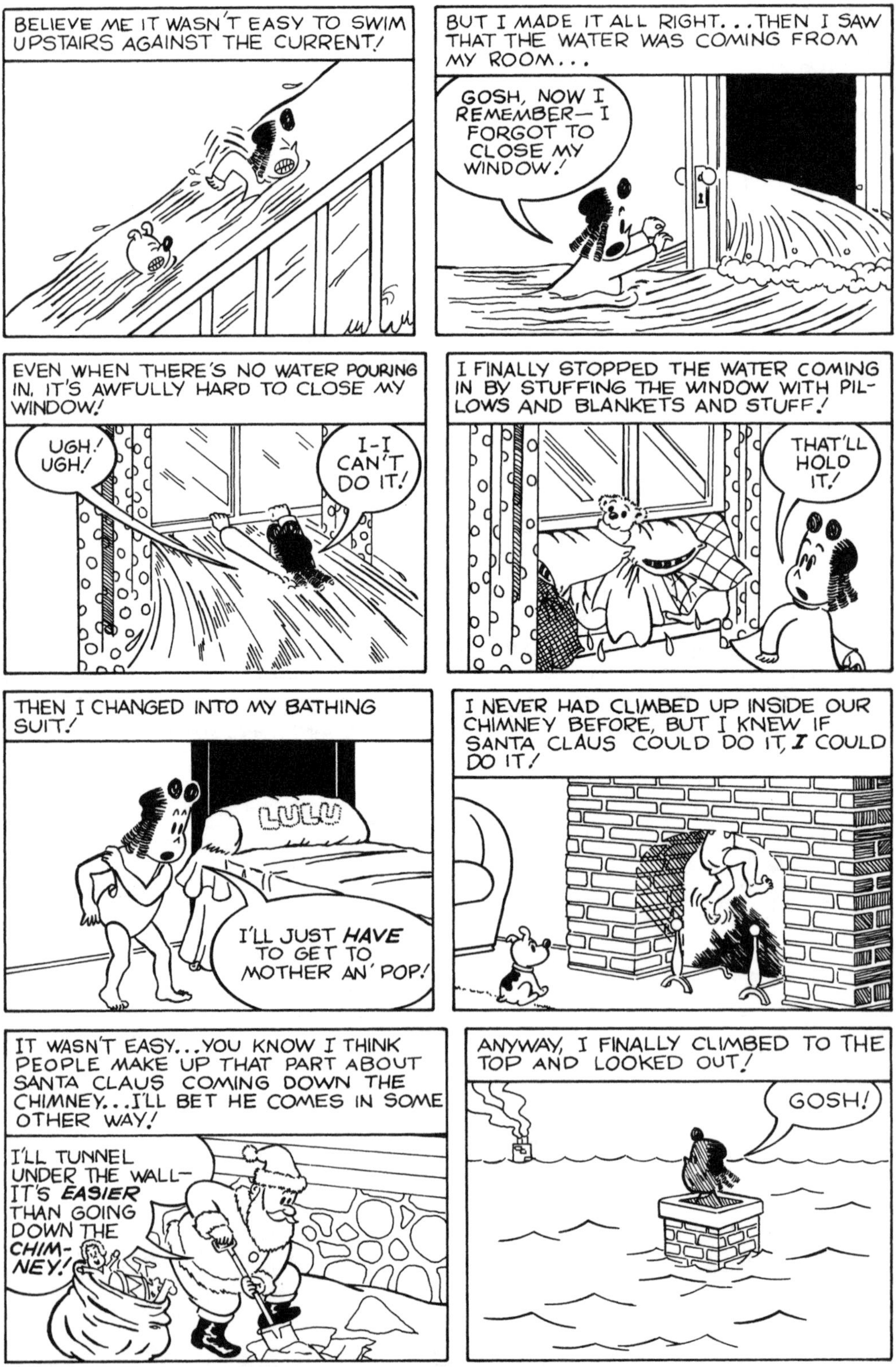

BELIEVE ME IT WASN'T EASY TO SWIM UPSTAIRS AGAINST THE CURRENT!
BUT I MADE IT ALL RIGHT. . . THEN I SAW THAT THE WATER WAS COMING FROM MY ROOM . . .
GOSH, NOW I REMEMBER— I FORGOT TO CLOSE MY WINDOW!
EVEN WHEN THERE'S NO WATER POURING IN, IT'S AWFULLY HARD TO CLOSE MY WINDOW!
UGH! UGH!
I-I CAN'T DO IT!
I FINALLY STOPPED THE WATER COMING IN BY STUFFING THE WINDOW WITH PILLOWS AND BLANKETS AND STUFF!
THAT'LL HOLD IT!
THEN I CHANGED INTO MY BATHING SUIT!
LULU
I'LL JUST HAVE TO GET TO MOTHER AN' POP!
I NEVER HAD CLIMBED UP INSIDE OUR CHIMNEY BEFORE, BUT I KNEW IF SANTA CLAUS COULD DO IT, I COULD DO IT!
IT WASN'T EASY... YOU KNOW I THINK PEOPLE MAKE UP THAT PART ABOUT SANTA CLAUS COMING DOWN THE CHIMNEY... I'LL BET HE COMES IN SOME OTHER WAY!
I'LL TUNNEL UNDER THE WALL— IT'S EASIER THAN GOING DOWN THE CHIMNEY!
ANYWAY, I FINALLY CLIMBED TO THE TOP AND LOOKED OUT!
GOSH!

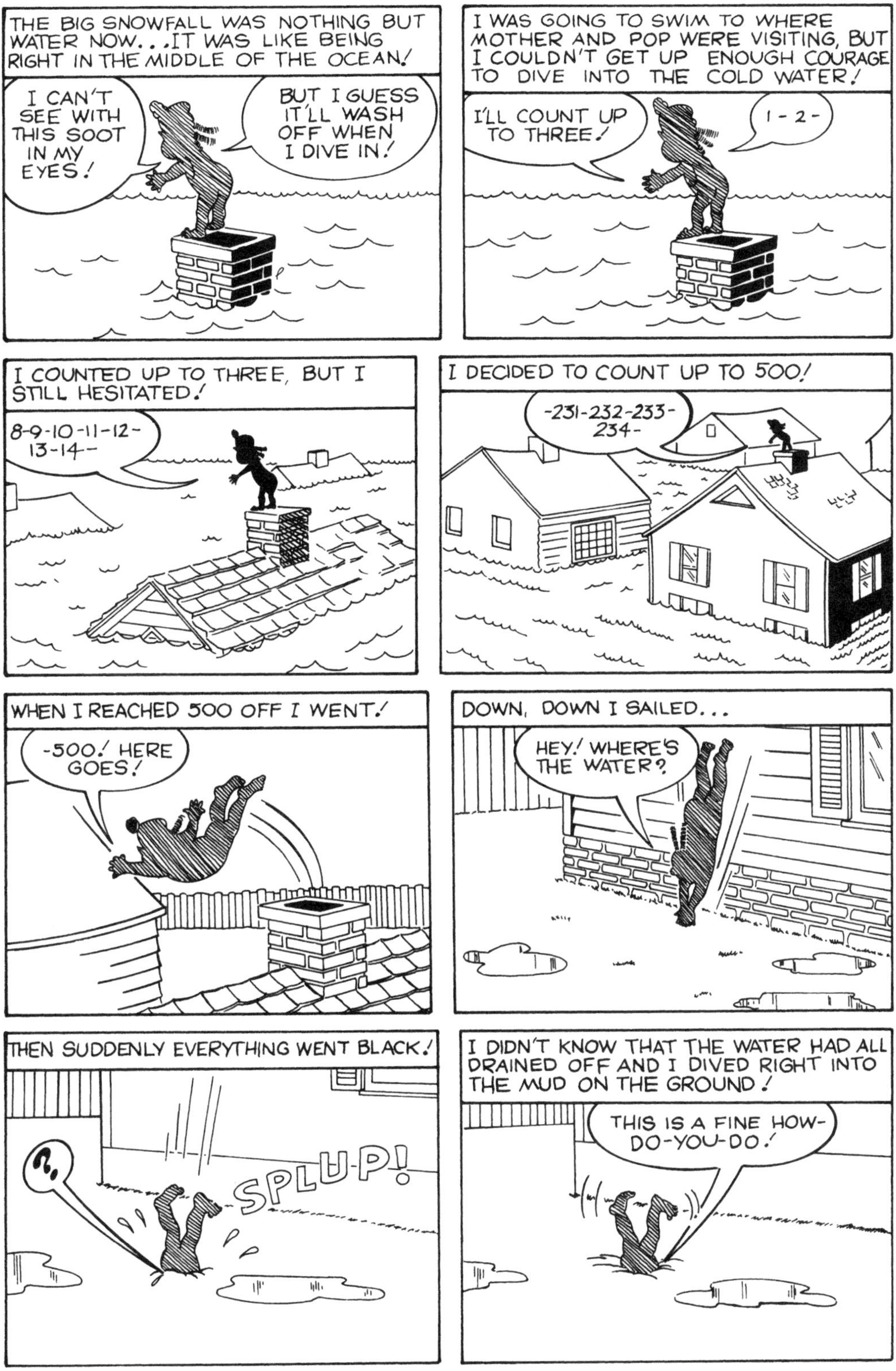
THE BIG SNOWFALL WAS NOTHING BUT WATER NOW. . .IT WAS LIKE BEING RIGHT IN THE MIDDLE OF THE OCEAN!
I CAN'T SEE WITH THIS SOOT IN MY EYES!
BUT I GUESS IT'LL WASH OFF WHEN I DIVE IN!
I WAS GOING TO SWIM TO WHERE MOTHER AND POP WERE VISITING, BUT I COULDN'T GET UP ENOUGH COURAGE TO DIVE INTO THE COLD WATER!
I'LL COUNT UP TO THREE!
1 - 2 -
I COUNTED UP TO THREE, BUT I STILL HESITATED!
8-9-10-11-12-13-14-
I DECIDED TO COUNT UP TO 500!
-231-232-233-234-
WHEN I REACHED 500 OFF I WENT!
-500! HERE GOES!
DOWN, DOWN I SAILED. . .
HEY! WHERE'S THE WATER?
THEN SUDDENLY EVERYTHING WENT BLACK!
?
SPLUP!
I DIDN'T KNOW THAT THE WATER HAD ALL DRAINED OFF AND I DIVED RIGHT INTO THE MUD ON THE GROUND!
THIS IS A FINE HOW-DO-YOU-DO!

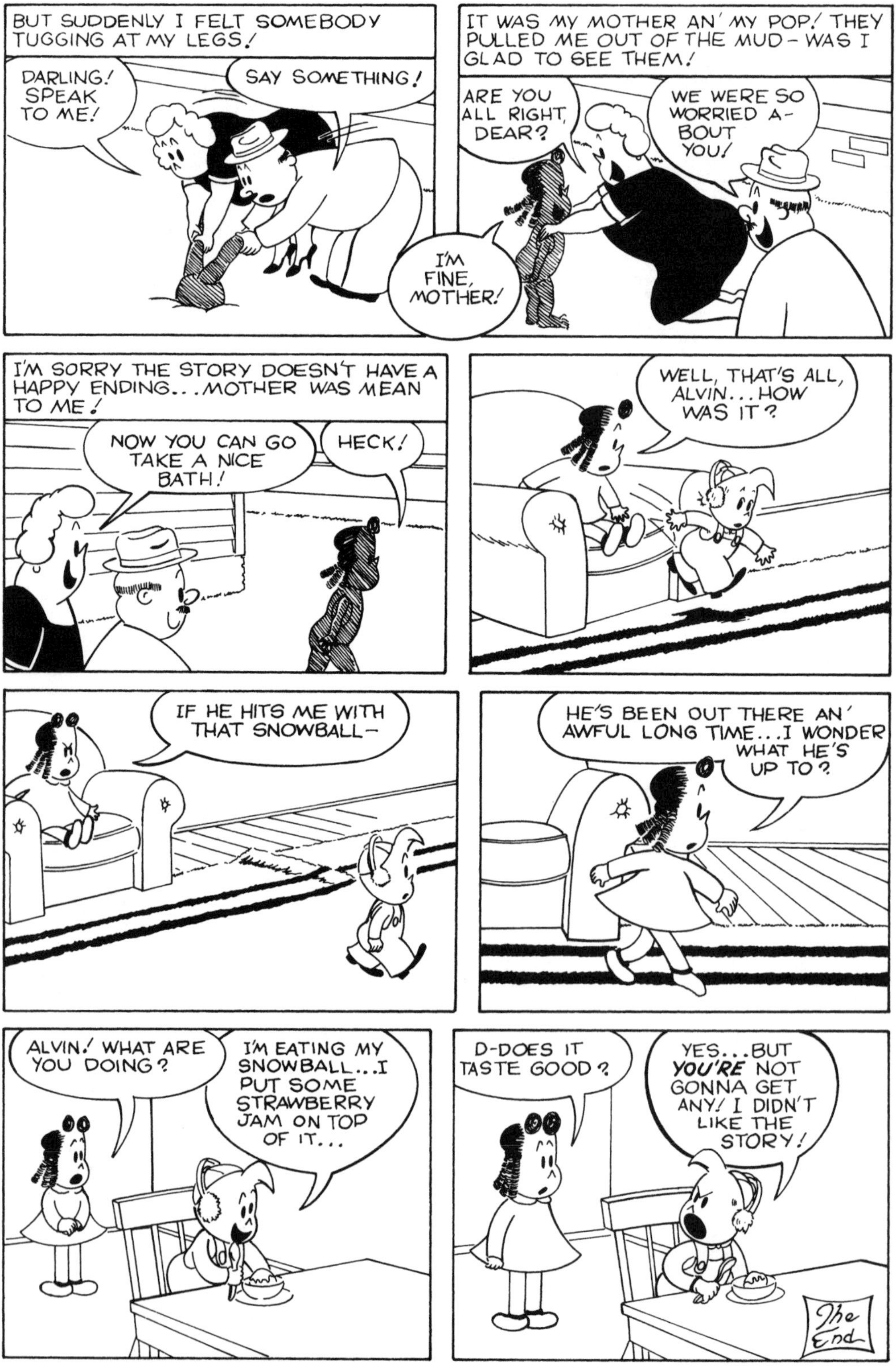
BUT SUDDENLY I FELT SOMEBODY TUGGING AT MY LEGS!
DARLING! SPEAK TO ME!
SAY SOMETHING!
IT WAS MY MOTHER AN' MY POP! THEY PULLED ME OUT OF THE MUD - WAS I GLAD TO SEE THEM!
ARE YOU ALL RIGHT, DEAR?
WE WERE SO WORRIED A-BOUT YOU!
I'M FINE, MOTHER!
I'M SORRY THE STORY DOESN'T HAVE A HAPPY ENDING...MOTHER WAS MEAN TO ME!
NOW YOU CAN GO TAKE A NICE BATH!
HECK!
WELL, THAT'S ALL, ALVIN...HOW WAS IT?
IF HE HITS ME WITH THAT SNOWBALL-
HE'S BEEN OUT THERE AN' AWFUL LONG TIME...I WONDER WHAT HE'S UP TO?
ALVIN! WHAT ARE YOU DOING?
I'M EATING MY SNOWBALL...I PUT SOME STRAWBERRY JAM ON TOP OF IT...
D-DOES IT TASTE GOOD?
YES...BUT ***YOU'RE*** NOT GONNA GET ANY! I DIDN'T LIKE THE STORY!
The End

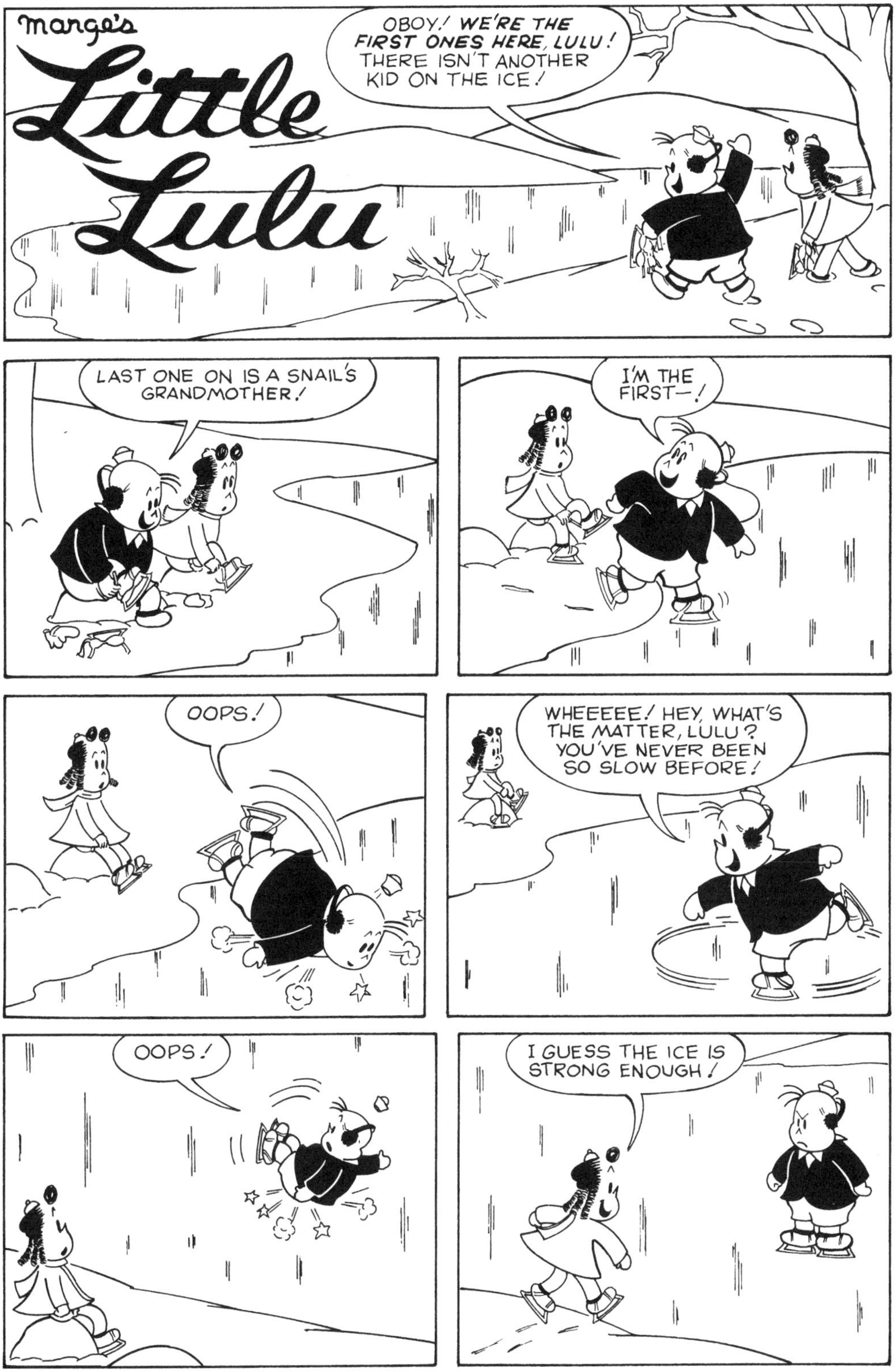
Marge's
Little Lulu
OBOY! WE'RE THE FIRST ONES HERE, LULU! THERE ISN'T ANOTHER KID ON THE ICE!
LAST ONE ON IS A SNAIL'S GRANDMOTHER!
I'M THE FIRST—!
OOPS!
WHEEEEE! HEY, WHAT'S THE MATTER, LULU? YOU'VE NEVER BEEN SO SLOW BEFORE!
OOPS!
I GUESS THE ICE IS STRONG ENOUGH!

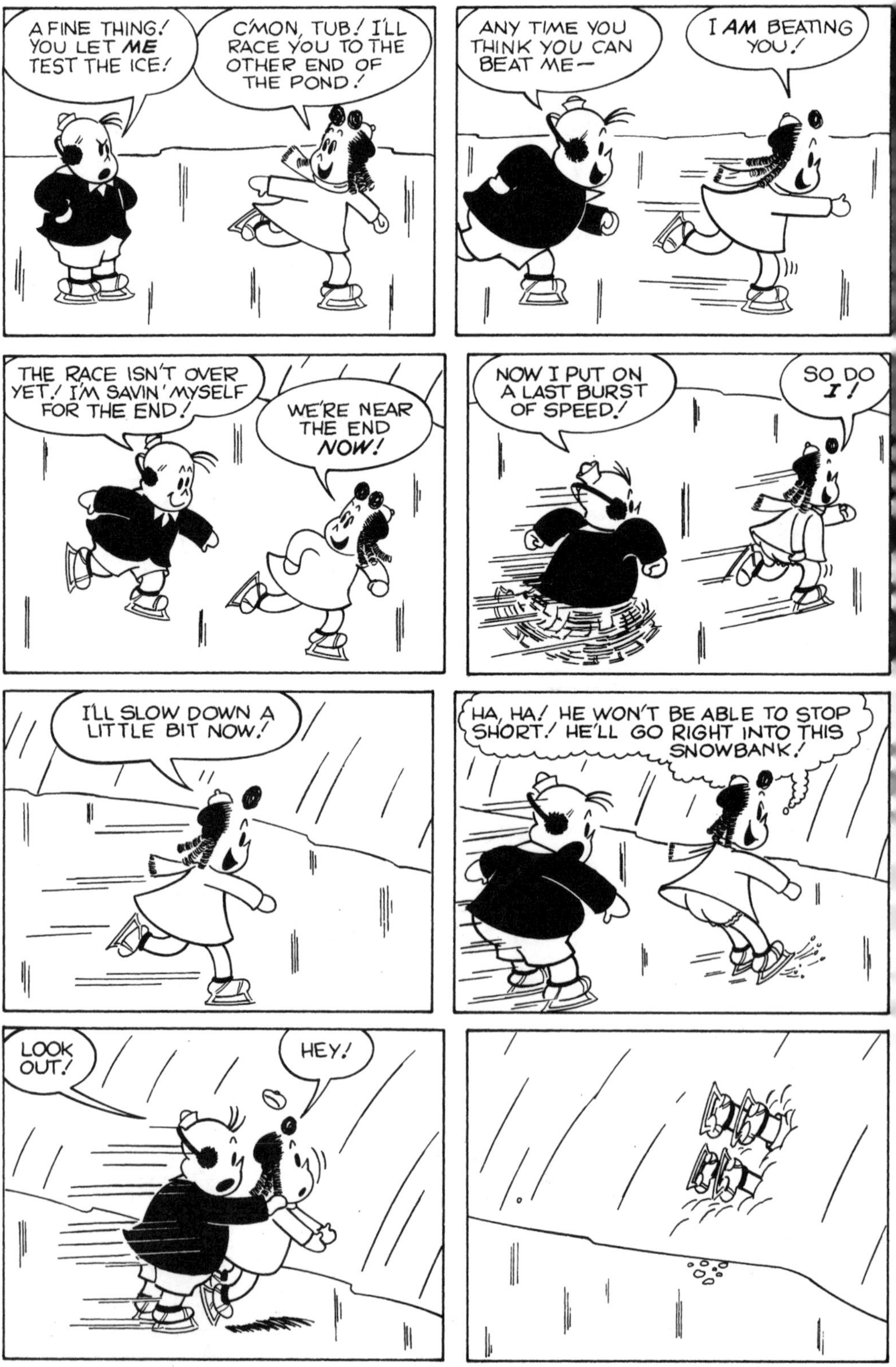
A FINE THING! YOU LET ME TEST THE ICE!
C'MON, TUB! I'LL RACE YOU TO THE OTHER END OF THE POND!
ANY TIME YOU THINK YOU CAN BEAT ME—
I AM BEATING YOU!
THE RACE ISN'T OVER YET! I'M SAVIN' MYSELF FOR THE END!
WE'RE NEAR THE END NOW!
NOW I PUT ON A LAST BURST OF SPEED!
SO DO I!
I'LL SLOW DOWN A LITTLE BIT NOW!
HA, HA! HE WON'T BE ABLE TO STOP SHORT! HE'LL GO RIGHT INTO THIS SNOWBANK!
LOOK OUT!
HEY!

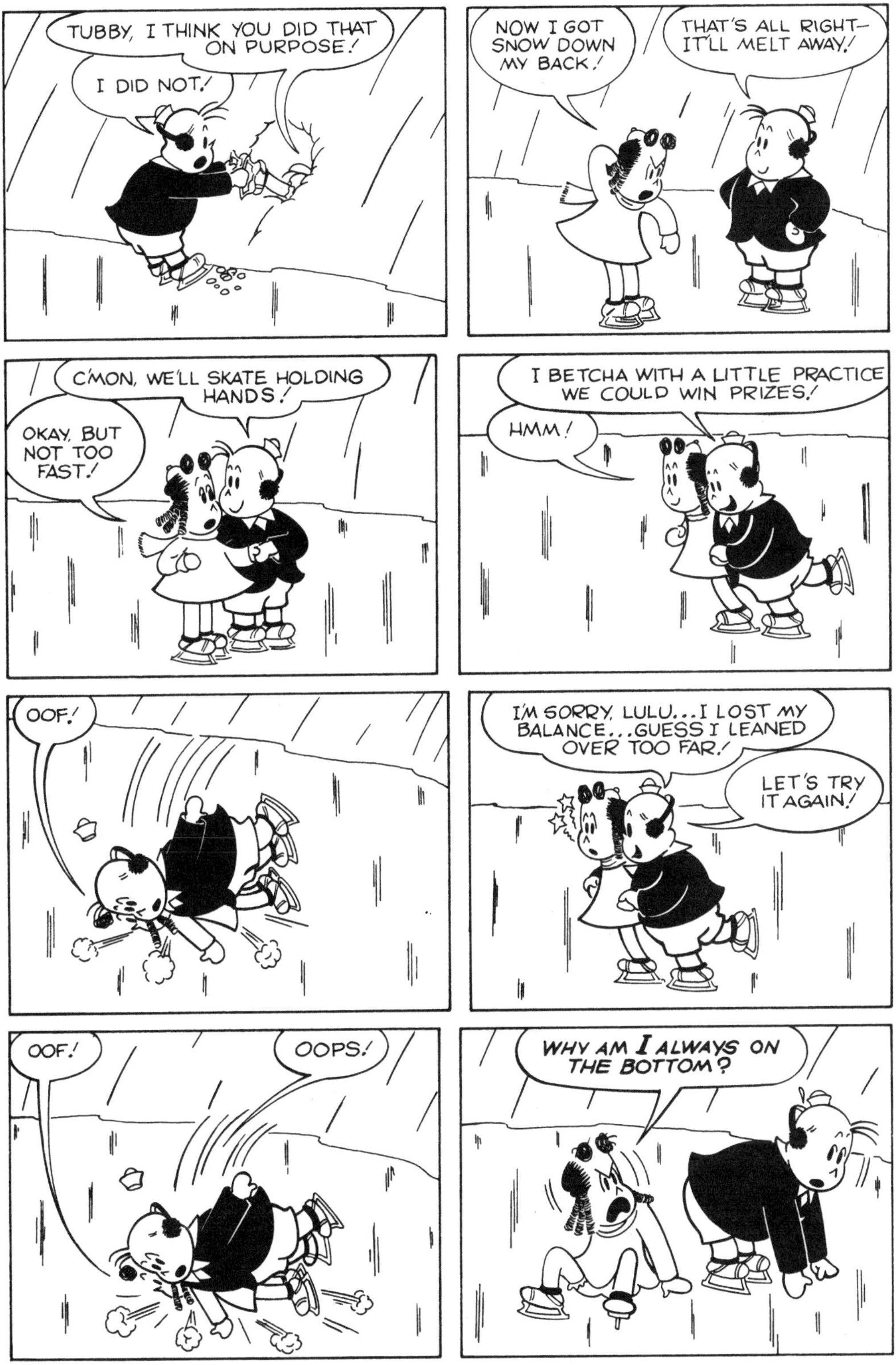
TUBBY, I THINK YOU DID THAT ON PURPOSE!
I DID NOT!
NOW I GOT SNOW DOWN MY BACK!
THAT'S ALL RIGHT— IT'LL MELT AWAY!
C'MON, WE'LL SKATE HOLDING HANDS!
OKAY, BUT NOT TOO FAST!
I BETCHA WITH A LITTLE PRACTICE WE COULD WIN PRIZES!
HMM!
OOF!
I'M SORRY, LULU...I LOST MY BALANCE...GUESS I LEANED OVER TOO FAR!
LET'S TRY IT AGAIN!
OOF!
OOPS!
WHY AM I ALWAYS ON THE BOTTOM?

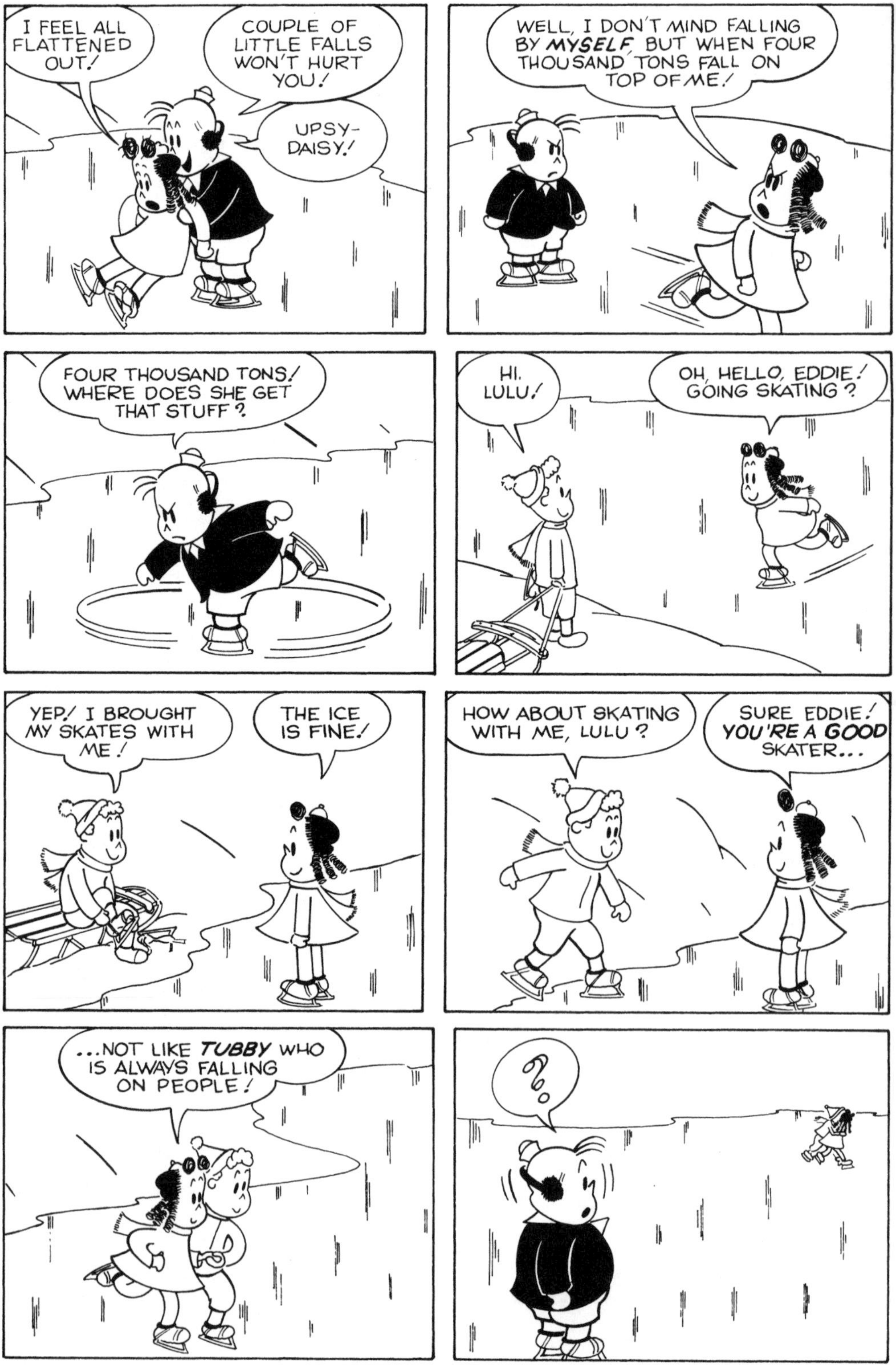
I FEEL ALL FLATTENED OUT!
COUPLE OF LITTLE FALLS WON'T HURT YOU!
UPSY-DAISY!
WELL, I DON'T MIND FALLING BY MYSELF, BUT WHEN FOUR THOUSAND TONS FALL ON TOP OF ME!
FOUR THOUSAND TONS! WHERE DOES SHE GET THAT STUFF?
HI, LULU!
OH, HELLO, EDDIE! GOING SKATING?
YEP! I BROUGHT MY SKATES WITH ME!
THE ICE IS FINE!
HOW ABOUT SKATING WITH ME, LULU?
SURE EDDIE! YOU'RE A GOOD SKATER...
...NOT LIKE TUBBY WHO IS ALWAYS FALLING ON PEOPLE!
?

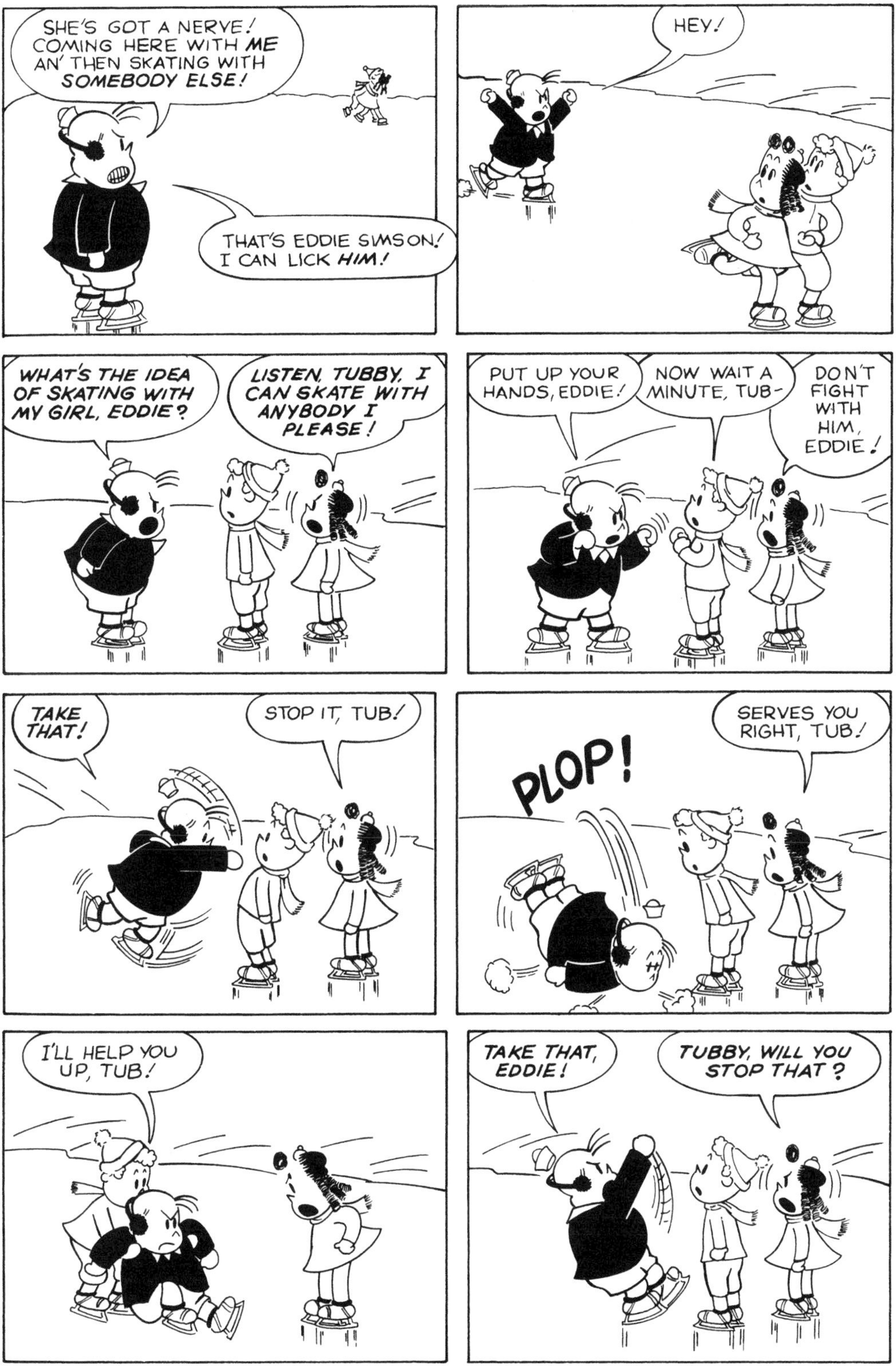
SHE'S GOT A NERVE! COMING HERE WITH **ME** AN' THEN SKATING WITH **SOMEBODY ELSE!**
THAT'S EDDIE SIMSON! I CAN LICK **HIM!**
HEY!
WHAT'S THE IDEA OF SKATING WITH MY GIRL, EDDIE?
LISTEN, TUBBY, I CAN SKATE WITH ANYBODY I PLEASE!
PUT UP YOUR HANDS, EDDIE!
NOW WAIT A MINUTE, TUB-
DON'T FIGHT WITH HIM, EDDIE!
TAKE THAT!
STOP IT, TUB!
PLOP!
SERVES YOU RIGHT, TUB!
I'LL HELP YOU UP, TUB!
TAKE THAT, EDDIE!
TUBBY, WILL YOU STOP THAT?

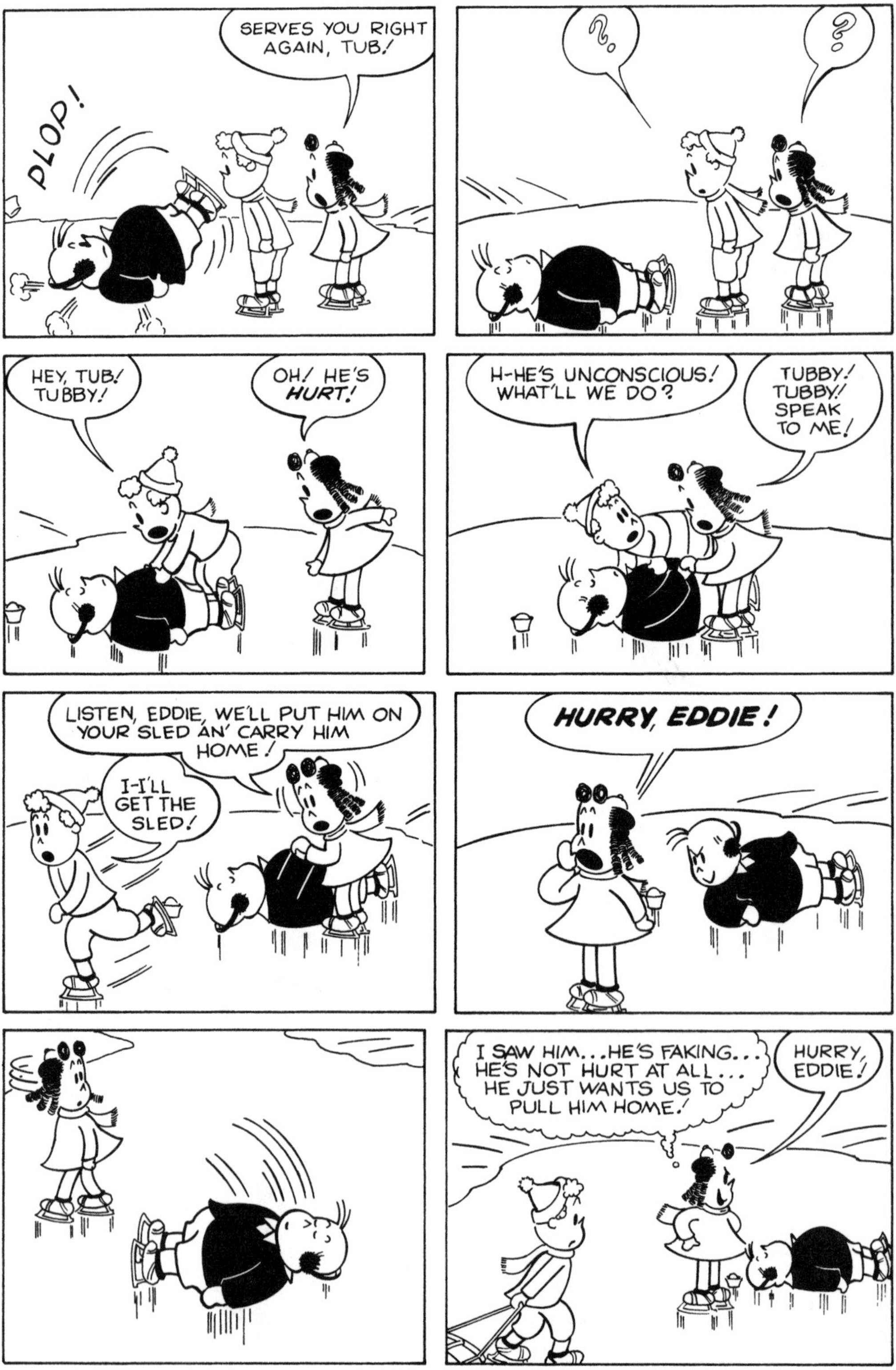

PLOP!
SERVES YOU RIGHT AGAIN, TUB!
?
?
HEY, TUB! TUBBY!
OH! HE'S HURT!
H-HE'S UNCONSCIOUS! WHAT'LL WE DO?
TUBBY! TUBBY! SPEAK TO ME!
LISTEN, EDDIE, WE'LL PUT HIM ON YOUR SLED AN' CARRY HIM HOME!
I-I'LL GET THE SLED!
HURRY, EDDIE!
I SAW HIM...HE'S FAKING... HE'S NOT HURT AT ALL... HE JUST WANTS US TO PULL HIM HOME!
HURRY, EDDIE!

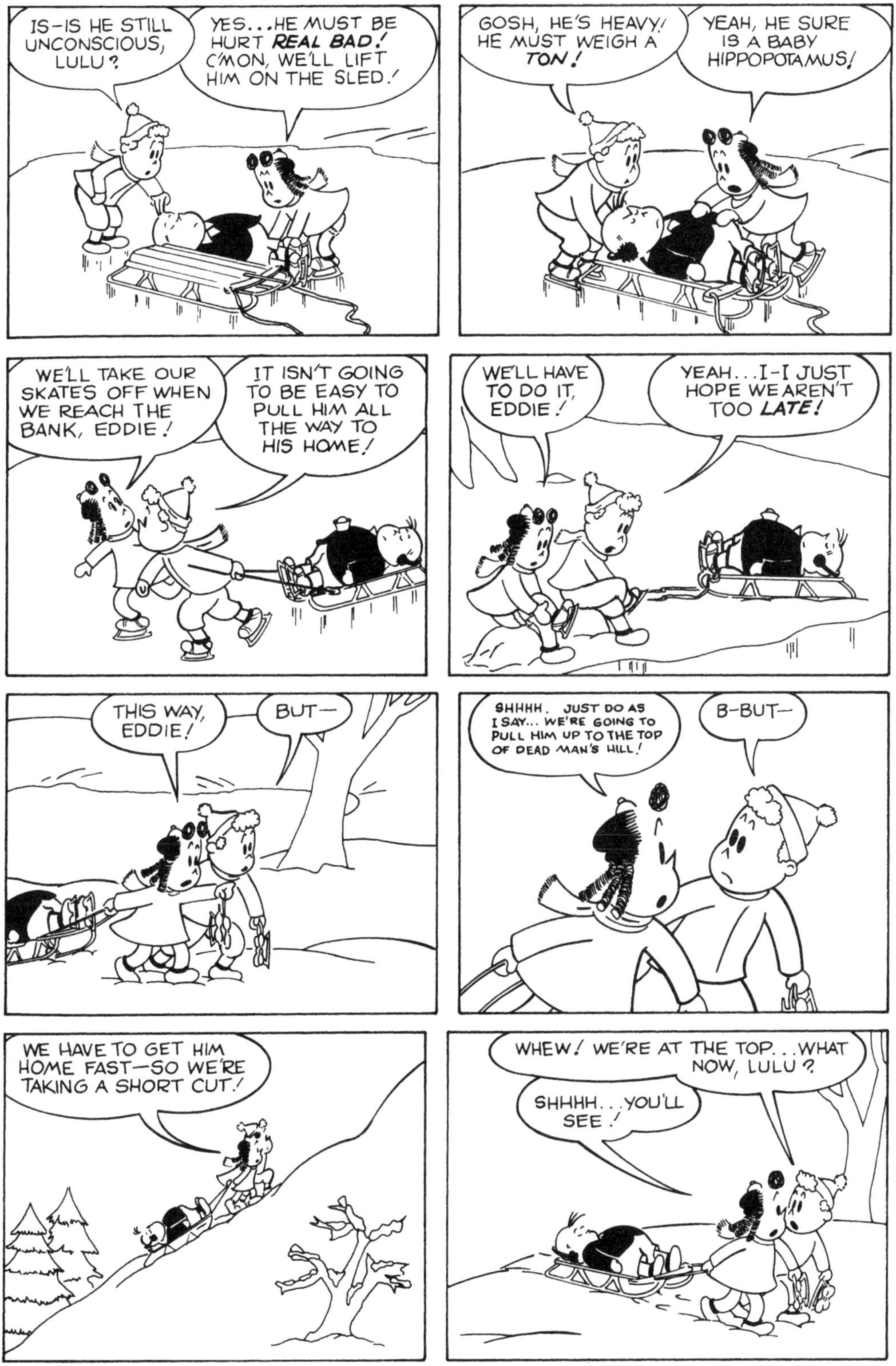
IS-IS HE STILL UNCONSCIOUS, LULU?
YES...HE MUST BE HURT REAL BAD! C'MON, WE'LL LIFT HIM ON THE SLED!
GOSH, HE'S HEAVY! HE MUST WEIGH A TON!
YEAH, HE SURE IS A BABY HIPPOPOTAMUS!
WE'LL TAKE OUR SKATES OFF WHEN WE REACH THE BANK, EDDIE!
IT ISN'T GOING TO BE EASY TO PULL HIM ALL THE WAY TO HIS HOME!
WE'LL HAVE TO DO IT, EDDIE!
YEAH...I-I JUST HOPE WE AREN'T TOO LATE!
THIS WAY, EDDIE!
BUT—
SHHHH. JUST DO AS I SAY... WE'RE GOING TO PULL HIM UP TO THE TOP OF DEAD MAN'S HILL!
B-BUT—
WE HAVE TO GET HIM HOME FAST—SO WE'RE TAKING A SHORT CUT!
WHEW! WE'RE AT THE TOP...WHAT NOW, LULU?
SHHHH...YOU'LL SEE!

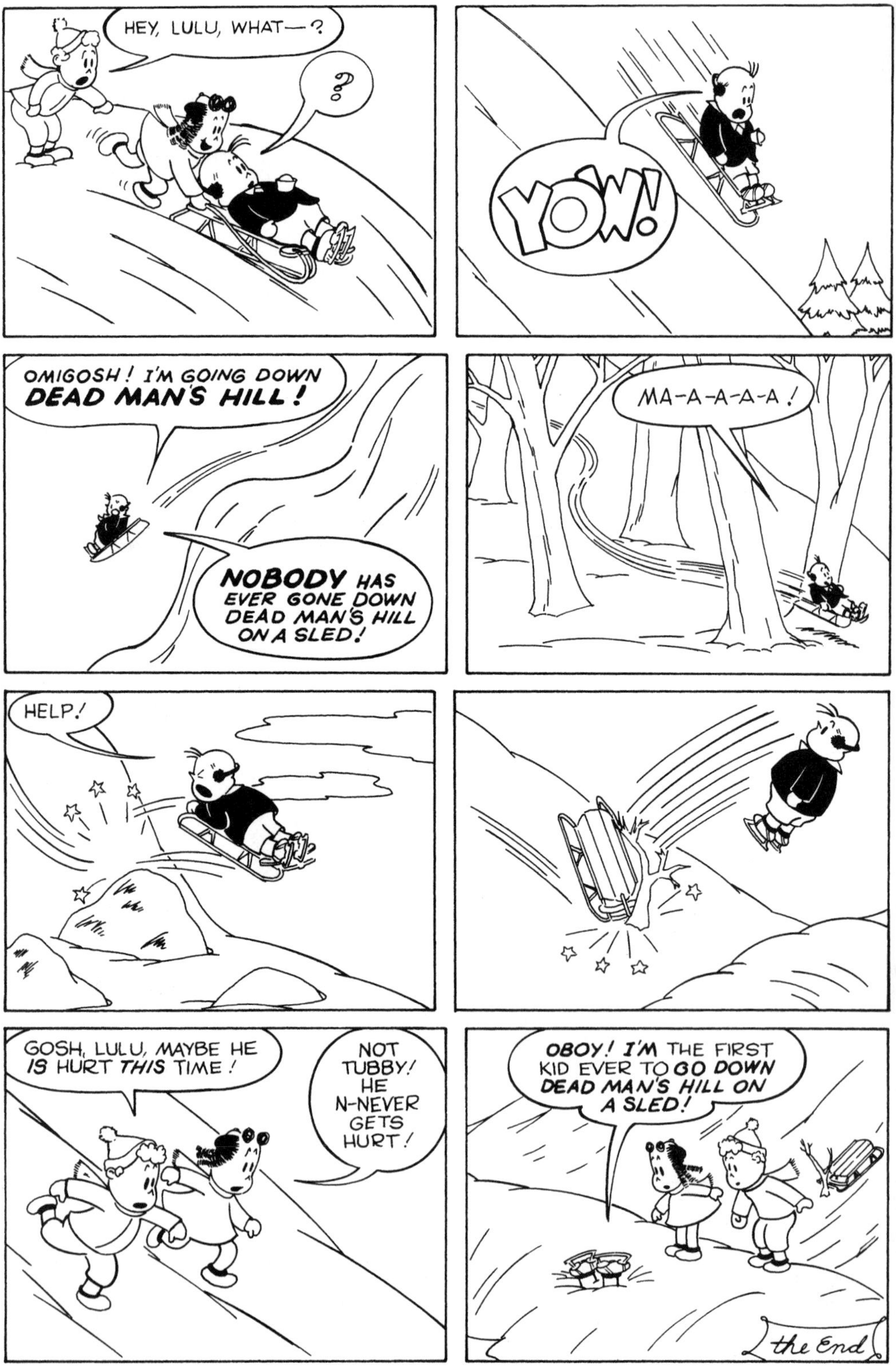
HEY, LULU, WHAT—?
?
YOW!
OMIGOSH! I'M GOING DOWN DEAD MAN'S HILL!
NOBODY HAS EVER GONE DOWN DEAD MAN'S HILL ON A SLED!
MA-A-A-A-A!
HELP!
GOSH, LULU, MAYBE HE IS HURT THIS TIME!
NOT TUBBY! HE N-NEVER GETS HURT!
OBOY! I'M THE FIRST KID EVER TO GO DOWN DEAD MAN'S HILL ON A SLED!
the End

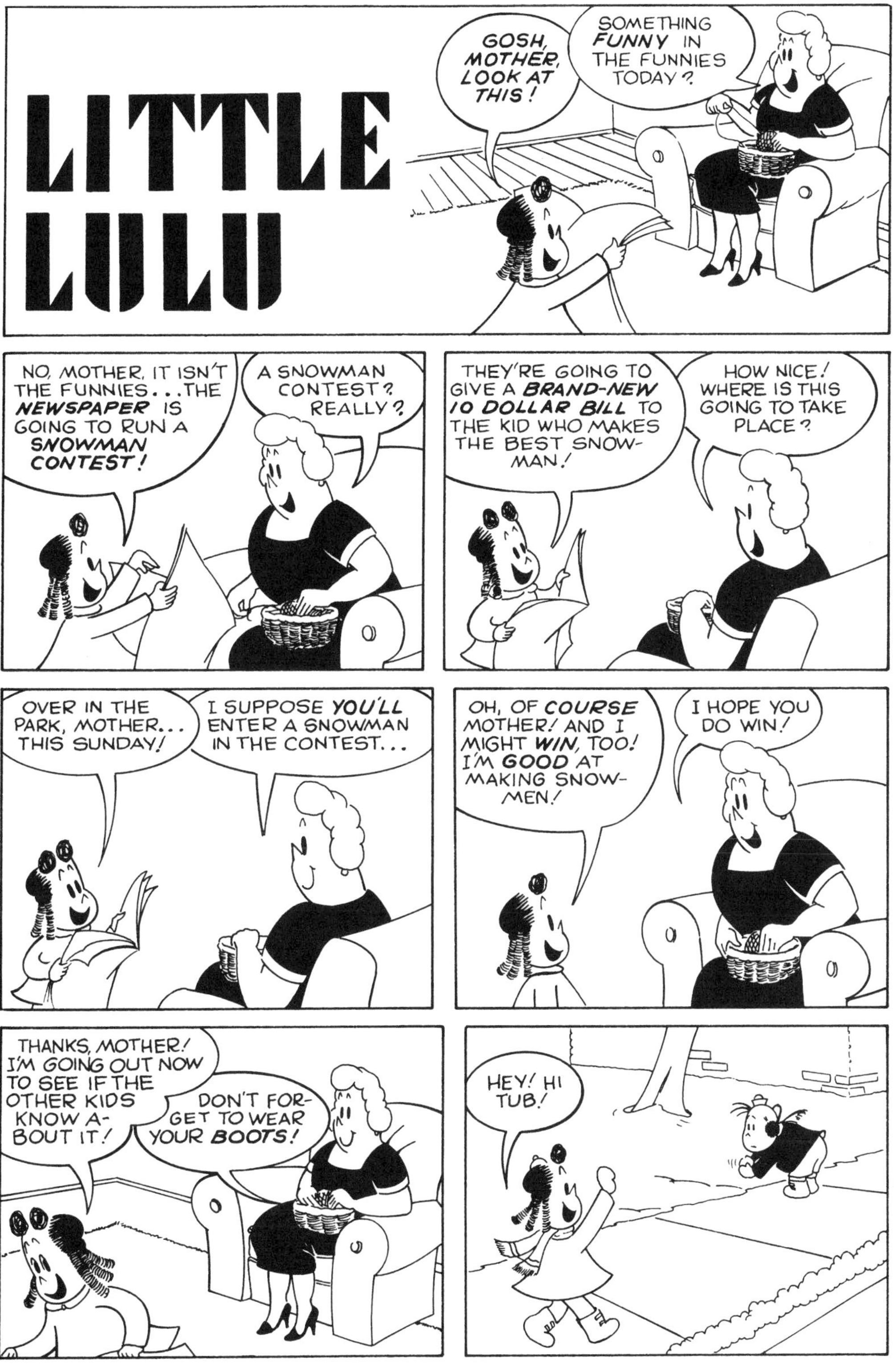
LITTLE LULU
GOSH, MOTHER, LOOK AT THIS!
SOMETHING FUNNY IN THE FUNNIES TODAY?
NO, MOTHER, IT ISN'T THE FUNNIES...THE NEWSPAPER IS GOING TO RUN A SNOWMAN CONTEST!
A SNOWMAN CONTEST? REALLY?
THEY'RE GOING TO GIVE A BRAND-NEW 10 DOLLAR BILL TO THE KID WHO MAKES THE BEST SNOW-MAN!
HOW NICE! WHERE IS THIS GOING TO TAKE PLACE?
OVER IN THE PARK, MOTHER... THIS SUNDAY!
I SUPPOSE YOU'LL ENTER A SNOWMAN IN THE CONTEST...
OH, OF COURSE MOTHER! AND I MIGHT WIN, TOO! I'M GOOD AT MAKING SNOW-MEN!
I HOPE YOU DO WIN!
THANKS, MOTHER! I'M GOING OUT NOW TO SEE IF THE OTHER KIDS KNOW A-BOUT IT!
DON'T FOR-GET TO WEAR YOUR BOOTS!
HEY! HI TUB!

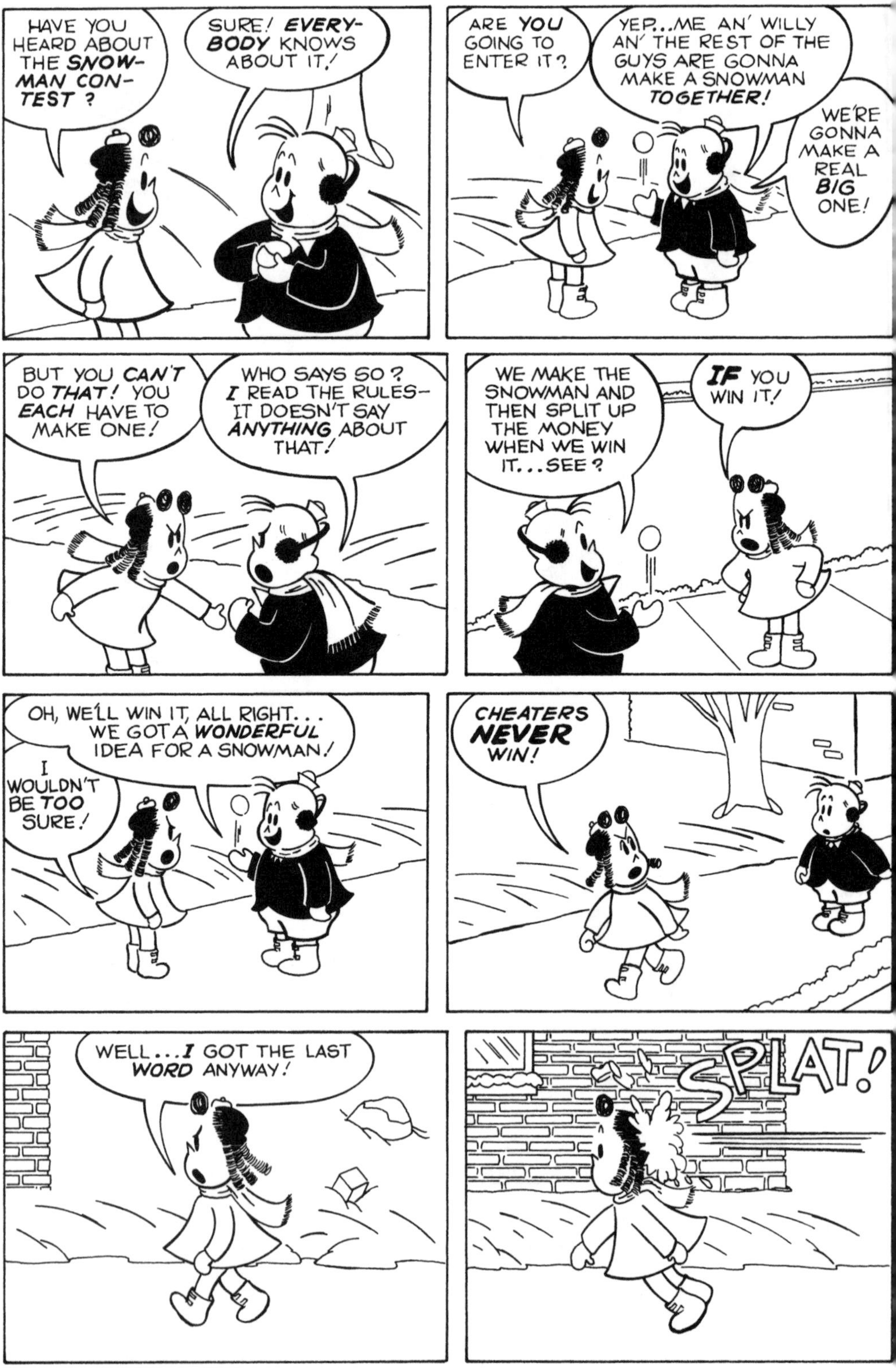
HAVE YOU HEARD ABOUT THE SNOWMAN CONTEST ?
SURE! EVERYBODY KNOWS ABOUT IT!
ARE YOU GOING TO ENTER IT?
YEP...ME AN' WILLY AN' THE REST OF THE GUYS ARE GONNA MAKE A SNOWMAN TOGETHER!
WE'RE GONNA MAKE A REAL BIG ONE!
BUT YOU CAN'T DO THAT! YOU EACH HAVE TO MAKE ONE!
WHO SAYS SO? I READ THE RULES- IT DOESN'T SAY ANYTHING ABOUT THAT!
WE MAKE THE SNOWMAN AND THEN SPLIT UP THE MONEY WHEN WE WIN IT...SEE?
IF YOU WIN IT!
OH, WE'LL WIN IT, ALL RIGHT... WE GOT A WONDERFUL IDEA FOR A SNOWMAN!
I WOULDN'T BE TOO SURE!
CHEATERS NEVER WIN!
WELL...I GOT THE LAST WORD ANYWAY!
SPLAT!

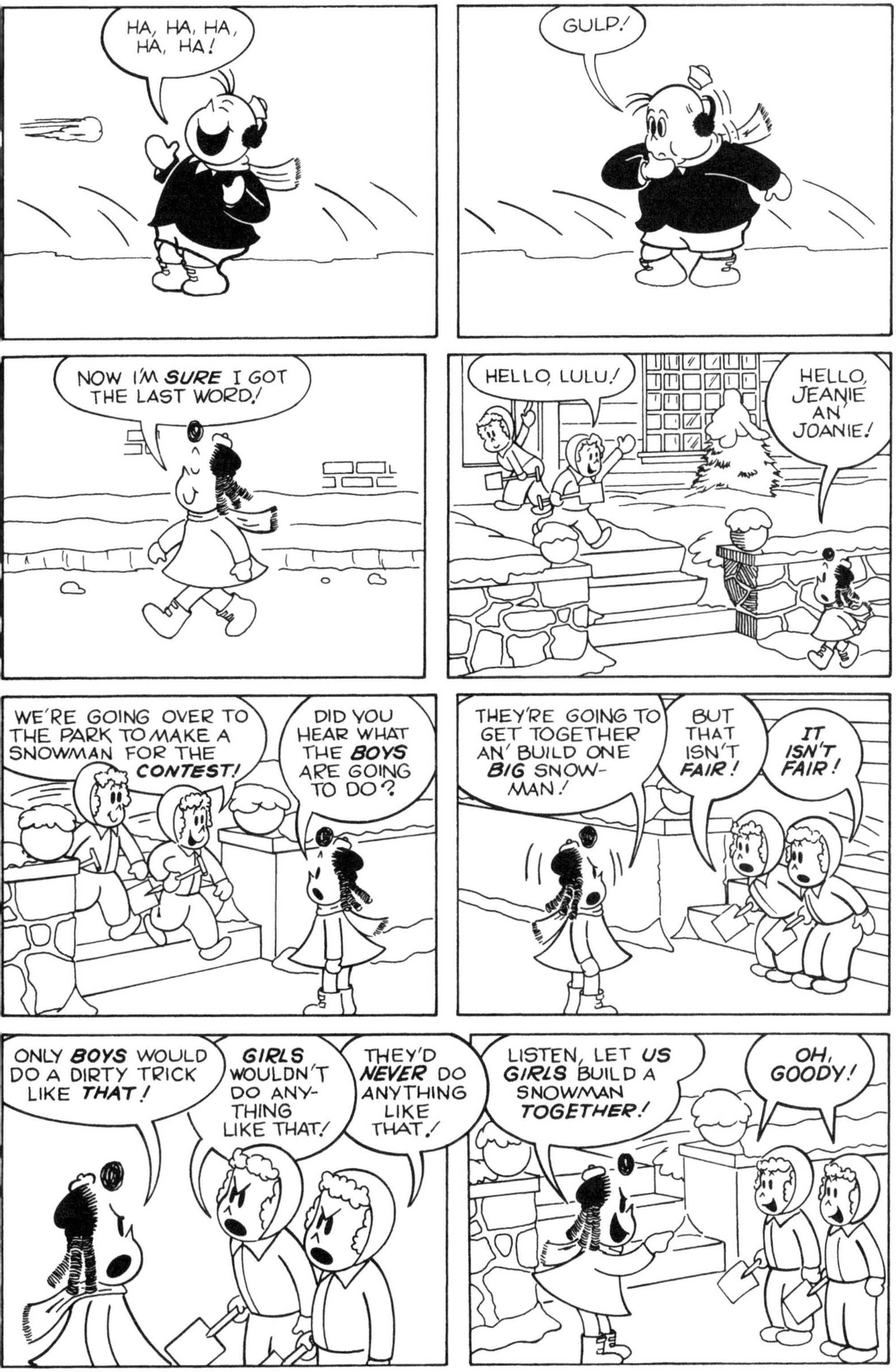
HA, HA, HA, HA, HA!
GULP!
NOW I'M SURE I GOT THE LAST WORD!
HELLO, LULU!
HELLO, JEANIE AN' JOANIE!
WE'RE GOING OVER TO THE PARK TO MAKE A SNOWMAN FOR THE CONTEST!
DID YOU HEAR WHAT THE BOYS ARE GOING TO DO?
THEY'RE GOING TO GET TOGETHER AN' BUILD ONE BIG SNOW-MAN!
BUT THAT ISN'T FAIR!
IT ISN'T FAIR!
ONLY BOYS WOULD DO A DIRTY TRICK LIKE THAT!
GIRLS WOULDN'T DO ANY-THING LIKE THAT!
THEY'D NEVER DO ANYTHING LIKE THAT!
LISTEN, LET US GIRLS BUILD A SNOWMAN TOGETHER!
OH, GOODY!

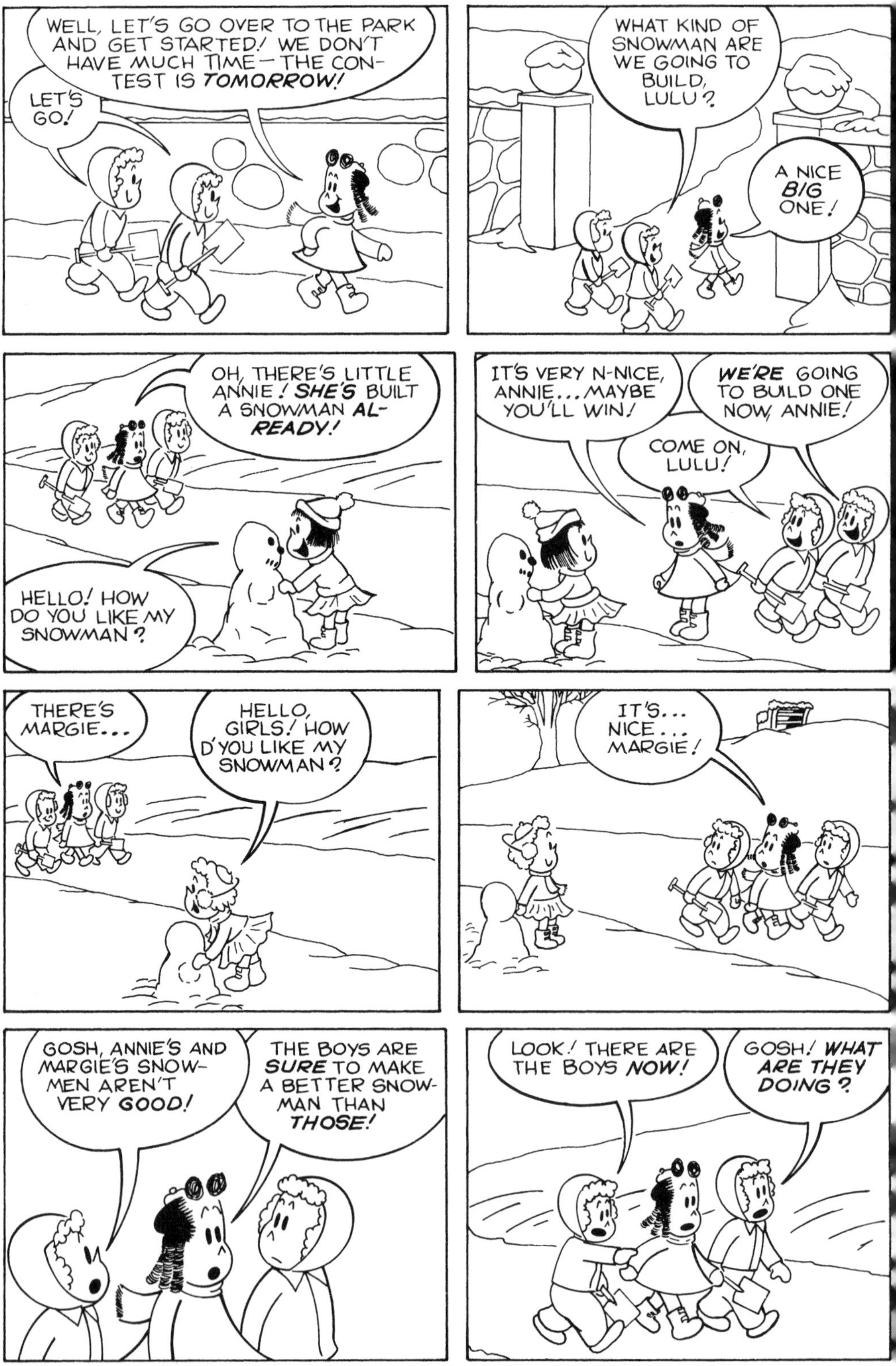
WELL, LET'S GO OVER TO THE PARK AND GET STARTED! WE DON'T HAVE MUCH TIME—THE CONTEST IS TOMORROW!
LET'S GO!
WHAT KIND OF SNOWMAN ARE WE GOING TO BUILD, LULU?
A NICE BIG ONE!
OH, THERE'S LITTLE ANNIE! SHE'S BUILT A SNOWMAN ALREADY!
HELLO! HOW DO YOU LIKE MY SNOWMAN?
IT'S VERY N-NICE, ANNIE... MAYBE YOU'LL WIN!
WE'RE GOING TO BUILD ONE NOW, ANNIE!
COME ON, LULU!
THERE'S MARGIE...
HELLO, GIRLS! HOW D'YOU LIKE MY SNOWMAN?
IT'S... NICE... MARGIE!
GOSH, ANNIE'S AND MARGIE'S SNOWMEN AREN'T VERY GOOD!
THE BOYS ARE SURE TO MAKE A BETTER SNOWMAN THAN THOSE!
LOOK! THERE ARE THE BOYS NOW!
GOSH! WHAT ARE THEY DOING?

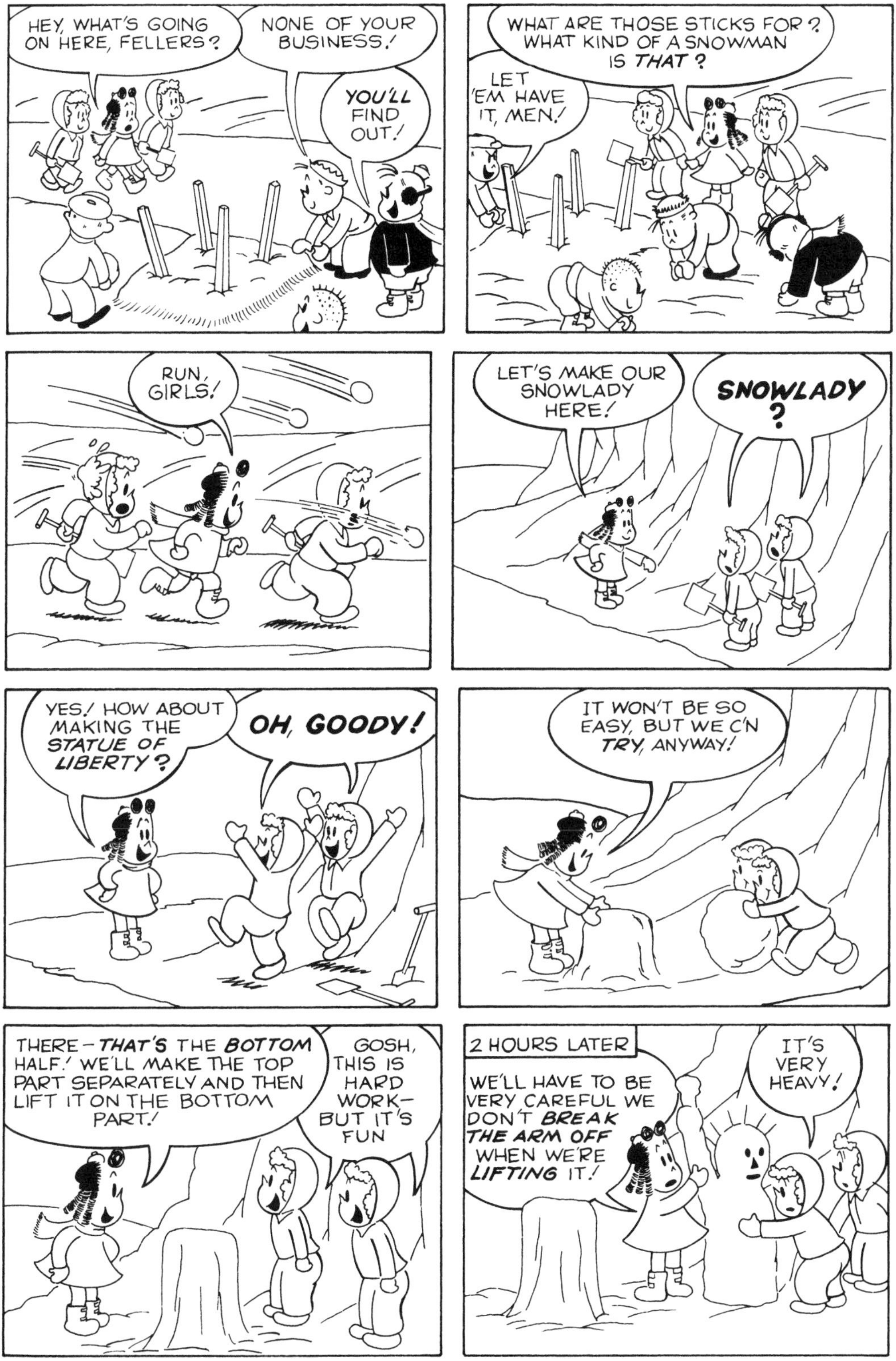
HEY, WHAT'S GOING ON HERE, FELLERS?
NONE OF YOUR BUSINESS!
YOU'LL FIND OUT!
WHAT ARE THOSE STICKS FOR? WHAT KIND OF A SNOWMAN IS THAT?
LET 'EM HAVE IT, MEN!
RUN, GIRLS!
LET'S MAKE OUR SNOWLADY HERE!
SNOWLADY?
YES! HOW ABOUT MAKING THE STATUE OF LIBERTY?
OH, GOODY!
IT WON'T BE SO EASY, BUT WE C'N TRY, ANYWAY!
THERE—THAT'S THE BOTTOM HALF! WE'LL MAKE THE TOP PART SEPARATELY AND THEN LIFT IT ON THE BOTTOM PART!
GOSH, THIS IS HARD WORK—BUT IT'S FUN
2 HOURS LATER
WE'LL HAVE TO BE VERY CAREFUL WE DON'T BREAK THE ARM OFF WHEN WE'RE LIFTING IT!
IT'S VERY HEAVY!

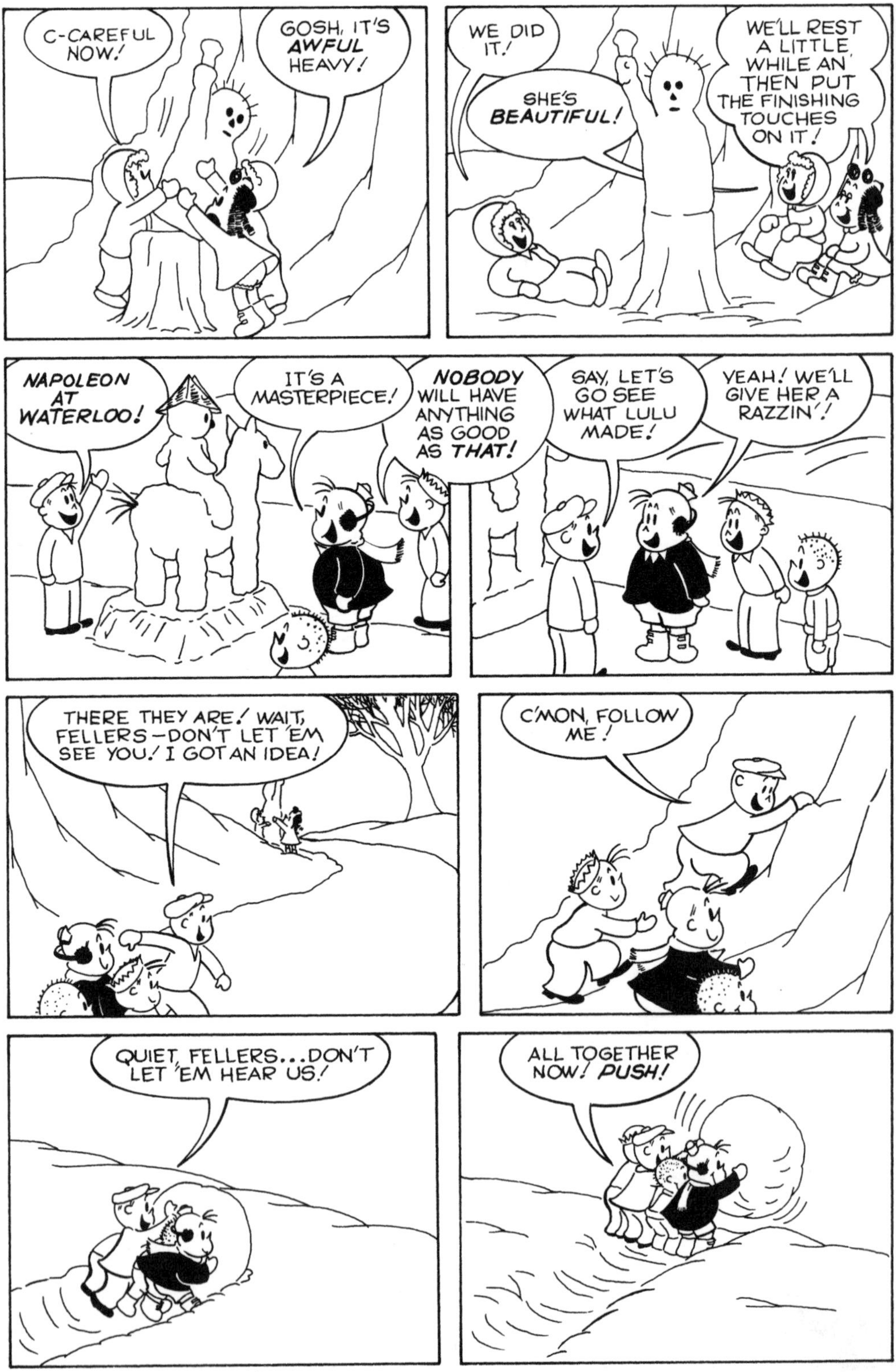

C-CAREFUL NOW!
GOSH, IT'S AWFUL HEAVY!
WE DID IT!
SHE'S BEAUTIFUL!
WE'LL REST A LITTLE WHILE AN' THEN PUT THE FINISHING TOUCHES ON IT!
NAPOLEON AT WATERLOO!
IT'S A MASTERPIECE!
NOBODY WILL HAVE ANYTHING AS GOOD AS THAT!
SAY, LET'S GO SEE WHAT LULU MADE!
YEAH! WE'LL GIVE HER A RAZZIN'!
THERE THEY ARE! WAIT, FELLERS—DON'T LET 'EM SEE YOU! I GOT AN IDEA!
C'MON, FOLLOW ME!
QUIET, FELLERS...DON'T LET 'EM HEAR US!
ALL TOGETHER NOW! PUSH!

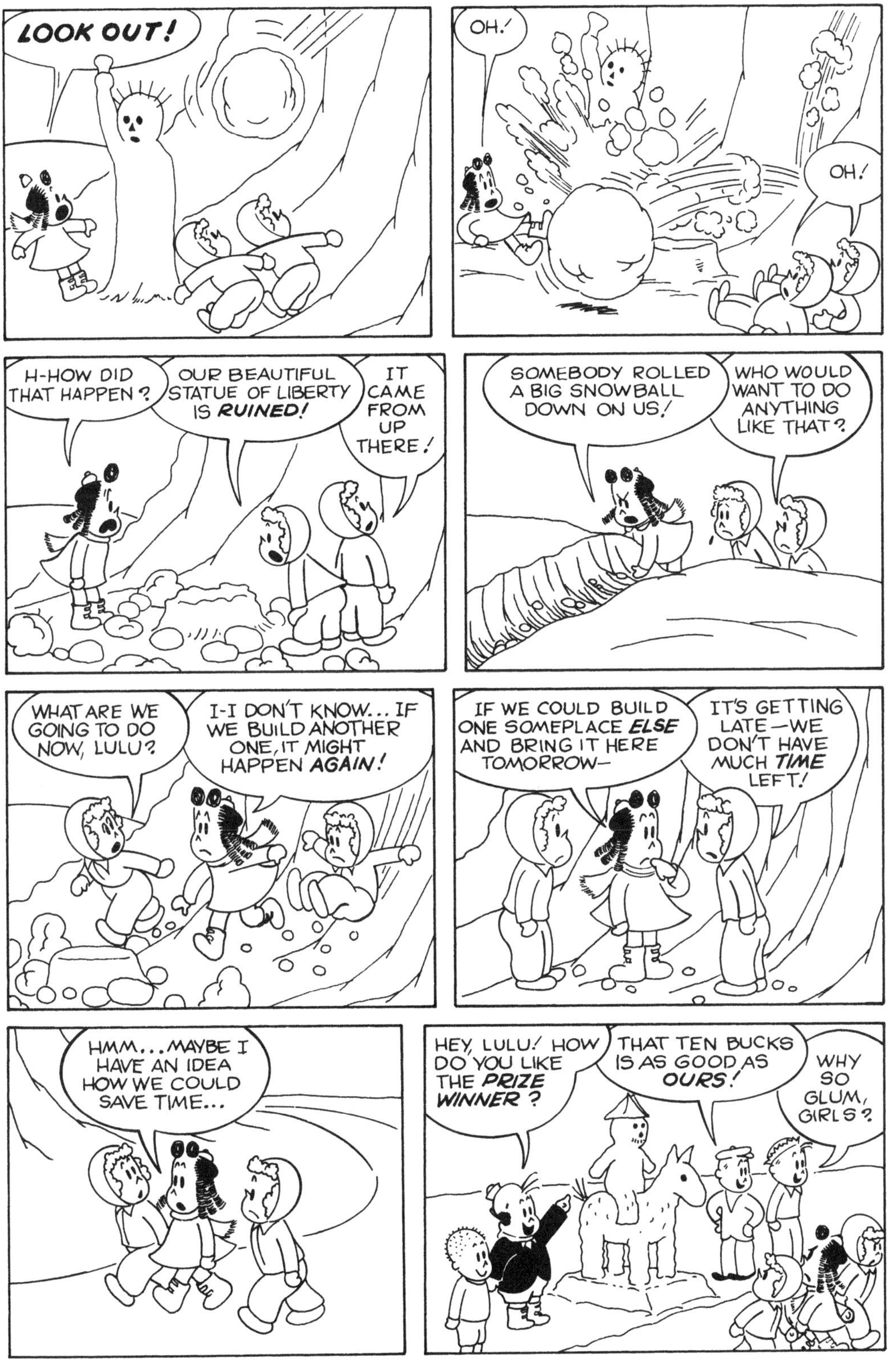
LOOK OUT!
OH!
OH!
H-HOW DID THAT HAPPEN?
OUR BEAUTIFUL STATUE OF LIBERTY IS RUINED!
IT CAME FROM UP THERE!
SOMEBODY ROLLED A BIG SNOWBALL DOWN ON US!
WHO WOULD WANT TO DO ANYTHING LIKE THAT?
WHAT ARE WE GOING TO DO NOW, LULU?
I-I DON'T KNOW... IF WE BUILD ANOTHER ONE, IT MIGHT HAPPEN AGAIN!
IF WE COULD BUILD ONE SOMEPLACE ELSE AND BRING IT HERE TOMORROW—
IT'S GETTING LATE—WE DON'T HAVE MUCH TIME LEFT!
HMM...MAYBE I HAVE AN IDEA HOW WE COULD SAVE TIME...
HEY, LULU! HOW DO YOU LIKE THE PRIZE WINNER?
THAT TEN BUCKS IS AS GOOD AS OURS!
WHY SO GLUM, GIRLS?

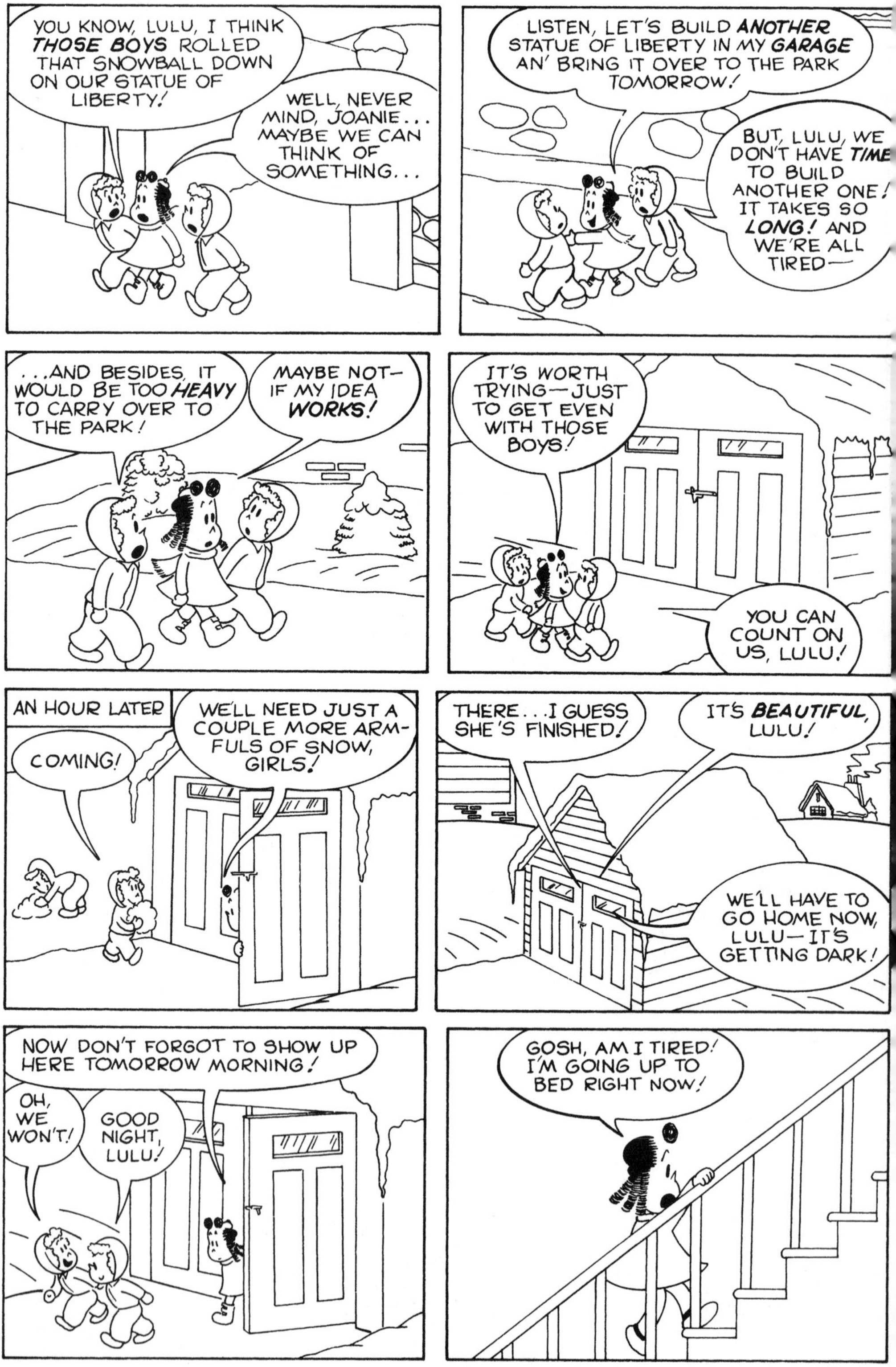
YOU KNOW, LULU, I THINK THOSE BOYS ROLLED THAT SNOWBALL DOWN ON OUR STATUE OF LIBERTY!
WELL, NEVER MIND, JOANIE... MAYBE WE CAN THINK OF SOMETHING...
LISTEN, LET'S BUILD ANOTHER STATUE OF LIBERTY IN MY GARAGE AN' BRING IT OVER TO THE PARK TOMORROW!
BUT, LULU, WE DON'T HAVE TIME TO BUILD ANOTHER ONE! IT TAKES SO LONG! AND WE'RE ALL TIRED—
...AND BESIDES, IT WOULD BE TOO HEAVY TO CARRY OVER TO THE PARK!
MAYBE NOT— IF MY IDEA WORKS!
IT'S WORTH TRYING—JUST TO GET EVEN WITH THOSE BOYS!
YOU CAN COUNT ON US, LULU!
AN HOUR LATER
COMING!
WE'LL NEED JUST A COUPLE MORE ARM-FULS OF SNOW, GIRLS!
THERE...I GUESS SHE'S FINISHED!
IT'S BEAUTIFUL, LULU!
WE'LL HAVE TO GO HOME NOW, LULU—IT'S GETTING DARK!
NOW DON'T FORGOT TO SHOW UP HERE TOMORROW MORNING!
OH, WE WON'T!
GOOD NIGHT, LULU!
GOSH, AM I TIRED! I'M GOING UP TO BED RIGHT NOW!

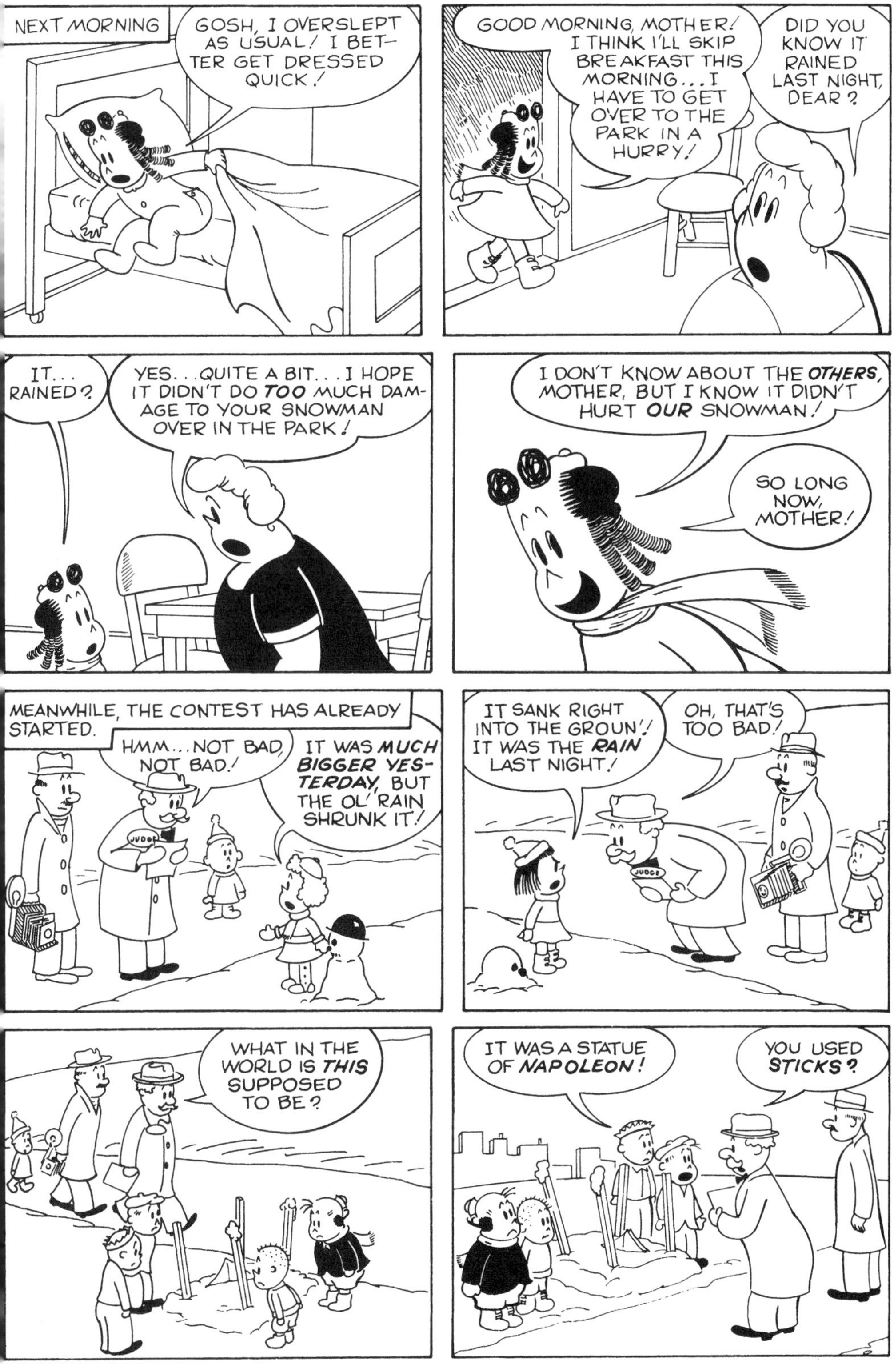
NEXT MORNING
GOSH, I OVERSLEPT AS USUAL! I BETTER GET DRESSED QUICK!
GOOD MORNING, MOTHER! I THINK I'LL SKIP BREAKFAST THIS MORNING... I HAVE TO GET OVER TO THE PARK IN A HURRY!
DID YOU KNOW IT RAINED LAST NIGHT, DEAR?
IT... RAINED?
YES... QUITE A BIT... I HOPE IT DIDN'T DO TOO MUCH DAMAGE TO YOUR SNOWMAN OVER IN THE PARK!
I DON'T KNOW ABOUT THE OTHERS, MOTHER, BUT I KNOW IT DIDN'T HURT OUR SNOWMAN!
SO LONG NOW, MOTHER!
MEANWHILE, THE CONTEST HAS ALREADY STARTED.
HMM... NOT BAD, NOT BAD!
IT WAS MUCH BIGGER YESTERDAY, BUT THE OL' RAIN SHRUNK IT!
JUDGE
IT SANK RIGHT INTO THE GROUN'! IT WAS THE RAIN LAST NIGHT!
OH, THAT'S TOO BAD!
JUDGE
WHAT IN THE WORLD IS THIS SUPPOSED TO BE?
IT WAS A STATUE OF NAPOLEON!
YOU USED STICKS?

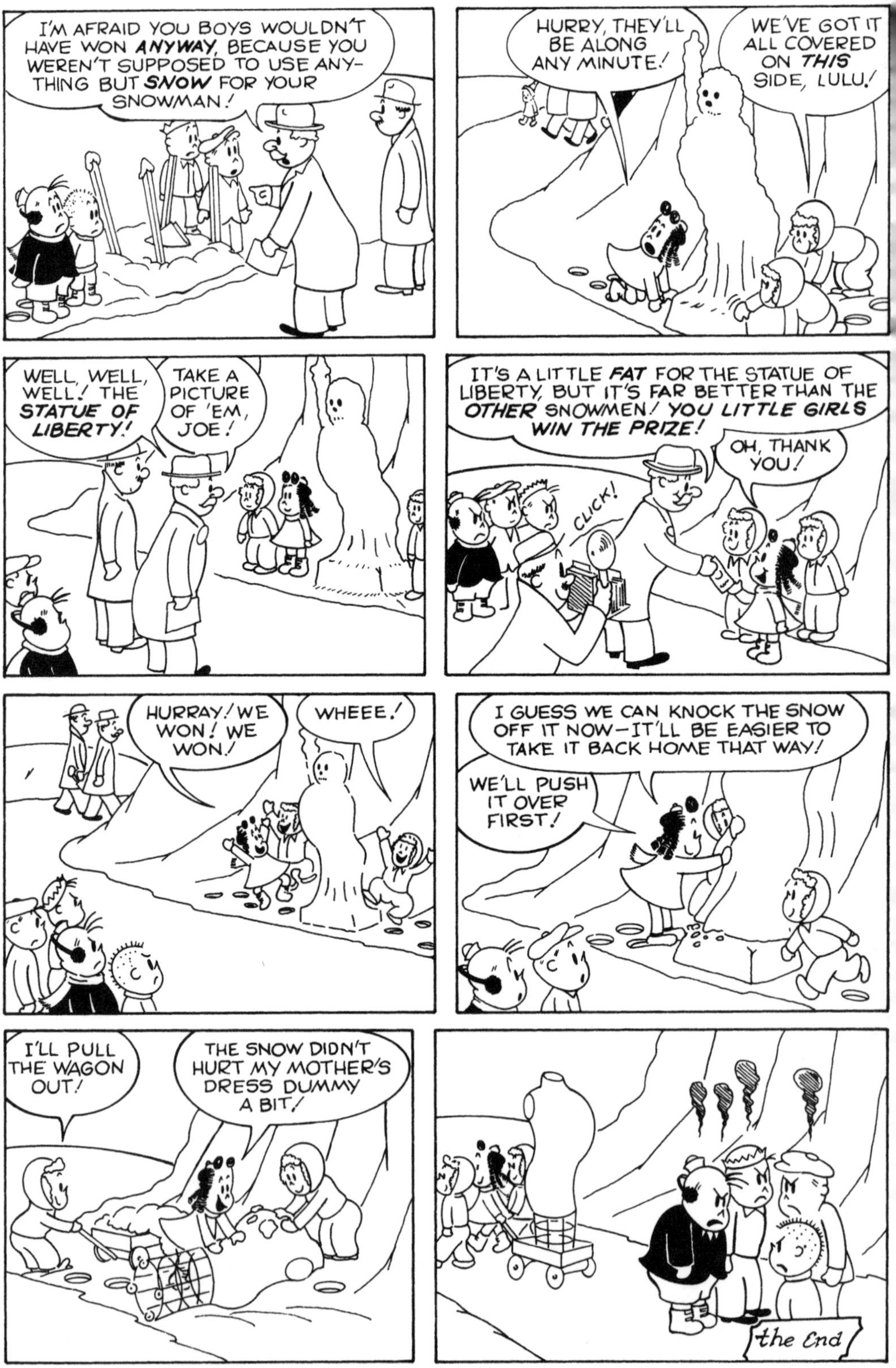
I'M AFRAID YOU BOYS WOULDN'T HAVE WON ANYWAY, BECAUSE YOU WEREN'T SUPPOSED TO USE ANYTHING BUT SNOW FOR YOUR SNOWMAN!
HURRY, THEY'LL BE ALONG ANY MINUTE!
WE'VE GOT IT ALL COVERED ON THIS SIDE, LULU!
WELL, WELL, WELL! THE STATUE OF LIBERTY!
TAKE A PICTURE OF 'EM, JOE!
IT'S A LITTLE FAT FOR THE STATUE OF LIBERTY, BUT IT'S FAR BETTER THAN THE OTHER SNOWMEN! YOU LITTLE GIRLS WIN THE PRIZE!
OH, THANK YOU!
CLICK!
HURRAY! WE WON! WE WON!
WHEEE!
I GUESS WE CAN KNOCK THE SNOW OFF IT NOW—IT'LL BE EASIER TO TAKE IT BACK HOME THAT WAY!
WE'LL PUSH IT OVER FIRST!
I'LL PULL THE WAGON OUT!
THE SNOW DIDN'T HURT MY MOTHER'S DRESS DUMMY A BIT!
the End

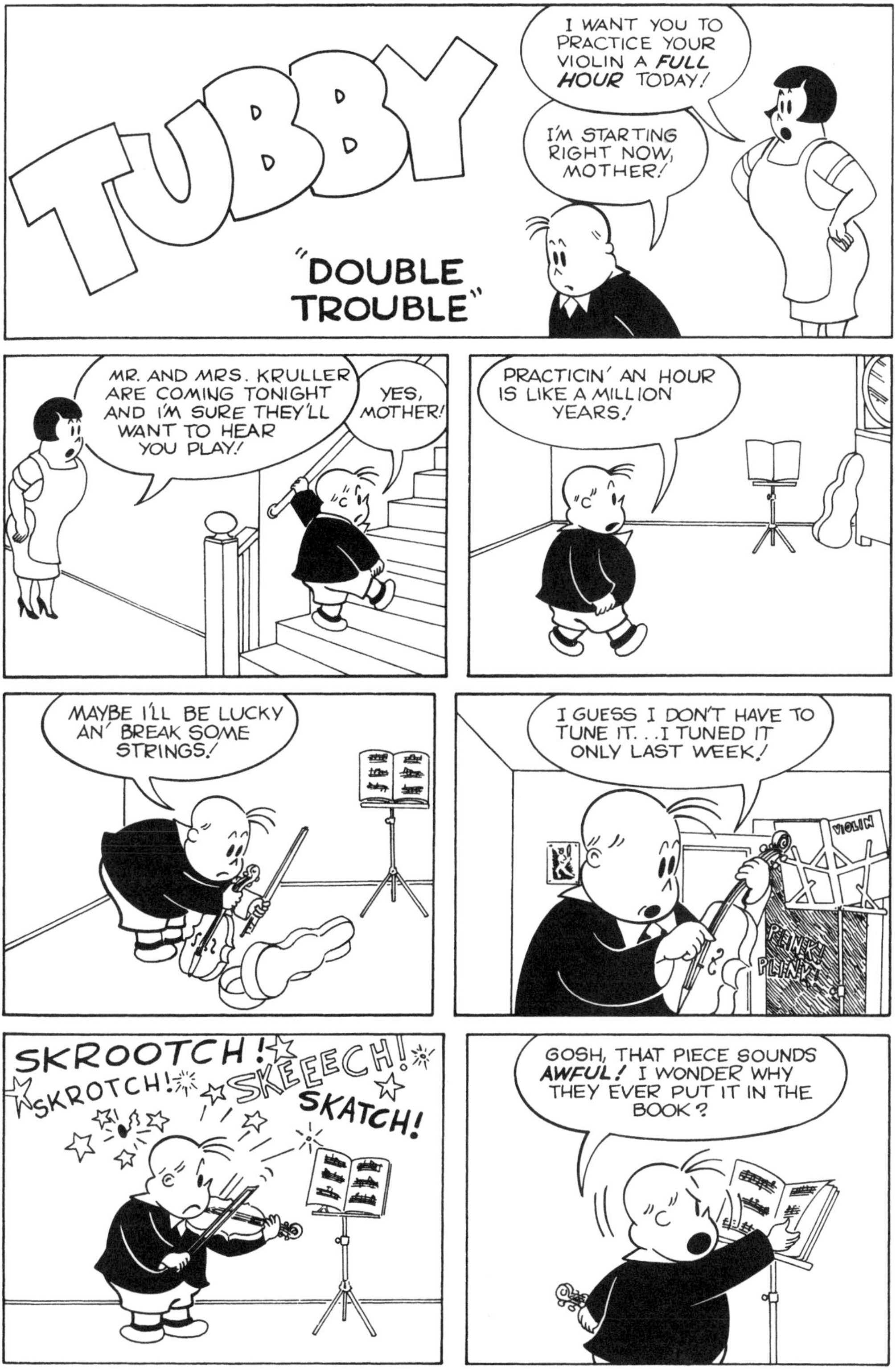
TUBBY
"DOUBLE TROUBLE"
I WANT YOU TO PRACTICE YOUR VIOLIN A **FULL HOUR** TODAY!
I'M STARTING RIGHT NOW, MOTHER!
MR. AND MRS. KRULLER ARE COMING TONIGHT AND I'M SURE THEY'LL WANT TO HEAR YOU PLAY!
YES, MOTHER!
PRACTICIN' AN HOUR IS LIKE A MILLION YEARS!
MAYBE I'LL BE LUCKY AN' BREAK SOME STRINGS!
I GUESS I DON'T HAVE TO TUNE IT. . .I TUNED IT ONLY LAST WEEK!
VIOLIN
PLINK! PLINK!
SKROOTCH!
SKROTCH!
SKEEEECH!
SKATCH!
GOSH, THAT PIECE SOUNDS **AWFUL!** I WONDER WHY THEY EVER PUT IT IN THE BOOK?

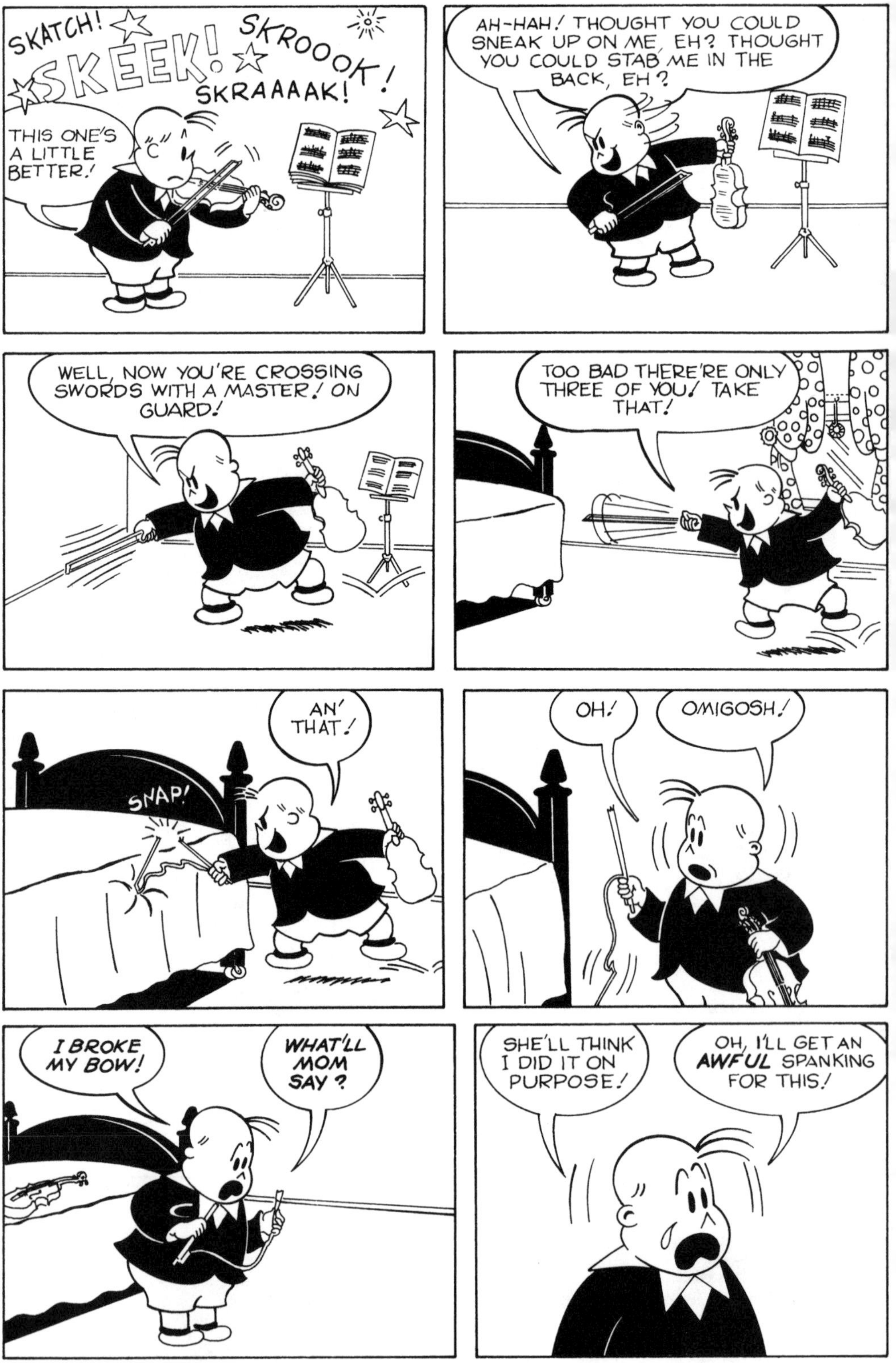
SKATCH!
SKEEK!
SKROOOOK!
SKRAAAAK!
THIS ONE'S A LITTLE BETTER!
AH-HAH! THOUGHT YOU COULD SNEAK UP ON ME, EH? THOUGHT YOU COULD STAB ME IN THE BACK, EH?
WELL, NOW YOU'RE CROSSING SWORDS WITH A MASTER! ON GUARD!
TOO BAD THERE'RE ONLY THREE OF YOU! TAKE THAT!
SNAP!
AN' THAT!
OH!
OMIGOSH!
I BROKE MY BOW!
WHAT'LL MOM SAY?
SHE'LL THINK I DID IT ON PURPOSE!
OH, I'LL GET AN AWFUL SPANKING FOR THIS!

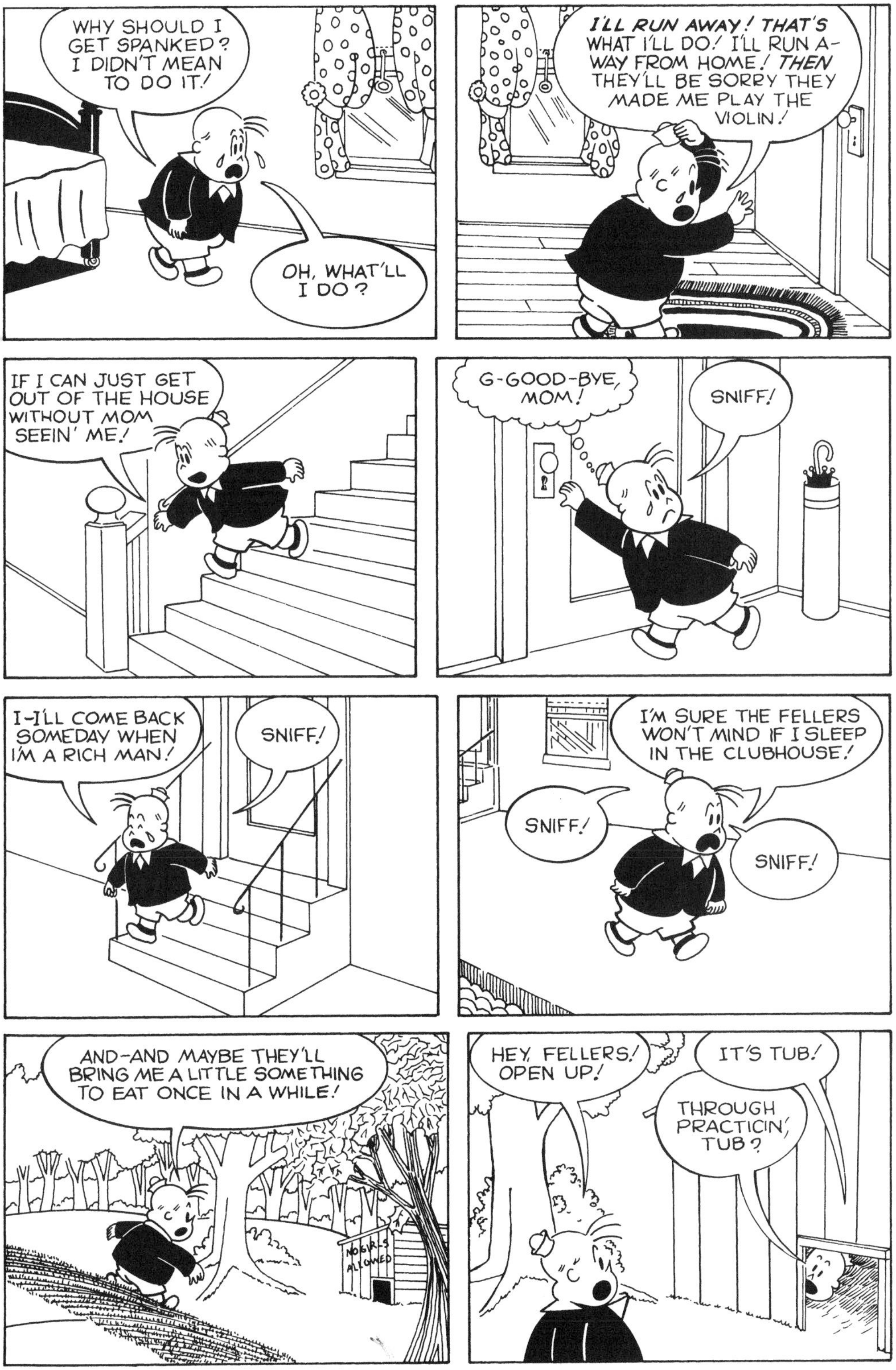
WHY SHOULD I GET SPANKED? I DIDN'T MEAN TO DO IT!
OH, WHAT'LL I DO?
I'LL RUN AWAY! THAT'S WHAT I'LL DO! I'LL RUN AWAY FROM HOME! THEN THEY'LL BE SORRY THEY MADE ME PLAY THE VIOLIN!
IF I CAN JUST GET OUT OF THE HOUSE WITHOUT MOM SEEIN' ME!
G-GOOD-BYE, MOM!
SNIFF!
I-I'LL COME BACK SOMEDAY WHEN I'M A RICH MAN!
SNIFF!
I'M SURE THE FELLERS WON'T MIND IF I SLEEP IN THE CLUBHOUSE!
SNIFF!
SNIFF!
AND-AND MAYBE THEY'LL BRING ME A LITTLE SOMETHING TO EAT ONCE IN A WHILE!
NO GIRLS ALLOWED
HEY, FELLERS! OPEN UP!
IT'S TUB!
THROUGH PRACTICIN', TUB?

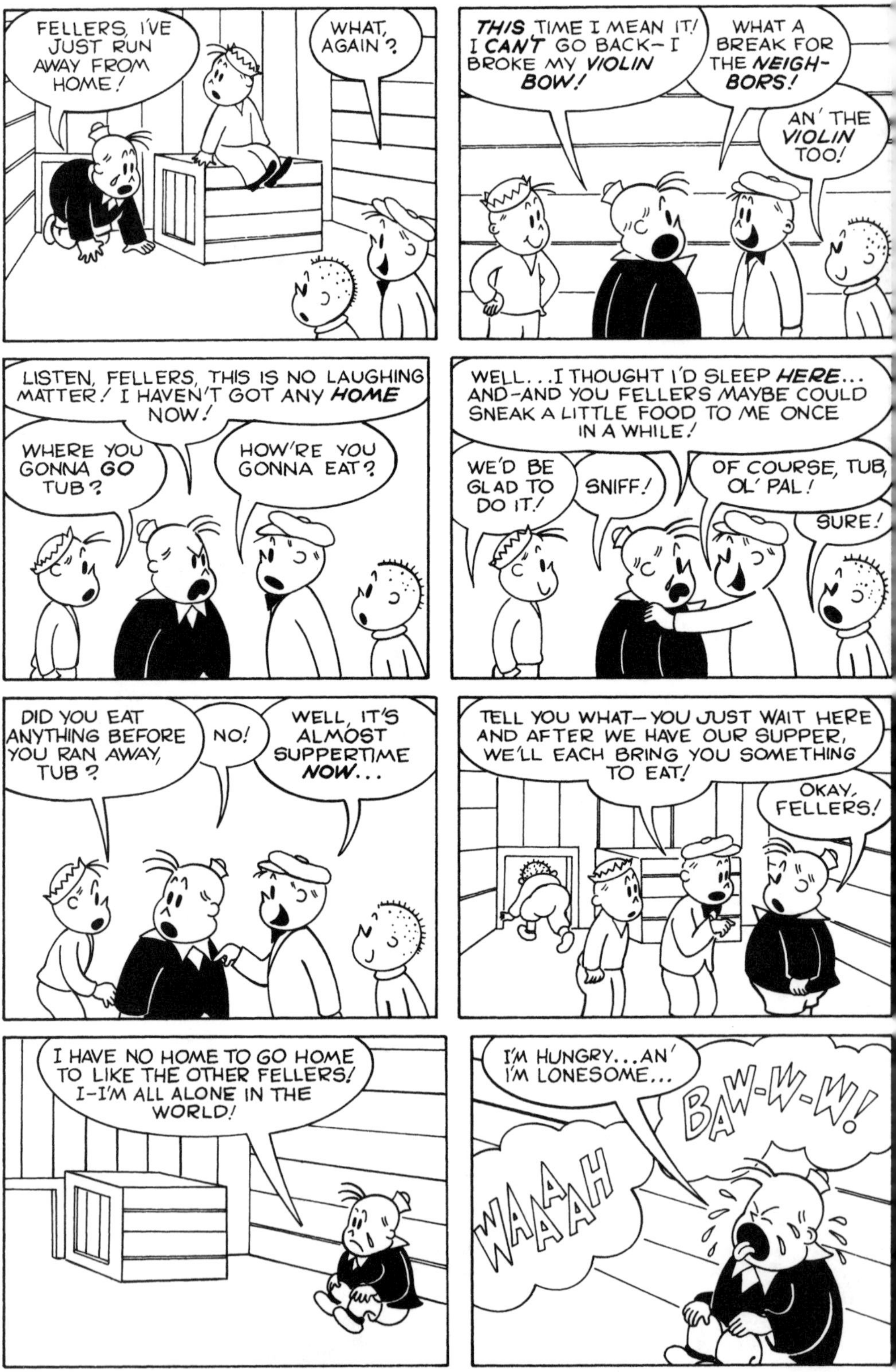
FELLERS, I'VE JUST RUN AWAY FROM HOME!
WHAT, AGAIN?
THIS TIME I MEAN IT! I CAN'T GO BACK—I BROKE MY VIOLIN BOW!
WHAT A BREAK FOR THE NEIGH-BORS!
AN' THE VIOLIN TOO!
LISTEN, FELLERS, THIS IS NO LAUGHING MATTER! I HAVEN'T GOT ANY HOME NOW!
WHERE YOU GONNA GO TUB?
HOW'RE YOU GONNA EAT?
WELL...I THOUGHT I'D SLEEP HERE... AND-AND YOU FELLERS MAYBE COULD SNEAK A LITTLE FOOD TO ME ONCE IN A WHILE!
WE'D BE GLAD TO DO IT!
SNIFF!
OF COURSE, TUB, OL' PAL!
SURE!
DID YOU EAT ANYTHING BEFORE YOU RAN AWAY, TUB?
NO!
WELL, IT'S ALMOST SUPPERTIME NOW...
TELL YOU WHAT—YOU JUST WAIT HERE AND AFTER WE HAVE OUR SUPPER, WE'LL EACH BRING YOU SOMETHING TO EAT!
OKAY, FELLERS!
I HAVE NO HOME TO GO HOME TO LIKE THE OTHER FELLERS! I-I'M ALL ALONE IN THE WORLD!
I'M HUNGRY...AN' I'M LONESOME...
BAW-W-W!
WAAAAH

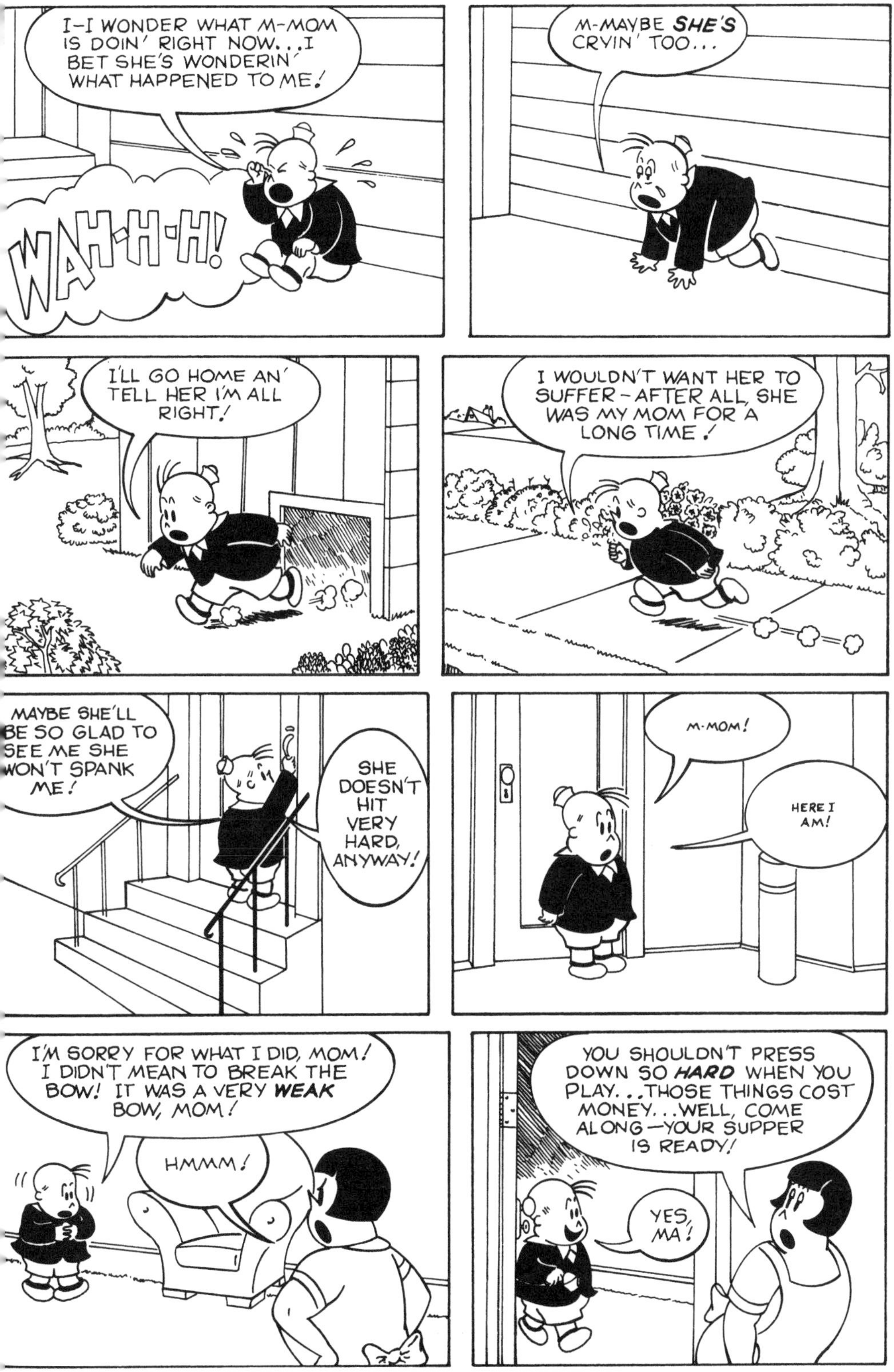
I-I WONDER WHAT M-MOM IS DOIN' RIGHT NOW...I BET SHE'S WONDERIN' WHAT HAPPENED TO ME!
WAH-H-H!
M-MAYBE **SHE'S** CRYIN' TOO...
I'LL GO HOME AN' TELL HER I'M ALL RIGHT!
I WOULDN'T WANT HER TO SUFFER—AFTER ALL, SHE WAS MY MOM FOR A LONG TIME!
MAYBE SHE'LL BE SO GLAD TO SEE ME SHE WON'T SPANK ME!
SHE DOESN'T HIT VERY HARD, ANYWAY!
M-MOM!
HERE I AM!
I'M SORRY FOR WHAT I DID, MOM! I DIDN'T MEAN TO BREAK THE BOW! IT WAS A VERY **WEAK** BOW, MOM!
HMMM!
YOU SHOULDN'T PRESS DOWN SO **HARD** WHEN YOU PLAY...THOSE THINGS COST MONEY...WELL, COME ALONG—YOUR SUPPER IS READY!
YES, MA!

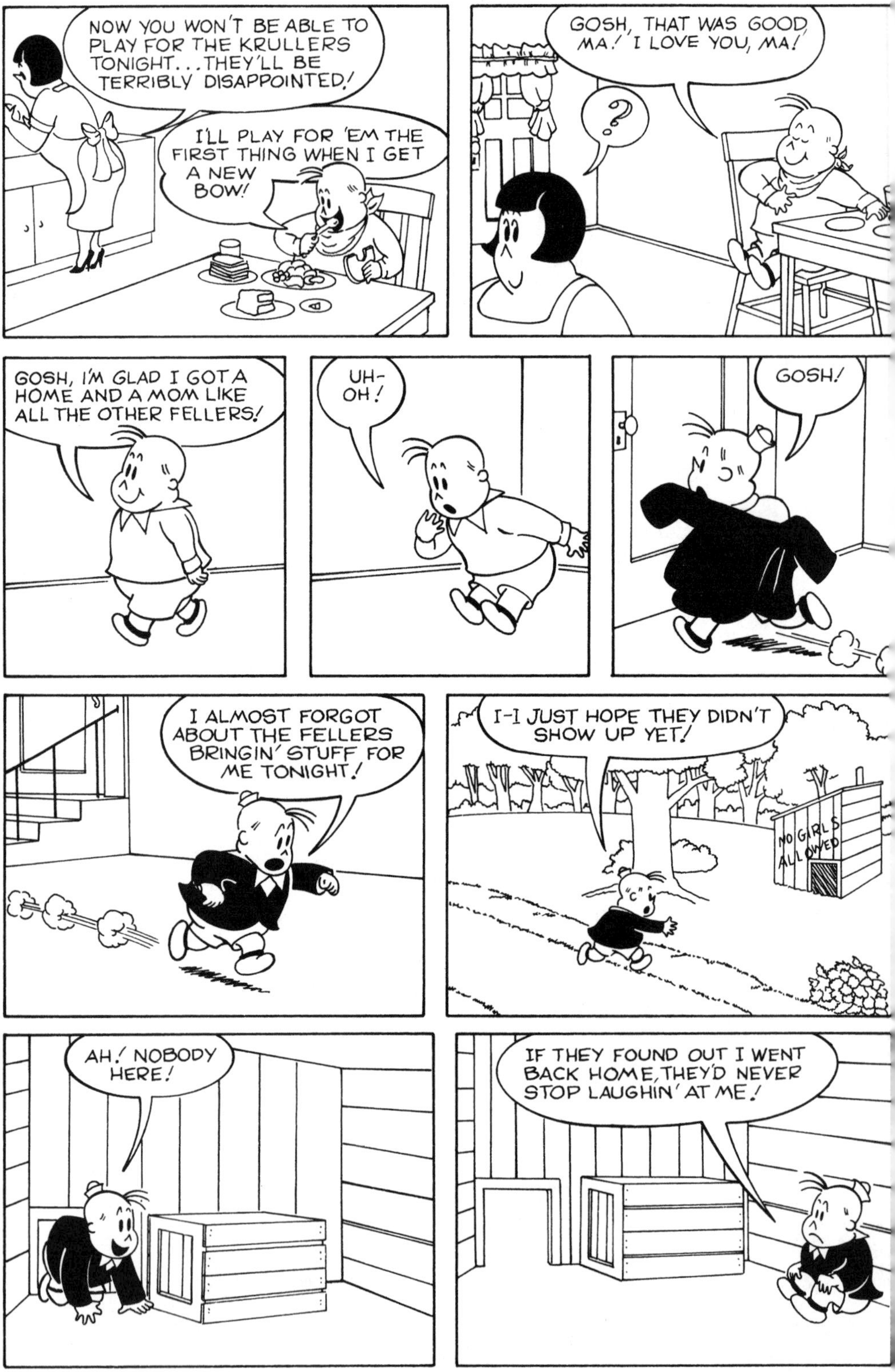
NOW YOU WON'T BE ABLE TO PLAY FOR THE KRULLERS TONIGHT... THEY'LL BE TERRIBLY DISAPPOINTED!
I'LL PLAY FOR 'EM THE FIRST THING WHEN I GET A NEW BOW!
GOSH, THAT WAS GOOD MA! I LOVE YOU, MA!
?
GOSH, I'M GLAD I GOT A HOME AND A MOM LIKE ALL THE OTHER FELLERS!
UH-OH!
GOSH!
I ALMOST FORGOT ABOUT THE FELLERS BRINGIN' STUFF FOR ME TONIGHT!
I-I JUST HOPE THEY DIDN'T SHOW UP YET!
NO GIRLS ALLOWED
AH! NOBODY HERE!
IF THEY FOUND OUT I WENT BACK HOME, THEY'D NEVER STOP LAUGHIN' AT ME!

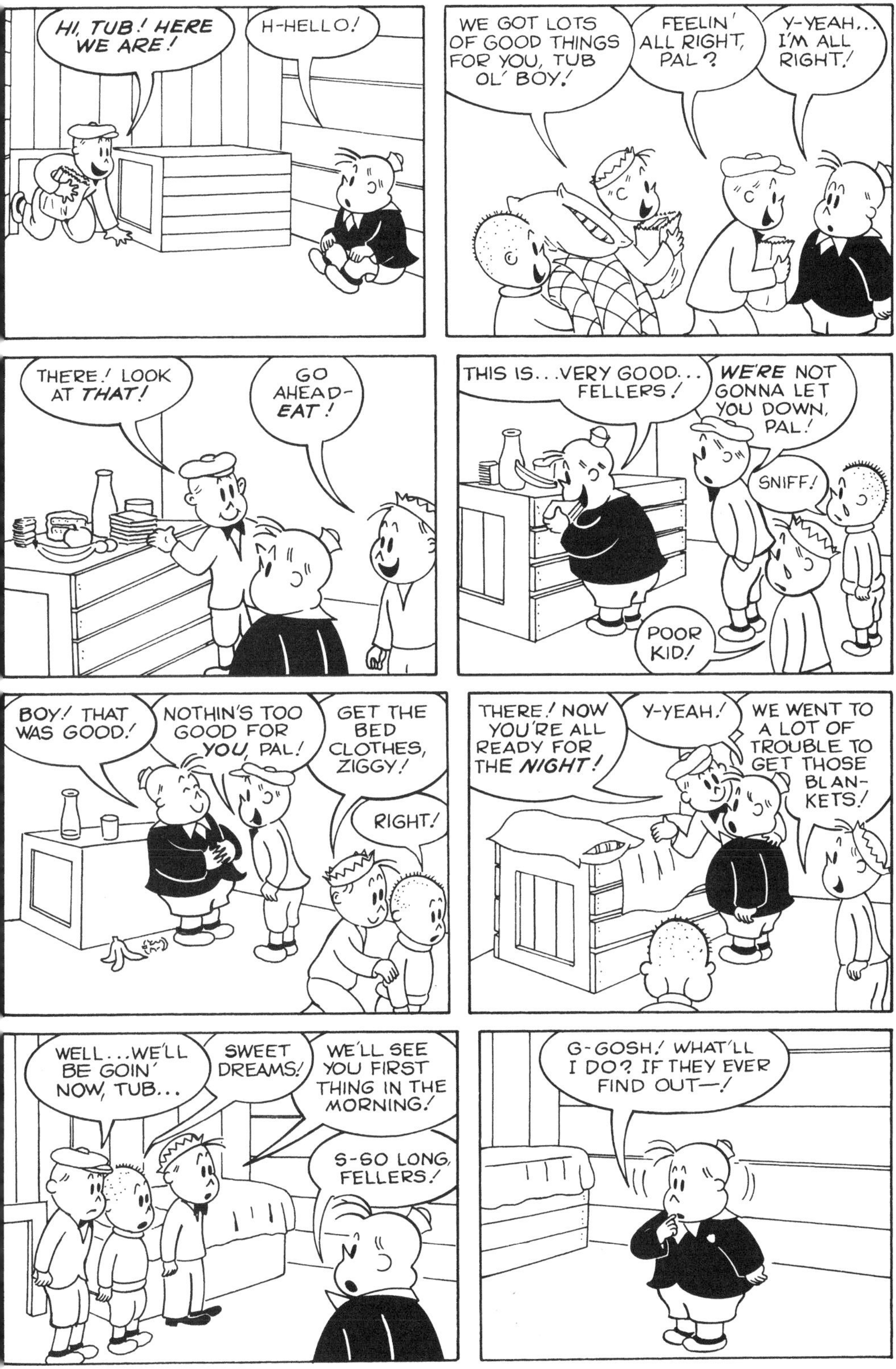
HI, TUB! HERE WE ARE!
H-HELLO!
WE GOT LOTS OF GOOD THINGS FOR YOU, TUB OL' BOY!
FEELIN' ALL RIGHT, PAL?
Y-YEAH... I'M ALL RIGHT!
THERE! LOOK AT THAT!
GO AHEAD- EAT!
THIS IS...VERY GOOD... FELLERS!
WE'RE NOT GONNA LET YOU DOWN, PAL!
SNIFF!
POOR KID!
BOY! THAT WAS GOOD!
NOTHIN'S TOO GOOD FOR YOU, PAL!
GET THE BED CLOTHES, ZIGGY!
RIGHT!
THERE! NOW YOU'RE ALL READY FOR THE NIGHT!
Y-YEAH!
WE WENT TO A LOT OF TROUBLE TO GET THOSE BLAN-KETS!
WELL...WE'LL BE GOIN' NOW, TUB...
SWEET DREAMS!
WE'LL SEE YOU FIRST THING IN THE MORNING!
S-SO LONG, FELLERS!
G-GOSH! WHAT'LL I DO? IF THEY EVER FIND OUT—!

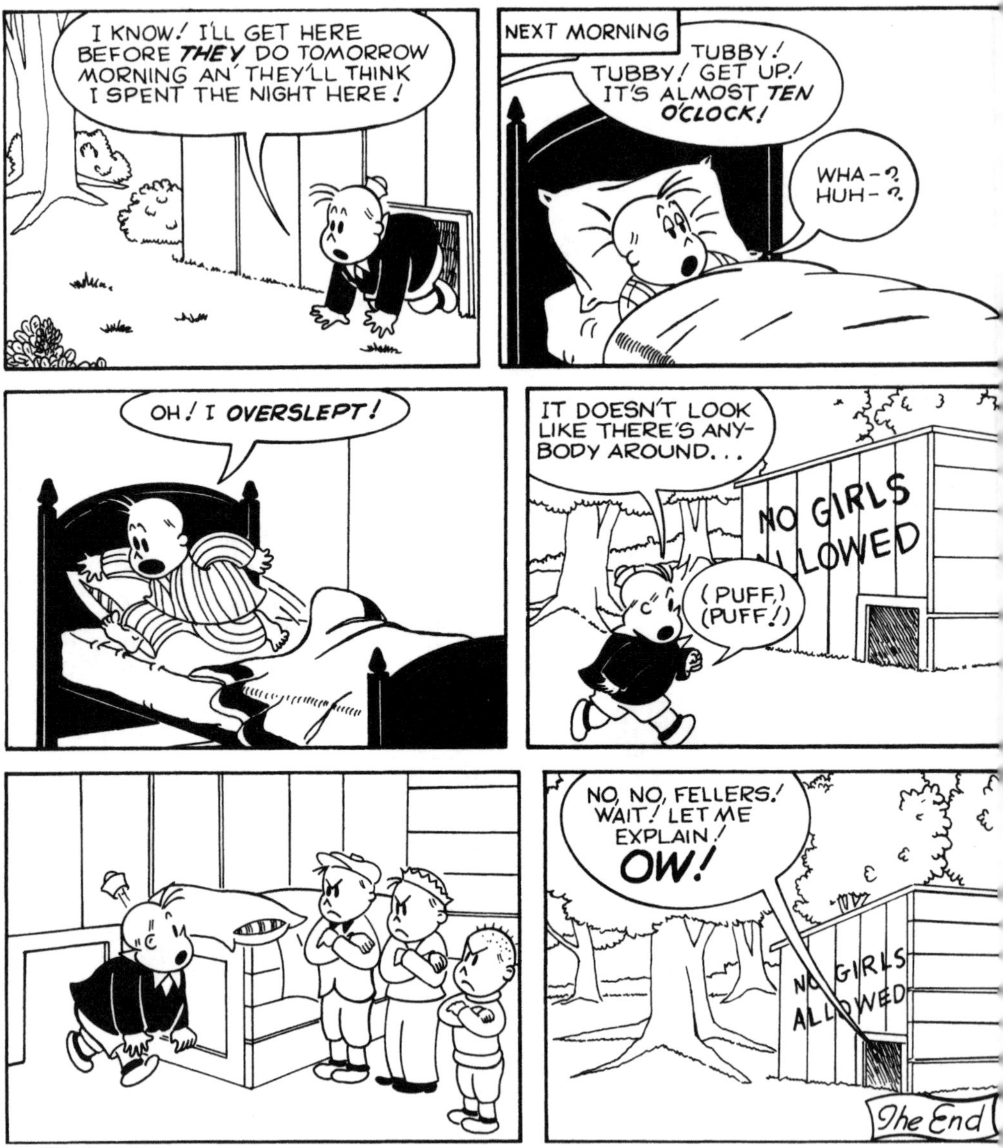
I KNOW! I'LL GET HERE BEFORE THEY DO TOMORROW MORNING AN' THEY'LL THINK I SPENT THE NIGHT HERE!
NEXT MORNING
TUBBY! TUBBY! GET UP! IT'S ALMOST TEN O'CLOCK!
WHA-? HUH-?
OH! I OVERSLEPT!
IT DOESN'T LOOK LIKE THERE'S ANY-BODY AROUND...
NO GIRLS ALLOWED
(PUFF!) (PUFF!)
NO, NO, FELLERS! WAIT! LET ME EXPLAIN! OW!
NO GIRLS ALLOWED
The End

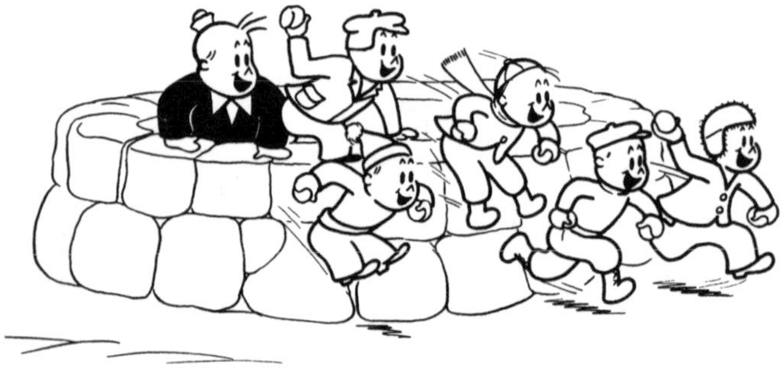

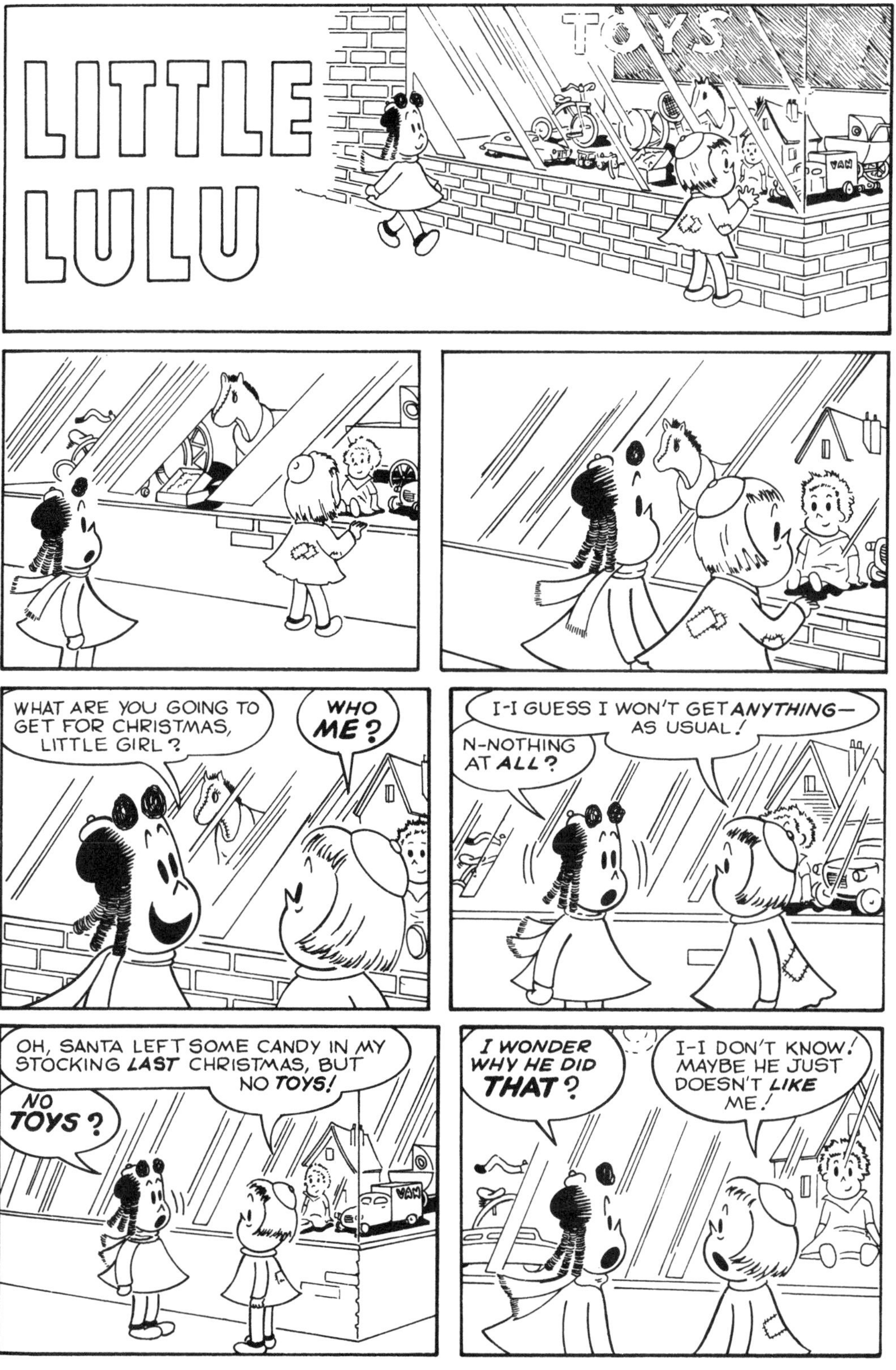
LITTLE LULU
TOYS
VAN
WHAT ARE YOU GOING TO GET FOR CHRISTMAS, LITTLE GIRL ?
WHO ME ?
I-I GUESS I WON'T GET ANYTHING— AS USUAL!
N-NOTHING AT ALL ?
OH, SANTA LEFT SOME CANDY IN MY STOCKING LAST CHRISTMAS, BUT NO TOYS!
NO TOYS ?
VAN
I WONDER WHY HE DID THAT ?
I-I DON'T KNOW! MAYBE HE JUST DOESN'T LIKE ME!

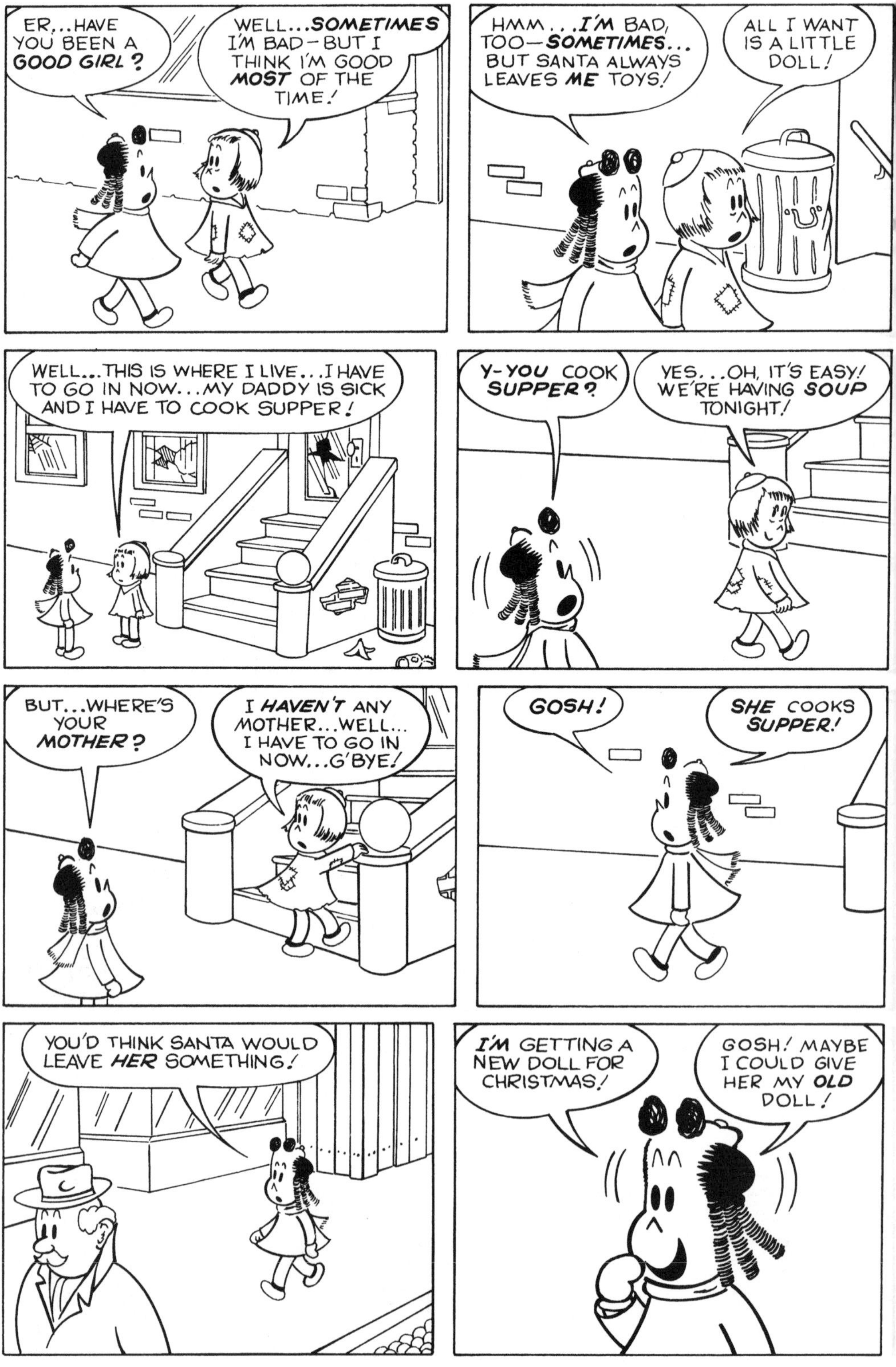
ER,..HAVE YOU BEEN A GOOD GIRL?
WELL...SOMETIMES I'M BAD-BUT I THINK I'M GOOD MOST OF THE TIME!
HMM...I'M BAD, TOO-SOMETIMES... BUT SANTA ALWAYS LEAVES ME TOYS!
ALL I WANT IS A LITTLE DOLL!
WELL...THIS IS WHERE I LIVE...I HAVE TO GO IN NOW...MY DADDY IS SICK AND I HAVE TO COOK SUPPER!
Y-YOU COOK SUPPER?
YES...OH, IT'S EASY! WE'RE HAVING SOUP TONIGHT!
BUT...WHERE'S YOUR MOTHER?
I HAVEN'T ANY MOTHER...WELL... I HAVE TO GO IN NOW...G'BYE!
GOSH!
SHE COOKS SUPPER!
YOU'D THINK SANTA WOULD LEAVE HER SOMETHING!
I'M GETTING A NEW DOLL FOR CHRISTMAS!
GOSH! MAYBE I COULD GIVE HER MY OLD DOLL!

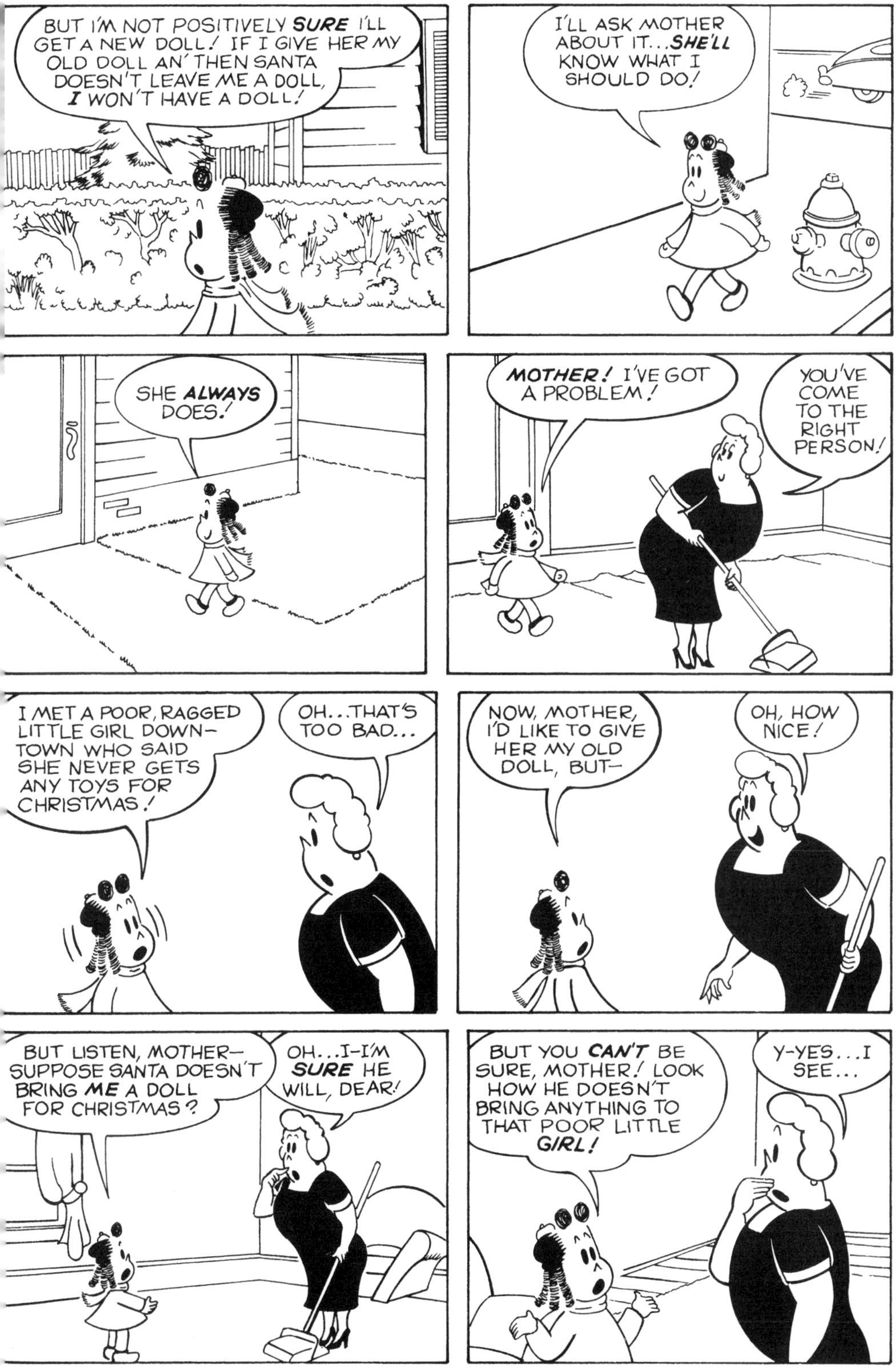
BUT I'M NOT POSITIVELY SURE I'LL GET A NEW DOLL! IF I GIVE HER MY OLD DOLL AN' THEN SANTA DOESN'T LEAVE ME A DOLL, I WON'T HAVE A DOLL!
I'LL ASK MOTHER ABOUT IT... SHE'LL KNOW WHAT I SHOULD DO!
SHE ALWAYS DOES!
MOTHER! I'VE GOT A PROBLEM!
YOU'VE COME TO THE RIGHT PERSON!
I MET A POOR, RAGGED LITTLE GIRL DOWN-TOWN WHO SAID SHE NEVER GETS ANY TOYS FOR CHRISTMAS!
OH... THAT'S TOO BAD...
NOW, MOTHER, I'D LIKE TO GIVE HER MY OLD DOLL, BUT–
OH, HOW NICE!
BUT LISTEN, MOTHER– SUPPOSE SANTA DOESN'T BRING ME A DOLL FOR CHRISTMAS?
OH... I-I'M SURE HE WILL, DEAR!
BUT YOU CAN'T BE SURE, MOTHER! LOOK HOW HE DOESN'T BRING ANYTHING TO THAT POOR LITTLE GIRL!
Y-YES... I SEE...

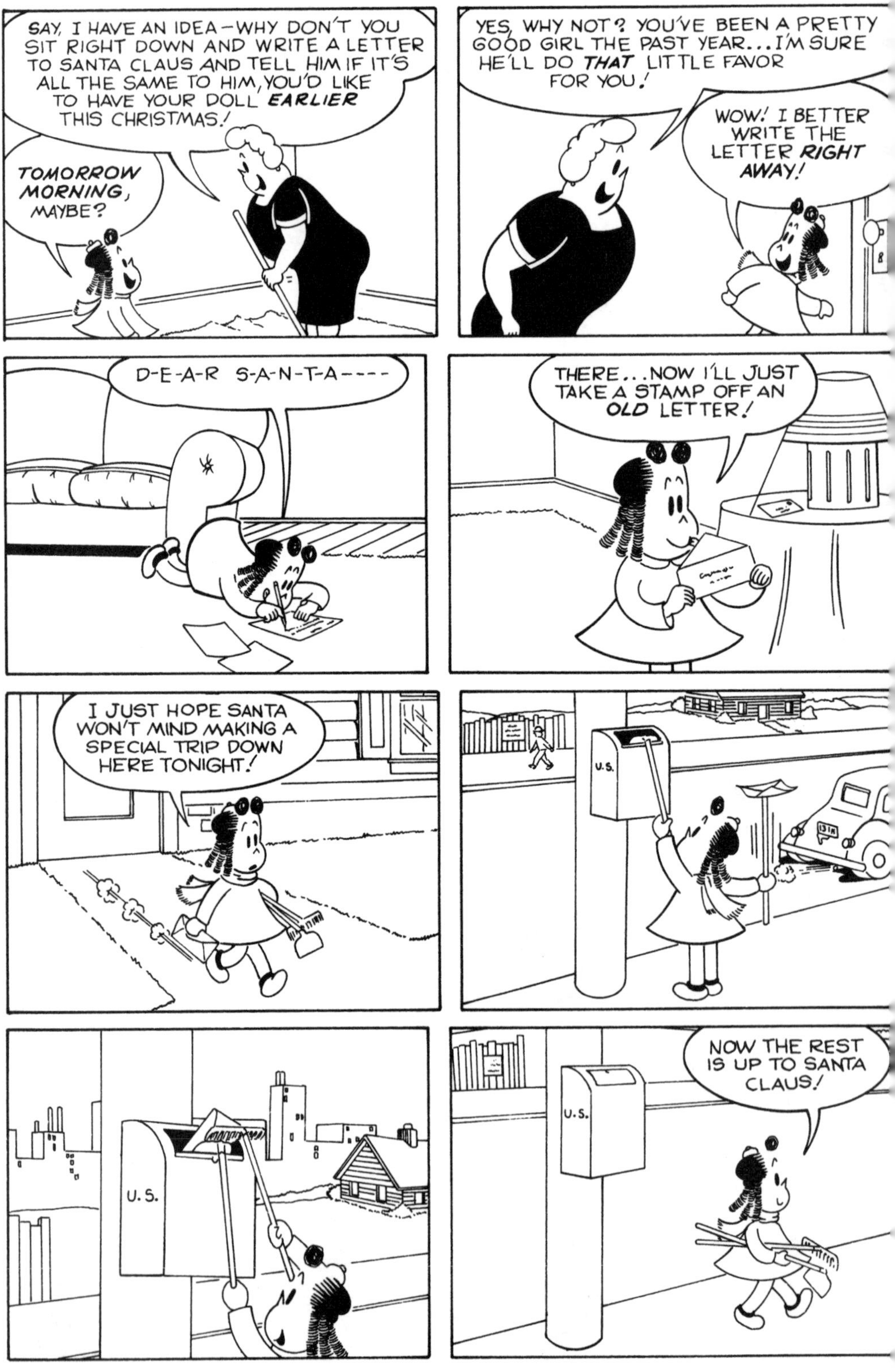
SAY, I HAVE AN IDEA—WHY DON'T YOU SIT RIGHT DOWN AND WRITE A LETTER TO SANTA CLAUS AND TELL HIM IF IT'S ALL THE SAME TO HIM, YOU'D LIKE TO HAVE YOUR DOLL EARLIER THIS CHRISTMAS!
TOMORROW MORNING, MAYBE?
YES, WHY NOT? YOU'VE BEEN A PRETTY GOOD GIRL THE PAST YEAR...I'M SURE HE'LL DO THAT LITTLE FAVOR FOR YOU!
WOW! I BETTER WRITE THE LETTER RIGHT AWAY!
D-E-A-R S-A-N-T-A----
THERE...NOW I'LL JUST TAKE A STAMP OFF AN OLD LETTER!
I JUST HOPE SANTA WON'T MIND MAKING A SPECIAL TRIP DOWN HERE TONIGHT!
U.S.
U.S.
U.S.
NOW THE REST IS UP TO SANTA CLAUS!

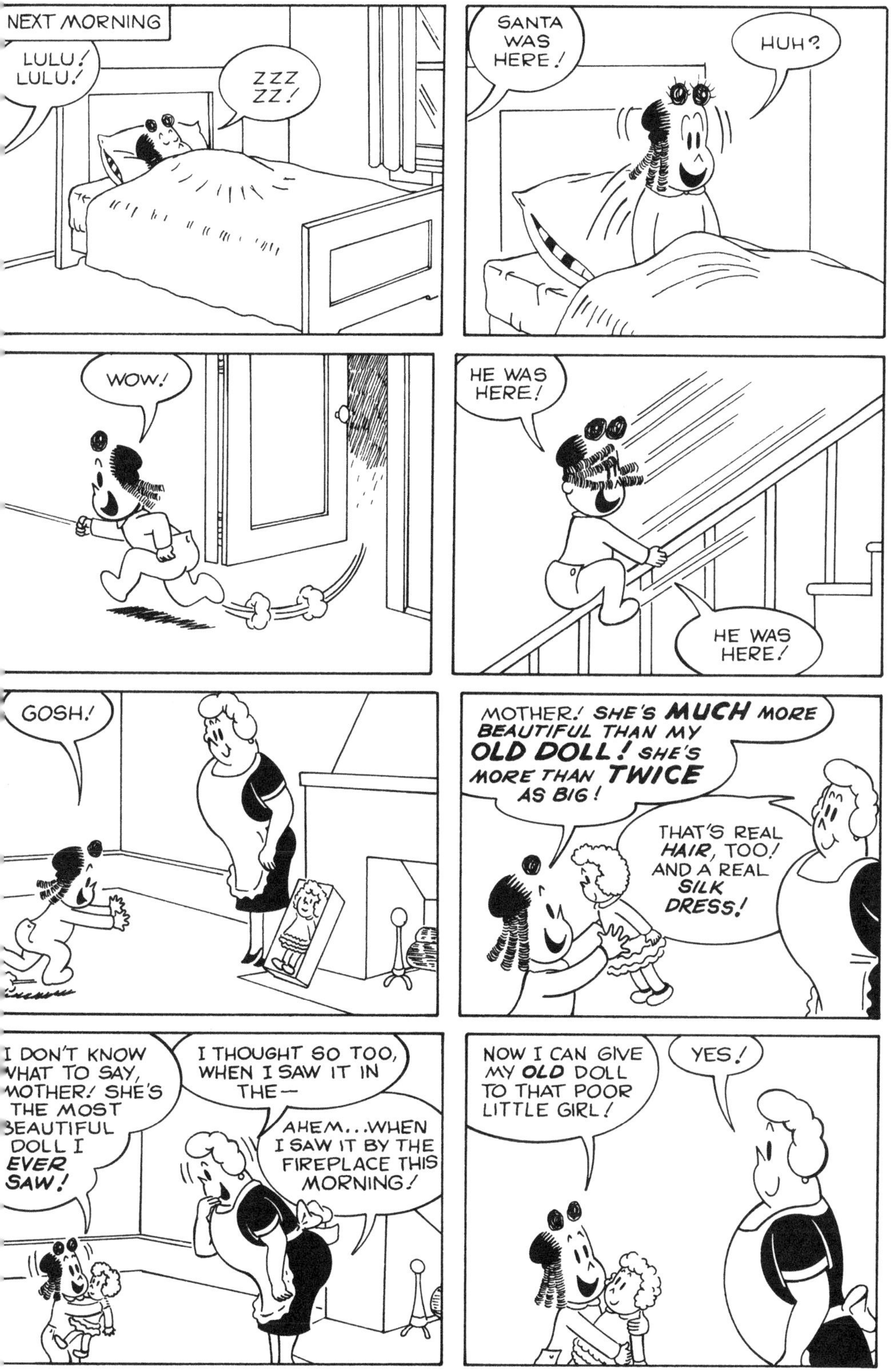
NEXT MORNING
LULU! LULU!
ZZZ ZZ!
SANTA WAS HERE!
HUH?
WOW!
HE WAS HERE!
HE WAS HERE!
GOSH!
MOTHER! SHE'S MUCH MORE BEAUTIFUL THAN MY OLD DOLL! SHE'S MORE THAN TWICE AS BIG!
THAT'S REAL HAIR, TOO! AND A REAL SILK DRESS!
I DON'T KNOW WHAT TO SAY, MOTHER! SHE'S THE MOST BEAUTIFUL DOLL I EVER SAW!
I THOUGHT SO TOO, WHEN I SAW IT IN THE—
AHEM...WHEN I SAW IT BY THE FIREPLACE THIS MORNING!
NOW I CAN GIVE MY OLD DOLL TO THAT POOR LITTLE GIRL!
YES!

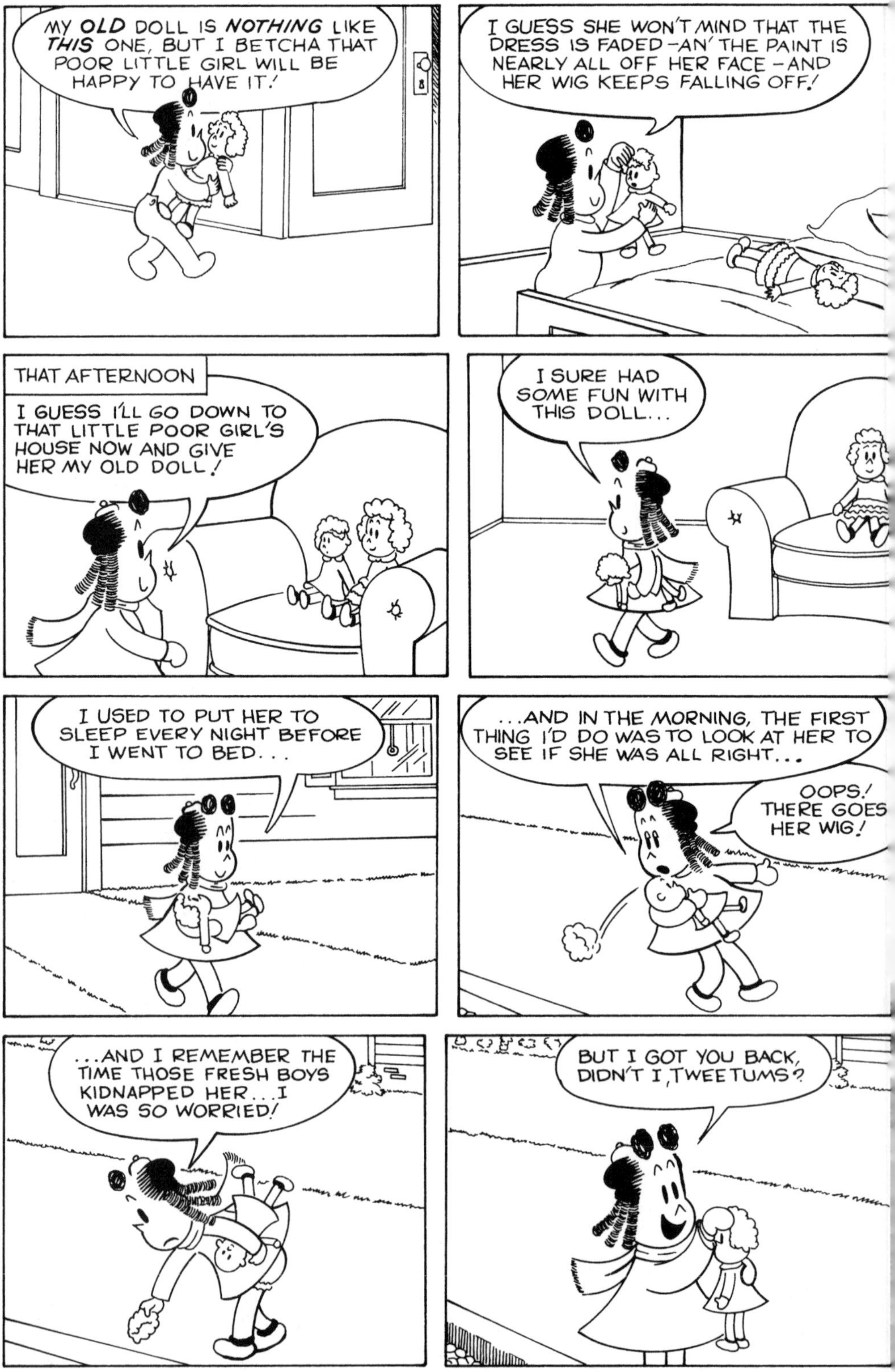

MY OLD DOLL IS NOTHING LIKE THIS ONE, BUT I BETCHA THAT POOR LITTLE GIRL WILL BE HAPPY TO HAVE IT!
I GUESS SHE WON'T MIND THAT THE DRESS IS FADED—AN' THE PAINT IS NEARLY ALL OFF HER FACE—AND HER WIG KEEPS FALLING OFF!
THAT AFTERNOON
I GUESS I'LL GO DOWN TO THAT LITTLE POOR GIRL'S HOUSE NOW AND GIVE HER MY OLD DOLL!
I SURE HAD SOME FUN WITH THIS DOLL...
I USED TO PUT HER TO SLEEP EVERY NIGHT BEFORE I WENT TO BED...
...AND IN THE MORNING, THE FIRST THING I'D DO WAS TO LOOK AT HER TO SEE IF SHE WAS ALL RIGHT...
OOPS! THERE GOES HER WIG!
...AND I REMEMBER THE TIME THOSE FRESH BOYS KIDNAPPED HER...I WAS SO WORRIED!
BUT I GOT YOU BACK, DIDN'T I, TWEETUMS?

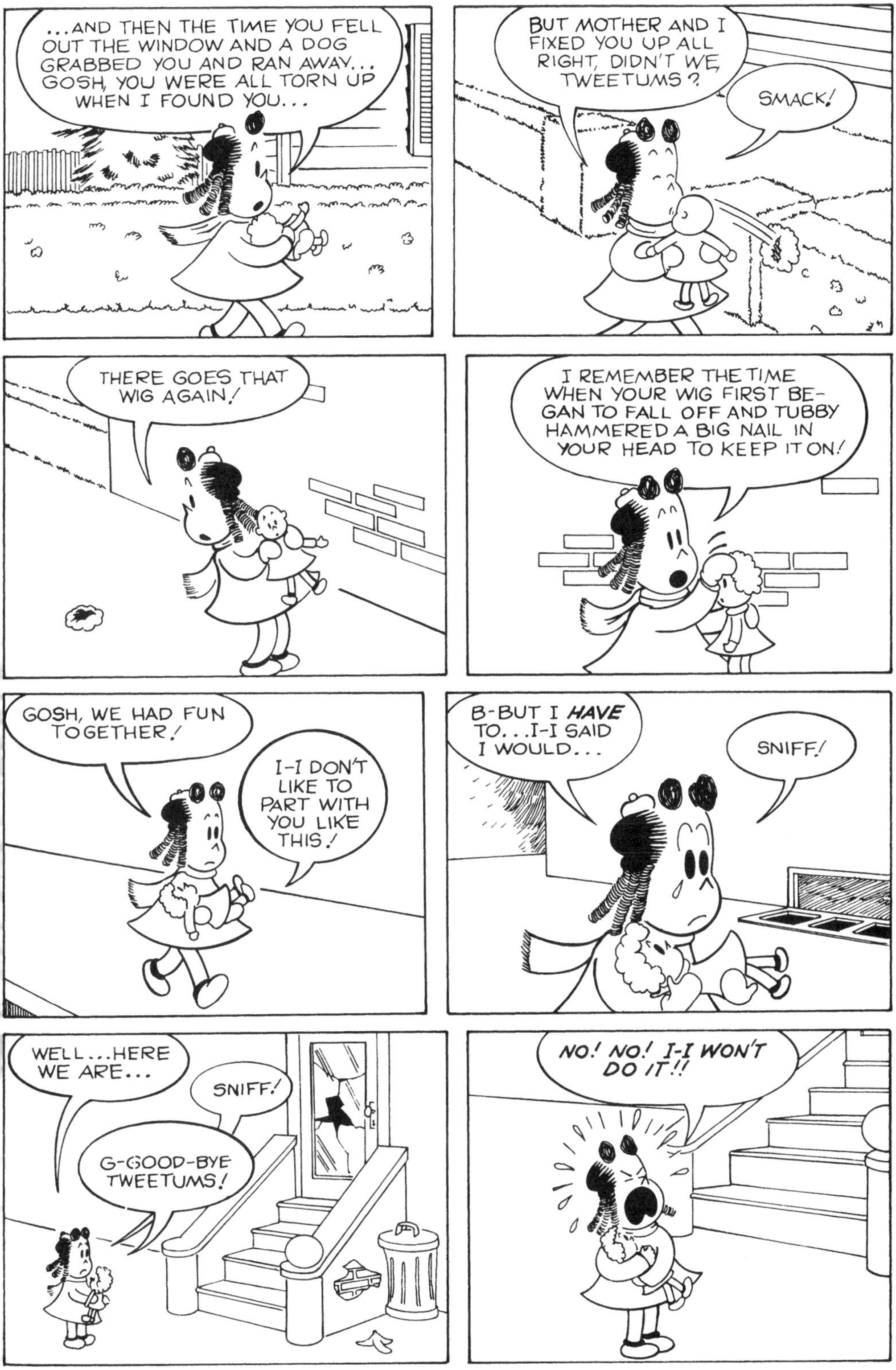
...AND THEN THE TIME YOU FELL OUT THE WINDOW AND A DOG GRABBED YOU AND RAN AWAY... GOSH, YOU WERE ALL TORN UP WHEN I FOUND YOU...
BUT MOTHER AND I FIXED YOU UP ALL RIGHT, DIDN'T WE, TWEETUMS?
SMACK!
THERE GOES THAT WIG AGAIN!
I REMEMBER THE TIME WHEN YOUR WIG FIRST BE-GAN TO FALL OFF AND TUBBY HAMMERED A BIG NAIL IN YOUR HEAD TO KEEP IT ON!
GOSH, WE HAD FUN TOGETHER!
I-I DON'T LIKE TO PART WITH YOU LIKE THIS!
B-BUT I *HAVE* TO...I-I SAID I WOULD...
SNIFF!
WELL...HERE WE ARE...
SNIFF!
G-GOOD-BYE TWEETUMS!
NO! NO! I-I WON'T DO IT!!

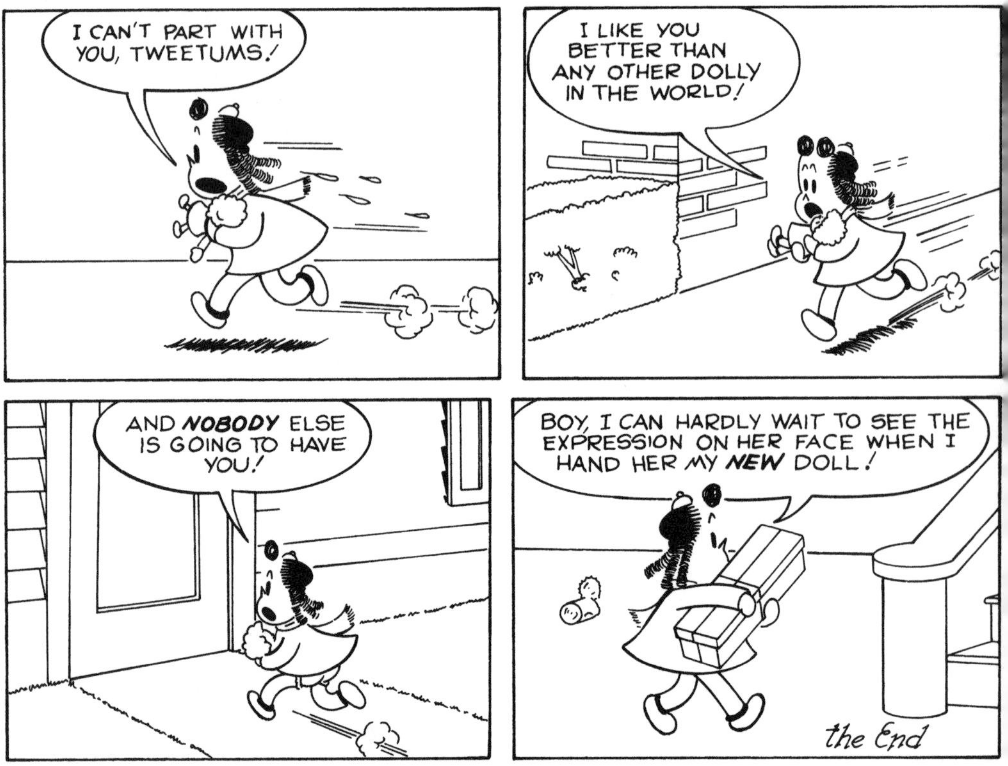
I CAN'T PART WITH YOU, TWEETUMS!
I LIKE YOU BETTER THAN ANY OTHER DOLLY IN THE WORLD!
AND NOBODY ELSE IS GOING TO HAVE YOU!
BOY, I CAN HARDLY WAIT TO SEE THE EXPRESSION ON HER FACE WHEN I HAND HER MY NEW DOLL!
the End

ALVIN

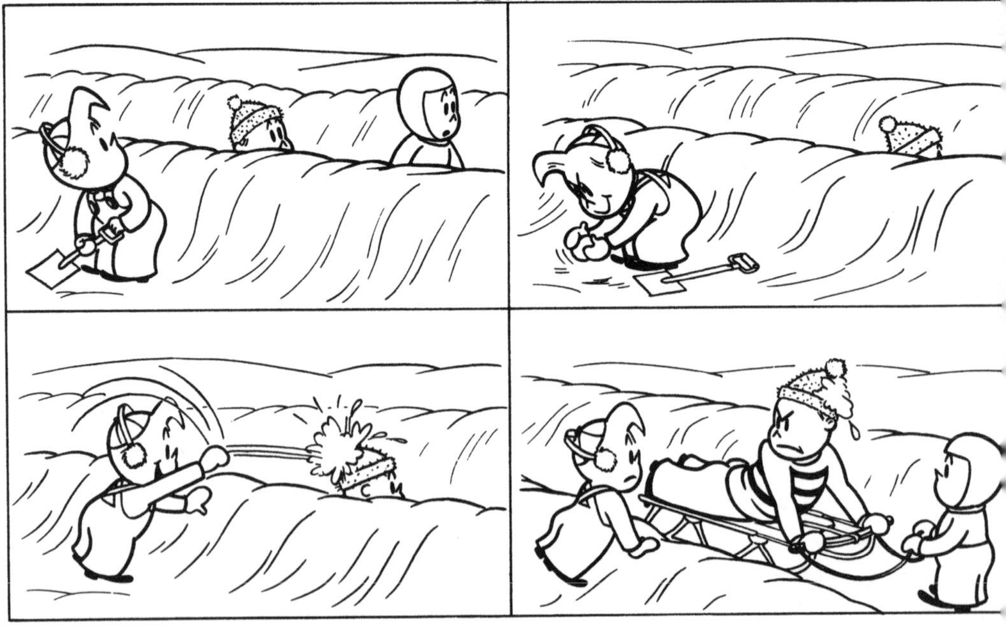

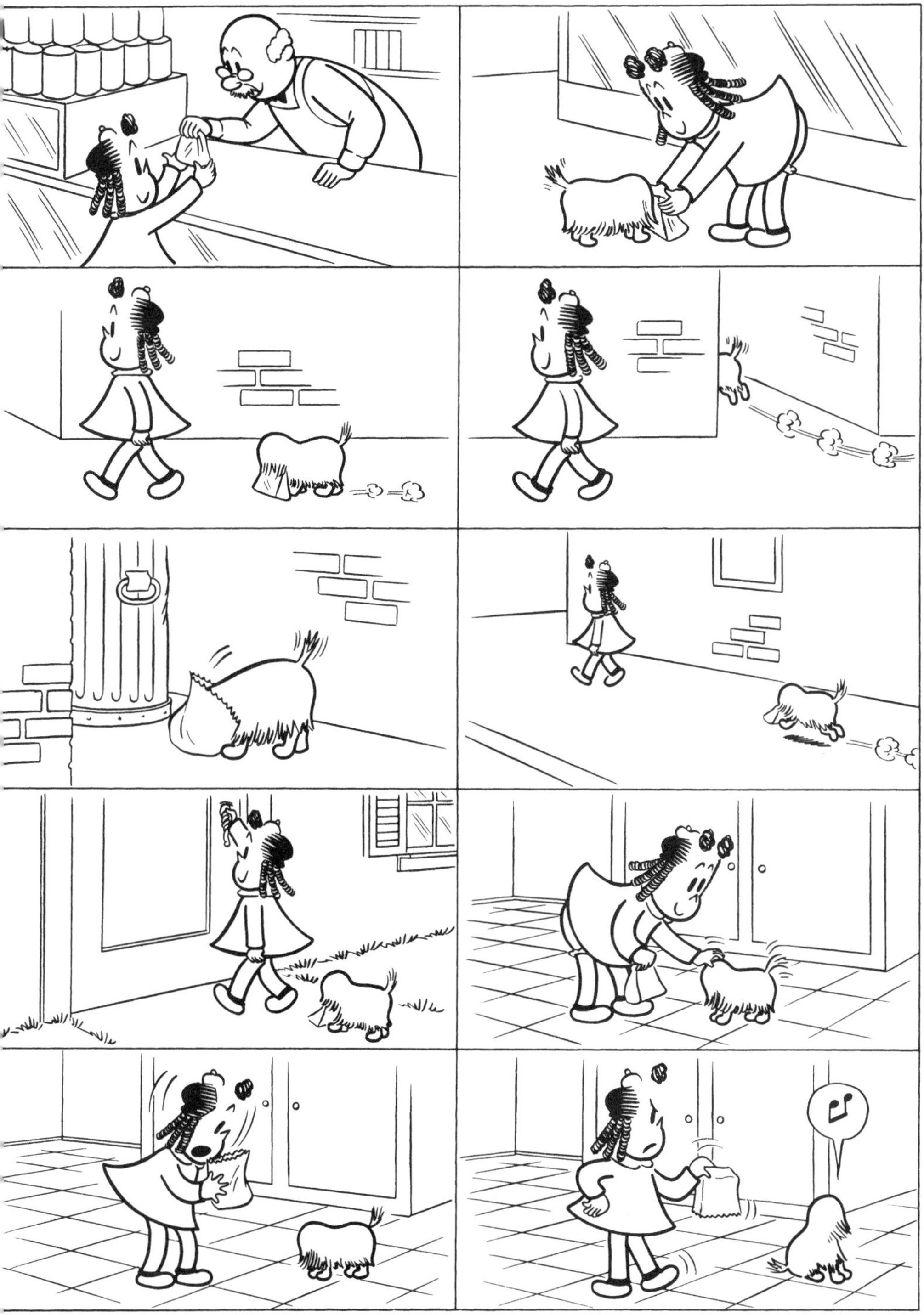

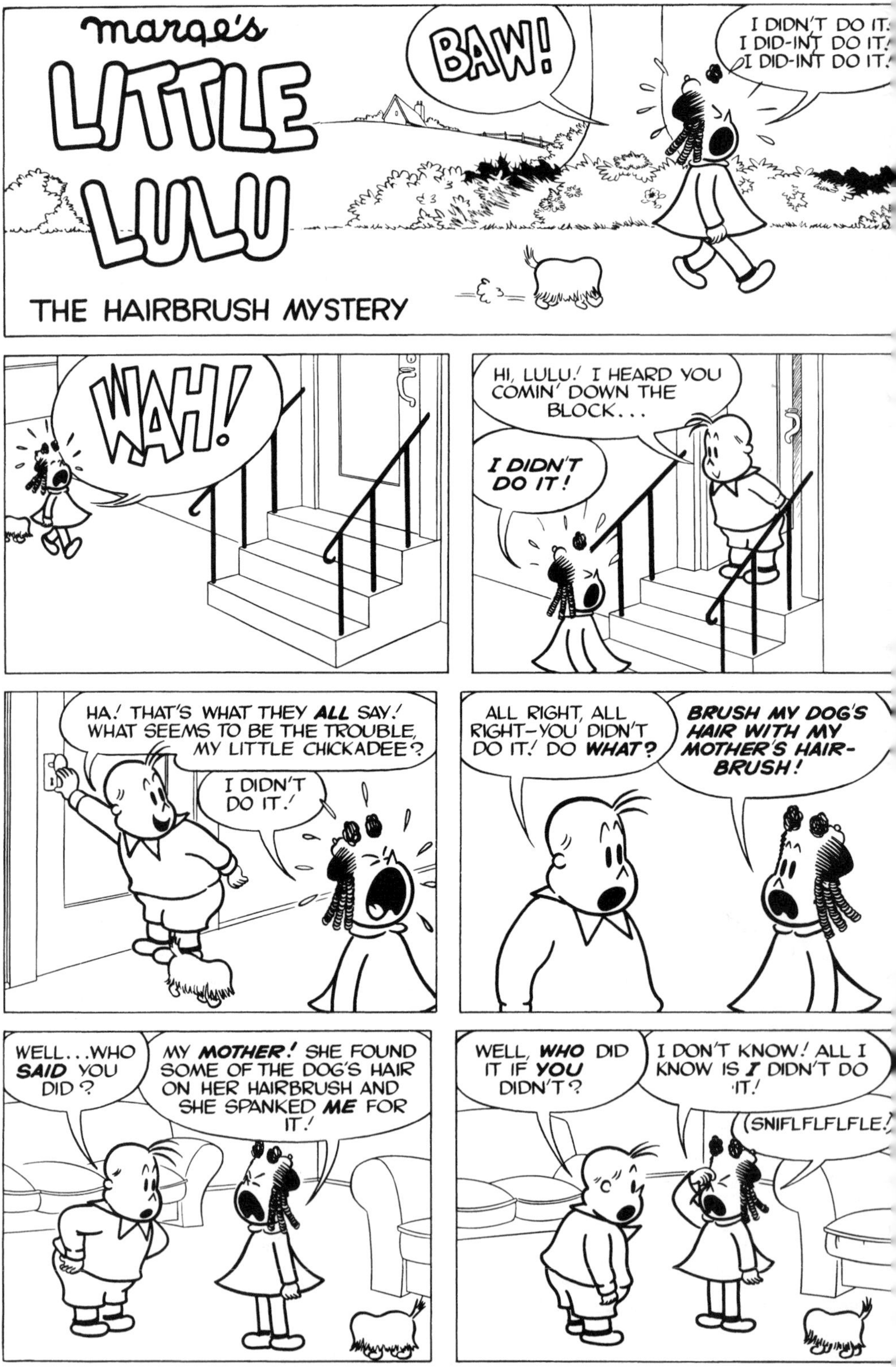
marge's
LITTLE LULU
THE HAIRBRUSH MYSTERY
BAW!
I DIDN'T DO IT! I DID-INT DO IT! I DID-INT DO IT!
WAH!
HI, LULU! I HEARD YOU COMIN' DOWN THE BLOCK...
I DIDN'T DO IT!
HA! THAT'S WHAT THEY ALL SAY! WHAT SEEMS TO BE THE TROUBLE, MY LITTLE CHICKADEE?
I DIDN'T DO IT!
ALL RIGHT, ALL RIGHT—YOU DIDN'T DO IT! DO WHAT?
BRUSH MY DOG'S HAIR WITH MY MOTHER'S HAIR-BRUSH!
WELL...WHO SAID YOU DID?
MY MOTHER! SHE FOUND SOME OF THE DOG'S HAIR ON HER HAIRBRUSH AND SHE SPANKED ME FOR IT!
WELL, WHO DID IT IF YOU DIDN'T?
I DON'T KNOW! ALL I KNOW IS I DIDN'T DO IT!
(SNIFLFLFLFLE!)

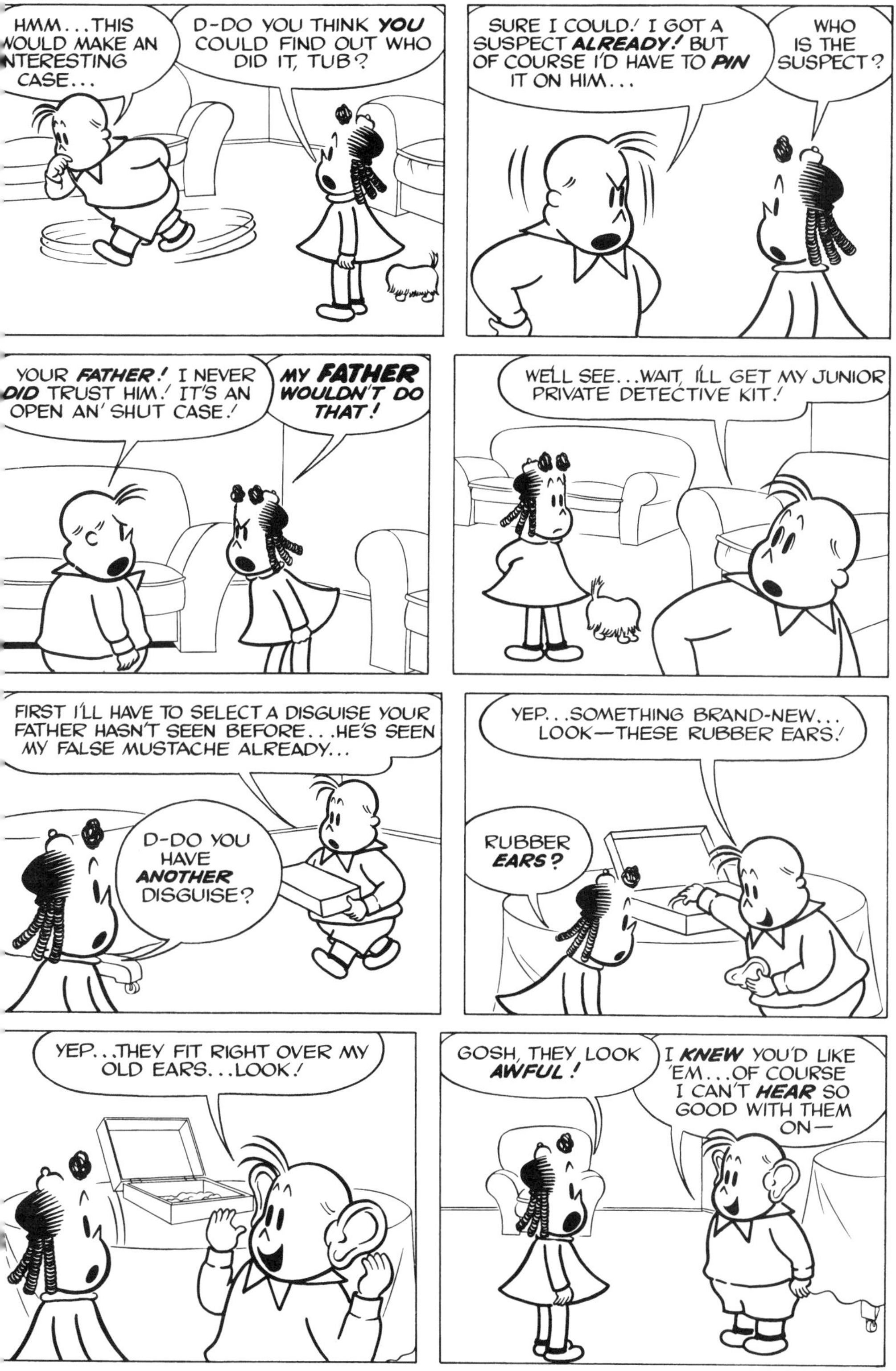

HMM...THIS WOULD MAKE AN INTERESTING CASE...
D-DO YOU THINK **YOU** COULD FIND OUT WHO DID IT, TUB?
SURE I COULD! I GOT A SUSPECT **ALREADY!** BUT OF COURSE I'D HAVE TO **PIN** IT ON HIM...
WHO IS THE SUSPECT?
YOUR **FATHER!** I NEVER **DID** TRUST HIM! IT'S AN OPEN AN' SHUT CASE!
MY FATHER WOULDN'T DO THAT!
WE'LL SEE...WAIT, I'LL GET MY JUNIOR PRIVATE DETECTIVE KIT!
FIRST I'LL HAVE TO SELECT A DISGUISE YOUR FATHER HASN'T SEEN BEFORE...HE'S SEEN MY FALSE MUSTACHE ALREADY...
D-DO YOU HAVE **ANOTHER** DISGUISE?
YEP...SOMETHING BRAND-NEW... LOOK—THESE RUBBER EARS!
RUBBER **EARS?**
YEP...THEY FIT RIGHT OVER MY OLD EARS...LOOK!
GOSH, THEY LOOK **AWFUL!**
I **KNEW** YOU'D LIKE 'EM...OF COURSE I CAN'T **HEAR** SO GOOD WITH THEM ON—

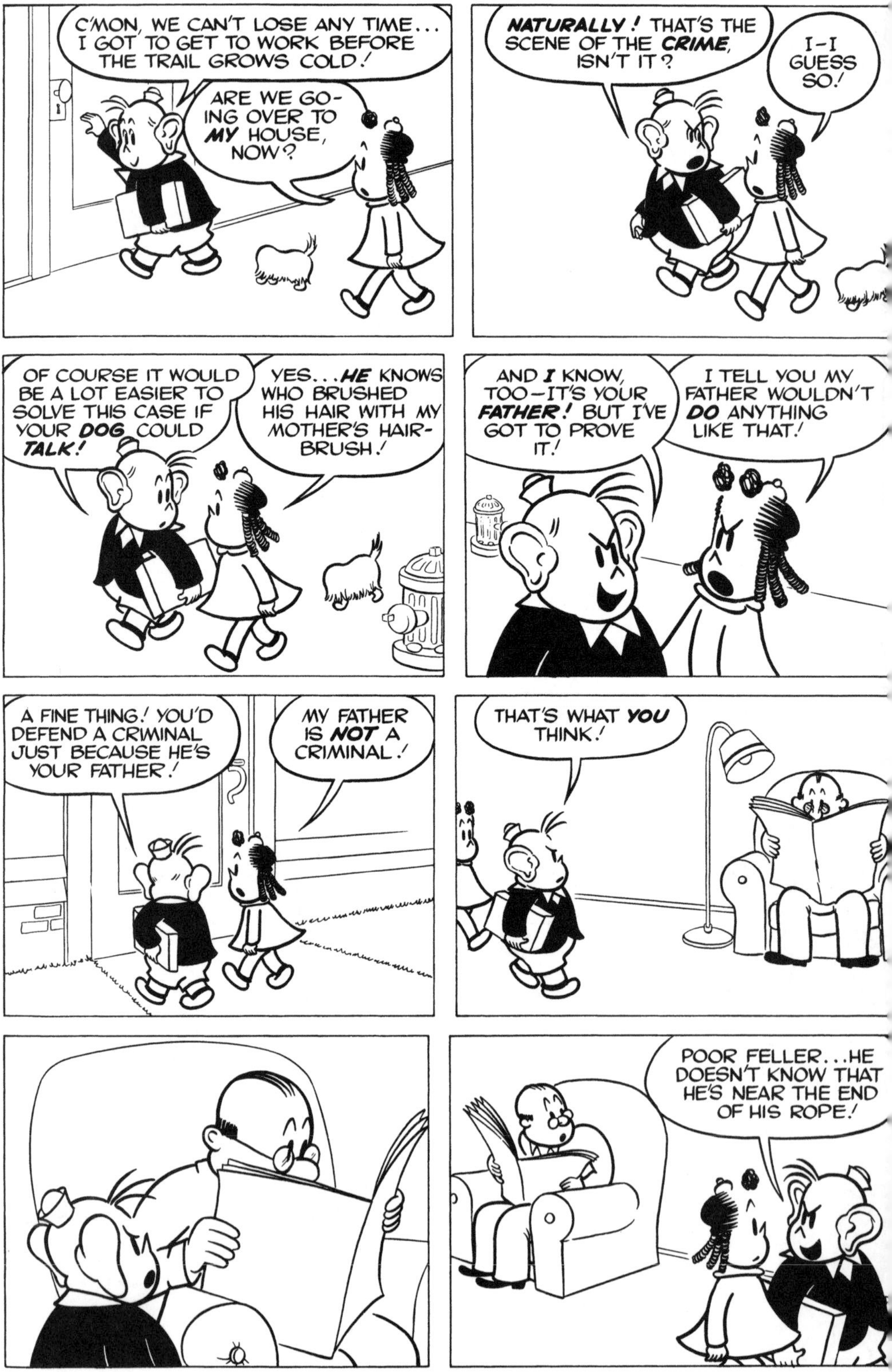
C'MON, WE CAN'T LOSE ANY TIME... I GOT TO GET TO WORK BEFORE THE TRAIL GROWS COLD!
ARE WE GOING OVER TO MY HOUSE, NOW?
NATURALLY! THAT'S THE SCENE OF THE CRIME, ISN'T IT?
I-I GUESS SO!
OF COURSE IT WOULD BE A LOT EASIER TO SOLVE THIS CASE IF YOUR DOG COULD TALK!
YES... HE KNOWS WHO BRUSHED HIS HAIR WITH MY MOTHER'S HAIR-BRUSH!
AND I KNOW, TOO—IT'S YOUR FATHER! BUT I'VE GOT TO PROVE IT!
I TELL YOU MY FATHER WOULDN'T DO ANYTHING LIKE THAT!
A FINE THING! YOU'D DEFEND A CRIMINAL JUST BECAUSE HE'S YOUR FATHER!
MY FATHER IS NOT A CRIMINAL!
THAT'S WHAT YOU THINK!
POOR FELLER...HE DOESN'T KNOW THAT HE'S NEAR THE END OF HIS ROPE!

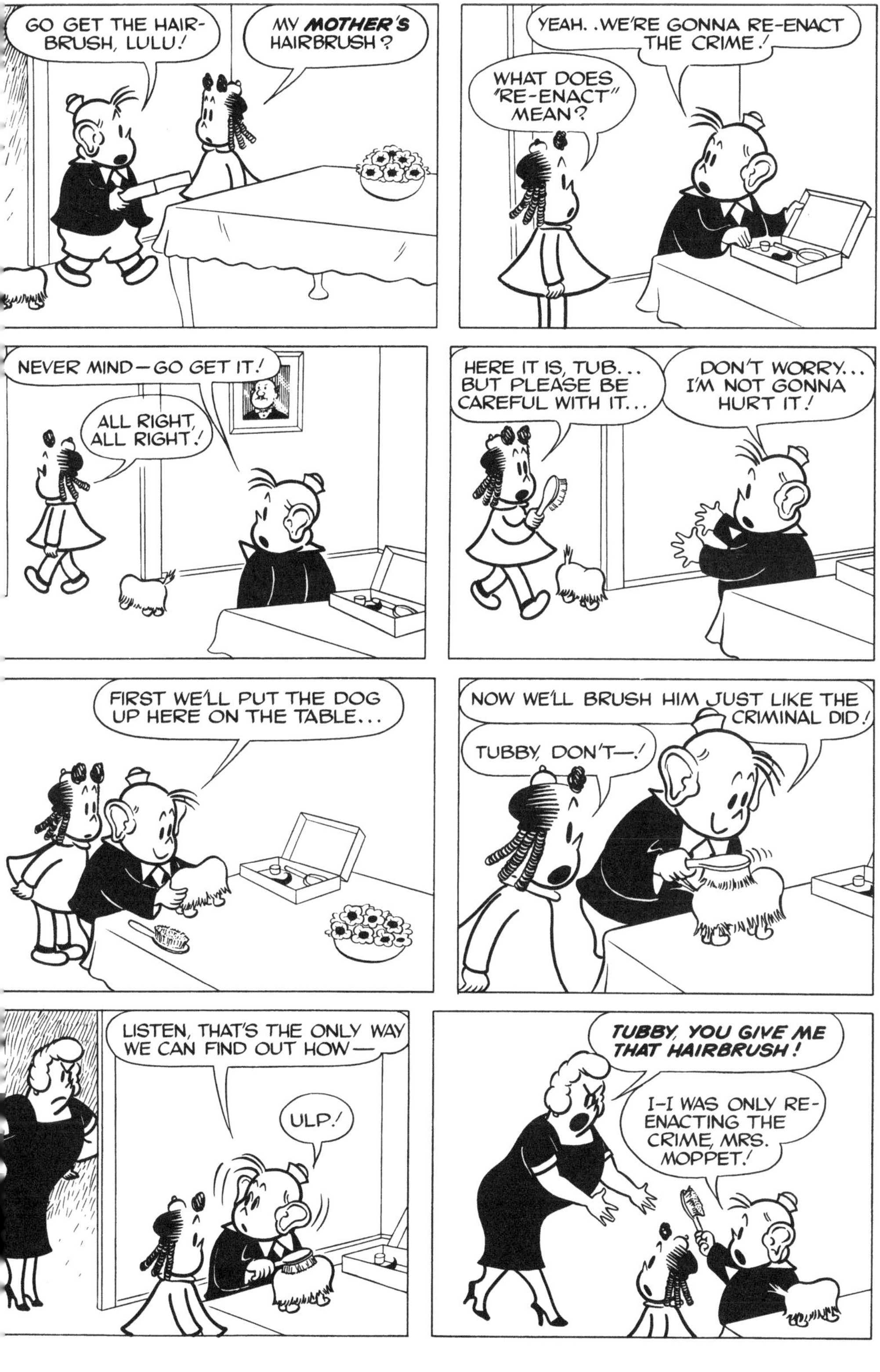
GO GET THE HAIR-BRUSH, LULU!
MY MOTHER'S HAIRBRUSH?
YEAH. .WE'RE GONNA RE-ENACT THE CRIME!
WHAT DOES "RE-ENACT" MEAN?
NEVER MIND—GO GET IT!
ALL RIGHT, ALL RIGHT!
HERE IT IS, TUB... BUT PLEASE BE CAREFUL WITH IT...
DON'T WORRY... I'M NOT GONNA HURT IT!
FIRST WE'LL PUT THE DOG UP HERE ON THE TABLE...
NOW WE'LL BRUSH HIM JUST LIKE THE CRIMINAL DID!
TUBBY, DON'T—!
LISTEN, THAT'S THE ONLY WAY WE CAN FIND OUT HOW—
ULP!
TUBBY, YOU GIVE ME THAT HAIRBRUSH!
I-I WAS ONLY RE-ENACTING THE CRIME, MRS. MOPPET!

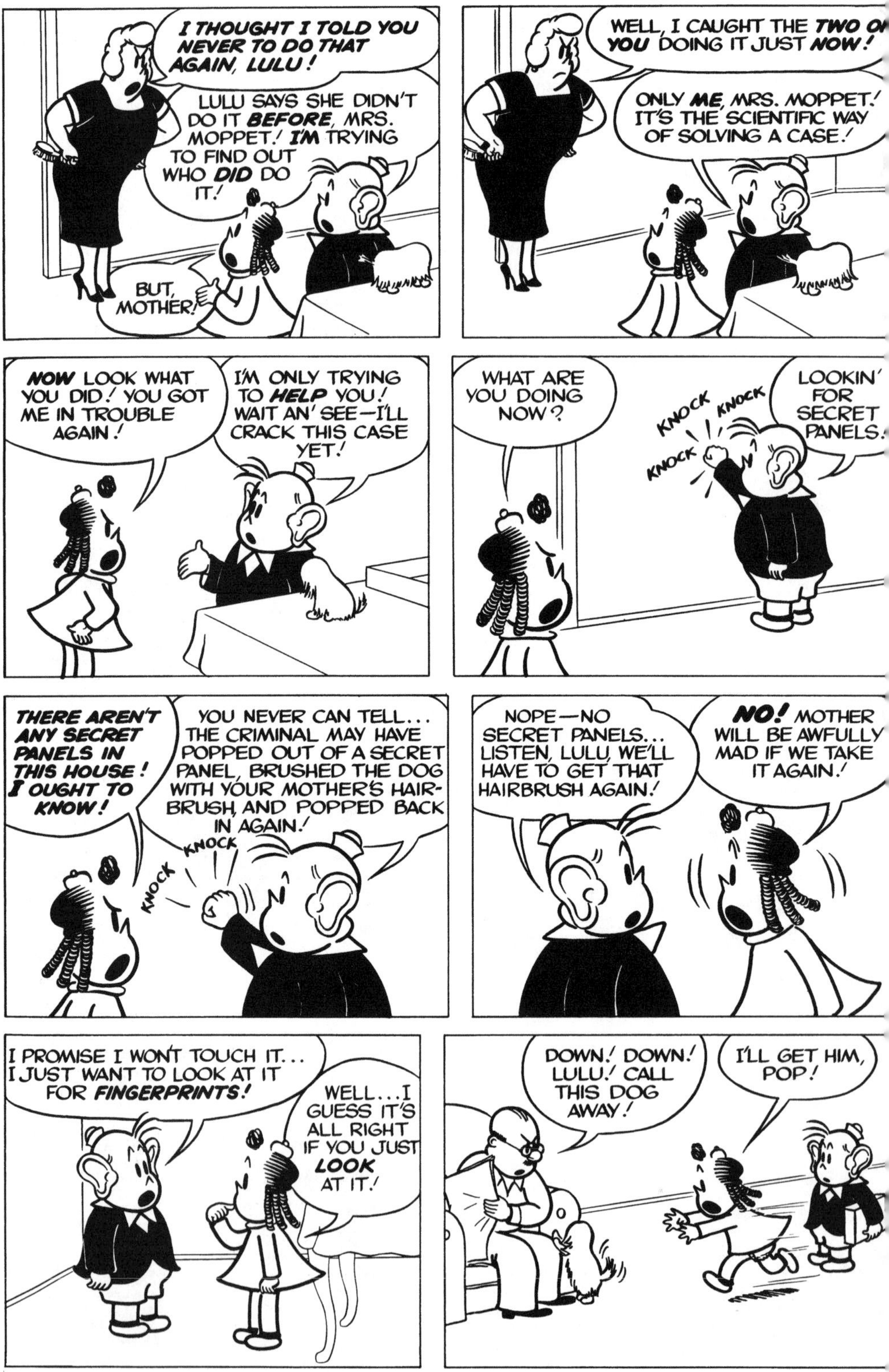
I THOUGHT I TOLD YOU NEVER TO DO THAT AGAIN, LULU!
LULU SAYS SHE DIDN'T DO IT BEFORE, MRS. MOPPET! I'M TRYING TO FIND OUT WHO DID DO IT!
BUT, MOTHER!
WELL, I CAUGHT THE TWO O
YOU DOING IT JUST NOW!
ONLY ME, MRS. MOPPET! IT'S THE SCIENTIFIC WAY OF SOLVING A CASE!
NOW LOOK WHAT YOU DID! YOU GOT ME IN TROUBLE AGAIN!
I'M ONLY TRYING TO HELP YOU! WAIT AN' SEE—I'LL CRACK THIS CASE YET!
WHAT ARE YOU DOING NOW?
KNOCK KNOCK KNOCK
LOOKIN' FOR SECRET PANELS.
THERE AREN'T ANY SECRET PANELS IN THIS HOUSE! I OUGHT TO KNOW!
YOU NEVER CAN TELL... THE CRIMINAL MAY HAVE POPPED OUT OF A SECRET PANEL, BRUSHED THE DOG WITH YOUR MOTHER'S HAIRBRUSH, AND POPPED BACK IN AGAIN!
KNOCK KNOCK
NOPE—NO SECRET PANELS... LISTEN, LULU, WE'LL HAVE TO GET THAT HAIRBRUSH AGAIN!
NO! MOTHER WILL BE AWFULLY MAD IF WE TAKE IT AGAIN!
I PROMISE I WON'T TOUCH IT... I JUST WANT TO LOOK AT IT FOR FINGERPRINTS!
WELL...I GUESS IT'S ALL RIGHT IF YOU JUST LOOK AT IT!
DOWN! DOWN! LULU! CALL THIS DOG AWAY!
I'LL GET HIM, POP!

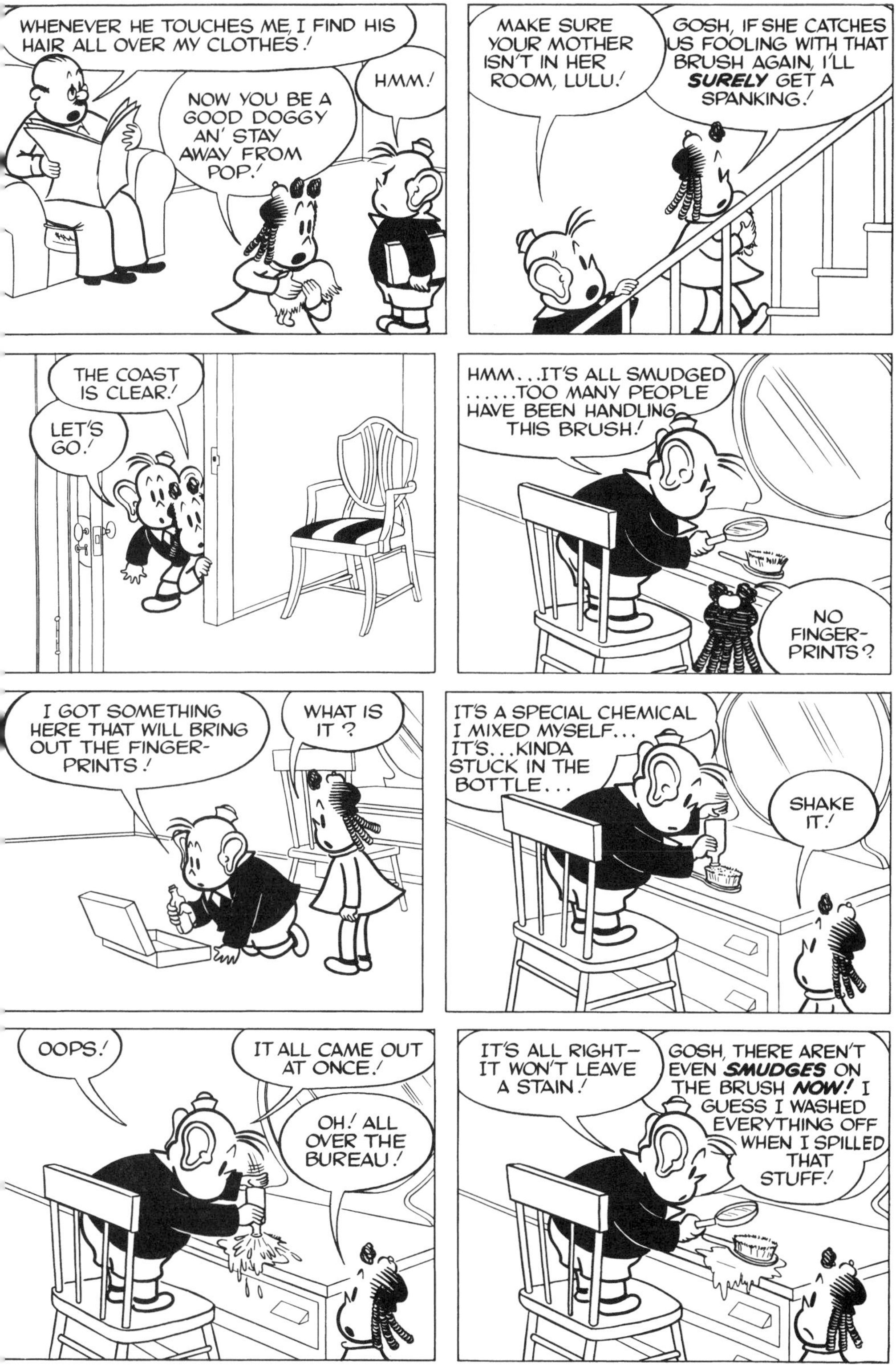
WHENEVER HE TOUCHES ME, I FIND HIS HAIR ALL OVER MY CLOTHES!
NOW YOU BE A GOOD DOGGY AN' STAY AWAY FROM POP!
HMM!
MAKE SURE YOUR MOTHER ISN'T IN HER ROOM, LULU!
GOSH, IF SHE CATCHES US FOOLING WITH THAT BRUSH AGAIN, I'LL **SURELY** GET A SPANKING!
THE COAST IS CLEAR!
LET'S GO!
HMM...IT'S ALL SMUDGED ......TOO MANY PEOPLE HAVE BEEN HANDLING THIS BRUSH!
NO FINGER-PRINTS?
I GOT SOMETHING HERE THAT WILL BRING OUT THE FINGER-PRINTS!
WHAT IS IT?
IT'S A SPECIAL CHEMICAL I MIXED MYSELF... IT'S...KINDA STUCK IN THE BOTTLE...
SHAKE IT!
OOPS!
IT ALL CAME OUT AT ONCE!
OH! ALL OVER THE BUREAU!
IT'S ALL RIGHT– IT WON'T LEAVE A STAIN!
GOSH, THERE AREN'T EVEN **SMUDGES** ON THE BRUSH **NOW!** I GUESS I WASHED EVERYTHING OFF WHEN I SPILLED THAT STUFF!

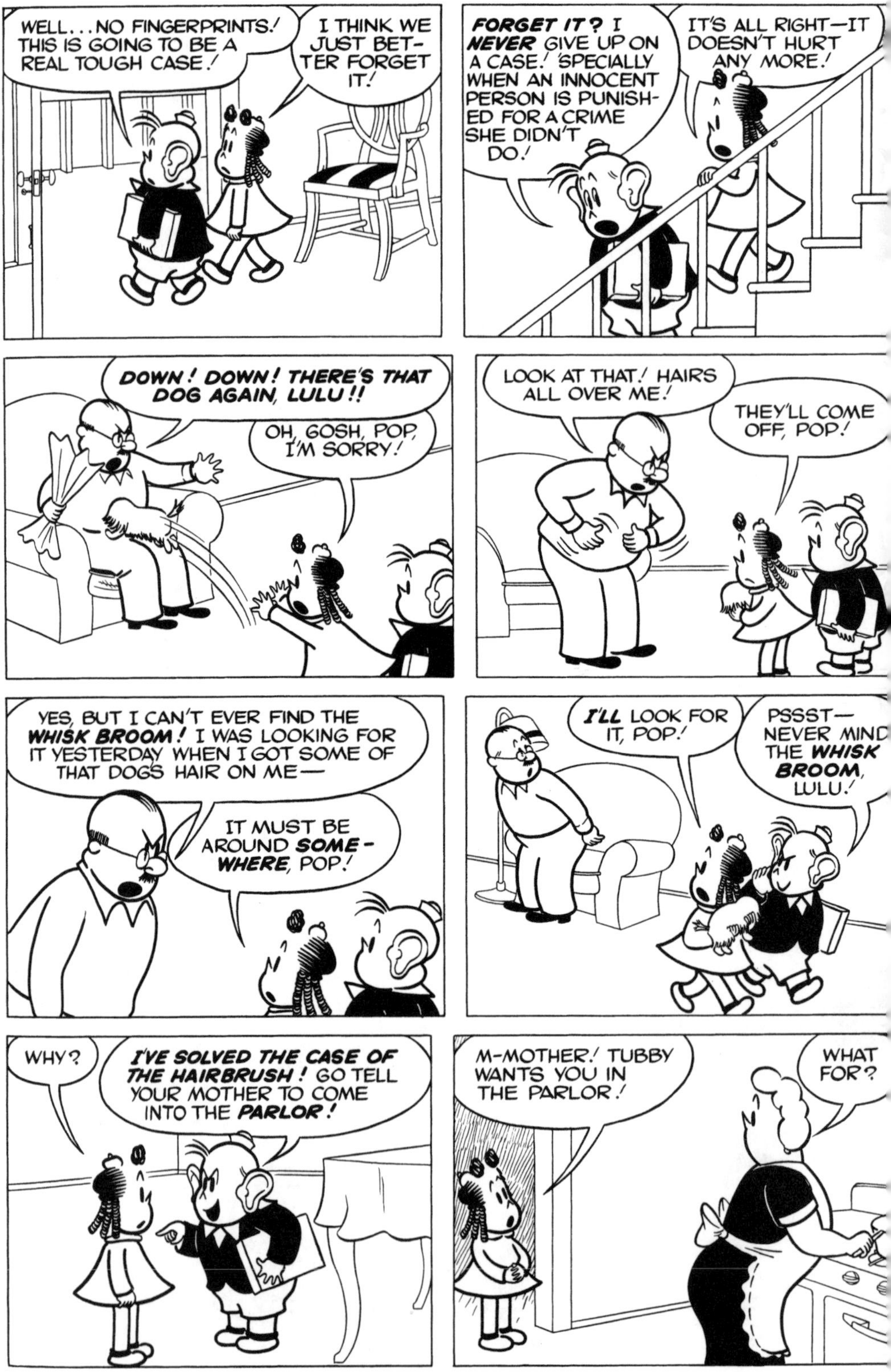
WELL...NO FINGERPRINTS! THIS IS GOING TO BE A REAL TOUGH CASE!
I THINK WE JUST BETTER FORGET IT!
FORGET IT? I NEVER GIVE UP ON A CASE! 'SPECIALLY WHEN AN INNOCENT PERSON IS PUNISHED FOR A CRIME SHE DIDN'T DO!
IT'S ALL RIGHT—IT DOESN'T HURT ANY MORE!
DOWN! DOWN! THERE'S THAT DOG AGAIN, LULU!!
OH, GOSH, POP, I'M SORRY!
LOOK AT THAT! HAIRS ALL OVER ME!
THEY'LL COME OFF, POP!
YES, BUT I CAN'T EVER FIND THE WHISK BROOM! I WAS LOOKING FOR IT YESTERDAY WHEN I GOT SOME OF THAT DOG'S HAIR ON ME—
IT MUST BE AROUND SOMEWHERE, POP!
I'LL LOOK FOR IT, POP!
PSSST— NEVER MIND THE WHISK BROOM, LULU!
WHY?
I'VE SOLVED THE CASE OF THE HAIRBRUSH! GO TELL YOUR MOTHER TO COME INTO THE PARLOR!
M-MOTHER! TUBBY WANTS YOU IN THE PARLOR!
WHAT FOR?

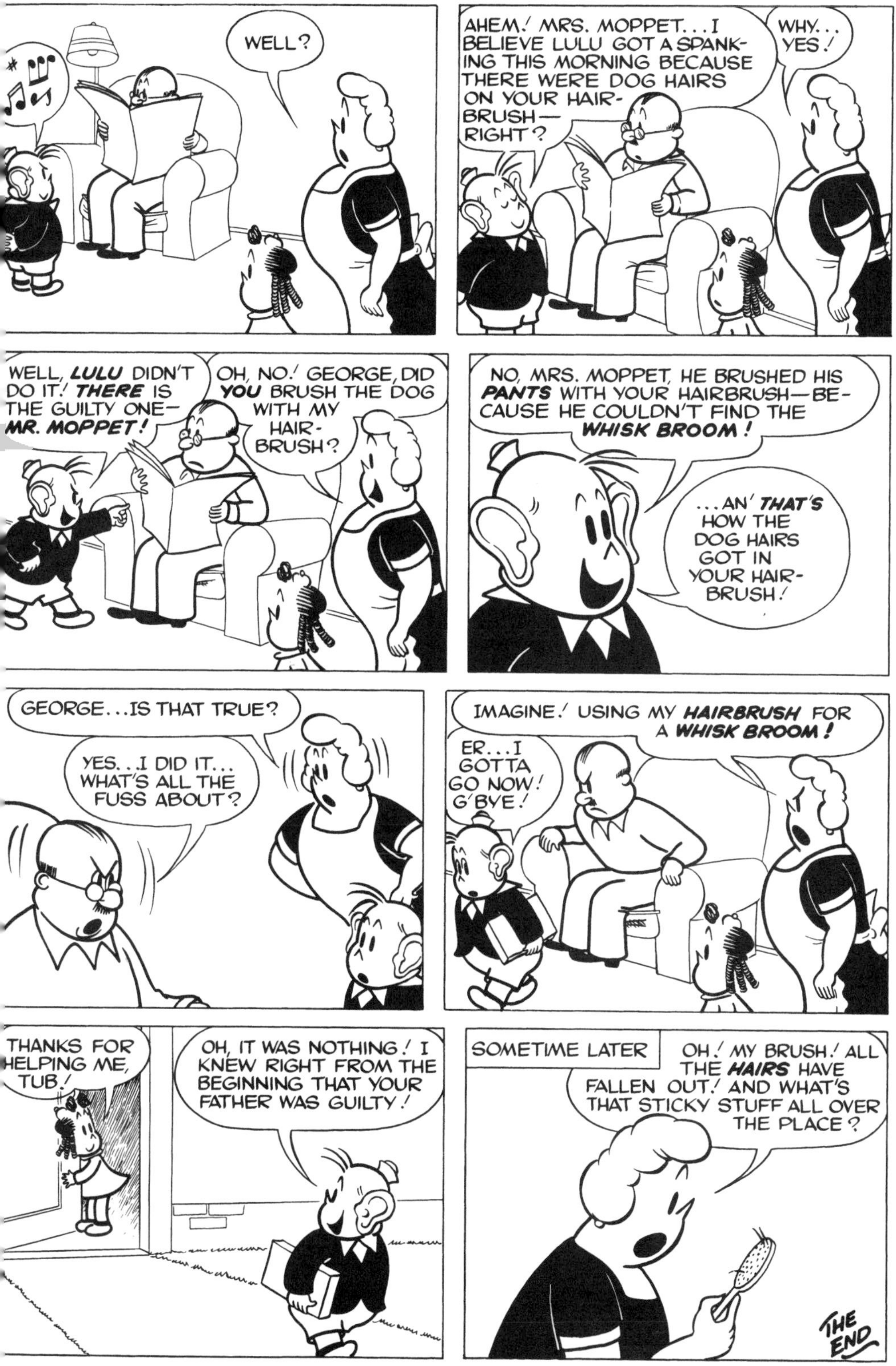
WELL?
AHEM! MRS. MOPPET...I BELIEVE LULU GOT A SPANKING THIS MORNING BECAUSE THERE WERE DOG HAIRS ON YOUR HAIRBRUSH— RIGHT?
WHY... YES!
WELL, LULU DIDN'T DO IT! THERE IS THE GUILTY ONE— MR. MOPPET!
OH, NO! GEORGE, DID YOU BRUSH THE DOG WITH MY HAIRBRUSH?
NO, MRS. MOPPET, HE BRUSHED HIS PANTS WITH YOUR HAIRBRUSH—BECAUSE HE COULDN'T FIND THE WHISK BROOM!
...AN' THAT'S HOW THE DOG HAIRS GOT IN YOUR HAIRBRUSH!
GEORGE...IS THAT TRUE?
YES...I DID IT... WHAT'S ALL THE FUSS ABOUT?
IMAGINE! USING MY HAIRBRUSH FOR A WHISK BROOM!
ER...I GOTTA GO NOW! G'BYE!
THANKS FOR HELPING ME, TUB!
OH, IT WAS NOTHING! I KNEW RIGHT FROM THE BEGINNING THAT YOUR FATHER WAS GUILTY!
SOMETIME LATER
OH! MY BRUSH! ALL THE HAIRS HAVE FALLEN OUT! AND WHAT'S THAT STICKY STUFF ALL OVER THE PLACE?
THE END

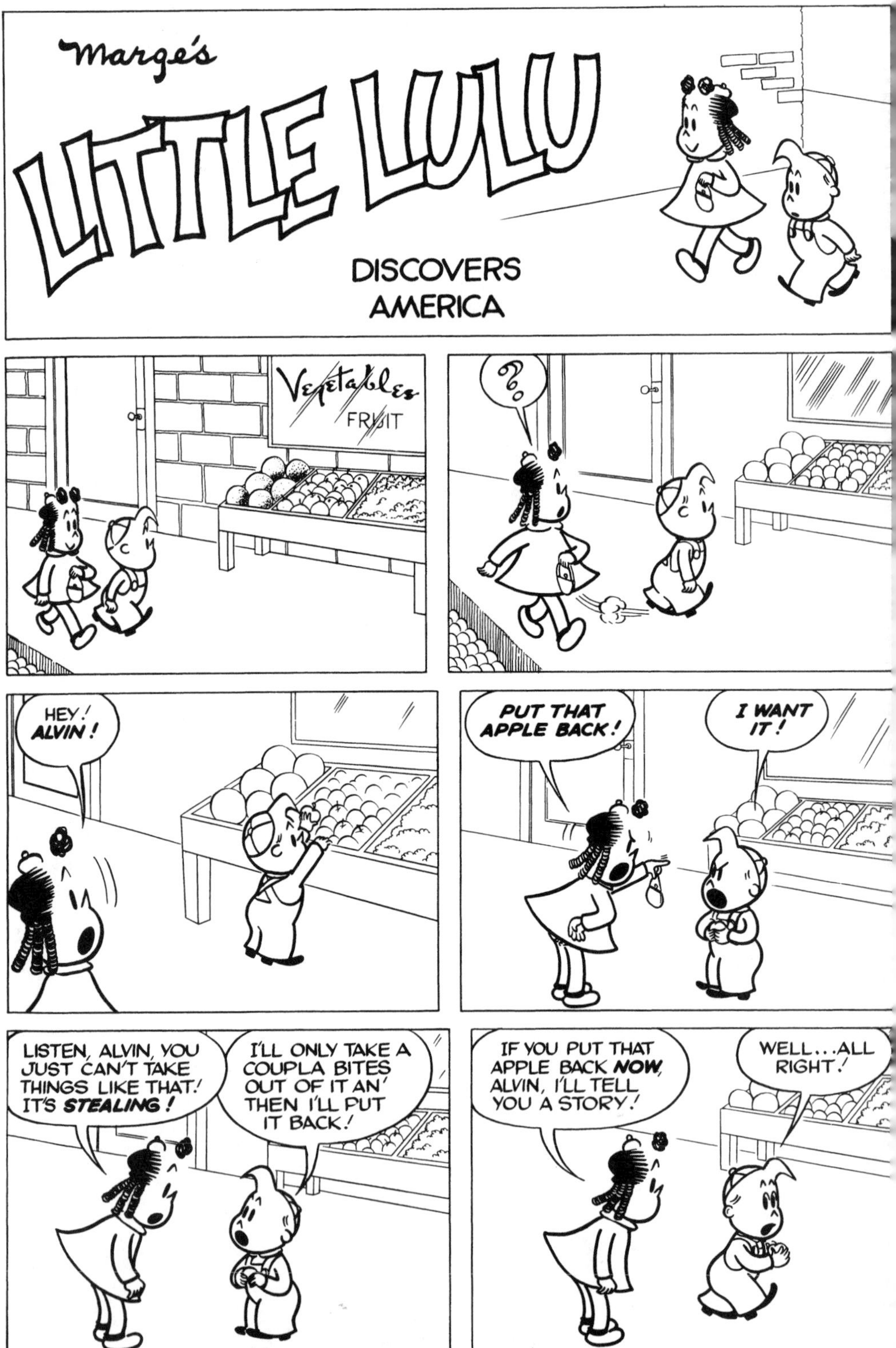
Marge's
LITTLE LULU
DISCOVERS AMERICA
Vegetables
FRUIT
?
HEY! ALVIN!
PUT THAT APPLE BACK!
I WANT IT!
LISTEN, ALVIN, YOU JUST CAN'T TAKE THINGS LIKE THAT! IT'S STEALING!
I'LL ONLY TAKE A COUPLA BITES OUT OF IT AN' THEN I'LL PUT IT BACK!
IF YOU PUT THAT APPLE BACK NOW, ALVIN, I'LL TELL YOU A STORY!
WELL...ALL RIGHT!

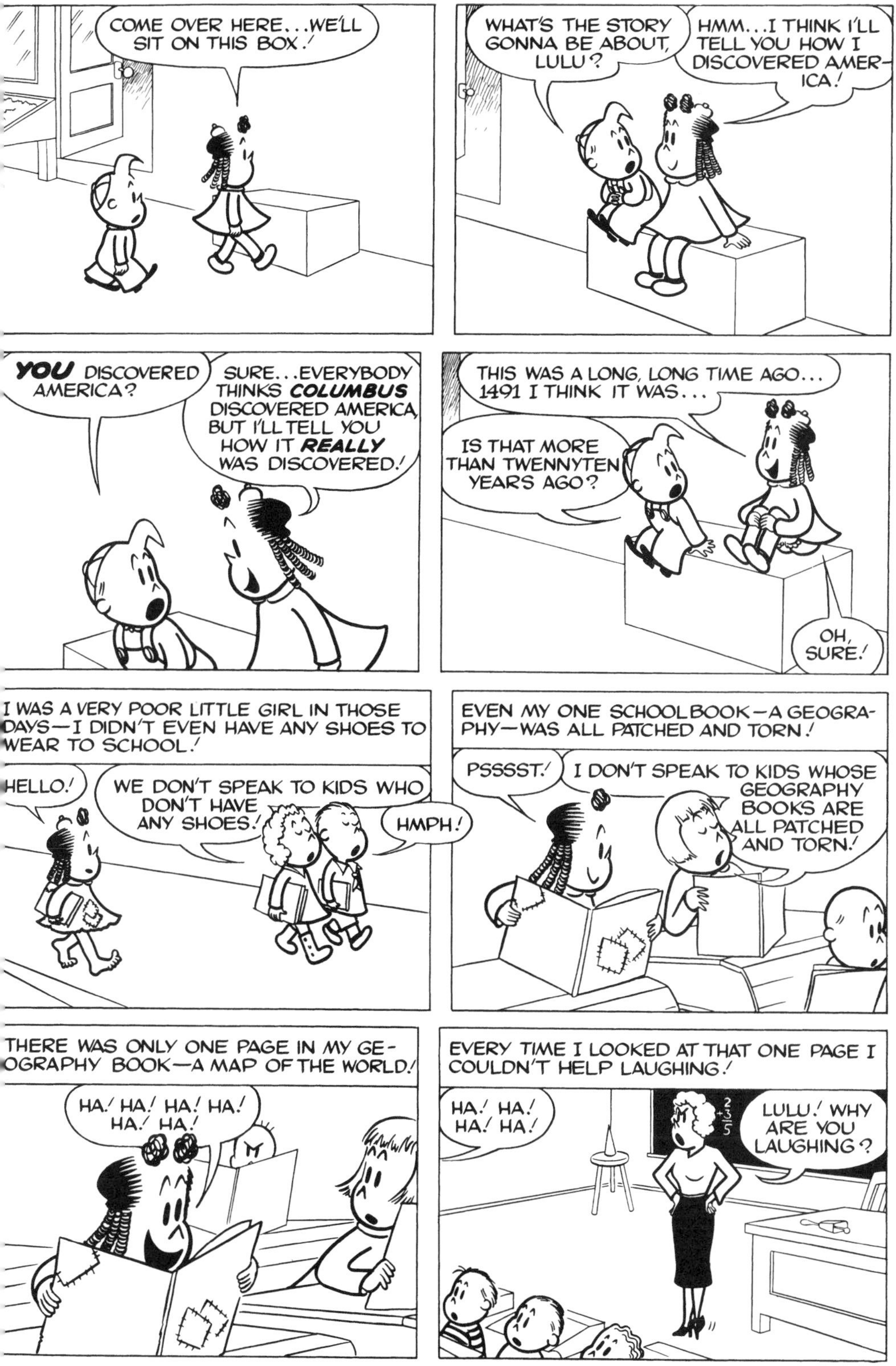
COME OVER HERE...WE'LL SIT ON THIS BOX.!
WHAT'S THE STORY GONNA BE ABOUT, LULU?
HMM...I THINK I'LL TELL YOU HOW I DISCOVERED AMERICA.!
YOU DISCOVERED AMERICA?
SURE...EVERYBODY THINKS COLUMBUS DISCOVERED AMERICA, BUT I'LL TELL YOU HOW IT REALLY WAS DISCOVERED.!
THIS WAS A LONG, LONG TIME AGO... 1491 I THINK IT WAS...
IS THAT MORE THAN TWENNYTEN YEARS AGO?
OH, SURE.!
I WAS A VERY POOR LITTLE GIRL IN THOSE DAYS—I DIDN'T EVEN HAVE ANY SHOES TO WEAR TO SCHOOL.!
HELLO.!
WE DON'T SPEAK TO KIDS WHO DON'T HAVE ANY SHOES.!
HMPH.!
EVEN MY ONE SCHOOLBOOK—A GEOGRAPHY—WAS ALL PATCHED AND TORN.!
PSSSST.!
I DON'T SPEAK TO KIDS WHOSE GEOGRAPHY BOOKS ARE ALL PATCHED AND TORN.!
THERE WAS ONLY ONE PAGE IN MY GEOGRAPHY BOOK—A MAP OF THE WORLD.!
HA.! HA.! HA.! HA.! HA.! HA.!
EVERY TIME I LOOKED AT THAT ONE PAGE I COULDN'T HELP LAUGHING.!
HA.! HA.! HA.! HA.!
LULU.! WHY ARE YOU LAUGHING?

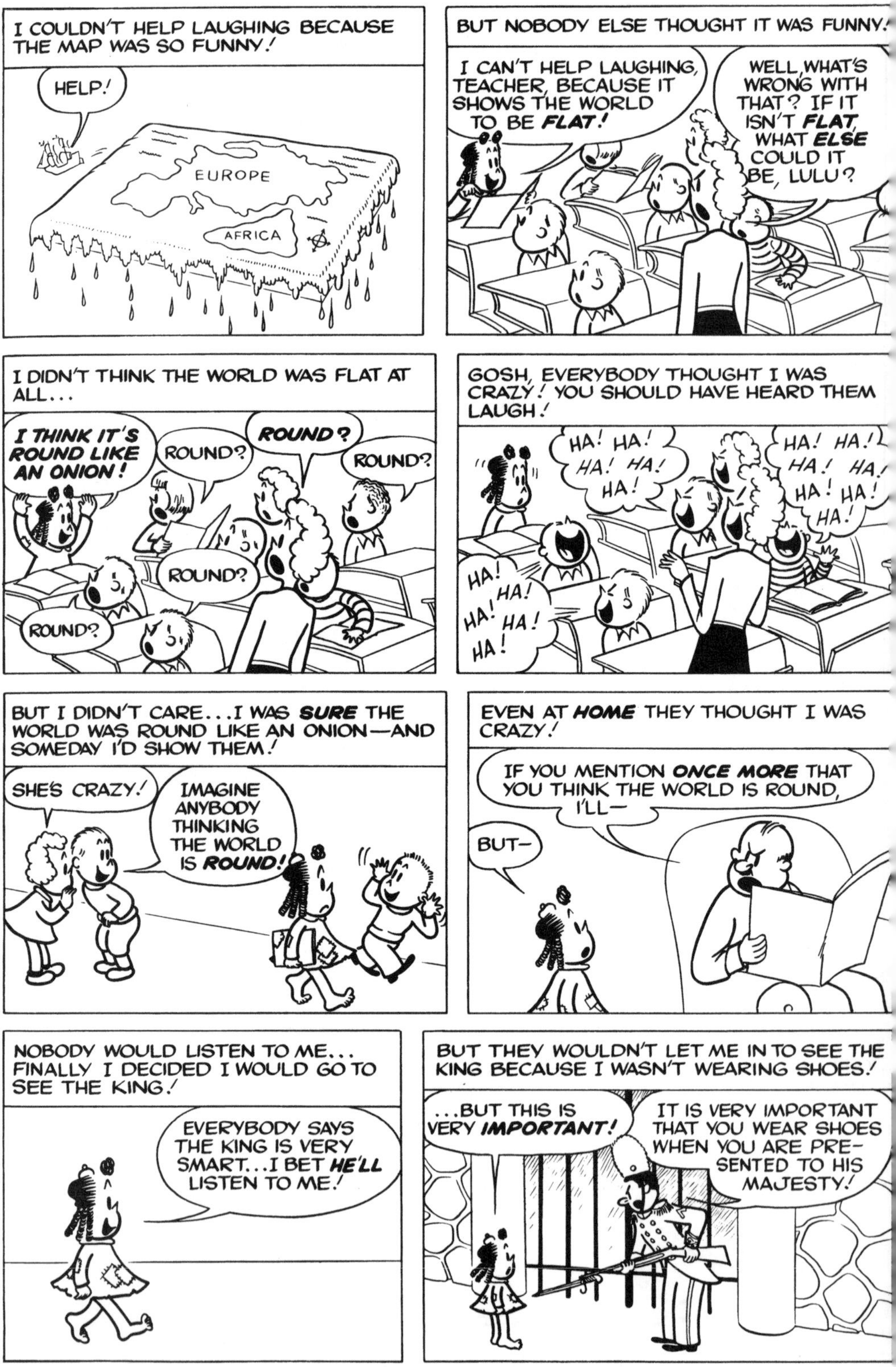

I COULDN'T HELP LAUGHING BECAUSE THE MAP WAS SO FUNNY!
HELP!
EUROPE
AFRICA
BUT NOBODY ELSE THOUGHT IT WAS FUNNY!
I CAN'T HELP LAUGHING, TEACHER, BECAUSE IT SHOWS THE WORLD TO BE **FLAT!**
WELL, WHAT'S WRONG WITH THAT? IF IT ISN'T **FLAT,** WHAT **ELSE** COULD IT BE, LULU?
I DIDN'T THINK THE WORLD WAS FLAT AT ALL...
I THINK IT'S ROUND LIKE AN ONION!
ROUND?
ROUND?
ROUND?
ROUND?
ROUND?
GOSH, EVERYBODY THOUGHT I WAS CRAZY! YOU SHOULD HAVE HEARD THEM LAUGH!
HA! HA! HA! HA! HA!
HA! HA! HA! HA! HA! HA! HA!
HA! HA! HA! HA! HA!
BUT I DIDN'T CARE...I WAS **SURE** THE WORLD WAS ROUND LIKE AN ONION—AND SOMEDAY I'D SHOW THEM!
SHE'S CRAZY!
IMAGINE ANYBODY THINKING THE WORLD IS **ROUND!**
EVEN AT **HOME** THEY THOUGHT I WAS CRAZY!
IF YOU MENTION **ONCE MORE** THAT YOU THINK THE WORLD IS ROUND, I'LL—
BUT—
NOBODY WOULD LISTEN TO ME... FINALLY I DECIDED I WOULD GO TO SEE THE KING!
EVERYBODY SAYS THE KING IS VERY SMART...I BET **HE'LL** LISTEN TO ME!
BUT THEY WOULDN'T LET ME IN TO SEE THE KING BECAUSE I WASN'T WEARING SHOES!
...BUT THIS IS VERY **IMPORTANT!**
IT IS VERY IMPORTANT THAT YOU WEAR SHOES WHEN YOU ARE PRESENTED TO HIS MAJESTY!

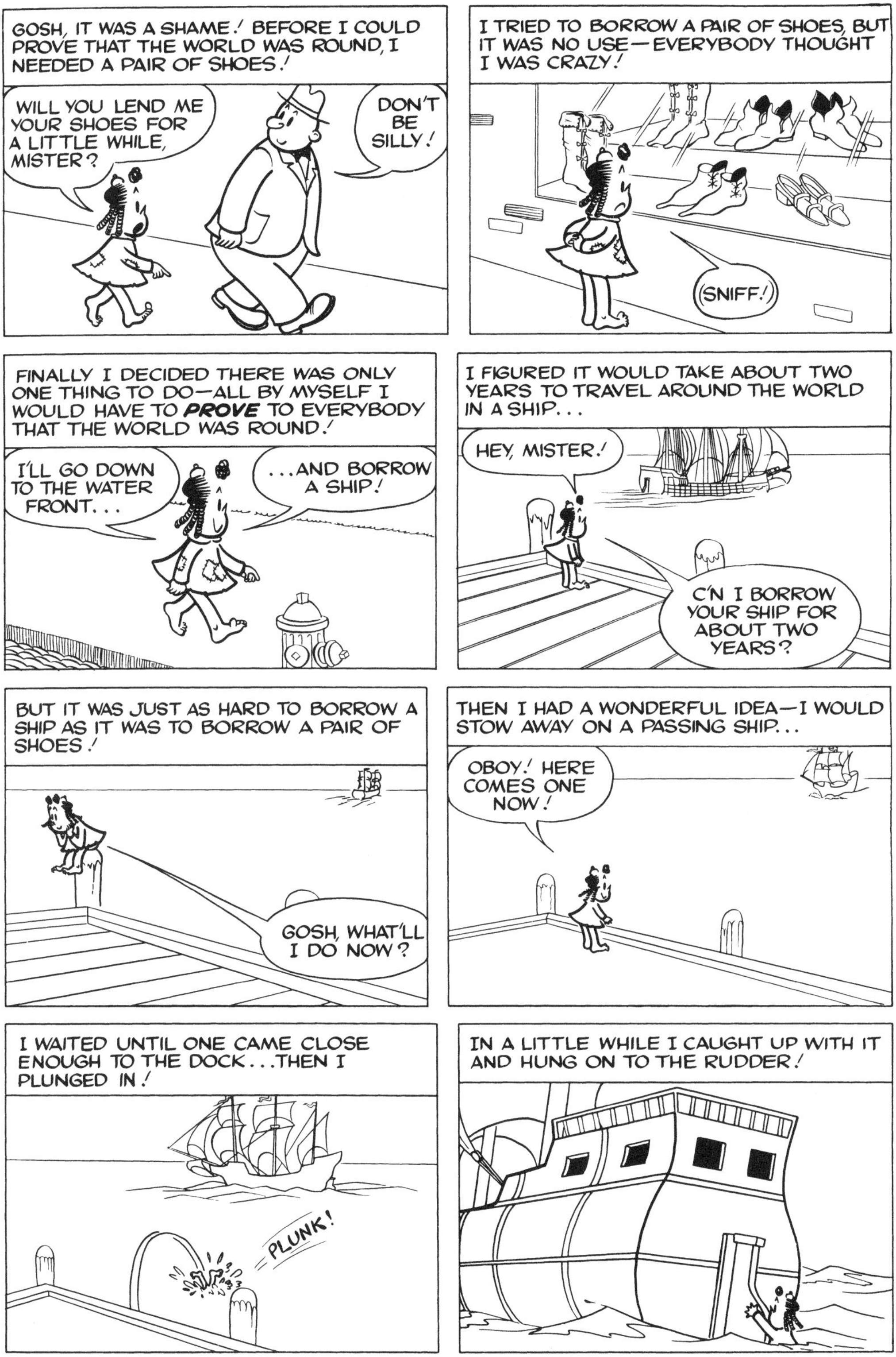
GOSH, IT WAS A SHAME! BEFORE I COULD PROVE THAT THE WORLD WAS ROUND, I NEEDED A PAIR OF SHOES!
WILL YOU LEND ME YOUR SHOES FOR A LITTLE WHILE, MISTER?
DON'T BE SILLY!
I TRIED TO BORROW A PAIR OF SHOES, BUT IT WAS NO USE—EVERYBODY THOUGHT I WAS CRAZY!
(SNIFF!)
FINALLY I DECIDED THERE WAS ONLY ONE THING TO DO—ALL BY MYSELF I WOULD HAVE TO **PROVE** TO EVERYBODY THAT THE WORLD WAS ROUND!
I'LL GO DOWN TO THE WATER FRONT...
...AND BORROW A SHIP!
I FIGURED IT WOULD TAKE ABOUT TWO YEARS TO TRAVEL AROUND THE WORLD IN A SHIP...
HEY, MISTER!
C'N I BORROW YOUR SHIP FOR ABOUT TWO YEARS?
BUT IT WAS JUST AS HARD TO BORROW A SHIP AS IT WAS TO BORROW A PAIR OF SHOES!
GOSH, WHAT'LL I DO NOW?
THEN I HAD A WONDERFUL IDEA—I WOULD STOW AWAY ON A PASSING SHIP...
OBOY! HERE COMES ONE NOW!
I WAITED UNTIL ONE CAME CLOSE ENOUGH TO THE DOCK...THEN I PLUNGED IN!
PLUNK!
IN A LITTLE WHILE I CAUGHT UP WITH IT AND HUNG ON TO THE RUDDER!

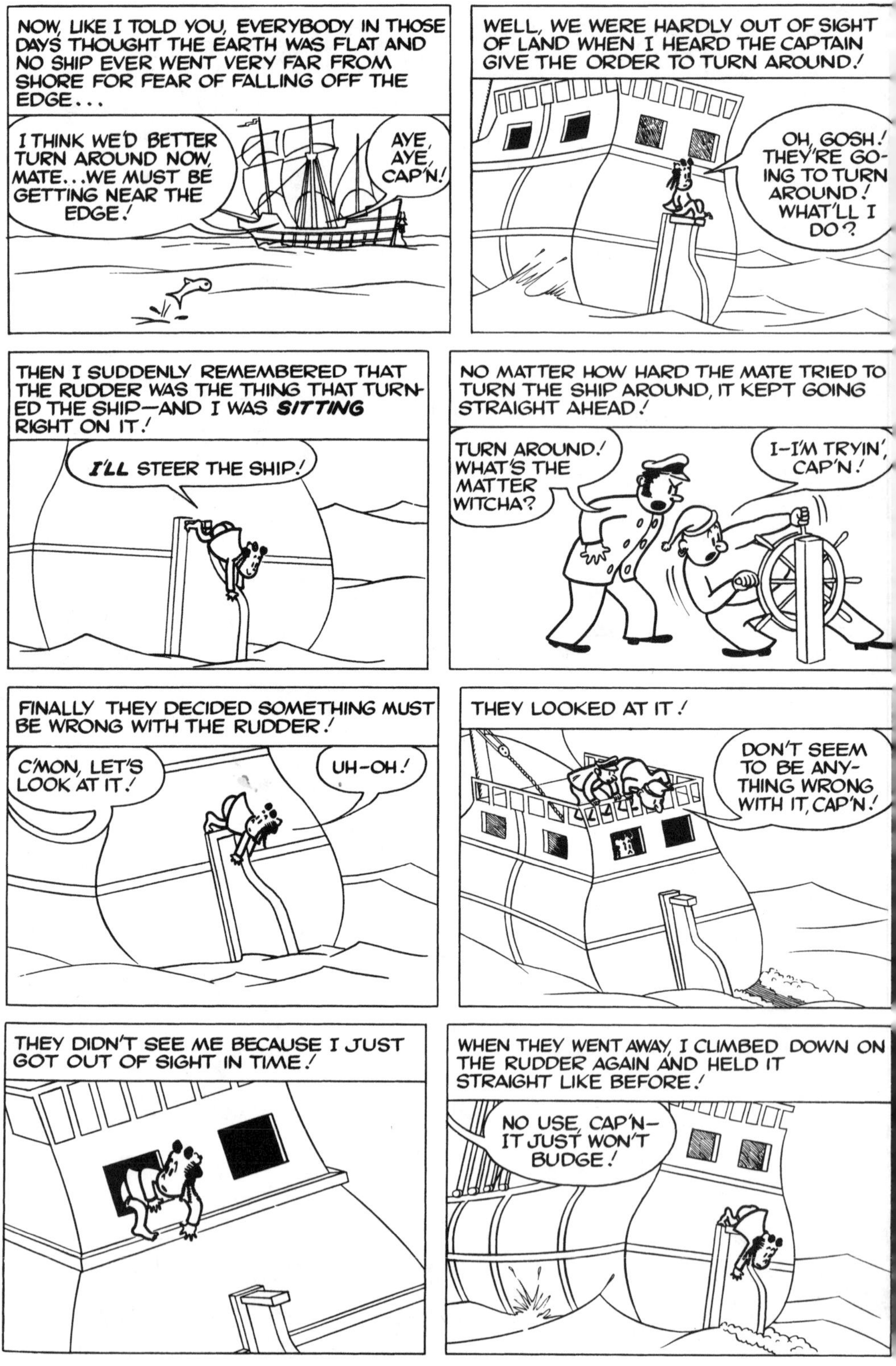
NOW, LIKE I TOLD YOU, EVERYBODY IN THOSE DAYS THOUGHT THE EARTH WAS FLAT AND NO SHIP EVER WENT VERY FAR FROM SHORE FOR FEAR OF FALLING OFF THE EDGE...
I THINK WE'D BETTER TURN AROUND NOW, MATE...WE MUST BE GETTING NEAR THE EDGE!
AYE, AYE, CAP'N!
WELL, WE WERE HARDLY OUT OF SIGHT OF LAND WHEN I HEARD THE CAPTAIN GIVE THE ORDER TO TURN AROUND!
OH, GOSH! THEY'RE GOING TO TURN AROUND! WHAT'LL I DO?
THEN I SUDDENLY REMEMBERED THAT THE RUDDER WAS THE THING THAT TURNED THE SHIP—AND I WAS SITTING RIGHT ON IT!
I'LL STEER THE SHIP!
NO MATTER HOW HARD THE MATE TRIED TO TURN THE SHIP AROUND, IT KEPT GOING STRAIGHT AHEAD!
TURN AROUND! WHAT'S THE MATTER WITCHA?
I-I'M TRYIN', CAP'N!
FINALLY THEY DECIDED SOMETHING MUST BE WRONG WITH THE RUDDER!
C'MON, LET'S LOOK AT IT!
UH-OH!
THEY LOOKED AT IT!
DON'T SEEM TO BE ANYTHING WRONG WITH IT, CAP'N!
THEY DIDN'T SEE ME BECAUSE I JUST GOT OUT OF SIGHT IN TIME!
WHEN THEY WENT AWAY, I CLIMBED DOWN ON THE RUDDER AGAIN AND HELD IT STRAIGHT LIKE BEFORE!
NO USE, CAP'N—IT JUST WON'T BUDGE!

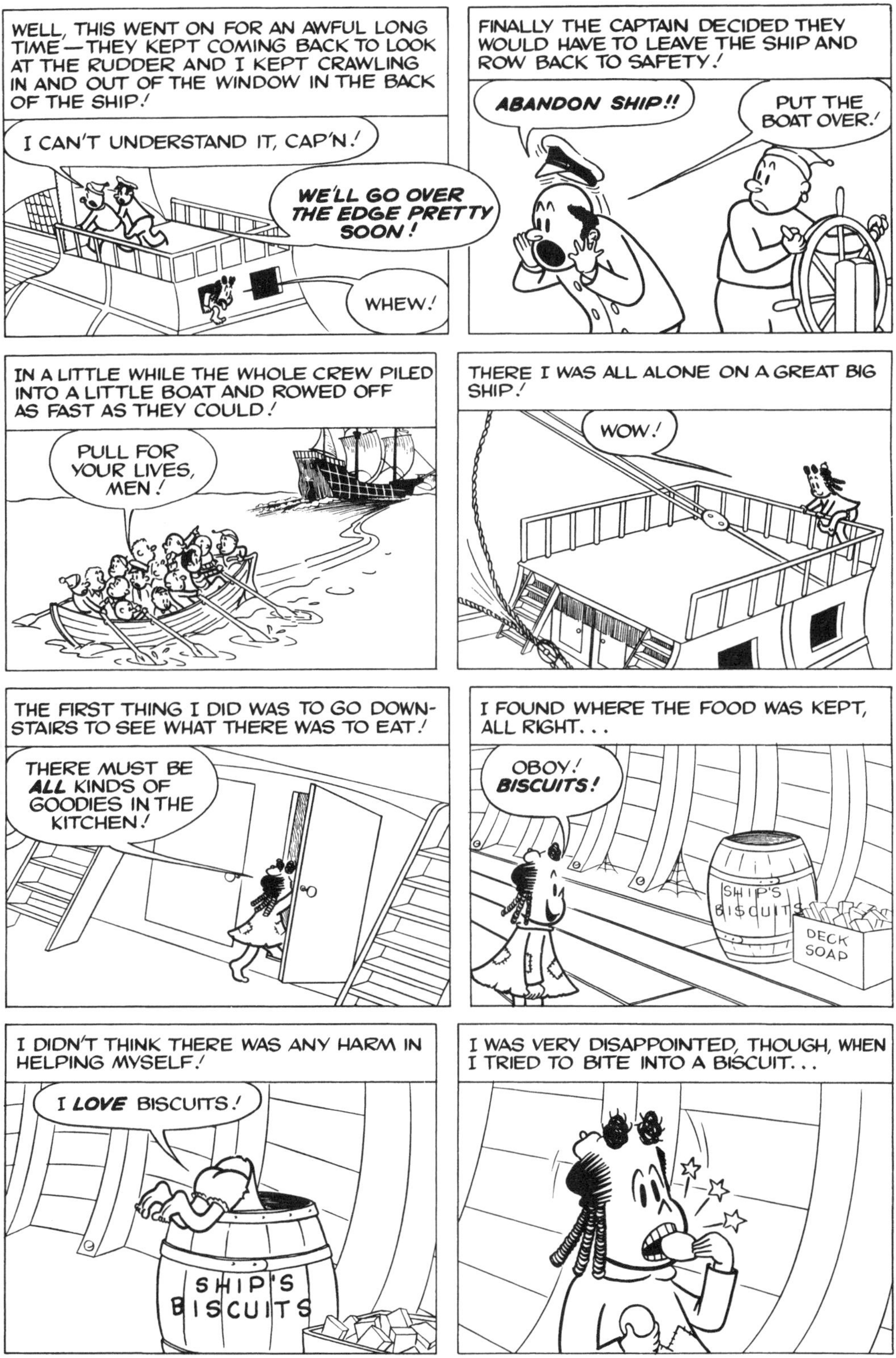
WELL, THIS WENT ON FOR AN AWFUL LONG TIME—THEY KEPT COMING BACK TO LOOK AT THE RUDDER AND I KEPT CRAWLING IN AND OUT OF THE WINDOW IN THE BACK OF THE SHIP!
I CAN'T UNDERSTAND IT, CAP'N.!
WE'LL GO OVER THE EDGE PRETTY SOON!
WHEW!
FINALLY THE CAPTAIN DECIDED THEY WOULD HAVE TO LEAVE THE SHIP AND ROW BACK TO SAFETY!
ABANDON SHIP!!
PUT THE BOAT OVER!
IN A LITTLE WHILE THE WHOLE CREW PILED INTO A LITTLE BOAT AND ROWED OFF AS FAST AS THEY COULD!
PULL FOR YOUR LIVES, MEN!
THERE I WAS ALL ALONE ON A GREAT BIG SHIP!
WOW!
THE FIRST THING I DID WAS TO GO DOWN-STAIRS TO SEE WHAT THERE WAS TO EAT!
THERE MUST BE ALL KINDS OF GOODIES IN THE KITCHEN!
I FOUND WHERE THE FOOD WAS KEPT, ALL RIGHT...
OBOY! BISCUITS!
SHIP'S BISCUITS
DECK SOAP
I DIDN'T THINK THERE WAS ANY HARM IN HELPING MYSELF!
I LOVE BISCUITS!
SHIP'S BISCUITS
I WAS VERY DISAPPOINTED, THOUGH, WHEN I TRIED TO BITE INTO A BISCUIT...

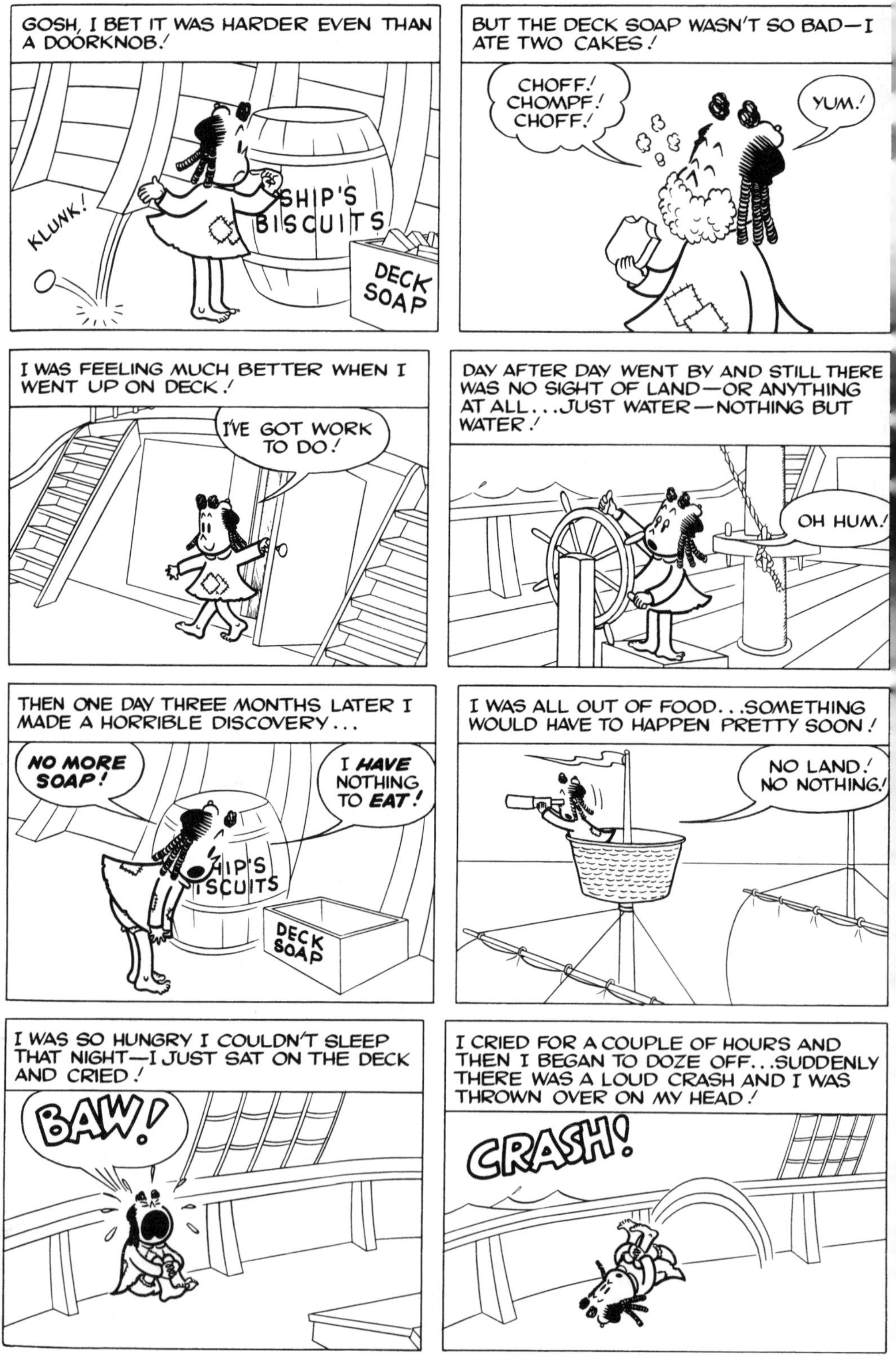
GOSH, I BET IT WAS HARDER EVEN THAN A DOORKNOB!
SHIP'S BISCUITS
KLUNK!
DECK SOAP
BUT THE DECK SOAP WASN'T SO BAD—I ATE TWO CAKES!
CHOFF! CHOMPF! CHOFF!
YUM!
I WAS FEELING MUCH BETTER WHEN I WENT UP ON DECK!
I'VE GOT WORK TO DO!
DAY AFTER DAY WENT BY AND STILL THERE WAS NO SIGHT OF LAND—OR ANYTHING AT ALL...JUST WATER—NOTHING BUT WATER!
OH HUM!
THEN ONE DAY THREE MONTHS LATER I MADE A HORRIBLE DISCOVERY...
NO MORE SOAP!
I HAVE NOTHING TO EAT!
SHIP'S BISCUITS
DECK SOAP
I WAS ALL OUT OF FOOD...SOMETHING WOULD HAVE TO HAPPEN PRETTY SOON!
NO LAND! NO NOTHING!
I WAS SO HUNGRY I COULDN'T SLEEP THAT NIGHT—I JUST SAT ON THE DECK AND CRIED!
BAW!
I CRIED FOR A COUPLE OF HOURS AND THEN I BEGAN TO DOZE OFF...SUDDENLY THERE WAS A LOUD CRASH AND I WAS THROWN OVER ON MY HEAD!
CRASH!

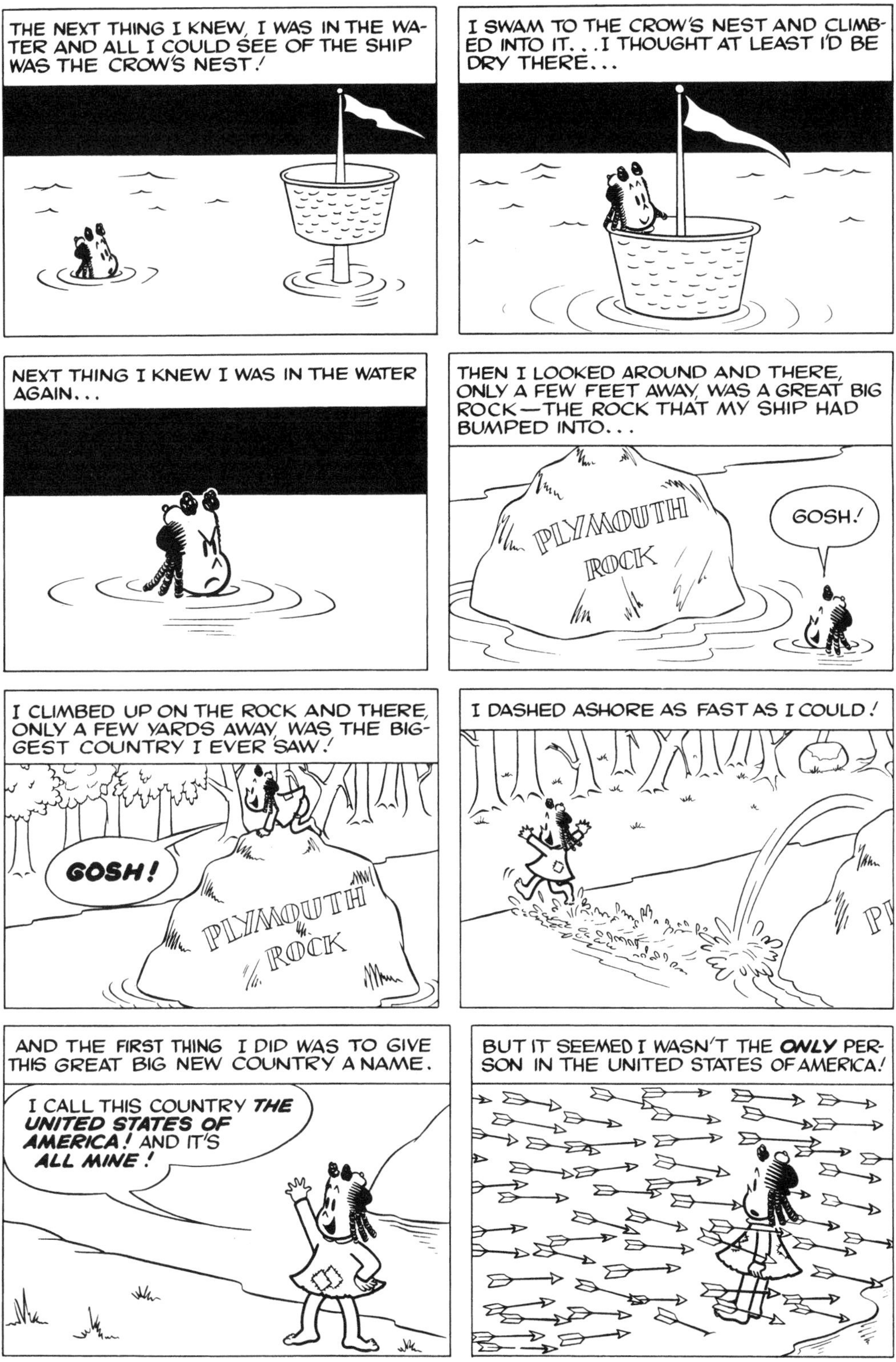
THE NEXT THING I KNEW, I WAS IN THE WATER AND ALL I COULD SEE OF THE SHIP WAS THE CROW'S NEST!
I SWAM TO THE CROW'S NEST AND CLIMBED INTO IT. . . I THOUGHT AT LEAST I'D BE DRY THERE. . .
NEXT THING I KNEW I WAS IN THE WATER AGAIN. . .
THEN I LOOKED AROUND AND THERE, ONLY A FEW FEET AWAY, WAS A GREAT BIG ROCK—THE ROCK THAT MY SHIP HAD BUMPED INTO. . .
PLYMOUTH ROCK
GOSH!
I CLIMBED UP ON THE ROCK AND THERE, ONLY A FEW YARDS AWAY, WAS THE BIGGEST COUNTRY I EVER SAW!
GOSH!
PLYMOUTH ROCK
I DASHED ASHORE AS FAST AS I COULD!
AND THE FIRST THING I DID WAS TO GIVE THIS GREAT BIG NEW COUNTRY A NAME.
I CALL THIS COUNTRY **THE UNITED STATES OF AMERICA!** AND IT'S **ALL MINE!**
BUT IT SEEMED I WASN'T THE **ONLY** PERSON IN THE UNITED STATES OF AMERICA!

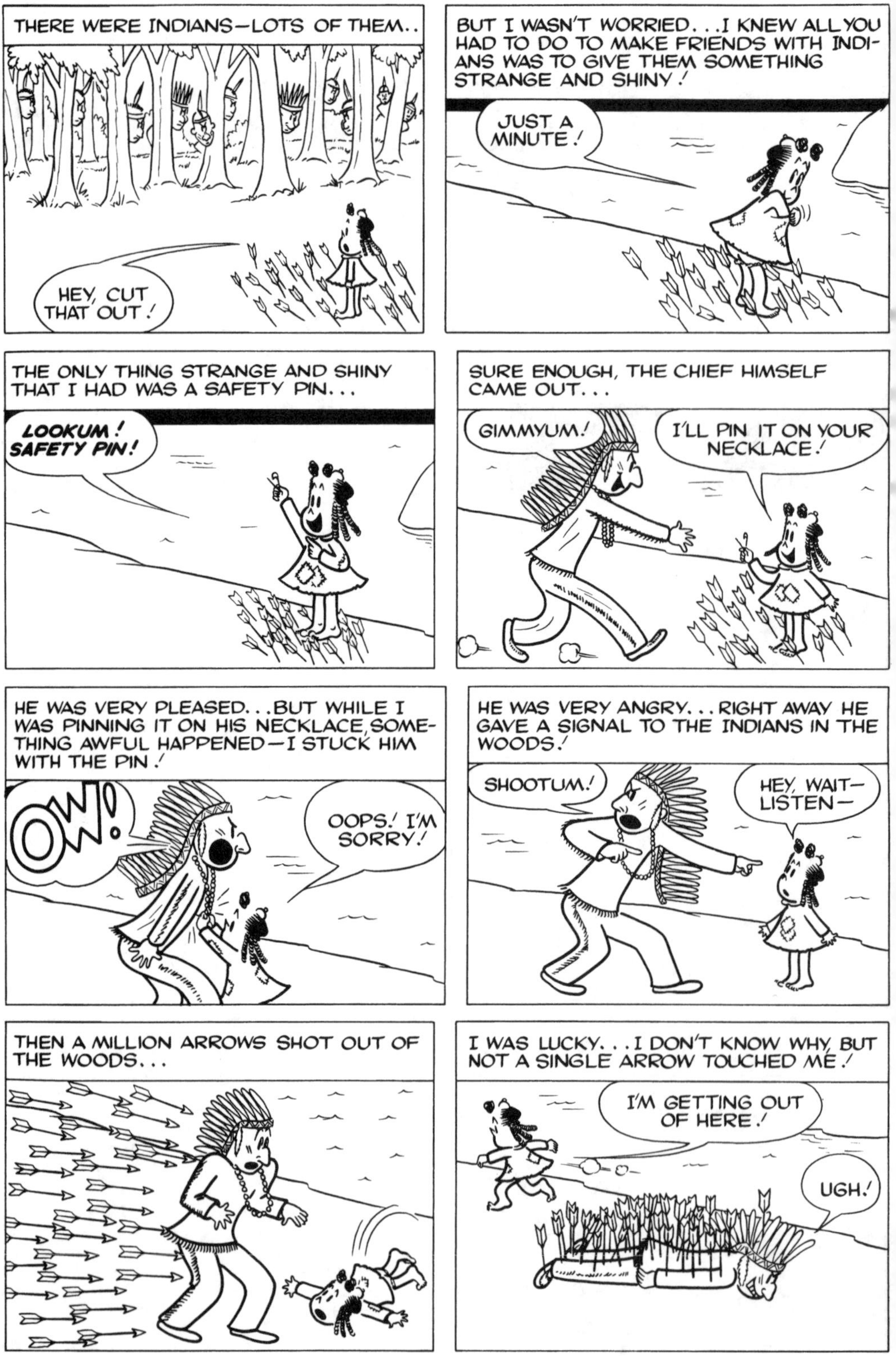
THERE WERE INDIANS—LOTS OF THEM..
HEY, CUT THAT OUT!
BUT I WASN'T WORRIED...I KNEW ALL YOU HAD TO DO TO MAKE FRIENDS WITH INDIANS WAS TO GIVE THEM SOMETHING STRANGE AND SHINY!
JUST A MINUTE!
THE ONLY THING STRANGE AND SHINY THAT I HAD WAS A SAFETY PIN...
LOOKUM! SAFETY PIN!
SURE ENOUGH, THE CHIEF HIMSELF CAME OUT...
GIMMYUM!
I'LL PIN IT ON YOUR NECKLACE!
HE WAS VERY PLEASED...BUT WHILE I WAS PINNING IT ON HIS NECKLACE, SOMETHING AWFUL HAPPENED—I STUCK HIM WITH THE PIN!
OW!
OOPS! I'M SORRY!
HE WAS VERY ANGRY...RIGHT AWAY HE GAVE A SIGNAL TO THE INDIANS IN THE WOODS!
SHOOTUM!
HEY, WAIT—LISTEN—
THEN A MILLION ARROWS SHOT OUT OF THE WOODS...
I WAS LUCKY...I DON'T KNOW WHY, BUT NOT A SINGLE ARROW TOUCHED ME!
I'M GETTING OUT OF HERE!
UGH!

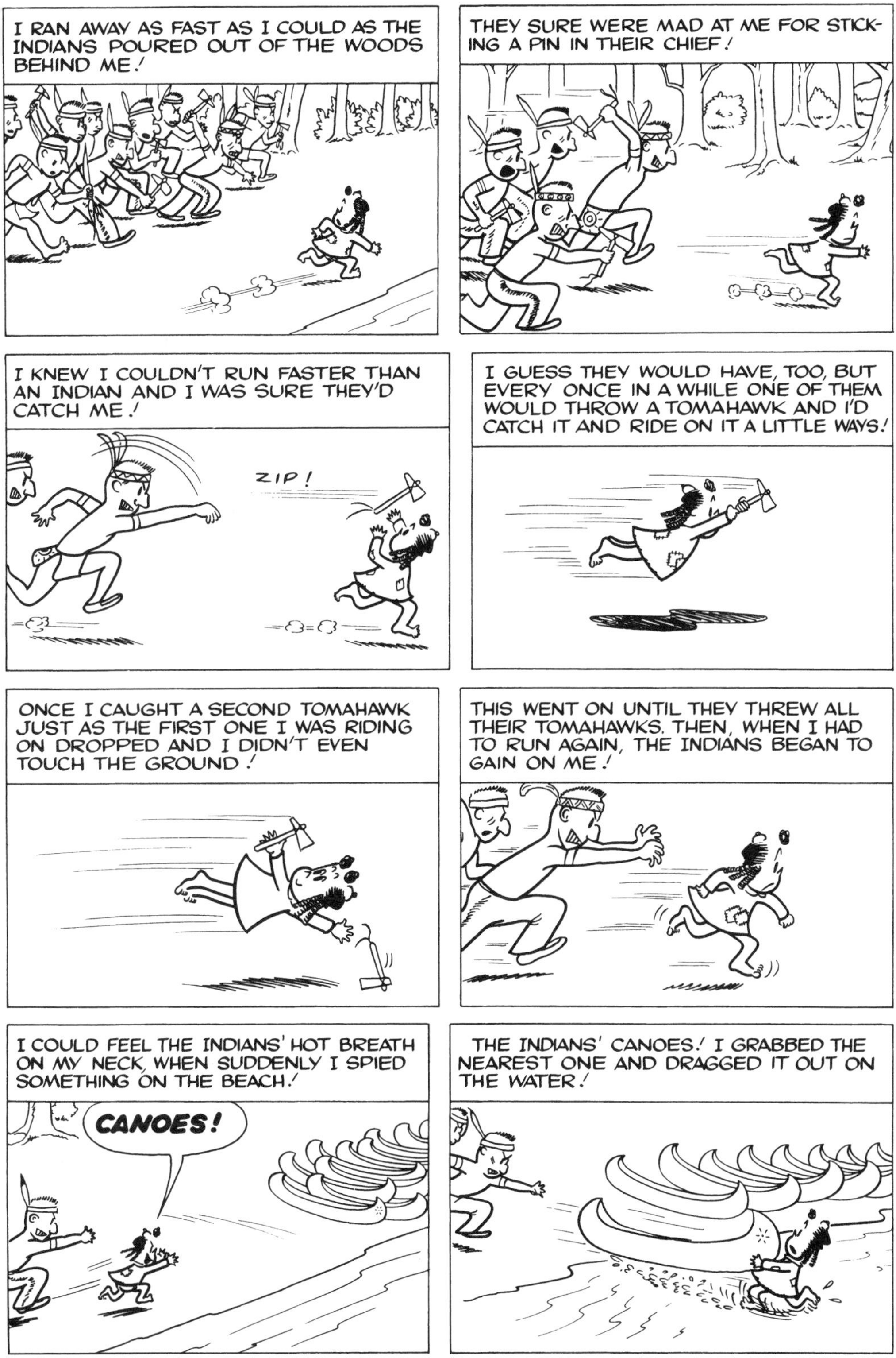
I RAN AWAY AS FAST AS I COULD AS THE INDIANS POURED OUT OF THE WOODS BEHIND ME!
THEY SURE WERE MAD AT ME FOR STICKING A PIN IN THEIR CHIEF!
I KNEW I COULDN'T RUN FASTER THAN AN INDIAN AND I WAS SURE THEY'D CATCH ME!
ZIP!
I GUESS THEY WOULD HAVE, TOO, BUT EVERY ONCE IN A WHILE ONE OF THEM WOULD THROW A TOMAHAWK AND I'D CATCH IT AND RIDE ON IT A LITTLE WAYS!
ONCE I CAUGHT A SECOND TOMAHAWK JUST AS THE FIRST ONE I WAS RIDING ON DROPPED AND I DIDN'T EVEN TOUCH THE GROUND!
THIS WENT ON UNTIL THEY THREW ALL THEIR TOMAHAWKS. THEN, WHEN I HAD TO RUN AGAIN, THE INDIANS BEGAN TO GAIN ON ME!
I COULD FEEL THE INDIANS' HOT BREATH ON MY NECK, WHEN SUDDENLY I SPIED SOMETHING ON THE BEACH!
CANOES!
THE INDIANS' CANOES! I GRABBED THE NEAREST ONE AND DRAGGED IT OUT ON THE WATER!

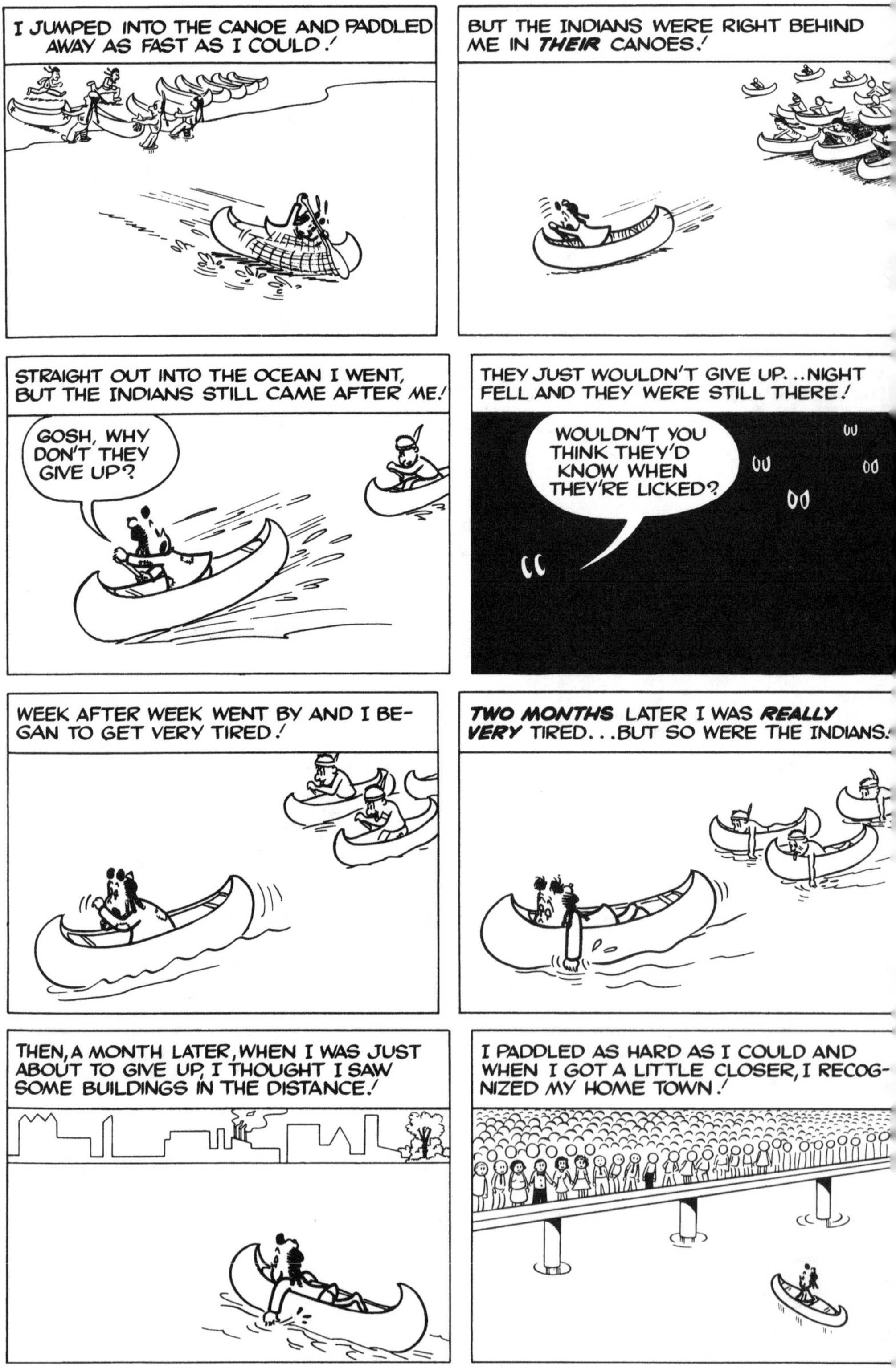
I JUMPED INTO THE CANOE AND PADDLED AWAY AS FAST AS I COULD!
BUT THE INDIANS WERE RIGHT BEHIND ME IN *THEIR* CANOES!
STRAIGHT OUT INTO THE OCEAN I WENT, BUT THE INDIANS STILL CAME AFTER ME!
GOSH, WHY DON'T THEY GIVE UP?
THEY JUST WOULDN'T GIVE UP...NIGHT FELL AND THEY WERE STILL THERE!
WOULDN'T YOU THINK THEY'D KNOW WHEN THEY'RE LICKED?
WEEK AFTER WEEK WENT BY AND I BE- GAN TO GET VERY TIRED!
TWO MONTHS LATER I WAS *REALLY VERY* TIRED...BUT SO WERE THE INDIANS!
THEN, A MONTH LATER, WHEN I WAS JUST ABOUT TO GIVE UP, I THOUGHT I SAW SOME BUILDINGS IN THE DISTANCE!
I PADDLED AS HARD AS I COULD AND WHEN I GOT A LITTLE CLOSER, I RECOG- NIZED MY HOME TOWN!

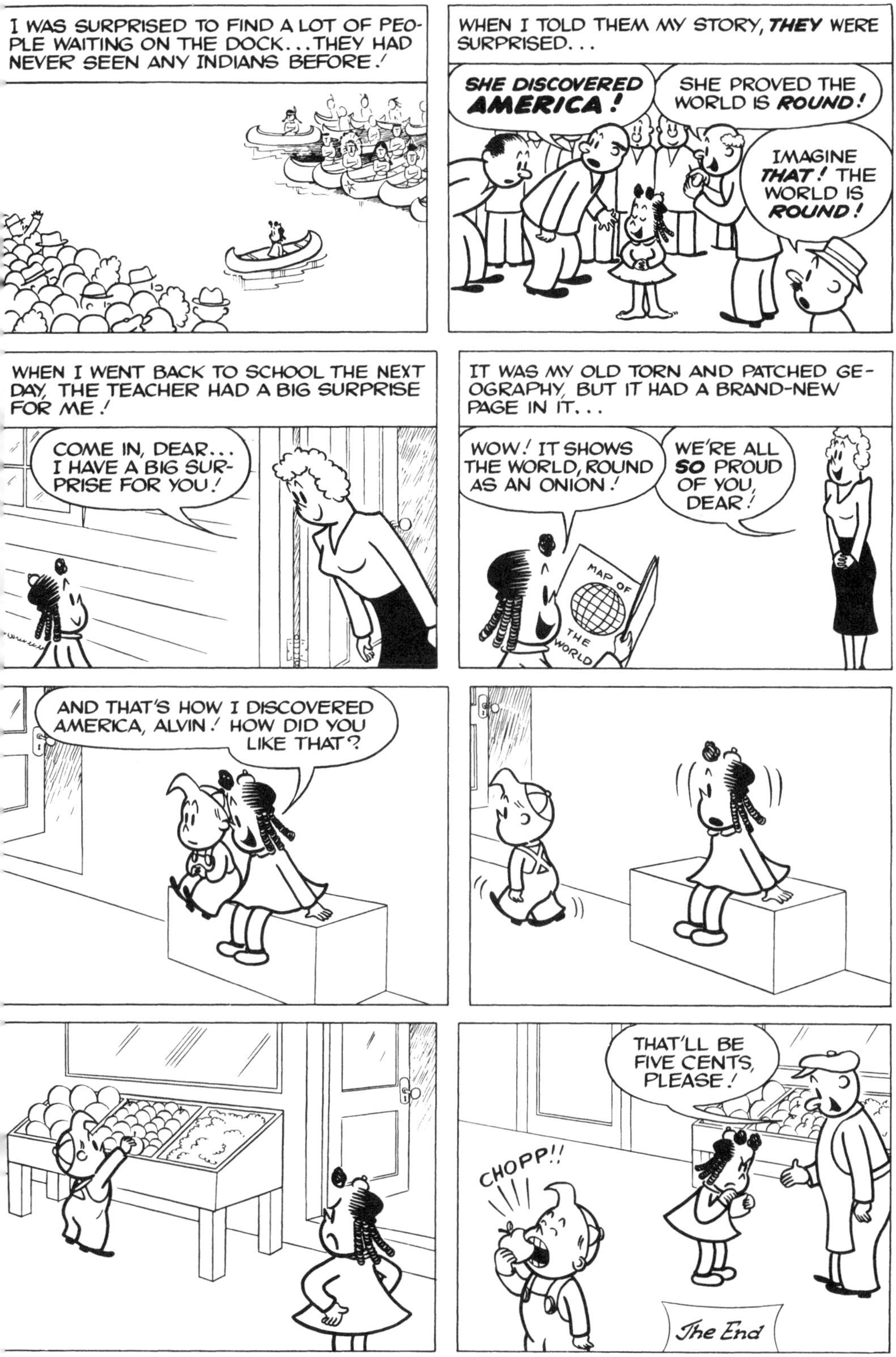
I WAS SURPRISED TO FIND A LOT OF PEOPLE WAITING ON THE DOCK...THEY HAD NEVER SEEN ANY INDIANS BEFORE!
WHEN I TOLD THEM MY STORY, THEY WERE SURPRISED...
SHE DISCOVERED AMERICA!
SHE PROVED THE WORLD IS ROUND!
IMAGINE THAT! THE WORLD IS ROUND!
WHEN I WENT BACK TO SCHOOL THE NEXT DAY, THE TEACHER HAD A BIG SURPRISE FOR ME!
COME IN, DEAR... I HAVE A BIG SURPRISE FOR YOU!
IT WAS MY OLD TORN AND PATCHED GEOGRAPHY, BUT IT HAD A BRAND-NEW PAGE IN IT...
WOW! IT SHOWS THE WORLD, ROUND AS AN ONION!
WE'RE ALL SO PROUD OF YOU, DEAR!
MAP OF THE WORLD
AND THAT'S HOW I DISCOVERED AMERICA, ALVIN! HOW DID YOU LIKE THAT?
THAT'LL BE FIVE CENTS, PLEASE!
CHOPP!!
The End

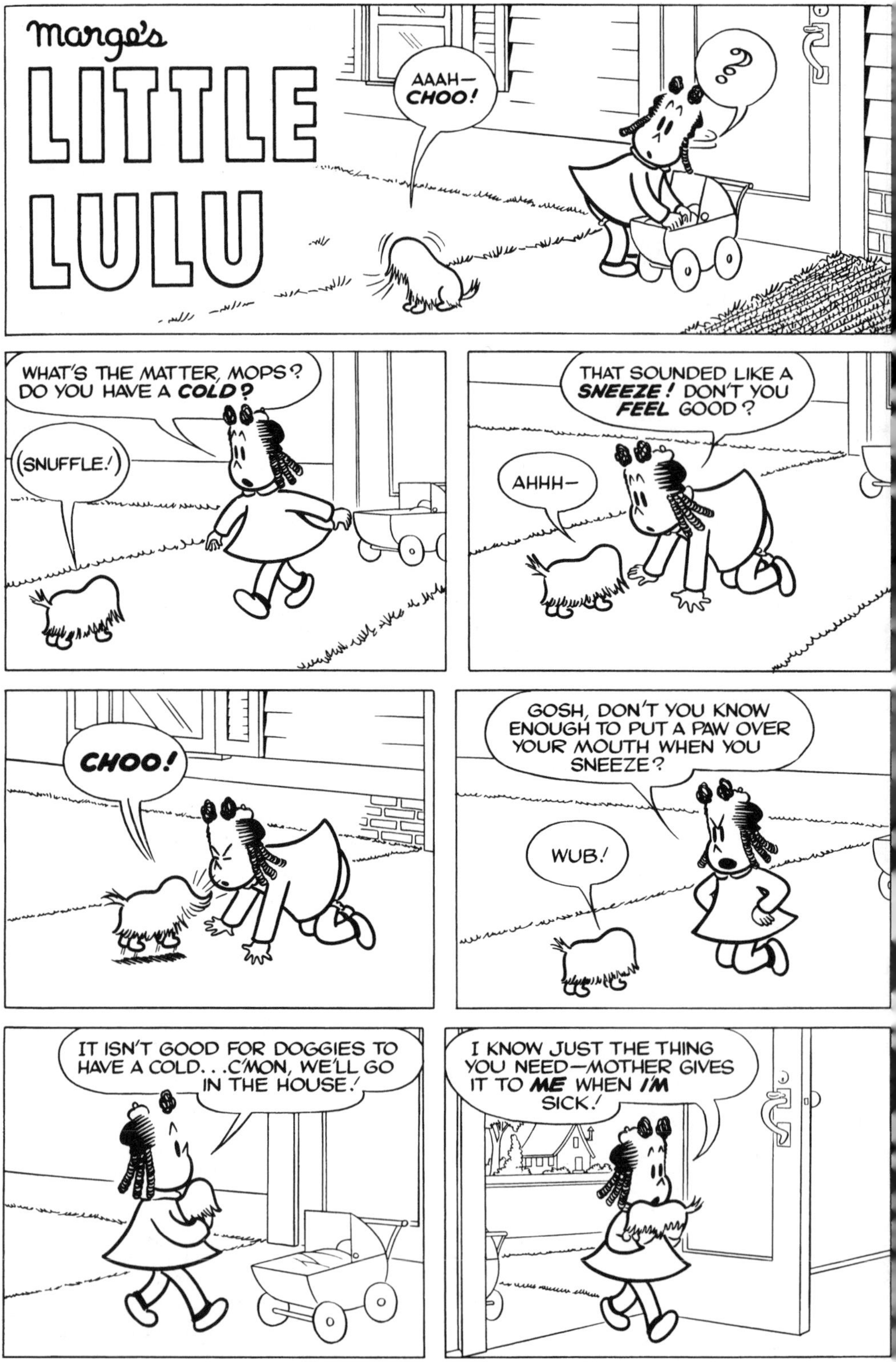
marge's
LITTLE LULU
AAAH—CHOO!
?
WHAT'S THE MATTER, MOPS? DO YOU HAVE A COLD?
(SNUFFLE!)
THAT SOUNDED LIKE A SNEEZE! DON'T YOU FEEL GOOD?
AHHH—
CHOO!
GOSH, DON'T YOU KNOW ENOUGH TO PUT A PAW OVER YOUR MOUTH WHEN YOU SNEEZE?
WUB!
IT ISN'T GOOD FOR DOGGIES TO HAVE A COLD. . .C'MON, WE'LL GO IN THE HOUSE!
I KNOW JUST THE THING YOU NEED—MOTHER GIVES IT TO ME WHEN I'M SICK!

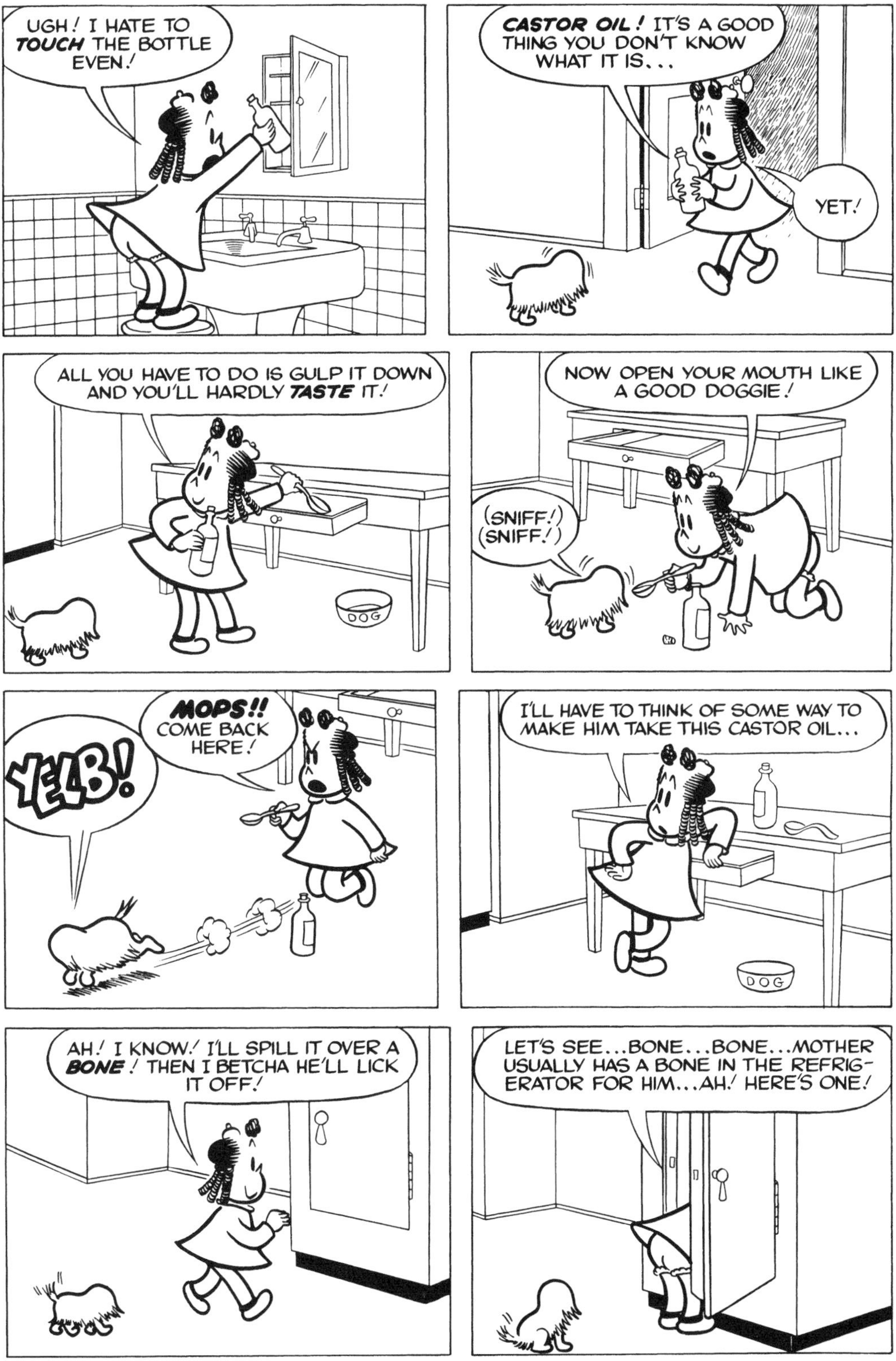
UGH! I HATE TO TOUCH THE BOTTLE EVEN!
CASTOR OIL! IT'S A GOOD THING YOU DON'T KNOW WHAT IT IS...
YET!
ALL YOU HAVE TO DO IS GULP IT DOWN AND YOU'LL HARDLY TASTE IT!
DOG
NOW OPEN YOUR MOUTH LIKE A GOOD DOGGIE!
(SNIFF!) (SNIFF!)
YELB!
MOPS!! COME BACK HERE!
I'LL HAVE TO THINK OF SOME WAY TO MAKE HIM TAKE THIS CASTOR OIL...
DOG
AH! I KNOW! I'LL SPILL IT OVER A BONE! THEN I BETCHA HE'LL LICK IT OFF!
LET'S SEE...BONE...BONE...MOTHER USUALLY HAS A BONE IN THE REFRIGERATOR FOR HIM...AH! HERE'S ONE!

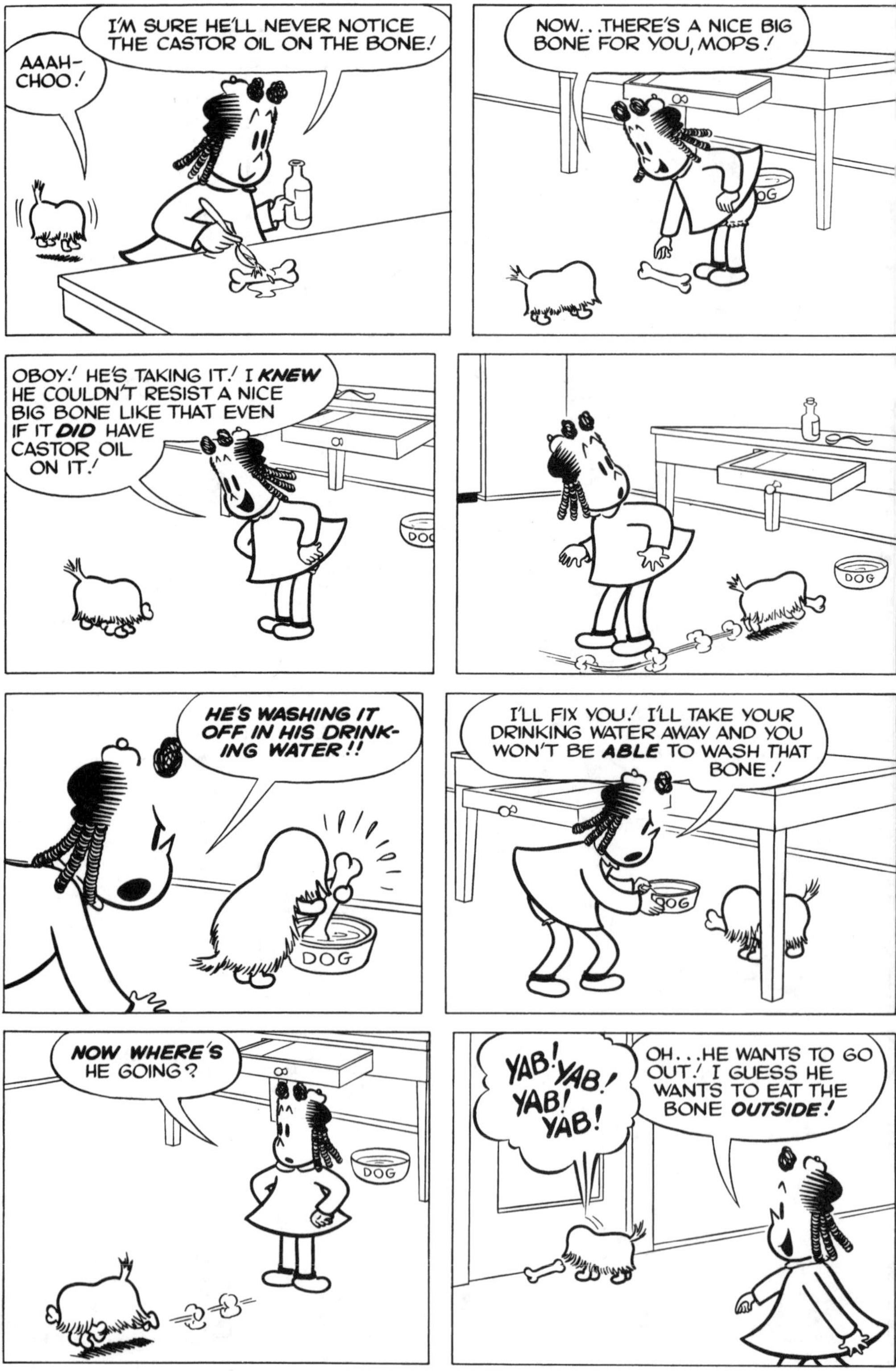
AAAH-CHOO.!
I'M SURE HE'LL NEVER NOTICE THE CASTOR OIL ON THE BONE.!
NOW. . .THERE'S A NICE BIG BONE FOR YOU, MOPS.!
DOG
OBOY.! HE'S TAKING IT.! I KNEW HE COULDN'T RESIST A NICE BIG BONE LIKE THAT EVEN IF IT DID HAVE CASTOR OIL ON IT.!
DOG
DOG
HE'S WASHING IT OFF IN HIS DRINK-ING WATER!!
DOG
I'LL FIX YOU.! I'LL TAKE YOUR DRINKING WATER AWAY AND YOU WON'T BE ABLE TO WASH THAT BONE.!
DOG
NOW WHERE'S HE GOING?
DOG
YAB! YAB! YAB! YAB!
OH. . .HE WANTS TO GO OUT.! I GUESS HE WANTS TO EAT THE BONE OUTSIDE.!

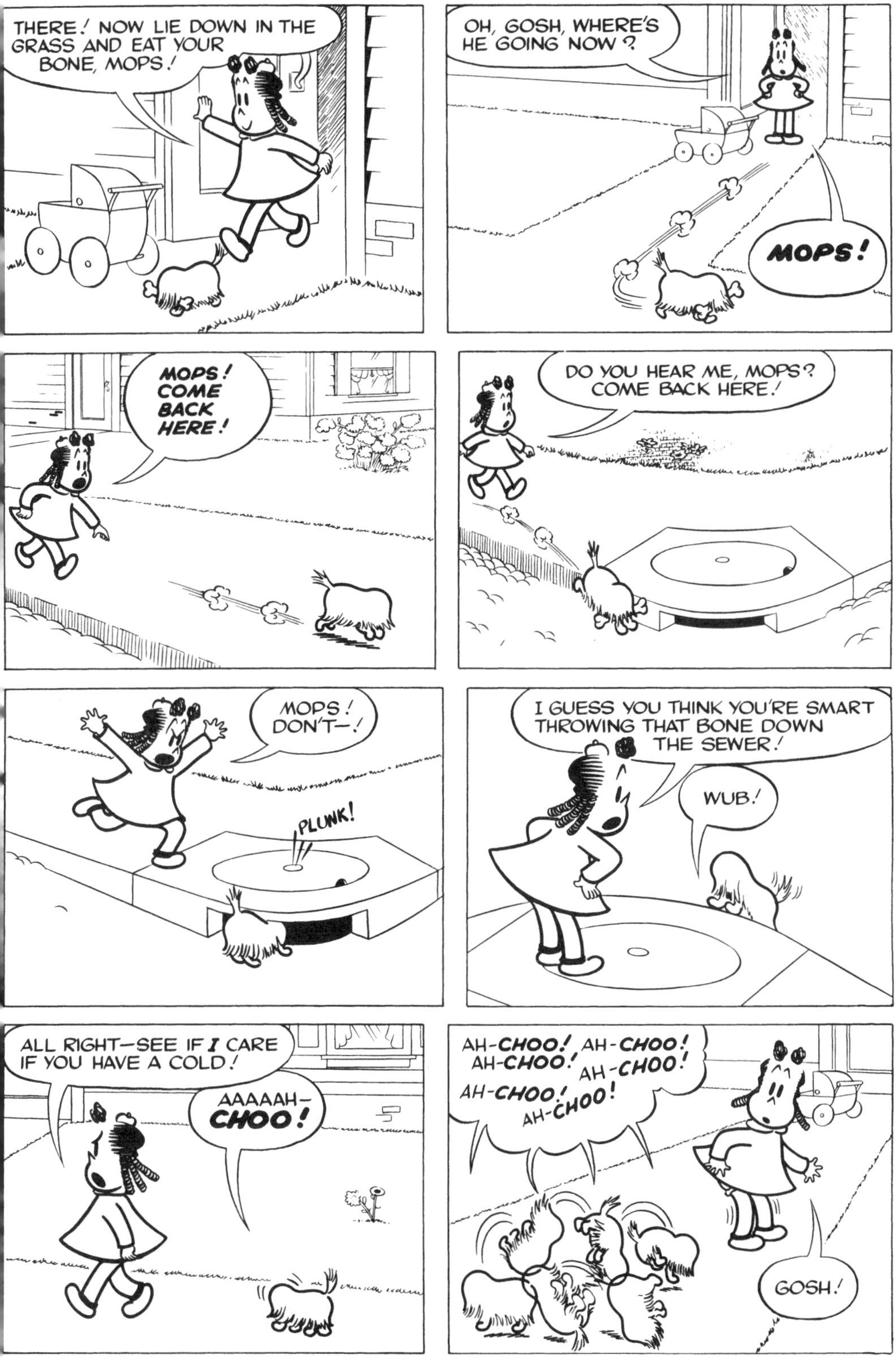
THERE! NOW LIE DOWN IN THE GRASS AND EAT YOUR BONE, MOPS!
OH, GOSH, WHERE'S HE GOING NOW?
MOPS!
MOPS! COME BACK HERE!
DO YOU HEAR ME, MOPS? COME BACK HERE!
MOPS! DON'T—!
PLUNK!
I GUESS YOU THINK YOU'RE SMART THROWING THAT BONE DOWN THE SEWER!
WUB!
ALL RIGHT—SEE IF I CARE IF YOU HAVE A COLD!
AAAAAH-CHOO!
AH-CHOO! AH-CHOO! AH-CHOO! AH-CHOO! AH-CHOO! AH-CHOO!
GOSH!

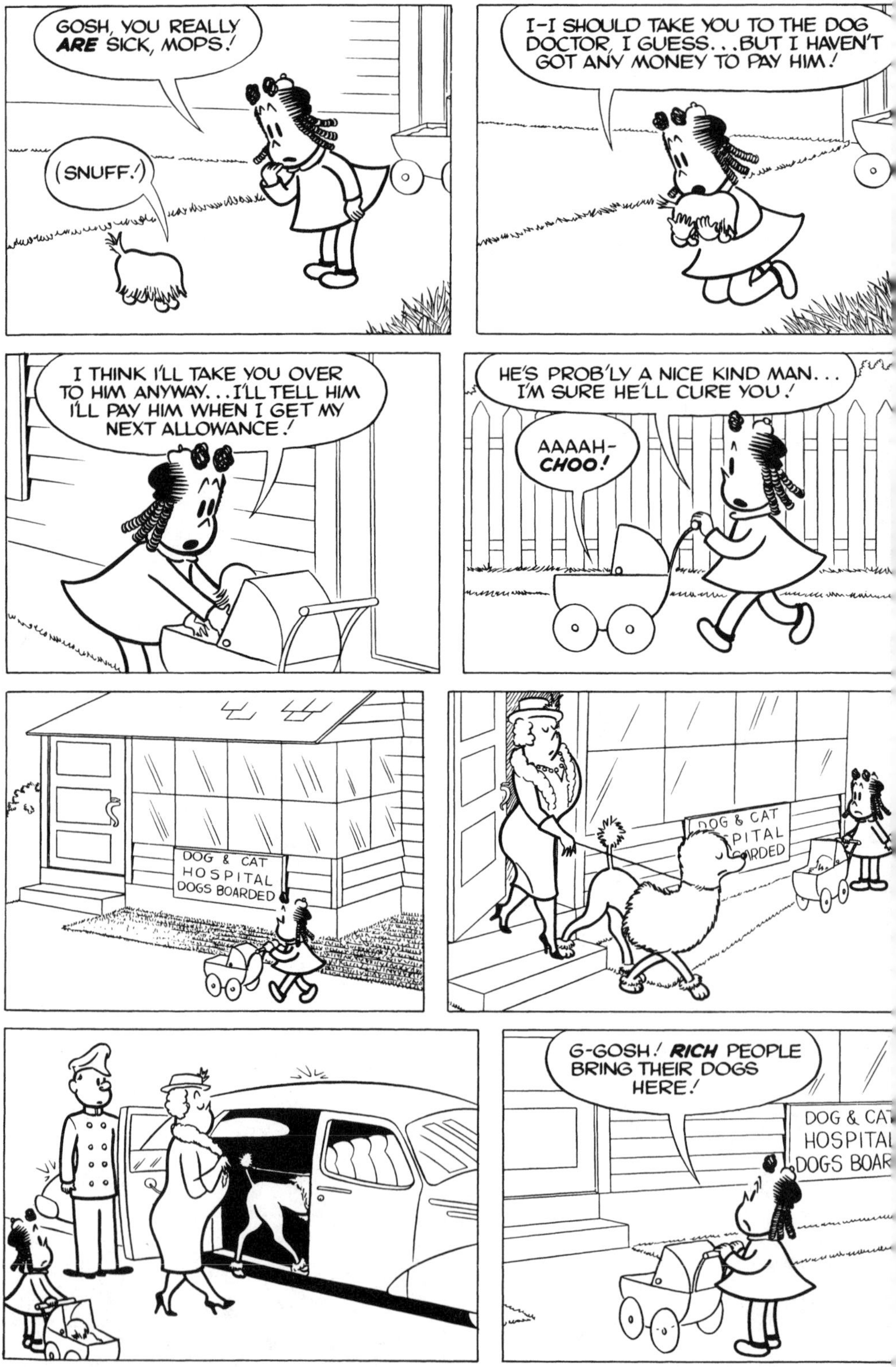
GOSH, YOU REALLY ARE SICK, MOPS!
(SNUFF!)
I-I SHOULD TAKE YOU TO THE DOG DOCTOR, I GUESS...BUT I HAVEN'T GOT ANY MONEY TO PAY HIM!
I THINK I'LL TAKE YOU OVER TO HIM ANYWAY...I'LL TELL HIM I'LL PAY HIM WHEN I GET MY NEXT ALLOWANCE!
HE'S PROB'LY A NICE KIND MAN... I'M SURE HE'LL CURE YOU!
AAAAH-CHOO!
DOG & CAT HOSPITAL DOGS BOARDED
G-GOSH! RICH PEOPLE BRING THEIR DOGS HERE!

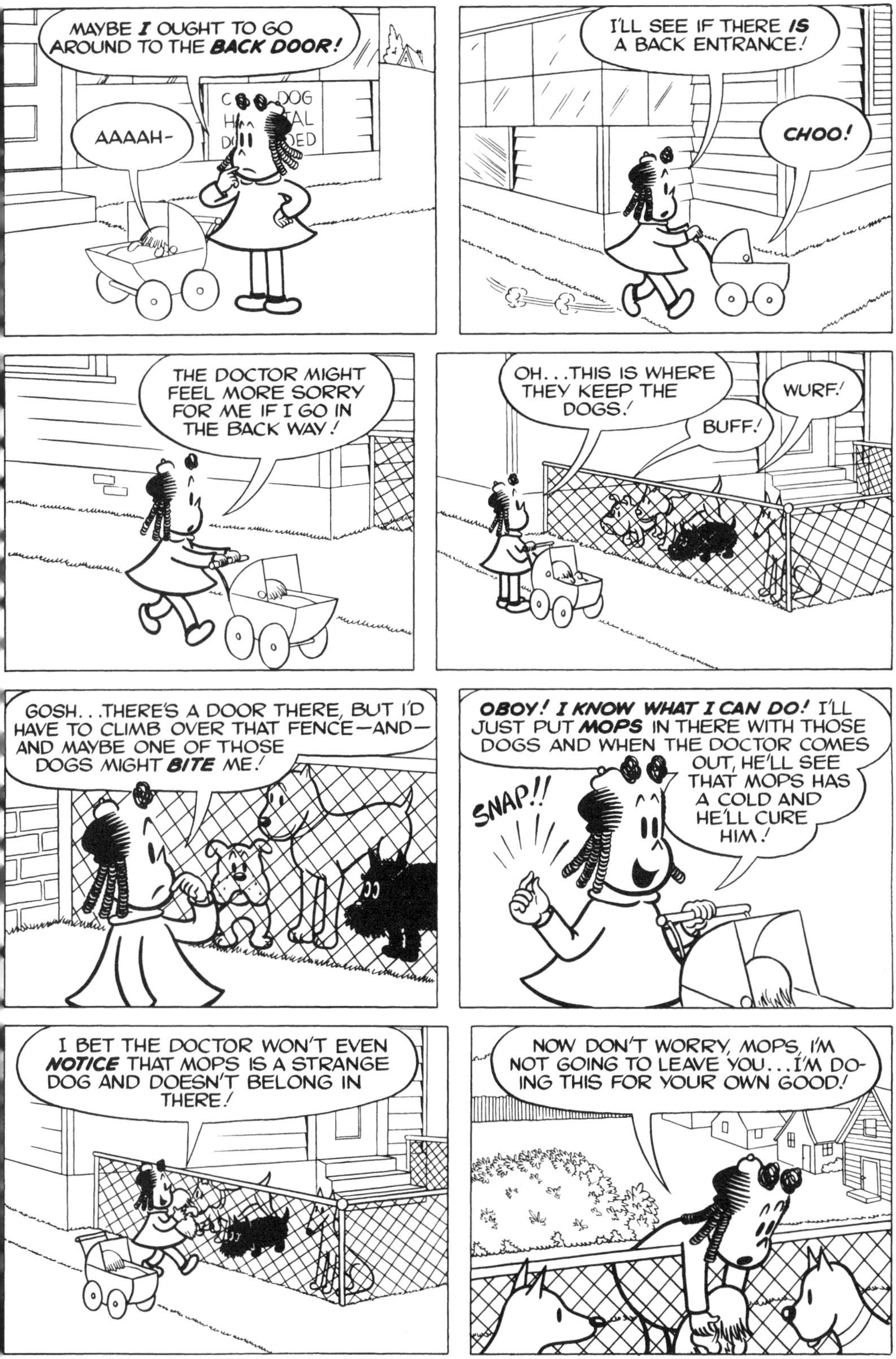
MAYBE I OUGHT TO GO AROUND TO THE BACK DOOR!
AAAAH-
I'LL SEE IF THERE IS A BACK ENTRANCE!
CHOO!
THE DOCTOR MIGHT FEEL MORE SORRY FOR ME IF I GO IN THE BACK WAY!
OH...THIS IS WHERE THEY KEEP THE DOGS!
BUFF!
WURF!
GOSH...THERE'S A DOOR THERE, BUT I'D HAVE TO CLIMB OVER THAT FENCE—AND—AND MAYBE ONE OF THOSE DOGS MIGHT BITE ME!
OBOY! I KNOW WHAT I CAN DO! I'LL JUST PUT MOPS IN THERE WITH THOSE DOGS AND WHEN THE DOCTOR COMES OUT, HE'LL SEE THAT MOPS HAS A COLD AND HE'LL CURE HIM!
SNAP!!
I BET THE DOCTOR WON'T EVEN NOTICE THAT MOPS IS A STRANGE DOG AND DOESN'T BELONG IN THERE!
NOW DON'T WORRY, MOPS, I'M NOT GOING TO LEAVE YOU...I'M DOING THIS FOR YOUR OWN GOOD!

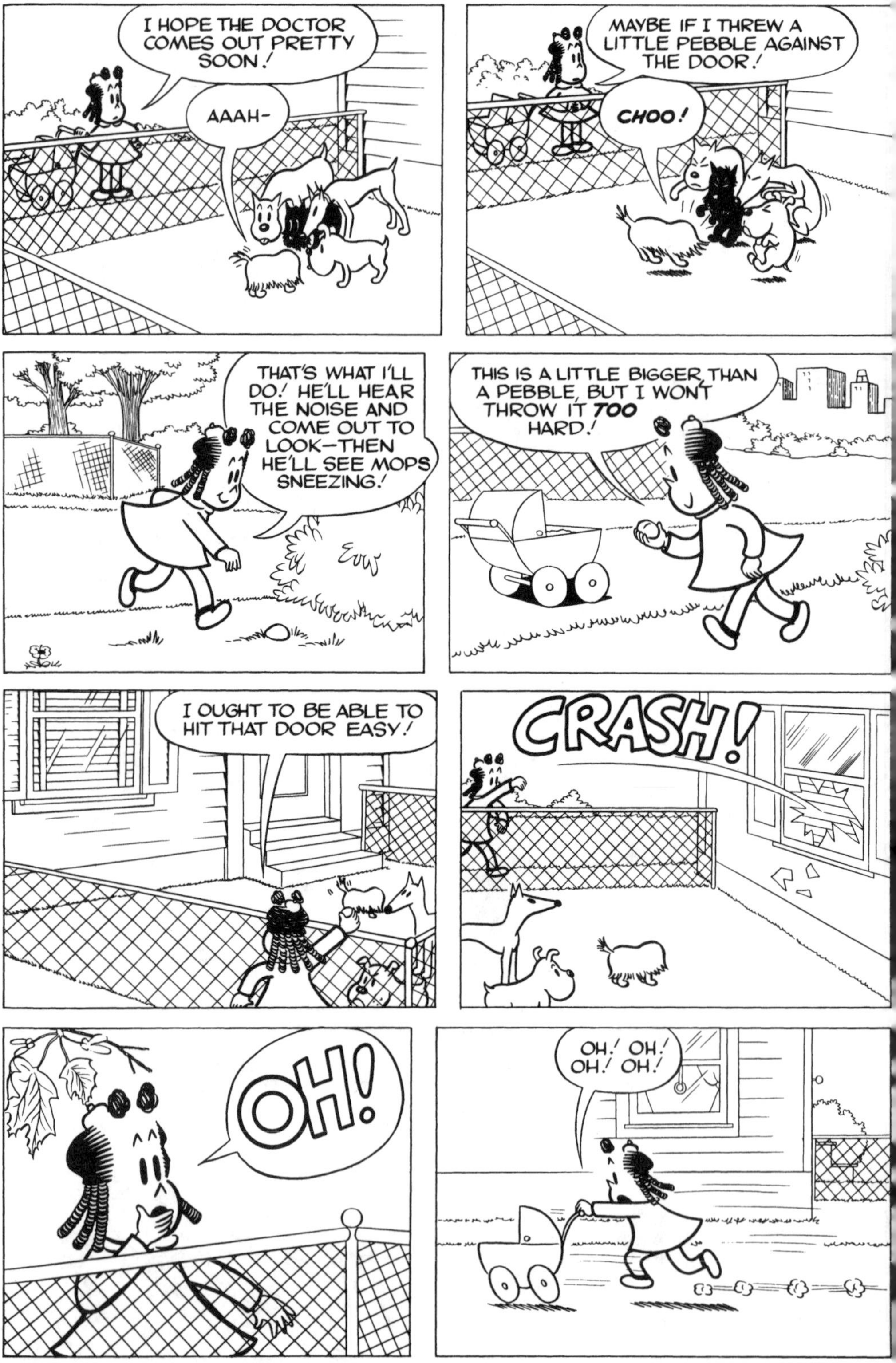
I HOPE THE DOCTOR COMES OUT PRETTY SOON!
AAAH-
MAYBE IF I THREW A LITTLE PEBBLE AGAINST THE DOOR!
CHOO!
THAT'S WHAT I'LL DO! HE'LL HEAR THE NOISE AND COME OUT TO LOOK—THEN HE'LL SEE MOPS SNEEZING!
THIS IS A LITTLE BIGGER THAN A PEBBLE, BUT I WON'T THROW IT *TOO* HARD!
I OUGHT TO BE ABLE TO HIT THAT DOOR EASY!
CRASH!
OH!
OH! OH! OH! OH!

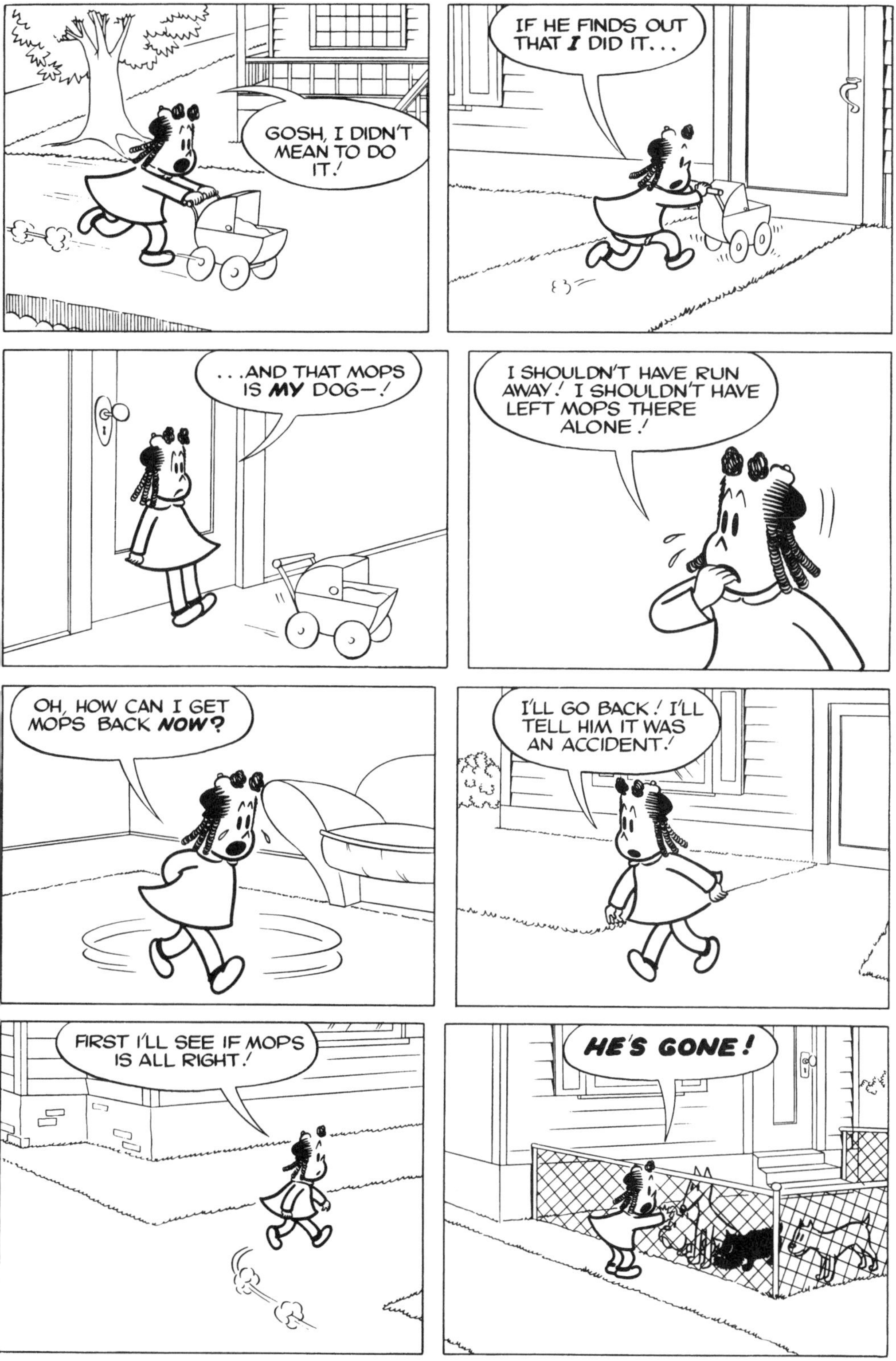
GOSH, I DIDN'T MEAN TO DO IT!
IF HE FINDS OUT THAT I DID IT...
...AND THAT MOPS IS MY DOG—!
I SHOULDN'T HAVE RUN AWAY! I SHOULDN'T HAVE LEFT MOPS THERE ALONE!
OH, HOW CAN I GET MOPS BACK NOW?
I'LL GO BACK! I'LL TELL HIM IT WAS AN ACCIDENT!
FIRST I'LL SEE IF MOPS IS ALL RIGHT!
HE'S GONE!

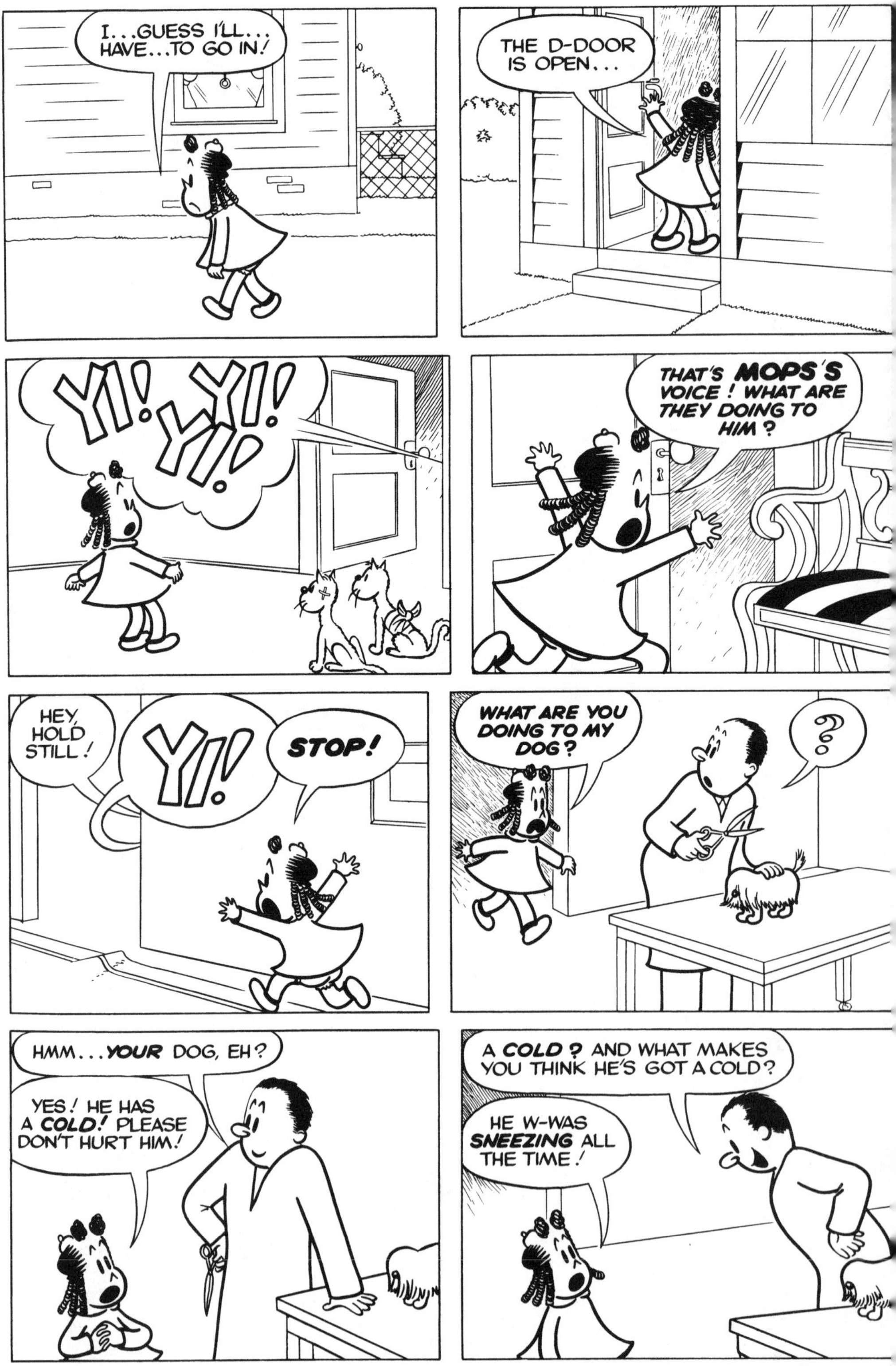
I...GUESS I'LL... HAVE...TO GO IN!
THE D-DOOR IS OPEN...
YI! YI! YI!
THAT'S MOPS'S VOICE! WHAT ARE THEY DOING TO HIM?
HEY, HOLD STILL!
YI!
STOP!
WHAT ARE YOU DOING TO MY DOG?
?
HMM...YOUR DOG, EH?
YES! HE HAS A COLD! PLEASE DON'T HURT HIM!
A COLD? AND WHAT MAKES YOU THINK HE'S GOT A COLD?
HE W-WAS SNEEZING ALL THE TIME!

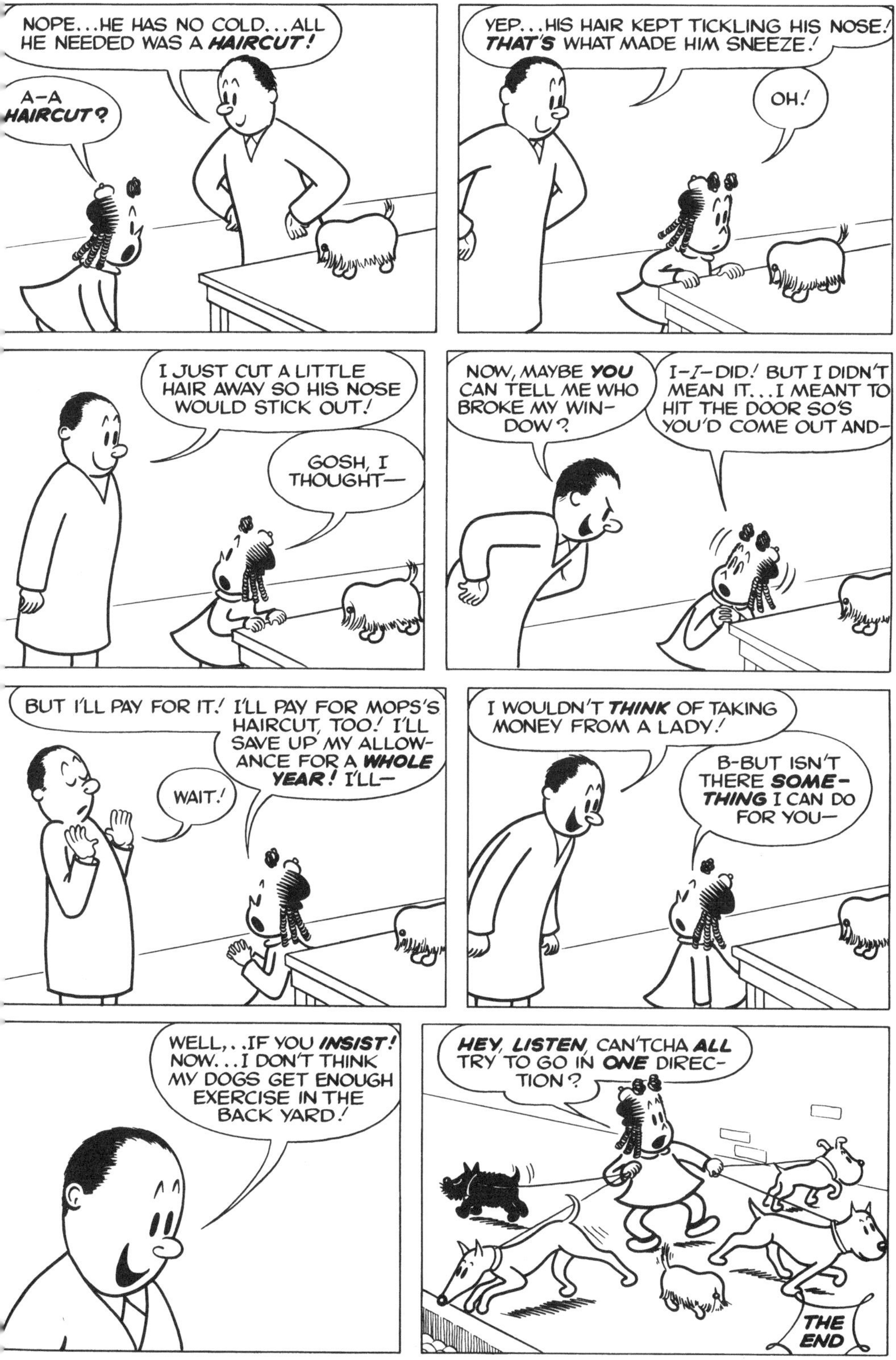
NOPE...HE HAS NO COLD...ALL HE NEEDED WAS A ***HAIRCUT!***
A-A ***HAIRCUT?***
YEP...HIS HAIR KEPT TICKLING HIS NOSE! ***THAT'S*** WHAT MADE HIM SNEEZE!
OH!
I JUST CUT A LITTLE HAIR AWAY SO HIS NOSE WOULD STICK OUT!
GOSH, I THOUGHT—
NOW, MAYBE ***YOU*** CAN TELL ME WHO BROKE MY WIN-DOW?
I-*I*-DID! BUT I DIDN'T MEAN IT...I MEANT TO HIT THE DOOR SO'S YOU'D COME OUT AND-
BUT I'LL PAY FOR IT! I'LL PAY FOR MOPS'S HAIRCUT, TOO! I'LL SAVE UP MY ALLOW-ANCE FOR A ***WHOLE YEAR!*** I'LL—
WAIT!
I WOULDN'T ***THINK*** OF TAKING MONEY FROM A LADY!
B-BUT ISN'T THERE ***SOME-THING*** I CAN DO FOR YOU—
WELL,..IF YOU ***INSIST!*** NOW...I DON'T THINK MY DOGS GET ENOUGH EXERCISE IN THE BACK YARD!
HEY, LISTEN, CAN'TCHA ***ALL*** TRY TO GO IN ***ONE*** DIREC-TION?
THE END

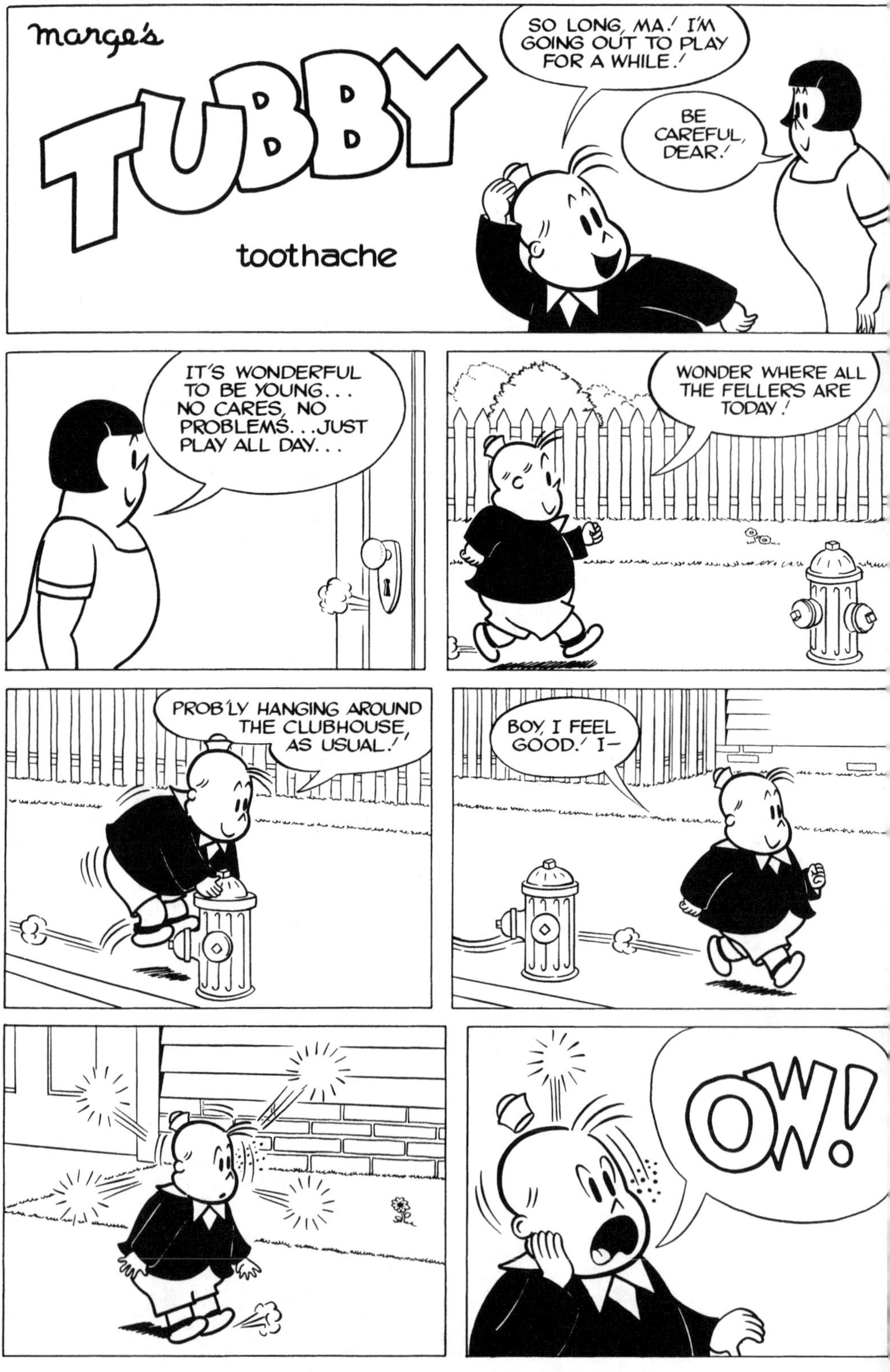
marge's
TUBBY
toothache
SO LONG, MA.! I'M GOING OUT TO PLAY FOR A WHILE.!
BE CAREFUL, DEAR.!
IT'S WONDERFUL TO BE YOUNG... NO CARES, NO PROBLEMS...JUST PLAY ALL DAY...
WONDER WHERE ALL THE FELLERS ARE TODAY.!
PROB'LY HANGING AROUND THE CLUBHOUSE, AS USUAL.!
BOY, I FEEL GOOD.! I—
OW!

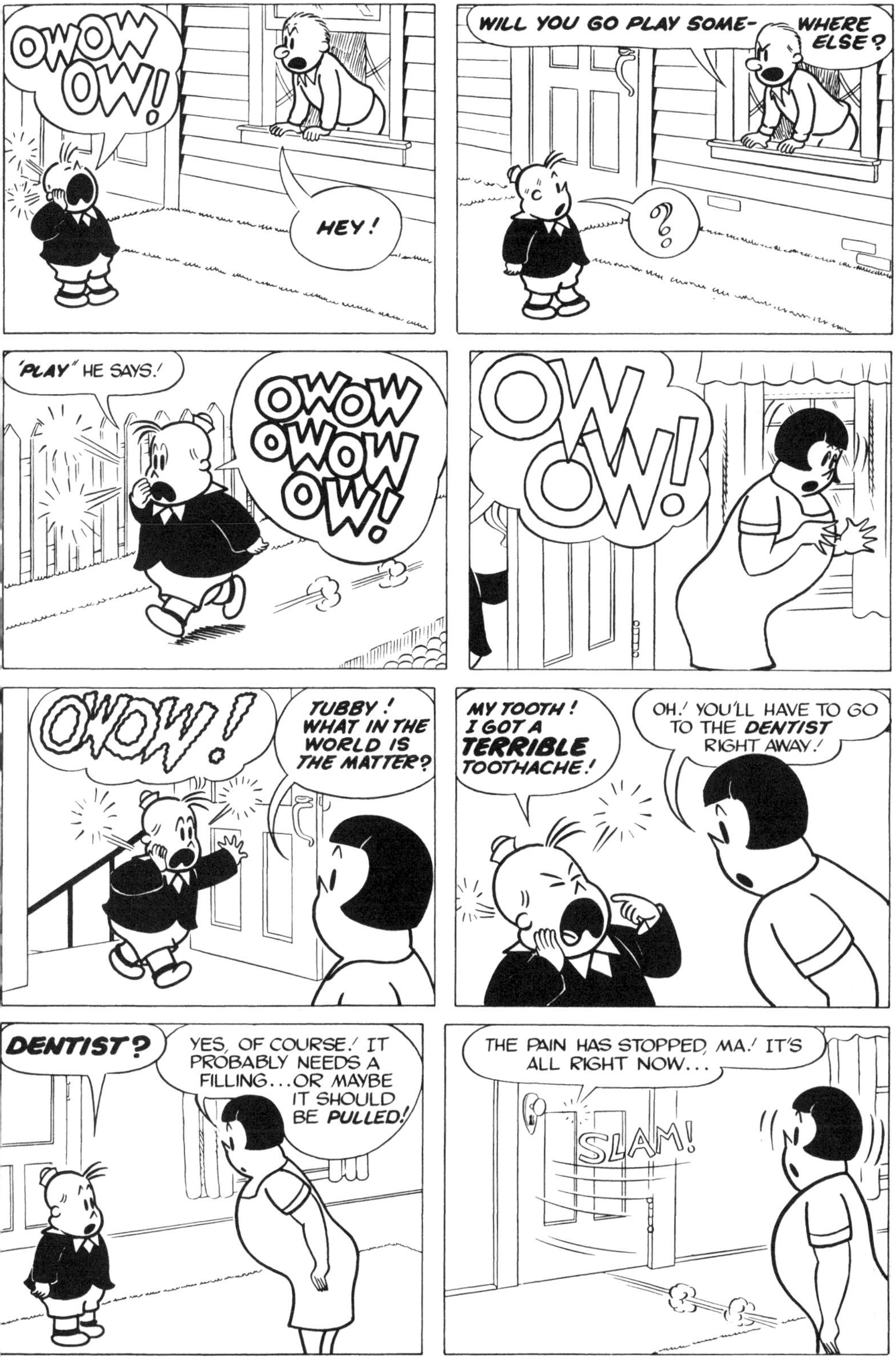
OWOW OW!
HEY!
WILL YOU GO PLAY SOME- WHERE ELSE?
?
"PLAY" HE SAYS!
OWOW OWOW OWOW OW!
OW OW OW!
OWOW!
TUBBY! WHAT IN THE WORLD IS THE MATTER?
MY TOOTH! I GOT A TERRIBLE TOOTHACHE!
OH! YOU'LL HAVE TO GO TO THE DENTIST RIGHT AWAY!
DENTIST?
YES, OF COURSE! IT PROBABLY NEEDS A FILLING...OR MAYBE IT SHOULD BE PULLED!
THE PAIN HAS STOPPED, MA! IT'S ALL RIGHT NOW...
SLAM!

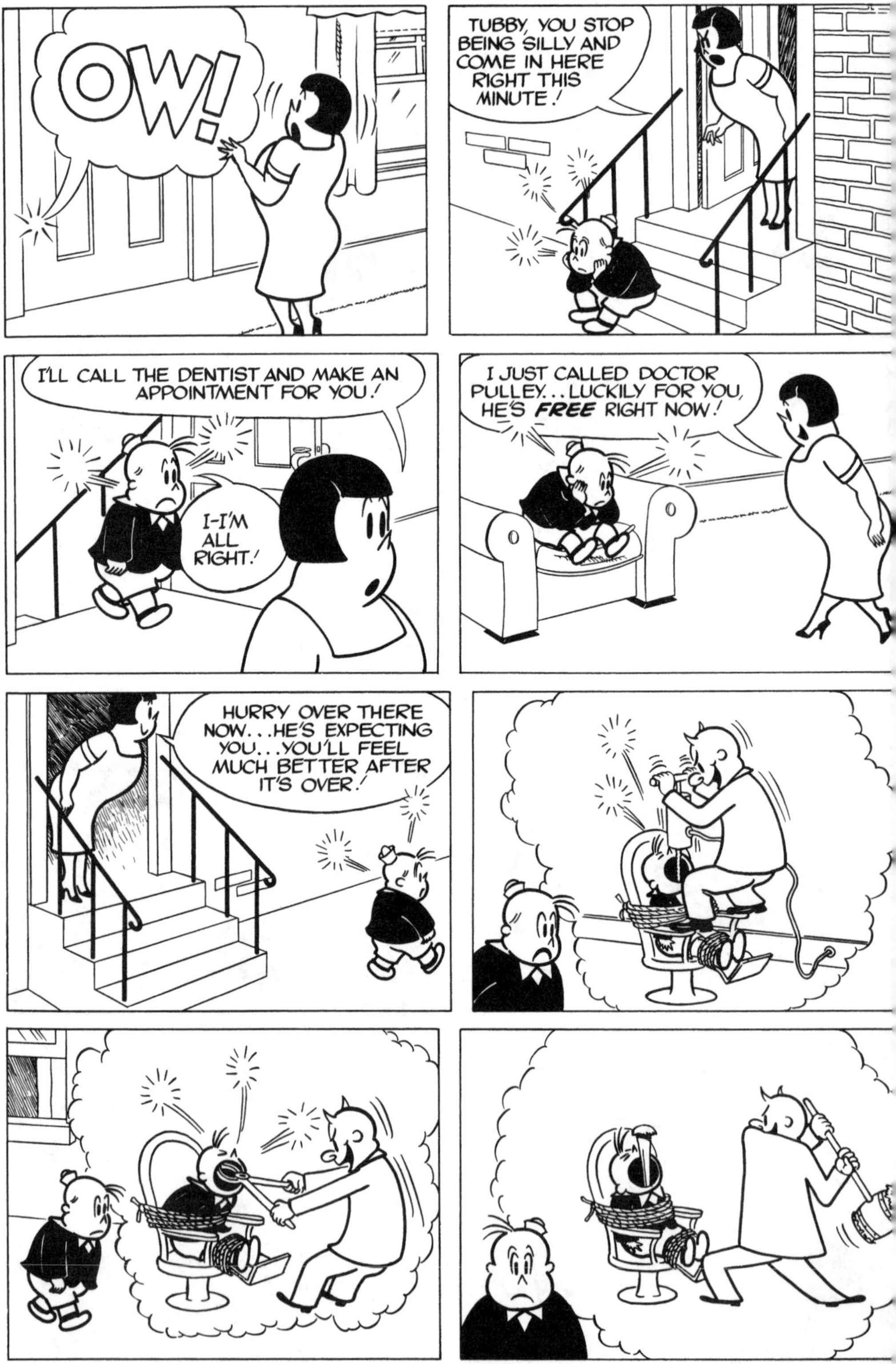
OW!
TUBBY, YOU STOP BEING SILLY AND COME IN HERE RIGHT THIS MINUTE!
I'LL CALL THE DENTIST AND MAKE AN APPOINTMENT FOR YOU!
I-I'M ALL RIGHT!
I JUST CALLED DOCTOR PULLEY... LUCKILY FOR YOU, HE'S FREE RIGHT NOW!
HURRY OVER THERE NOW... HE'S EXPECTING YOU... YOU'LL FEEL MUCH BETTER AFTER IT'S OVER!

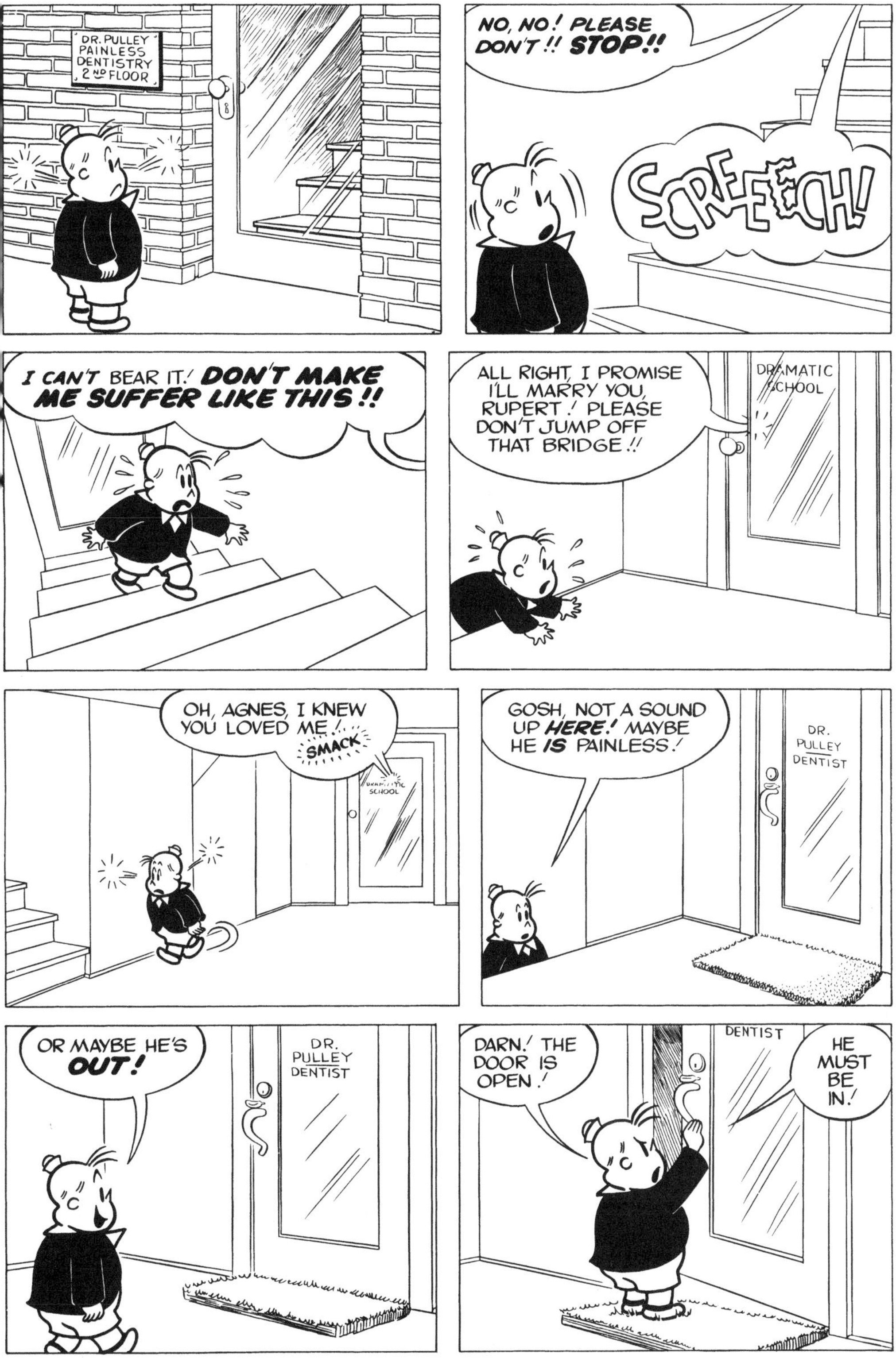
DR. PULLEY PAINLESS DENTISTRY 2ND FLOOR
NO, NO! PLEASE DON'T!! STOP!!
SCREEECH!
I CAN'T BEAR IT! DON'T MAKE ME SUFFER LIKE THIS!!
ALL RIGHT, I PROMISE I'LL MARRY YOU, RUPERT! PLEASE DON'T JUMP OFF THAT BRIDGE!!
DRAMATIC SCHOOL
OH, AGNES, I KNEW YOU LOVED ME!
SMACK
GOSH, NOT A SOUND UP HERE! MAYBE HE IS PAINLESS!
DR. PULLEY DENTIST
OR MAYBE HE'S OUT!
DR. PULLEY DENTIST
DARN! THE DOOR IS OPEN!
DENTIST
HE MUST BE IN!

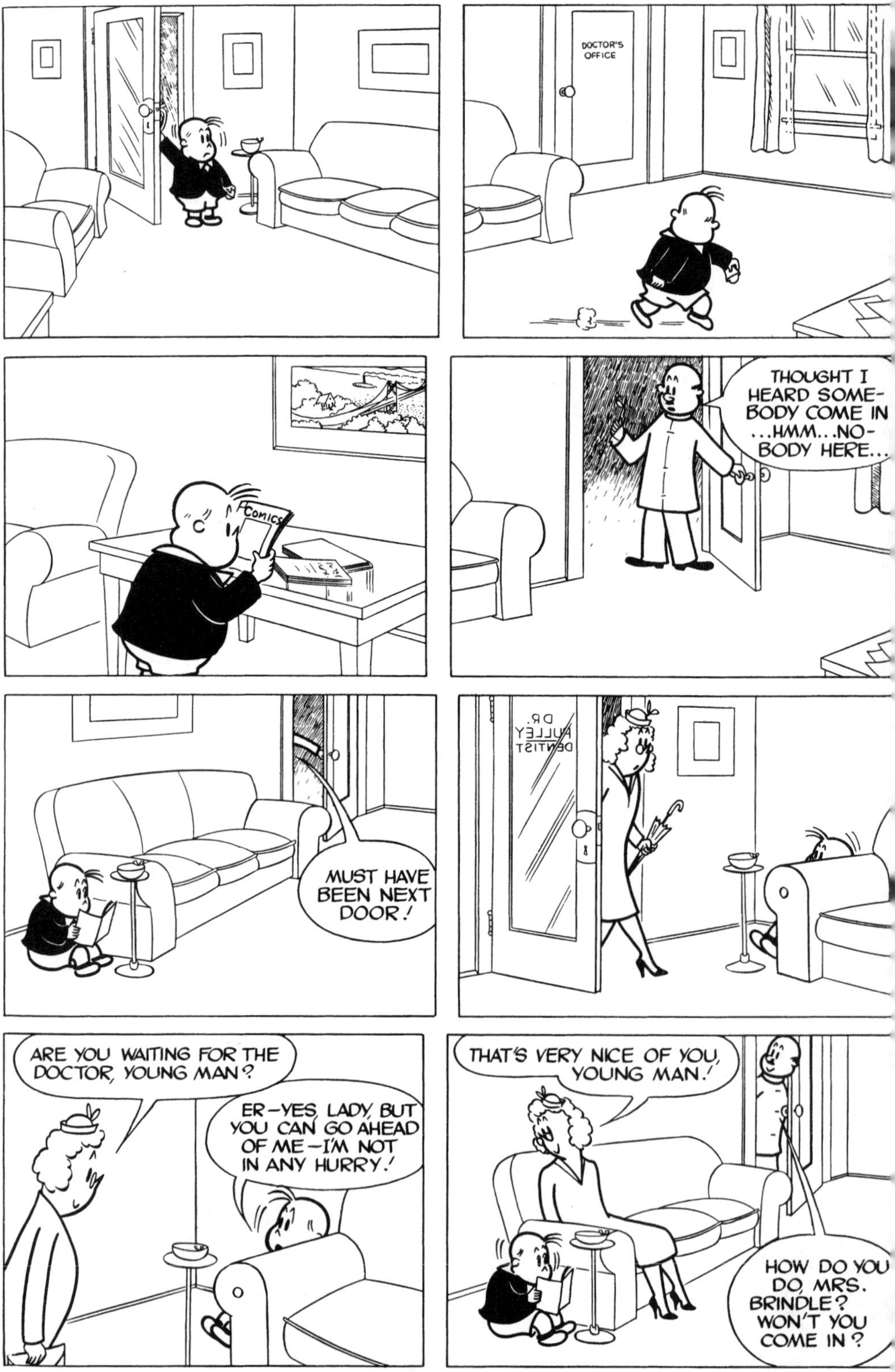
DOCTOR'S OFFICE
COMICS
THOUGHT I HEARD SOMEBODY COME IN ...HMM...NOBODY HERE...
MUST HAVE BEEN NEXT DOOR!
DR. PULLEY DENTIST
ARE YOU WAITING FOR THE DOCTOR, YOUNG MAN?
ER—YES LADY, BUT YOU CAN GO AHEAD OF ME—I'M NOT IN ANY HURRY!
THAT'S VERY NICE OF YOU, YOUNG MAN!
HOW DO YOU DO, MRS. BRINDLE? WON'T YOU COME IN?

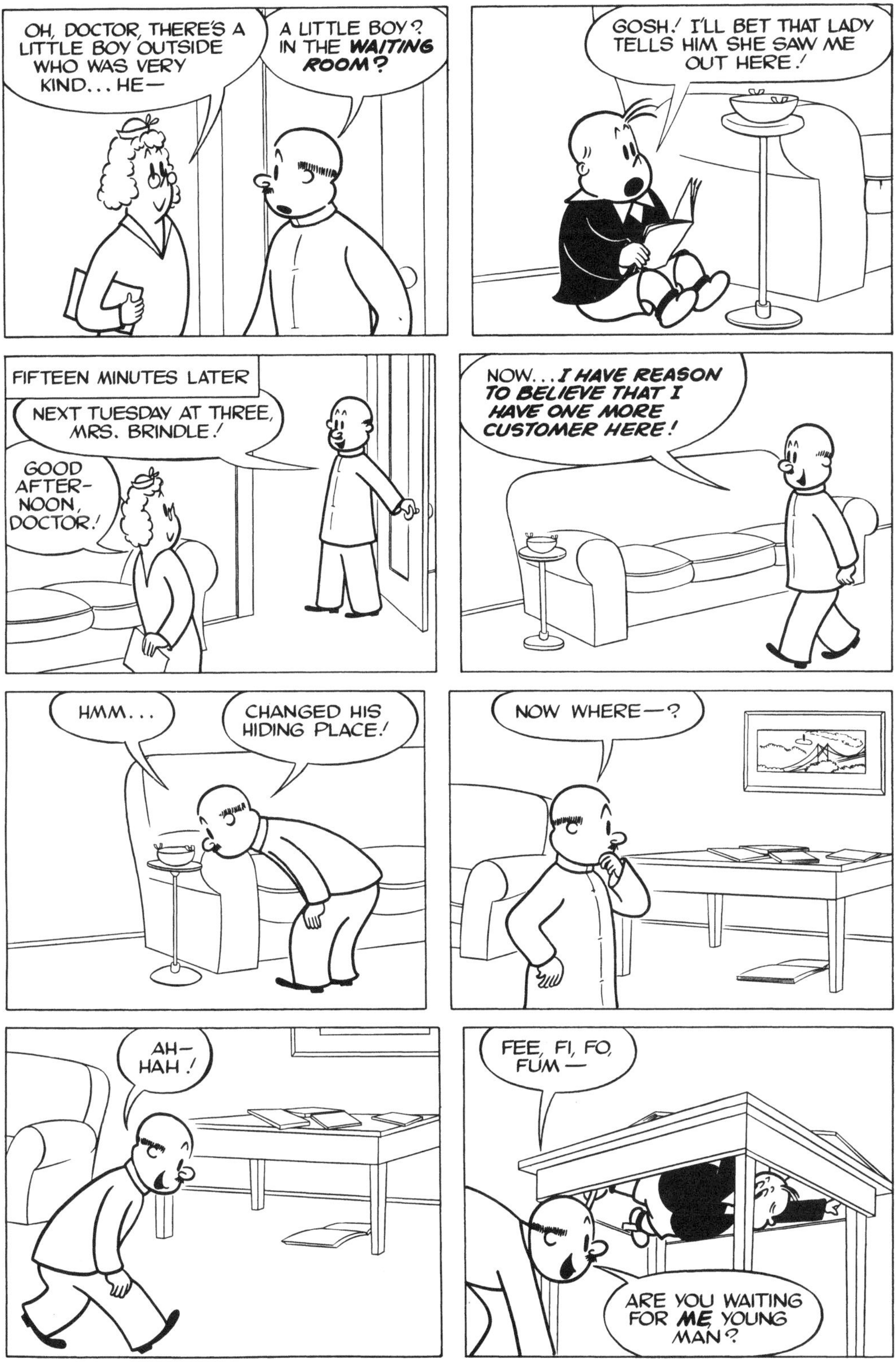

OH, DOCTOR, THERE'S A LITTLE BOY OUTSIDE WHO WAS VERY KIND... HE—
A LITTLE BOY? IN THE **WAITING ROOM?**
GOSH! I'LL BET THAT LADY TELLS HIM SHE SAW ME OUT HERE!
FIFTEEN MINUTES LATER
NEXT TUESDAY AT THREE, MRS. BRINDLE!
GOOD AFTER-NOON, DOCTOR!
NOW... ***I HAVE REASON TO BELIEVE THAT I HAVE ONE MORE CUSTOMER HERE!***
HMM...
CHANGED HIS HIDING PLACE!
NOW WHERE—?
AH-HAH!
FEE, FI, FO, FUM—
ARE YOU WAITING FOR **ME**, YOUNG MAN?

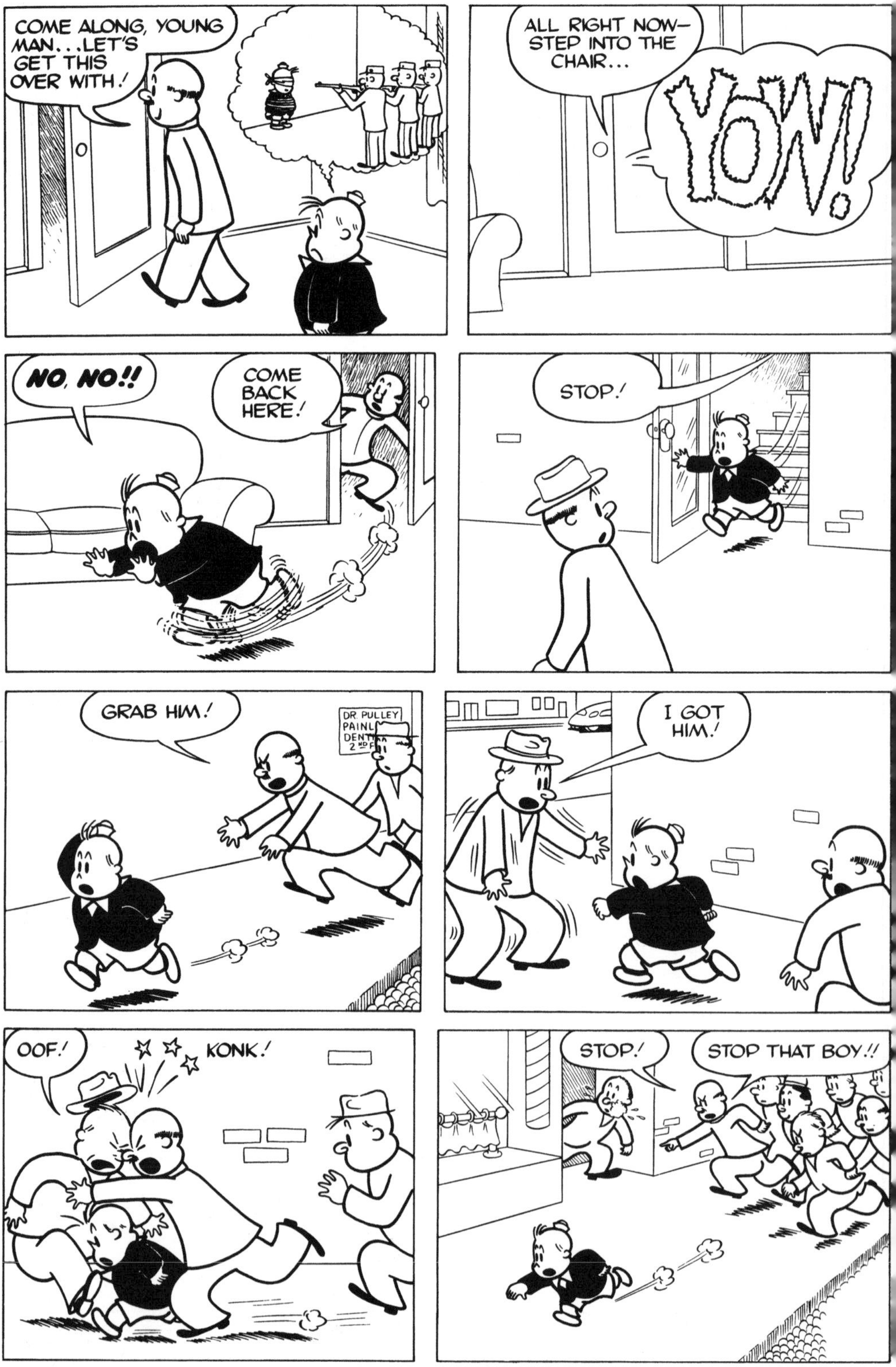
COME ALONG, YOUNG MAN...LET'S GET THIS OVER WITH!
ALL RIGHT NOW— STEP INTO THE CHAIR...
YOW!
NO, NO!!
COME BACK HERE!
STOP!
GRAB HIM!
DR. PULLEY PAINL DENT 2ND F
I GOT HIM!
OOF!
KONK!
STOP!
STOP THAT BOY!!

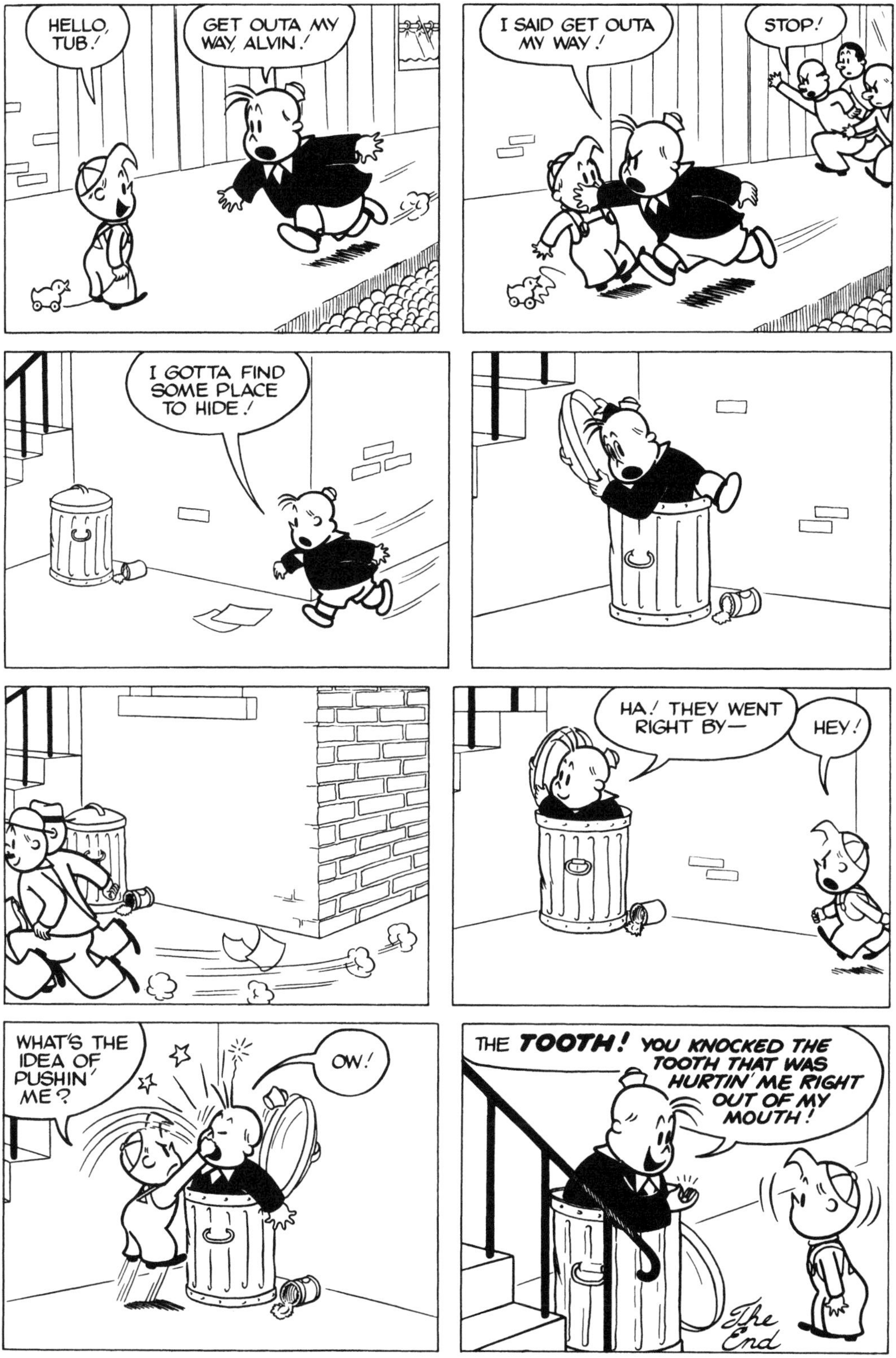
HELLO, TUB!
GET OUTA MY WAY, ALVIN!
I SAID GET OUTA MY WAY!
STOP!
I GOTTA FIND SOME PLACE TO HIDE!
HA! THEY WENT RIGHT BY—
HEY!
WHAT'S THE IDEA OF PUSHIN' ME?
OW!
THE TOOTH! YOU KNOCKED THE TOOTH THAT WAS HURTIN' ME RIGHT OUT OF MY MOUTH!
The End

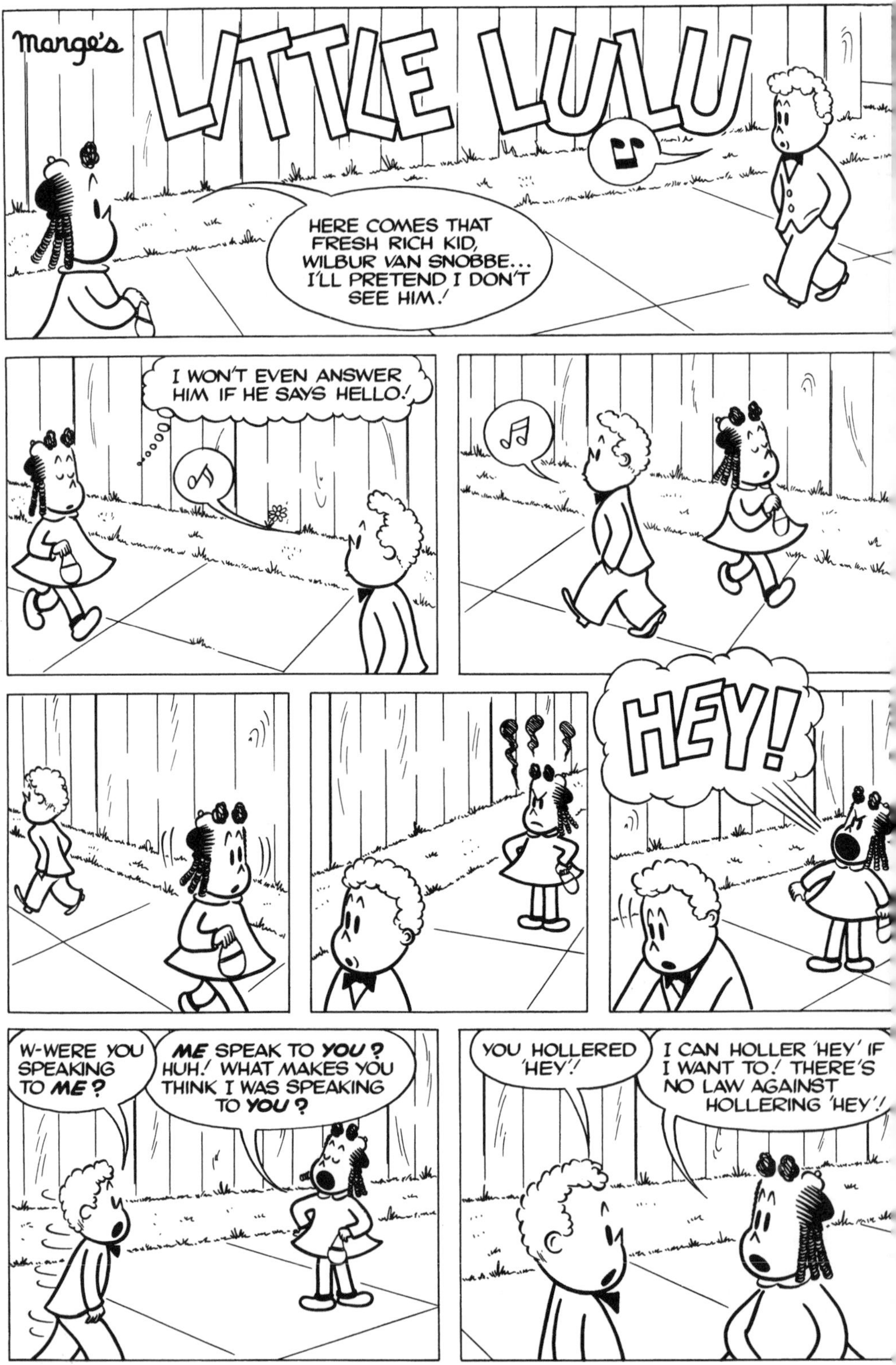
Marge's
LITTLE LULU
HERE COMES THAT FRESH RICH KID, WILBUR VAN SNOBBE... I'LL PRETEND I DON'T SEE HIM!
I WON'T EVEN ANSWER HIM IF HE SAYS HELLO!
HEY!
W-WERE YOU SPEAKING TO ME?
ME SPEAK TO YOU? HUH! WHAT MAKES YOU THINK I WAS SPEAKING TO YOU?
YOU HOLLERED 'HEY'!
I CAN HOLLER 'HEY' IF I WANT TO! THERE'S NO LAW AGAINST HOLLERING 'HEY'!

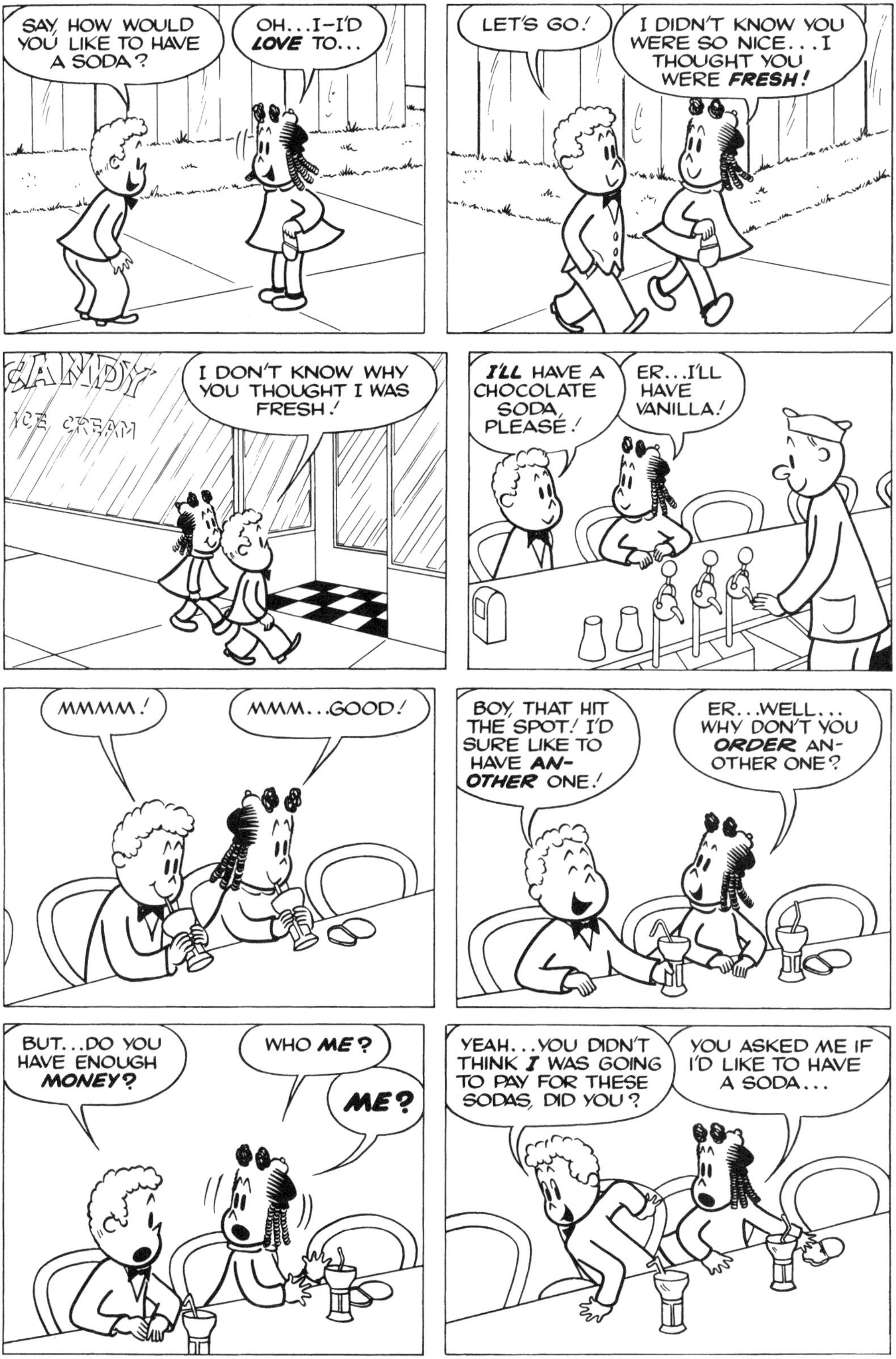
SAY, HOW WOULD YOU LIKE TO HAVE A SODA?
OH...I–I'D LOVE TO...
LET'S GO!
I DIDN'T KNOW YOU WERE SO NICE...I THOUGHT YOU WERE FRESH!
CANDY
ICE CREAM
I DON'T KNOW WHY YOU THOUGHT I WAS FRESH!
I'LL HAVE A CHOCOLATE SODA, PLEASE!
ER...I'LL HAVE VANILLA!
MMMM!
MMM...GOOD!
BOY, THAT HIT THE SPOT! I'D SURE LIKE TO HAVE ANOTHER ONE!
ER...WELL...WHY DON'T YOU ORDER ANOTHER ONE?
BUT...DO YOU HAVE ENOUGH MONEY?
WHO ME?
ME?
YEAH...YOU DIDN'T THINK I WAS GOING TO PAY FOR THESE SODAS, DID YOU?
YOU ASKED ME IF I'D LIKE TO HAVE A SODA...

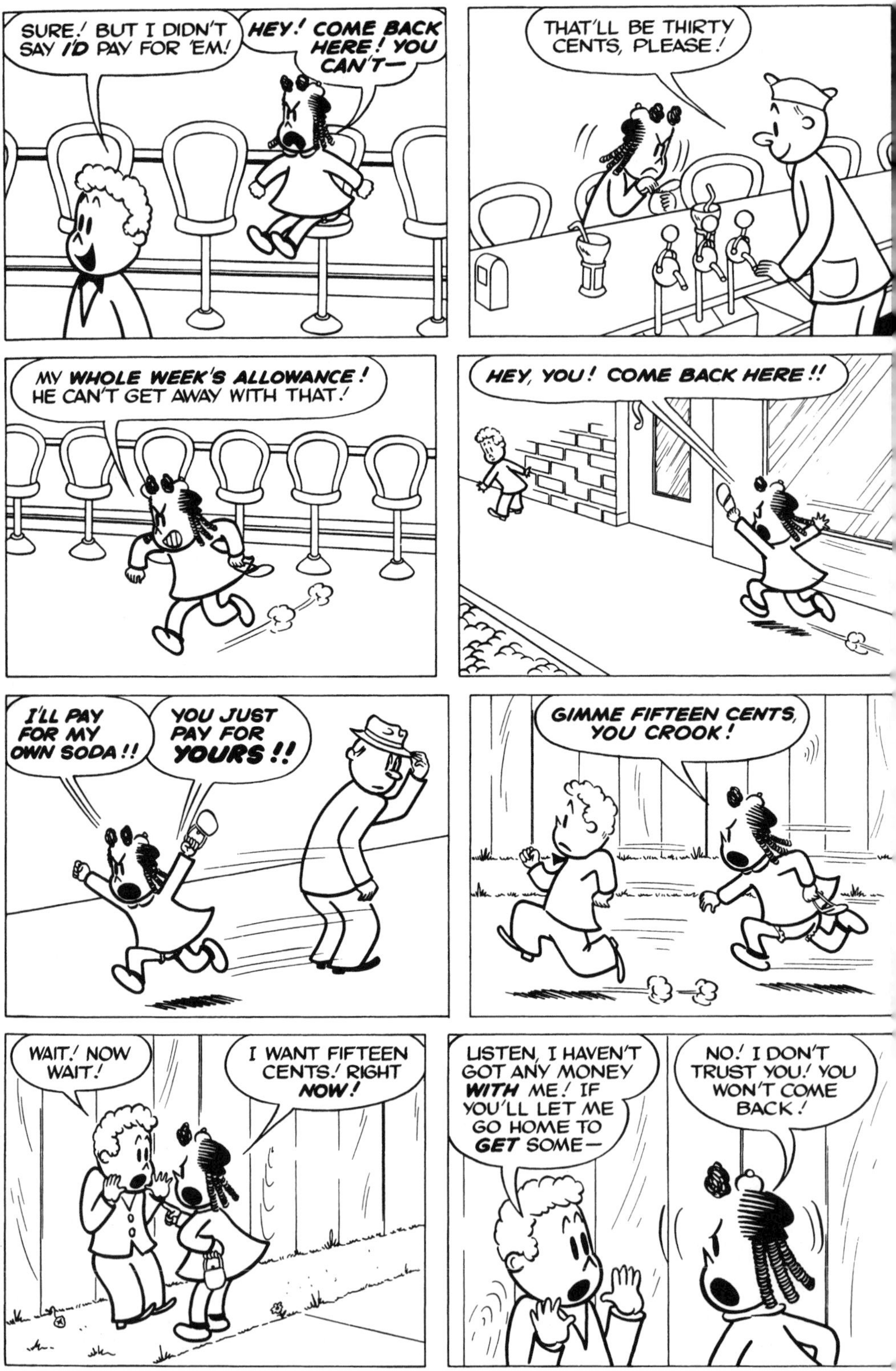
SURE! BUT I DIDN'T SAY I'D PAY FOR 'EM!
HEY! COME BACK HERE! YOU CAN'T—
THAT'LL BE THIRTY CENTS, PLEASE!
MY WHOLE WEEK'S ALLOWANCE! HE CAN'T GET AWAY WITH THAT!
HEY, YOU! COME BACK HERE!!
I'LL PAY FOR MY OWN SODA!!
YOU JUST PAY FOR YOURS!!
GIMME FIFTEEN CENTS, YOU CROOK!
WAIT! NOW WAIT!
I WANT FIFTEEN CENTS! RIGHT NOW!
LISTEN, I HAVEN'T GOT ANY MONEY WITH ME! IF YOU'LL LET ME GO HOME TO GET SOME—
NO! I DON'T TRUST YOU! YOU WON'T COME BACK!

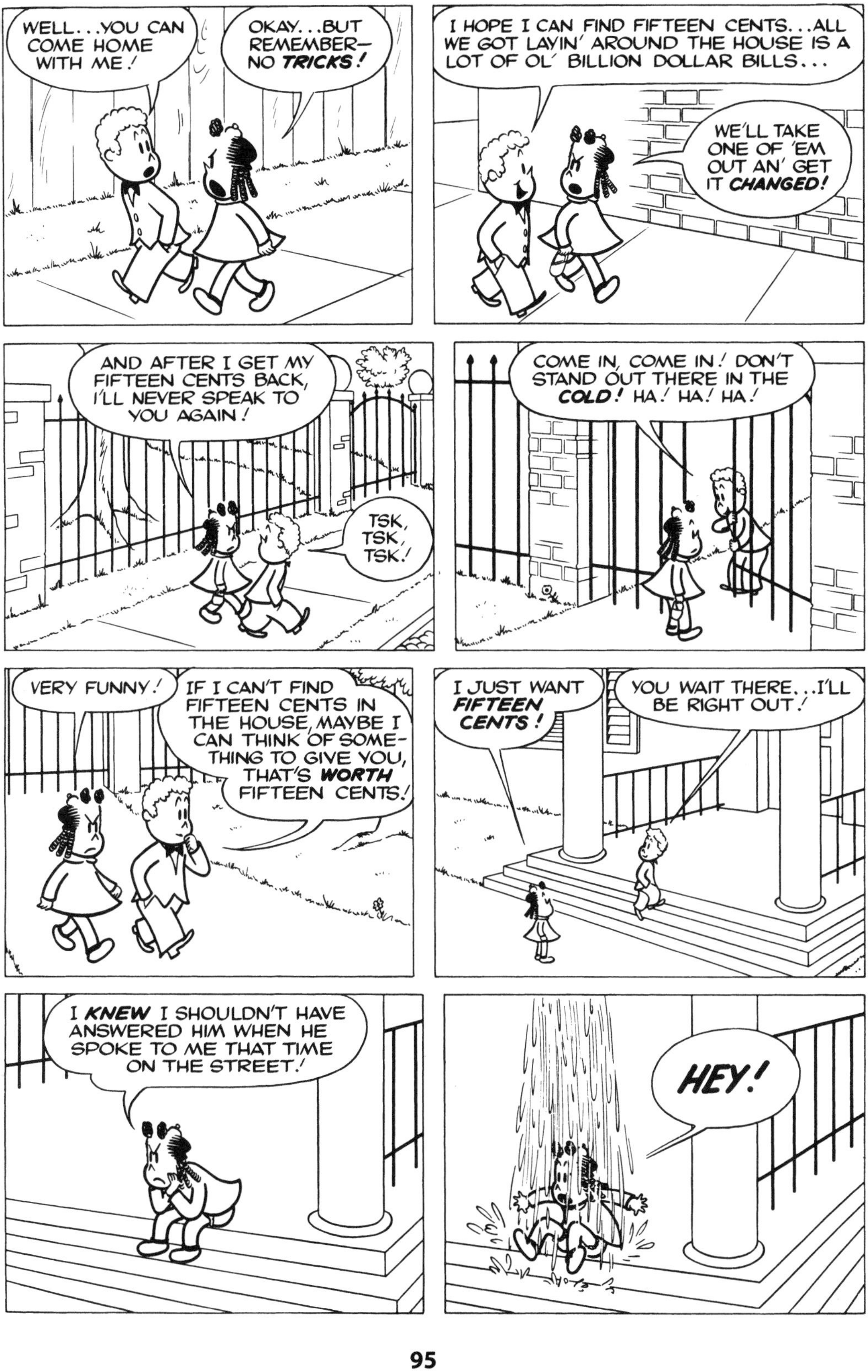
WELL...YOU CAN COME HOME WITH ME!
OKAY...BUT REMEMBER— NO TRICKS!
I HOPE I CAN FIND FIFTEEN CENTS...ALL WE GOT LAYIN' AROUND THE HOUSE IS A LOT OF OL' BILLION DOLLAR BILLS...
WE'LL TAKE ONE OF 'EM OUT AN' GET IT CHANGED!
AND AFTER I GET MY FIFTEEN CENTS BACK, I'LL NEVER SPEAK TO YOU AGAIN!
TSK, TSK, TSK!
COME IN, COME IN! DON'T STAND OUT THERE IN THE COLD! HA! HA! HA!
VERY FUNNY!
IF I CAN'T FIND FIFTEEN CENTS IN THE HOUSE, MAYBE I CAN THINK OF SOMETHING TO GIVE YOU, THAT'S WORTH FIFTEEN CENTS!
I JUST WANT FIFTEEN CENTS!
YOU WAIT THERE...I'LL BE RIGHT OUT!
I KNEW I SHOULDN'T HAVE ANSWERED HIM WHEN HE SPOKE TO ME THAT TIME ON THE STREET!
HEY!

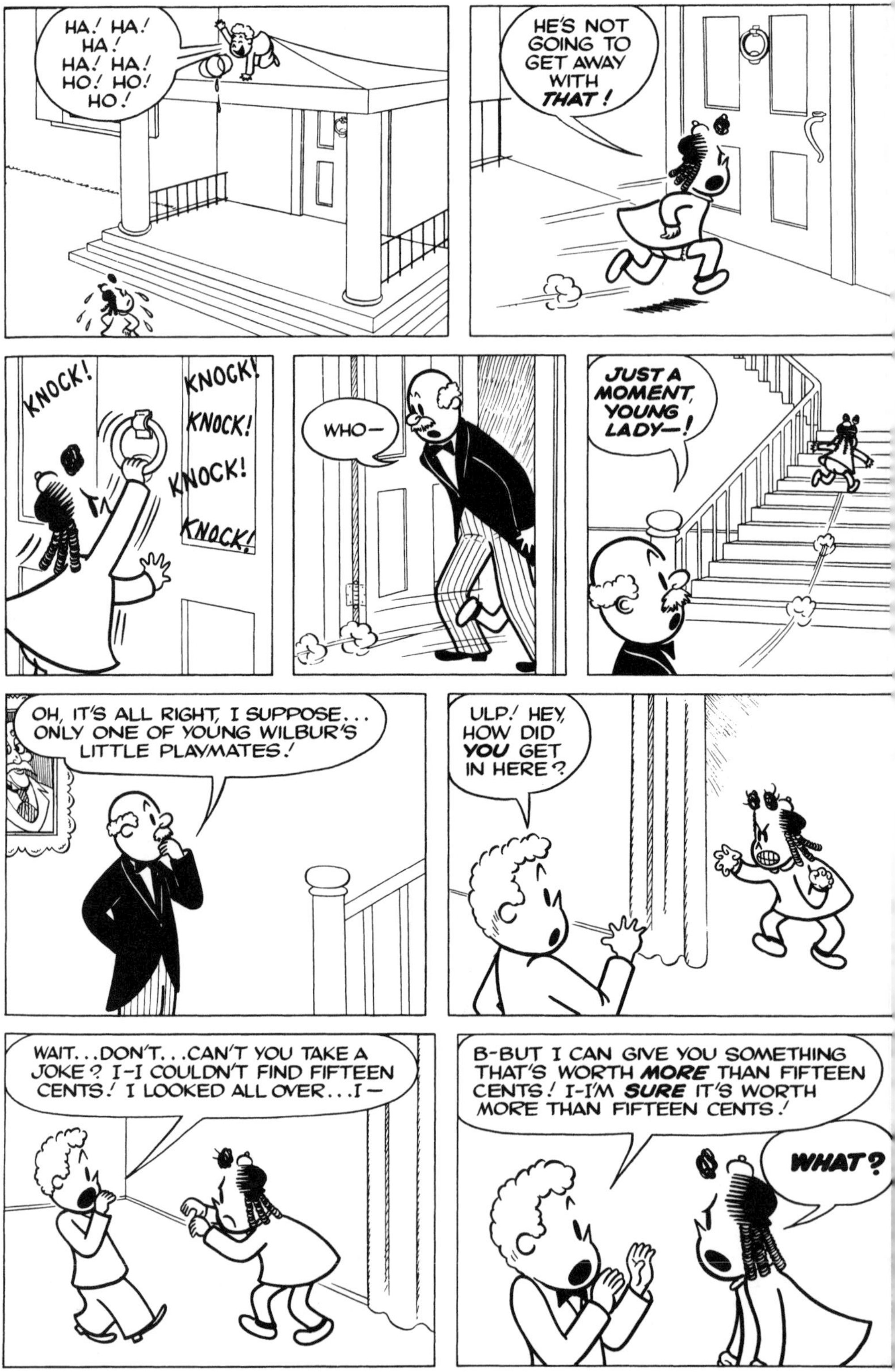
HA! HA! HA! HA! HA! HO! HO! HO!
HE'S NOT GOING TO GET AWAY WITH THAT!
KNOCK! KNOCK! KNOCK! KNOCK! KNOCK!
WHO—
JUST A MOMENT, YOUNG LADY—!
OH, IT'S ALL RIGHT, I SUPPOSE... ONLY ONE OF YOUNG WILBUR'S LITTLE PLAYMATES!
ULP! HEY, HOW DID YOU GET IN HERE?
WAIT...DON'T...CAN'T YOU TAKE A JOKE? I-I COULDN'T FIND FIFTEEN CENTS! I LOOKED ALL OVER...I—
B-BUT I CAN GIVE YOU SOMETHING THAT'S WORTH MORE THAN FIFTEEN CENTS! I-I'M SURE IT'S WORTH MORE THAN FIFTEEN CENTS!
WHAT?

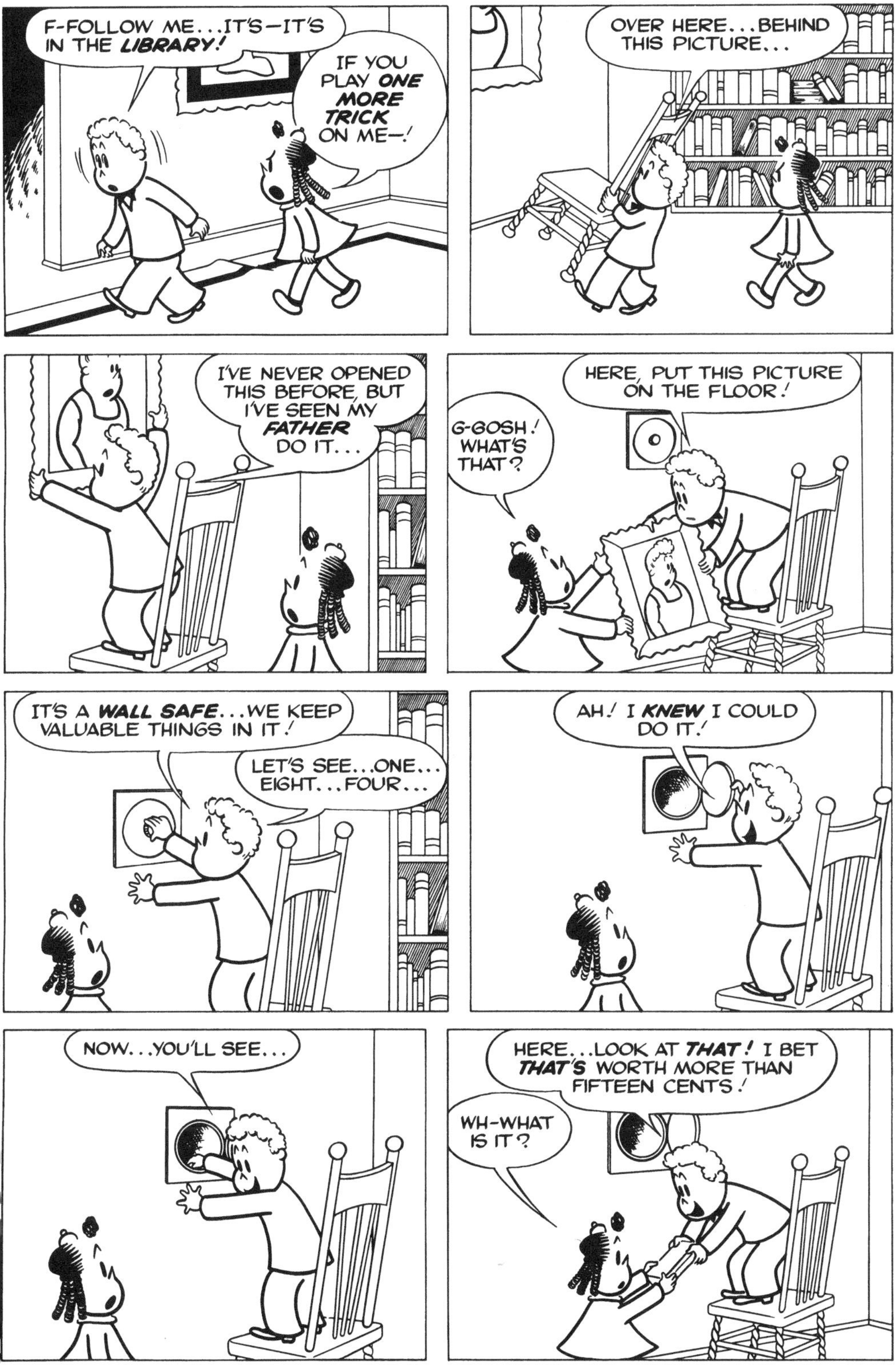
F-FOLLOW ME...IT'S—IT'S IN THE **LIBRARY!**
IF YOU PLAY **ONE MORE TRICK** ON ME—!
OVER HERE...BEHIND THIS PICTURE...
I'VE NEVER OPENED THIS BEFORE, BUT I'VE SEEN MY **FATHER** DO IT...
HERE, PUT THIS PICTURE ON THE FLOOR!
G-GOSH! WHAT'S THAT?
IT'S A **WALL SAFE**...WE KEEP VALUABLE THINGS IN IT!
LET'S SEE...ONE... EIGHT...FOUR...
AH! I **KNEW** I COULD DO IT!
NOW...YOU'LL SEE...
HERE...LOOK AT **THAT!** I BET **THAT'S** WORTH MORE THAN FIFTEEN CENTS!
WH-WHAT IS IT?

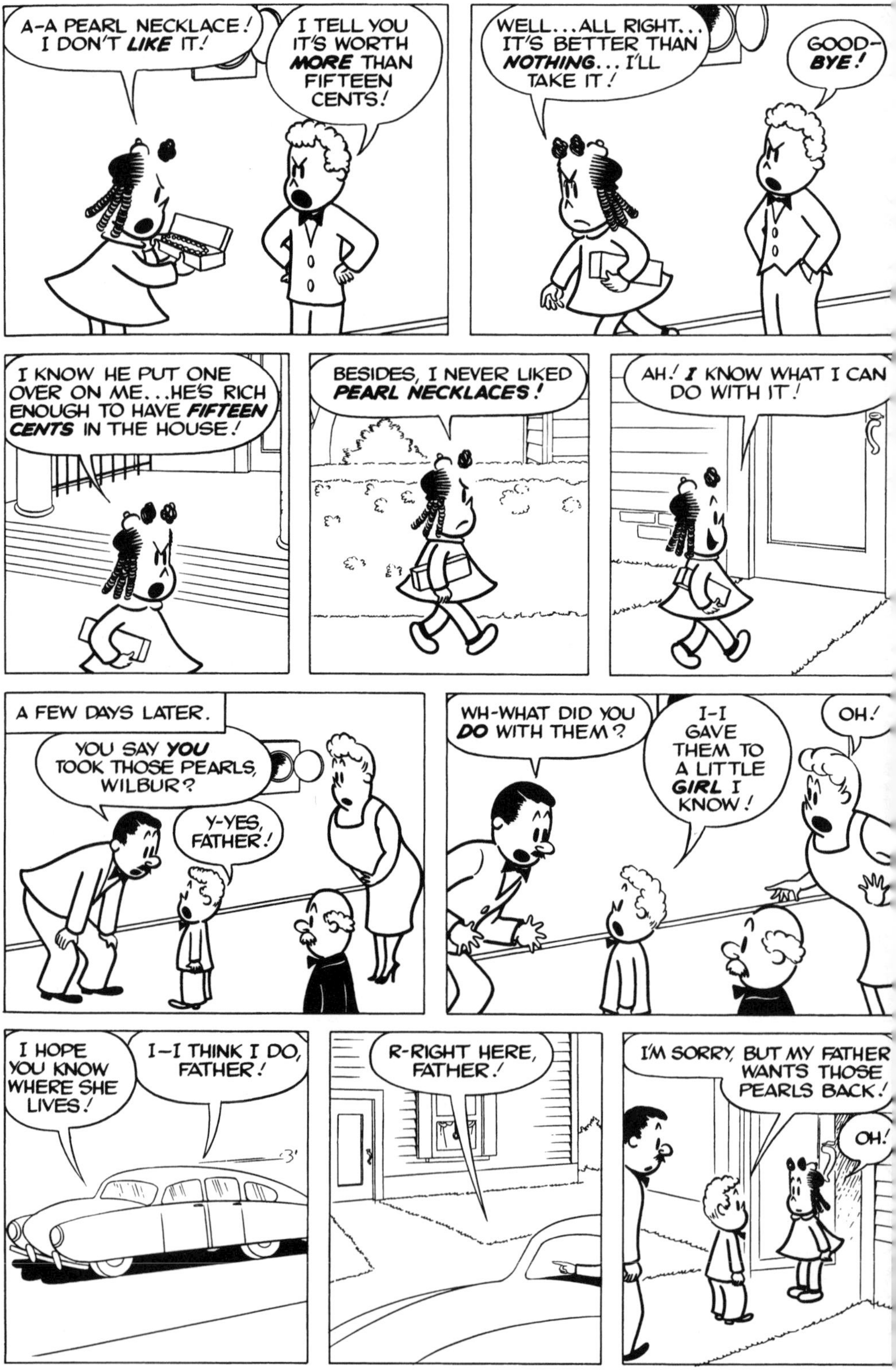
A-A PEARL NECKLACE! I DON'T LIKE IT!
I TELL YOU IT'S WORTH MORE THAN FIFTEEN CENTS!
WELL...ALL RIGHT... IT'S BETTER THAN NOTHING... I'LL TAKE IT!
GOOD-BYE!
I KNOW HE PUT ONE OVER ON ME...HE'S RICH ENOUGH TO HAVE FIFTEEN CENTS IN THE HOUSE!
BESIDES, I NEVER LIKED PEARL NECKLACES!
AH! I KNOW WHAT I CAN DO WITH IT!
A FEW DAYS LATER.
YOU SAY YOU TOOK THOSE PEARLS, WILBUR?
Y-YES, FATHER!
WH-WHAT DID YOU DO WITH THEM?
I-I GAVE THEM TO A LITTLE GIRL I KNOW!
OH!
I HOPE YOU KNOW WHERE SHE LIVES!
I-I THINK I DO, FATHER!
R-RIGHT HERE, FATHER!
I'M SORRY, BUT MY FATHER WANTS THOSE PEARLS BACK!
OH!

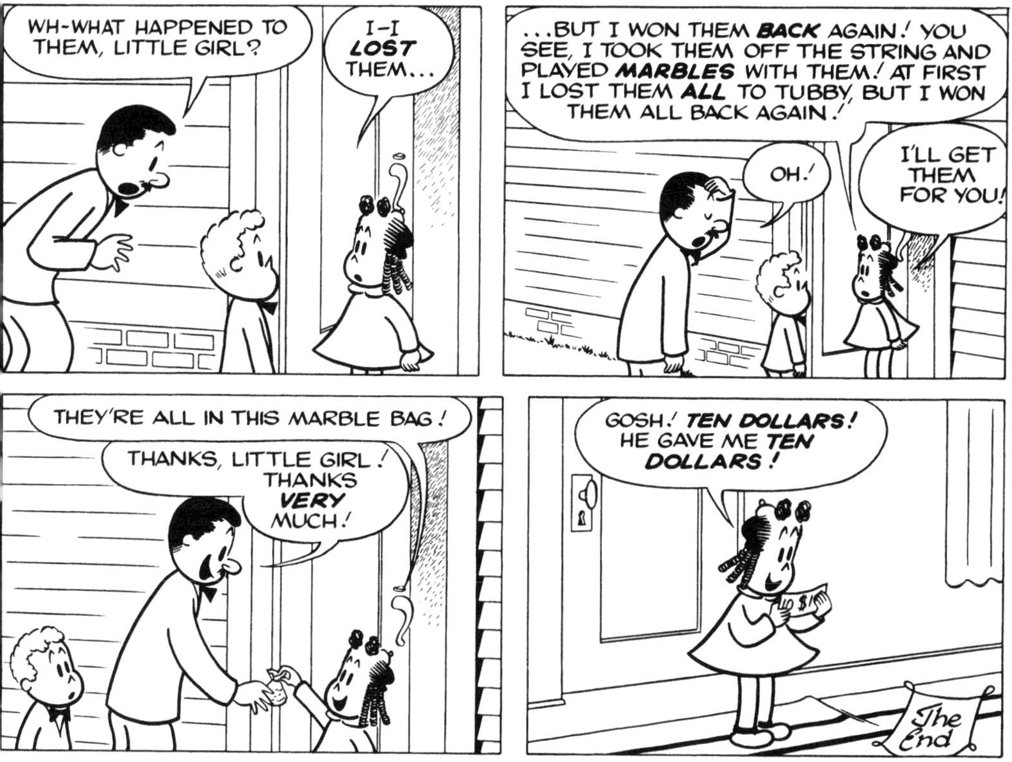
WH-WHAT HAPPENED TO THEM, LITTLE GIRL?
I-I **LOST** THEM...
...BUT I WON THEM **BACK** AGAIN! YOU SEE, I TOOK THEM OFF THE STRING AND PLAYED **MARBLES** WITH THEM! AT FIRST I LOST THEM **ALL** TO TUBBY, BUT I WON THEM ALL BACK AGAIN!
OH!
I'LL GET THEM FOR YOU!
THEY'RE ALL IN THIS MARBLE BAG!
THANKS, LITTLE GIRL! THANKS **VERY** MUCH!
GOSH! **TEN DOLLARS!** HE GAVE ME **TEN DOLLARS!**
The End

ALVIN

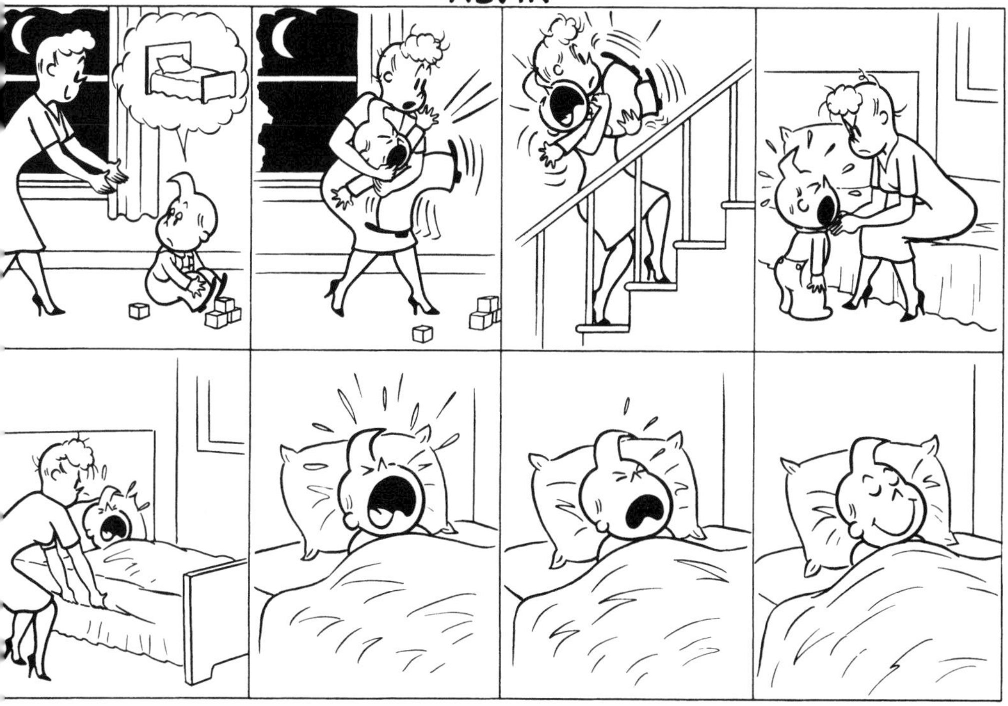

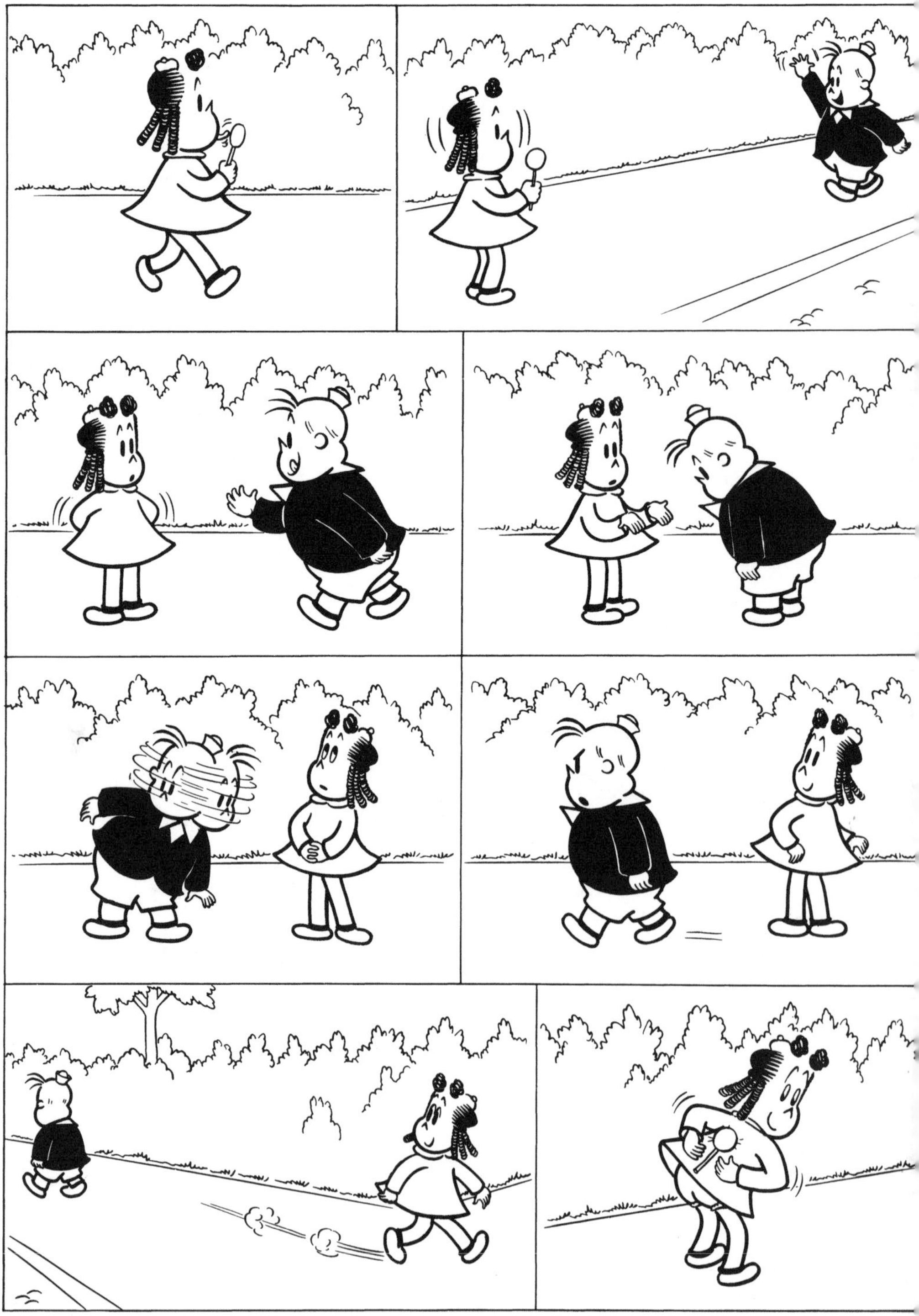

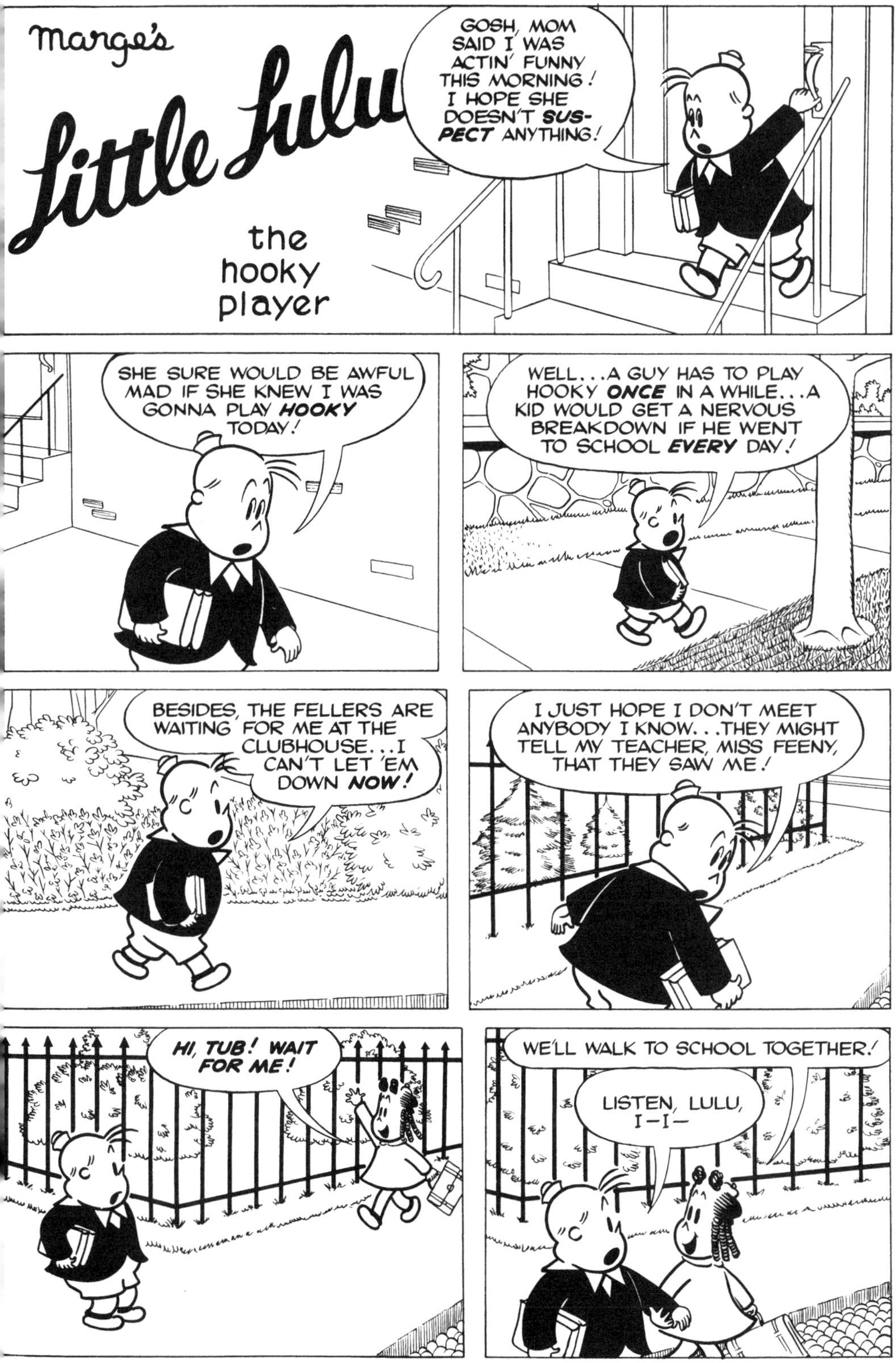
marge's
Little Lulu
the hooky player
GOSH, MOM SAID I WAS ACTIN' FUNNY THIS MORNING! I HOPE SHE DOESN'T SUSPECT ANYTHING!
SHE SURE WOULD BE AWFUL MAD IF SHE KNEW I WAS GONNA PLAY HOOKY TODAY!
WELL...A GUY HAS TO PLAY HOOKY ONCE IN A WHILE...A KID WOULD GET A NERVOUS BREAKDOWN IF HE WENT TO SCHOOL EVERY DAY!
BESIDES, THE FELLERS ARE WAITING FOR ME AT THE CLUBHOUSE...I CAN'T LET 'EM DOWN NOW!
I JUST HOPE I DON'T MEET ANYBODY I KNOW...THEY MIGHT TELL MY TEACHER, MISS FEENY, THAT THEY SAW ME!
HI, TUB! WAIT FOR ME!
WE'LL WALK TO SCHOOL TOGETHER!
LISTEN, LULU, I—I—

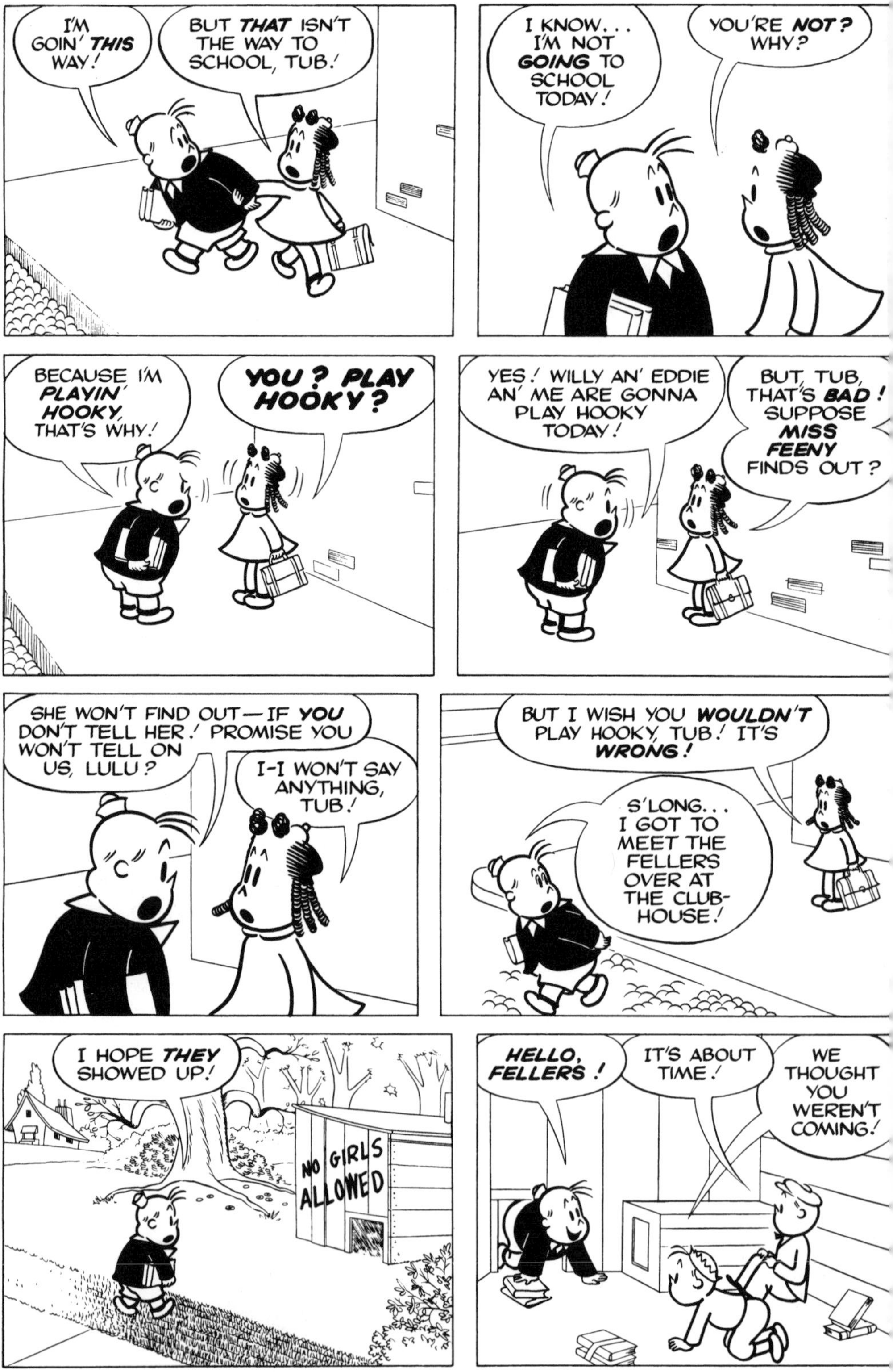
I'M GOIN' THIS WAY!
BUT THAT ISN'T THE WAY TO SCHOOL, TUB!
I KNOW... I'M NOT GOING TO SCHOOL TODAY!
YOU'RE NOT? WHY?
BECAUSE I'M PLAYIN' HOOKY, THAT'S WHY!
YOU? PLAY HOOKY?
YES! WILLY AN' EDDIE AN' ME ARE GONNA PLAY HOOKY TODAY!
BUT, TUB, THAT'S BAD! SUPPOSE MISS FEENY FINDS OUT?
SHE WON'T FIND OUT—IF YOU DON'T TELL HER! PROMISE YOU WON'T TELL ON US, LULU?
I-I WON'T SAY ANYTHING, TUB!
BUT I WISH YOU WOULDN'T PLAY HOOKY, TUB! IT'S WRONG!
S'LONG... I GOT TO MEET THE FELLERS OVER AT THE CLUB-HOUSE!
I HOPE THEY SHOWED UP!
NO GIRLS ALLOWED
HELLO, FELLERS!
IT'S ABOUT TIME!
WE THOUGHT YOU WEREN'T COMING!

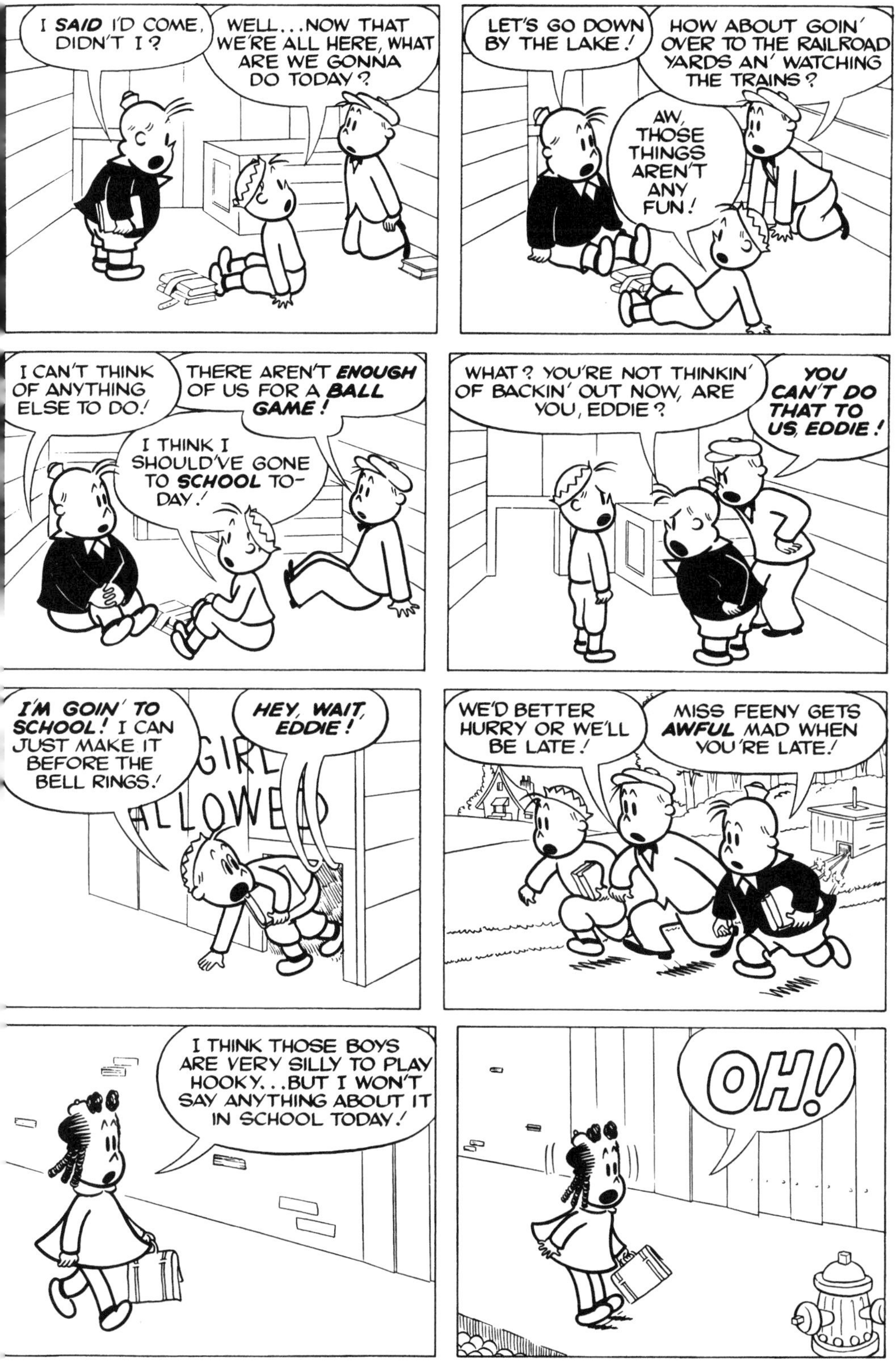
I SAID I'D COME, DIDN'T I?
WELL...NOW THAT WE'RE ALL HERE, WHAT ARE WE GONNA DO TODAY?
LET'S GO DOWN BY THE LAKE!
HOW ABOUT GOIN' OVER TO THE RAILROAD YARDS AN' WATCHING THE TRAINS?
AW, THOSE THINGS AREN'T ANY FUN!
I CAN'T THINK OF ANYTHING ELSE TO DO!
THERE AREN'T ENOUGH OF US FOR A BALL GAME!
I THINK I SHOULD'VE GONE TO SCHOOL TO-DAY!
WHAT? YOU'RE NOT THINKIN' OF BACKIN' OUT NOW, ARE YOU, EDDIE?
YOU CAN'T DO THAT TO US, EDDIE!
I'M GOIN' TO SCHOOL! I CAN JUST MAKE IT BEFORE THE BELL RINGS!
HEY, WAIT, EDDIE!
WE'D BETTER HURRY OR WE'LL BE LATE!
MISS FEENY GETS AWFUL MAD WHEN YOU'RE LATE!
I THINK THOSE BOYS ARE VERY SILLY TO PLAY HOOKY...BUT I WON'T SAY ANYTHING ABOUT IT IN SCHOOL TODAY!
OH!

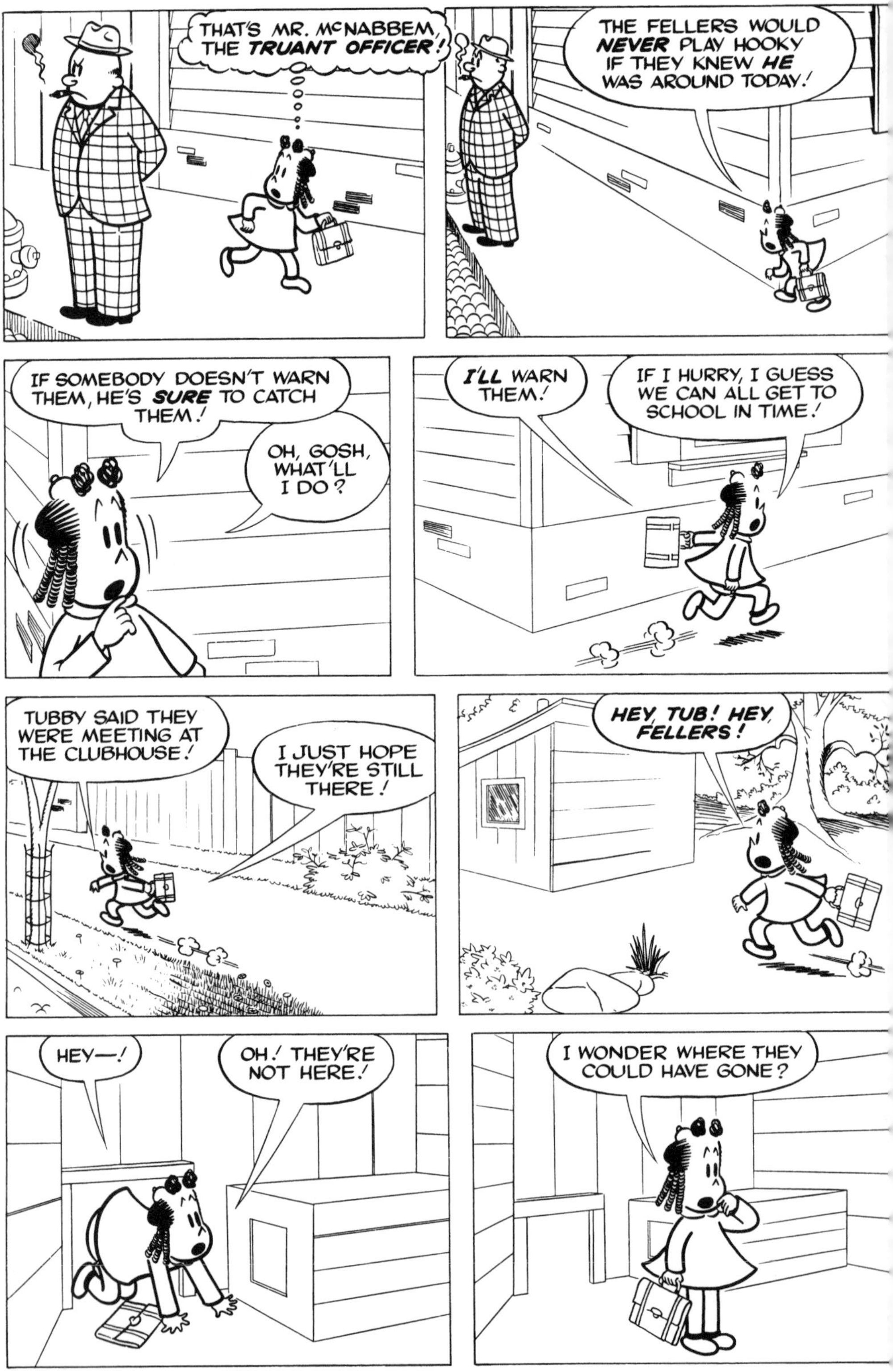
THAT'S MR. McNABBEM, THE TRUANT OFFICER!
THE FELLERS WOULD NEVER PLAY HOOKY IF THEY KNEW HE WAS AROUND TODAY!
IF SOMEBODY DOESN'T WARN THEM, HE'S SURE TO CATCH THEM!
OH, GOSH, WHAT'LL I DO?
I'LL WARN THEM!
IF I HURRY, I GUESS WE CAN ALL GET TO SCHOOL IN TIME!
TUBBY SAID THEY WERE MEETING AT THE CLUBHOUSE!
I JUST HOPE THEY'RE STILL THERE!
HEY, TUB! HEY, FELLERS!
HEY—!
OH! THEY'RE NOT HERE!
I WONDER WHERE THEY COULD HAVE GONE?

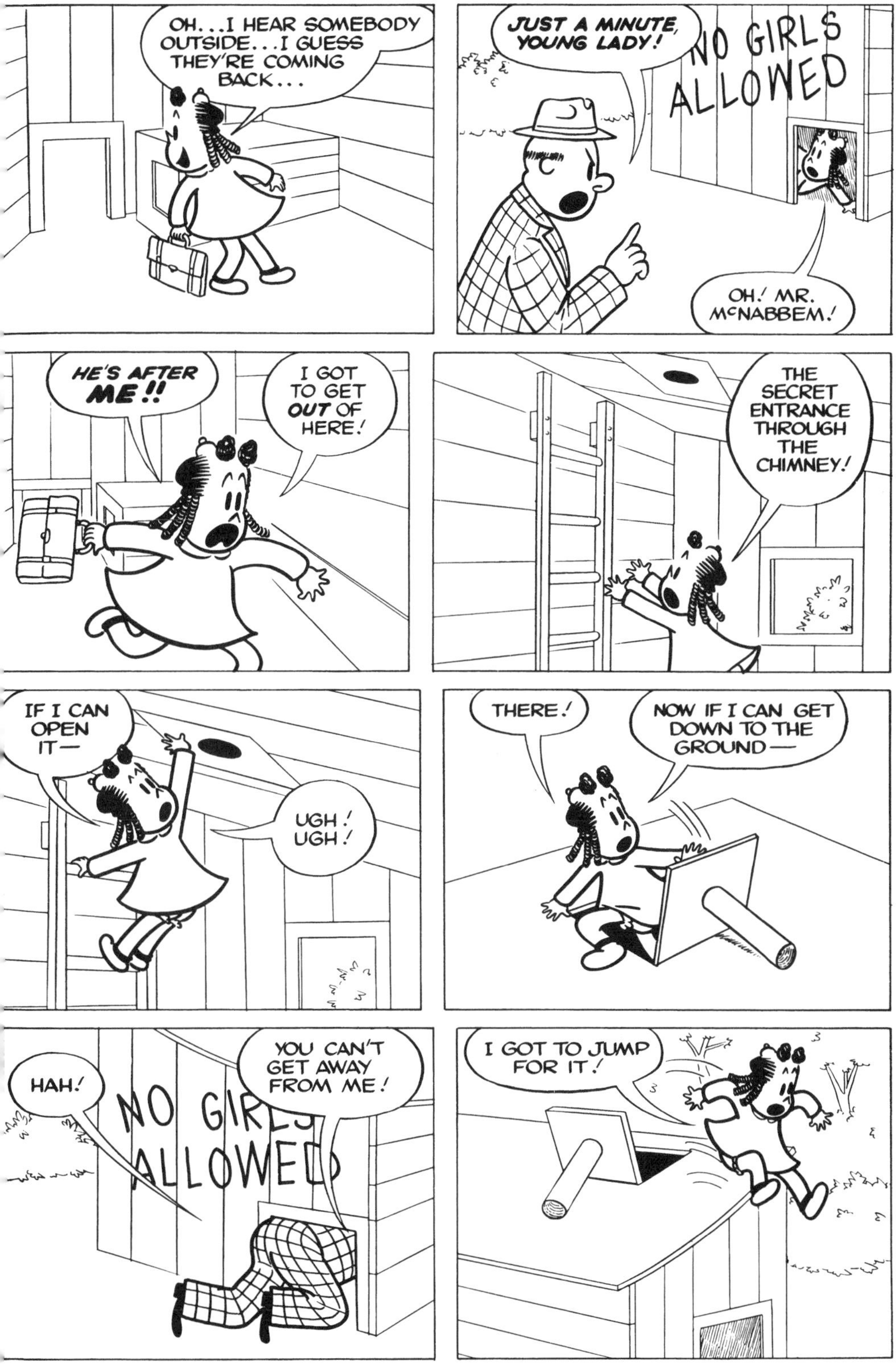

OH...I HEAR SOMEBODY OUTSIDE...I GUESS THEY'RE COMING BACK...
JUST A MINUTE, YOUNG LADY!
NO GIRLS ALLOWED
OH! MR. McNABBEM!
HE'S AFTER ME!!
I GOT TO GET OUT OF HERE!
THE SECRET ENTRANCE THROUGH THE CHIMNEY!
IF I CAN OPEN IT—
UGH! UGH!
THERE!
NOW IF I CAN GET DOWN TO THE GROUND—
HAH!
YOU CAN'T GET AWAY FROM ME!
I GOT TO JUMP FOR IT!

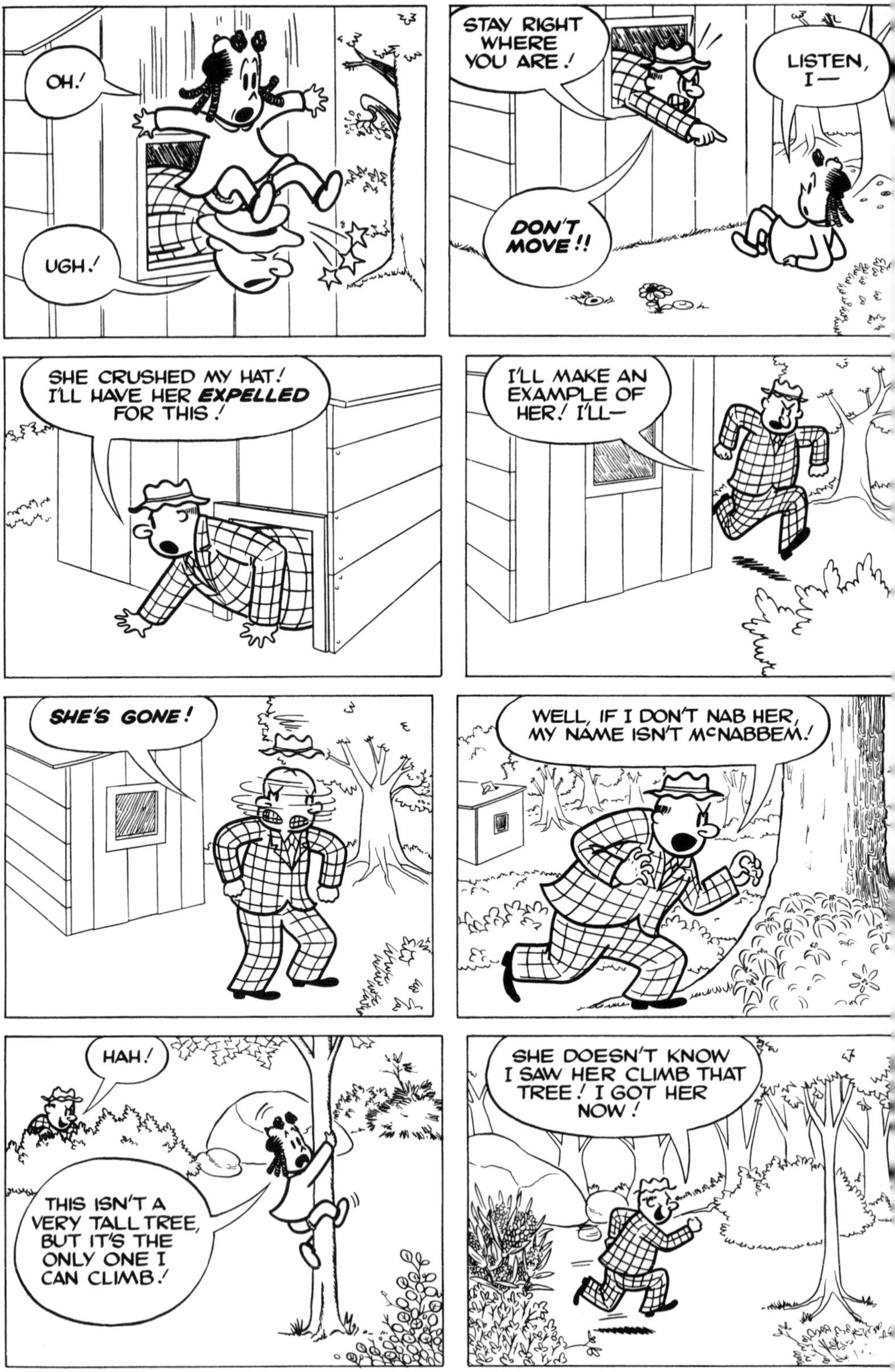
OH!
UGH!
STAY RIGHT WHERE YOU ARE!
LISTEN, I—
DON'T MOVE!!
SHE CRUSHED MY HAT! I'LL HAVE HER **EXPELLED** FOR THIS!
I'LL MAKE AN EXAMPLE OF HER! I'LL—
SHE'S GONE!
WELL, IF I DON'T NAB HER, MY NAME ISN'T McNABBEM!
HAH!
THIS ISN'T A VERY TALL TREE, BUT IT'S THE ONLY ONE I CAN CLIMB!
SHE DOESN'T KNOW I SAW HER CLIMB THAT TREE! I GOT HER NOW!

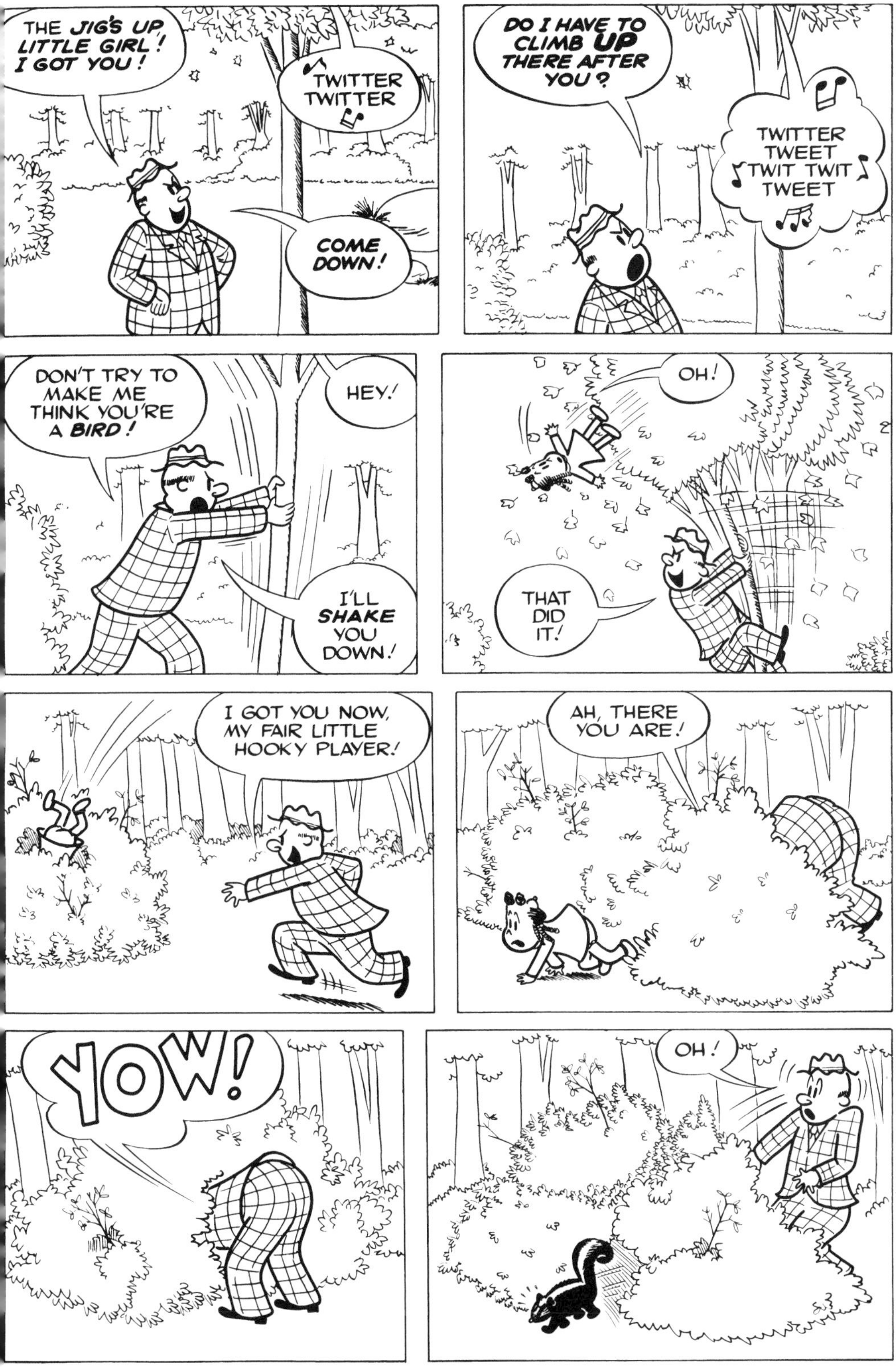
THE JIG'S UP, LITTLE GIRL! I GOT YOU!
TWITTER TWITTER
COME DOWN!
DO I HAVE TO CLIMB UP THERE AFTER YOU?
TWITTER TWEET TWIT TWIT TWEET
DON'T TRY TO MAKE ME THINK YOU'RE A BIRD!
HEY!
I'LL SHAKE YOU DOWN!
OH!
THAT DID IT!
I GOT YOU NOW, MY FAIR LITTLE HOOKY PLAYER!
AH, THERE YOU ARE!
YOW!
OH!

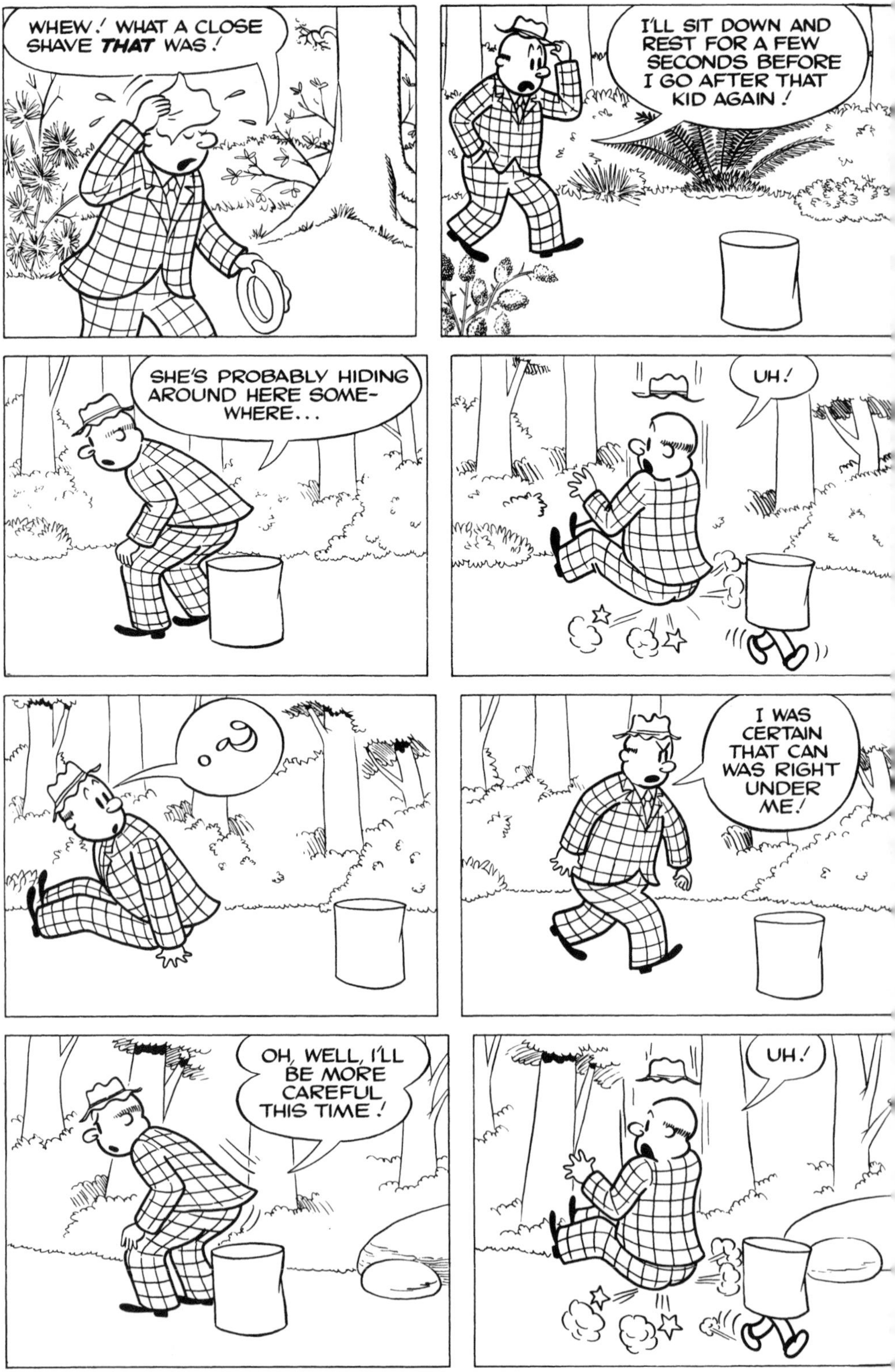
WHEW! WHAT A CLOSE SHAVE THAT WAS!
I'LL SIT DOWN AND REST FOR A FEW SECONDS BEFORE I GO AFTER THAT KID AGAIN!
SHE'S PROBABLY HIDING AROUND HERE SOME-WHERE...
UH!
?
I WAS CERTAIN THAT CAN WAS RIGHT UNDER ME!
OH, WELL, I'LL BE MORE CAREFUL THIS TIME!
UH!

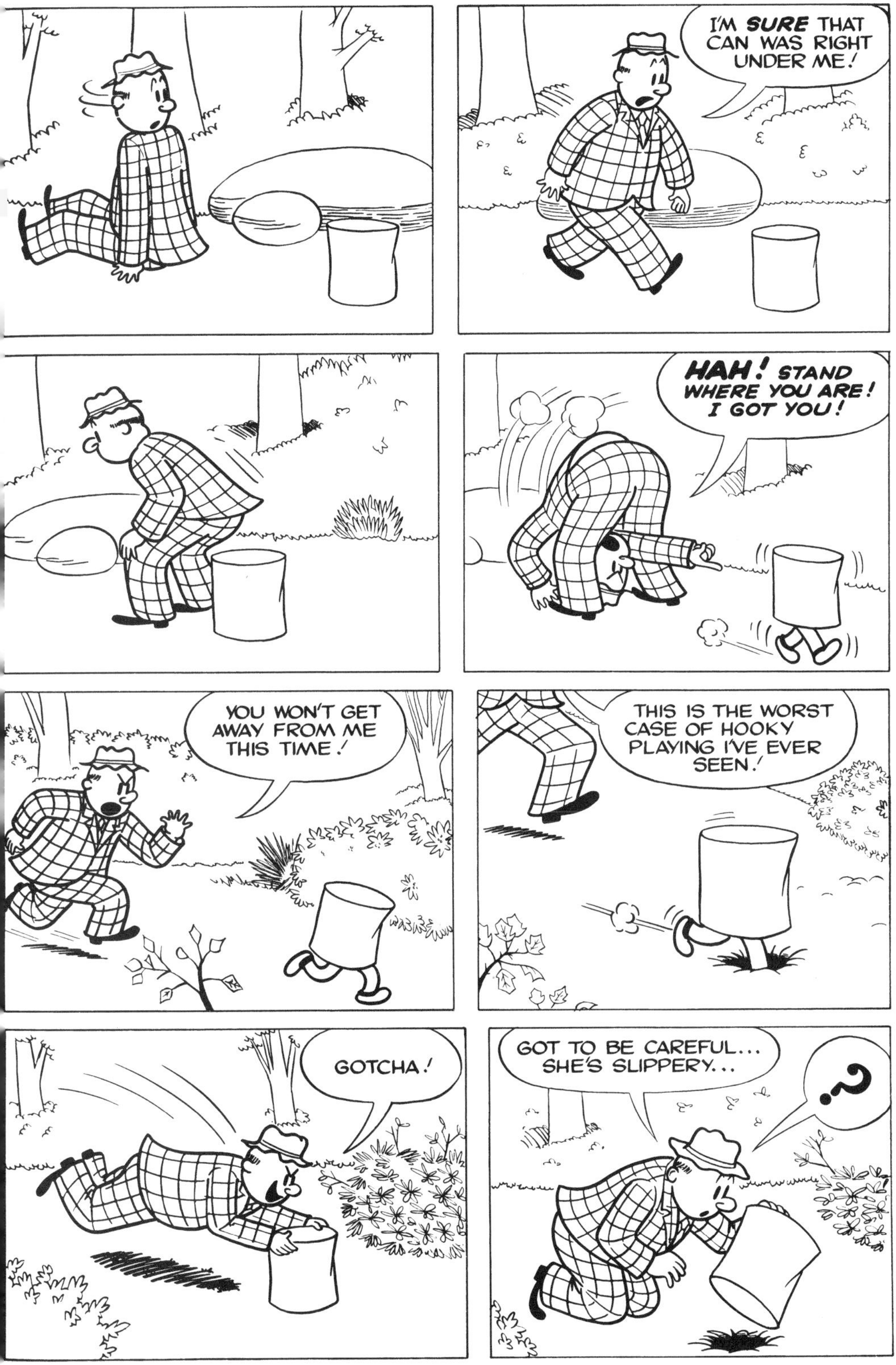
I'M **SURE** THAT CAN WAS RIGHT UNDER ME!
HAH! STAND WHERE YOU ARE! I GOT YOU!
YOU WON'T GET AWAY FROM ME THIS TIME!
THIS IS THE WORST CASE OF HOOKY PLAYING I'VE EVER SEEN!
GOTCHA!
GOT TO BE CAREFUL... SHE'S SLIPPERY...
?

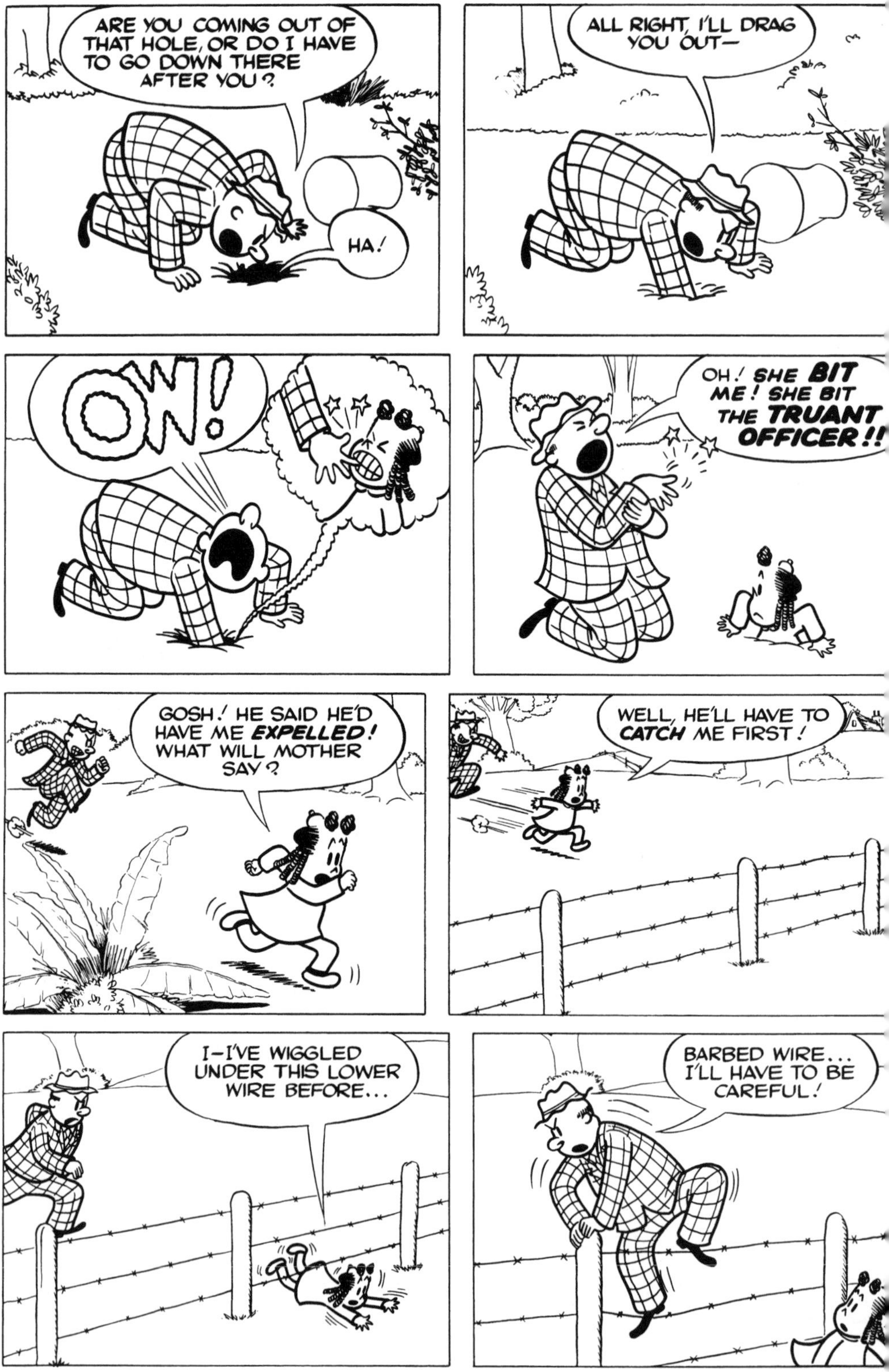
ARE YOU COMING OUT OF THAT HOLE, OR DO I HAVE TO GO DOWN THERE AFTER YOU?
HA!
ALL RIGHT, I'LL DRAG YOU OUT—
OW!
OH! SHE BIT ME! SHE BIT THE TRUANT OFFICER!!
GOSH! HE SAID HE'D HAVE ME EXPELLED! WHAT WILL MOTHER SAY?
WELL, HE'LL HAVE TO CATCH ME FIRST!
I-I'VE WIGGLED UNDER THIS LOWER WIRE BEFORE...
BARBED WIRE... I'LL HAVE TO BE CAREFUL!

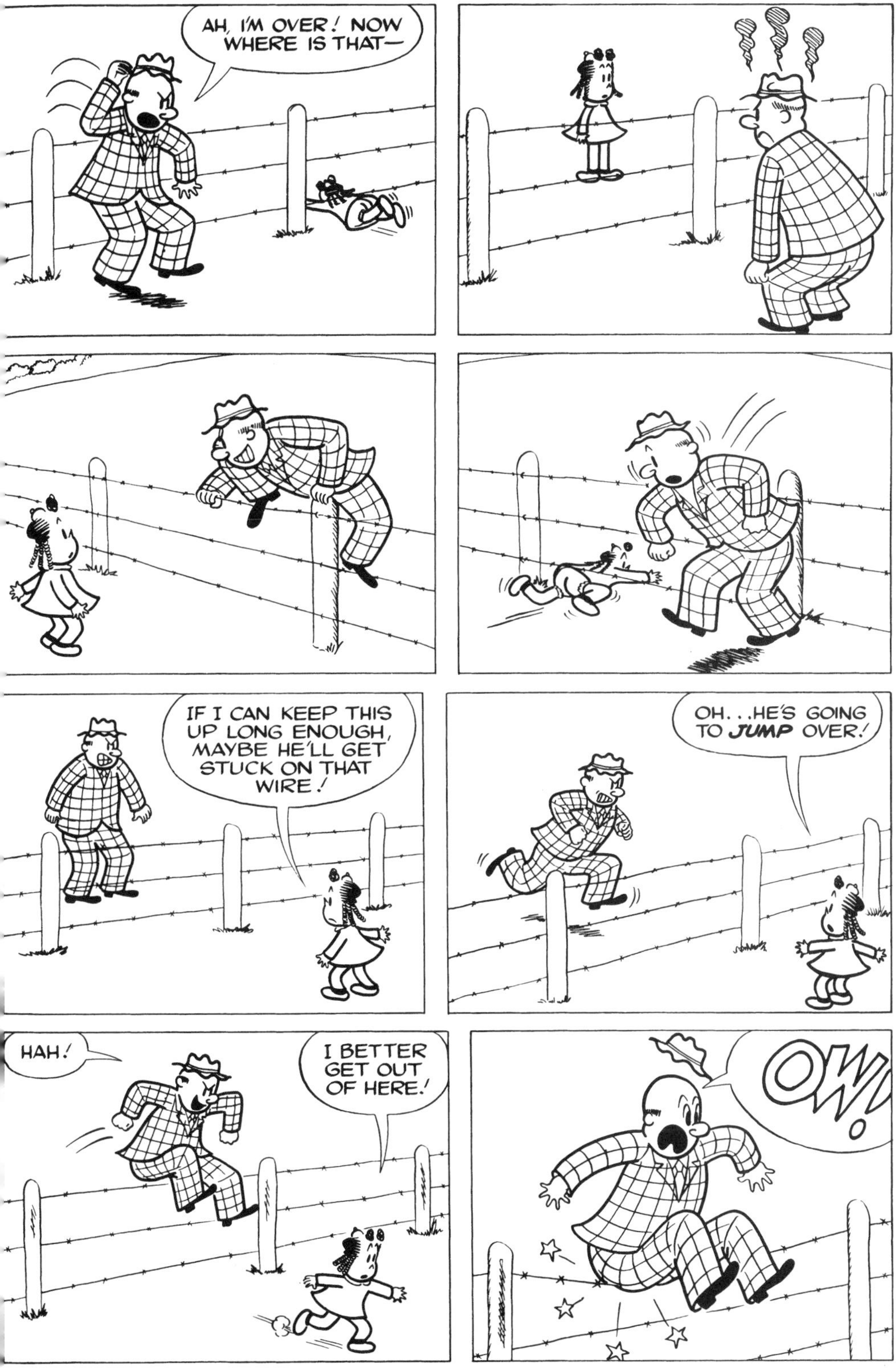
AH, I'M OVER! NOW WHERE IS THAT—
IF I CAN KEEP THIS UP LONG ENOUGH, MAYBE HE'LL GET STUCK ON THAT WIRE!
OH...HE'S GOING TO JUMP OVER!
HAH!
I BETTER GET OUT OF HERE!
OW!

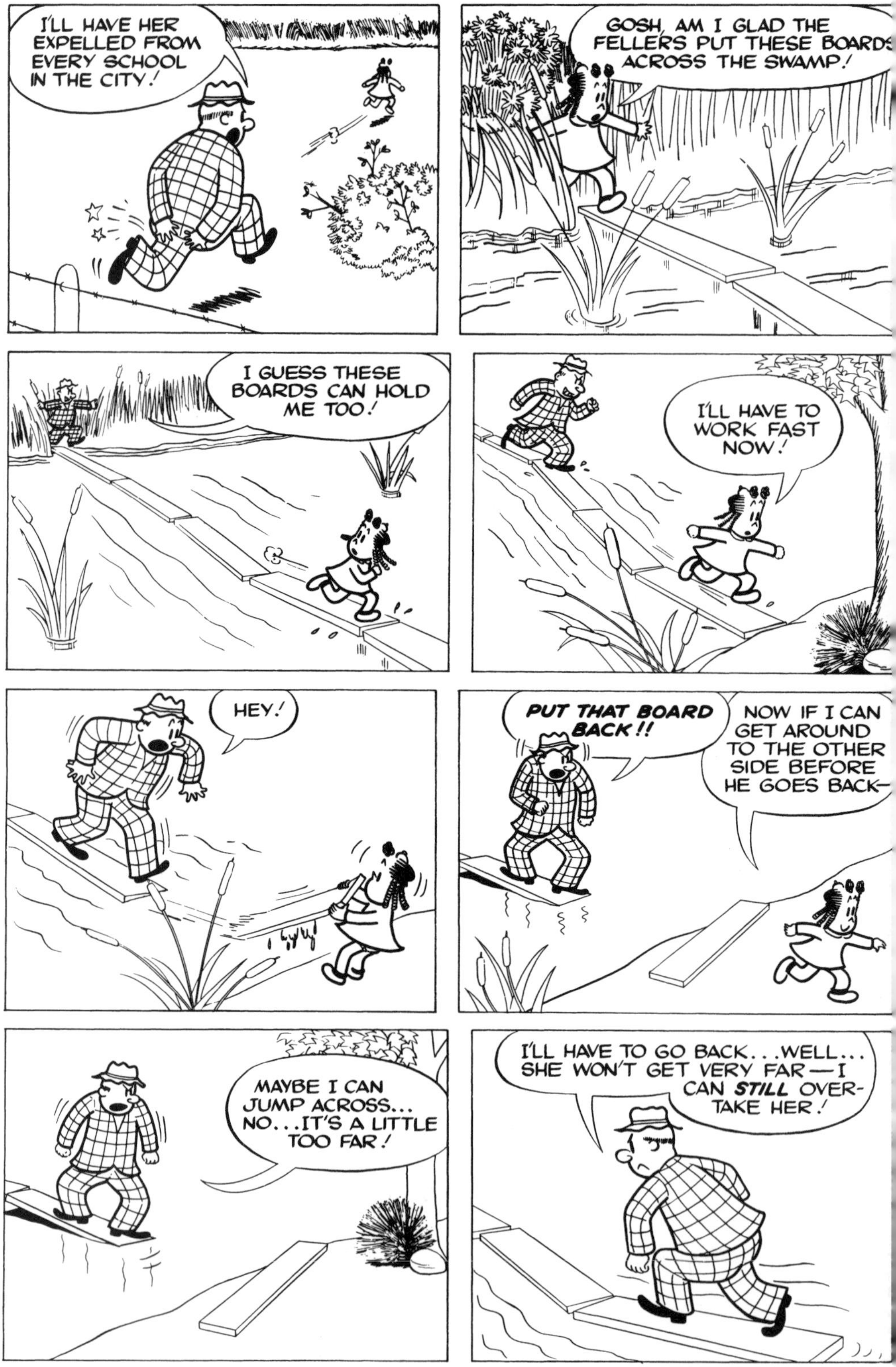

I'LL HAVE HER EXPELLED FROM EVERY SCHOOL IN THE CITY!
GOSH, AM I GLAD THE FELLERS PUT THESE BOARDS ACROSS THE SWAMP!
I GUESS THESE BOARDS CAN HOLD ME TOO!
I'LL HAVE TO WORK FAST NOW!
HEY!
PUT THAT BOARD BACK!!
NOW IF I CAN GET AROUND TO THE OTHER SIDE BEFORE HE GOES BACK—
MAYBE I CAN JUMP ACROSS... NO...IT'S A LITTLE TOO FAR!
I'LL HAVE TO GO BACK...WELL... SHE WON'T GET VERY FAR—I CAN STILL OVER-TAKE HER!

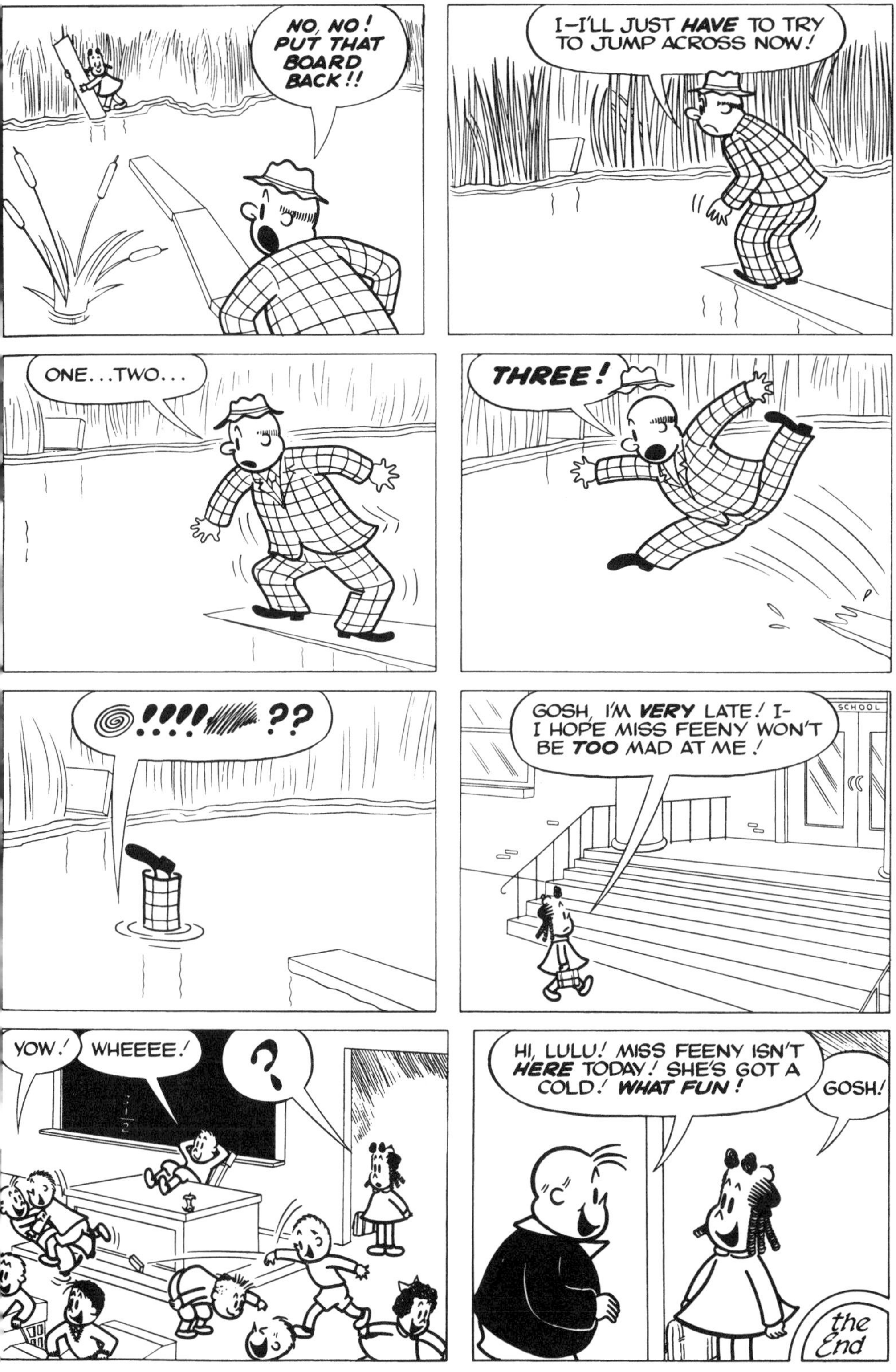
NO, NO! PUT THAT BOARD BACK!!
I-I'LL JUST HAVE TO TRY TO JUMP ACROSS NOW!
ONE...TWO...
THREE!
!!!!??
SCHOOL
GOSH, I'M VERY LATE! I-I HOPE MISS FEENY WON'T BE TOO MAD AT ME!
YOW!
WHEEEE!
?
HI, LULU! MISS FEENY ISN'T HERE TODAY! SHE'S GOT A COLD! WHAT FUN!
GOSH!
the End

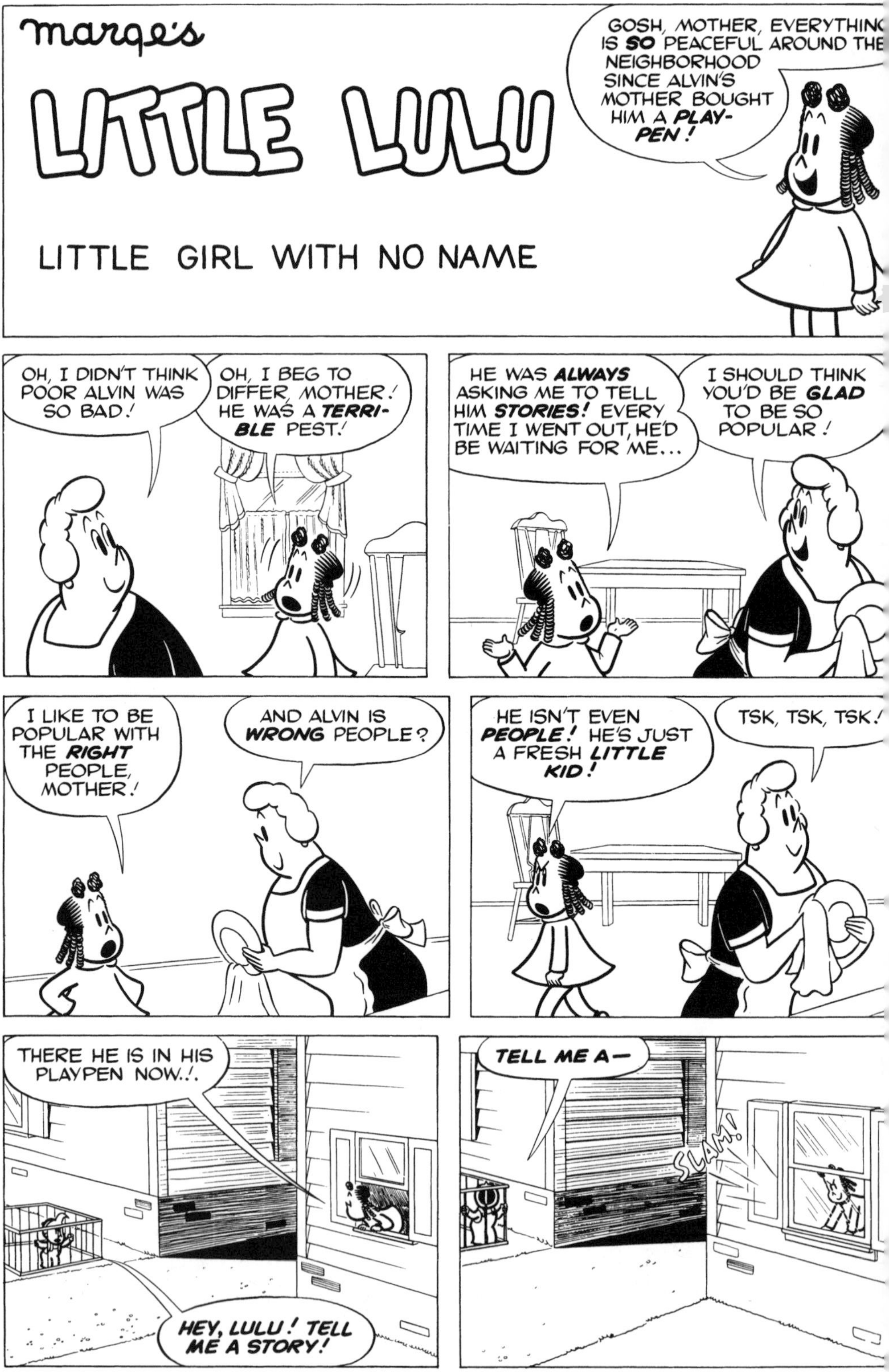
marge's
LITTLE LULU
LITTLE GIRL WITH NO NAME
GOSH, MOTHER, EVERYTHIN IS SO PEACEFUL AROUND THE NEIGHBORHOOD SINCE ALVIN'S MOTHER BOUGHT HIM A PLAY-PEN!
OH, I DIDN'T THINK POOR ALVIN WAS SO BAD!
OH, I BEG TO DIFFER, MOTHER! HE WAS A TERRIBLE PEST!
HE WAS ALWAYS ASKING ME TO TELL HIM STORIES! EVERY TIME I WENT OUT, HE'D BE WAITING FOR ME...
I SHOULD THINK YOU'D BE GLAD TO BE SO POPULAR!
I LIKE TO BE POPULAR WITH THE RIGHT PEOPLE, MOTHER!
AND ALVIN IS WRONG PEOPLE?
HE ISN'T EVEN PEOPLE! HE'S JUST A FRESH LITTLE KID!
TSK, TSK, TSK!
THERE HE IS IN HIS PLAYPEN NOW..!.
HEY, LULU! TELL ME A STORY!
TELL ME A—
SLAM!

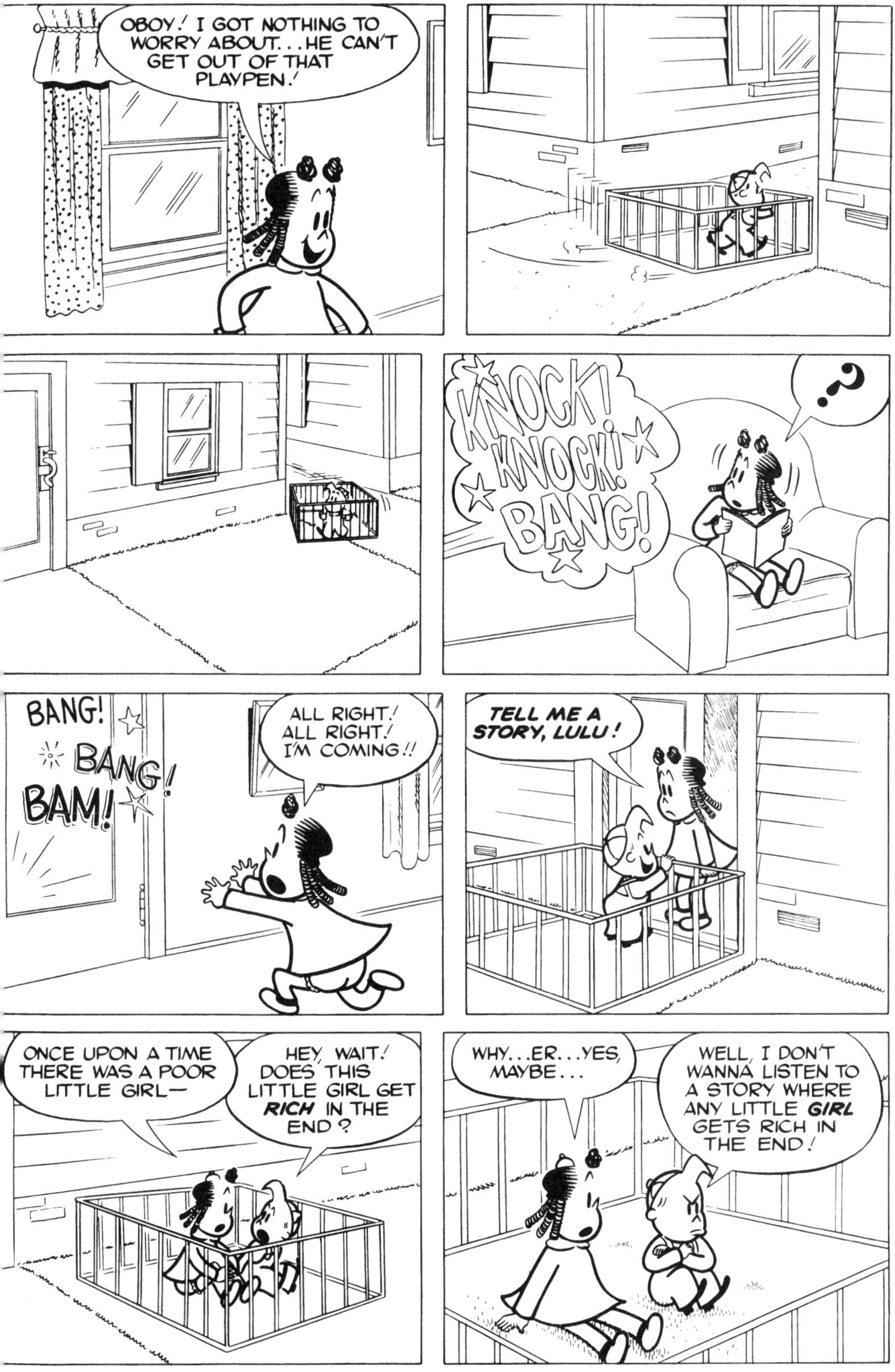
OBOY! I GOT NOTHING TO WORRY ABOUT...HE CAN'T GET OUT OF THAT PLAYPEN!
KNOCK! KNOCK! BANG!
?
BANG!
BANG!
BAM!
ALL RIGHT! ALL RIGHT! I'M COMING!!
TELL ME A STORY, LULU!
ONCE UPON A TIME THERE WAS A POOR LITTLE GIRL—
HEY, WAIT! DOES THIS LITTLE GIRL GET RICH IN THE END?
WHY...ER...YES, MAYBE...
WELL, I DON'T WANNA LISTEN TO A STORY WHERE ANY LITTLE GIRL GETS RICH IN THE END!

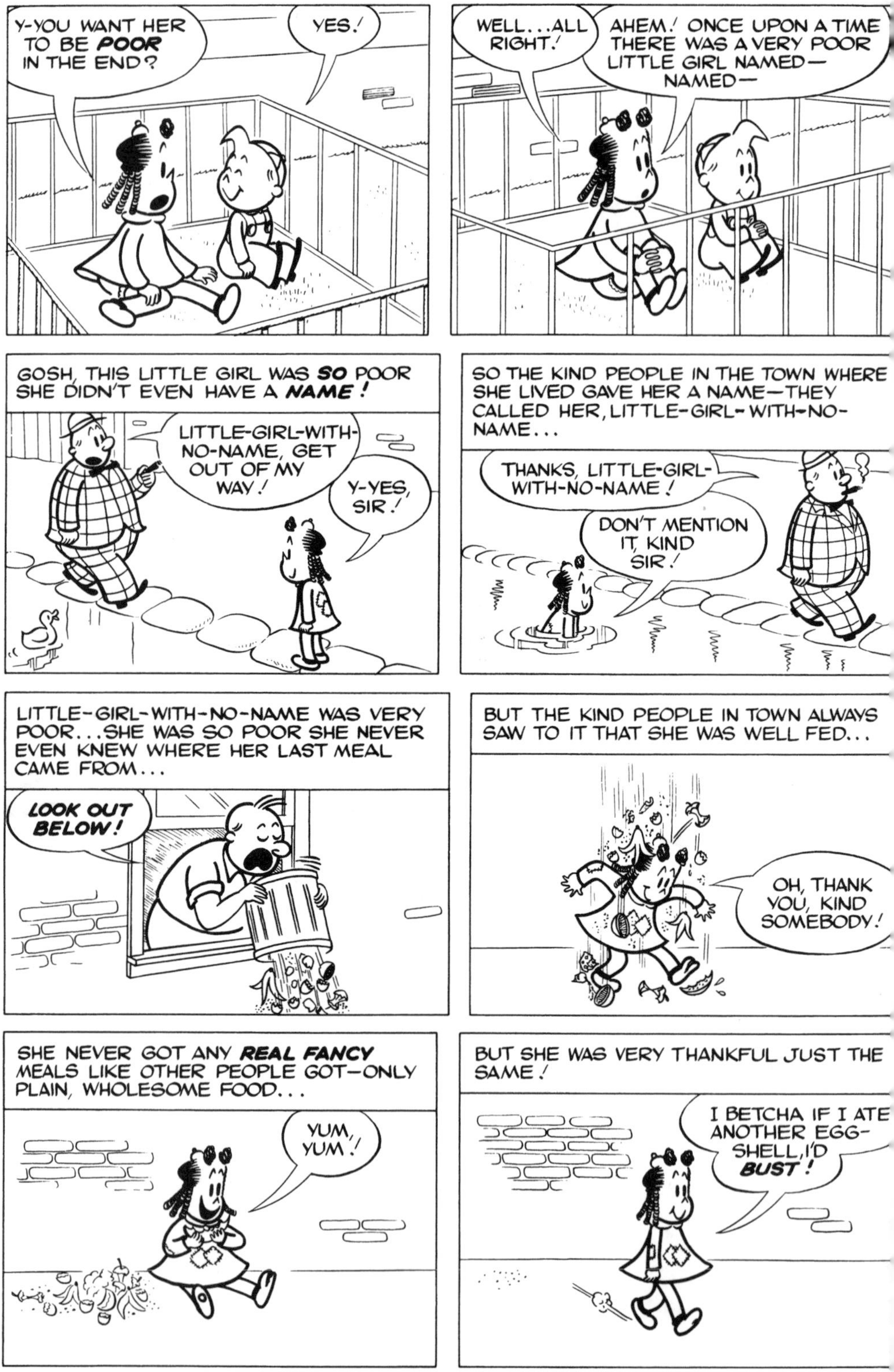
Y-YOU WANT HER TO BE POOR IN THE END?
YES!
WELL...ALL RIGHT!
AHEM! ONCE UPON A TIME THERE WAS A VERY POOR LITTLE GIRL NAMED— NAMED—
GOSH, THIS LITTLE GIRL WAS SO POOR SHE DIDN'T EVEN HAVE A NAME!
LITTLE-GIRL-WITH-NO-NAME, GET OUT OF MY WAY!
Y-YES, SIR!
SO THE KIND PEOPLE IN THE TOWN WHERE SHE LIVED GAVE HER A NAME—THEY CALLED HER, LITTLE-GIRL-WITH-NO-NAME...
THANKS, LITTLE-GIRL-WITH-NO-NAME!
DON'T MENTION IT, KIND SIR!
LITTLE-GIRL-WITH-NO-NAME WAS VERY POOR...SHE WAS SO POOR SHE NEVER EVEN KNEW WHERE HER LAST MEAL CAME FROM...
LOOK OUT BELOW!
BUT THE KIND PEOPLE IN TOWN ALWAYS SAW TO IT THAT SHE WAS WELL FED...
OH, THANK YOU, KIND SOMEBODY!
SHE NEVER GOT ANY REAL FANCY MEALS LIKE OTHER PEOPLE GOT—ONLY PLAIN, WHOLESOME FOOD...
YUM, YUM!
BUT SHE WAS VERY THANKFUL JUST THE SAME!
I BETCHA IF I ATE ANOTHER EGG-SHELL, I'D BUST!

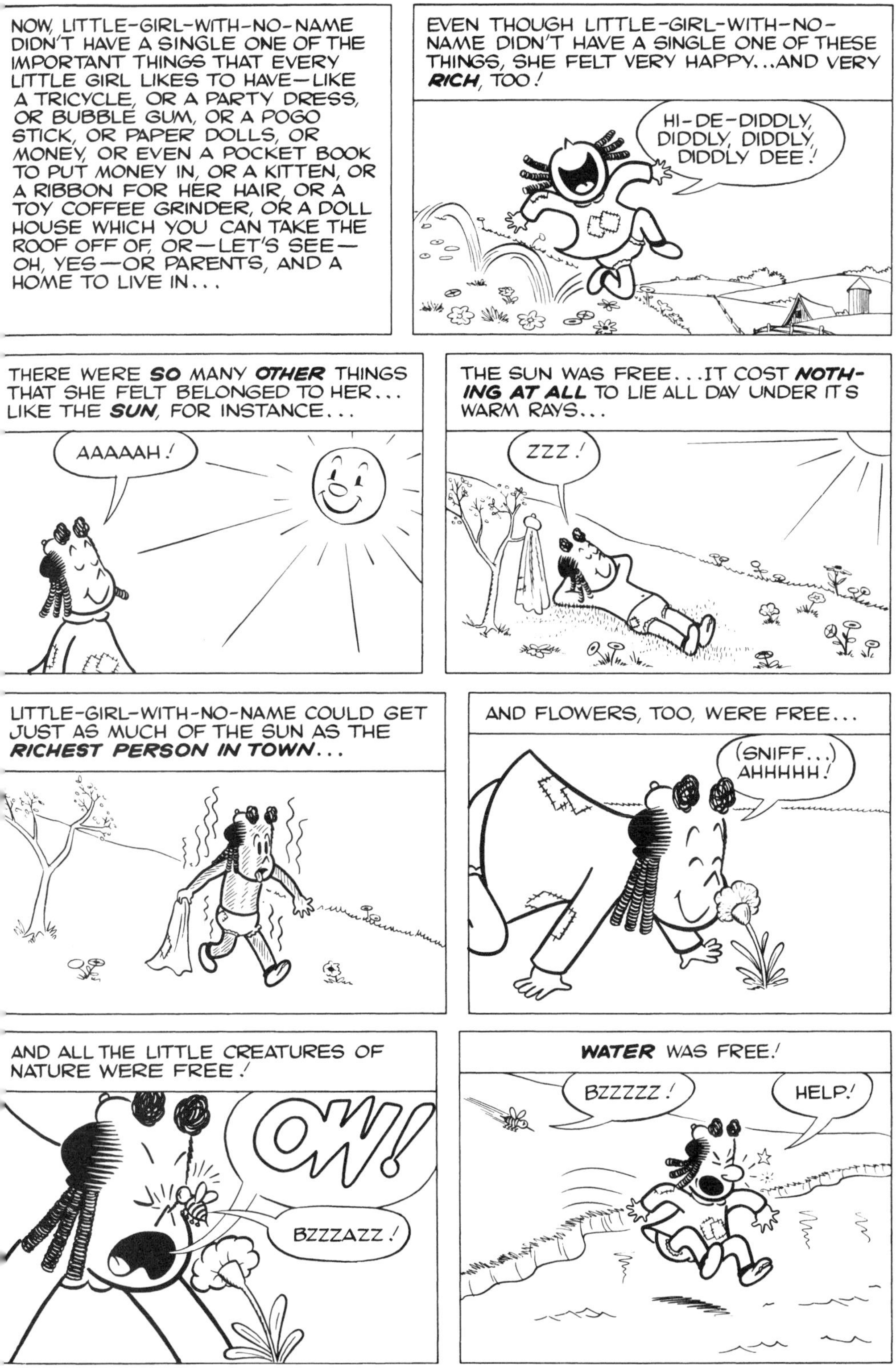
NOW, LITTLE-GIRL-WITH-NO-NAME DIDN'T HAVE A SINGLE ONE OF THE IMPORTANT THINGS THAT EVERY LITTLE GIRL LIKES TO HAVE—LIKE A TRICYCLE, OR A PARTY DRESS, OR BUBBLE GUM, OR A POGO STICK, OR PAPER DOLLS, OR MONEY, OR EVEN A POCKET BOOK TO PUT MONEY IN, OR A KITTEN, OR A RIBBON FOR HER HAIR, OR A TOY COFFEE GRINDER, OR A DOLL HOUSE WHICH YOU CAN TAKE THE ROOF OFF OF, OR—LET'S SEE—OH, YES—OR PARENTS, AND A HOME TO LIVE IN...
EVEN THOUGH LITTLE-GIRL-WITH-NO-NAME DIDN'T HAVE A SINGLE ONE OF THESE THINGS, SHE FELT VERY HAPPY...AND VERY RICH, TOO!
HI-DE-DIDDLY, DIDDLY, DIDDLY, DIDDLY DEE!
THERE WERE SO MANY OTHER THINGS THAT SHE FELT BELONGED TO HER... LIKE THE SUN, FOR INSTANCE...
AAAAAH!
THE SUN WAS FREE...IT COST NOTHING AT ALL TO LIE ALL DAY UNDER IT'S WARM RAYS...
ZZZ!
LITTLE-GIRL-WITH-NO-NAME COULD GET JUST AS MUCH OF THE SUN AS THE RICHEST PERSON IN TOWN...
AND FLOWERS, TOO, WERE FREE...
(SNIFF...) AHHHHH!
AND ALL THE LITTLE CREATURES OF NATURE WERE FREE!
OW!
BZZZAZZ!
WATER WAS FREE!
BZZZZZ!
HELP!

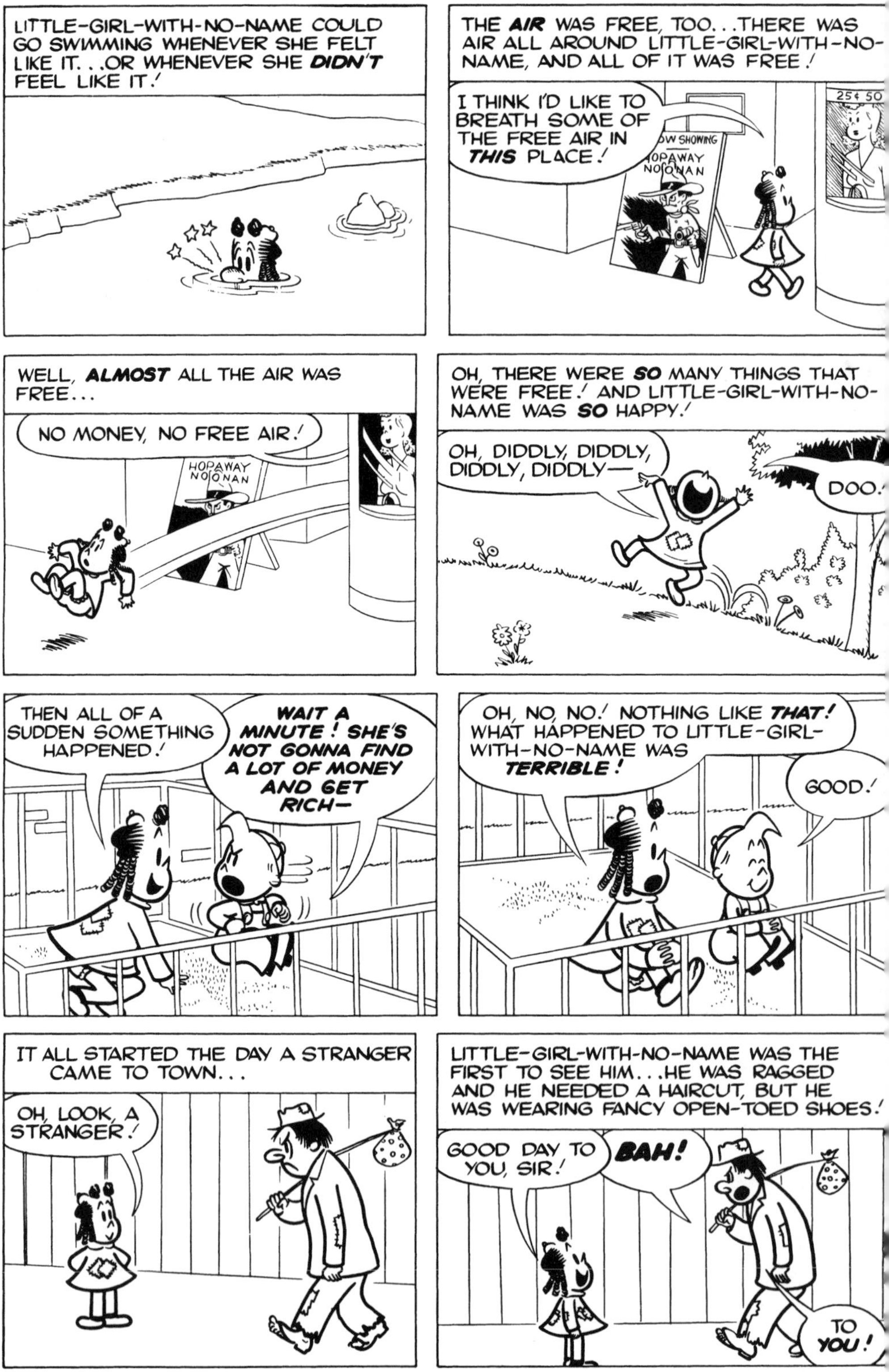

LITTLE-GIRL-WITH-NO-NAME COULD GO SWIMMING WHENEVER SHE FELT LIKE IT. . .OR WHENEVER SHE DIDN'T FEEL LIKE IT.!
THE AIR WAS FREE, TOO. . .THERE WAS AIR ALL AROUND LITTLE-GIRL-WITH-NO-NAME, AND ALL OF IT WAS FREE.!
I THINK I'D LIKE TO BREATH SOME OF THE FREE AIR IN THIS PLACE.!
OW SHOWING
HOPAWAY NO NAN
25¢ 50
WELL, ALMOST ALL THE AIR WAS FREE...
NO MONEY, NO FREE AIR.!
HOPAWAY NO NAN
OH, THERE WERE SO MANY THINGS THAT WERE FREE.! AND LITTLE-GIRL-WITH-NO-NAME WAS SO HAPPY.!
OH, DIDDLY, DIDDLY, DIDDLY, DIDDLY—
DOO.
THEN ALL OF A SUDDEN SOMETHING HAPPENED.!
WAIT A MINUTE! SHE'S NOT GONNA FIND A LOT OF MONEY AND GET RICH—
OH, NO, NO.! NOTHING LIKE THAT! WHAT HAPPENED TO LITTLE-GIRL-WITH-NO-NAME WAS TERRIBLE!
GOOD.!
IT ALL STARTED THE DAY A STRANGER CAME TO TOWN...
OH, LOOK, A STRANGER.!
LITTLE-GIRL-WITH-NO-NAME WAS THE FIRST TO SEE HIM. . .HE WAS RAGGED AND HE NEEDED A HAIRCUT, BUT HE WAS WEARING FANCY OPEN-TOED SHOES.!
GOOD DAY TO YOU, SIR.!
BAH!
TO YOU!

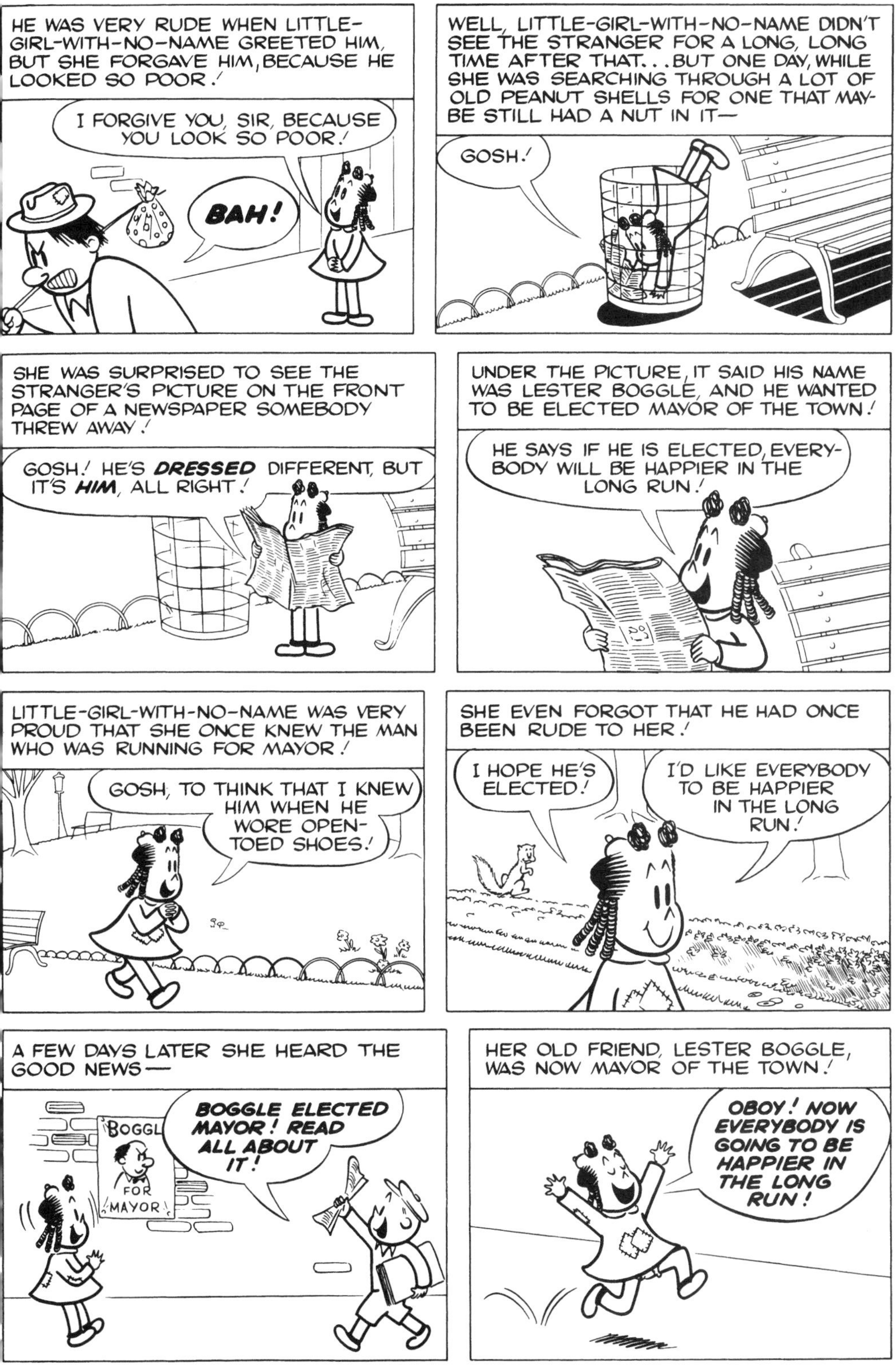
HE WAS VERY RUDE WHEN LITTLE-GIRL-WITH-NO-NAME GREETED HIM, BUT SHE FORGAVE HIM, BECAUSE HE LOOKED SO POOR!
I FORGIVE YOU, SIR, BECAUSE YOU LOOK SO POOR!
BAH!
WELL, LITTLE-GIRL-WITH-NO-NAME DIDN'T SEE THE STRANGER FOR A LONG, LONG TIME AFTER THAT...BUT ONE DAY, WHILE SHE WAS SEARCHING THROUGH A LOT OF OLD PEANUT SHELLS FOR ONE THAT MAY-BE STILL HAD A NUT IN IT—
GOSH!
SHE WAS SURPRISED TO SEE THE STRANGER'S PICTURE ON THE FRONT PAGE OF A NEWSPAPER SOMEBODY THREW AWAY!
GOSH! HE'S ***DRESSED*** DIFFERENT, BUT IT'S ***HIM***, ALL RIGHT!
UNDER THE PICTURE, IT SAID HIS NAME WAS LESTER BOGGLE, AND HE WANTED TO BE ELECTED MAYOR OF THE TOWN!
HE SAYS IF HE IS ELECTED, EVERY-BODY WILL BE HAPPIER IN THE LONG RUN!
LITTLE-GIRL-WITH-NO-NAME WAS VERY PROUD THAT SHE ONCE KNEW THE MAN WHO WAS RUNNING FOR MAYOR!
GOSH, TO THINK THAT I KNEW HIM WHEN HE WORE OPEN-TOED SHOES!
SHE EVEN FORGOT THAT HE HAD ONCE BEEN RUDE TO HER!
I HOPE HE'S ELECTED!
I'D LIKE EVERYBODY TO BE HAPPIER IN THE LONG RUN!
A FEW DAYS LATER SHE HEARD THE GOOD NEWS—
BOGGL
FOR MAYOR
BOGGLE ELECTED MAYOR! READ ALL ABOUT IT!
HER OLD FRIEND, LESTER BOGGLE, WAS NOW MAYOR OF THE TOWN!
OBOY! NOW EVERYBODY IS GOING TO BE HAPPIER IN THE LONG RUN!

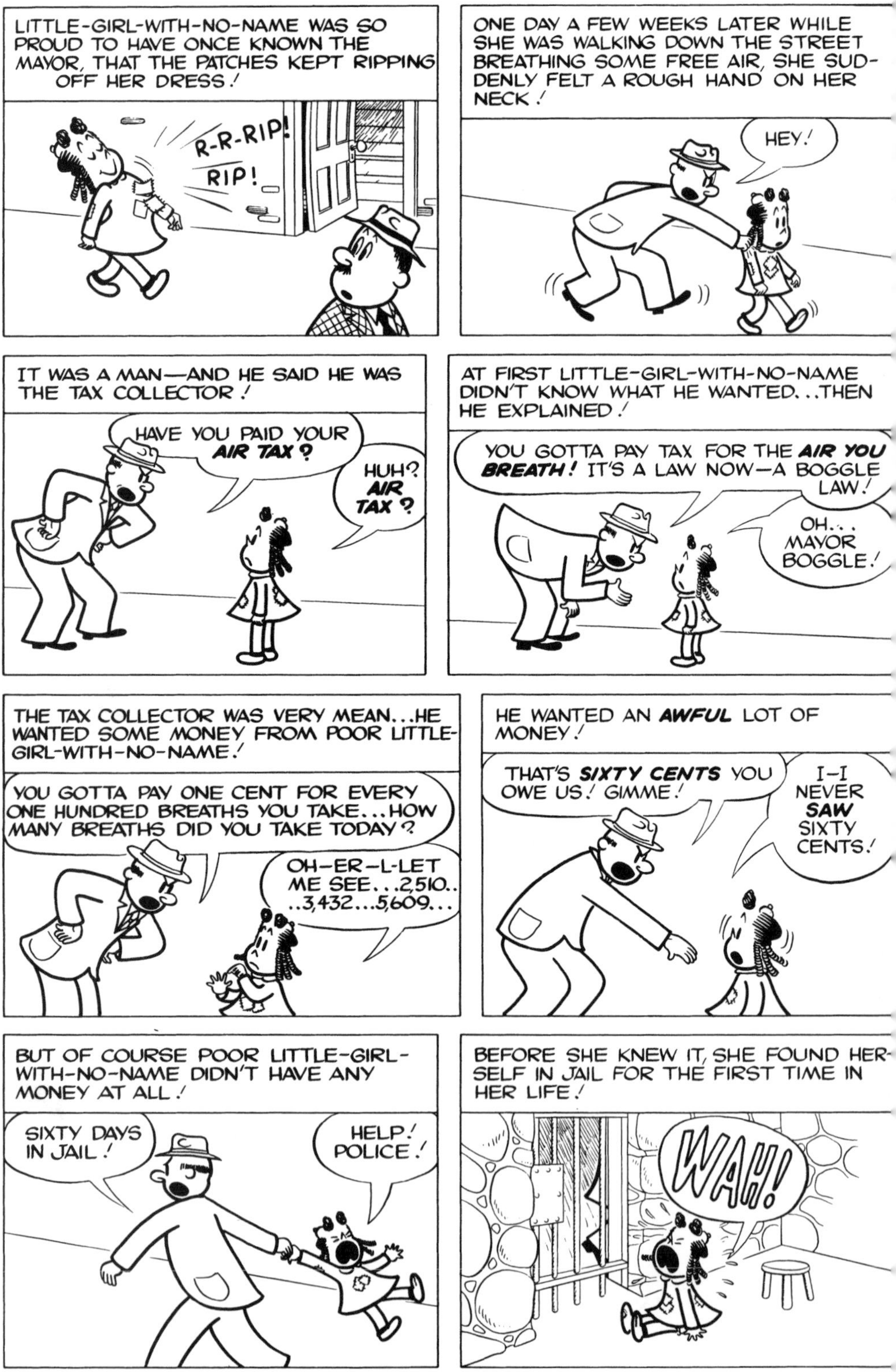
LITTLE-GIRL-WITH-NO-NAME WAS SO PROUD TO HAVE ONCE KNOWN THE MAYOR, THAT THE PATCHES KEPT RIPPING OFF HER DRESS!
R-R-RIP!
RIP!
ONE DAY A FEW WEEKS LATER WHILE SHE WAS WALKING DOWN THE STREET BREATHING SOME FREE AIR, SHE SUDDENLY FELT A ROUGH HAND ON HER NECK!
HEY!
IT WAS A MAN—AND HE SAID HE WAS THE TAX COLLECTOR!
HAVE YOU PAID YOUR AIR TAX?
HUH? AIR TAX?
AT FIRST LITTLE-GIRL-WITH-NO-NAME DIDN'T KNOW WHAT HE WANTED...THEN HE EXPLAINED!
YOU GOTTA PAY TAX FOR THE AIR YOU BREATH! IT'S A LAW NOW—A BOGGLE LAW!
OH... MAYOR BOGGLE!
THE TAX COLLECTOR WAS VERY MEAN...HE WANTED SOME MONEY FROM POOR LITTLE-GIRL-WITH-NO-NAME!
YOU GOTTA PAY ONE CENT FOR EVERY ONE HUNDRED BREATHS YOU TAKE...HOW MANY BREATHS DID YOU TAKE TODAY?
OH—ER—L-LET ME SEE...2,510... ...3,432...5,609...
HE WANTED AN AWFUL LOT OF MONEY!
THAT'S SIXTY CENTS YOU OWE US! GIMME!
I—I NEVER SAW SIXTY CENTS!
BUT OF COURSE POOR LITTLE-GIRL-WITH-NO-NAME DIDN'T HAVE ANY MONEY AT ALL!
SIXTY DAYS IN JAIL!
HELP! POLICE!
BEFORE SHE KNEW IT, SHE FOUND HERSELF IN JAIL FOR THE FIRST TIME IN HER LIFE!
WAH!

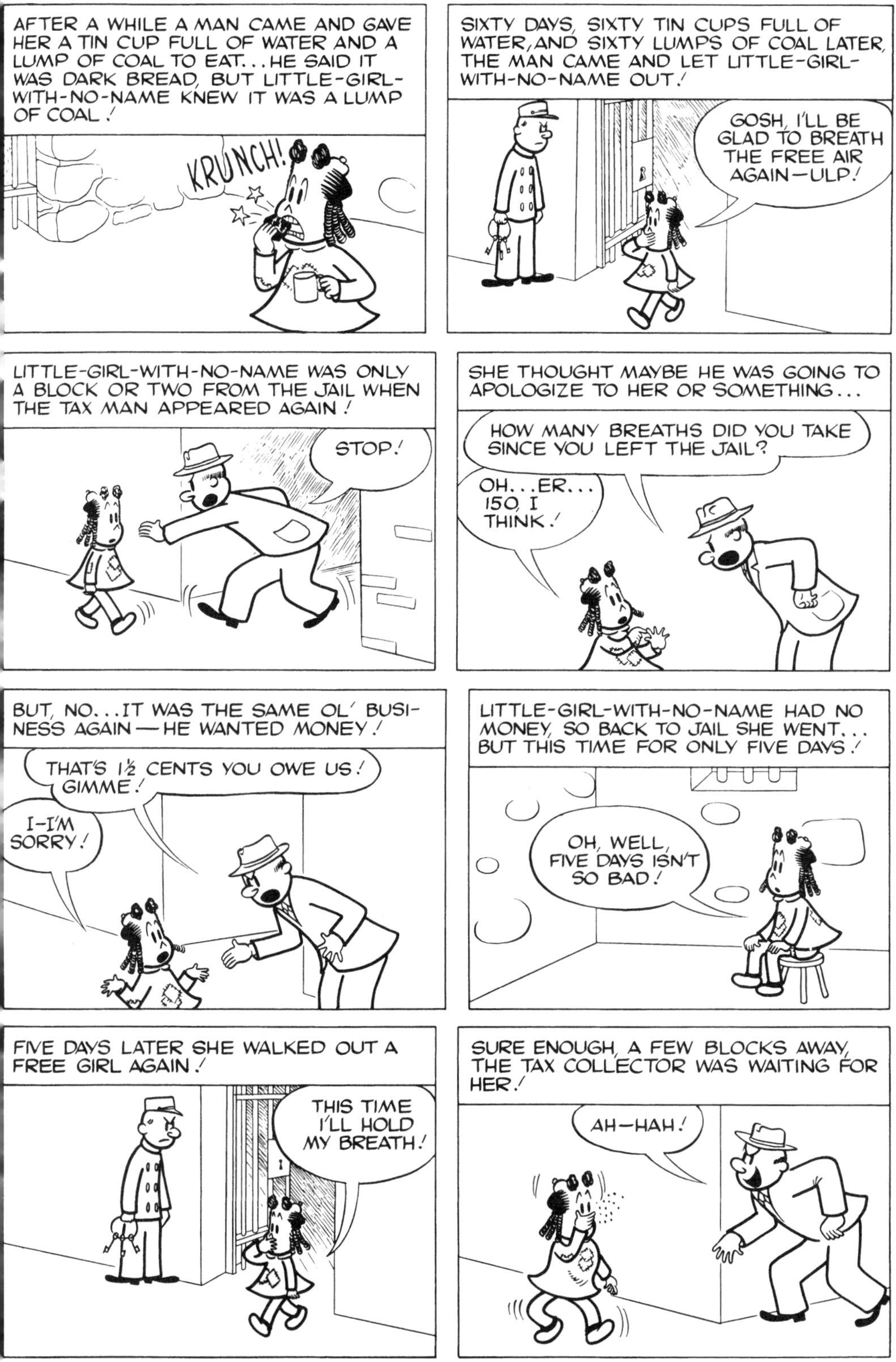
AFTER A WHILE A MAN CAME AND GAVE HER A TIN CUP FULL OF WATER AND A LUMP OF COAL TO EAT... HE SAID IT WAS DARK BREAD, BUT LITTLE-GIRL-WITH-NO-NAME KNEW IT WAS A LUMP OF COAL!
KRUNCH!
SIXTY DAYS, SIXTY TIN CUPS FULL OF WATER, AND SIXTY LUMPS OF COAL LATER, THE MAN CAME AND LET LITTLE-GIRL-WITH-NO-NAME OUT!
GOSH, I'LL BE GLAD TO BREATH THE FREE AIR AGAIN—ULP!
LITTLE-GIRL-WITH-NO-NAME WAS ONLY A BLOCK OR TWO FROM THE JAIL WHEN THE TAX MAN APPEARED AGAIN!
STOP!
SHE THOUGHT MAYBE HE WAS GOING TO APOLOGIZE TO HER OR SOMETHING...
HOW MANY BREATHS DID YOU TAKE SINCE YOU LEFT THE JAIL?
OH...ER... 150, I THINK!
BUT, NO...IT WAS THE SAME OL' BUSINESS AGAIN—HE WANTED MONEY!
THAT'S 1½ CENTS YOU OWE US! GIMME!
I-I'M SORRY!
LITTLE-GIRL-WITH-NO-NAME HAD NO MONEY, SO BACK TO JAIL SHE WENT... BUT THIS TIME FOR ONLY FIVE DAYS!
OH, WELL, FIVE DAYS ISN'T SO BAD!
FIVE DAYS LATER SHE WALKED OUT A FREE GIRL AGAIN!
THIS TIME I'LL HOLD MY BREATH!
SURE ENOUGH, A FEW BLOCKS AWAY, THE TAX COLLECTOR WAS WAITING FOR HER!
AH—HAH!

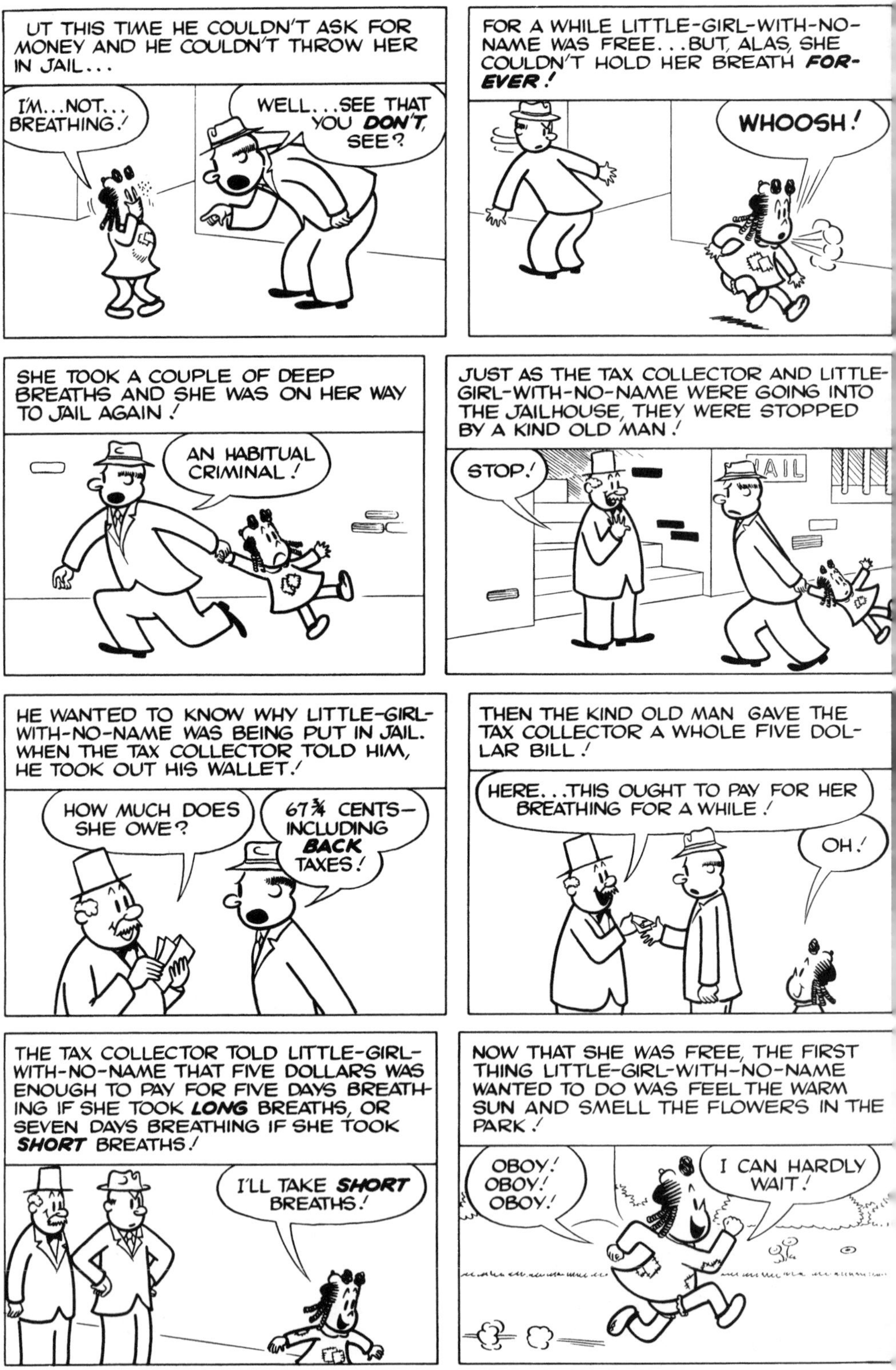
UT THIS TIME HE COULDN'T ASK FOR MONEY AND HE COULDN'T THROW HER IN JAIL...
I'M...NOT... BREATHING.!
WELL...SEE THAT YOU DON'T, SEE?
FOR A WHILE LITTLE-GIRL-WITH-NO-NAME WAS FREE...BUT, ALAS, SHE COULDN'T HOLD HER BREATH FOR-EVER!
WHOOSH!
SHE TOOK A COUPLE OF DEEP BREATHS AND SHE WAS ON HER WAY TO JAIL AGAIN!
AN HABITUAL CRIMINAL!
JUST AS THE TAX COLLECTOR AND LITTLE-GIRL-WITH-NO-NAME WERE GOING INTO THE JAILHOUSE, THEY WERE STOPPED BY A KIND OLD MAN!
STOP!
JAIL
HE WANTED TO KNOW WHY LITTLE-GIRL-WITH-NO-NAME WAS BEING PUT IN JAIL. WHEN THE TAX COLLECTOR TOLD HIM, HE TOOK OUT HIS WALLET!
HOW MUCH DOES SHE OWE?
67¾ CENTS—INCLUDING BACK TAXES!
THEN THE KIND OLD MAN GAVE THE TAX COLLECTOR A WHOLE FIVE DOLLAR BILL!
HERE...THIS OUGHT TO PAY FOR HER BREATHING FOR A WHILE!
OH!
THE TAX COLLECTOR TOLD LITTLE-GIRL-WITH-NO-NAME THAT FIVE DOLLARS WAS ENOUGH TO PAY FOR FIVE DAYS BREATHING IF SHE TOOK LONG BREATHS, OR SEVEN DAYS BREATHING IF SHE TOOK SHORT BREATHS!
I'LL TAKE SHORT BREATHS!
NOW THAT SHE WAS FREE, THE FIRST THING LITTLE-GIRL-WITH-NO-NAME WANTED TO DO WAS FEEL THE WARM SUN AND SMELL THE FLOWERS IN THE PARK!
OBOY! OBOY! OBOY!
I CAN HARDLY WAIT!

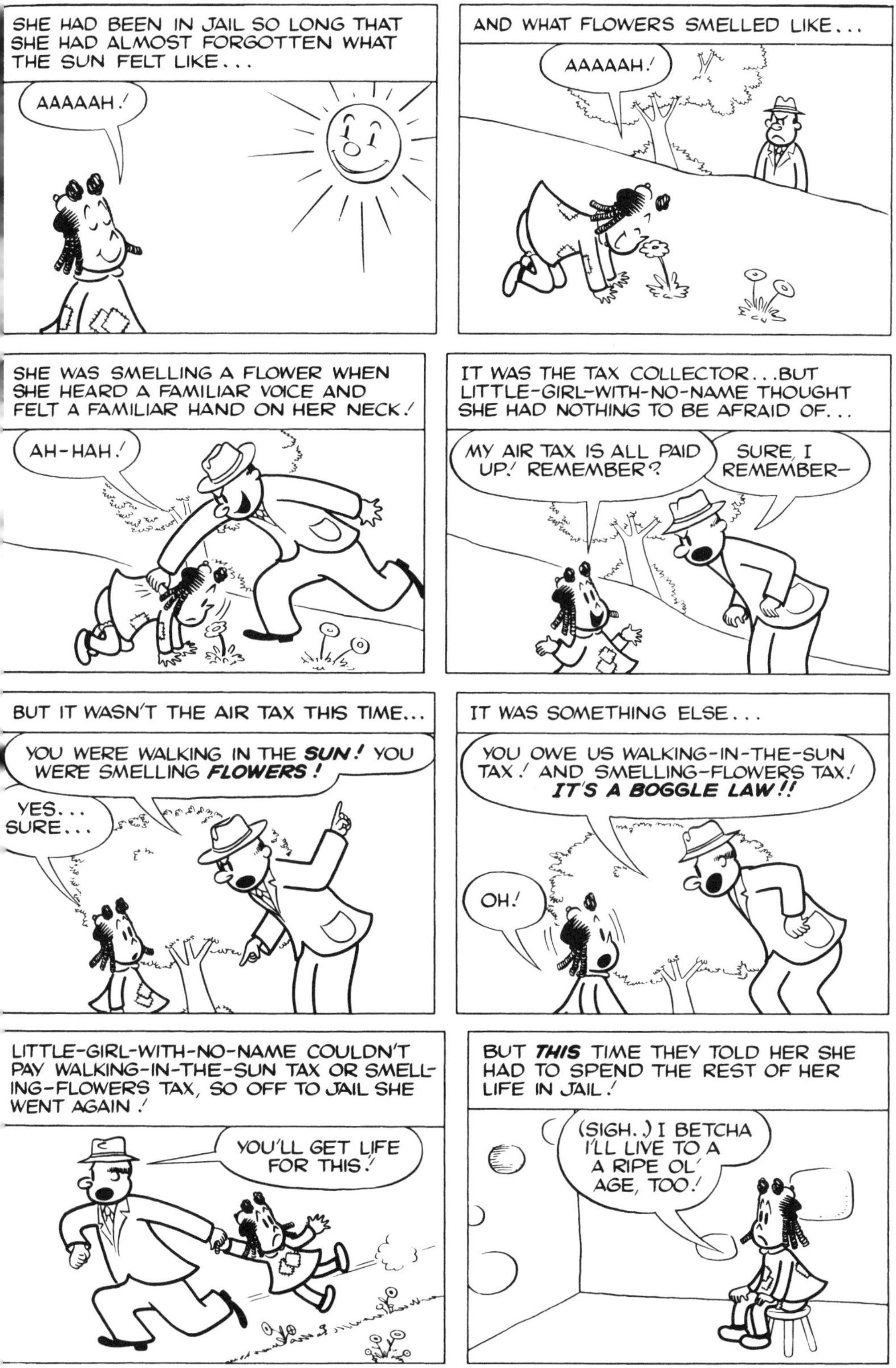

SHE HAD BEEN IN JAIL SO LONG THAT SHE HAD ALMOST FORGOTTEN WHAT THE SUN FELT LIKE...
AAAAAH!
AND WHAT FLOWERS SMELLED LIKE...
AAAAAH!
SHE WAS SMELLING A FLOWER WHEN SHE HEARD A FAMILIAR VOICE AND FELT A FAMILIAR HAND ON HER NECK!
AH-HAH!
IT WAS THE TAX COLLECTOR...BUT LITTLE-GIRL-WITH-NO-NAME THOUGHT SHE HAD NOTHING TO BE AFRAID OF...
MY AIR TAX IS ALL PAID UP! REMEMBER?
SURE, I REMEMBER–
BUT IT WASN'T THE AIR TAX THIS TIME...
YOU WERE WALKING IN THE **SUN!** YOU WERE SMELLING **FLOWERS!**
YES... SURE...
IT WAS SOMETHING ELSE...
YOU OWE US WALKING-IN-THE-SUN TAX! AND SMELLING-FLOWERS TAX! ***IT'S A BOGGLE LAW!!***
OH!
LITTLE-GIRL-WITH-NO-NAME COULDN'T PAY WALKING-IN-THE-SUN TAX OR SMELLING-FLOWERS TAX, SO OFF TO JAIL SHE WENT AGAIN!
YOU'LL GET LIFE FOR THIS!
BUT ***THIS*** TIME THEY TOLD HER SHE HAD TO SPEND THE REST OF HER LIFE IN JAIL!
(SIGH.) I BETCHA I'LL LIVE TO A A RIPE OL' AGE, TOO!

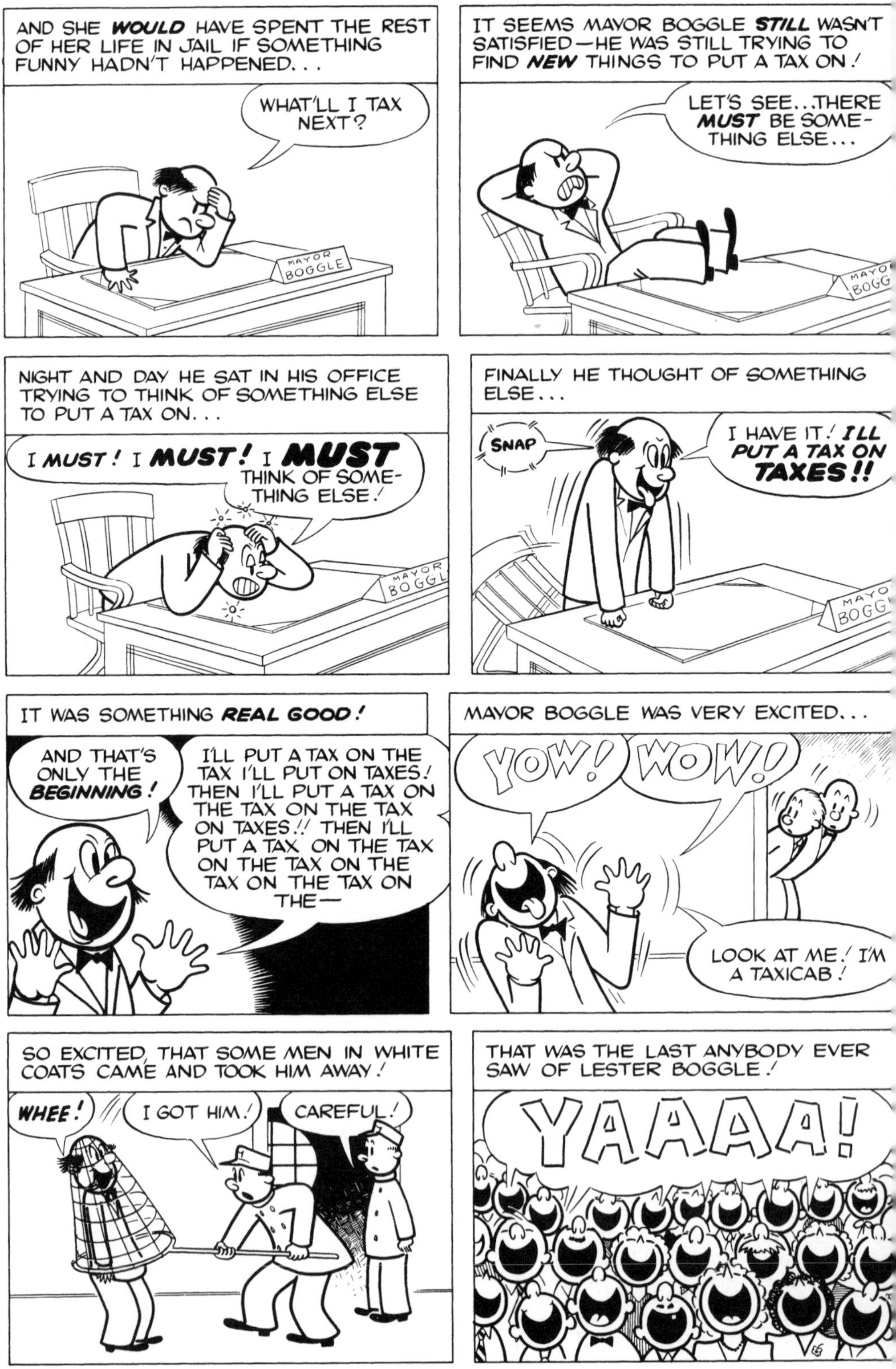

AND SHE WOULD HAVE SPENT THE REST OF HER LIFE IN JAIL IF SOMETHING FUNNY HADN'T HAPPENED...
WHAT'LL I TAX NEXT?
MAYOR BOGGLE
IT SEEMS MAYOR BOGGLE STILL WASN'T SATISFIED—HE WAS STILL TRYING TO FIND NEW THINGS TO PUT A TAX ON!
LET'S SEE...THERE MUST BE SOME-THING ELSE...
NIGHT AND DAY HE SAT IN HIS OFFICE TRYING TO THINK OF SOMETHING ELSE TO PUT A TAX ON...
I MUST! I MUST! I MUST THINK OF SOME-THING ELSE!
FINALLY HE THOUGHT OF SOMETHING ELSE...
SNAP
I HAVE IT! I'LL PUT A TAX ON TAXES!!
IT WAS SOMETHING REAL GOOD!
AND THAT'S ONLY THE BEGINNING!
I'LL PUT A TAX ON THE TAX I'LL PUT ON TAXES! THEN I'LL PUT A TAX ON THE TAX ON THE TAX ON TAXES!! THEN I'LL PUT A TAX ON THE TAX ON THE TAX ON THE TAX ON THE TAX ON THE—
MAYOR BOGGLE WAS VERY EXCITED...
YOW! WOW!
LOOK AT ME! I'M A TAXICAB!
SO EXCITED, THAT SOME MEN IN WHITE COATS CAME AND TOOK HIM AWAY!
WHEE!
I GOT HIM!
CAREFUL!
THAT WAS THE LAST ANYBODY EVER SAW OF LESTER BOGGLE!
YAAAA!

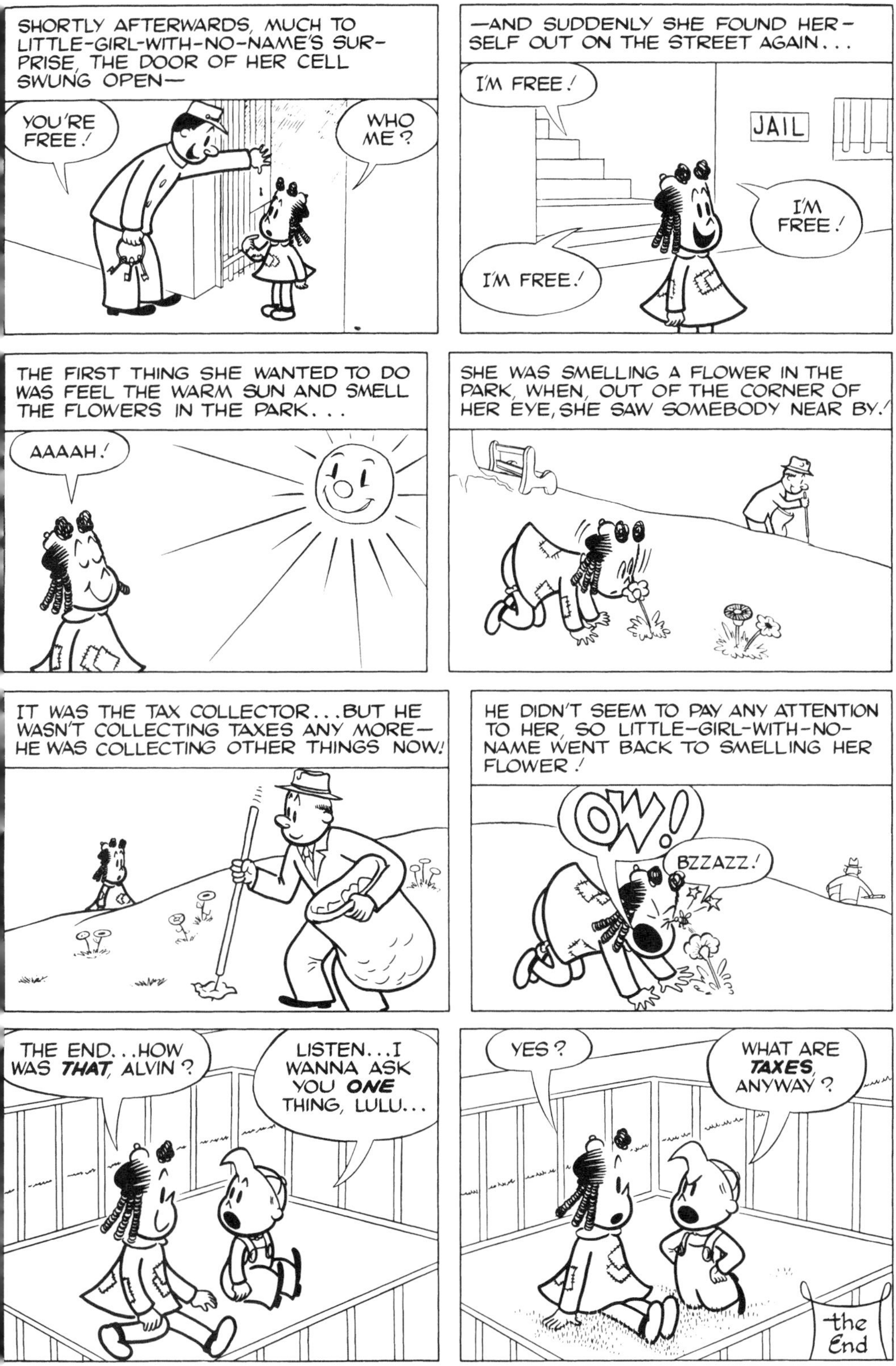

SHORTLY AFTERWARDS, MUCH TO LITTLE-GIRL-WITH-NO-NAME'S SURPRISE, THE DOOR OF HER CELL SWUNG OPEN—
YOU'RE FREE!
WHO ME?
—AND SUDDENLY SHE FOUND HERSELF OUT ON THE STREET AGAIN...
I'M FREE!
JAIL
I'M FREE!
I'M FREE!
THE FIRST THING SHE WANTED TO DO WAS FEEL THE WARM SUN AND SMELL THE FLOWERS IN THE PARK...
AAAAH!
SHE WAS SMELLING A FLOWER IN THE PARK, WHEN, OUT OF THE CORNER OF HER EYE, SHE SAW SOMEBODY NEAR BY!
IT WAS THE TAX COLLECTOR...BUT HE WASN'T COLLECTING TAXES ANY MORE—HE WAS COLLECTING OTHER THINGS NOW!
HE DIDN'T SEEM TO PAY ANY ATTENTION TO HER, SO LITTLE-GIRL-WITH-NO-NAME WENT BACK TO SMELLING HER FLOWER!
OW!
BZZAZZ!
THE END...HOW WAS **THAT**, ALVIN?
LISTEN...I WANNA ASK YOU **ONE** THING, LULU...
YES?
WHAT ARE **TAXES**, ANYWAY?
the End

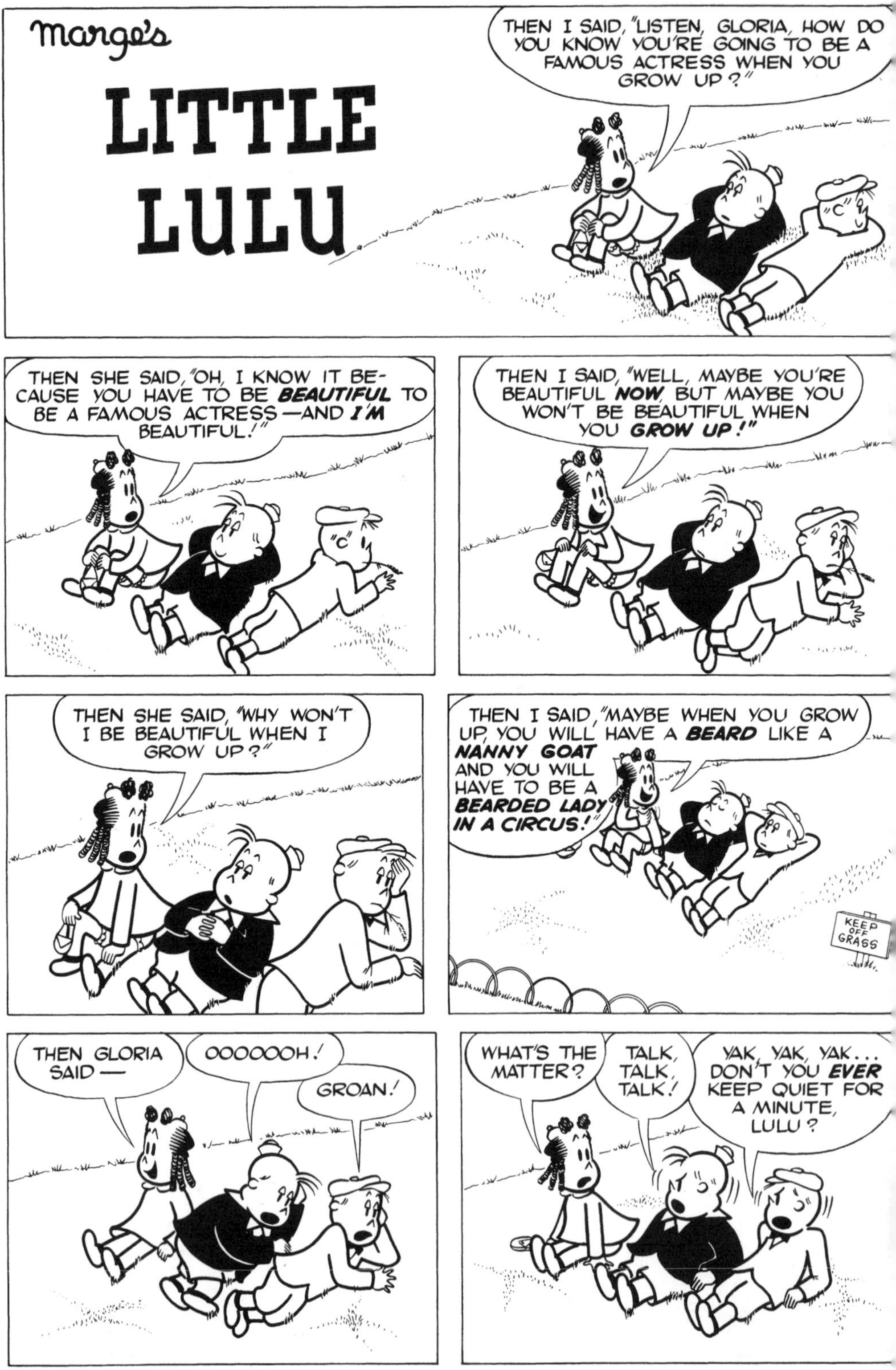
marge's
LITTLE LULU
THEN I SAID, "LISTEN, GLORIA, HOW DO YOU KNOW YOU'RE GOING TO BE A FAMOUS ACTRESS WHEN YOU GROW UP?"
THEN SHE SAID, "OH, I KNOW IT BECAUSE YOU HAVE TO BE **BEAUTIFUL** TO BE A FAMOUS ACTRESS—AND **I'M** BEAUTIFUL!"
THEN I SAID, "WELL, MAYBE YOU'RE BEAUTIFUL **NOW**, BUT MAYBE YOU WON'T BE BEAUTIFUL WHEN YOU **GROW UP!**"
THEN SHE SAID, "WHY WON'T I BE BEAUTIFUL WHEN I GROW UP?"
THEN I SAID, "MAYBE WHEN YOU GROW UP, YOU WILL HAVE A **BEARD** LIKE A **NANNY GOAT** AND YOU WILL HAVE TO BE A **BEARDED LADY IN A CIRCUS!**"
KEEP OFF GRASS
THEN GLORIA SAID—
OOOOOOH!
GROAN!
WHAT'S THE MATTER?
TALK, TALK, TALK!
YAK, YAK, YAK... DON'T YOU **EVER** KEEP QUIET FOR A MINUTE, LULU?

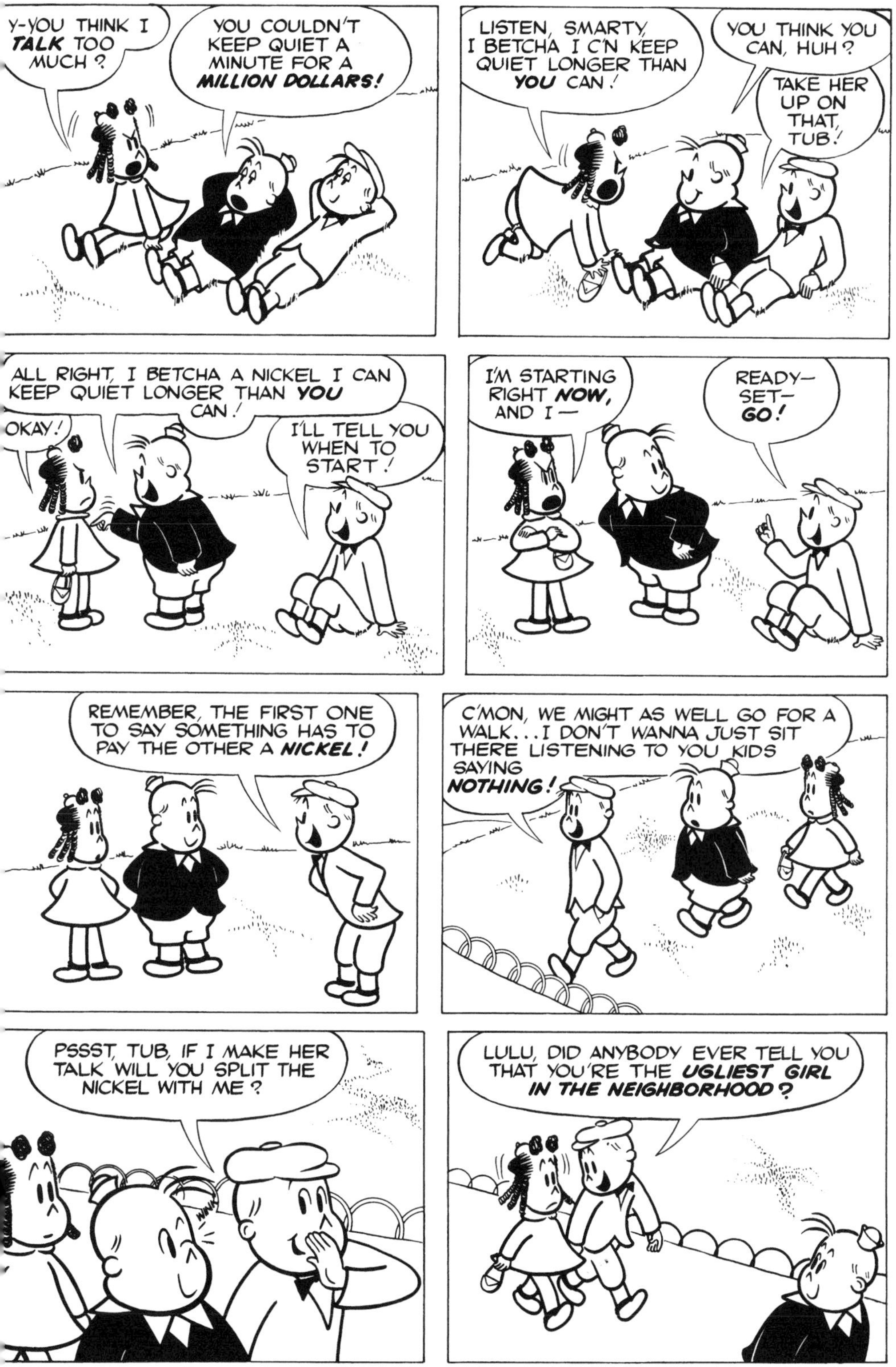
Y-YOU THINK I TALK TOO MUCH ?
YOU COULDN'T KEEP QUIET A MINUTE FOR A MILLION DOLLARS!
LISTEN, SMARTY, I BETCHA I C'N KEEP QUIET LONGER THAN YOU CAN!
YOU THINK YOU CAN, HUH ?
TAKE HER UP ON THAT, TUB!
ALL RIGHT, I BETCHA A NICKEL I CAN KEEP QUIET LONGER THAN YOU CAN!
OKAY!
I'LL TELL YOU WHEN TO START!
I'M STARTING RIGHT NOW, AND I —
READY— SET— GO!
REMEMBER, THE FIRST ONE TO SAY SOMETHING HAS TO PAY THE OTHER A NICKEL!
C'MON, WE MIGHT AS WELL GO FOR A WALK...I DON'T WANNA JUST SIT THERE LISTENING TO YOU KIDS SAYING NOTHING!
PSSST, TUB, IF I MAKE HER TALK WILL YOU SPLIT THE NICKEL WITH ME ?
LULU, DID ANYBODY EVER TELL YOU THAT YOU'RE THE UGLIEST GIRL IN THE NEIGHBORHOOD ?

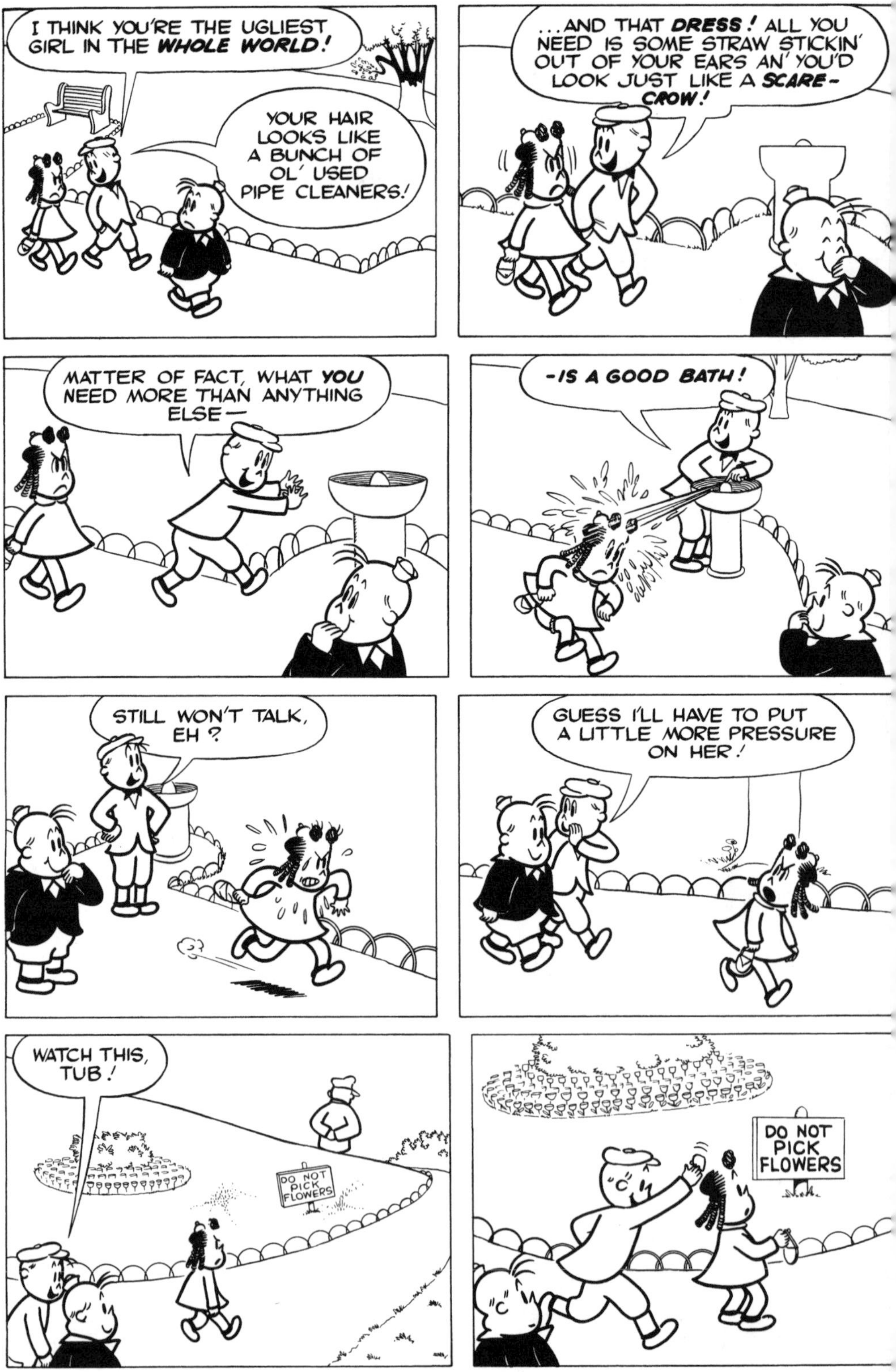

I THINK YOU'RE THE UGLIEST GIRL IN THE WHOLE WORLD!
YOUR HAIR LOOKS LIKE A BUNCH OF OL' USED PIPE CLEANERS!
...AND THAT DRESS! ALL YOU NEED IS SOME STRAW STICKIN' OUT OF YOUR EARS AN' YOU'D LOOK JUST LIKE A SCARE-CROW!
MATTER OF FACT, WHAT YOU NEED MORE THAN ANYTHING ELSE—
-IS A GOOD BATH!
STILL WON'T TALK, EH?
GUESS I'LL HAVE TO PUT A LITTLE MORE PRESSURE ON HER!
WATCH THIS, TUB!
DO NOT PICK FLOWERS
DO NOT PICK FLOWERS

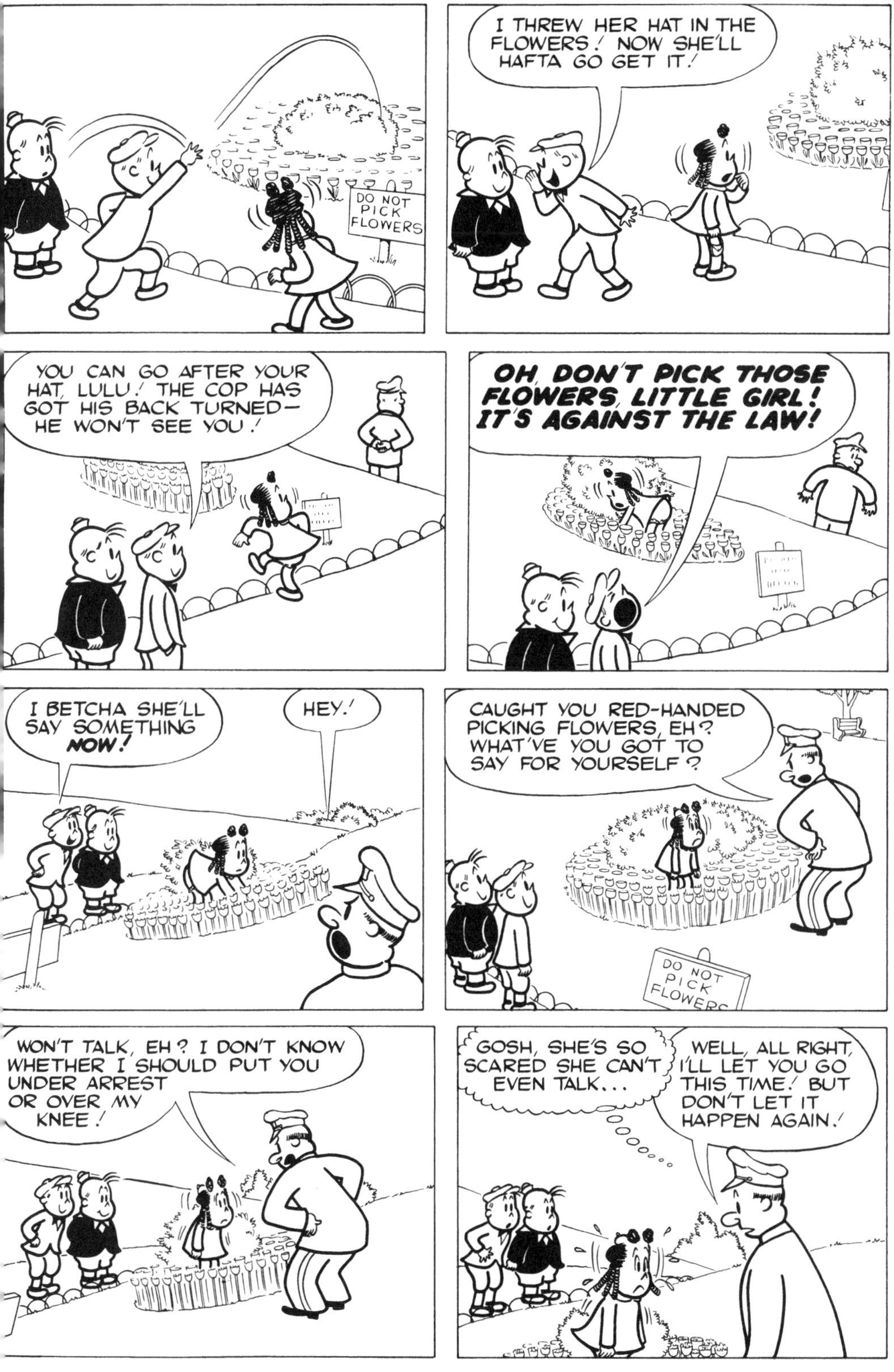
DO NOT PICK FLOWERS
I THREW HER HAT IN THE FLOWERS! NOW SHE'LL HAFTA GO GET IT!
YOU CAN GO AFTER YOUR HAT, LULU! THE COP HAS GOT HIS BACK TURNED— HE WON'T SEE YOU!
OH, DON'T PICK THOSE FLOWERS, LITTLE GIRL! IT'S AGAINST THE LAW!
I BETCHA SHE'LL SAY SOMETHING NOW!
HEY!
CAUGHT YOU RED-HANDED PICKING FLOWERS, EH? WHAT'VE YOU GOT TO SAY FOR YOURSELF?
DO NOT PICK FLOWERS
WON'T TALK, EH? I DON'T KNOW WHETHER I SHOULD PUT YOU UNDER ARREST OR OVER MY KNEE!
GOSH, SHE'S SO SCARED SHE CAN'T EVEN TALK...
WELL, ALL RIGHT, I'LL LET YOU GO THIS TIME! BUT DON'T LET IT HAPPEN AGAIN!

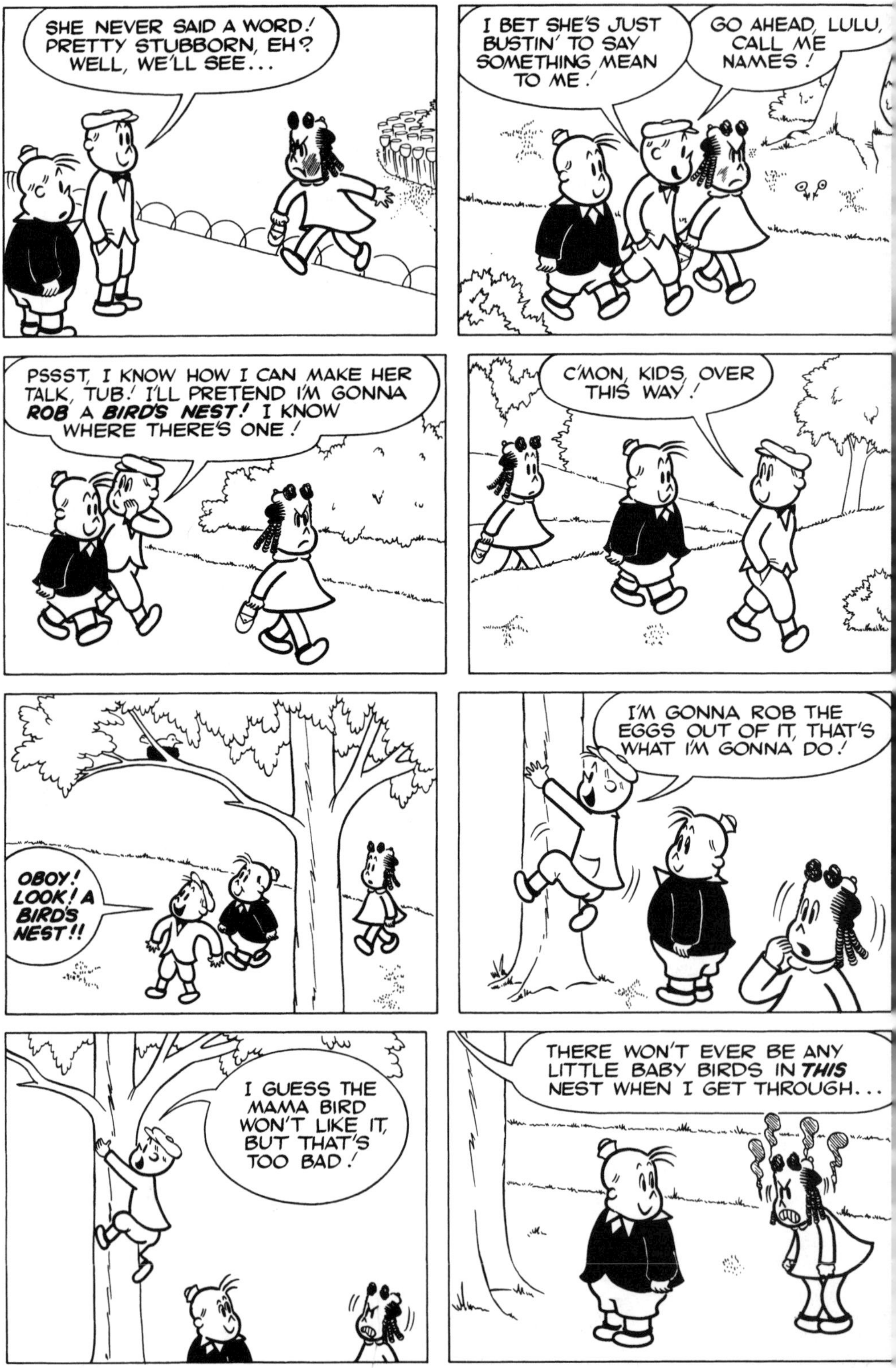
SHE NEVER SAID A WORD! PRETTY STUBBORN, EH? WELL, WE'LL SEE...
I BET SHE'S JUST BUSTIN' TO SAY SOMETHING MEAN TO ME!
GO AHEAD, LULU, CALL ME NAMES!
PSSST, I KNOW HOW I CAN MAKE HER TALK, TUB! I'LL PRETEND I'M GONNA ***ROB*** A ***BIRD'S NEST!*** I KNOW WHERE THERE'S ONE!
C'MON, KIDS, OVER THIS WAY!
OBOY! LOOK! A BIRD'S NEST!!
I'M GONNA ROB THE EGGS OUT OF IT, THAT'S WHAT I'M GONNA DO!
I GUESS THE MAMA BIRD WON'T LIKE IT, BUT THAT'S TOO BAD!
THERE WON'T EVER BE ANY LITTLE BABY BIRDS IN ***THIS*** NEST WHEN I GET THROUGH...

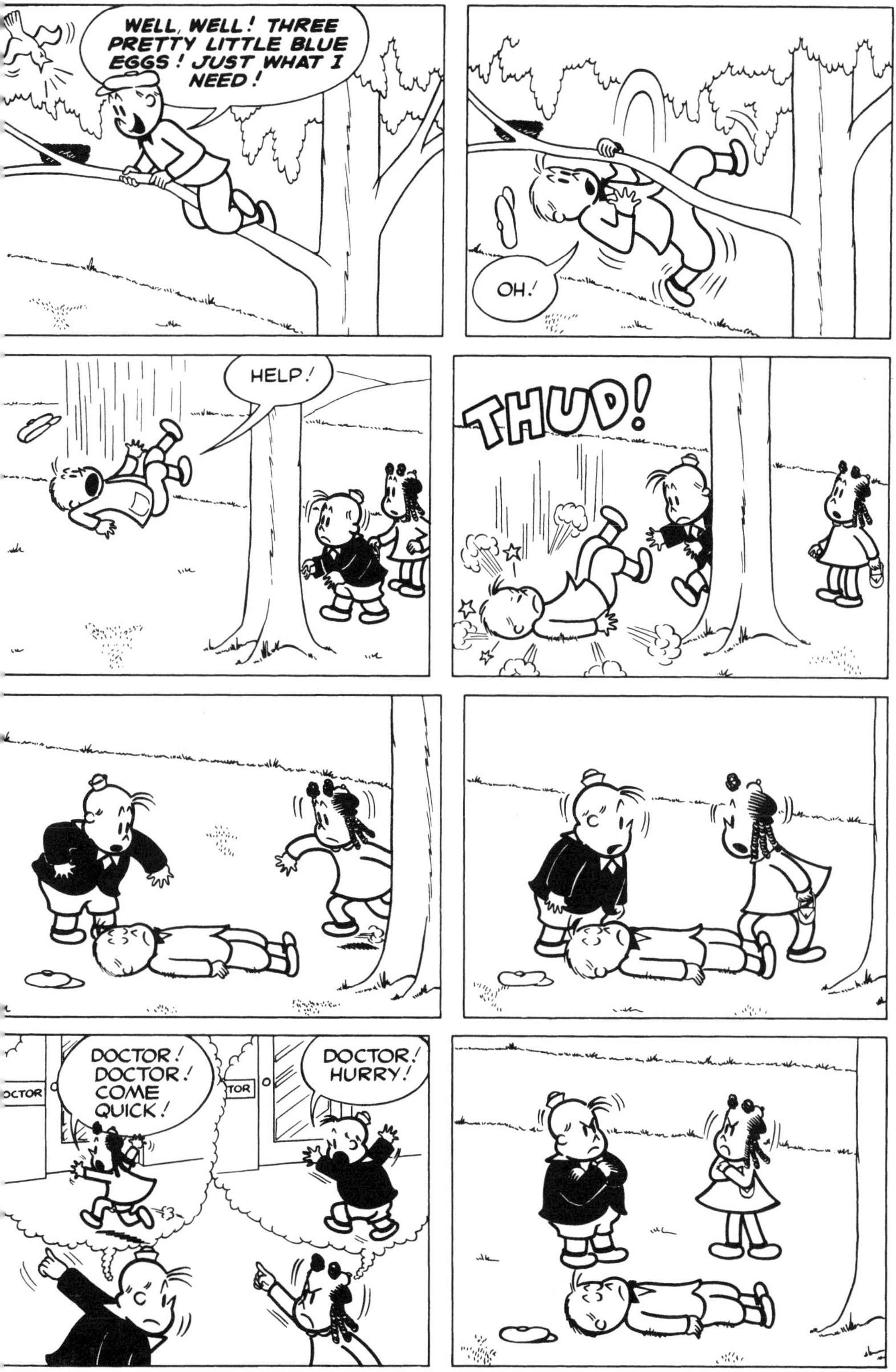
WELL, WELL! THREE PRETTY LITTLE BLUE EGGS! JUST WHAT I NEED!
OH!
HELP!
THUD!
DOCTOR! DOCTOR! COME QUICK!
DOCTOR! HURRY!

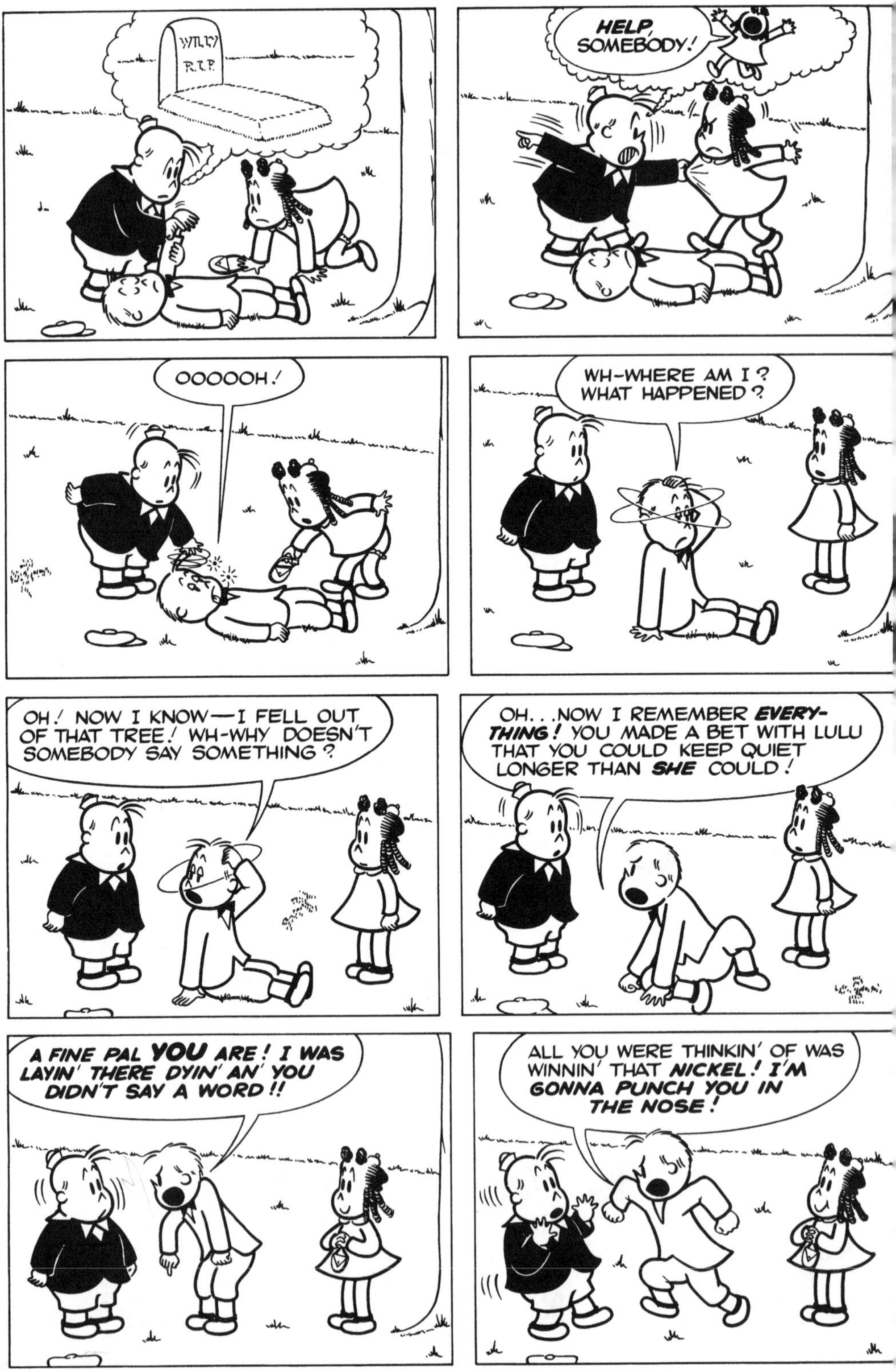

HELP, SOMEBODY!
OOOOOH!
WH-WHERE AM I? WHAT HAPPENED?
OH! NOW I KNOW—I FELL OUT OF THAT TREE! WH-WHY DOESN'T SOMEBODY SAY SOMETHING?
OH...NOW I REMEMBER EVERY-THING! YOU MADE A BET WITH LULU THAT YOU COULD KEEP QUIET LONGER THAN SHE COULD!
A FINE PAL YOU ARE! I WAS LAYIN' THERE DYIN' AN' YOU DIDN'T SAY A WORD!!
ALL YOU WERE THINKIN' OF WAS WINNIN' THAT NICKEL! I'M GONNA PUNCH YOU IN THE NOSE!

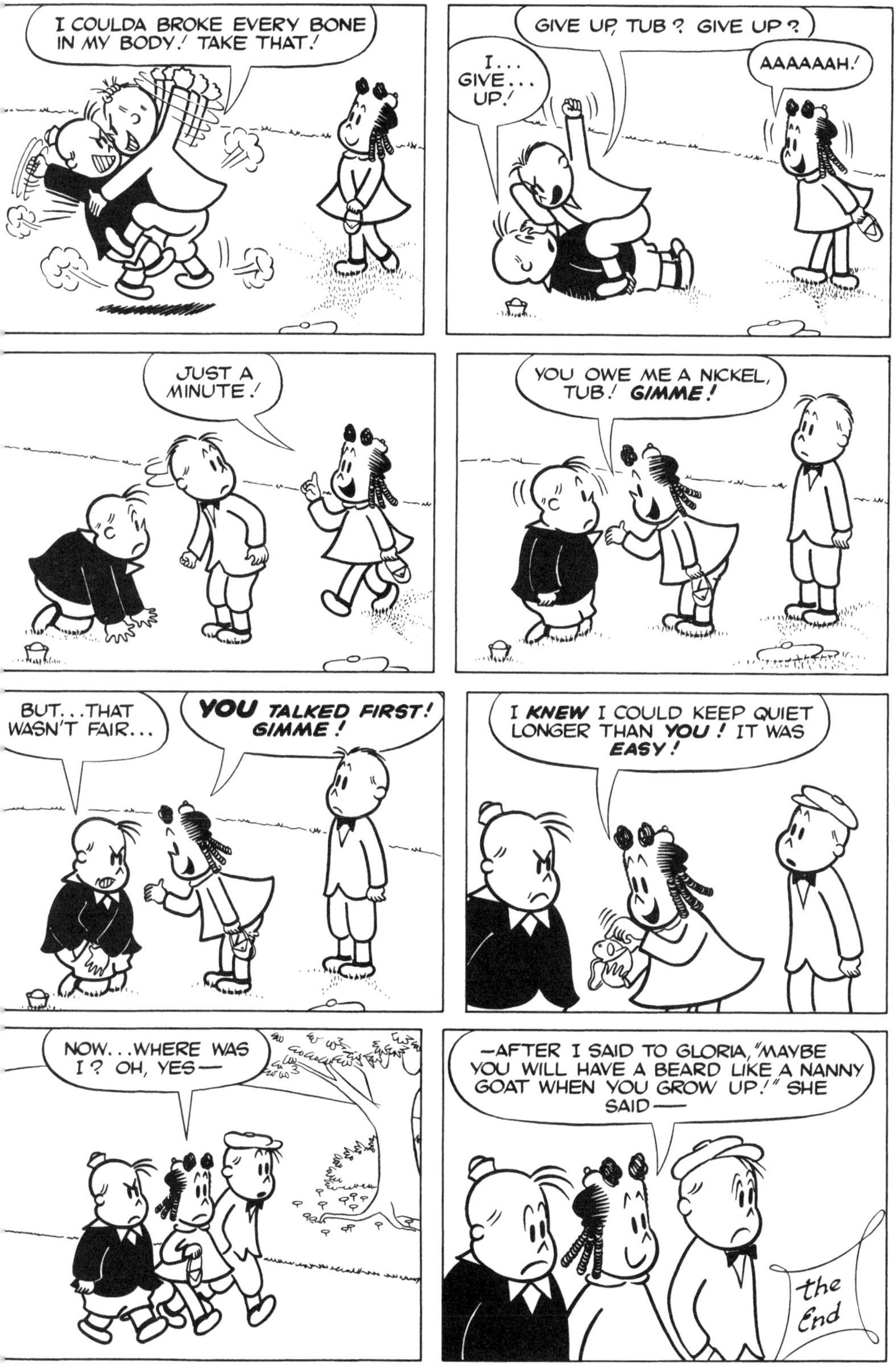
I COULDA BROKE EVERY BONE IN MY BODY! TAKE THAT!
GIVE UP, TUB? GIVE UP?
I... GIVE... UP!
AAAAAAH!
JUST A MINUTE!
YOU OWE ME A NICKEL, TUB! GIMME!
BUT...THAT WASN'T FAIR...
YOU TALKED FIRST! GIMME!
I KNEW I COULD KEEP QUIET LONGER THAN YOU! IT WAS EASY!
NOW...WHERE WAS I? OH, YES—
—AFTER I SAID TO GLORIA, "MAYBE YOU WILL HAVE A BEARD LIKE A NANNY GOAT WHEN YOU GROW UP!" SHE SAID—
the End

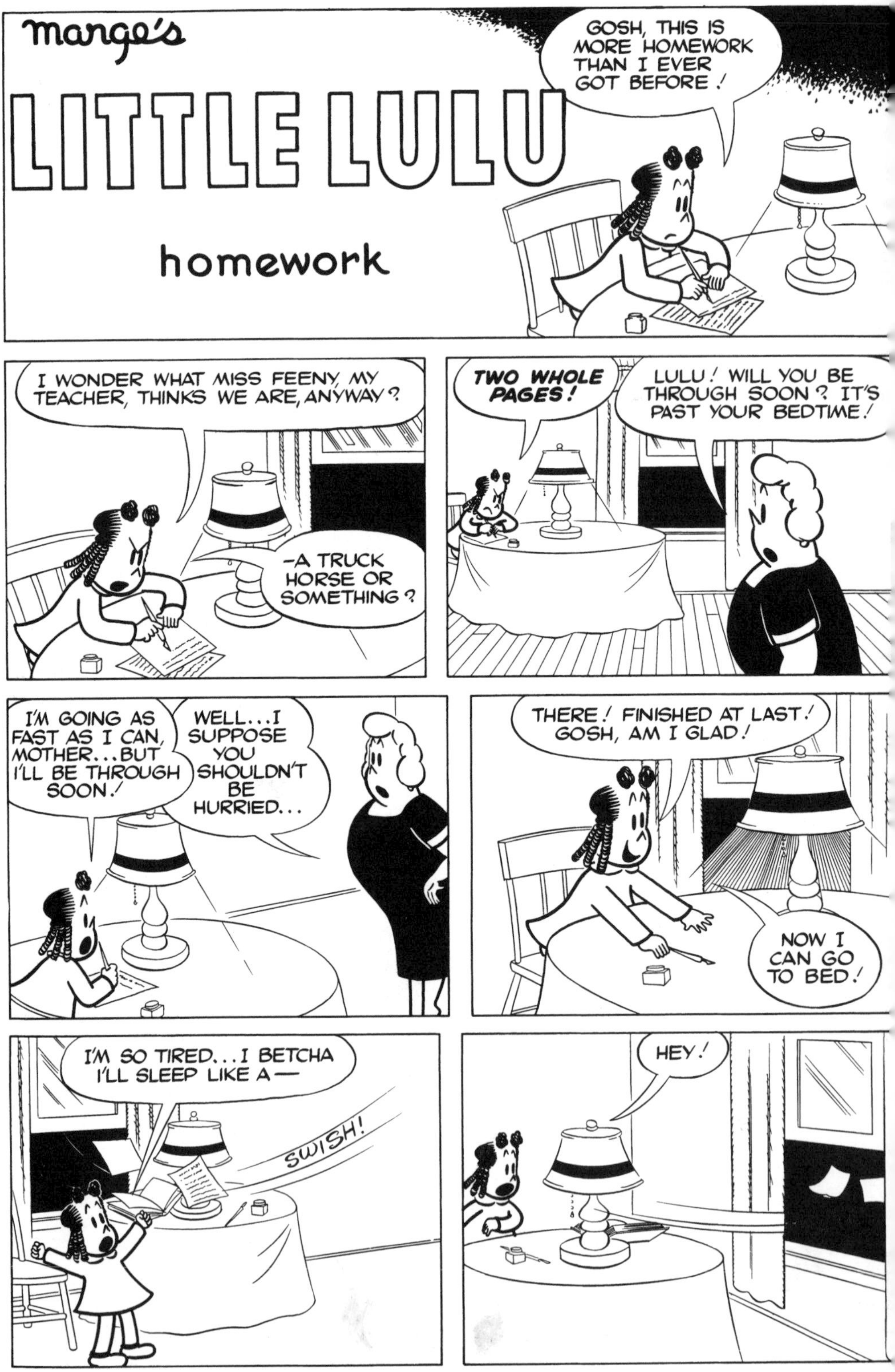
marge's
LITTLE LULU
homework
GOSH, THIS IS MORE HOMEWORK THAN I EVER GOT BEFORE!
I WONDER WHAT MISS FEENY, MY TEACHER, THINKS WE ARE, ANYWAY?
-A TRUCK HORSE OR SOMETHING?
TWO WHOLE PAGES!
LULU! WILL YOU BE THROUGH SOON? IT'S PAST YOUR BEDTIME!
I'M GOING AS FAST AS I CAN, MOTHER...BUT I'LL BE THROUGH SOON!
WELL...I SUPPOSE YOU SHOULDN'T BE HURRIED...
THERE! FINISHED AT LAST! GOSH, AM I GLAD!
NOW I CAN GO TO BED!
I'M SO TIRED...I BETCHA I'LL SLEEP LIKE A—
SWISH!
HEY!

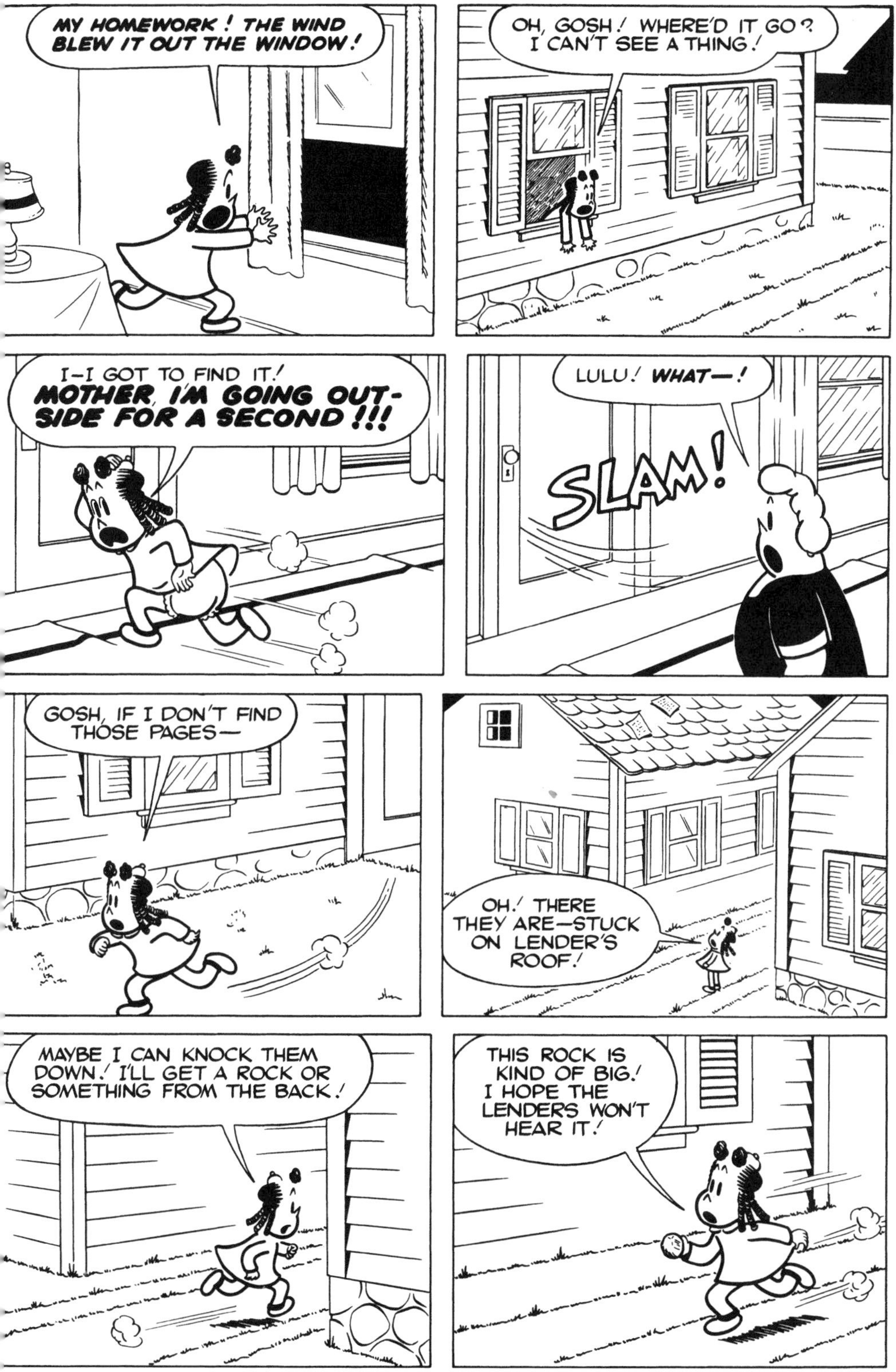
MY HOMEWORK! THE WIND BLEW IT OUT THE WINDOW!
OH, GOSH! WHERE'D IT GO? I CAN'T SEE A THING!
I-I GOT TO FIND IT! MOTHER, I'M GOING OUT-SIDE FOR A SECOND!!!
LULU! WHAT—!
SLAM!
GOSH, IF I DON'T FIND THOSE PAGES—
OH! THERE THEY ARE—STUCK ON LENDER'S ROOF!
MAYBE I CAN KNOCK THEM DOWN! I'LL GET A ROCK OR SOMETHING FROM THE BACK!
THIS ROCK IS KIND OF BIG! I HOPE THE LENDERS WON'T HEAR IT!

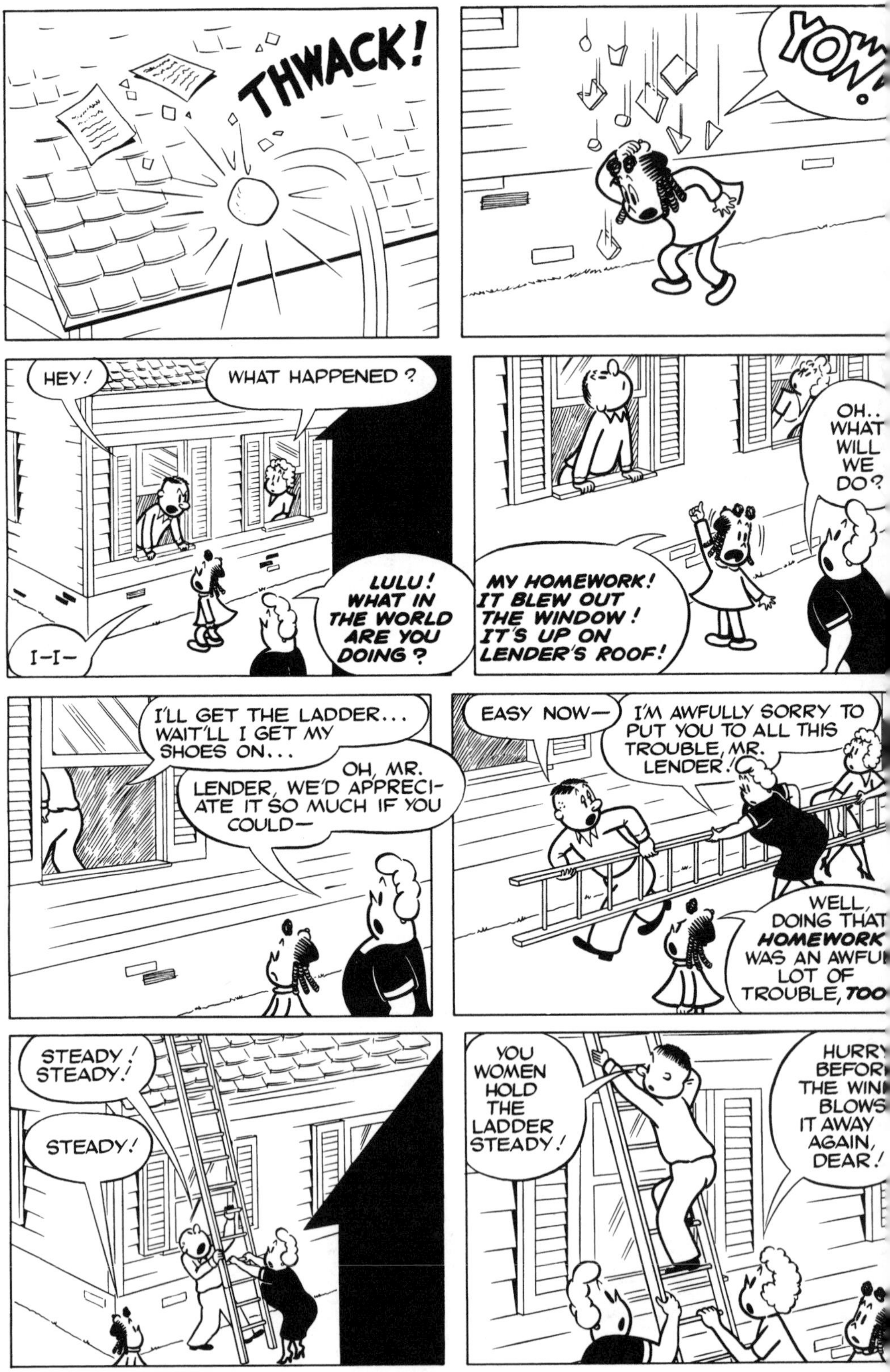
THWACK!
YOW!
HEY!
WHAT HAPPENED?
I-I-
LULU! WHAT IN THE WORLD ARE YOU DOING?
MY HOMEWORK! IT BLEW OUT THE WINDOW! IT'S UP ON LENDER'S ROOF!
OH.. WHAT WILL WE DO?
I'LL GET THE LADDER... WAIT'LL I GET MY SHOES ON...
OH, MR. LENDER, WE'D APPRECIATE IT SO MUCH IF YOU COULD—
EASY NOW—
I'M AWFULLY SORRY TO PUT YOU TO ALL THIS TROUBLE, MR. LENDER!
WELL, DOING THAT HOMEWORK WAS AN AWFU LOT OF TROUBLE, TOO
STEADY! STEADY!
STEADY!
YOU WOMEN HOLD THE LADDER STEADY!
HURRY BEFOR THE WIN BLOWS IT AWAY AGAIN, DEAR!

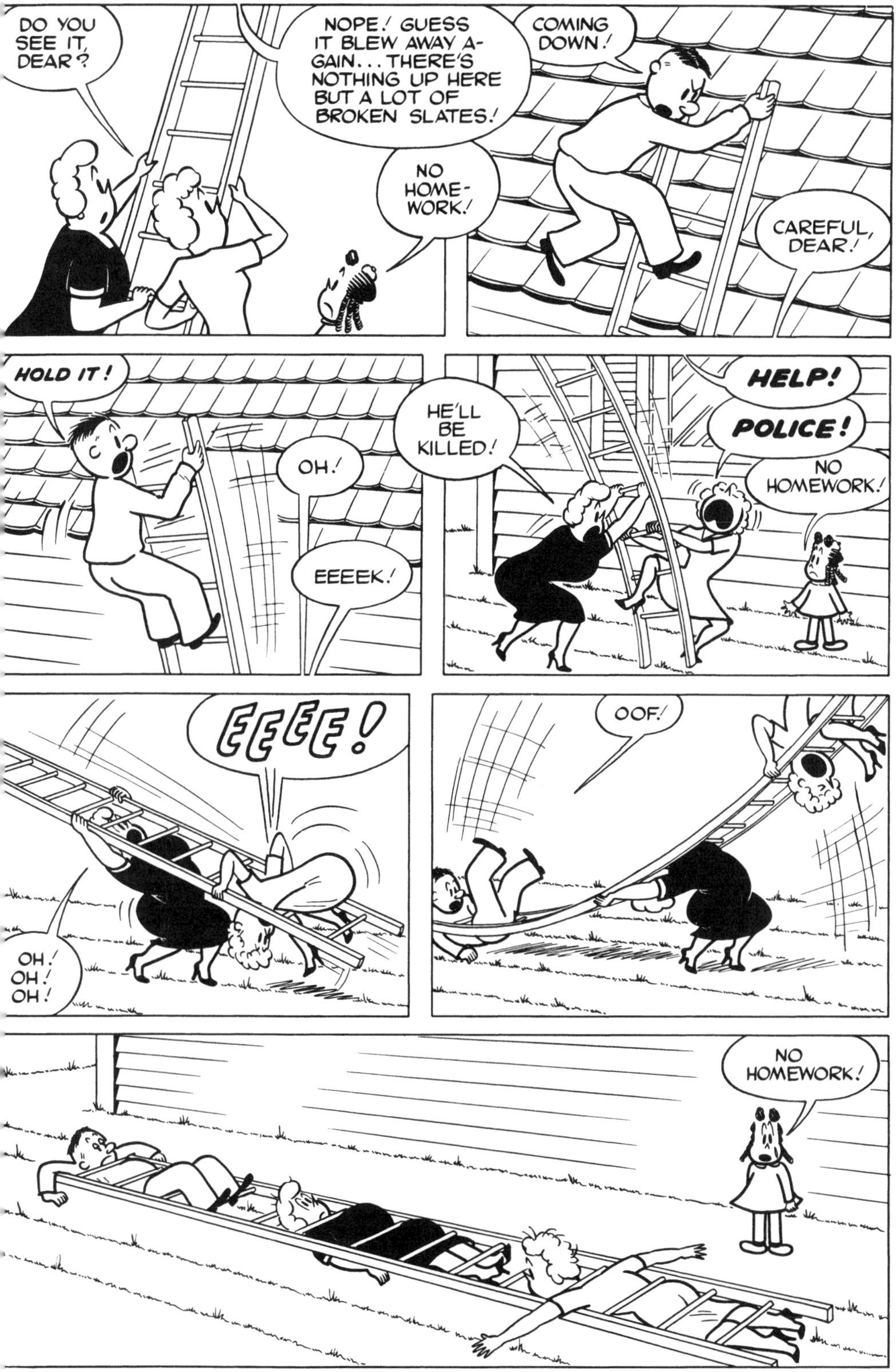
DO YOU SEE IT, DEAR?
NOPE! GUESS IT BLEW AWAY A-GAIN... THERE'S NOTHING UP HERE BUT A LOT OF BROKEN SLATES!
NO HOME-WORK!
COMING DOWN!
CAREFUL, DEAR!
HOLD IT!
OH!
EEEEK!
HE'LL BE KILLED!
HELP!
POLICE!
NO HOMEWORK!
EEEE!
OH! OH! OH!
OOF!
NO HOMEWORK!

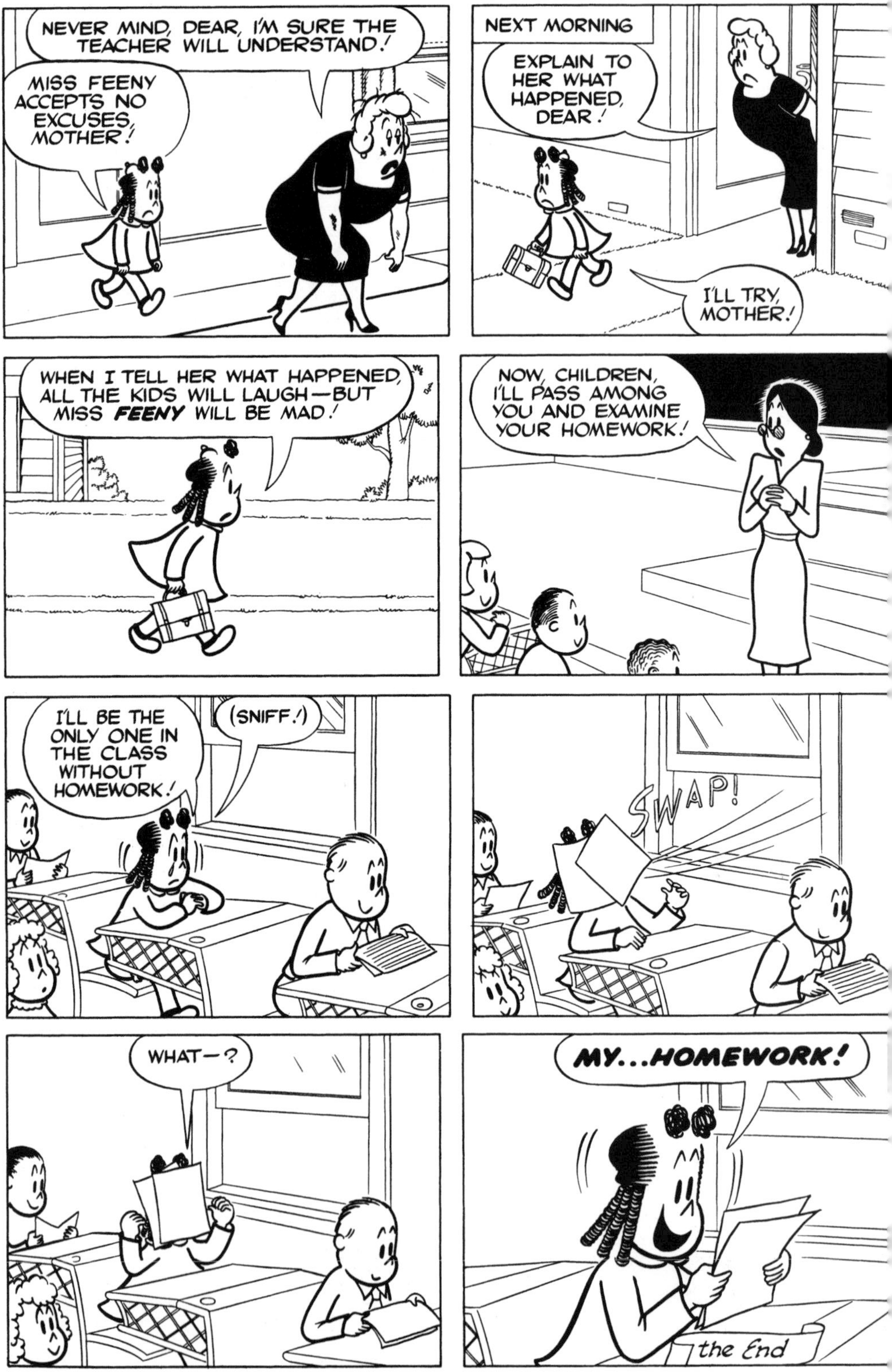
MISS FEENY ACCEPTS NO EXCUSES, MOTHER!
NEVER MIND, DEAR, I'M SURE THE TEACHER WILL UNDERSTAND!
NEXT MORNING
EXPLAIN TO HER WHAT HAPPENED, DEAR!
I'LL TRY, MOTHER!
WHEN I TELL HER WHAT HAPPENED, ALL THE KIDS WILL LAUGH—BUT MISS FEENY WILL BE MAD!
NOW, CHILDREN, I'LL PASS AMONG YOU AND EXAMINE YOUR HOMEWORK!
I'LL BE THE ONLY ONE IN THE CLASS WITHOUT HOMEWORK!
(SNIFF!)
SWAP!
WHAT—?
MY...HOMEWORK!
the End

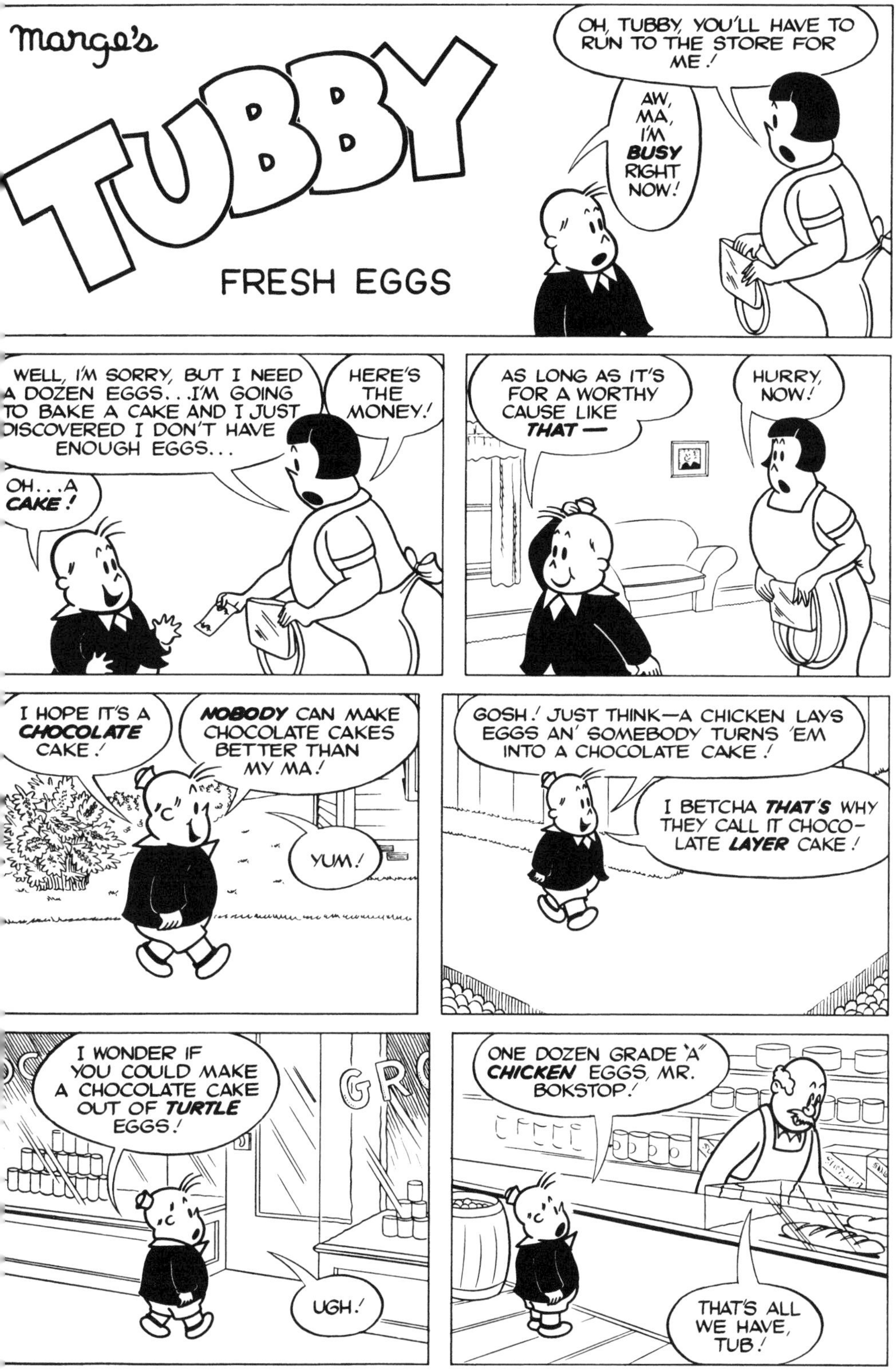
Marge's
TUBBY
FRESH EGGS
OH, TUBBY, YOU'LL HAVE TO RUN TO THE STORE FOR ME!
AW, MA, I'M BUSY RIGHT NOW!
WELL, I'M SORRY, BUT I NEED A DOZEN EGGS... I'M GOING TO BAKE A CAKE AND I JUST DISCOVERED I DON'T HAVE ENOUGH EGGS...
HERE'S THE MONEY!
OH... A CAKE!
AS LONG AS IT'S FOR A WORTHY CAUSE LIKE THAT—
HURRY, NOW!
I HOPE IT'S A CHOCOLATE CAKE!
NOBODY CAN MAKE CHOCOLATE CAKES BETTER THAN MY MA!
YUM!
GOSH! JUST THINK—A CHICKEN LAYS EGGS AN' SOMEBODY TURNS 'EM INTO A CHOCOLATE CAKE!
I BETCHA THAT'S WHY THEY CALL IT CHOCOLATE LAYER CAKE!
I WONDER IF YOU COULD MAKE A CHOCOLATE CAKE OUT OF TURTLE EGGS!
UGH!
ONE DOZEN GRADE "A" CHICKEN EGGS, MR. BOKSTOP!
THAT'S ALL WE HAVE, TUB!

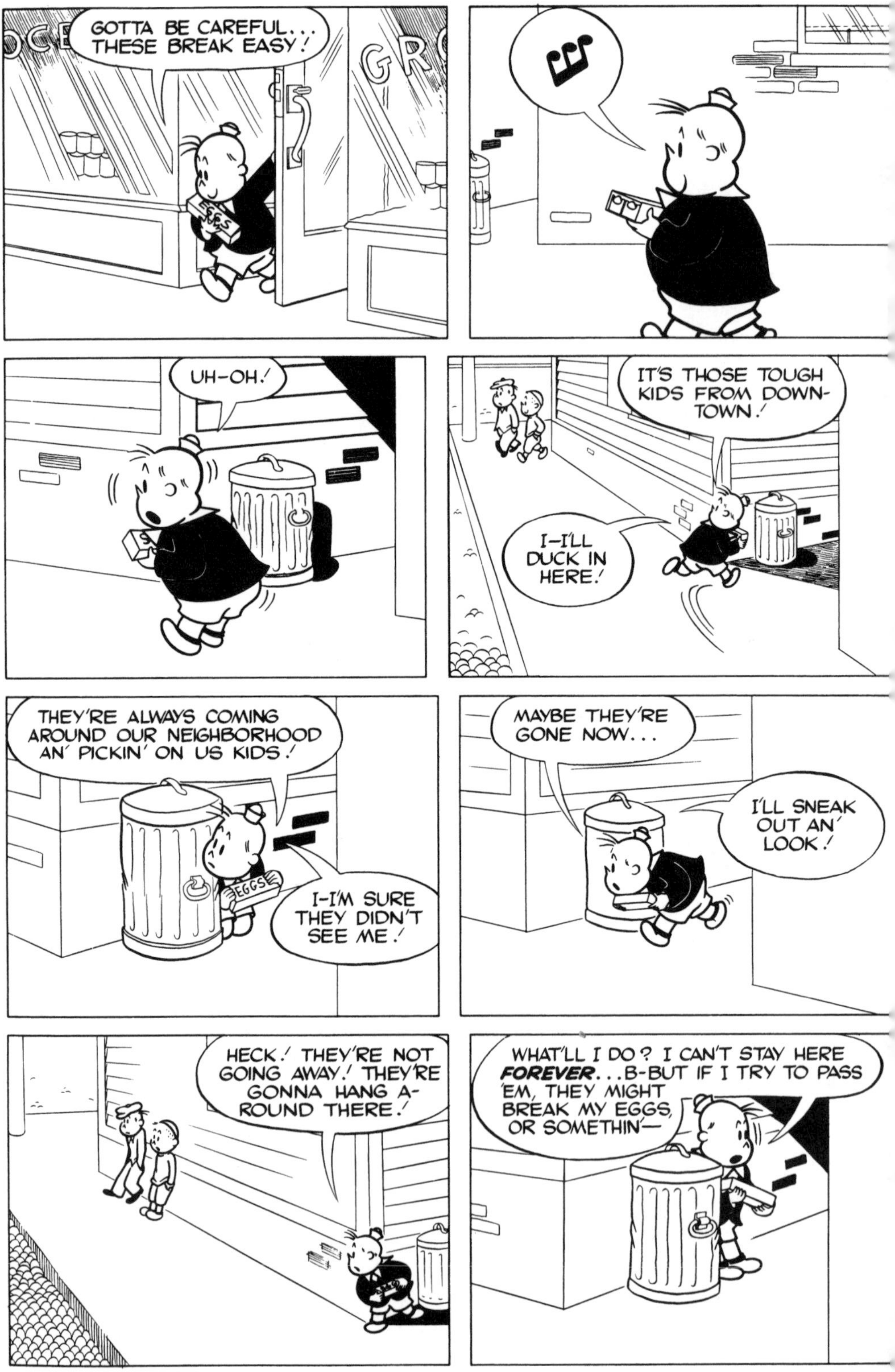

GOTTA BE CAREFUL... THESE BREAK EASY!
EGGS
UH-OH!
IT'S THOSE TOUGH KIDS FROM DOWN-TOWN!
I-I'LL DUCK IN HERE!
THEY'RE ALWAYS COMING AROUND OUR NEIGHBORHOOD AN' PICKIN' ON US KIDS!
EGGS
I-I'M SURE THEY DIDN'T SEE ME!
MAYBE THEY'RE GONE NOW...
I'LL SNEAK OUT AN' LOOK!
HECK! THEY'RE NOT GOING AWAY! THEY'RE GONNA HANG A-ROUND THERE!
WHAT'LL I DO? I CAN'T STAY HERE **FOREVER**...B-BUT IF I TRY TO PASS 'EM, THEY MIGHT BREAK MY EGGS, OR SOMETHIN'—

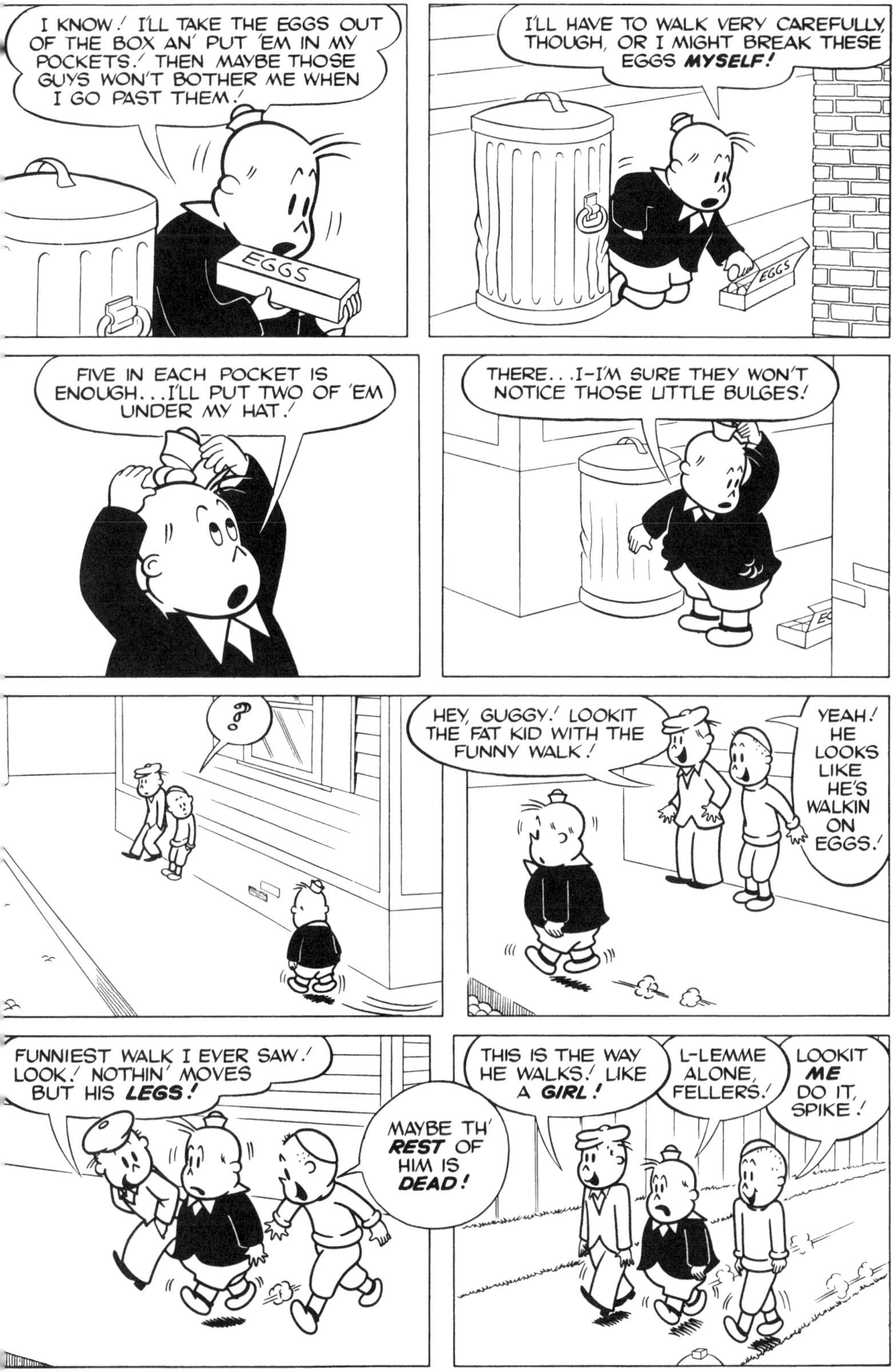
I KNOW! I'LL TAKE THE EGGS OUT OF THE BOX AN' PUT 'EM IN MY POCKETS! THEN MAYBE THOSE GUYS WON'T BOTHER ME WHEN I GO PAST THEM!
EGGS
I'LL HAVE TO WALK VERY CAREFULLY, THOUGH, OR I MIGHT BREAK THESE EGGS **MYSELF**!
EGGS
FIVE IN EACH POCKET IS ENOUGH...I'LL PUT TWO OF 'EM UNDER MY HAT!
THERE...I-I'M SURE THEY WON'T NOTICE THOSE LITTLE BULGES!
?
HEY, GUGGY! LOOKIT THE FAT KID WITH THE FUNNY WALK!
YEAH! HE LOOKS LIKE HE'S WALKIN ON EGGS!
FUNNIEST WALK I EVER SAW! LOOK! NOTHIN' MOVES BUT HIS **LEGS**!
MAYBE TH' **REST** OF HIM IS **DEAD**!
THIS IS THE WAY HE WALKS! LIKE A **GIRL**!
L-LEMME ALONE, FELLERS!
LOOKIT **ME** DO IT, SPIKE!

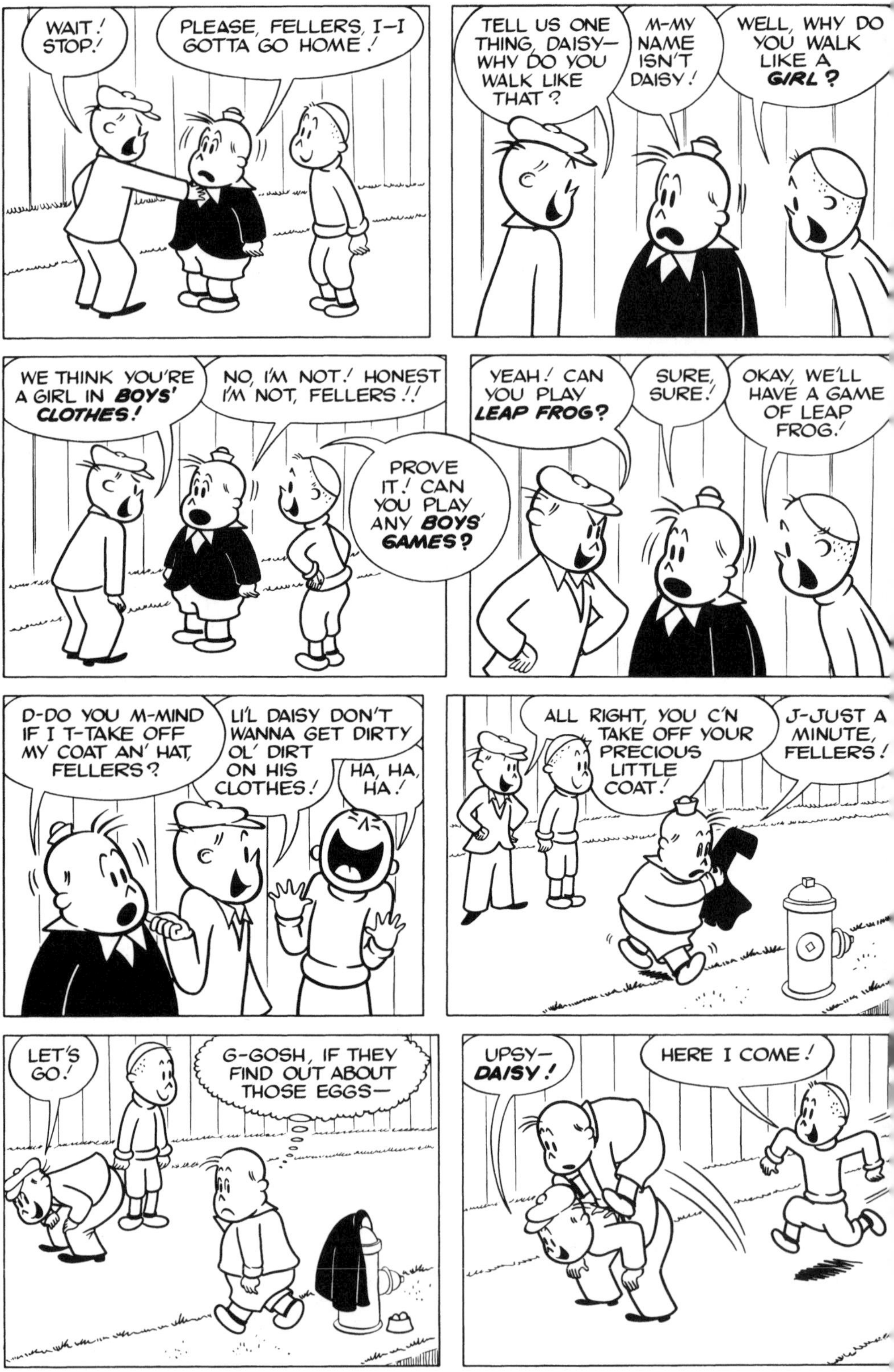
WAIT! STOP!
PLEASE, FELLERS, I-I GOTTA GO HOME!
TELL US ONE THING, DAISY— WHY DO YOU WALK LIKE THAT?
M-MY NAME ISN'T DAISY!
WELL, WHY DO YOU WALK LIKE A GIRL?
WE THINK YOU'RE A GIRL IN BOYS' CLOTHES!
NO, I'M NOT! HONEST I'M NOT, FELLERS!!
PROVE IT! CAN YOU PLAY ANY BOYS' GAMES?
YEAH! CAN YOU PLAY LEAP FROG?
SURE, SURE!
OKAY, WE'LL HAVE A GAME OF LEAP FROG!
D-DO YOU M-MIND IF I T-TAKE OFF MY COAT AN' HAT, FELLERS?
LI'L DAISY DON'T WANNA GET DIRTY OL' DIRT ON HIS CLOTHES!
HA, HA, HA!
ALL RIGHT, YOU C'N TAKE OFF YOUR PRECIOUS LITTLE COAT!
J-JUST A MINUTE, FELLERS!
LET'S GO!
G-GOSH, IF THEY FIND OUT ABOUT THOSE EGGS—
UPSY— DAISY!
HERE I COME!

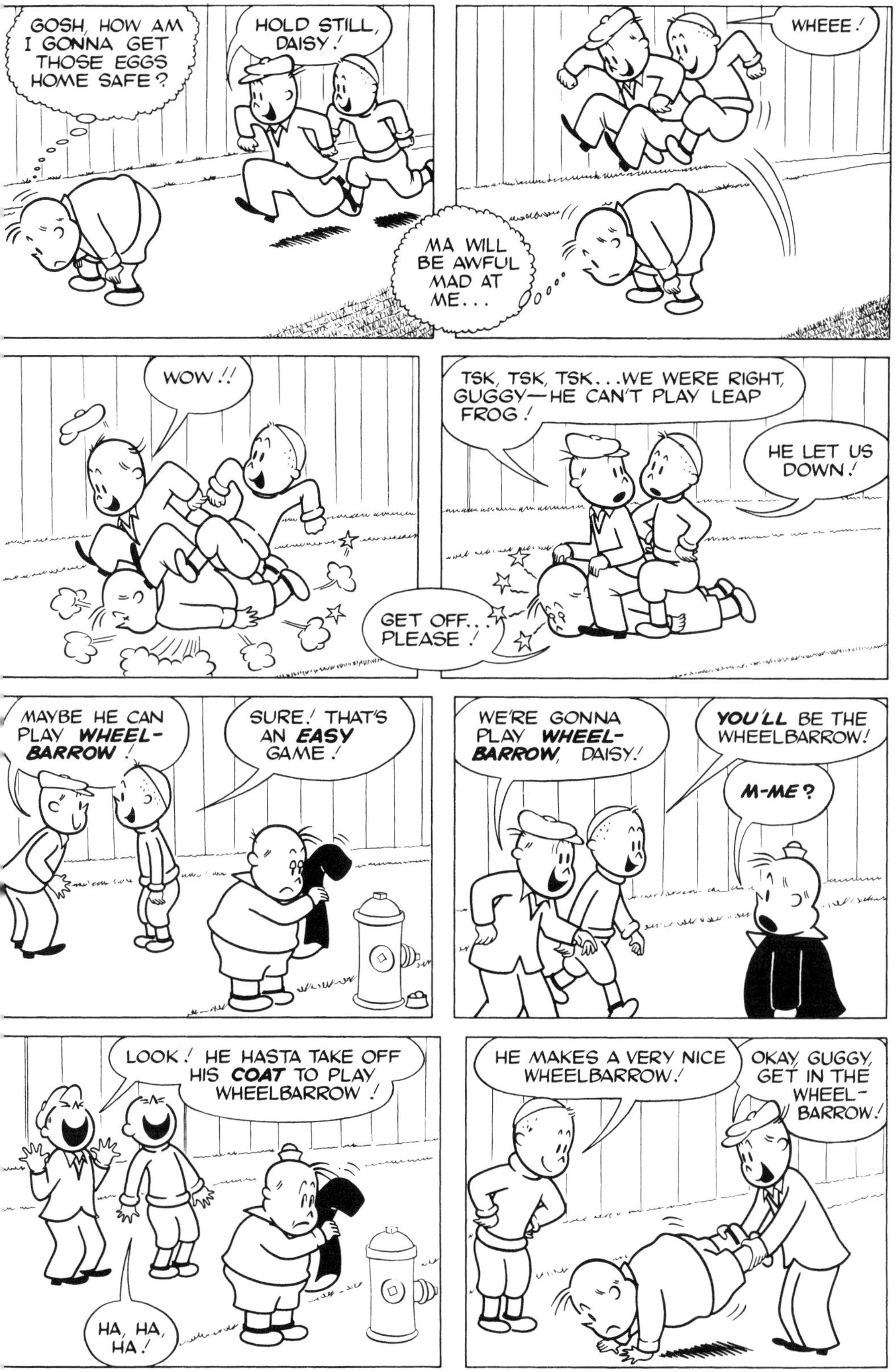
GOSH, HOW AM I GONNA GET THOSE EGGS HOME SAFE?
HOLD STILL, DAISY!
WHEEE!
MA WILL BE AWFUL MAD AT ME...
WOW!!
TSK, TSK, TSK...WE WERE RIGHT, GUGGY—HE CAN'T PLAY LEAP FROG!
HE LET US DOWN!
GET OFF... PLEASE!
MAYBE HE CAN PLAY **WHEEL-BARROW**!
SURE! THAT'S AN **EASY** GAME!
WE'RE GONNA PLAY **WHEEL-BARROW**, DAISY!
YOU'LL BE THE WHEELBARROW!
M-ME?
LOOK! HE HASTA TAKE OFF HIS **COAT** TO PLAY WHEELBARROW!
HA, HA, HA!
HE MAKES A VERY NICE WHEELBARROW!
OKAY, GUGGY, GET IN THE WHEEL-BARROW!

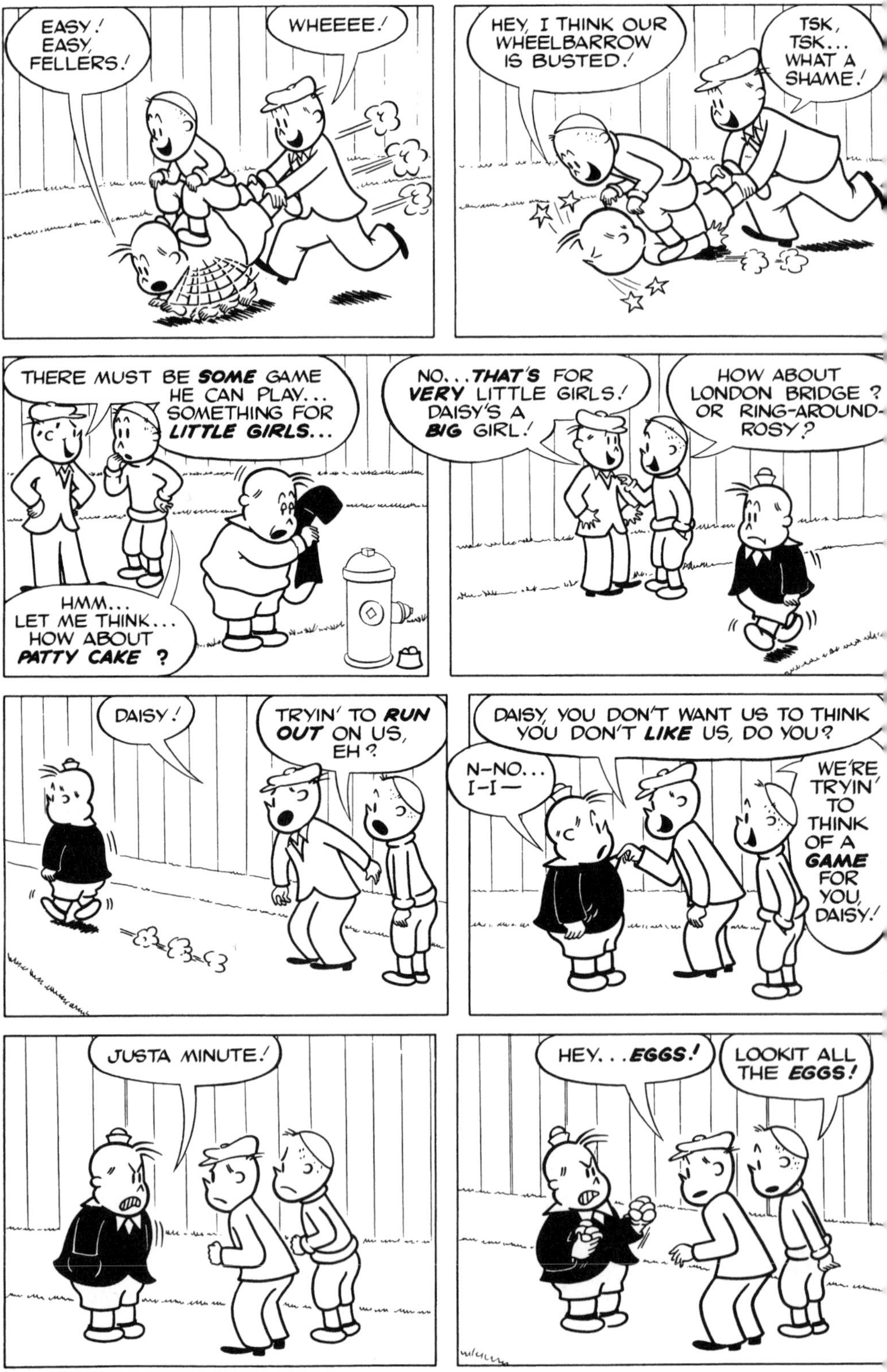
EASY! EASY, FELLERS!
WHEEEE!
HEY, I THINK OUR WHEELBARROW IS BUSTED!
TSK, TSK... WHAT A SHAME!
THERE MUST BE SOME GAME HE CAN PLAY... SOMETHING FOR LITTLE GIRLS...
HMM... LET ME THINK... HOW ABOUT PATTY CAKE ?
NO...THAT'S FOR VERY LITTLE GIRLS! DAISY'S A BIG GIRL!
HOW ABOUT LONDON BRIDGE ? OR RING-AROUND-ROSY?
DAISY!
TRYIN' TO RUN OUT ON US, EH?
DAISY, YOU DON'T WANT US TO THINK YOU DON'T LIKE US, DO YOU?
N-NO... I-I—
WE'RE TRYIN' TO THINK OF A GAME FOR YOU, DAISY!
JUSTA MINUTE!
HEY...EGGS!
LOOKIT ALL THE EGGS!

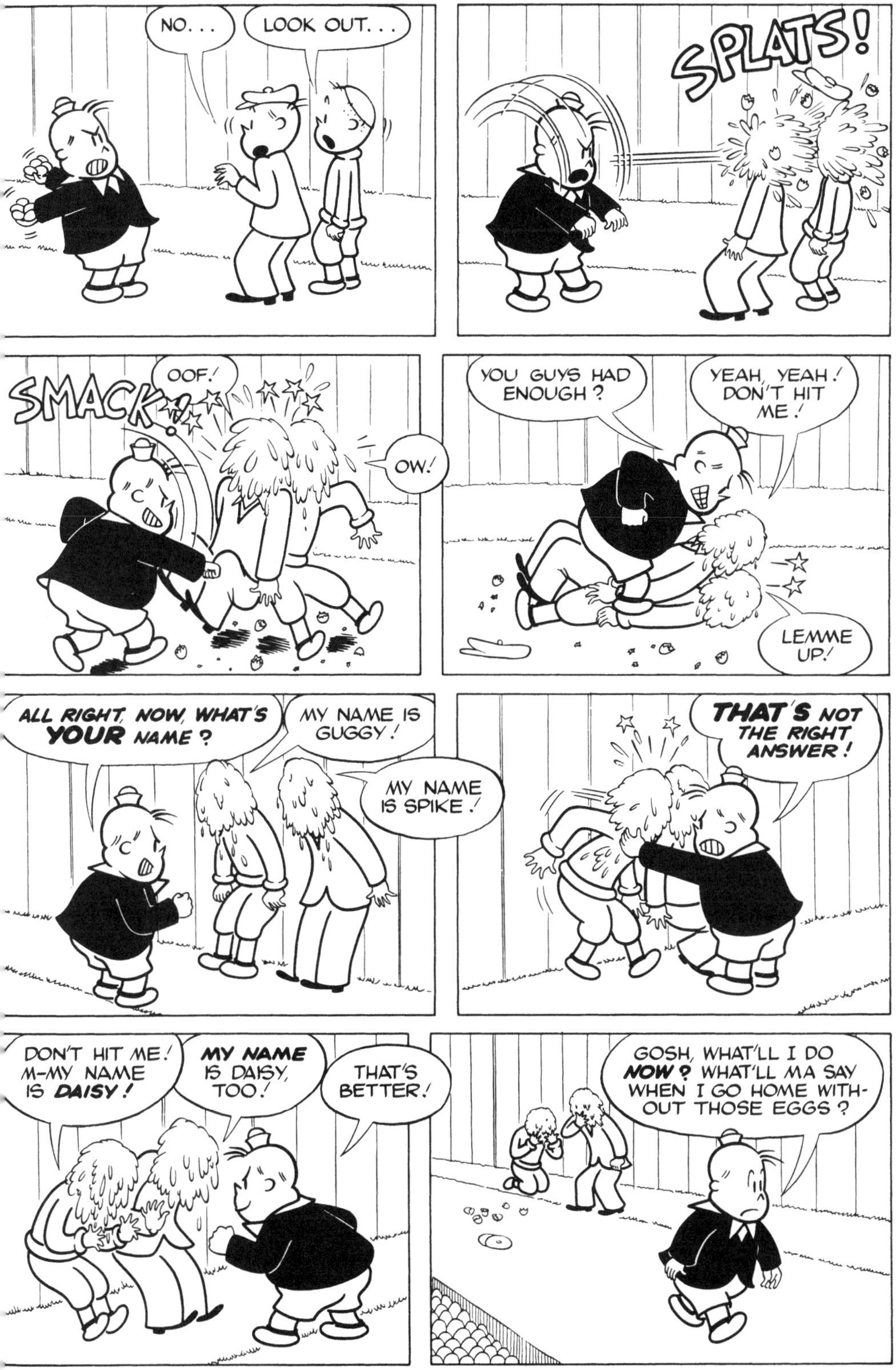
NO. . .
LOOK OUT. . .
SPLATS!
SMACK
OOF!
OW!
YOU GUYS HAD ENOUGH?
YEAH, YEAH! DON'T HIT ME!
LEMME UP!
ALL RIGHT, NOW, WHAT'S YOUR NAME?
MY NAME IS GUGGY!
MY NAME IS SPIKE!
THAT'S NOT THE RIGHT ANSWER!
DON'T HIT ME! M-MY NAME IS DAISY!
MY NAME IS DAISY, TOO!
THAT'S BETTER!
GOSH, WHAT'LL I DO NOW? WHAT'LL MA SAY WHEN I GO HOME WITH-OUT THOSE EGGS?

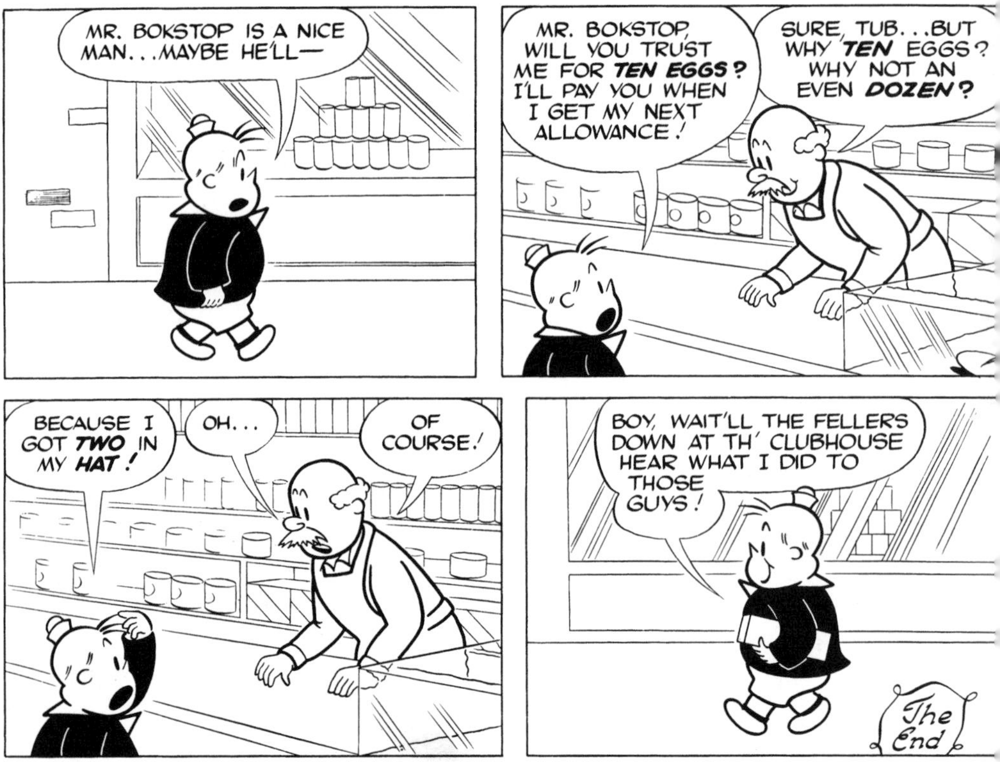
MR. BOKSTOP IS A NICE MAN...MAYBE HE'LL—
MR. BOKSTOP, WILL YOU TRUST ME FOR TEN EGGS? I'LL PAY YOU WHEN I GET MY NEXT ALLOWANCE!
SURE, TUB...BUT WHY TEN EGGS? WHY NOT AN EVEN DOZEN?
BECAUSE I GOT TWO IN MY HAT!
OH...
OF COURSE!
BOY, WAIT'LL THE FELLERS DOWN AT TH' CLUBHOUSE HEAR WHAT I DID TO THOSE GUYS!
The End

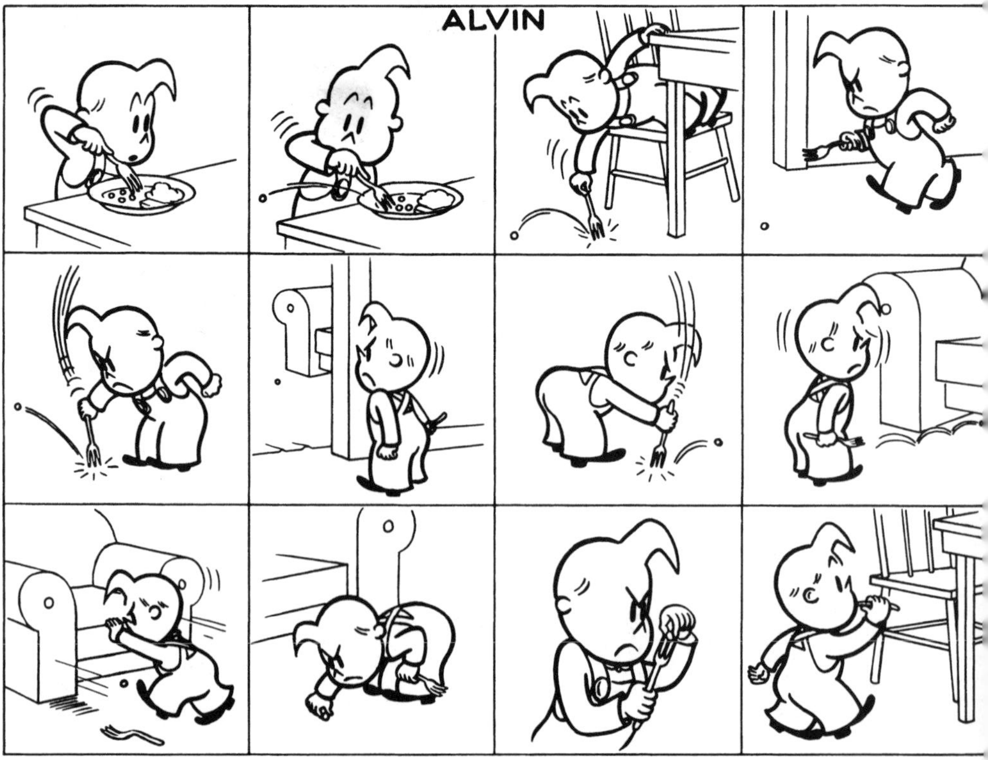
ALVIN

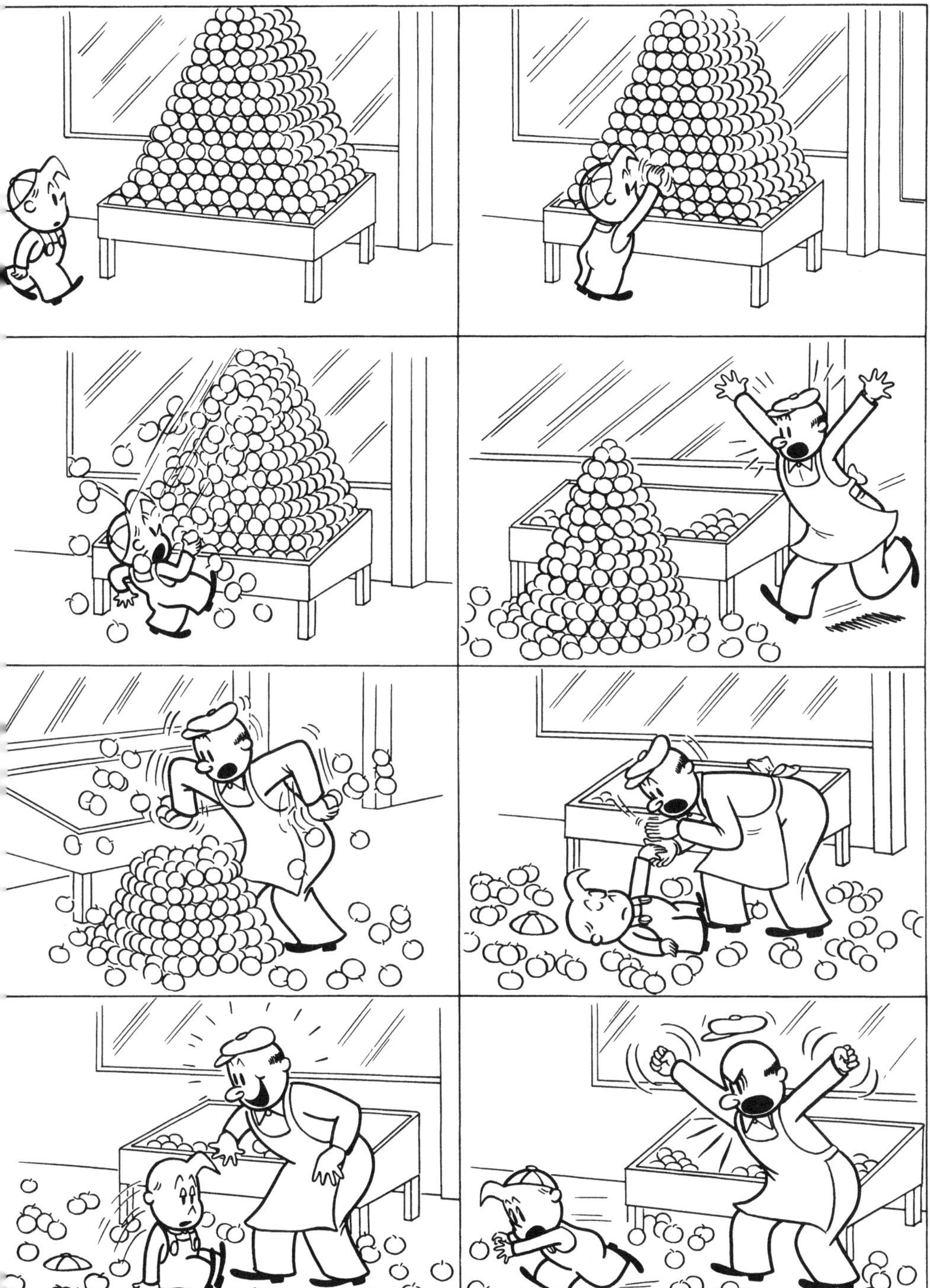

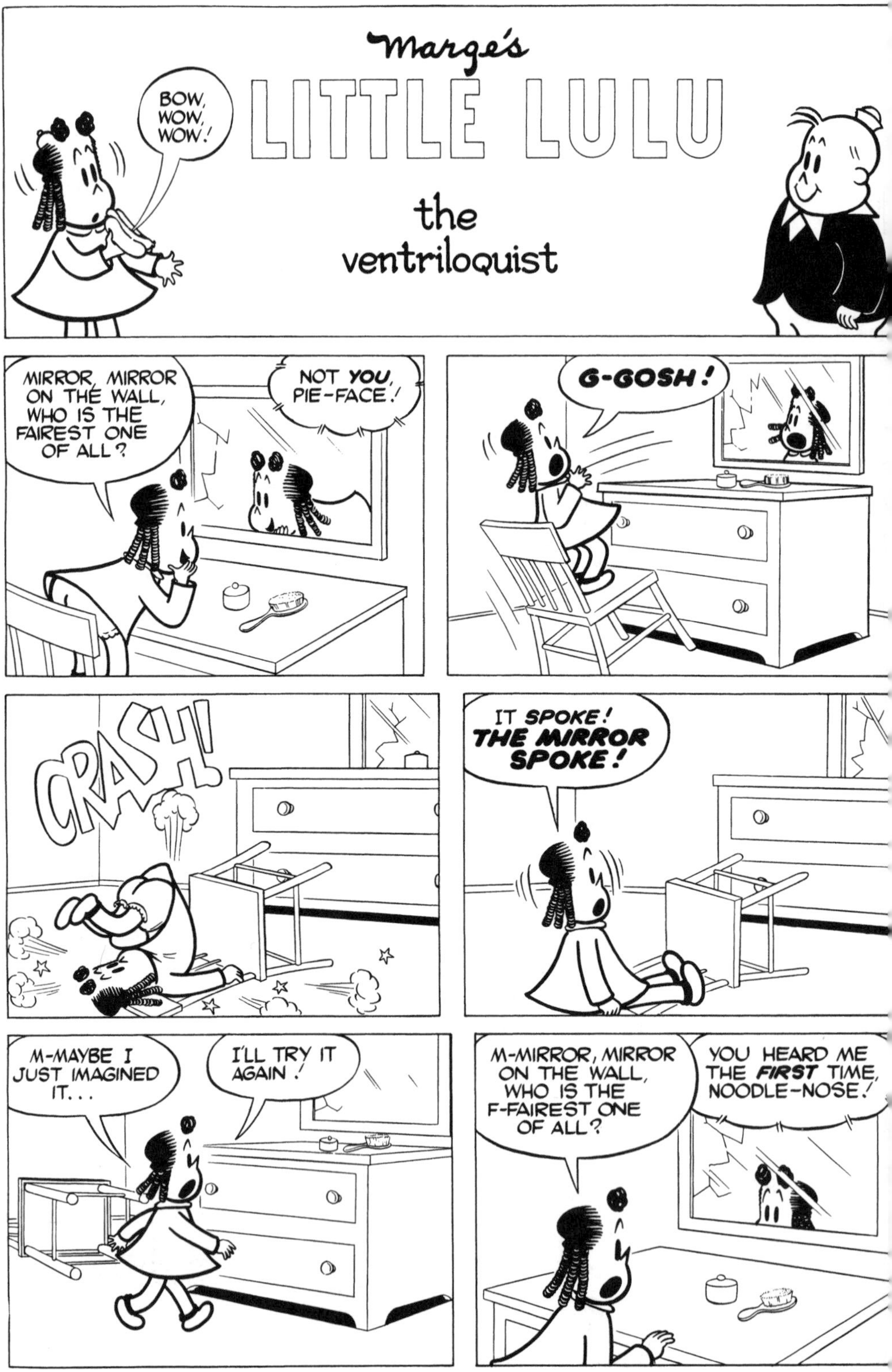
Marge's
LITTLE LULU
the ventriloquist
BOW, WOW, WOW!
MIRROR, MIRROR ON THE WALL, WHO IS THE FAIREST ONE OF ALL?
NOT YOU, PIE-FACE!
G-GOSH!
CRASH!
IT SPOKE! THE MIRROR SPOKE!
M-MAYBE I JUST IMAGINED IT...
I'LL TRY IT AGAIN!
M-MIRROR, MIRROR ON THE WALL, WHO IS THE F-FAIREST ONE OF ALL?
YOU HEARD ME THE FIRST TIME, NOODLE-NOSE!

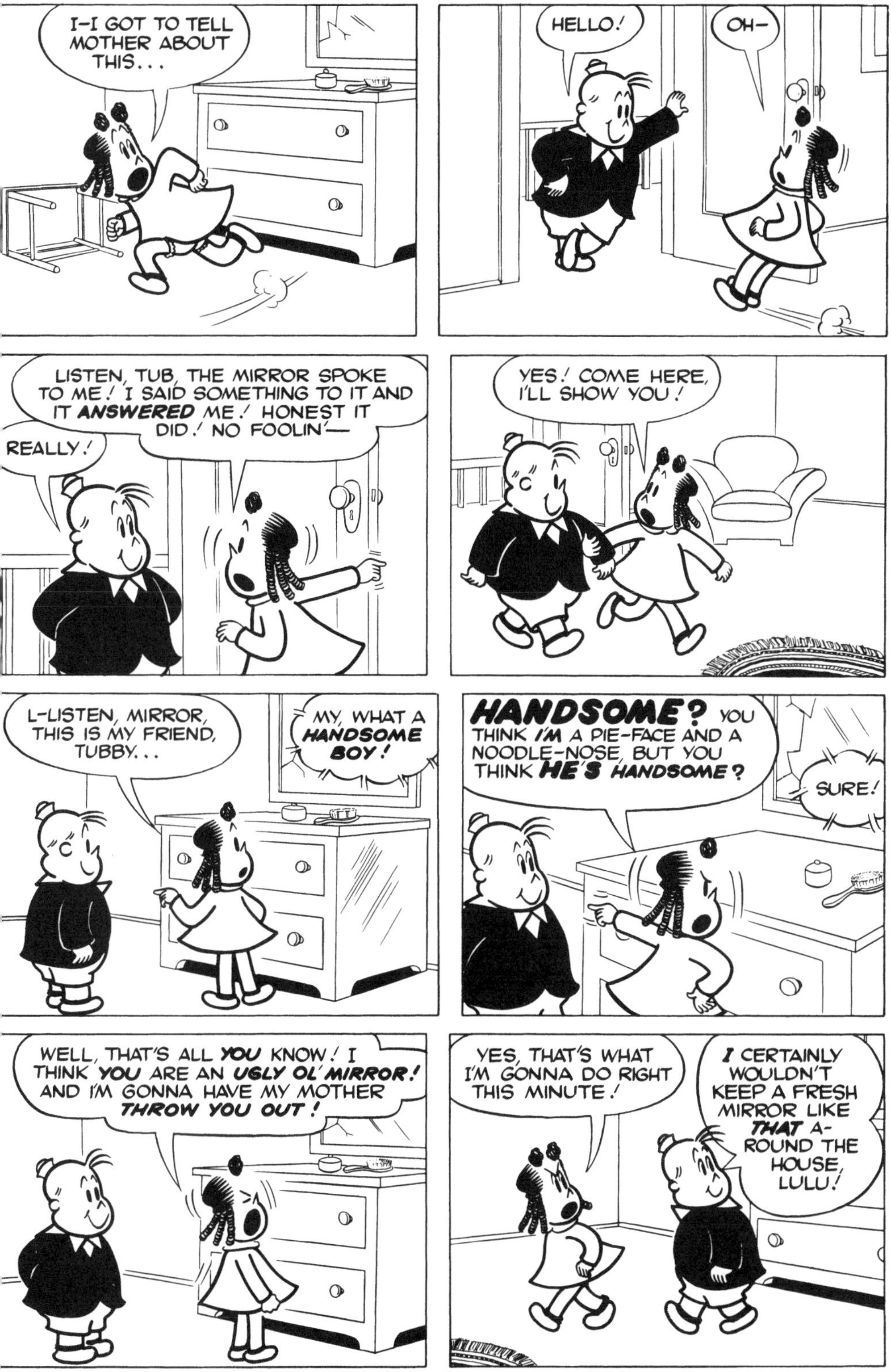
I-I GOT TO TELL MOTHER ABOUT THIS...
HELLO!
OH-
LISTEN, TUB, THE MIRROR SPOKE TO ME! I SAID SOMETHING TO IT AND IT ANSWERED ME! HONEST IT DID! NO FOOLIN'—
REALLY!
YES! COME HERE, I'LL SHOW YOU!
L-LISTEN, MIRROR, THIS IS MY FRIEND, TUBBY...
MY, WHAT A HANDSOME BOY!
HANDSOME? YOU THINK I'M A PIE-FACE AND A NOODLE-NOSE, BUT YOU THINK HE'S HANDSOME?
SURE!
WELL, THAT'S ALL YOU KNOW! I THINK YOU ARE AN UGLY OL' MIRROR! AND I'M GONNA HAVE MY MOTHER THROW YOU OUT!
YES, THAT'S WHAT I'M GONNA DO RIGHT THIS MINUTE!
I CERTAINLY WOULDN'T KEEP A FRESH MIRROR LIKE THAT A-ROUND THE HOUSE, LULU!

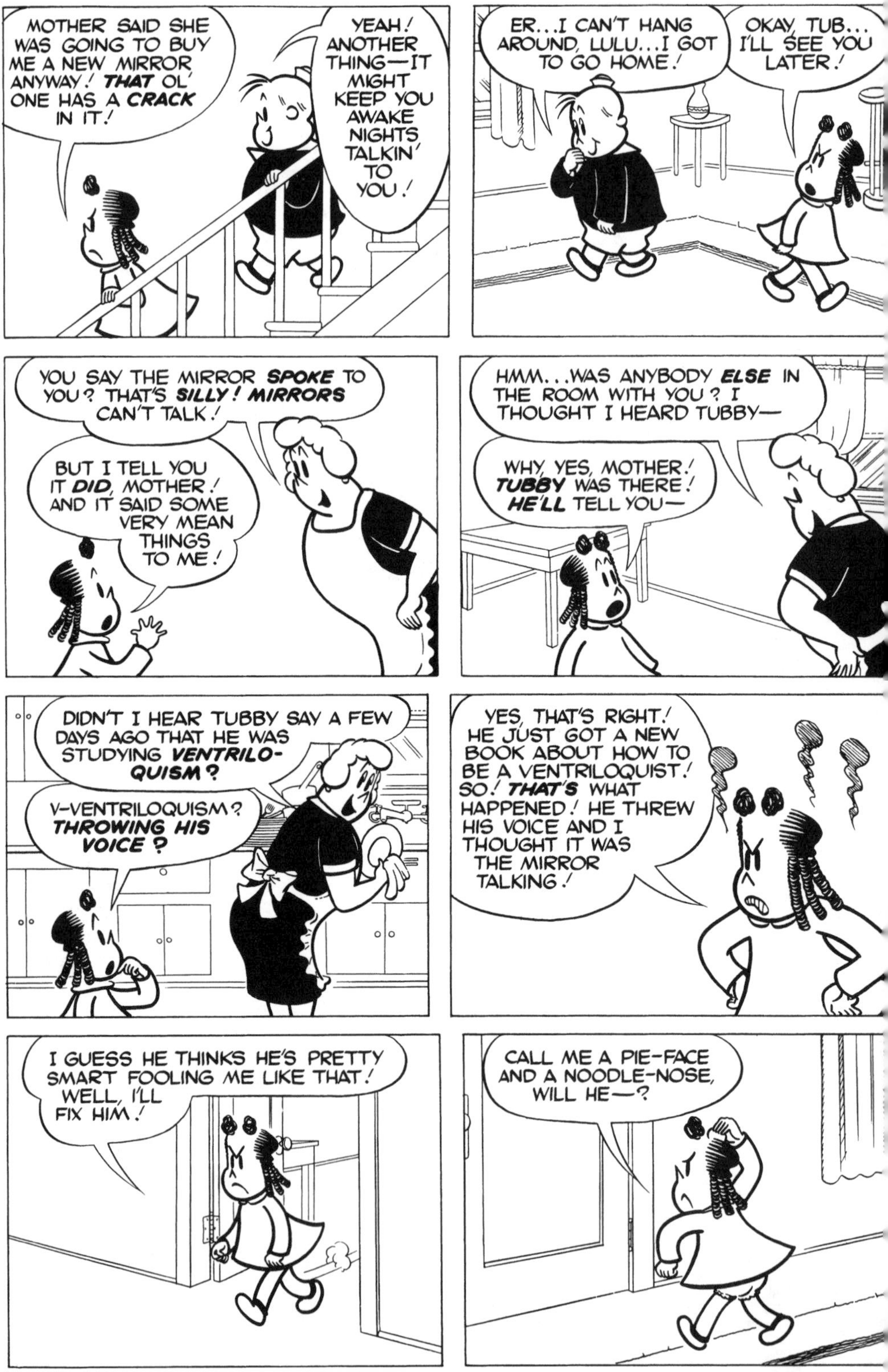

MOTHER SAID SHE WAS GOING TO BUY ME A NEW MIRROR ANYWAY! THAT OL' ONE HAS A CRACK IN IT!
YEAH! ANOTHER THING—IT MIGHT KEEP YOU AWAKE NIGHTS TALKIN' TO YOU!
ER...I CAN'T HANG AROUND, LULU...I GOT TO GO HOME!
OKAY, TUB... I'LL SEE YOU LATER!
YOU SAY THE MIRROR SPOKE TO YOU? THAT'S SILLY! MIRRORS CAN'T TALK!
BUT I TELL YOU IT DID, MOTHER! AND IT SAID SOME VERY MEAN THINGS TO ME!
HMM...WAS ANYBODY ELSE IN THE ROOM WITH YOU? I THOUGHT I HEARD TUBBY—
WHY, YES, MOTHER! TUBBY WAS THERE! HE'LL TELL YOU—
DIDN'T I HEAR TUBBY SAY A FEW DAYS AGO THAT HE WAS STUDYING VENTRILO-QUISM?
V-VENTRILOQUISM? THROWING HIS VOICE?
YES, THAT'S RIGHT! HE JUST GOT A NEW BOOK ABOUT HOW TO BE A VENTRILOQUIST! SO! THAT'S WHAT HAPPENED! HE THREW HIS VOICE AND I THOUGHT IT WAS THE MIRROR TALKING!
I GUESS HE THINKS HE'S PRETTY SMART FOOLING ME LIKE THAT! WELL, I'LL FIX HIM!
CALL ME A PIE-FACE AND A NOODLE-NOSE, WILL HE—?

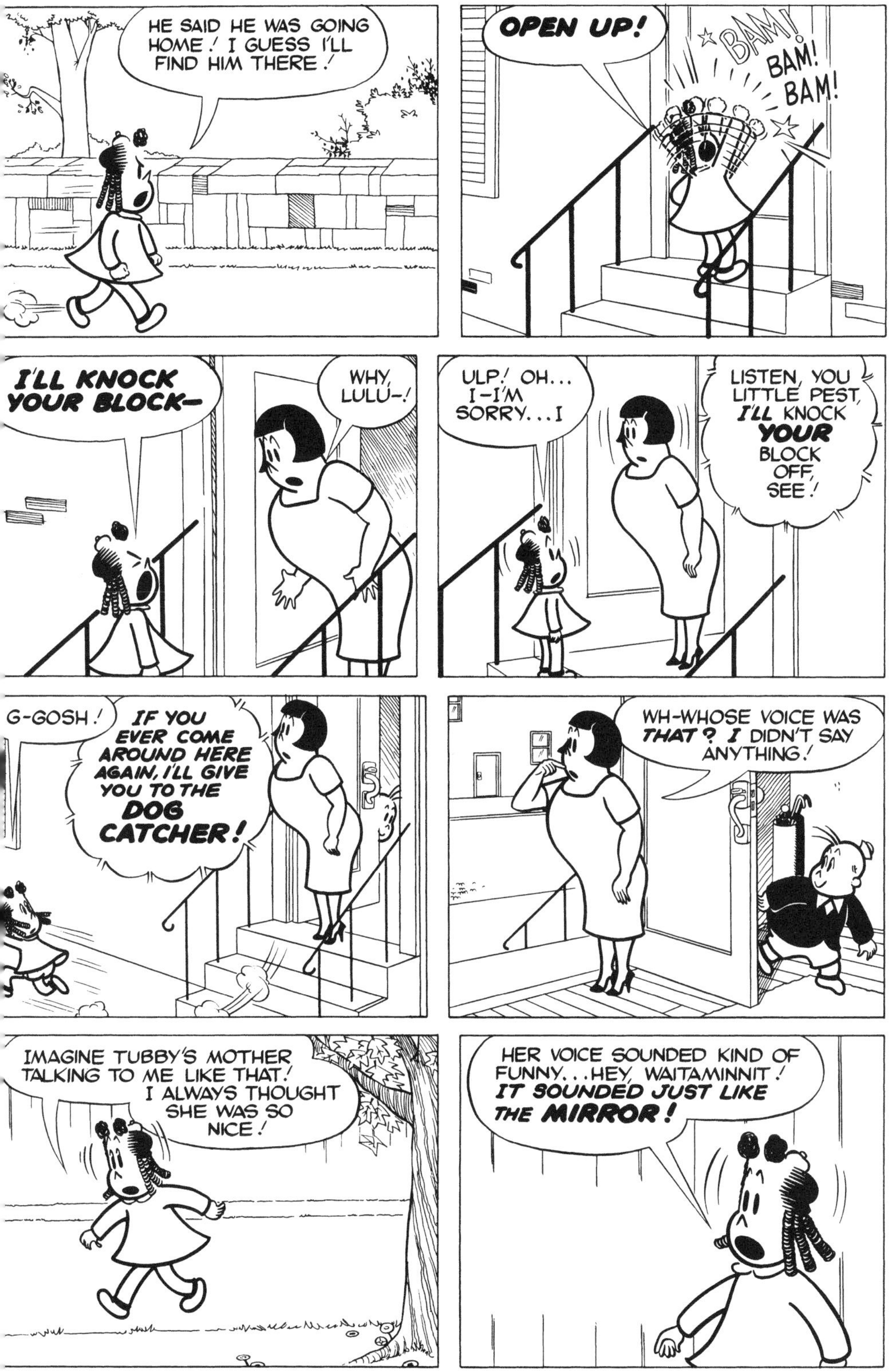
HE SAID HE WAS GOING HOME! I GUESS I'LL FIND HIM THERE!
OPEN UP!
BAM! BAM! BAM!
I'LL KNOCK YOUR BLOCK—
WHY, LULU—!
ULP! OH... I-I'M SORRY... I
LISTEN, YOU LITTLE PEST, I'LL KNOCK YOUR BLOCK OFF, SEE!
G-GOSH!
IF YOU EVER COME AROUND HERE AGAIN, I'LL GIVE YOU TO THE DOG CATCHER!
WH-WHOSE VOICE WAS THAT? I DIDN'T SAY ANYTHING!
IMAGINE TUBBY'S MOTHER TALKING TO ME LIKE THAT! I ALWAYS THOUGHT SHE WAS SO NICE!
HER VOICE SOUNDED KIND OF FUNNY...HEY, WAITAMINNIT! IT SOUNDED JUST LIKE THE MIRROR!

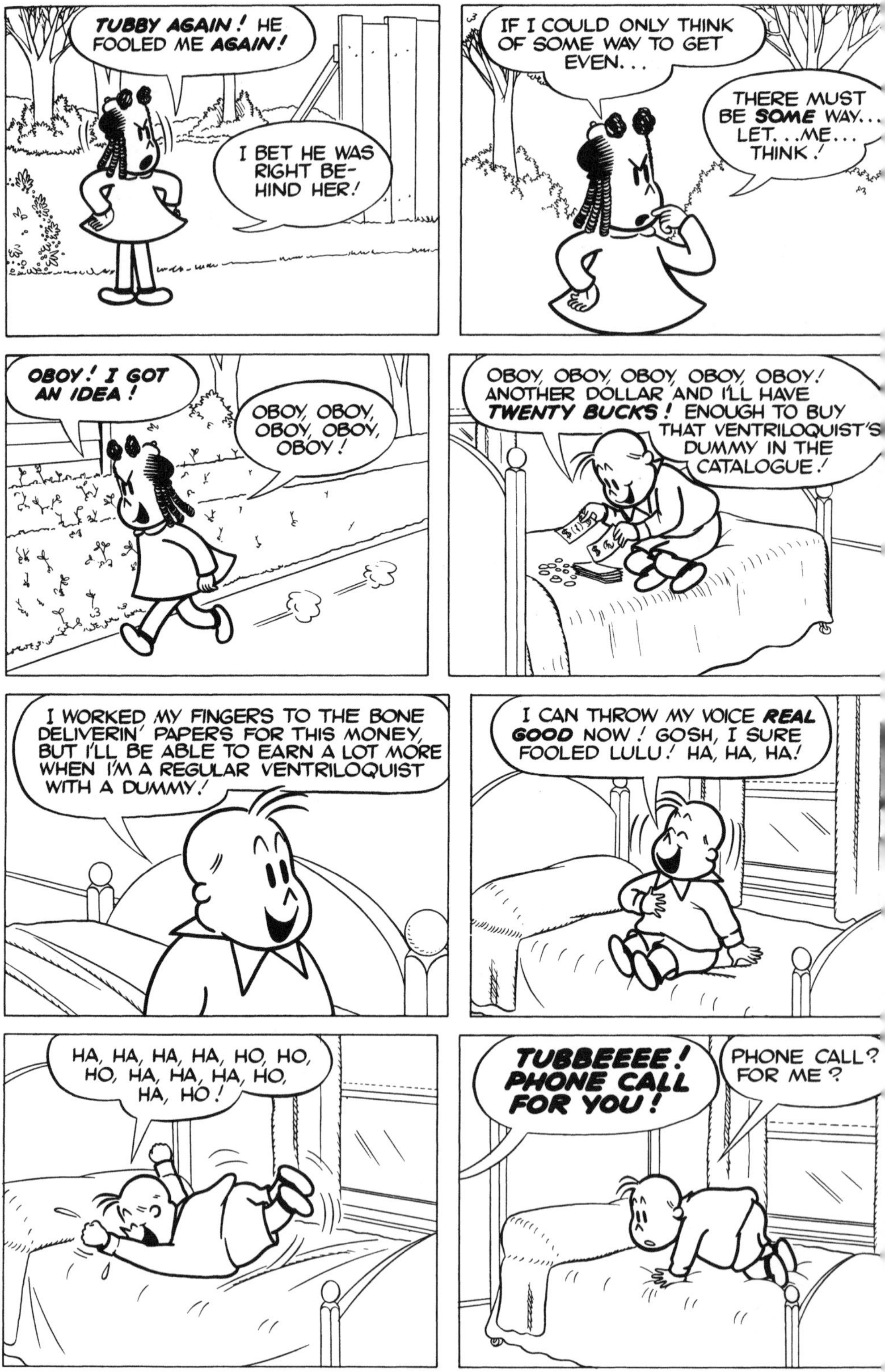
TUBBY AGAIN! HE FOOLED ME AGAIN!
I BET HE WAS RIGHT BE-HIND HER!
IF I COULD ONLY THINK OF SOME WAY TO GET EVEN...
THERE MUST BE SOME WAY... LET...ME... THINK!
OBOY! I GOT AN IDEA!
OBOY, OBOY, OBOY, OBOY, OBOY!
OBOY, OBOY, OBOY, OBOY, OBOY! ANOTHER DOLLAR AND I'LL HAVE TWENTY BUCKS! ENOUGH TO BUY THAT VENTRILOQUIST'S DUMMY IN THE CATALOGUE!
I WORKED MY FINGERS TO THE BONE DELIVERIN' PAPERS FOR THIS MONEY, BUT I'LL BE ABLE TO EARN A LOT MORE WHEN I'M A REGULAR VENTRILOQUIST WITH A DUMMY!
I CAN THROW MY VOICE REAL GOOD NOW! GOSH, I SURE FOOLED LULU! HA, HA, HA!
HA, HA, HA, HA, HO, HO, HO, HA, HA, HA, HO, HA, HO!
TUBBEEEE! PHONE CALL FOR YOU!
PHONE CALL? FOR ME?

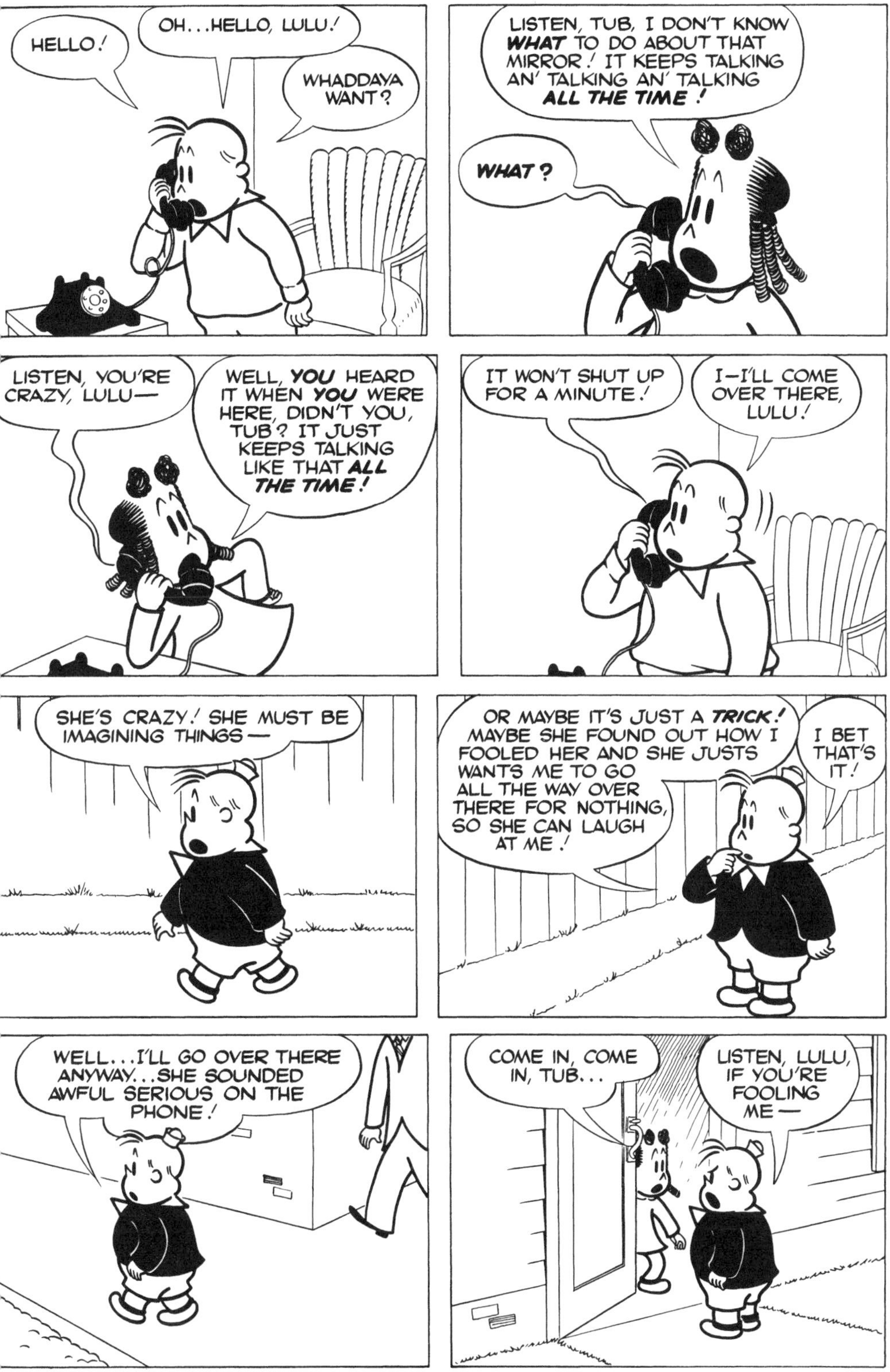
HELLO!
OH...HELLO, LULU!
WHADDAYA WANT?
LISTEN, TUB, I DON'T KNOW WHAT TO DO ABOUT THAT MIRROR! IT KEEPS TALKING AN' TALKING AN' TALKING ALL THE TIME!
WHAT?
LISTEN, YOU'RE CRAZY, LULU—
WELL, YOU HEARD IT WHEN YOU WERE HERE, DIDN'T YOU, TUB? IT JUST KEEPS TALKING LIKE THAT ALL THE TIME!
IT WON'T SHUT UP FOR A MINUTE!
I—I'LL COME OVER THERE, LULU!
SHE'S CRAZY! SHE MUST BE IMAGINING THINGS—
OR MAYBE IT'S JUST A TRICK! MAYBE SHE FOUND OUT HOW I FOOLED HER AND SHE JUSTS WANTS ME TO GO ALL THE WAY OVER THERE FOR NOTHING, SO SHE CAN LAUGH AT ME!
I BET THAT'S IT!
WELL...I'LL GO OVER THERE ANYWAY...SHE SOUNDED AWFUL SERIOUS ON THE PHONE!
COME IN, COME IN, TUB...
LISTEN, LULU, IF YOU'RE FOOLING ME—

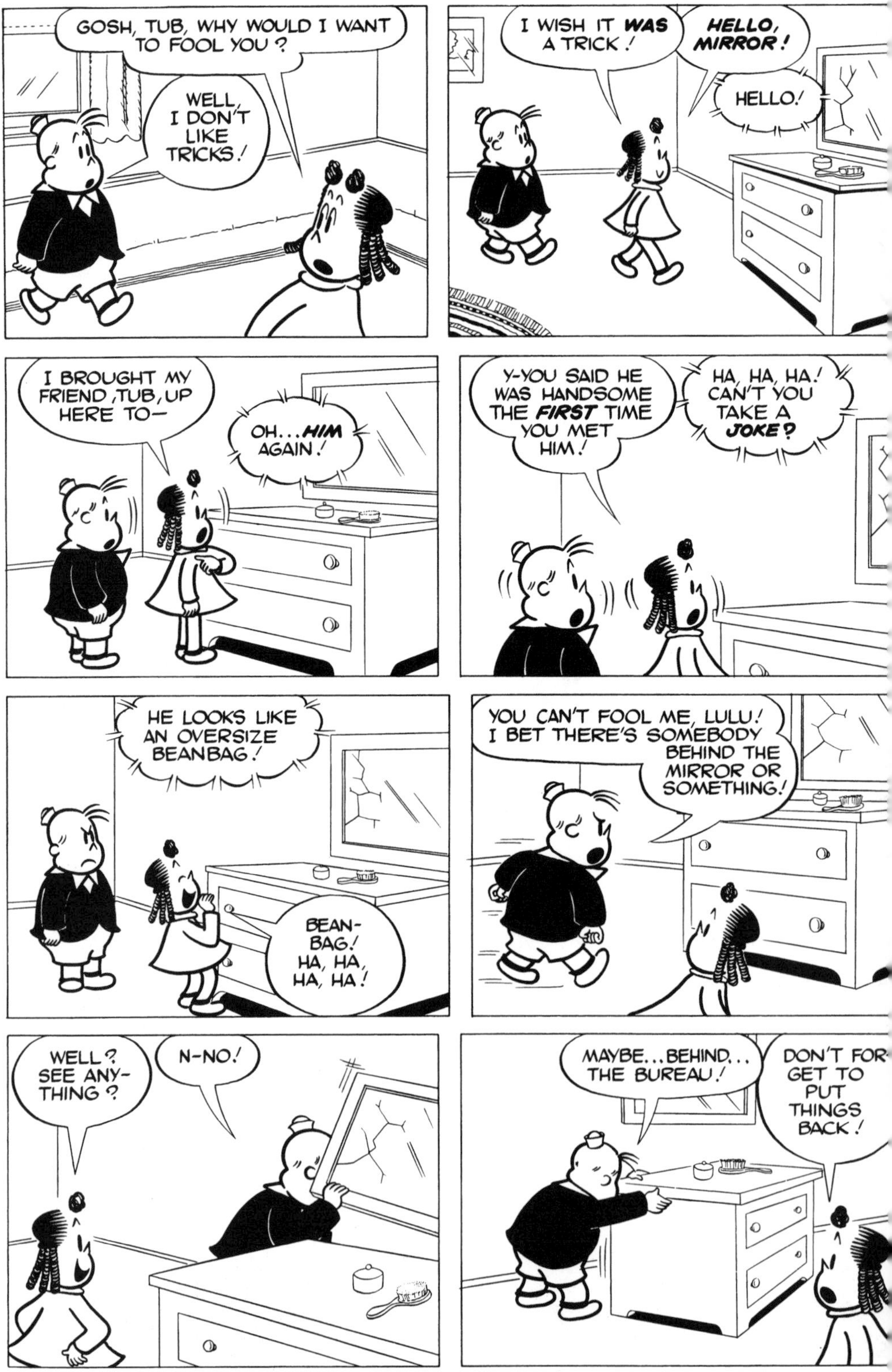
GOSH, TUB, WHY WOULD I WANT TO FOOL YOU?
WELL, I DON'T LIKE TRICKS!
I WISH IT WAS A TRICK!
HELLO, MIRROR!
HELLO!
I BROUGHT MY FRIEND, TUB, UP HERE TO—
OH...HIM AGAIN!
Y-YOU SAID HE WAS HANDSOME THE FIRST TIME YOU MET HIM!
HA, HA, HA! CAN'T YOU TAKE A JOKE?
HE LOOKS LIKE AN OVERSIZE BEANBAG!
BEAN-BAG! HA, HA, HA, HA!
YOU CAN'T FOOL ME, LULU! I BET THERE'S SOMEBODY BEHIND THE MIRROR OR SOMETHING!
WELL? SEE ANY-THING?
N-NO!
MAYBE...BEHIND... THE BUREAU!
DON'T FOR-GET TO PUT THINGS BACK!

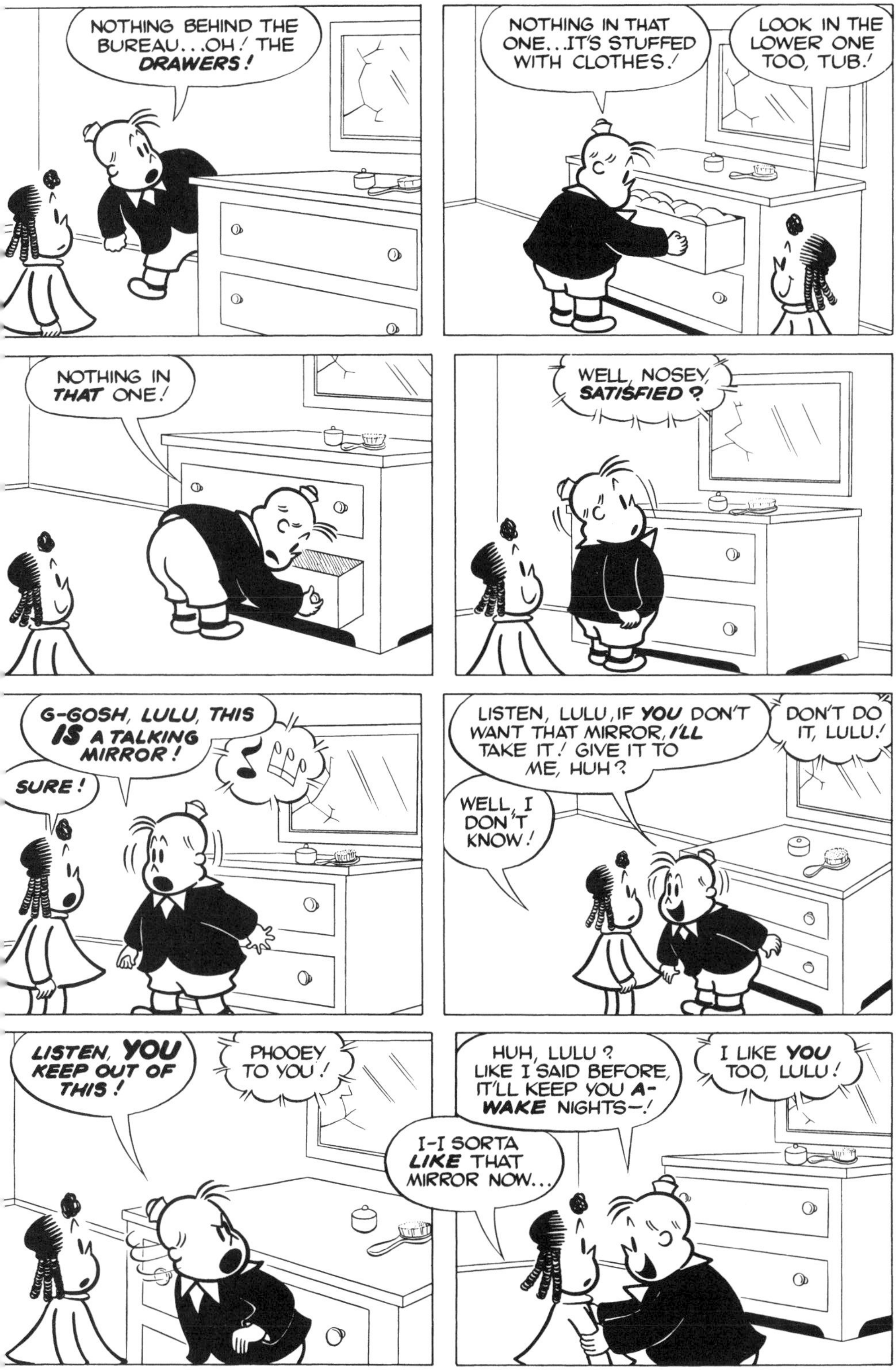

NOTHING BEHIND THE BUREAU...OH! THE DRAWERS!
NOTHING IN THAT ONE...IT'S STUFFED WITH CLOTHES!
LOOK IN THE LOWER ONE TOO, TUB!
NOTHING IN THAT ONE!
WELL, NOSEY, SATISFIED?
G-GOSH, LULU, THIS IS A TALKING MIRROR!
SURE!
LISTEN, LULU, IF YOU DON'T WANT THAT MIRROR, I'LL TAKE IT! GIVE IT TO ME, HUH?
DON'T DO IT, LULU!
WELL, I DON'T KNOW!
LISTEN, YOU KEEP OUT OF THIS!
PHOOEY TO YOU!
HUH, LULU? LIKE I SAID BEFORE, IT'LL KEEP YOU A-WAKE NIGHTS—!
I LIKE YOU TOO, LULU!
I-I SORTA LIKE THAT MIRROR NOW...

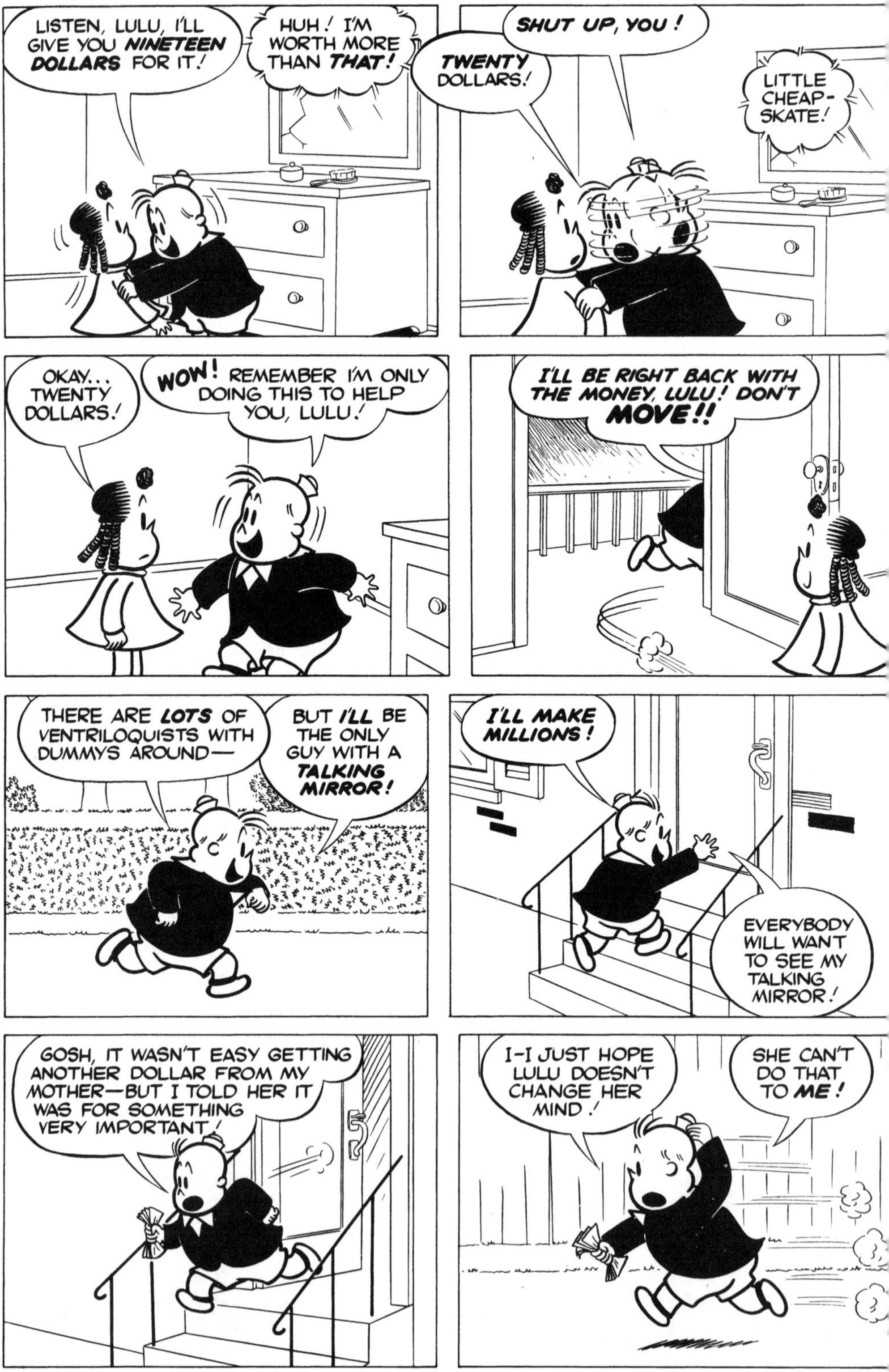
LISTEN, LULU, I'LL GIVE YOU NINETEEN DOLLARS FOR IT!
HUH! I'M WORTH MORE THAN THAT!
SHUT UP, YOU!
TWENTY DOLLARS!
LITTLE CHEAP-SKATE!
OKAY... TWENTY DOLLARS!
WOW! REMEMBER I'M ONLY DOING THIS TO HELP YOU, LULU!
I'LL BE RIGHT BACK WITH THE MONEY, LULU! DON'T MOVE!!
THERE ARE LOTS OF VENTRILOQUISTS WITH DUMMYS AROUND—
BUT I'LL BE THE ONLY GUY WITH A TALKING MIRROR!
I'LL MAKE MILLIONS!
EVERYBODY WILL WANT TO SEE MY TALKING MIRROR!
GOSH, IT WASN'T EASY GETTING ANOTHER DOLLAR FROM MY MOTHER—BUT I TOLD HER IT WAS FOR SOMETHING VERY IMPORTANT!
I-I JUST HOPE LULU DOESN'T CHANGE HER MIND!
SHE CAN'T DO THAT TO ME!

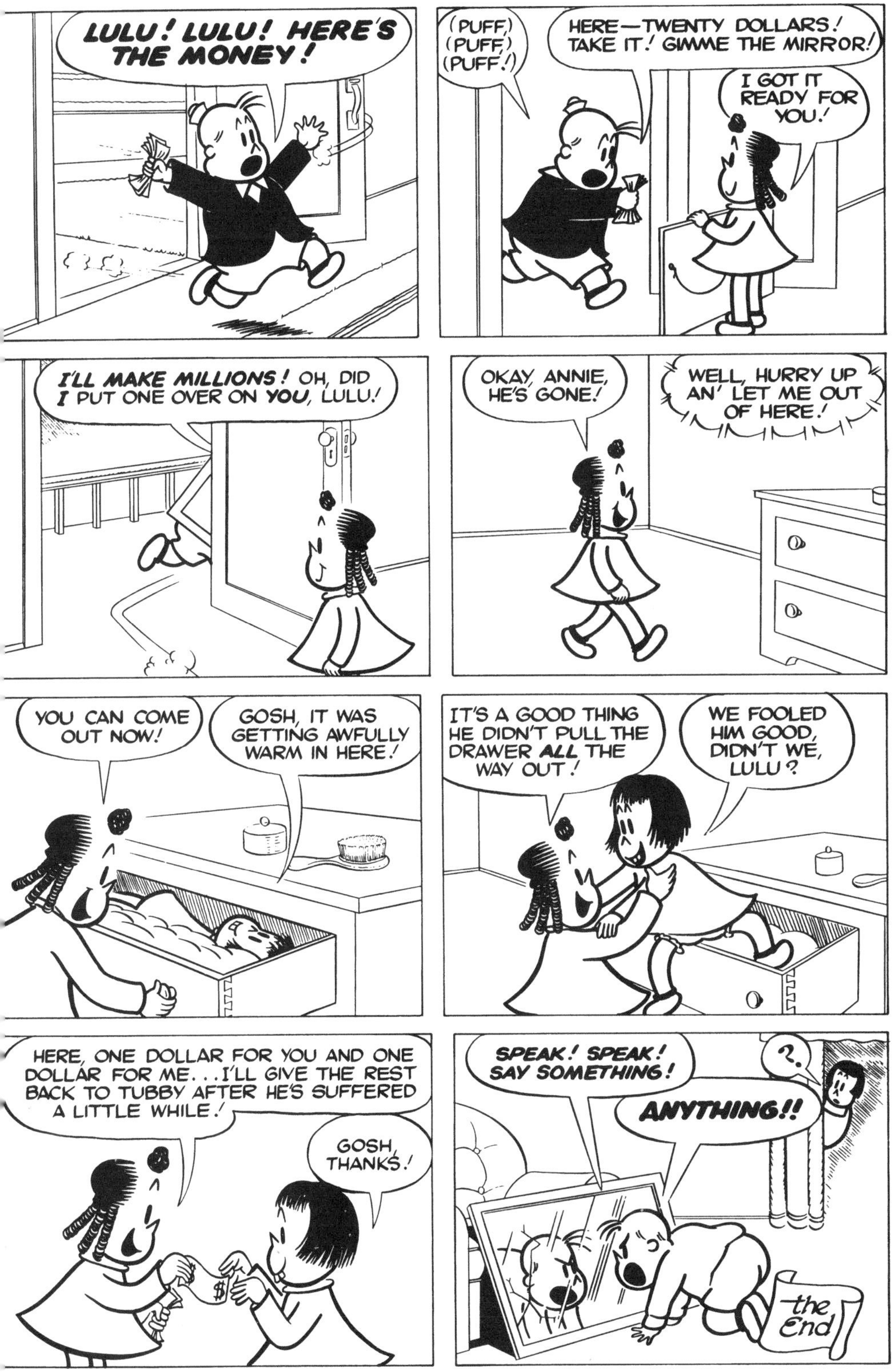
LULU! LULU! HERE'S THE MONEY!
(PUFF) (PUFF) (PUFF!)
HERE—TWENTY DOLLARS! TAKE IT! GIMME THE MIRROR!
I GOT IT READY FOR YOU!
I'LL MAKE MILLIONS! OH, DID I PUT ONE OVER ON YOU, LULU!
OKAY, ANNIE, HE'S GONE!
WELL, HURRY UP AN' LET ME OUT OF HERE!
YOU CAN COME OUT NOW!
GOSH, IT WAS GETTING AWFULLY WARM IN HERE!
IT'S A GOOD THING HE DIDN'T PULL THE DRAWER ALL THE WAY OUT!
WE FOOLED HIM GOOD, DIDN'T WE, LULU?
HERE, ONE DOLLAR FOR YOU AND ONE DOLLAR FOR ME...I'LL GIVE THE REST BACK TO TUBBY AFTER HE'S SUFFERED A LITTLE WHILE!
GOSH, THANKS!
SPEAK! SPEAK! SAY SOMETHING!
ANYTHING!!
?
the End

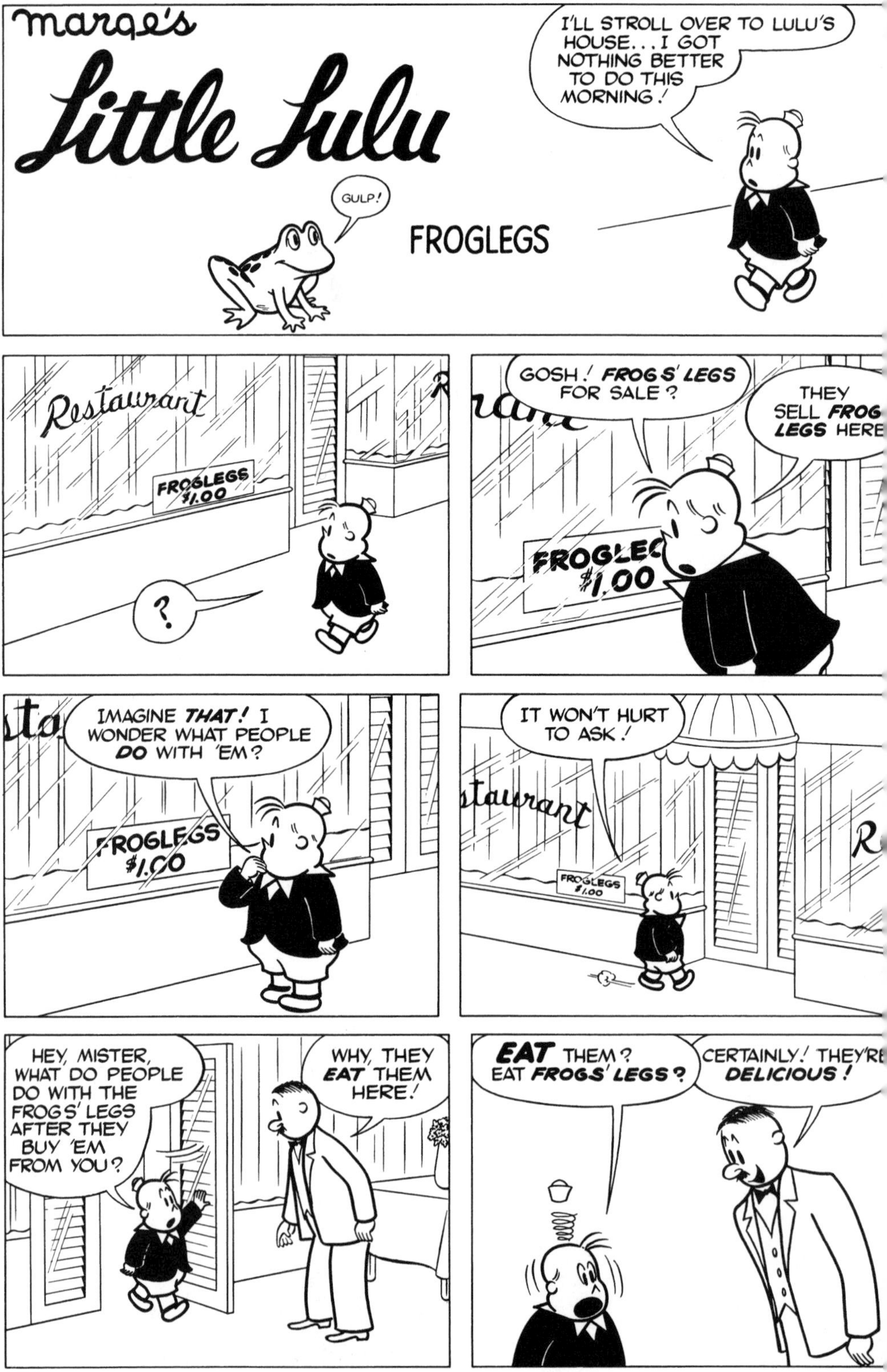
marge's
Little Lulu
I'LL STROLL OVER TO LULU'S HOUSE...I GOT NOTHING BETTER TO DO THIS MORNING!
GULP!
FROGLEGS
Restaurant
FROGLEGS $1.00
?
GOSH! FROGS' LEGS FOR SALE?
THEY SELL FROG LEGS HERE
FROGLEG $1.00
IMAGINE THAT! I WONDER WHAT PEOPLE DO WITH 'EM?
FROGLEGS $1.00
IT WON'T HURT TO ASK!
staurant
FROGLEGS $1.00
HEY, MISTER, WHAT DO PEOPLE DO WITH THE FROGS' LEGS AFTER THEY BUY 'EM FROM YOU?
WHY, THEY EAT THEM HERE!
EAT THEM? EAT FROGS' LEGS?
CERTAINLY! THEY'RE DELICIOUS!

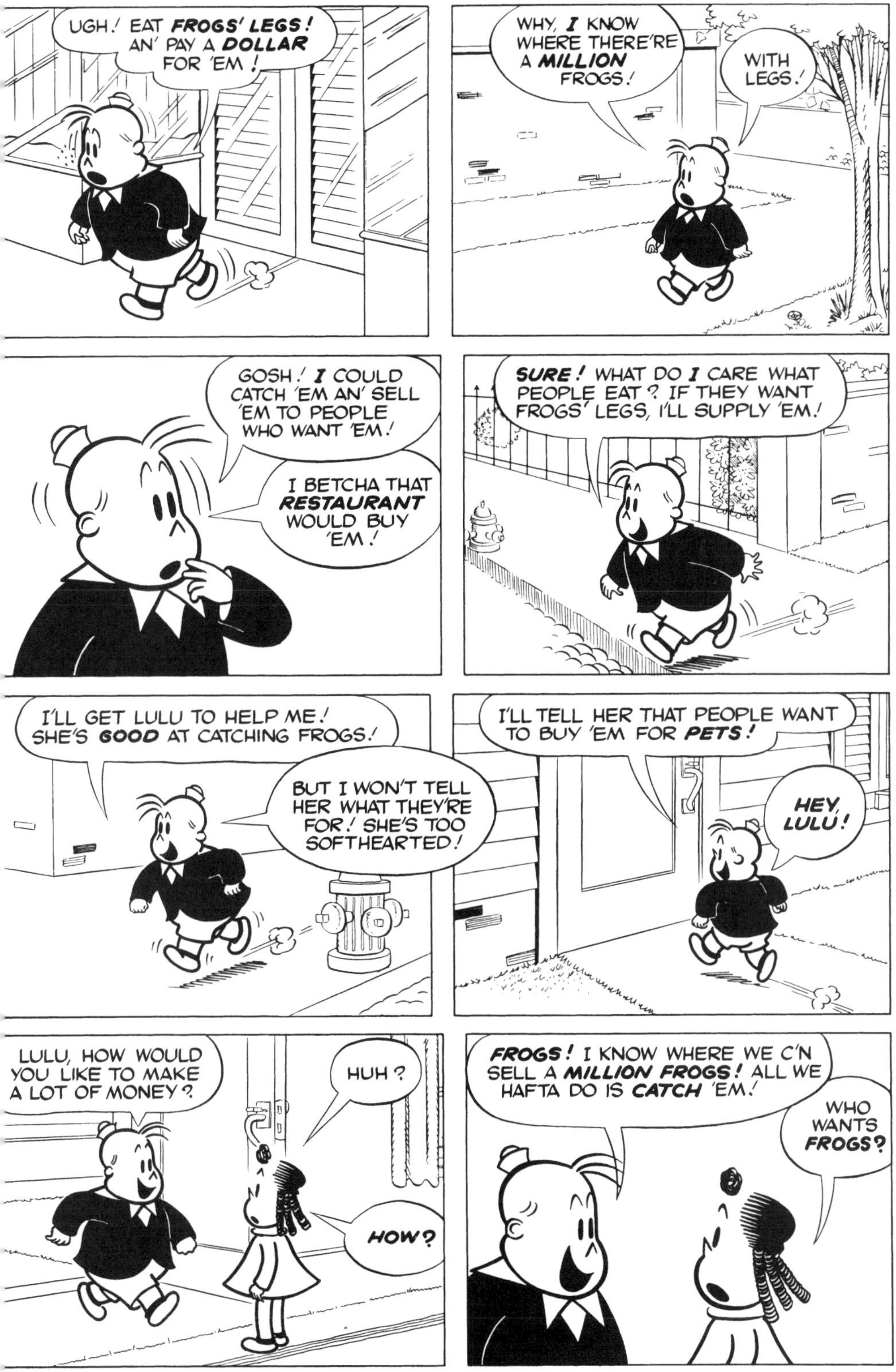
UGH! EAT FROGS' LEGS! AN' PAY A DOLLAR FOR 'EM!
WHY, I KNOW WHERE THERE'RE A MILLION FROGS!
WITH LEGS!
GOSH! I COULD CATCH 'EM AN' SELL 'EM TO PEOPLE WHO WANT 'EM!
I BETCHA THAT RESTAURANT WOULD BUY 'EM!
SURE! WHAT DO I CARE WHAT PEOPLE EAT? IF THEY WANT FROGS' LEGS, I'LL SUPPLY 'EM!
I'LL GET LULU TO HELP ME! SHE'S GOOD AT CATCHING FROGS!
BUT I WON'T TELL HER WHAT THEY'RE FOR! SHE'S TOO SOFTHEARTED!
I'LL TELL HER THAT PEOPLE WANT TO BUY 'EM FOR PETS!
HEY, LULU!
LULU, HOW WOULD YOU LIKE TO MAKE A LOT OF MONEY?
HUH?
HOW?
FROGS! I KNOW WHERE WE C'N SELL A MILLION FROGS! ALL WE HAFTA DO IS CATCH 'EM!
WHO WANTS FROGS?

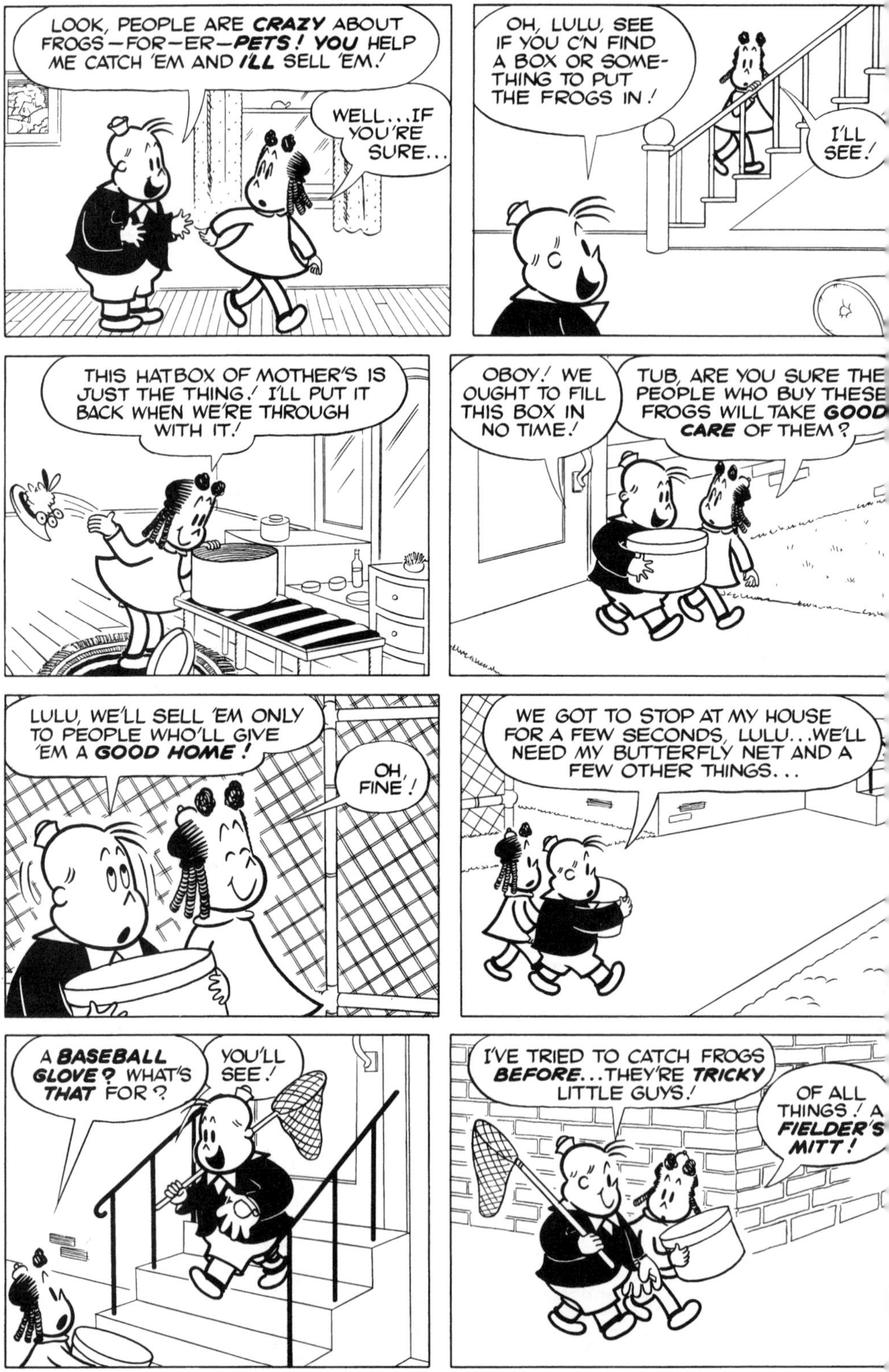
LOOK, PEOPLE ARE CRAZY ABOUT FROGS—FOR—ER—PETS! YOU HELP ME CATCH 'EM AND I'LL SELL 'EM!
WELL...IF YOU'RE SURE...
OH, LULU, SEE IF YOU C'N FIND A BOX OR SOME-THING TO PUT THE FROGS IN!
I'LL SEE!
THIS HATBOX OF MOTHER'S IS JUST THE THING! I'LL PUT IT BACK WHEN WE'RE THROUGH WITH IT!
OBOY! WE OUGHT TO FILL THIS BOX IN NO TIME!
TUB, ARE YOU SURE THE PEOPLE WHO BUY THESE FROGS WILL TAKE GOOD CARE OF THEM?
LULU, WE'LL SELL 'EM ONLY TO PEOPLE WHO'LL GIVE 'EM A GOOD HOME!
OH, FINE!
WE GOT TO STOP AT MY HOUSE FOR A FEW SECONDS, LULU...WE'LL NEED MY BUTTERFLY NET AND A FEW OTHER THINGS...
A BASEBALL GLOVE? WHAT'S THAT FOR?
YOU'LL SEE!
I'VE TRIED TO CATCH FROGS BEFORE...THEY'RE TRICKY LITTLE GUYS!
OF ALL THINGS! A FIELDER'S MITT!

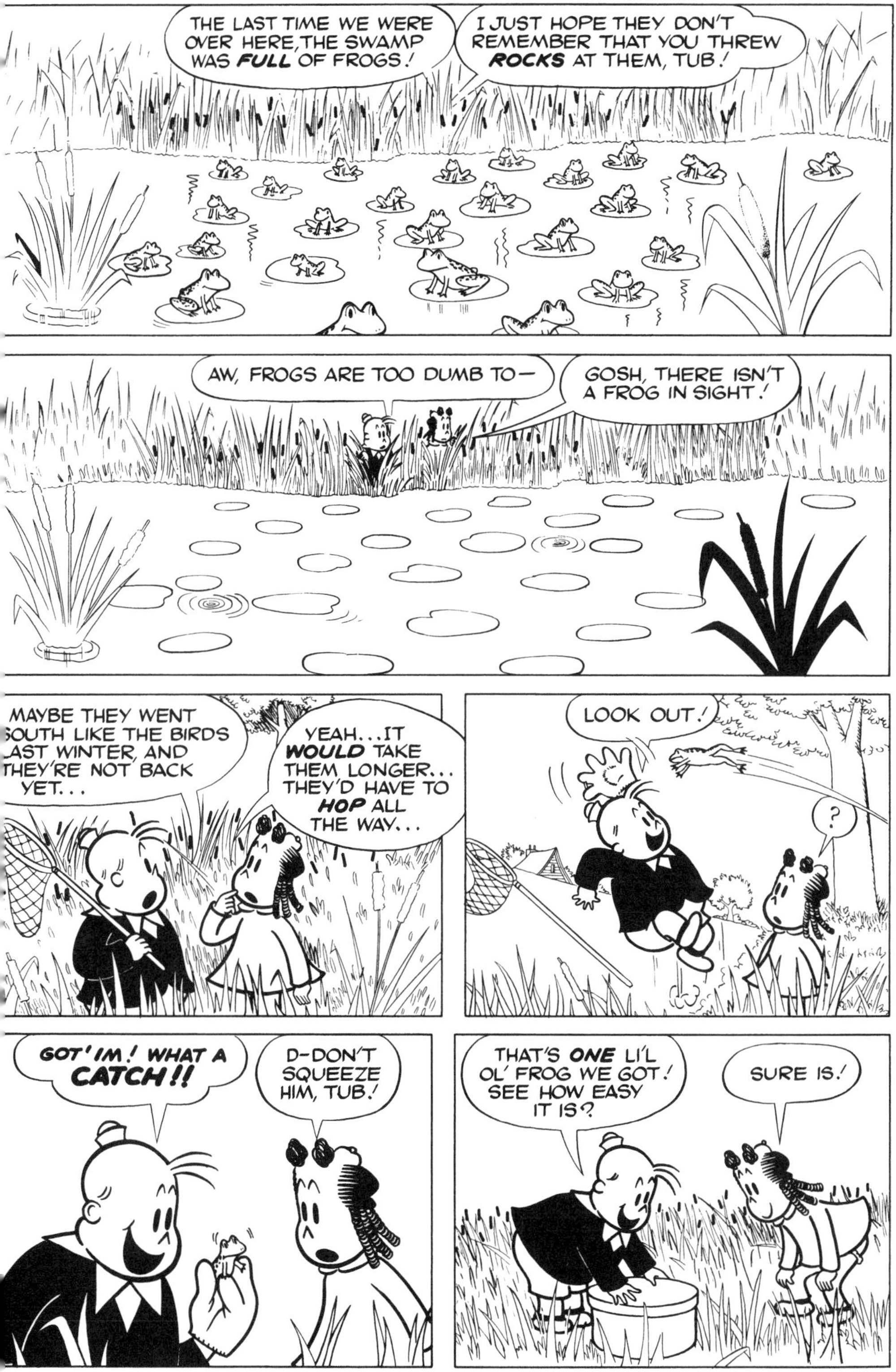
THE LAST TIME WE WERE OVER HERE, THE SWAMP WAS FULL OF FROGS!
I JUST HOPE THEY DON'T REMEMBER THAT YOU THREW ROCKS AT THEM, TUB!
AW, FROGS ARE TOO DUMB TO—
GOSH, THERE ISN'T A FROG IN SIGHT!
MAYBE THEY WENT SOUTH LIKE THE BIRDS LAST WINTER, AND THEY'RE NOT BACK YET...
YEAH...IT WOULD TAKE THEM LONGER... THEY'D HAVE TO HOP ALL THE WAY...
LOOK OUT!
?
GOT'IM! WHAT A CATCH!!
D-DON'T SQUEEZE HIM, TUB!
THAT'S ONE LI'L OL' FROG WE GOT! SEE HOW EASY IT IS?
SURE IS!

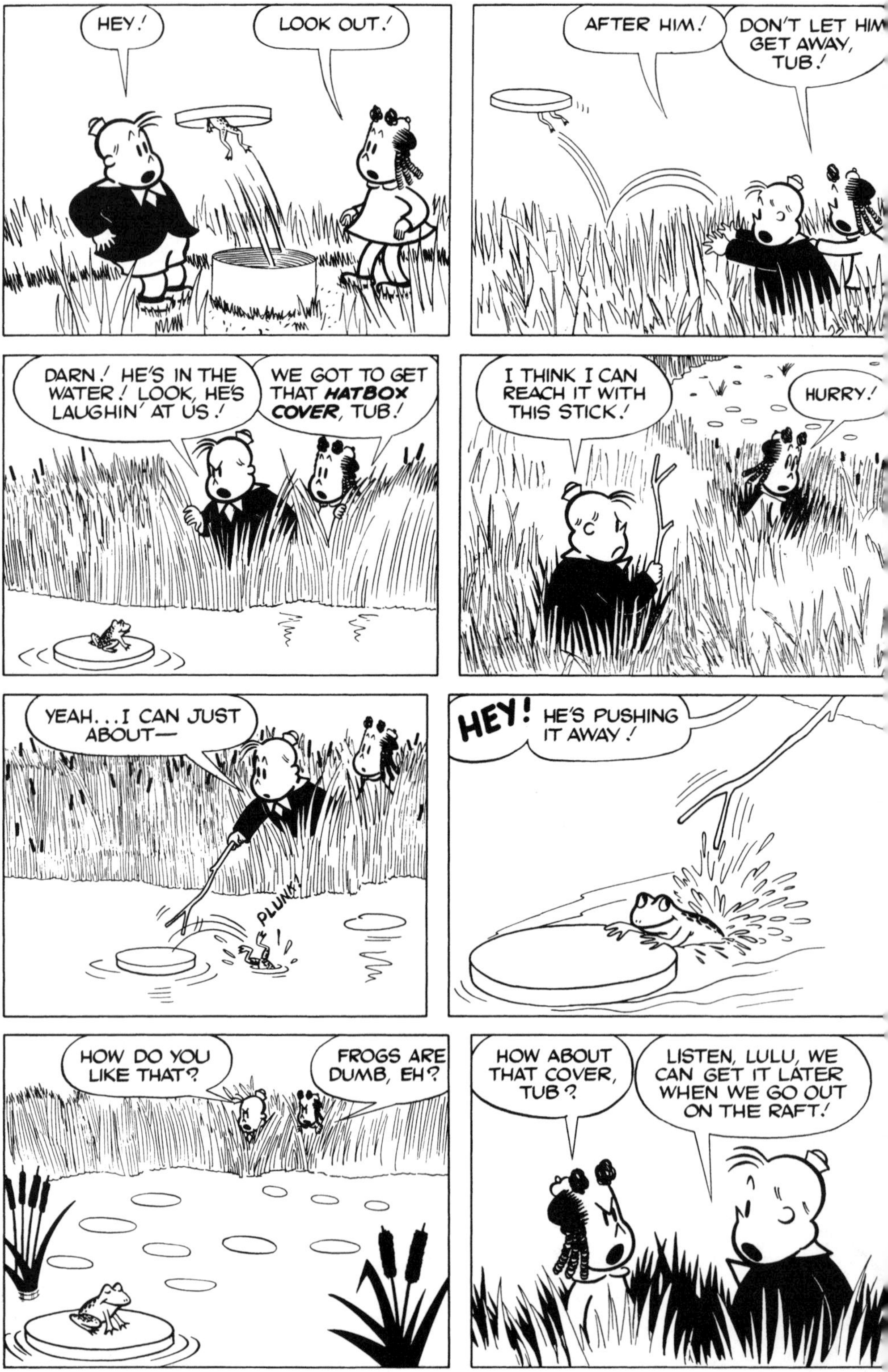
HEY!
LOOK OUT!
AFTER HIM!
DON'T LET HIM GET AWAY, TUB!
DARN! HE'S IN THE WATER! LOOK, HE'S LAUGHIN' AT US!
WE GOT TO GET THAT **HATBOX COVER**, TUB!
I THINK I CAN REACH IT WITH THIS STICK!
HURRY!
YEAH...I CAN JUST ABOUT—
PLUNK!
HEY! HE'S PUSHING IT AWAY!
HOW DO YOU LIKE THAT?
FROGS ARE DUMB, EH?
HOW ABOUT THAT COVER, TUB?
LISTEN, LULU, WE CAN GET IT LATER WHEN WE GO OUT ON THE RAFT!

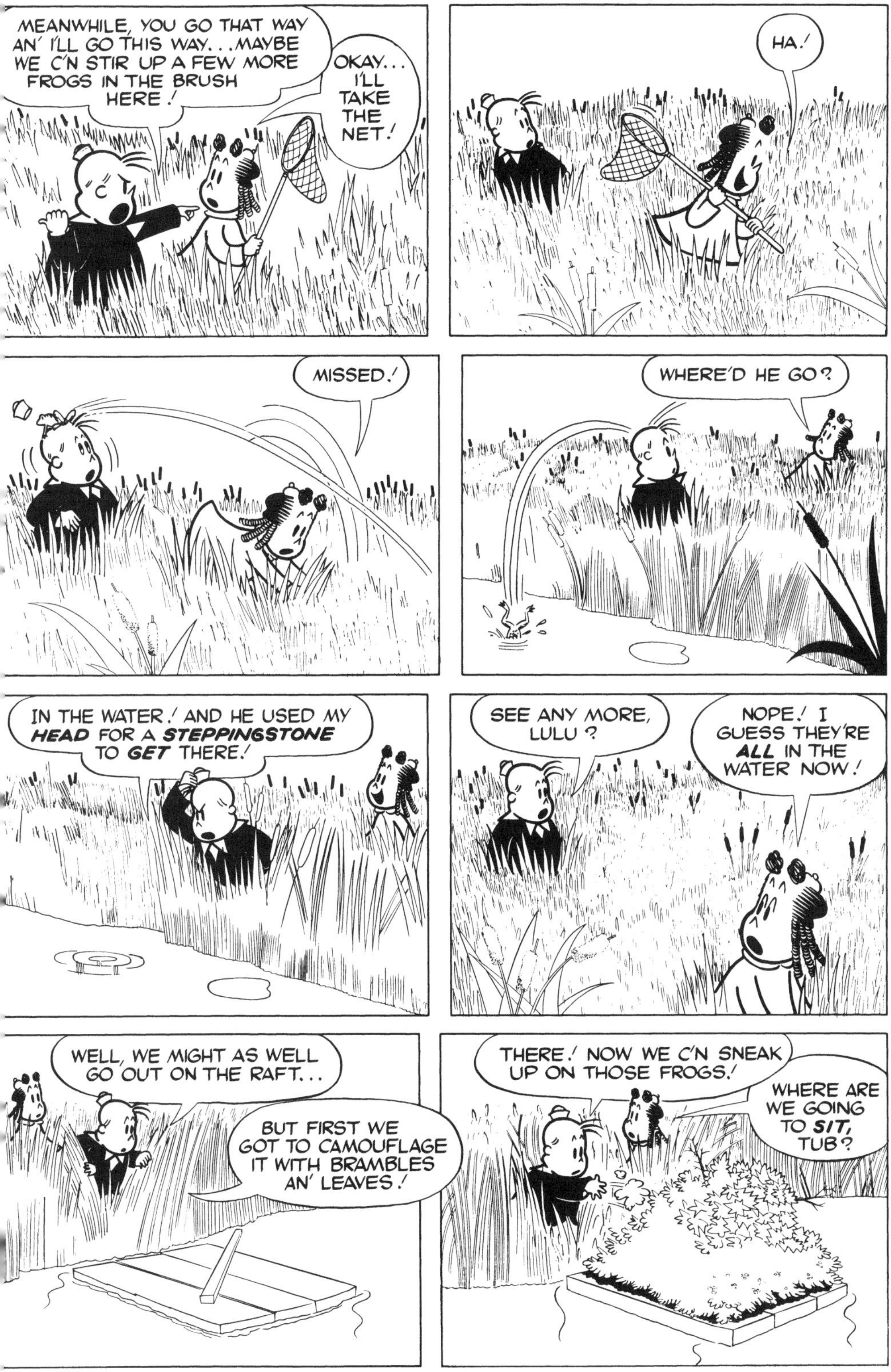
MEANWHILE, YOU GO THAT WAY AN' I'LL GO THIS WAY. . . MAYBE WE C'N STIR UP A FEW MORE FROGS IN THE BRUSH HERE!
OKAY. . . I'LL TAKE THE NET!
HA!
MISSED!
WHERE'D HE GO?
IN THE WATER! AND HE USED MY **HEAD** FOR A **STEPPINGSTONE** TO **GET** THERE!
SEE ANY MORE, LULU?
NOPE! I GUESS THEY'RE **ALL** IN THE WATER NOW!
WELL, WE MIGHT AS WELL GO OUT ON THE RAFT. . .
BUT FIRST WE GOT TO CAMOUFLAGE IT WITH BRAMBLES AN' LEAVES!
THERE! NOW WE C'N SNEAK UP ON THOSE FROGS!
WHERE ARE WE GOING TO **SIT,** TUB?

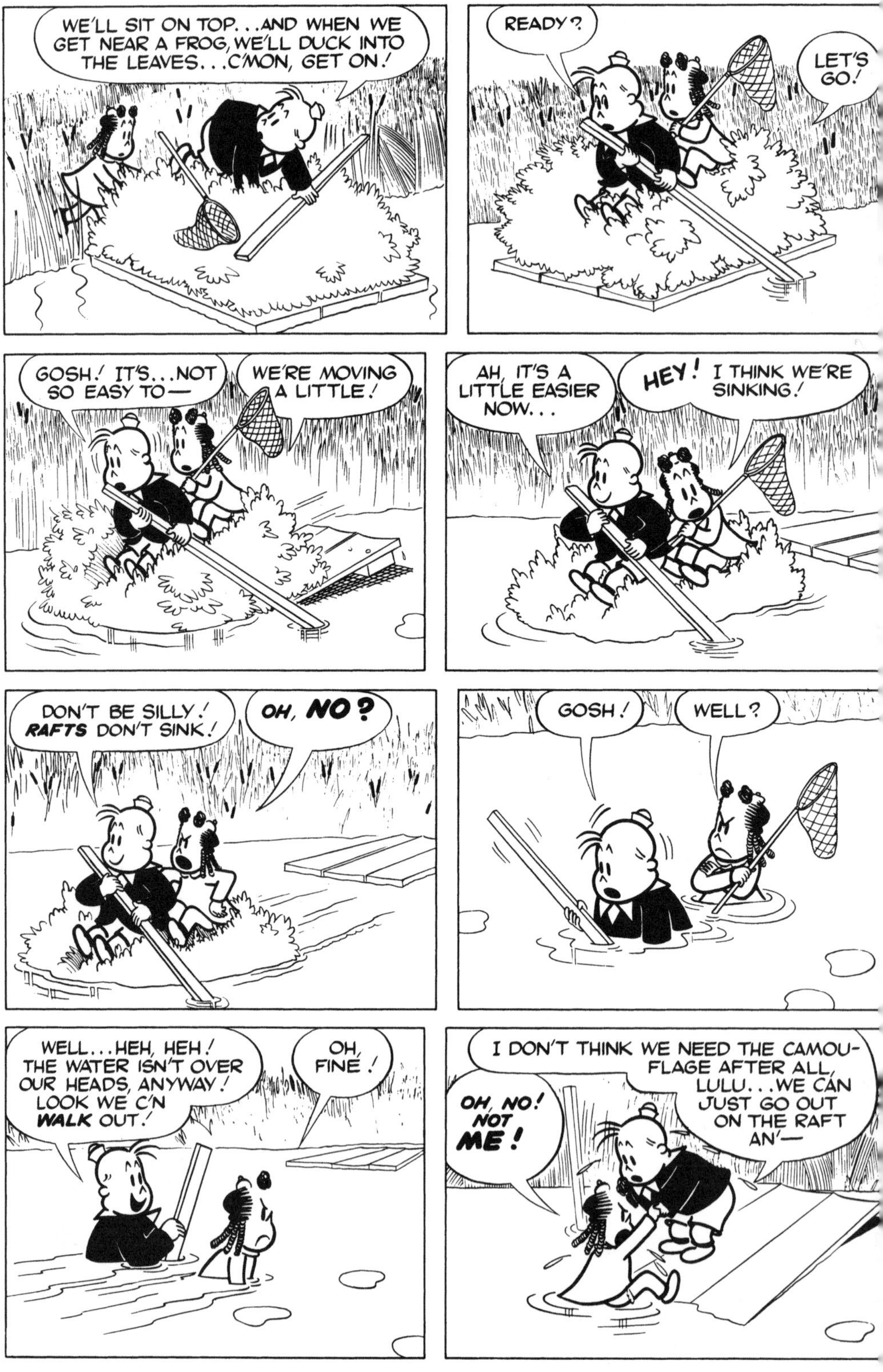

WE'LL SIT ON TOP...AND WHEN WE GET NEAR A FROG, WE'LL DUCK INTO THE LEAVES...C'MON, GET ON!
READY?
LET'S GO!
GOSH! IT'S...NOT SO EASY TO—
WE'RE MOVING A LITTLE!
AH, IT'S A LITTLE EASIER NOW...
HEY! I THINK WE'RE SINKING!
DON'T BE SILLY! RAFTS DON'T SINK!
OH, NO?
GOSH!
WELL?
WELL...HEH, HEH! THE WATER ISN'T OVER OUR HEADS, ANYWAY! LOOK WE C'N WALK OUT!
OH, FINE!
I DON'T THINK WE NEED THE CAMOUFLAGE AFTER ALL, LULU...WE CAN JUST GO OUT ON THE RAFT AN'—
OH, NO! NOT ME!

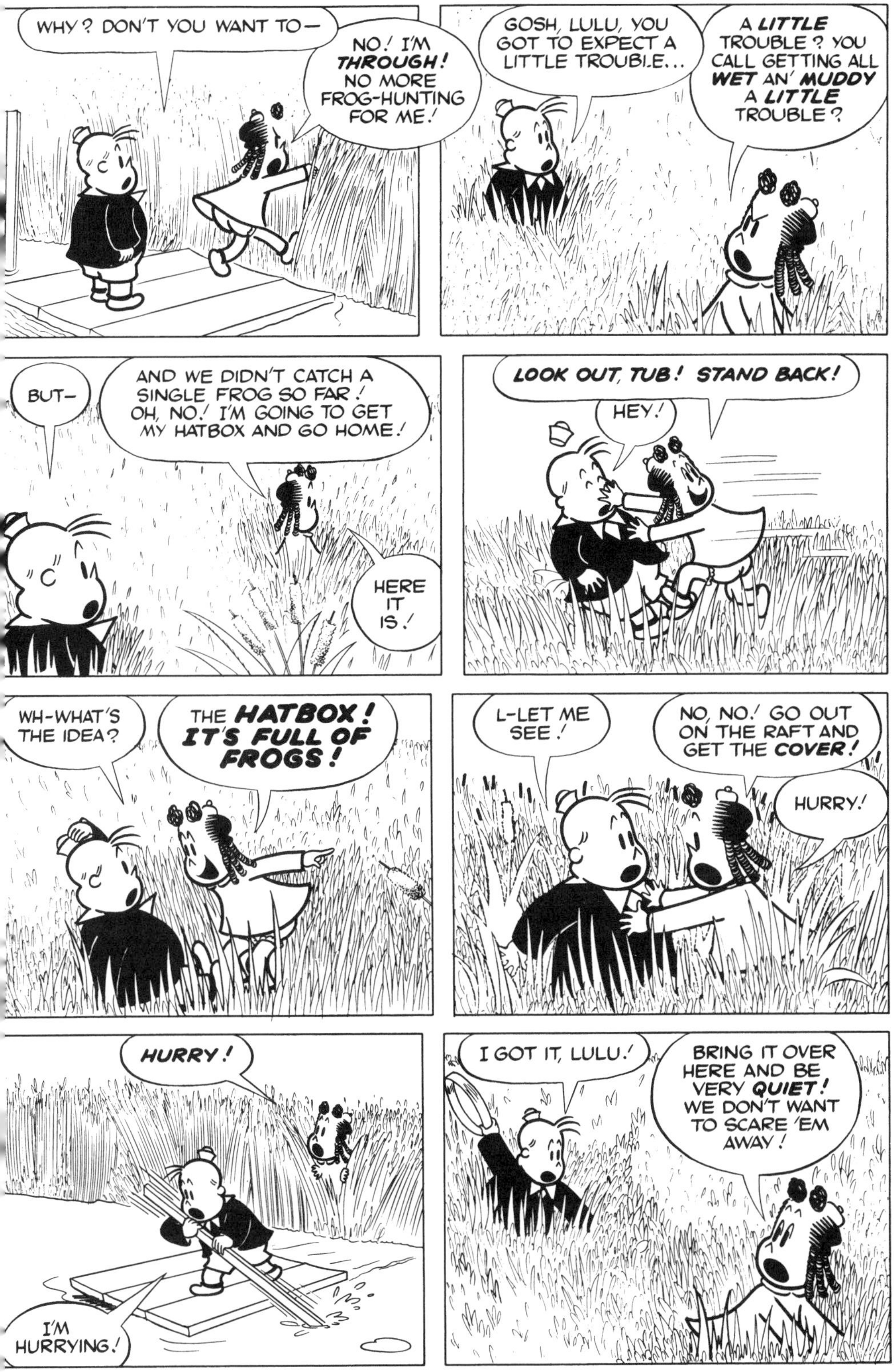
WHY? DON'T YOU WANT TO—
NO! I'M **THROUGH!** NO MORE FROG-HUNTING FOR ME!
GOSH, LULU, YOU GOT TO EXPECT A LITTLE TROUBLE...
A **LITTLE** TROUBLE? YOU CALL GETTING ALL **WET** AN' **MUDDY** A **LITTLE** TROUBLE?
BUT—
AND WE DIDN'T CATCH A SINGLE FROG SO FAR! OH, NO! I'M GOING TO GET MY HATBOX AND GO HOME!
HERE IT IS!
LOOK OUT, TUB! STAND BACK!
HEY!
WH-WHAT'S THE IDEA?
THE **HATBOX! IT'S FULL OF FROGS!**
L-LET ME SEE!
NO, NO! GO OUT ON THE RAFT AND GET THE **COVER!**
HURRY!
HURRY!
I'M HURRYING!
I GOT IT, LULU!
BRING IT OVER HERE AND BE VERY **QUIET!** WE DON'T WANT TO SCARE 'EM AWAY!

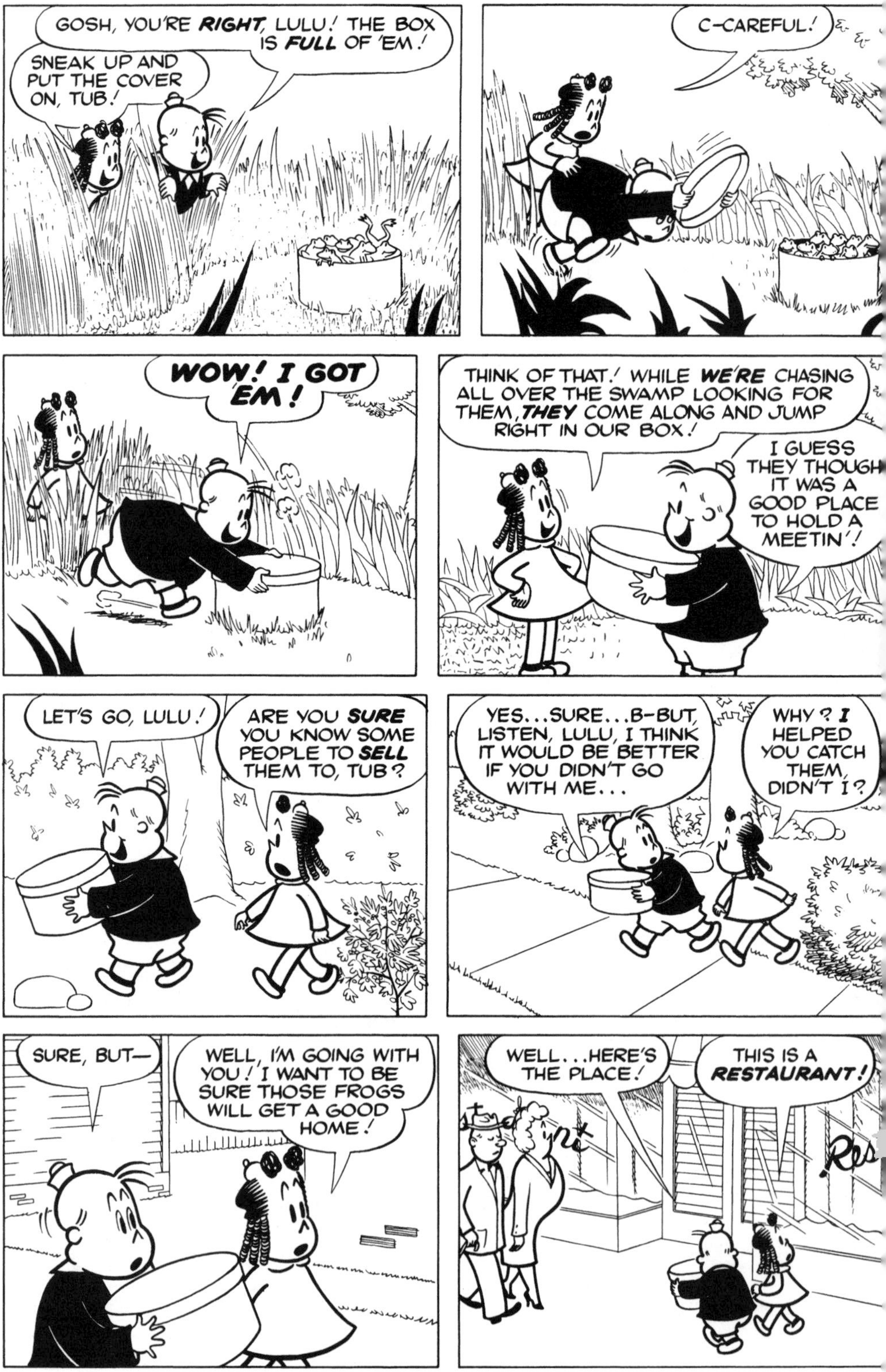
GOSH, YOU'RE RIGHT, LULU! THE BOX IS FULL OF 'EM!
SNEAK UP AND PUT THE COVER ON, TUB!
C-CAREFUL!
WOW! I GOT 'EM!
THINK OF THAT! WHILE WE'RE CHASING ALL OVER THE SWAMP LOOKING FOR THEM, THEY COME ALONG AND JUMP RIGHT IN OUR BOX!
I GUESS THEY THOUGH IT WAS A GOOD PLACE TO HOLD A MEETIN'!
LET'S GO, LULU!
ARE YOU SURE YOU KNOW SOME PEOPLE TO SELL THEM TO, TUB?
YES...SURE...B-BUT, LISTEN, LULU, I THINK IT WOULD BE BETTER IF YOU DIDN'T GO WITH ME...
WHY? I HELPED YOU CATCH THEM, DIDN'T I?
SURE, BUT—
WELL, I'M GOING WITH YOU! I WANT TO BE SURE THOSE FROGS WILL GET A GOOD HOME!
WELL...HERE'S THE PLACE!
THIS IS A RESTAURANT!

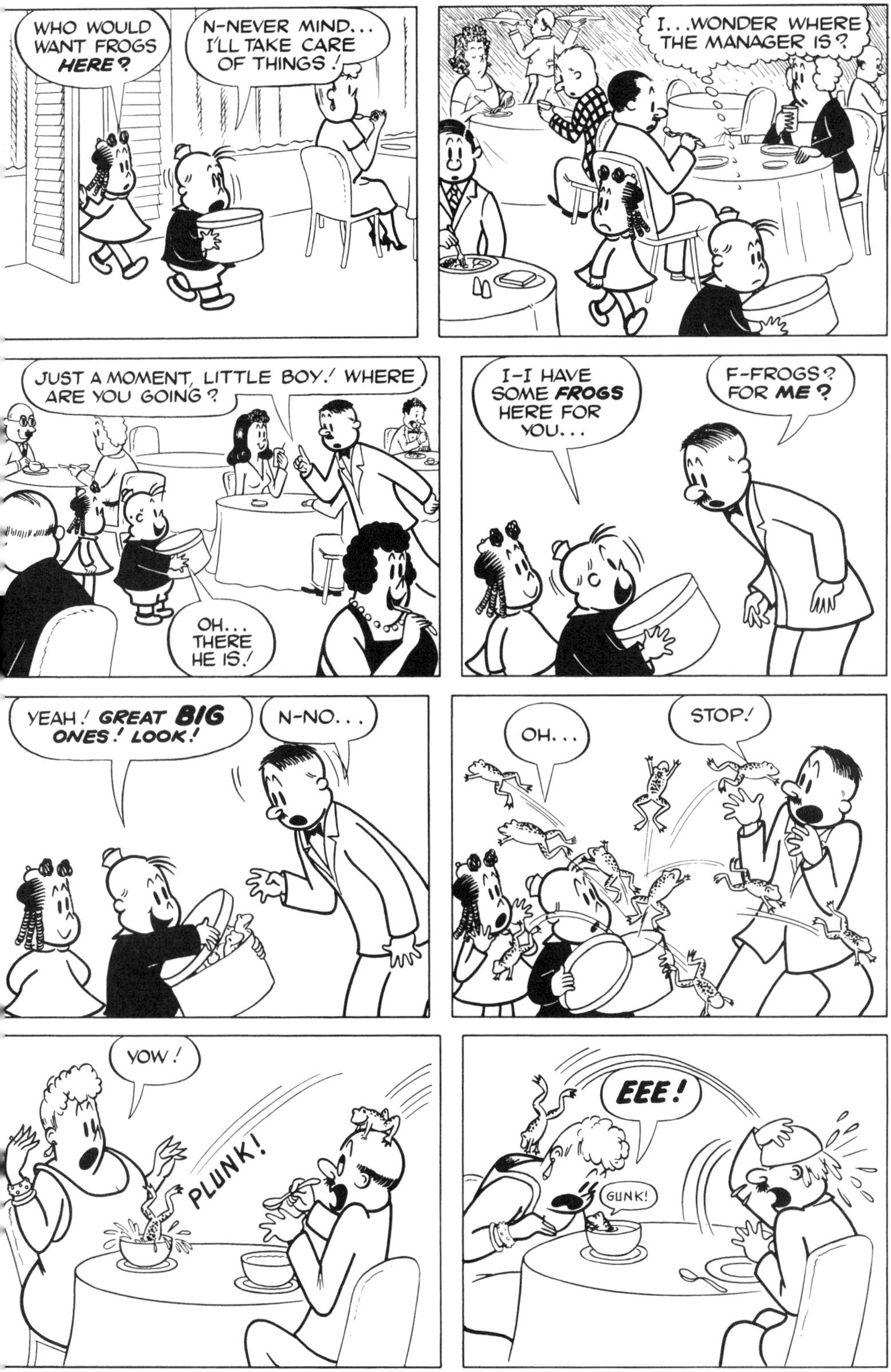
WHO WOULD WANT FROGS HERE?
N-NEVER MIND... I'LL TAKE CARE OF THINGS!
I...WONDER WHERE THE MANAGER IS?
JUST A MOMENT, LITTLE BOY! WHERE ARE YOU GOING?
OH... THERE HE IS!
I-I HAVE SOME FROGS HERE FOR YOU...
F-FROGS? FOR ME?
YEAH! GREAT BIG ONES! LOOK!
N-NO...
OH...
STOP!
YOW!
PLUNK!
EEE!
GUNK!

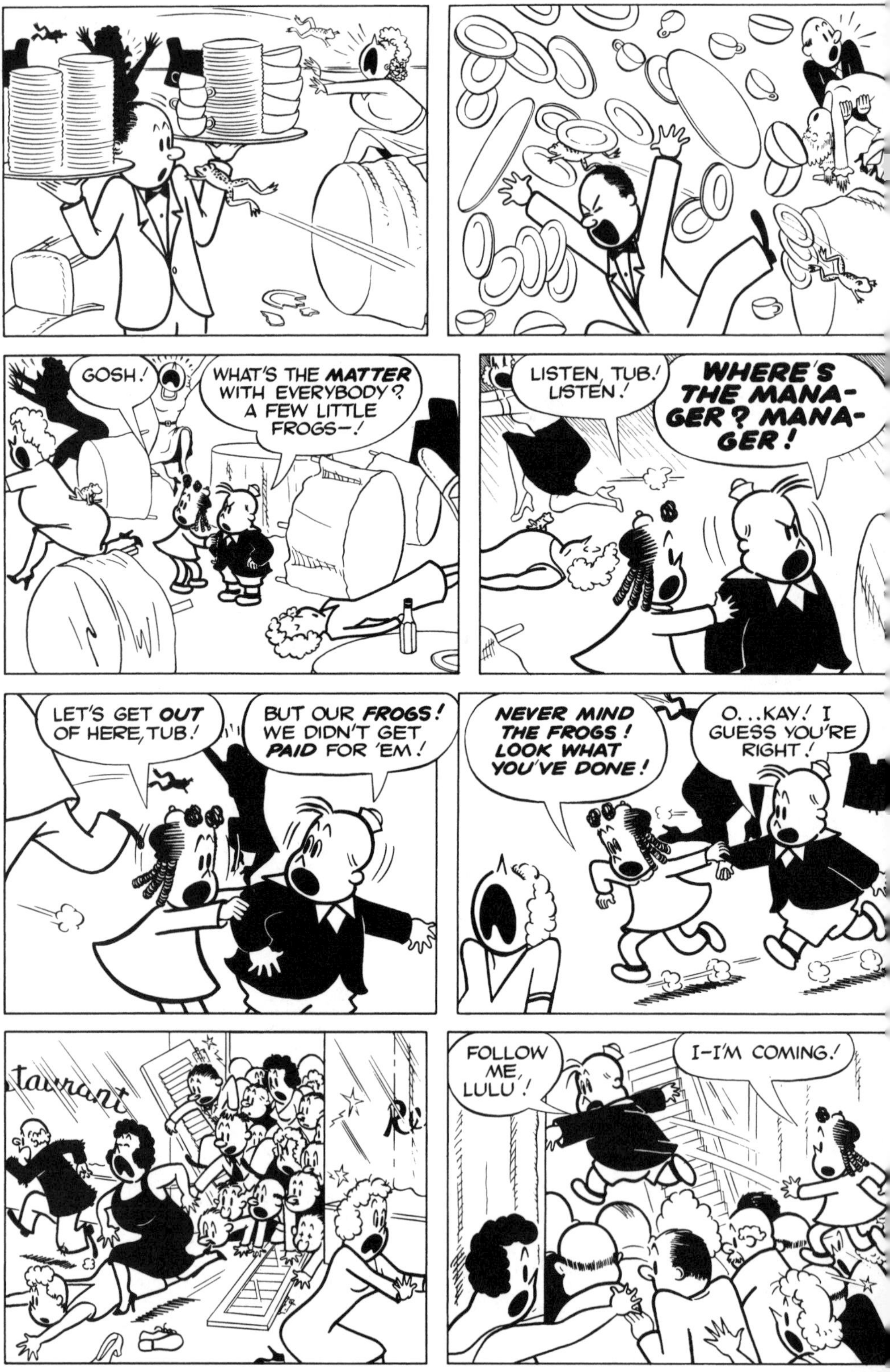
GOSH!
WHAT'S THE MATTER WITH EVERYBODY? A FEW LITTLE FROGS-!
LISTEN, TUB! LISTEN!
WHERE'S THE MANAGER? MANAGER!
LET'S GET OUT OF HERE, TUB!
BUT OUR FROGS! WE DIDN'T GET PAID FOR 'EM!
NEVER MIND THE FROGS! LOOK WHAT YOU'VE DONE!
O...KAY! I GUESS YOU'RE RIGHT!
FOLLOW ME, LULU!
I-I'M COMING!

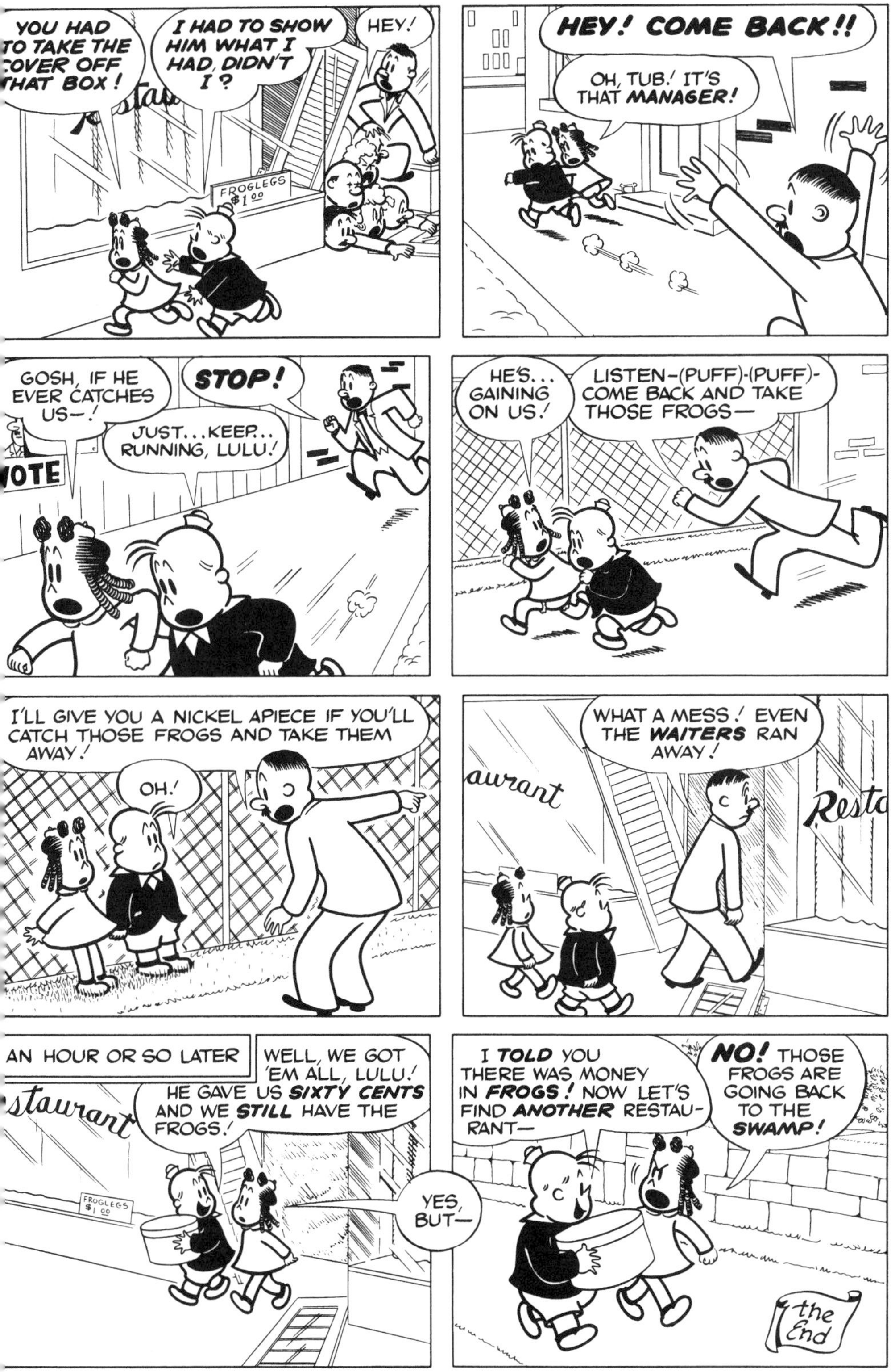
YOU HAD TO TAKE THE COVER OFF THAT BOX!
I HAD TO SHOW HIM WHAT I HAD, DIDN'T I?
HEY!
FROGLEGS $1.00
HEY! COME BACK!!
OH, TUB! IT'S THAT MANAGER!
GOSH, IF HE EVER CATCHES US—!
STOP!
JUST...KEEP...RUNNING, LULU!
HE'S... GAINING ON US!
LISTEN—(PUFF)-(PUFF)-COME BACK AND TAKE THOSE FROGS—
I'LL GIVE YOU A NICKEL APIECE IF YOU'LL CATCH THOSE FROGS AND TAKE THEM AWAY!
OH!
WHAT A MESS! EVEN THE WAITERS RAN AWAY!
AN HOUR OR SO LATER
WELL, WE GOT 'EM ALL, LULU! HE GAVE US SIXTY CENTS AND WE STILL HAVE THE FROGS!
FROGLEGS $1.00
YES, BUT—
I TOLD YOU THERE WAS MONEY IN FROGS! NOW LET'S FIND ANOTHER RESTAU-RANT—
NO! THOSE FROGS ARE GOING BACK TO THE SWAMP!
the End

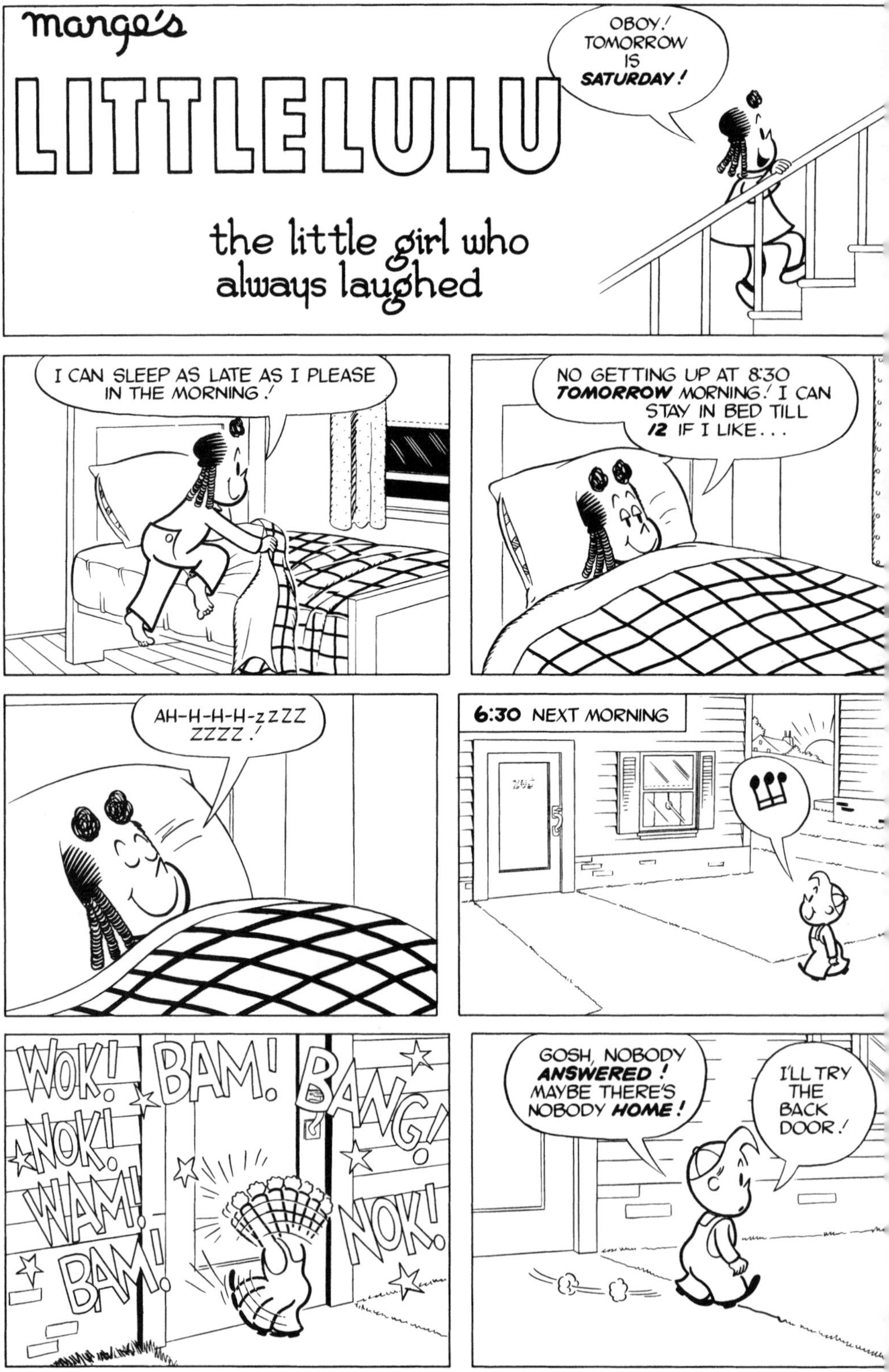
marge's
LITTLE LULU
OBOY! TOMORROW IS SATURDAY!
the little girl who always laughed
I CAN SLEEP AS LATE AS I PLEASE IN THE MORNING!
NO GETTING UP AT 8:30 TOMORROW MORNING! I CAN STAY IN BED TILL 12 IF I LIKE...
AH-H-H-H-zZZZ ZZZZ!
6:30 NEXT MORNING
WOK! BAM! BANG! NOK! WAM! BAM! NOK!
GOSH, NOBODY ANSWERED! MAYBE THERE'S NOBODY HOME!
I'LL TRY THE BACK DOOR!

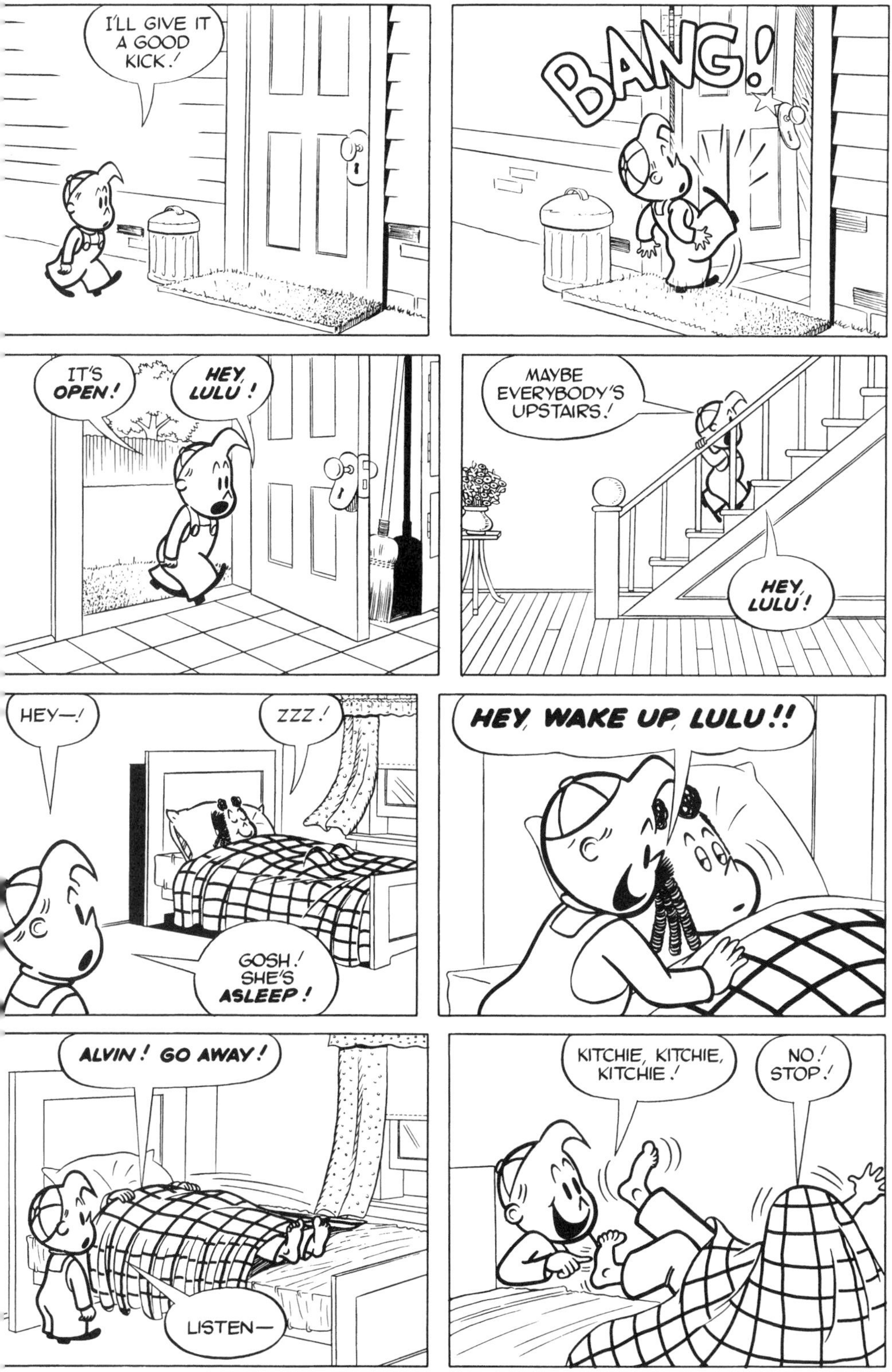
I'LL GIVE IT A GOOD KICK.!
BANG!
IT'S OPEN!
HEY, LULU!
MAYBE EVERYBODY'S UPSTAIRS!
HEY, LULU!
HEY—!
ZZZ!
GOSH! SHE'S ASLEEP!
HEY, WAKE UP, LULU!!
ALVIN! GO AWAY!
LISTEN—
KITCHIE, KITCHIE, KITCHIE!
NO! STOP!

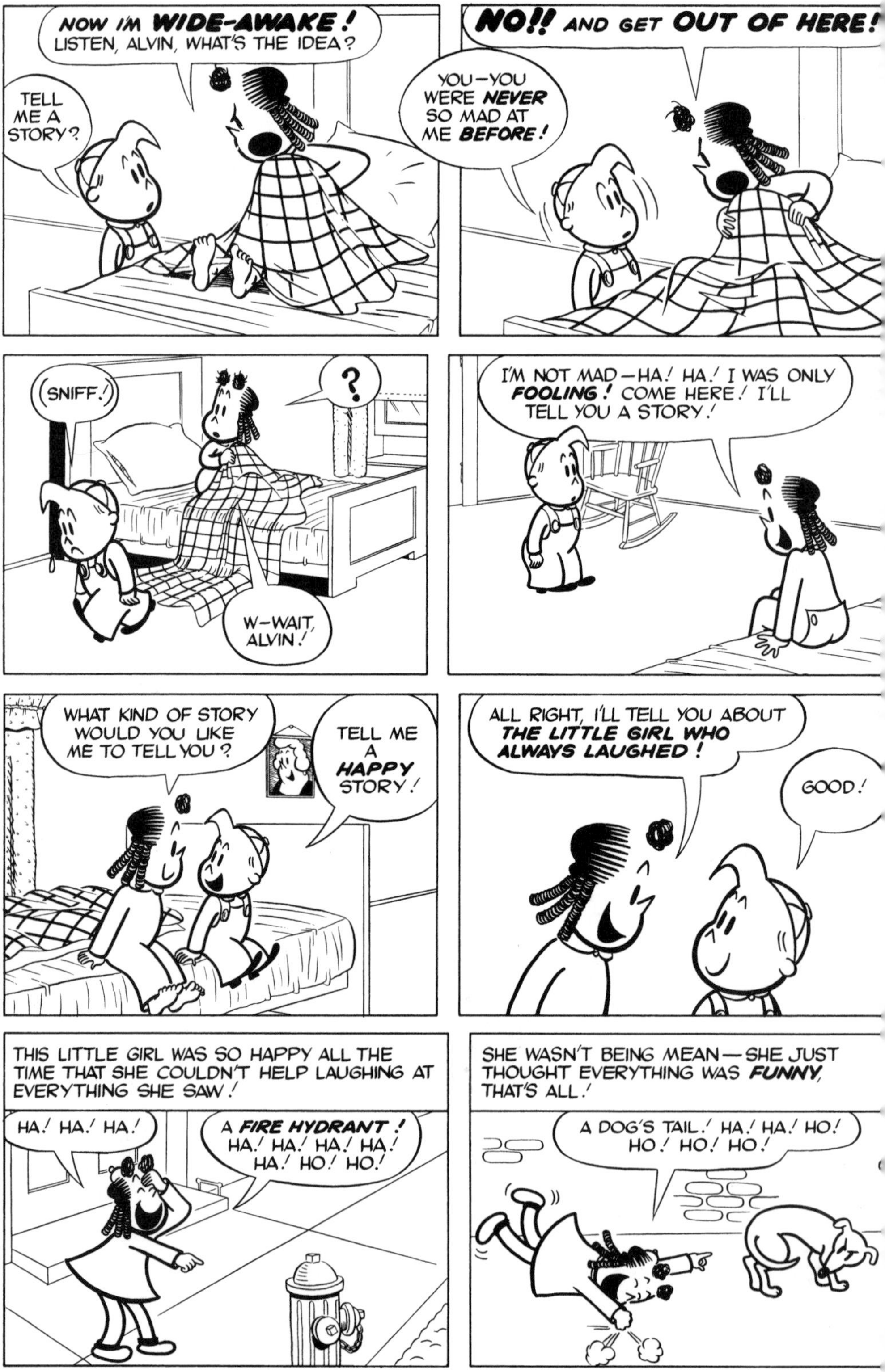
NOW I'M WIDE-AWAKE! LISTEN, ALVIN, WHAT'S THE IDEA?
TELL ME A STORY?
NO!! AND GET OUT OF HERE!
YOU—YOU WERE NEVER SO MAD AT ME BEFORE!
(SNIFF!)
?
W-WAIT, ALVIN!
I'M NOT MAD—HA! HA! I WAS ONLY FOOLING! COME HERE! I'LL TELL YOU A STORY!
WHAT KIND OF STORY WOULD YOU LIKE ME TO TELL YOU?
TELL ME A HAPPY STORY!
ALL RIGHT, I'LL TELL YOU ABOUT THE LITTLE GIRL WHO ALWAYS LAUGHED!
GOOD!
THIS LITTLE GIRL WAS SO HAPPY ALL THE TIME THAT SHE COULDN'T HELP LAUGHING AT EVERYTHING SHE SAW!
HA! HA! HA!
A FIRE HYDRANT! HA! HA! HA! HA! HA! HO! HO!
SHE WASN'T BEING MEAN—SHE JUST THOUGHT EVERYTHING WAS FUNNY, THAT'S ALL!
A DOG'S TAIL! HA! HA! HO! HO! HO! HO!

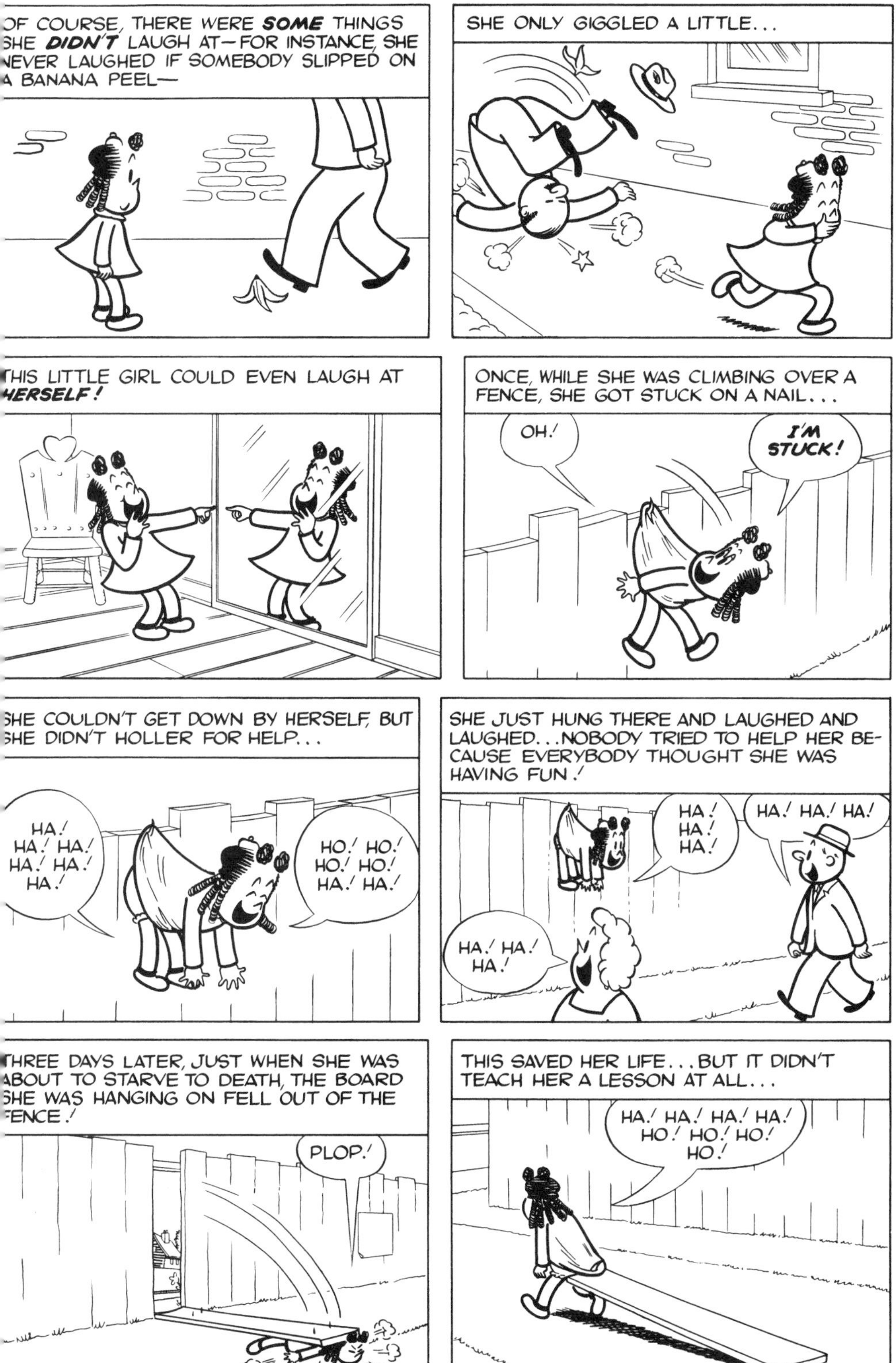
OF COURSE, THERE WERE SOME THINGS SHE DIDN'T LAUGH AT—FOR INSTANCE, SHE NEVER LAUGHED IF SOMEBODY SLIPPED ON A BANANA PEEL—
SHE ONLY GIGGLED A LITTLE...
THIS LITTLE GIRL COULD EVEN LAUGH AT HERSELF!
ONCE, WHILE SHE WAS CLIMBING OVER A FENCE, SHE GOT STUCK ON A NAIL...
OH!
I'M STUCK!
SHE COULDN'T GET DOWN BY HERSELF, BUT SHE DIDN'T HOLLER FOR HELP...
HA! HA! HA! HA! HA! HA! HA!
HO! HO! HO! HO! HA! HA!
SHE JUST HUNG THERE AND LAUGHED AND LAUGHED...NOBODY TRIED TO HELP HER BECAUSE EVERYBODY THOUGHT SHE WAS HAVING FUN!
HA! HA! HA!
HA! HA! HA!
HA! HA! HA!
THREE DAYS LATER, JUST WHEN SHE WAS ABOUT TO STARVE TO DEATH, THE BOARD SHE WAS HANGING ON FELL OUT OF THE FENCE!
PLOP!
THIS SAVED HER LIFE...BUT IT DIDN'T TEACH HER A LESSON AT ALL...
HA! HA! HA! HA! HO! HO! HO! HO!

SHE JUST WENT RIGHT ON LAUGHING AT EVERYTHING AND EVERYBODY INCLUDING HERSELF!

WELL, ONE DAY IT WAS ANNOUNCED IN ALL THE NEWSPAPERS THAT THE KING WAS GOING TO MARCH IN A BIG PARADE DOWN THE MAIN STREET!

GOSH! THE *KING HIMSELF!*

DID YOU READ IT? WE'RE GOING TO SEE THE *KING!*

EVERYBODY WAS *VERY* EXCITED BECAUSE, BELIEVE IT OR NOT, *NOBODY* HAD *EVER* SEEN THE KING BEFORE!

I WONDER WHAT HE *LOOKS* LIKE?

I'M *DYING* TO SEE HIM!

I'M *SURE* HE'S VERY HANDSOME!

FOR YEARS THE PEOPLE WONDERED WHY THE KING NEVER SHOWED HIMSELF TO ANYONE, AND NOBODY WAS EVER ALLOWED TO ENTER THE GREAT CASTLE IN THE MIDDLE OF THE CITY!

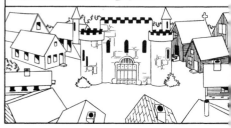

EVEN THE *SERVANTS* IN THE *CASTLE* HAD NEVER SEEN HIM!

THE KING'S TEA...TAKE IT UP TO HIM AT ONCE!

YES, SIR!

WHEN SOMETHING HAD TO BE TAKEN TO THE KING, THE SERVANT ALWAYS ENTERED THE ROOM BACKWARDS!

YOUR TEA, SIR!

COME IN! COME IN!

KNOCK!
KNOCK!

IF A SERVANT SO MUCH AS STOLE A LOOK AT THE KING, THE PUNISHMENT WAS DEATH!

PUT IT DOWN OVER HERE!

THE REASON FOR ALL THIS WAS BECAUSE THE KING HAD THE BIGGEST *NOSE* YOU EVER SAW...

WHAT A BUGLE!

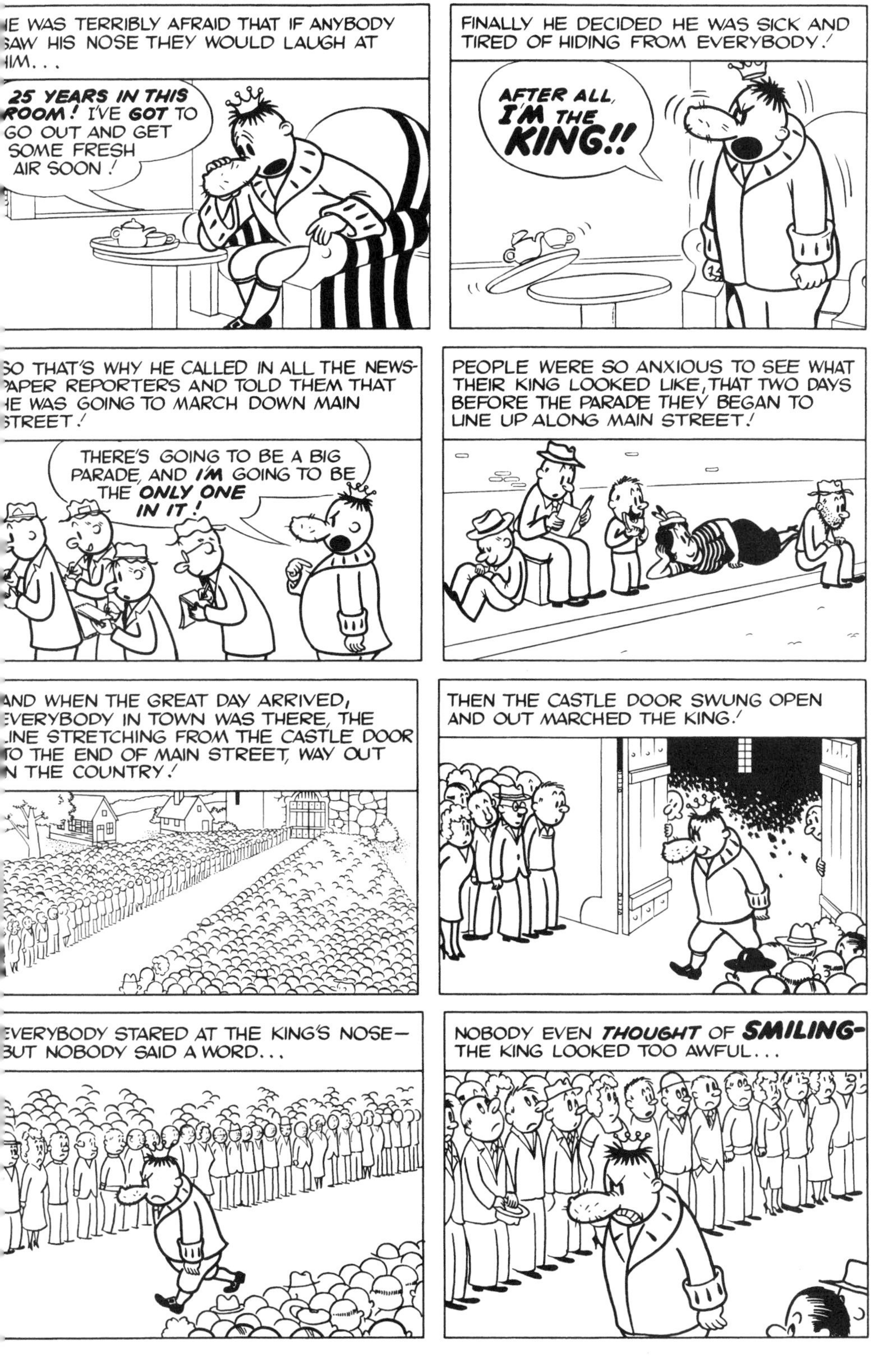

IE WAS TERRIBLY AFRAID THAT IF ANYBODY SAW HIS NOSE THEY WOULD LAUGH AT IM...
25 YEARS IN THIS ROOM! I'VE GOT TO GO OUT AND GET SOME FRESH AIR SOON!
FINALLY HE DECIDED HE WAS SICK AND TIRED OF HIDING FROM EVERYBODY!
AFTER ALL, I'M THE KING!!
SO THAT'S WHY HE CALLED IN ALL THE NEWS-PAPER REPORTERS AND TOLD THEM THAT IE WAS GOING TO MARCH DOWN MAIN STREET!
THERE'S GOING TO BE A BIG PARADE, AND I'M GOING TO BE THE ONLY ONE IN IT!
PEOPLE WERE SO ANXIOUS TO SEE WHAT THEIR KING LOOKED LIKE, THAT TWO DAYS BEFORE THE PARADE THEY BEGAN TO LINE UP ALONG MAIN STREET!
AND WHEN THE GREAT DAY ARRIVED, EVERYBODY IN TOWN WAS THERE, THE LINE STRETCHING FROM THE CASTLE DOOR TO THE END OF MAIN STREET, WAY OUT N THE COUNTRY!
THEN THE CASTLE DOOR SWUNG OPEN AND OUT MARCHED THE KING!
EVERYBODY STARED AT THE KING'S NOSE— BUT NOBODY SAID A WORD...
NOBODY EVEN THOUGHT OF SMILING- THE KING LOOKED TOO AWFUL...

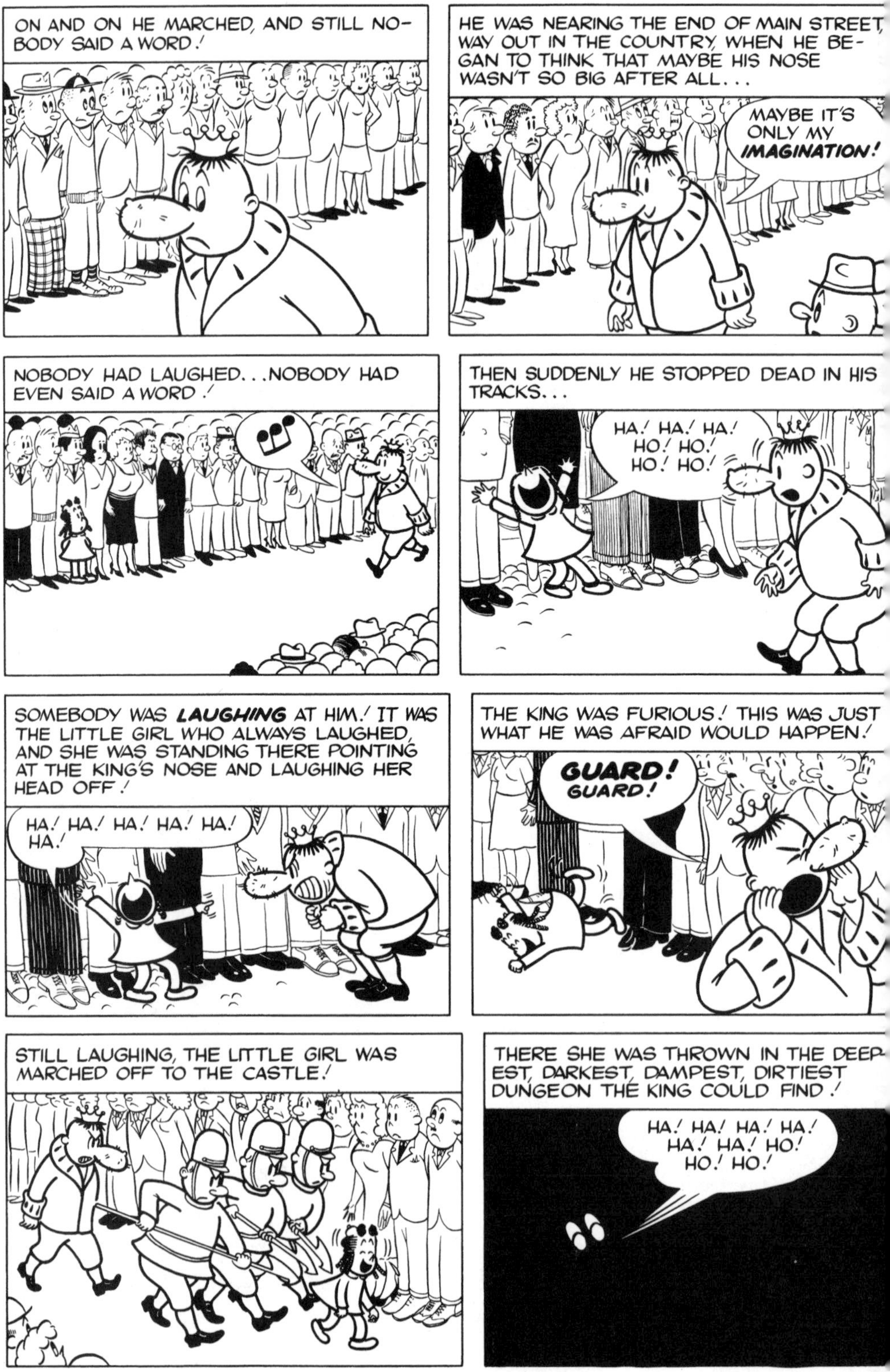
ON AND ON HE MARCHED, AND STILL NOBODY SAID A WORD!
HE WAS NEARING THE END OF MAIN STREET, WAY OUT IN THE COUNTRY, WHEN HE BEGAN TO THINK THAT MAYBE HIS NOSE WASN'T SO BIG AFTER ALL...
MAYBE IT'S ONLY MY IMAGINATION!
NOBODY HAD LAUGHED...NOBODY HAD EVEN SAID A WORD!
THEN SUDDENLY HE STOPPED DEAD IN HIS TRACKS...
HA! HA! HA! HO! HO! HO! HO!
SOMEBODY WAS LAUGHING AT HIM! IT WAS THE LITTLE GIRL WHO ALWAYS LAUGHED, AND SHE WAS STANDING THERE POINTING AT THE KING'S NOSE AND LAUGHING HER HEAD OFF!
HA! HA! HA! HA! HA! HA!
THE KING WAS FURIOUS! THIS WAS JUST WHAT HE WAS AFRAID WOULD HAPPEN!
GUARD! GUARD!
STILL LAUGHING, THE LITTLE GIRL WAS MARCHED OFF TO THE CASTLE!
THERE SHE WAS THROWN IN THE DEEPEST, DARKEST, DAMPEST, DIRTIEST DUNGEON THE KING COULD FIND!
HA! HA! HA! HA! HA! HA! HO! HO! HO!

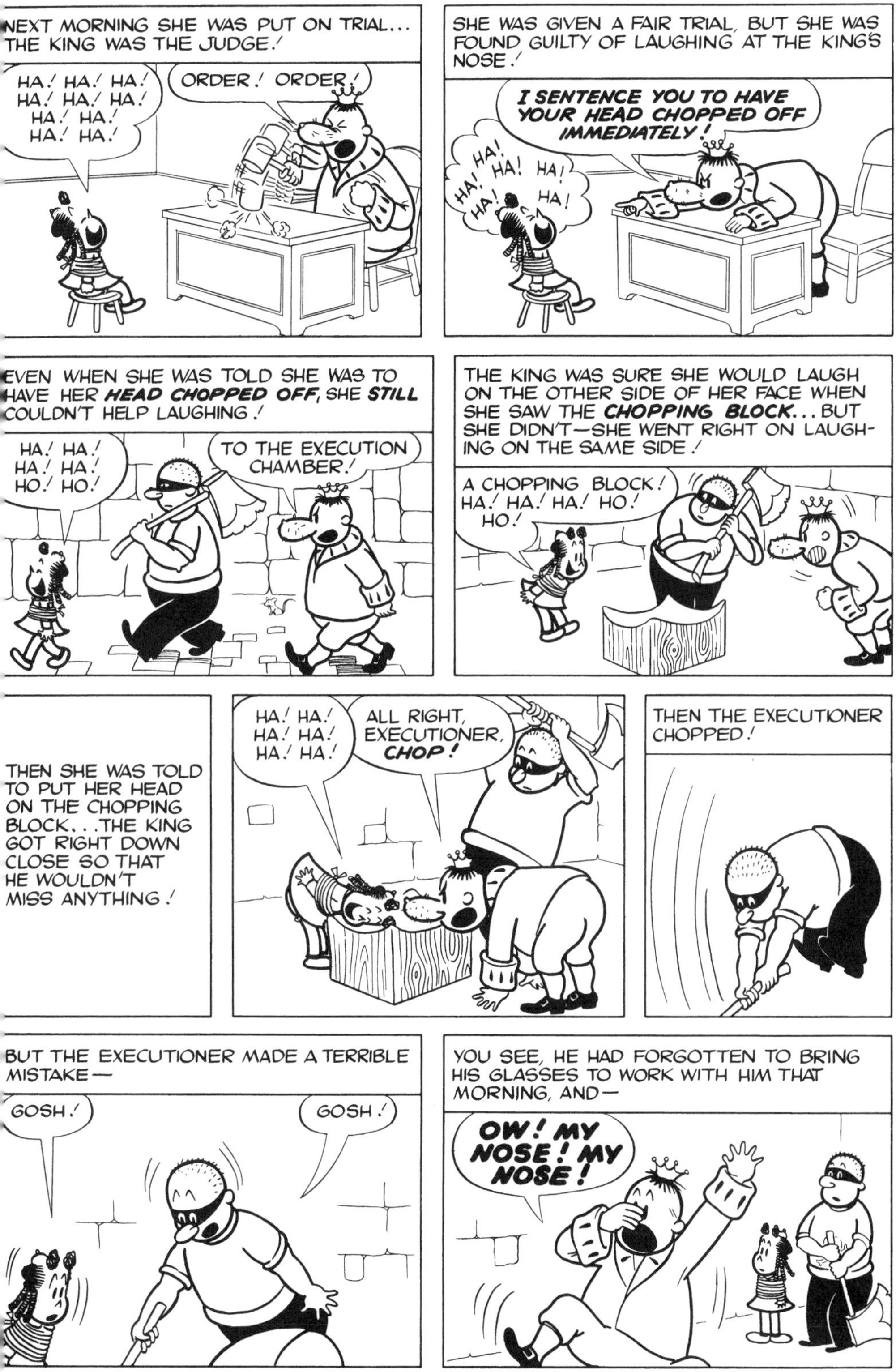
NEXT MORNING SHE WAS PUT ON TRIAL... THE KING WAS THE JUDGE!
HA! HA! HA! HA! HA! HA! HA! HA! HA! HA!
ORDER! ORDER!
SHE WAS GIVEN A FAIR TRIAL, BUT SHE WAS FOUND GUILTY OF LAUGHING AT THE KING'S NOSE!
I SENTENCE YOU TO HAVE YOUR HEAD CHOPPED OFF IMMEDIATELY!
HA! HA! HA! HA! HA! HA!
EVEN WHEN SHE WAS TOLD SHE WAS TO HAVE HER HEAD CHOPPED OFF, SHE STILL COULDN'T HELP LAUGHING!
HA! HA! HA! HA! HO! HO!
TO THE EXECUTION CHAMBER!
THE KING WAS SURE SHE WOULD LAUGH ON THE OTHER SIDE OF HER FACE WHEN SHE SAW THE CHOPPING BLOCK... BUT SHE DIDN'T—SHE WENT RIGHT ON LAUGHING ON THE SAME SIDE!
A CHOPPING BLOCK! HA! HA! HA! HO! HO!
THEN SHE WAS TOLD TO PUT HER HEAD ON THE CHOPPING BLOCK... THE KING GOT RIGHT DOWN CLOSE SO THAT HE WOULDN'T MISS ANYTHING!
HA! HA! HA! HA! HA! HA!
ALL RIGHT, EXECUTIONER, CHOP!
THEN THE EXECUTIONER CHOPPED!
BUT THE EXECUTIONER MADE A TERRIBLE MISTAKE—
GOSH!
GOSH!
YOU SEE, HE HAD FORGOTTEN TO BRING HIS GLASSES TO WORK WITH HIM THAT MORNING, AND—
OW! MY NOSE! MY NOSE!

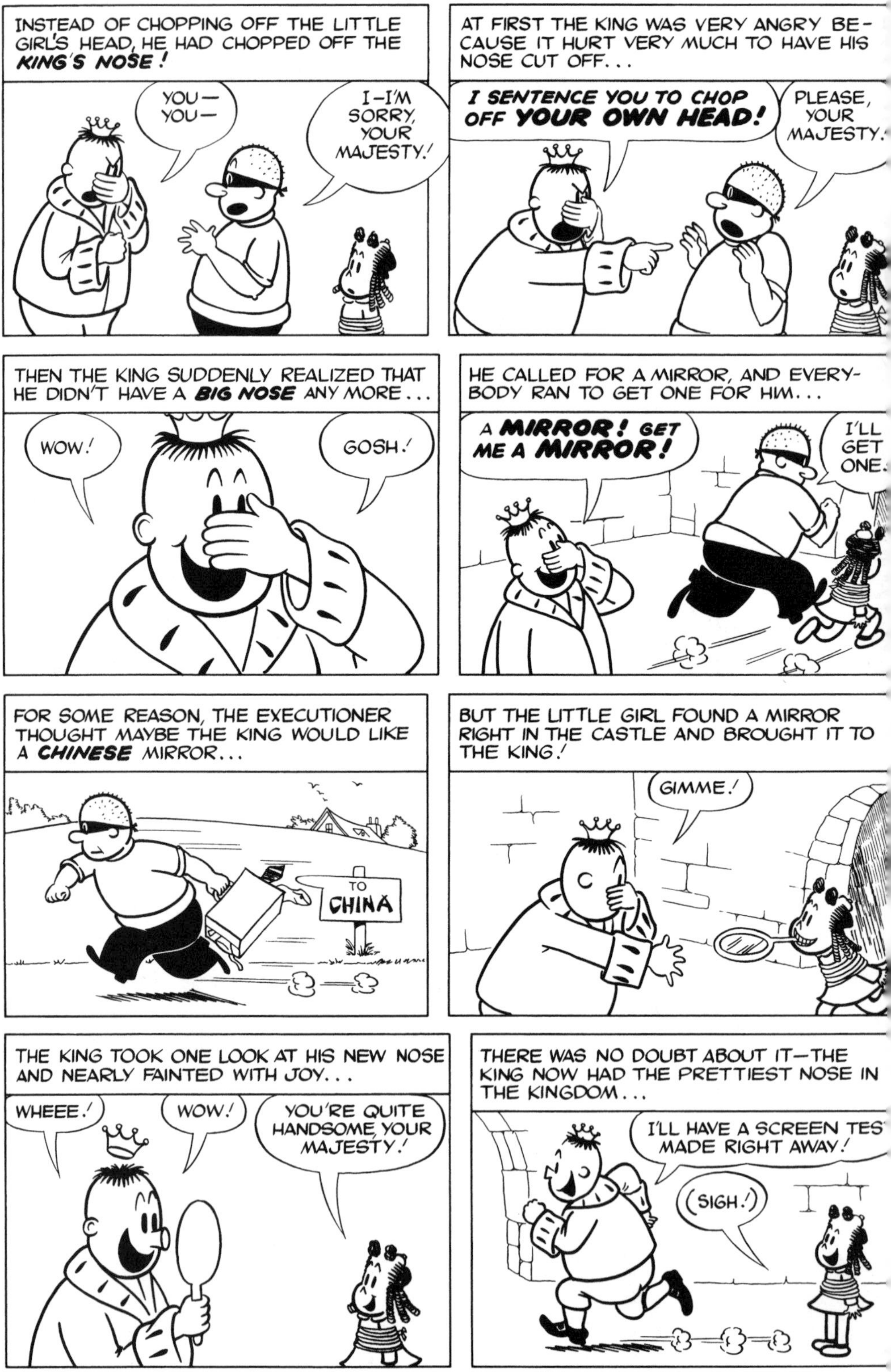
INSTEAD OF CHOPPING OFF THE LITTLE GIRL'S HEAD, HE HAD CHOPPED OFF THE KING'S NOSE!
YOU— YOU—
I-I'M SORRY, YOUR MAJESTY!
AT FIRST THE KING WAS VERY ANGRY BECAUSE IT HURT VERY MUCH TO HAVE HIS NOSE CUT OFF...
I SENTENCE YOU TO CHOP OFF YOUR OWN HEAD!
PLEASE, YOUR MAJESTY!
THEN THE KING SUDDENLY REALIZED THAT HE DIDN'T HAVE A BIG NOSE ANY MORE...
WOW!
GOSH!
HE CALLED FOR A MIRROR, AND EVERYBODY RAN TO GET ONE FOR HIM...
A MIRROR! GET ME A MIRROR!
I'LL GET ONE!
FOR SOME REASON, THE EXECUTIONER THOUGHT MAYBE THE KING WOULD LIKE A CHINESE MIRROR...
TO CHINA
BUT THE LITTLE GIRL FOUND A MIRROR RIGHT IN THE CASTLE AND BROUGHT IT TO THE KING!
GIMME!
THE KING TOOK ONE LOOK AT HIS NEW NOSE AND NEARLY FAINTED WITH JOY...
WHEEE!
WOW!
YOU'RE QUITE HANDSOME, YOUR MAJESTY!
THERE WAS NO DOUBT ABOUT IT—THE KING NOW HAD THE PRETTIEST NOSE IN THE KINGDOM...
I'LL HAVE A SCREEN TES
MADE RIGHT AWAY!
(SIGH!)

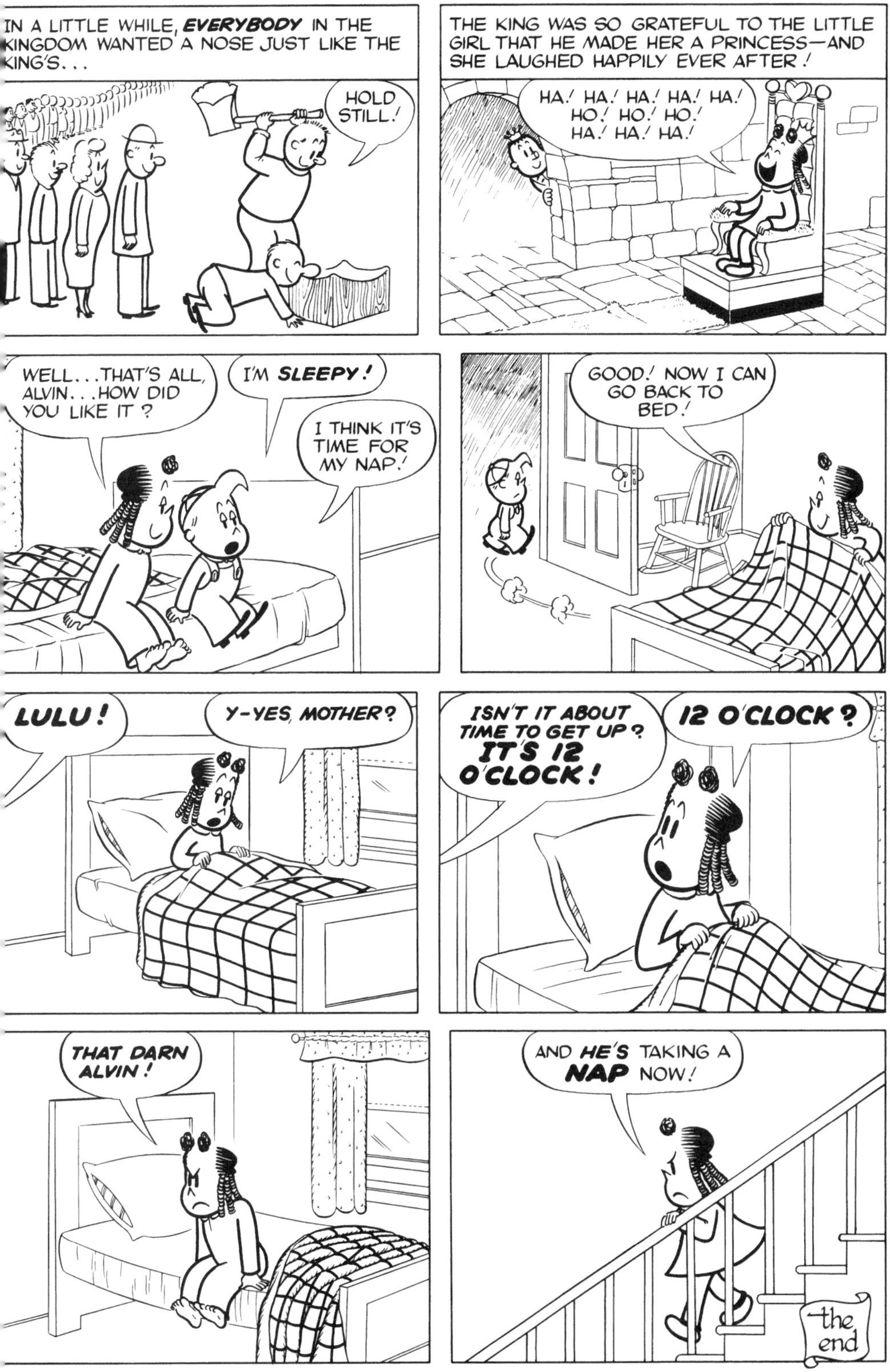
IN A LITTLE WHILE, EVERYBODY IN THE KINGDOM WANTED A NOSE JUST LIKE THE KING'S...
HOLD STILL!
THE KING WAS SO GRATEFUL TO THE LITTLE GIRL THAT HE MADE HER A PRINCESS—AND SHE LAUGHED HAPPILY EVER AFTER!
HA! HA! HA! HA! HA! HO! HO! HO! HA! HA! HA!
WELL...THAT'S ALL, ALVIN...HOW DID YOU LIKE IT?
I'M SLEEPY!
I THINK IT'S TIME FOR MY NAP!
GOOD! NOW I CAN GO BACK TO BED!
LULU!
Y-YES, MOTHER?
ISN'T IT ABOUT TIME TO GET UP? IT'S 12 O'CLOCK!
12 O'CLOCK?
THAT DARN ALVIN!
AND HE'S TAKING A NAP NOW!
the end

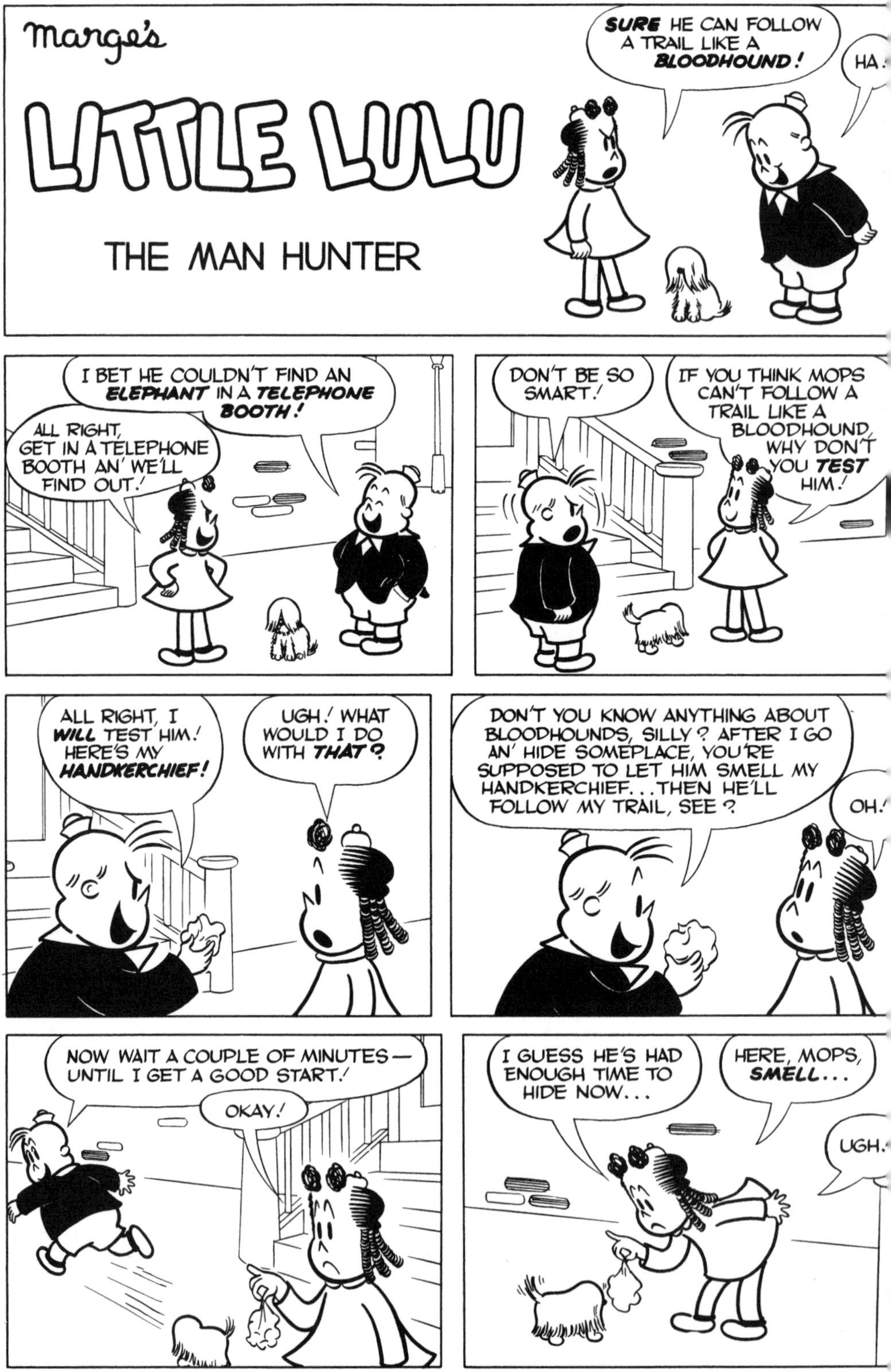
marge's
LITTLE LULU
THE MAN HUNTER
SURE HE CAN FOLLOW A TRAIL LIKE A BLOODHOUND!
HA.
I BET HE COULDN'T FIND AN ELEPHANT IN A TELEPHONE BOOTH!
ALL RIGHT, GET IN A TELEPHONE BOOTH AN' WE'LL FIND OUT!
DON'T BE SO SMART!
IF YOU THINK MOPS CAN'T FOLLOW A TRAIL LIKE A BLOODHOUND, WHY DON'T YOU TEST HIM!
ALL RIGHT, I WILL TEST HIM! HERE'S MY HANDKERCHIEF!
UGH! WHAT WOULD I DO WITH THAT?
DON'T YOU KNOW ANYTHING ABOUT BLOODHOUNDS, SILLY? AFTER I GO AN' HIDE SOMEPLACE, YOU'RE SUPPOSED TO LET HIM SMELL MY HANDKERCHIEF...THEN HE'LL FOLLOW MY TRAIL, SEE?
OH!
NOW WAIT A COUPLE OF MINUTES— UNTIL I GET A GOOD START!
OKAY!
I GUESS HE'S HAD ENOUGH TIME TO HIDE NOW...
HERE, MOPS, SMELL...
UGH.

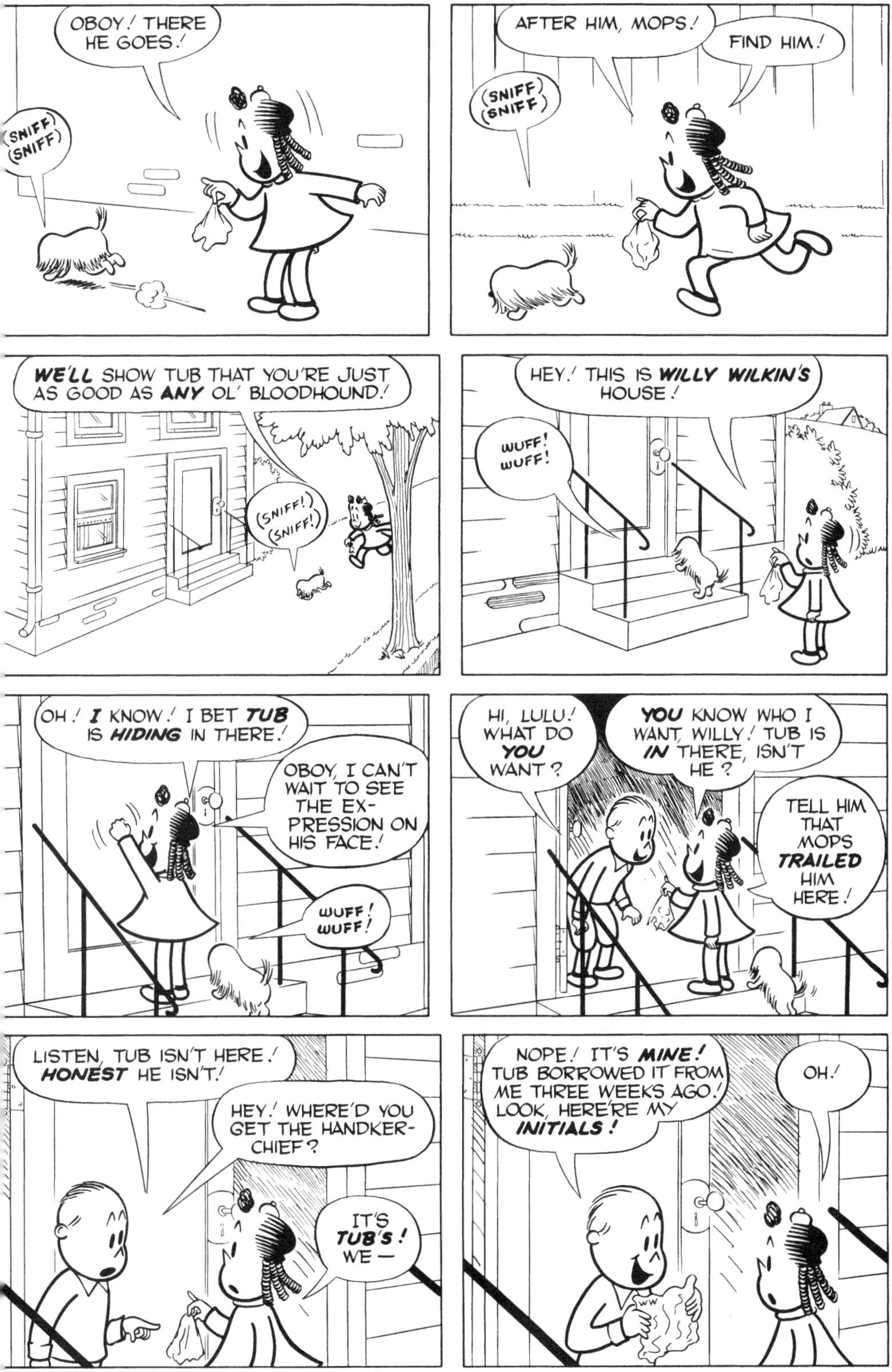

OBOY! THERE HE GOES!
(SNIFF) (SNIFF)
AFTER HIM, MOPS!
FIND HIM!
(SNIFF) (SNIFF)
WE'LL SHOW TUB THAT YOU'RE JUST AS GOOD AS ANY OL' BLOODHOUND!
(SNIFF!) (SNIFF!)
HEY! THIS IS WILLY WILKIN'S HOUSE!
WUFF! WUFF!
OH! I KNOW! I BET TUB IS HIDING IN THERE!
OBOY, I CAN'T WAIT TO SEE THE EX-PRESSION ON HIS FACE!
WUFF! WUFF!
HI, LULU! WHAT DO YOU WANT?
YOU KNOW WHO I WANT, WILLY! TUB IS IN THERE, ISN'T HE?
TELL HIM THAT MOPS TRAILED HIM HERE!
LISTEN, TUB ISN'T HERE! HONEST HE ISN'T!
HEY! WHERE'D YOU GET THE HANDKER-CHIEF?
IT'S TUB'S! WE—
NOPE! IT'S MINE! TUB BORROWED IT FROM ME THREE WEEKS AGO! LOOK, HERE'RE MY INITIALS!
OH!
WW

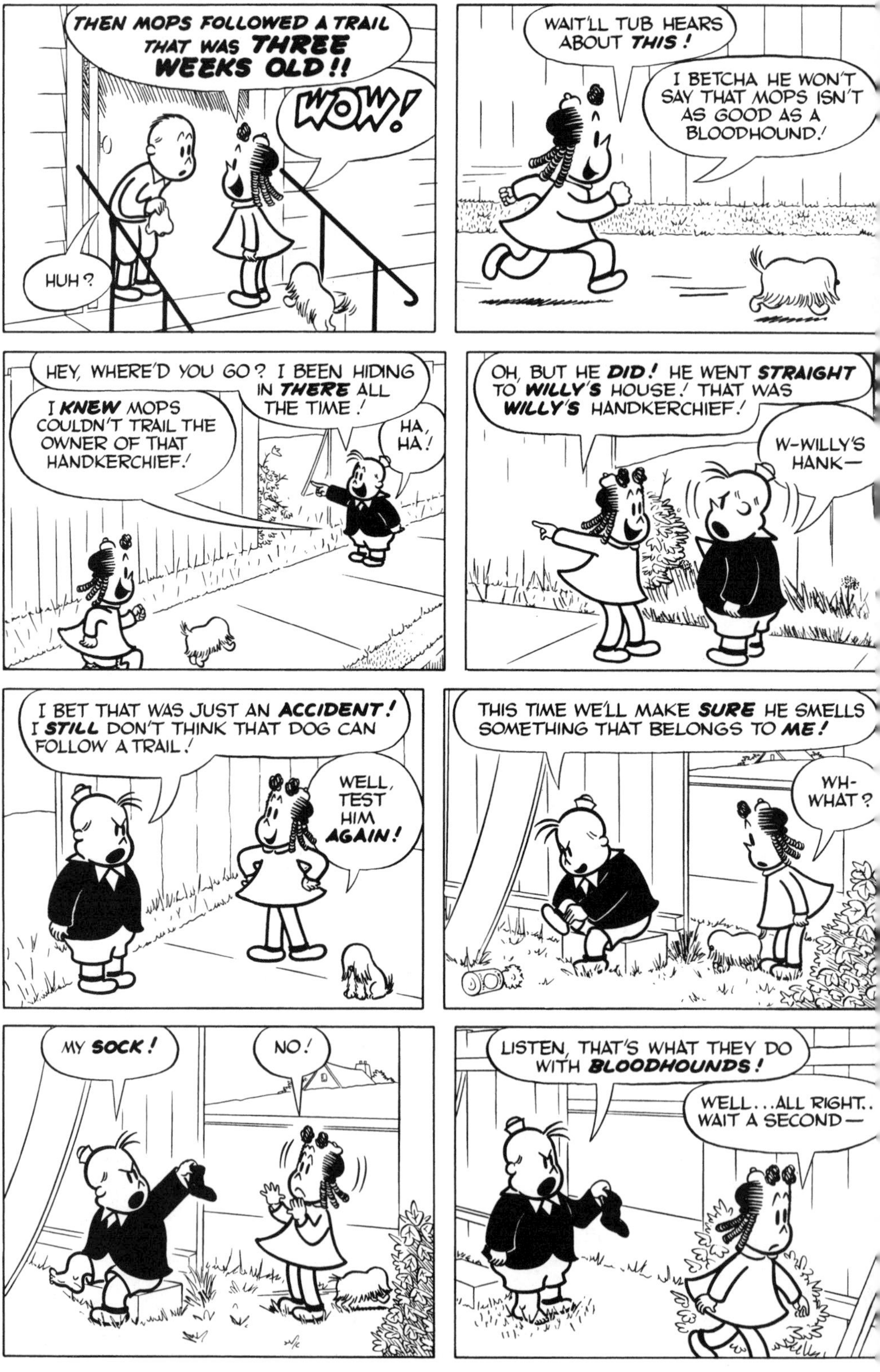
THEN MOPS FOLLOWED A TRAIL THAT WAS THREE WEEKS OLD!!
WOW!
HUH?
WAIT'LL TUB HEARS ABOUT THIS!
I BETCHA HE WON'T SAY THAT MOPS ISN'T AS GOOD AS A BLOODHOUND!
HEY, WHERE'D YOU GO? I BEEN HIDING IN THERE ALL THE TIME!
I KNEW MOPS COULDN'T TRAIL THE OWNER OF THAT HANDKERCHIEF!
HA, HA!
OH, BUT HE DID! HE WENT STRAIGHT TO WILLY'S HOUSE! THAT WAS WILLY'S HANDKERCHIEF!
W-WILLY'S HANK—
I BET THAT WAS JUST AN ACCIDENT! I STILL DON'T THINK THAT DOG CAN FOLLOW A TRAIL!
WELL, TEST HIM AGAIN!
THIS TIME WE'LL MAKE SURE HE SMELLS SOMETHING THAT BELONGS TO ME!
WH- WHAT?
MY SOCK!
NO!
LISTEN, THAT'S WHAT THEY DO WITH BLOODHOUNDS!
WELL...ALL RIGHT.. WAIT A SECOND—

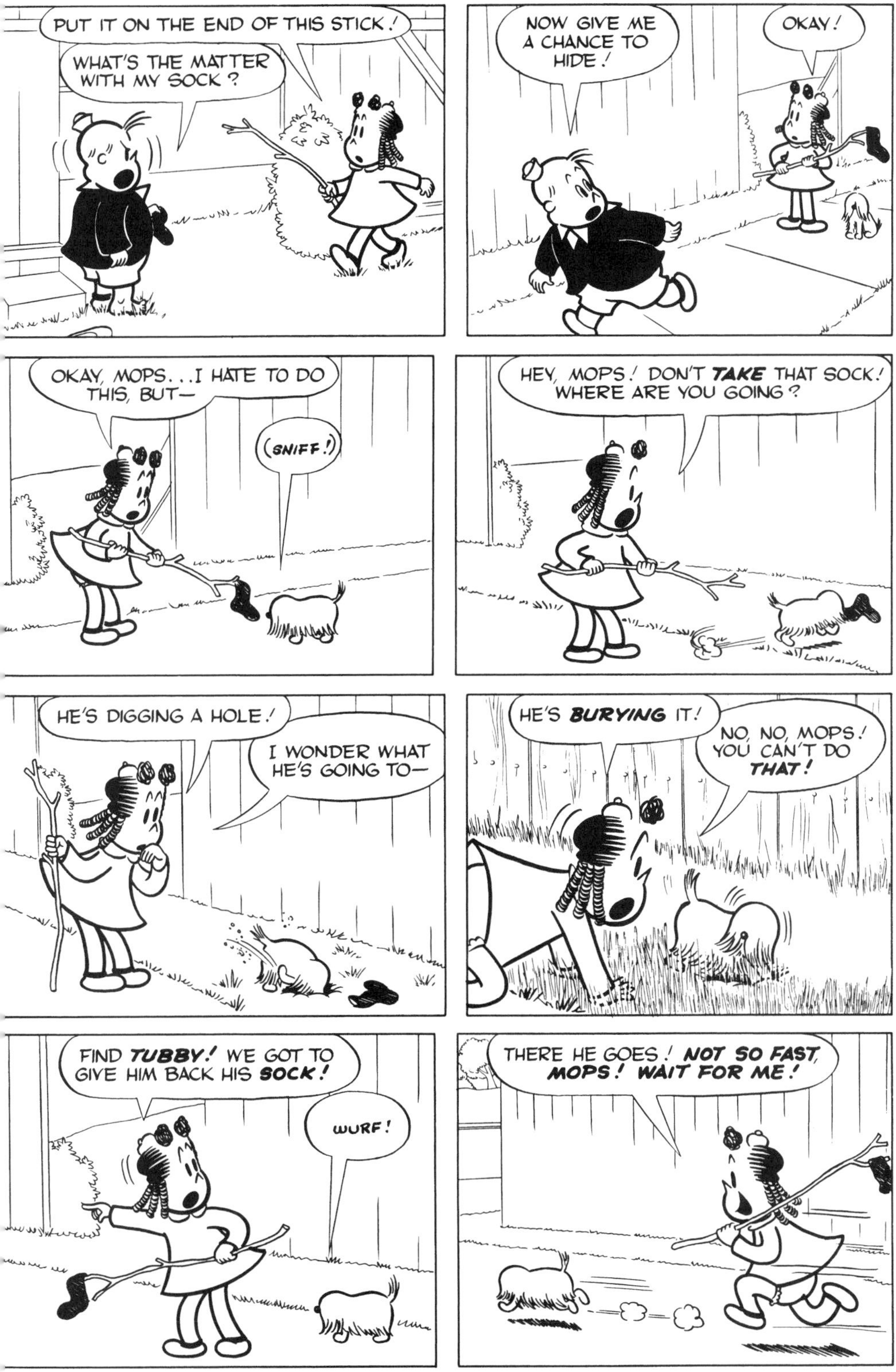
PUT IT ON THE END OF THIS STICK!
WHAT'S THE MATTER WITH MY SOCK?
NOW GIVE ME A CHANCE TO HIDE!
OKAY!
OKAY, MOPS...I HATE TO DO THIS, BUT—
(SNIFF!)
HEY, MOPS! DON'T TAKE THAT SOCK! WHERE ARE YOU GOING?
HE'S DIGGING A HOLE!
I WONDER WHAT HE'S GOING TO—
HE'S BURYING IT!
NO, NO, MOPS! YOU CAN'T DO THAT!
FIND TUBBY! WE GOT TO GIVE HIM BACK HIS SOCK!
WURF!
THERE HE GOES! NOT SO FAST, MOPS! WAIT FOR ME!

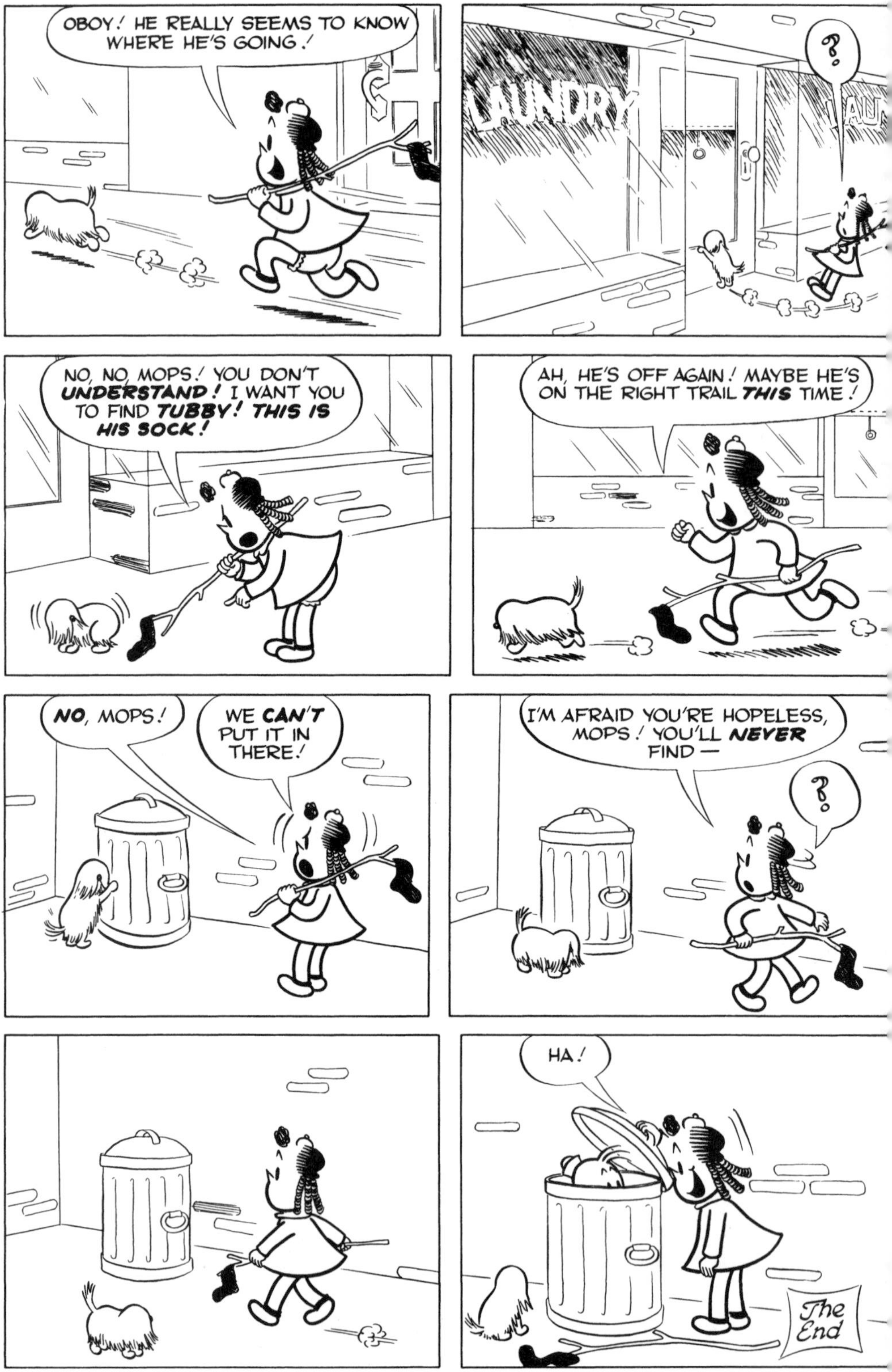
OBOY! HE REALLY SEEMS TO KNOW WHERE HE'S GOING!
LAUNDRY
?
NO, NO, MOPS! YOU DON'T UNDERSTAND! I WANT YOU TO FIND TUBBY! THIS IS HIS SOCK!
AH, HE'S OFF AGAIN! MAYBE HE'S ON THE RIGHT TRAIL THIS TIME!
NO, MOPS!
WE CAN'T PUT IT IN THERE!
I'M AFRAID YOU'RE HOPELESS, MOPS! YOU'LL NEVER FIND —
?
HA!
The End

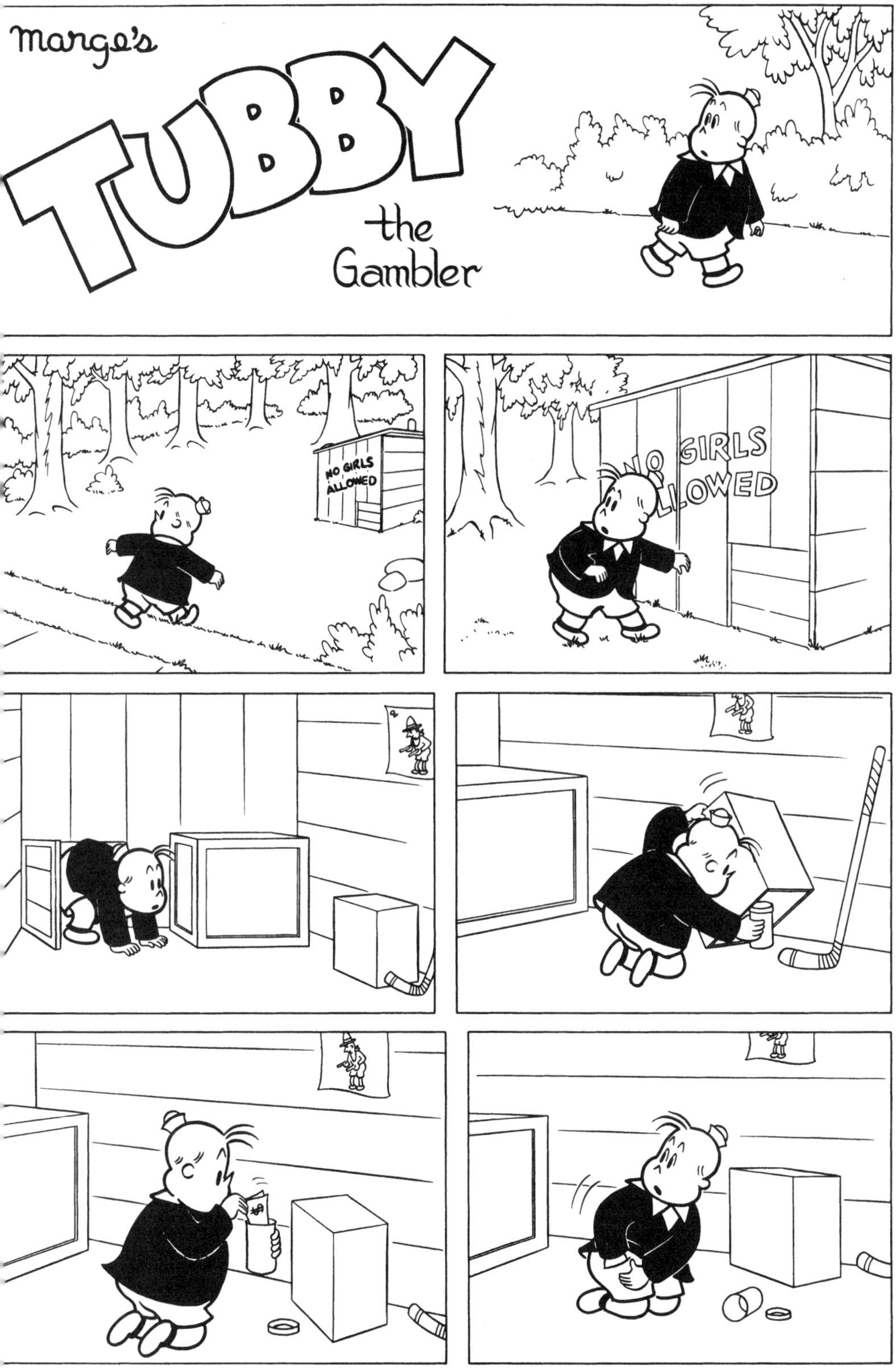
marge's
TUBBY
the Gambler
NO GIRLS ALLOWED
NO GIRLS
LLOWED

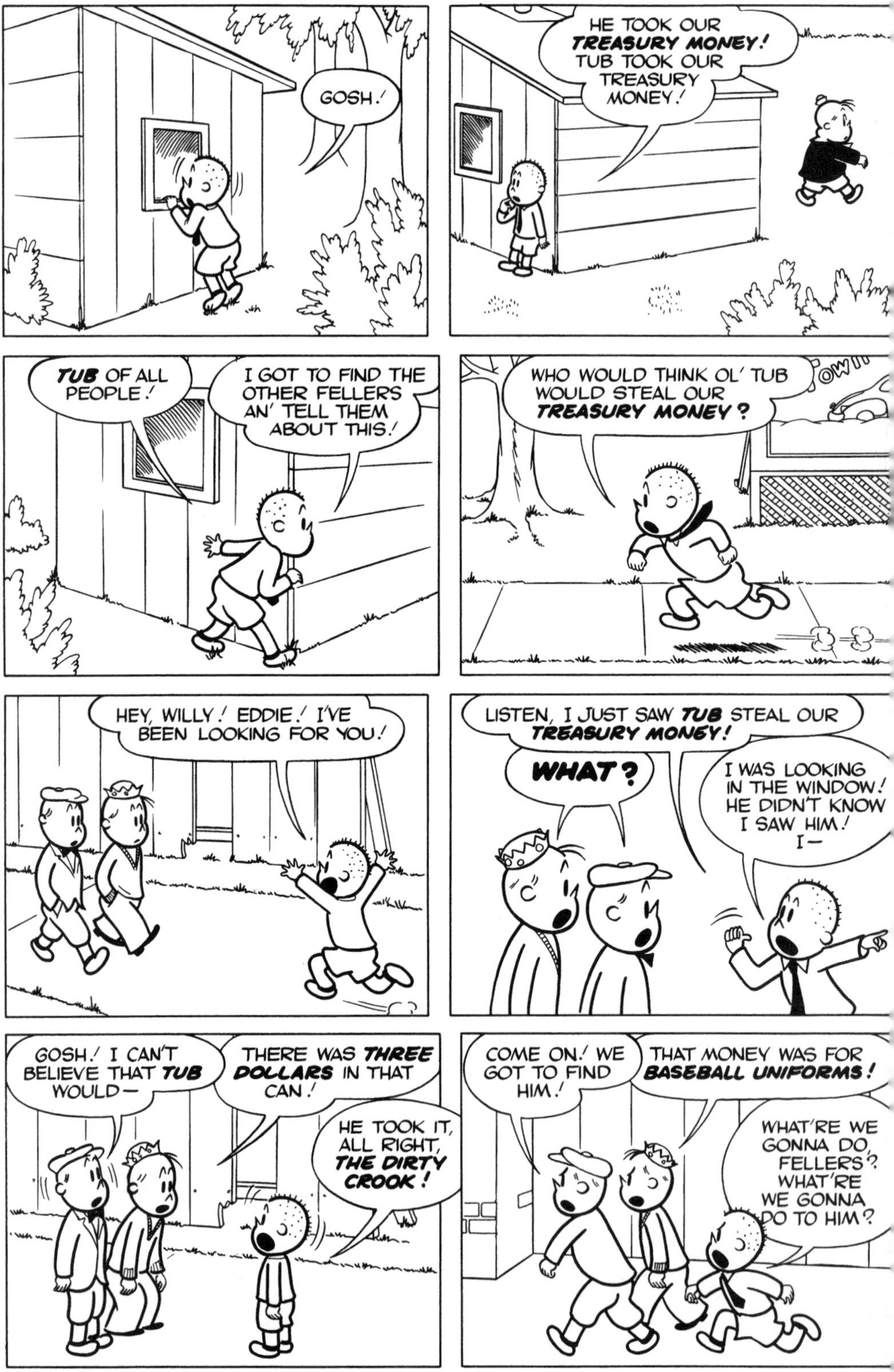
GOSH!
HE TOOK OUR TREASURY MONEY! TUB TOOK OUR TREASURY MONEY!
TUB OF ALL PEOPLE!
I GOT TO FIND THE OTHER FELLERS AN' TELL THEM ABOUT THIS!
WHO WOULD THINK OL' TUB WOULD STEAL OUR TREASURY MONEY?
HEY, WILLY! EDDIE! I'VE BEEN LOOKING FOR YOU!
LISTEN, I JUST SAW TUB STEAL OUR TREASURY MONEY!
WHAT?
I WAS LOOKING IN THE WINDOW! HE DIDN'T KNOW I SAW HIM! I—
GOSH! I CAN'T BELIEVE THAT TUB WOULD—
THERE WAS THREE DOLLARS IN THAT CAN!
HE TOOK IT, ALL RIGHT, THE DIRTY CROOK!
COME ON! WE GOT TO FIND HIM!
THAT MONEY WAS FOR BASEBALL UNIFORMS!
WHAT'RE WE GONNA DO, FELLERS? WHAT'RE WE GONNA DO TO HIM?

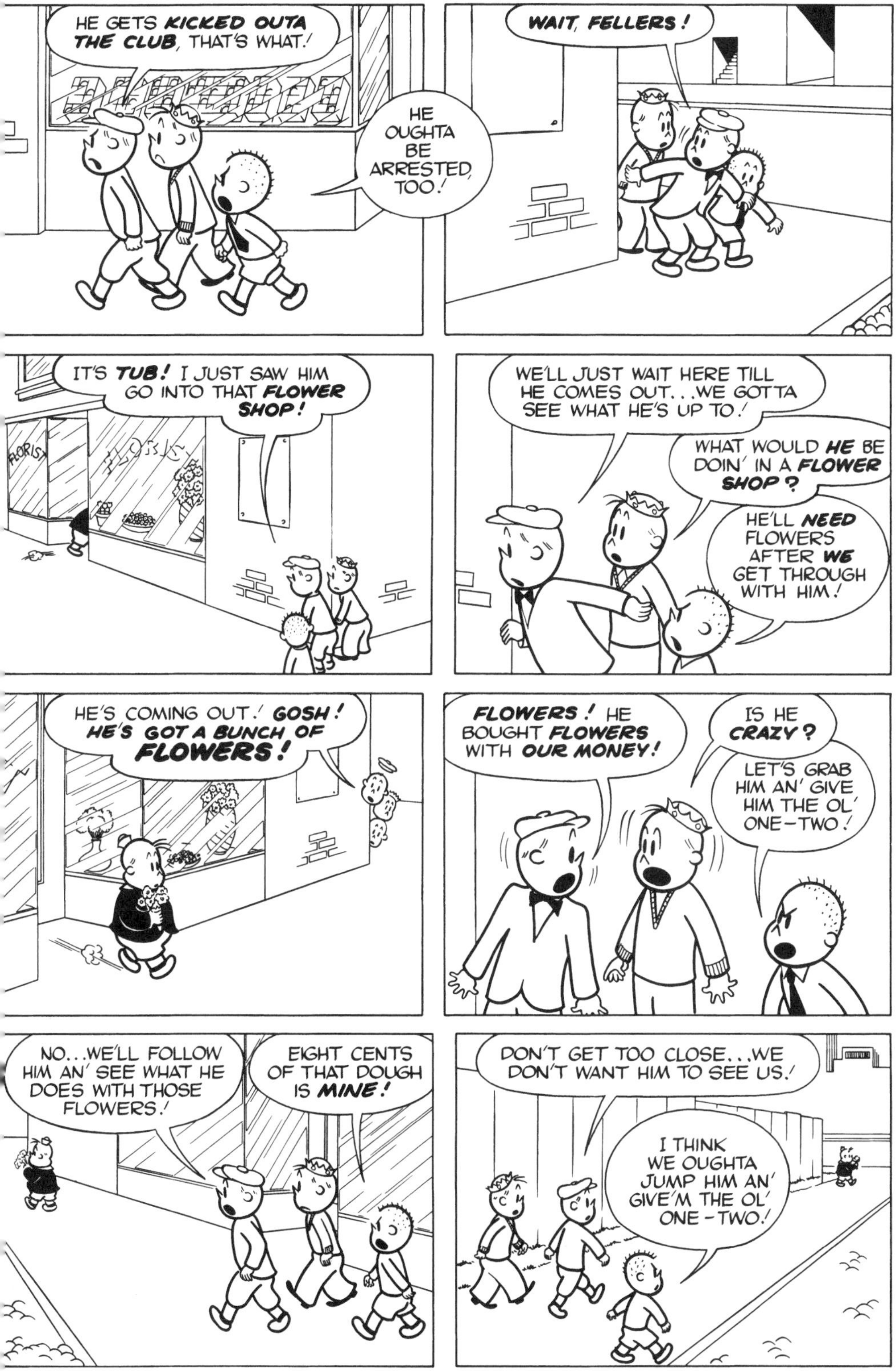
HE GETS KICKED OUTA THE CLUB, THAT'S WHAT!
HE OUGHTA BE ARRESTED, TOO!
WAIT, FELLERS!
IT'S TUB! I JUST SAW HIM GO INTO THAT FLOWER SHOP!
WE'LL JUST WAIT HERE TILL HE COMES OUT...WE GOTTA SEE WHAT HE'S UP TO!
WHAT WOULD HE BE DOIN' IN A FLOWER SHOP?
HE'LL NEED FLOWERS AFTER WE GET THROUGH WITH HIM!
HE'S COMING OUT! GOSH! HE'S GOT A BUNCH OF FLOWERS!
FLOWERS! HE BOUGHT FLOWERS WITH OUR MONEY!
IS HE CRAZY?
LET'S GRAB HIM AN' GIVE HIM THE OL' ONE-TWO!
NO...WE'LL FOLLOW HIM AN' SEE WHAT HE DOES WITH THOSE FLOWERS!
EIGHT CENTS OF THAT DOUGH IS MINE!
DON'T GET TOO CLOSE...WE DON'T WANT HIM TO SEE US!
I THINK WE OUGHTA JUMP HIM AN' GIVE'M THE OL' ONE-TWO!

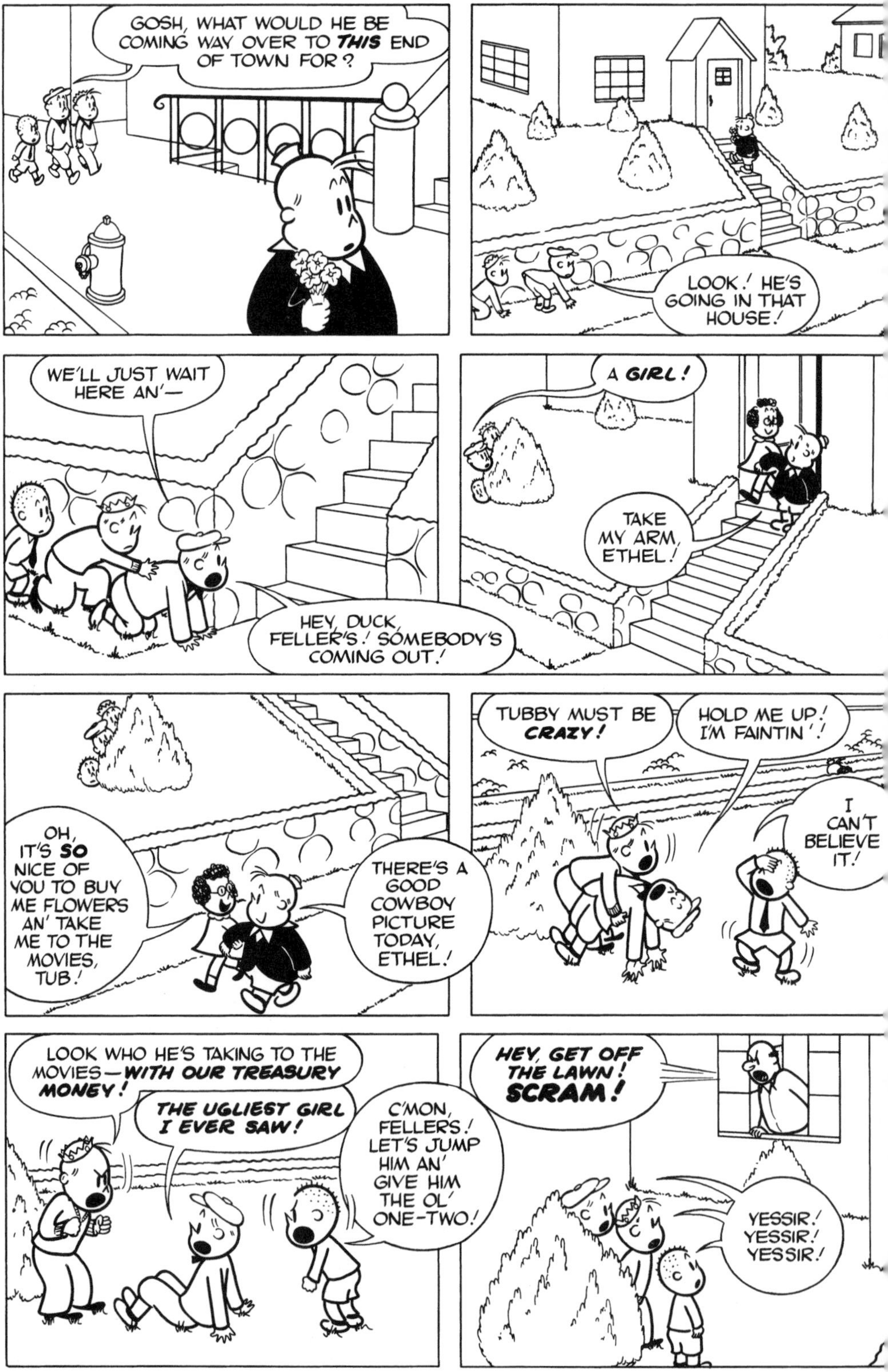
GOSH, WHAT WOULD HE BE COMING WAY OVER TO THIS END OF TOWN FOR?
LOOK! HE'S GOING IN THAT HOUSE!
WE'LL JUST WAIT HERE AN'—
HEY, DUCK, FELLER'S! SOMEBODY'S COMING OUT!
A GIRL!
TAKE MY ARM, ETHEL!
OH, IT'S SO NICE OF YOU TO BUY ME FLOWERS AN' TAKE ME TO THE MOVIES, TUB!
THERE'S A GOOD COWBOY PICTURE TODAY, ETHEL!
TUBBY MUST BE CRAZY!
HOLD ME UP! I'M FAINTIN'!
I CAN'T BELIEVE IT!
LOOK WHO HE'S TAKING TO THE MOVIES—WITH OUR TREASURY MONEY!
THE UGLIEST GIRL I EVER SAW!
C'MON, FELLERS! LET'S JUMP HIM AN' GIVE HIM THE OL' ONE-TWO!
HEY, GET OFF THE LAWN! SCRAM!
YESSIR! YESSIR! YESSIR!

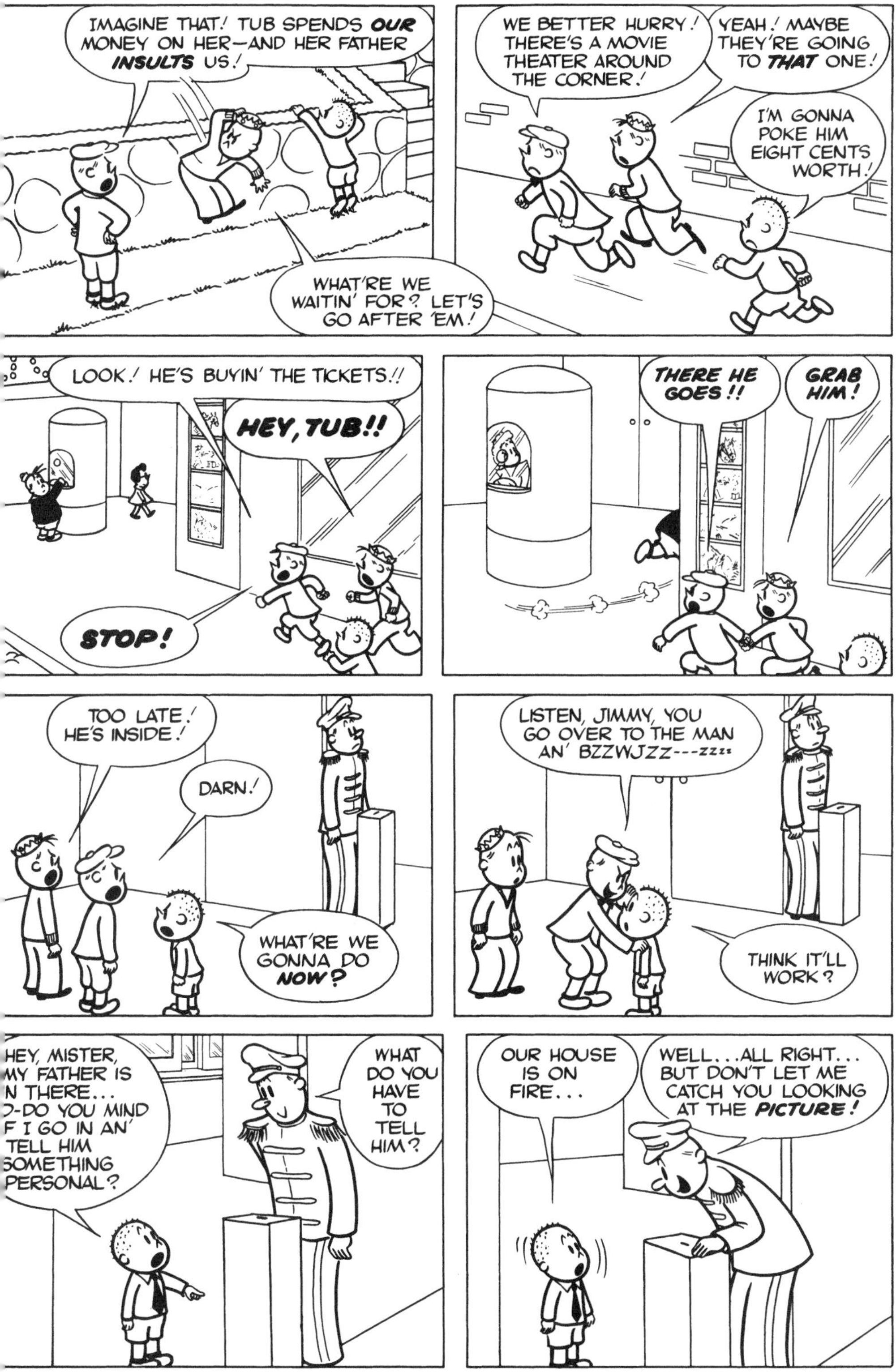

IMAGINE THAT! TUB SPENDS OUR MONEY ON HER—AND HER FATHER INSULTS US!
WHAT'RE WE WAITIN' FOR? LET'S GO AFTER 'EM!
WE BETTER HURRY! THERE'S A MOVIE THEATER AROUND THE CORNER!
YEAH! MAYBE THEY'RE GOING TO THAT ONE!
I'M GONNA POKE HIM EIGHT CENTS WORTH!
LOOK! HE'S BUYIN' THE TICKETS!!
HEY, TUB!!
STOP!
THERE HE GOES!!
GRAB HIM!
TOO LATE! HE'S INSIDE!
DARN!
WHAT'RE WE GONNA DO NOW?
LISTEN, JIMMY, YOU GO OVER TO THE MAN AN' BZZWJZZ---zzzz
THINK IT'LL WORK?
HEY, MISTER, MY FATHER IS IN THERE... D-DO YOU MIND IF I GO IN AN' TELL HIM SOMETHING PERSONAL?
WHAT DO YOU HAVE TO TELL HIM?
OUR HOUSE IS ON FIRE...
WELL...ALL RIGHT... BUT DON'T LET ME CATCH YOU LOOKING AT THE PICTURE!

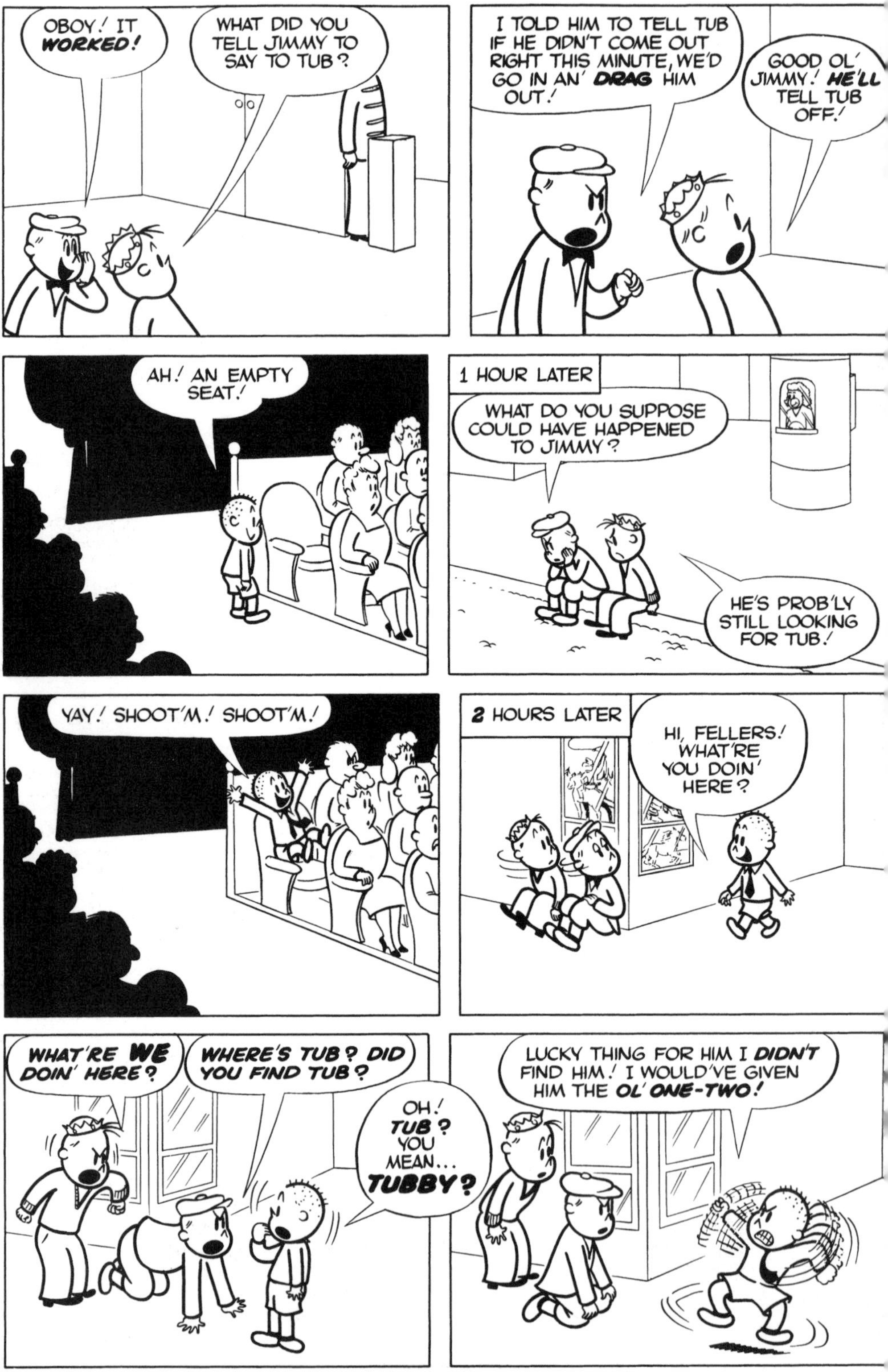
OBOY! IT WORKED!
WHAT DID YOU TELL JIMMY TO SAY TO TUB?
I TOLD HIM TO TELL TUB IF HE DIDN'T COME OUT RIGHT THIS MINUTE, WE'D GO IN AN' DRAG HIM OUT!
GOOD OL' JIMMY! HE'LL TELL TUB OFF!
AH! AN EMPTY SEAT!
1 HOUR LATER
WHAT DO YOU SUPPOSE COULD HAVE HAPPENED TO JIMMY?
HE'S PROB'LY STILL LOOKING FOR TUB!
YAY! SHOOT'M! SHOOT'M!
2 HOURS LATER
HI, FELLERS! WHAT'RE YOU DOIN' HERE?
WHAT'RE WE DOIN' HERE?
WHERE'S TUB? DID YOU FIND TUB?
OH! TUB? YOU MEAN... TUBBY?
LUCKY THING FOR HIM I DIDN'T FIND HIM! I WOULD'VE GIVEN HIM THE OL' ONE-TWO!

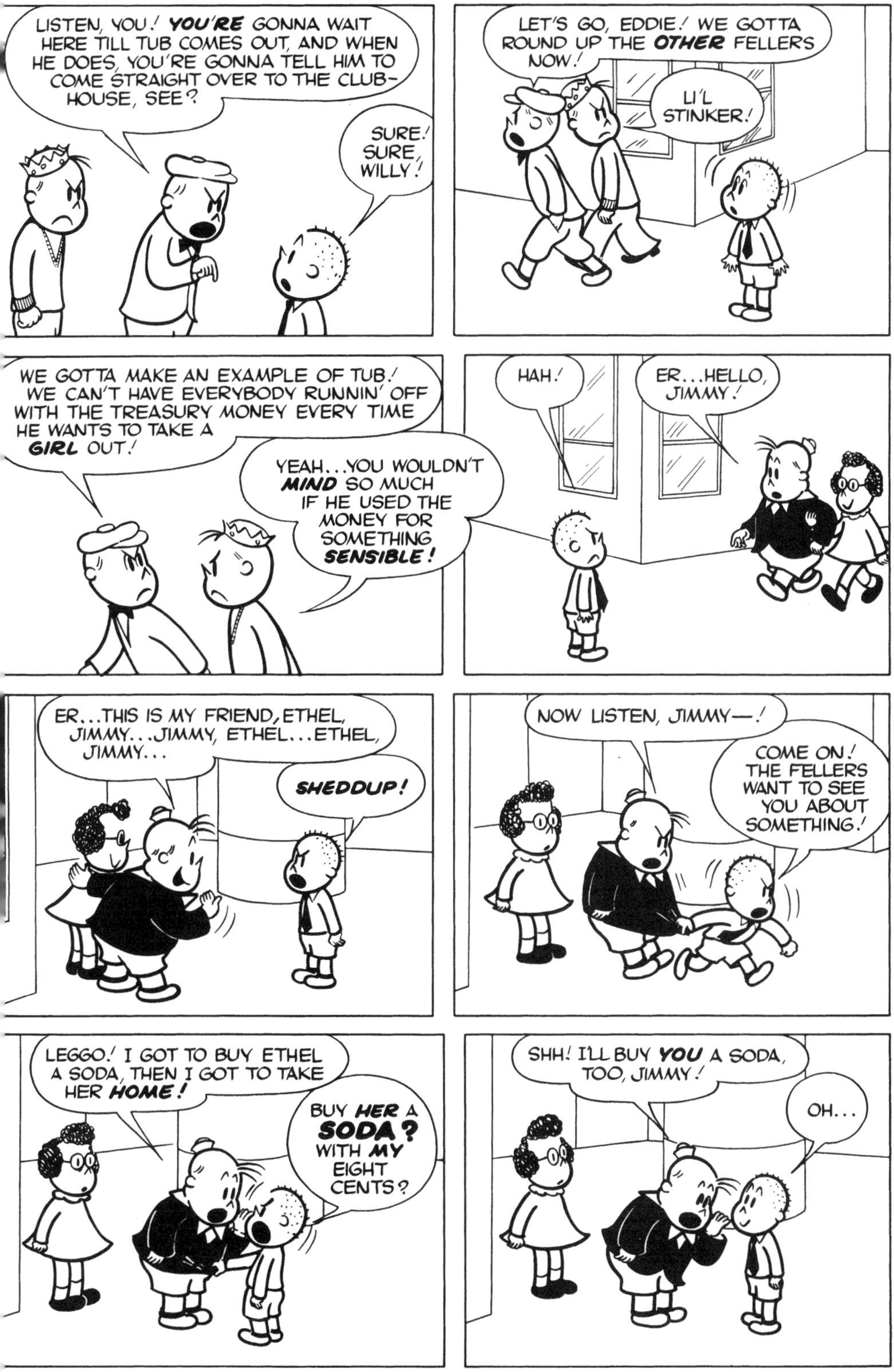
LISTEN, YOU! YOU'RE GONNA WAIT HERE TILL TUB COMES OUT, AND WHEN HE DOES, YOU'RE GONNA TELL HIM TO COME STRAIGHT OVER TO THE CLUB-HOUSE, SEE?
SURE! SURE, WILLY!
LET'S GO, EDDIE! WE GOTTA ROUND UP THE OTHER FELLERS NOW!
LI'L STINKER!
WE GOTTA MAKE AN EXAMPLE OF TUB! WE CAN'T HAVE EVERYBODY RUNNIN' OFF WITH THE TREASURY MONEY EVERY TIME HE WANTS TO TAKE A GIRL OUT!
YEAH...YOU WOULDN'T MIND SO MUCH IF HE USED THE MONEY FOR SOMETHING SENSIBLE!
HAH!
ER...HELLO, JIMMY!
ER...THIS IS MY FRIEND, ETHEL, JIMMY...JIMMY, ETHEL...ETHEL, JIMMY...
SHEDDUP!
NOW LISTEN, JIMMY—!
COME ON! THE FELLERS WANT TO SEE YOU ABOUT SOMETHING!
LEGGO! I GOT TO BUY ETHEL A SODA, THEN I GOT TO TAKE HER HOME!
BUY HER A SODA? WITH MY EIGHT CENTS?
SHH! I'LL BUY YOU A SODA, TOO, JIMMY!
OH...

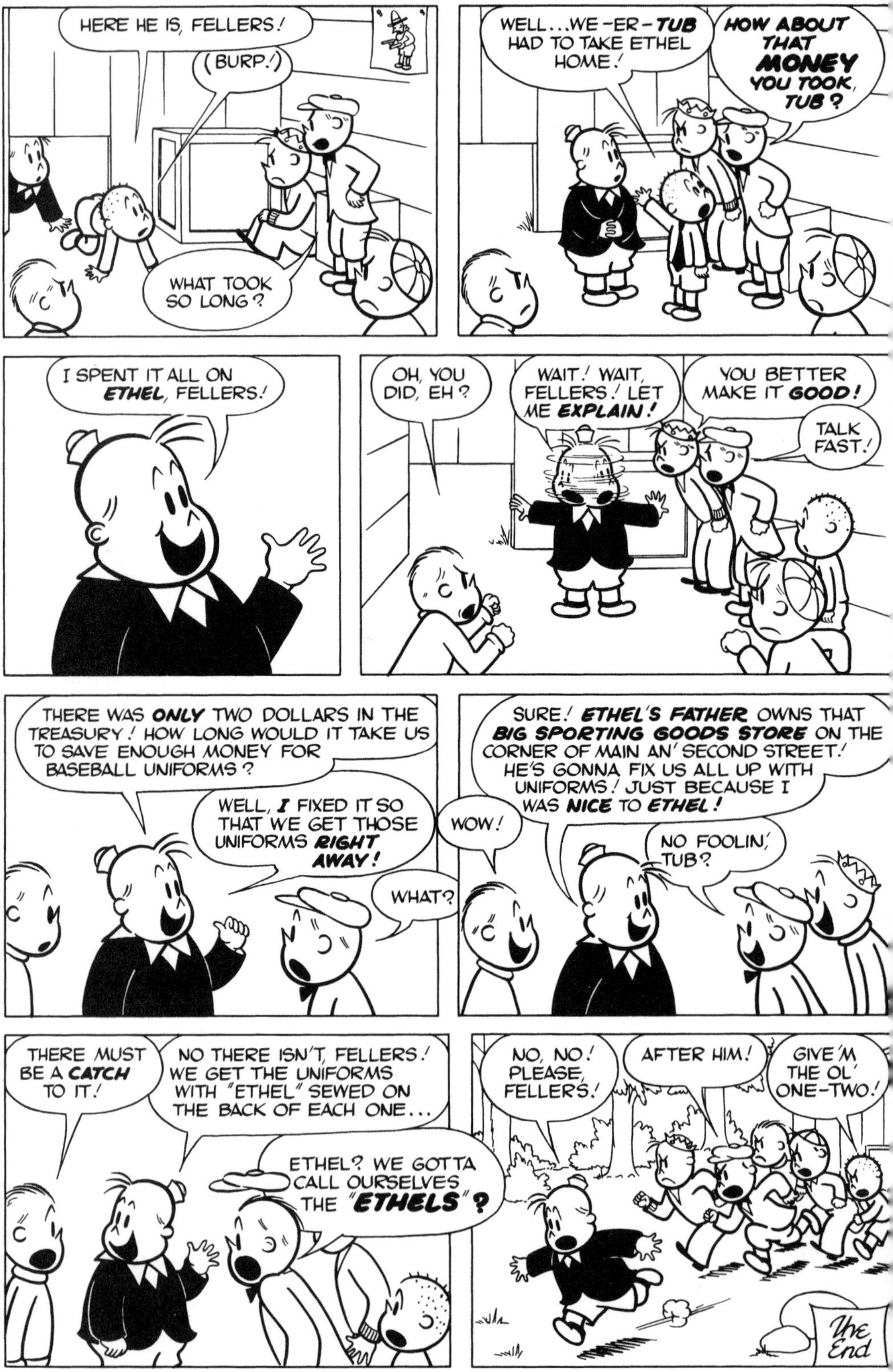
HERE HE IS, FELLERS!
(BURP!)
WHAT TOOK SO LONG?
WELL...WE-ER-TUB HAD TO TAKE ETHEL HOME!
HOW ABOUT THAT MONEY YOU TOOK, TUB?
I SPENT IT ALL ON ETHEL, FELLERS!
OH, YOU DID, EH?
WAIT! WAIT, FELLERS! LET ME EXPLAIN!
YOU BETTER MAKE IT GOOD!
TALK FAST!
THERE WAS ONLY TWO DOLLARS IN THE TREASURY! HOW LONG WOULD IT TAKE US TO SAVE ENOUGH MONEY FOR BASEBALL UNIFORMS?
WELL, I FIXED IT SO THAT WE GET THOSE UNIFORMS RIGHT AWAY!
WHAT?
WOW!
SURE! ETHEL'S FATHER OWNS THAT BIG SPORTING GOODS STORE ON THE CORNER OF MAIN AN' SECOND STREET! HE'S GONNA FIX US ALL UP WITH UNIFORMS! JUST BECAUSE I WAS NICE TO ETHEL!
NO FOOLIN', TUB?
THERE MUST BE A CATCH TO IT!
NO THERE ISN'T, FELLERS! WE GET THE UNIFORMS WITH "ETHEL" SEWED ON THE BACK OF EACH ONE...
ETHEL? WE GOTTA CALL OURSELVES THE "ETHELS"?
NO, NO! PLEASE, FELLERS!
AFTER HIM!
GIVE 'M THE OL' ONE-TWO!
The End

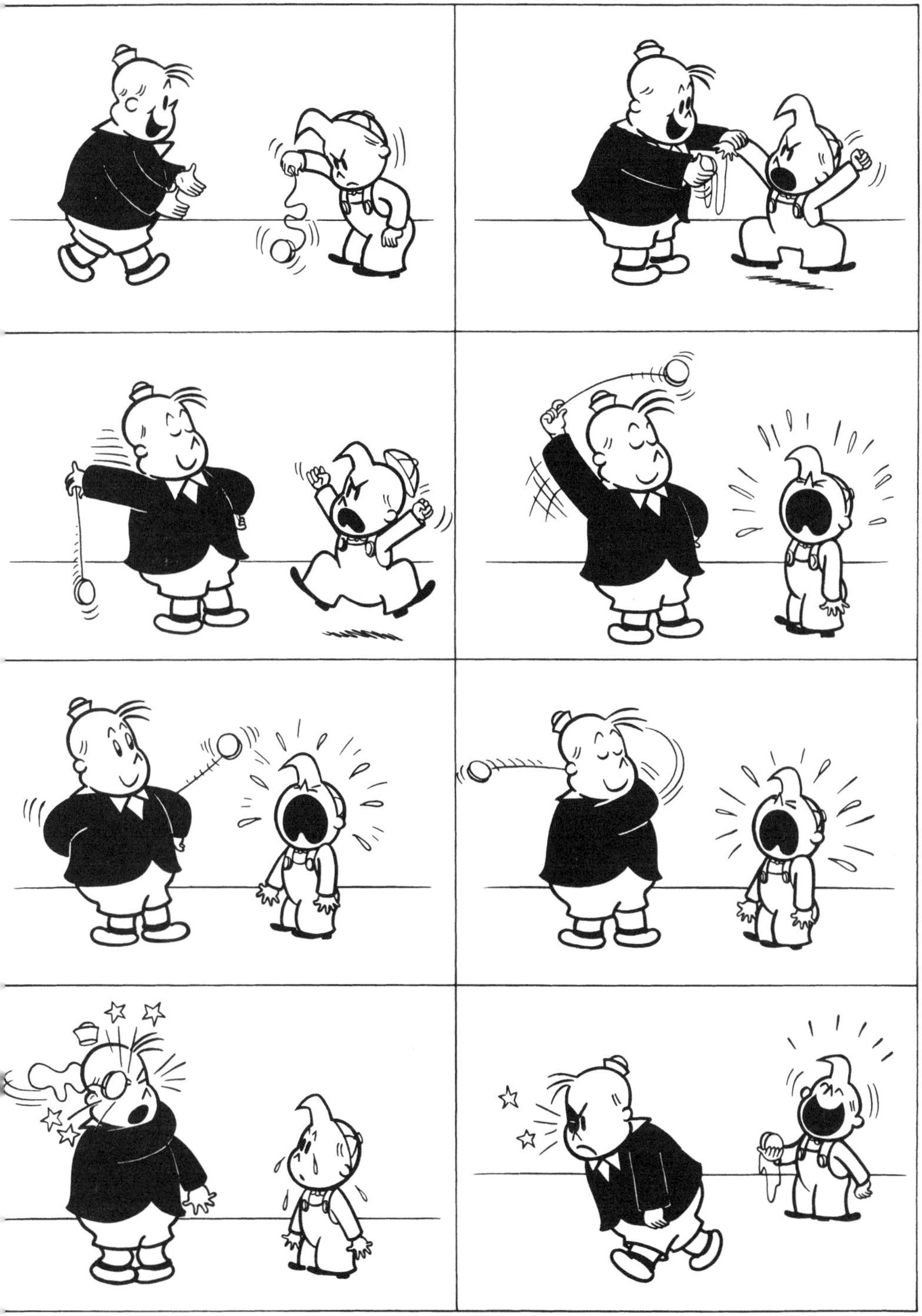

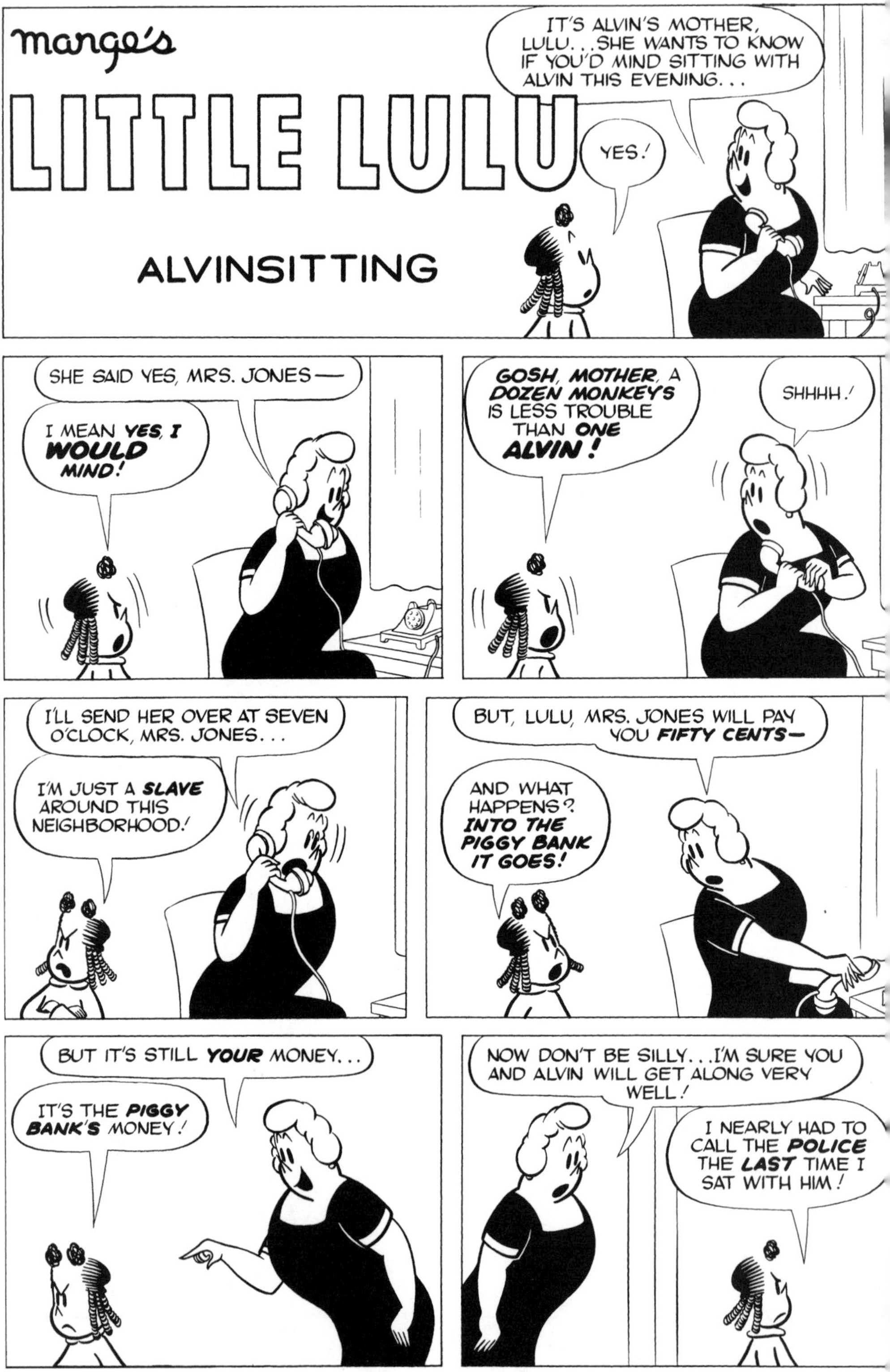
marge's
LITTLE LULU
ALVINSITTING
IT'S ALVIN'S MOTHER, LULU. . .SHE WANTS TO KNOW IF YOU'D MIND SITTING WITH ALVIN THIS EVENING. . .
YES!
SHE SAID YES, MRS. JONES—
I MEAN YES, I WOULD MIND!
GOSH, MOTHER, A DOZEN MONKEYS IS LESS TROUBLE THAN ONE ALVIN!
SHHHH!
I'LL SEND HER OVER AT SEVEN O'CLOCK, MRS. JONES. . .
I'M JUST A SLAVE AROUND THIS NEIGHBORHOOD!
BUT, LULU, MRS. JONES WILL PAY YOU FIFTY CENTS—
AND WHAT HAPPENS? INTO THE PIGGY BANK IT GOES!
BUT IT'S STILL YOUR MONEY. . .
IT'S THE PIGGY BANK'S MONEY!
NOW DON'T BE SILLY. . .I'M SURE YOU AND ALVIN WILL GET ALONG VERY WELL!
I NEARLY HAD TO CALL THE POLICE THE LAST TIME I SAT WITH HIM!

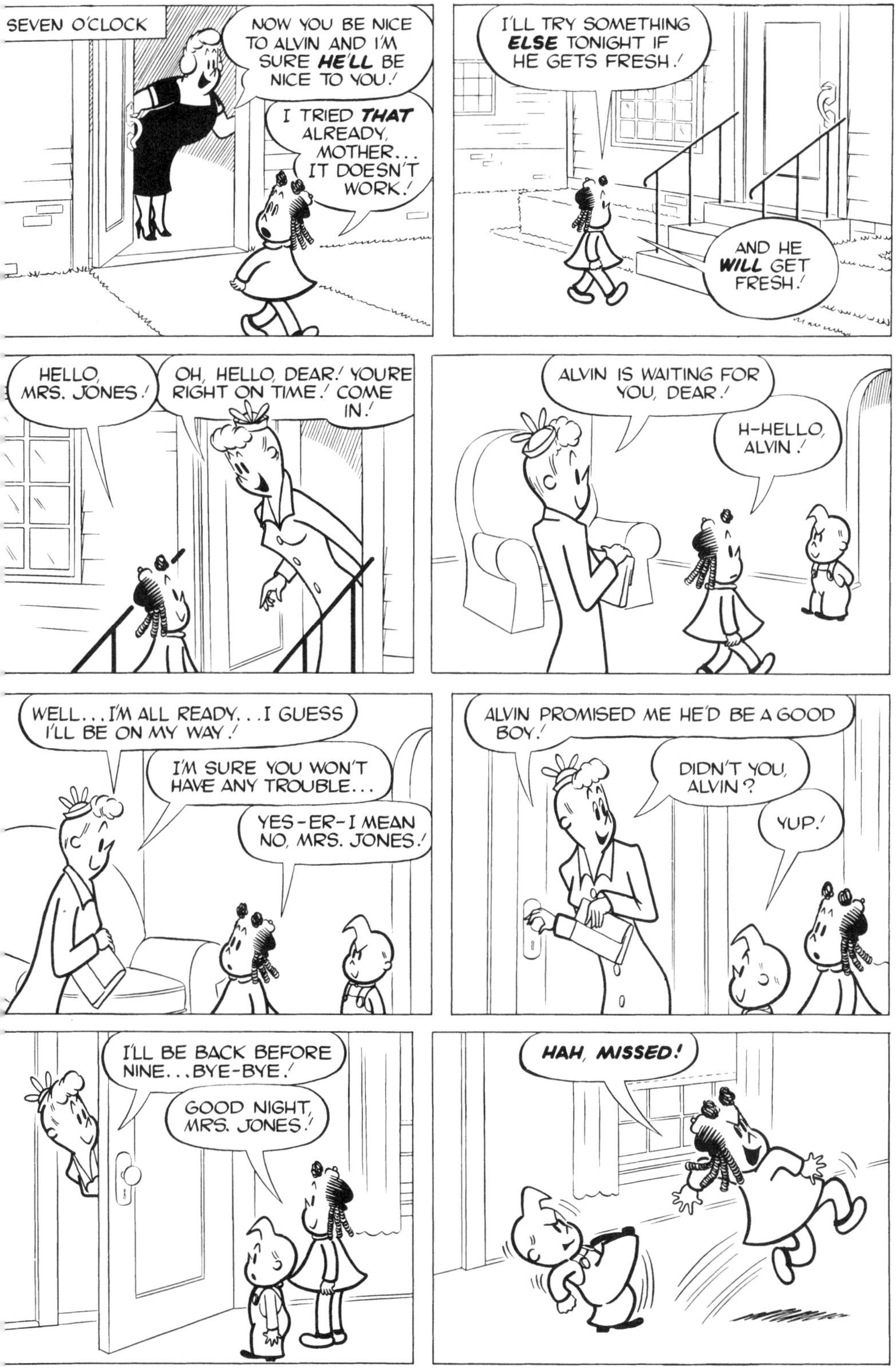
SEVEN O'CLOCK
NOW YOU BE NICE TO ALVIN AND I'M SURE HE'LL BE NICE TO YOU!
I TRIED THAT ALREADY, MOTHER... IT DOESN'T WORK!
I'LL TRY SOMETHING ELSE TONIGHT IF HE GETS FRESH!
AND HE WILL GET FRESH!
HELLO, MRS. JONES!
OH, HELLO, DEAR! YOU'RE RIGHT ON TIME! COME IN!
ALVIN IS WAITING FOR YOU, DEAR!
H-HELLO, ALVIN!
WELL... I'M ALL READY... I GUESS I'LL BE ON MY WAY!
I'M SURE YOU WON'T HAVE ANY TROUBLE...
YES-ER-I MEAN NO, MRS. JONES!
ALVIN PROMISED ME HE'D BE A GOOD BOY!
DIDN'T YOU, ALVIN?
YUP!
I'LL BE BACK BEFORE NINE... BYE-BYE!
GOOD NIGHT, MRS. JONES!
HAH, MISSED!

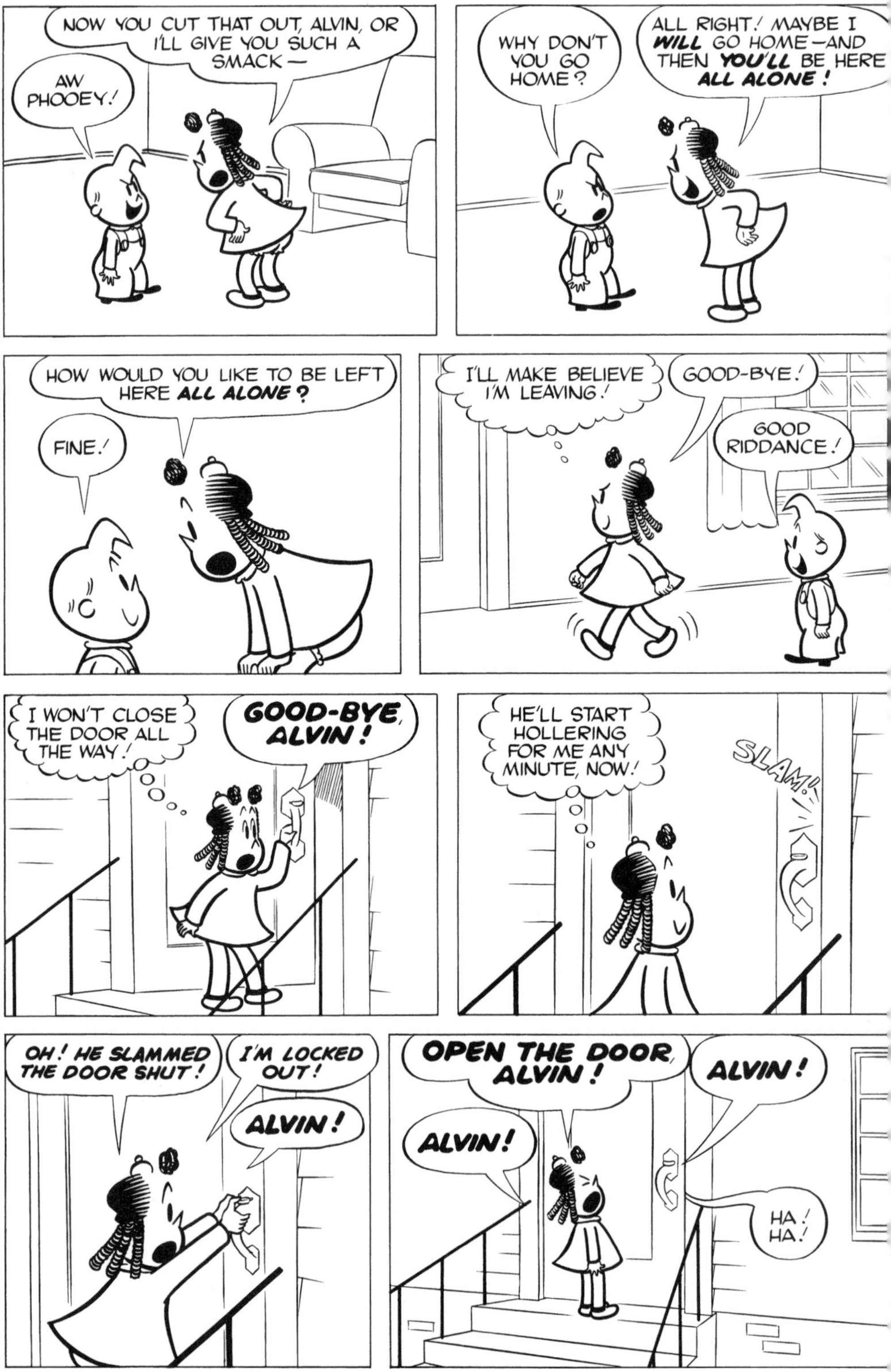
NOW YOU CUT THAT OUT, ALVIN, OR I'LL GIVE YOU SUCH A SMACK—
AW PHOOEY!
WHY DON'T YOU GO HOME?
ALL RIGHT! MAYBE I WILL GO HOME—AND THEN YOU'LL BE HERE ALL ALONE!
HOW WOULD YOU LIKE TO BE LEFT HERE ALL ALONE?
FINE!
I'LL MAKE BELIEVE I'M LEAVING!
GOOD-BYE!
GOOD RIDDANCE!
I WON'T CLOSE THE DOOR ALL THE WAY!
GOOD-BYE, ALVIN!
HE'LL START HOLLERING FOR ME ANY MINUTE, NOW!
SLAM!
OH! HE SLAMMED THE DOOR SHUT!
I'M LOCKED OUT!
ALVIN!
OPEN THE DOOR, ALVIN!
ALVIN!
ALVIN!
HA! HA!

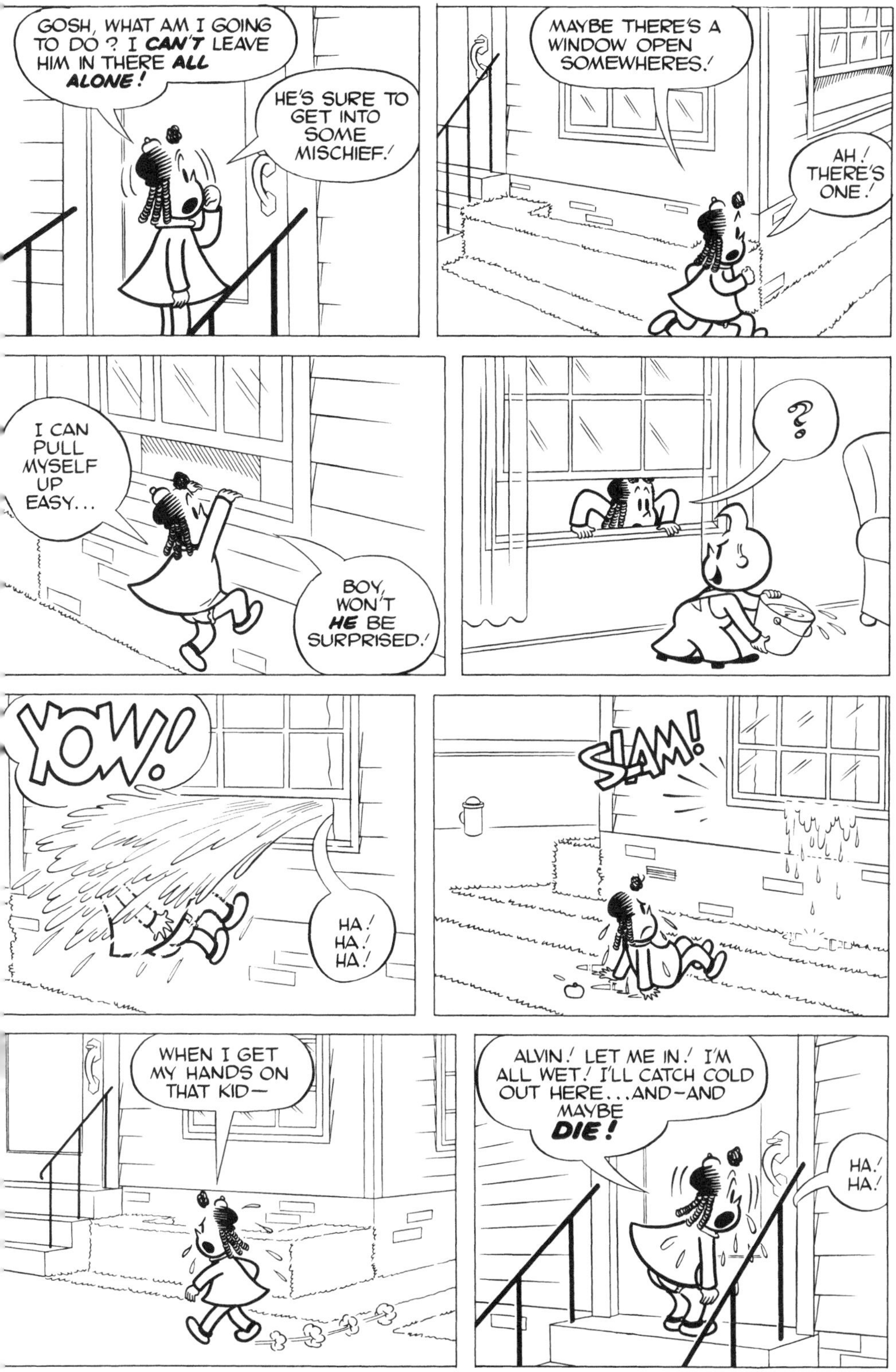
GOSH, WHAT AM I GOING TO DO ? I CAN'T LEAVE HIM IN THERE ALL ALONE !
HE'S SURE TO GET INTO SOME MISCHIEF!
MAYBE THERE'S A WINDOW OPEN SOMEWHERES!
AH! THERE'S ONE!
I CAN PULL MYSELF UP EASY...
BOY, WON'T HE BE SURPRISED!
?
YOW!
HA! HA! HA!
SLAM!
WHEN I GET MY HANDS ON THAT KID—
ALVIN! LET ME IN! I'M ALL WET! I'LL CATCH COLD OUT HERE...AND-AND MAYBE DIE!
HA! HA!

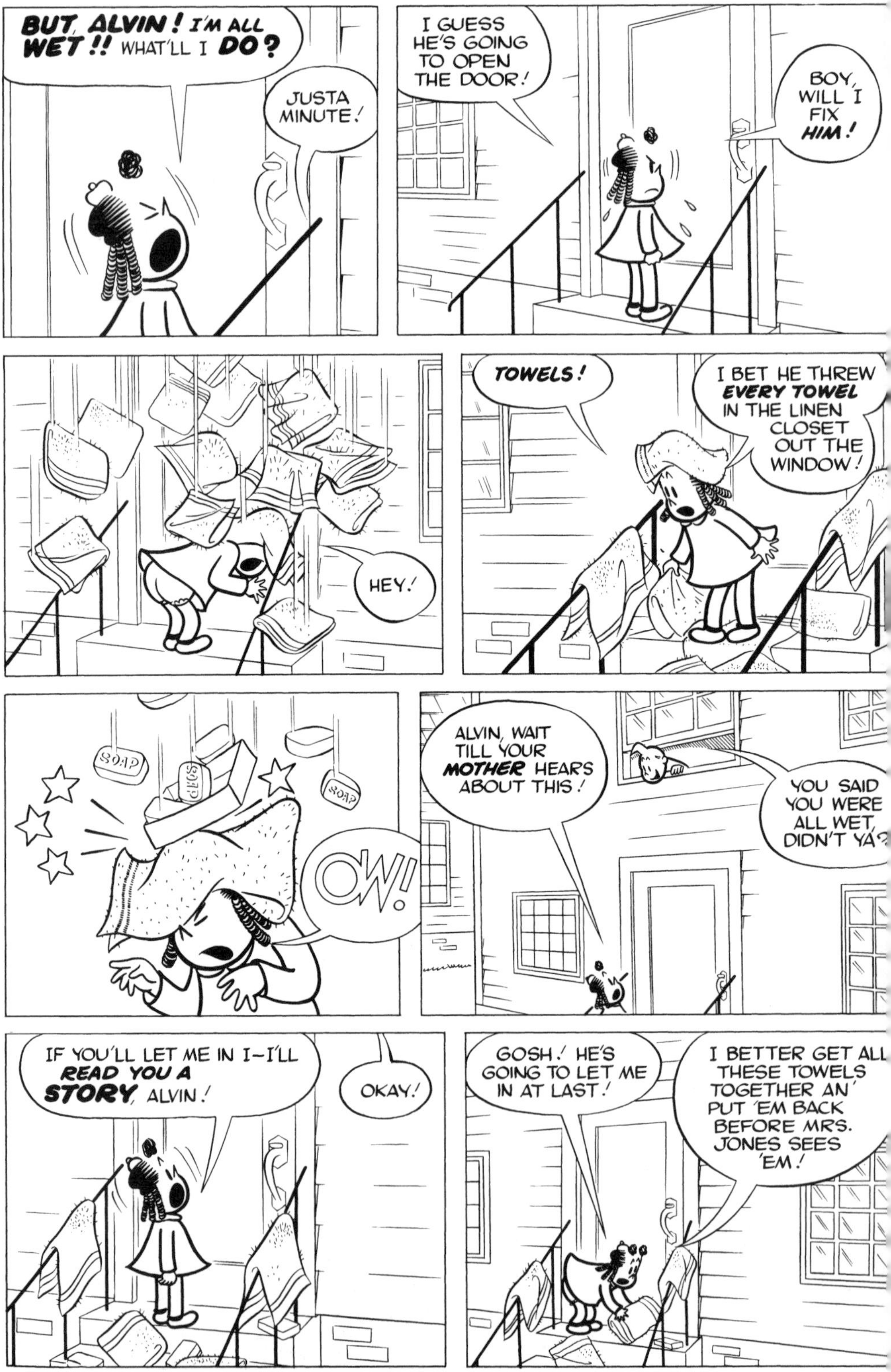
BUT, ALVIN! I'M ALL WET!! WHAT'LL I DO?
JUSTA MINUTE!
I GUESS HE'S GOING TO OPEN THE DOOR!
BOY, WILL I FIX HIM!
HEY!
TOWELS!
I BET HE THREW EVERY TOWEL IN THE LINEN CLOSET OUT THE WINDOW!
SOAP
SOAP
SOAP
OW!
ALVIN, WAIT TILL YOUR MOTHER HEARS ABOUT THIS!
YOU SAID YOU WERE ALL WET, DIDN'T YA?
IF YOU'LL LET ME IN I–I'LL READ YOU A STORY, ALVIN!
OKAY!
GOSH! HE'S GOING TO LET ME IN AT LAST!
I BETTER GET ALL THESE TOWELS TOGETHER AN' PUT 'EM BACK BEFORE MRS. JONES SEES 'EM!

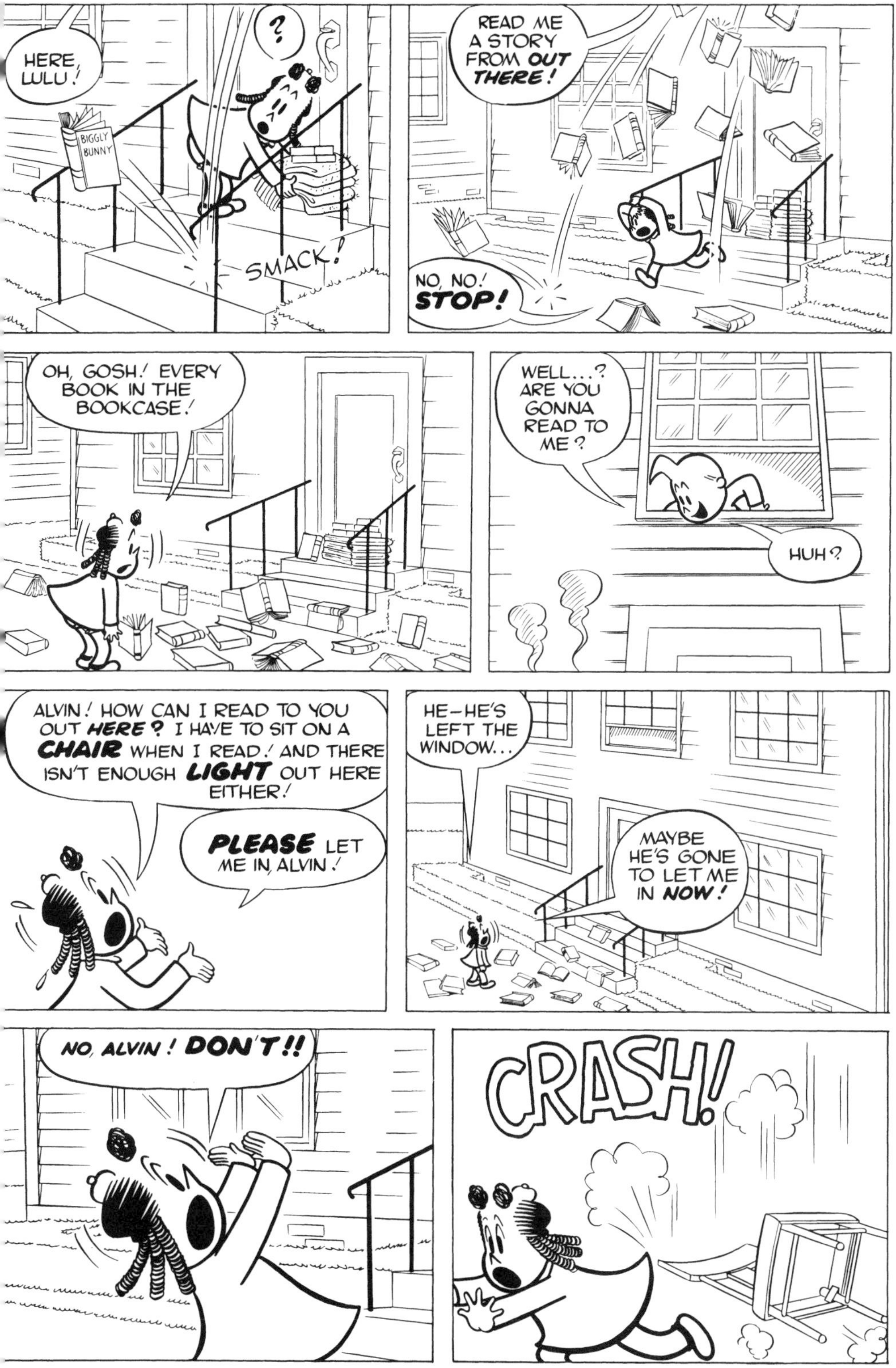
HERE, LULU!
?
BIGGLY BUNNY
SMACK!
READ ME A STORY FROM OUT THERE!
NO, NO! STOP!
OH, GOSH! EVERY BOOK IN THE BOOKCASE!
WELL...? ARE YOU GONNA READ TO ME?
HUH?
ALVIN! HOW CAN I READ TO YOU OUT HERE? I HAVE TO SIT ON A CHAIR WHEN I READ! AND THERE ISN'T ENOUGH LIGHT OUT HERE EITHER!
PLEASE LET ME IN, ALVIN!
HE-HE'S LEFT THE WINDOW...
MAYBE HE'S GONE TO LET ME IN NOW!
NO, ALVIN! DON'T!!
CRASH!

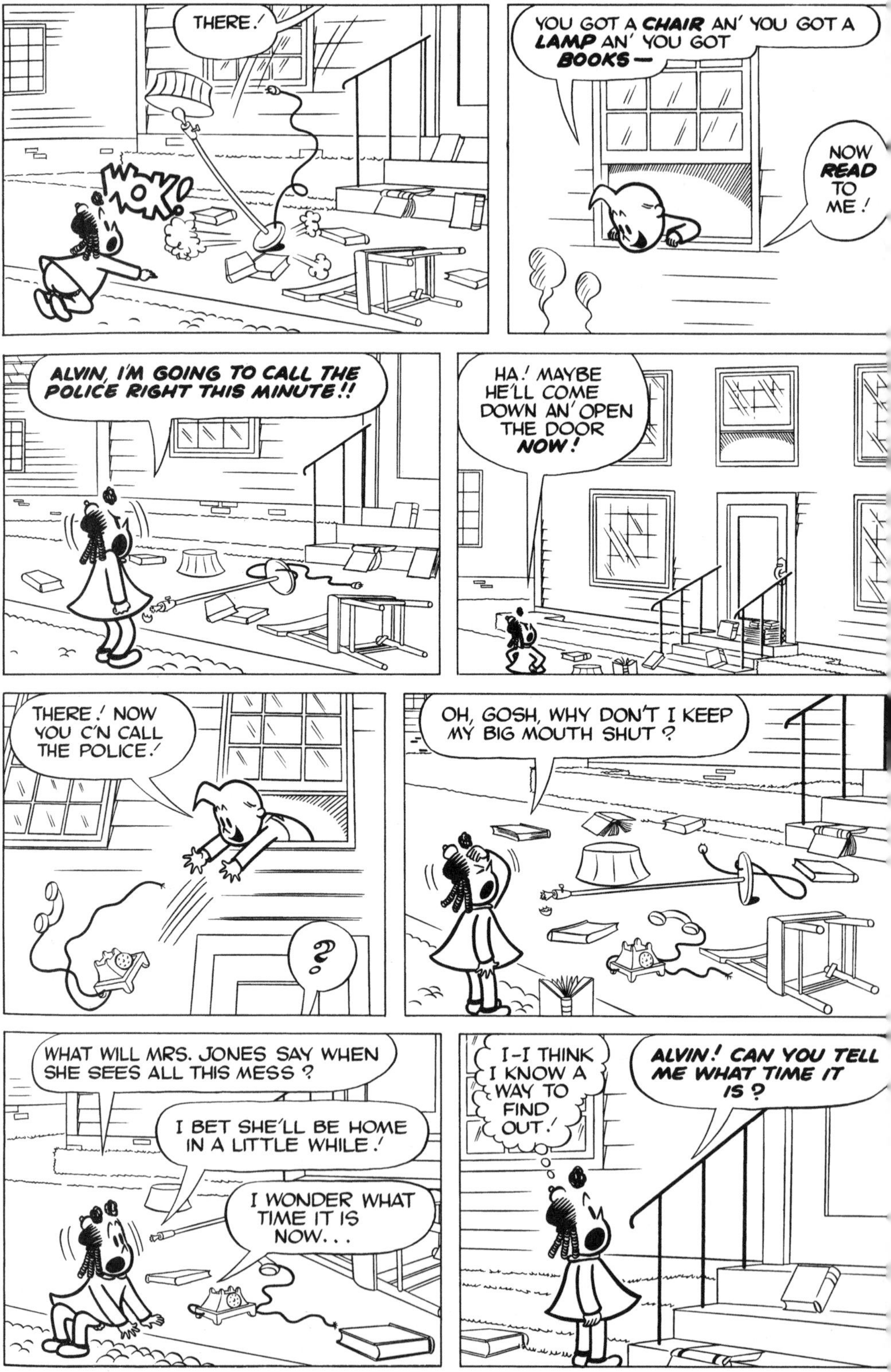
THERE!
WOK!
YOU GOT A CHAIR AN' YOU GOT A LAMP AN' YOU GOT BOOKS—
NOW READ TO ME!
ALVIN, I'M GOING TO CALL THE POLICE RIGHT THIS MINUTE!!
HA! MAYBE HE'LL COME DOWN AN' OPEN THE DOOR NOW!
THERE! NOW YOU C'N CALL THE POLICE!
?
OH, GOSH, WHY DON'T I KEEP MY BIG MOUTH SHUT?
WHAT WILL MRS. JONES SAY WHEN SHE SEES ALL THIS MESS?
I BET SHE'LL BE HOME IN A LITTLE WHILE!
I WONDER WHAT TIME IT IS NOW...
I-I THINK I KNOW A WAY TO FIND OUT!
ALVIN! CAN YOU TELL ME WHAT TIME IT IS?

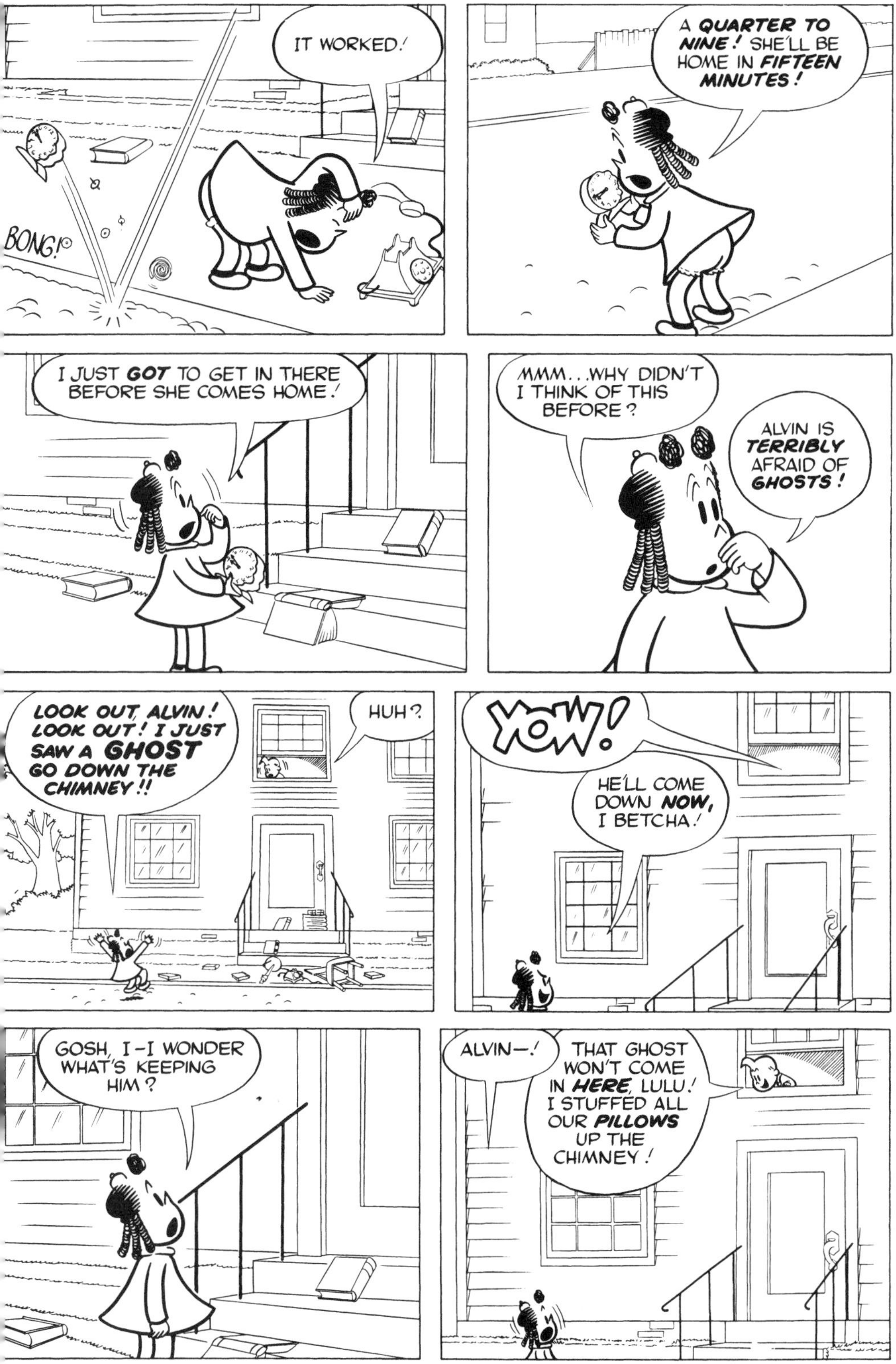
IT WORKED!
BONG!
A QUARTER TO NINE! SHE'LL BE HOME IN FIFTEEN MINUTES!
I JUST GOT TO GET IN THERE BEFORE SHE COMES HOME!
MMM...WHY DIDN'T I THINK OF THIS BEFORE?
ALVIN IS TERRIBLY AFRAID OF GHOSTS!
LOOK OUT, ALVIN! LOOK OUT! I JUST SAW A GHOST GO DOWN THE CHIMNEY!!
HUH?
YOW!
HE'LL COME DOWN NOW, I BETCHA!
GOSH, I-I WONDER WHAT'S KEEPING HIM?
ALVIN—!
THAT GHOST WON'T COME IN HERE, LULU! I STUFFED ALL OUR PILLOWS UP THE CHIMNEY!

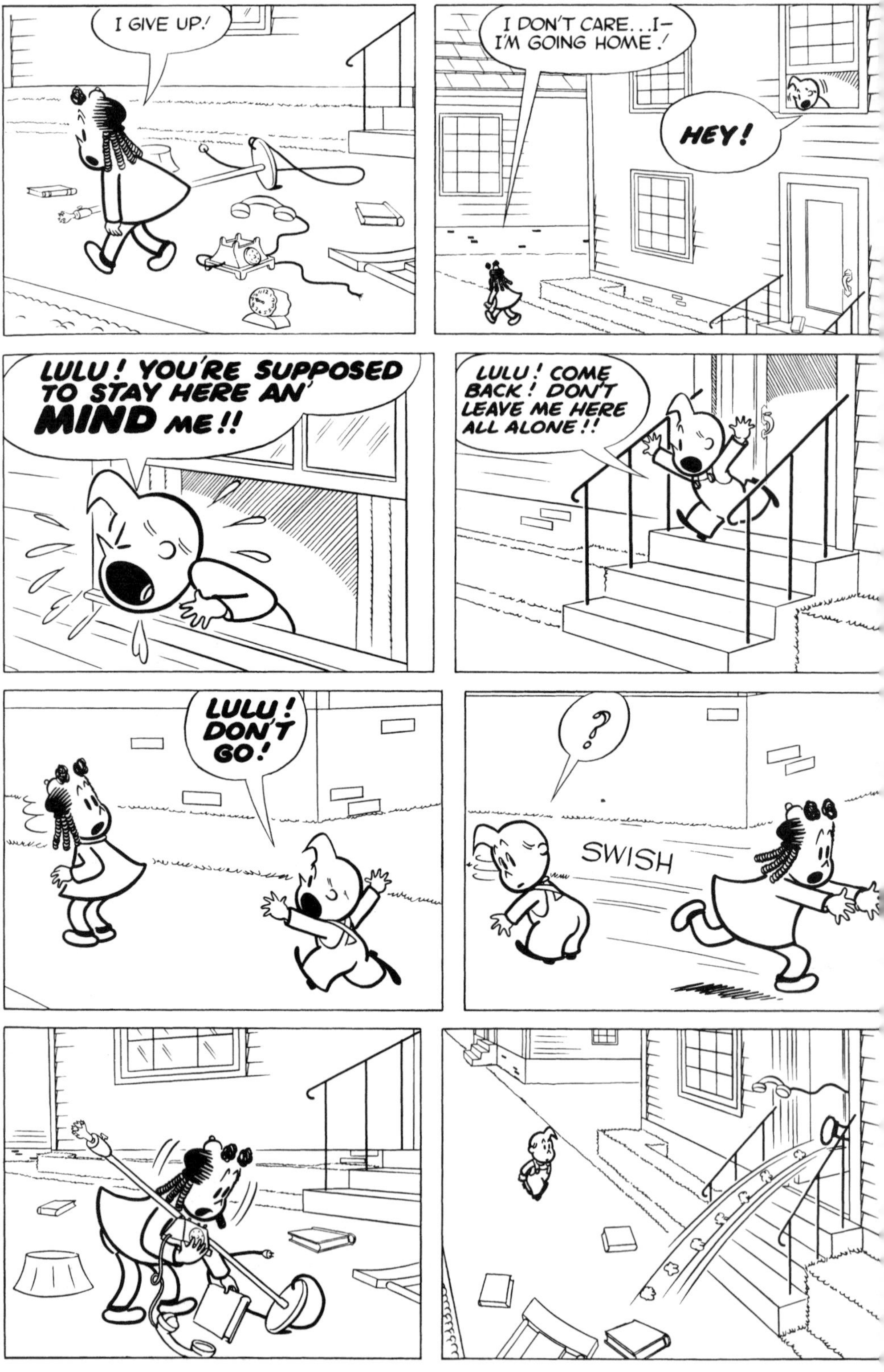
I GIVE UP!
I DON'T CARE...I— I'M GOING HOME!
HEY!
LULU! YOU'RE SUPPOSED TO STAY HERE AN' MIND ME!!
LULU! COME BACK! DON'T LEAVE ME HERE ALL ALONE!!
LULU! DON'T GO!
?
SWISH

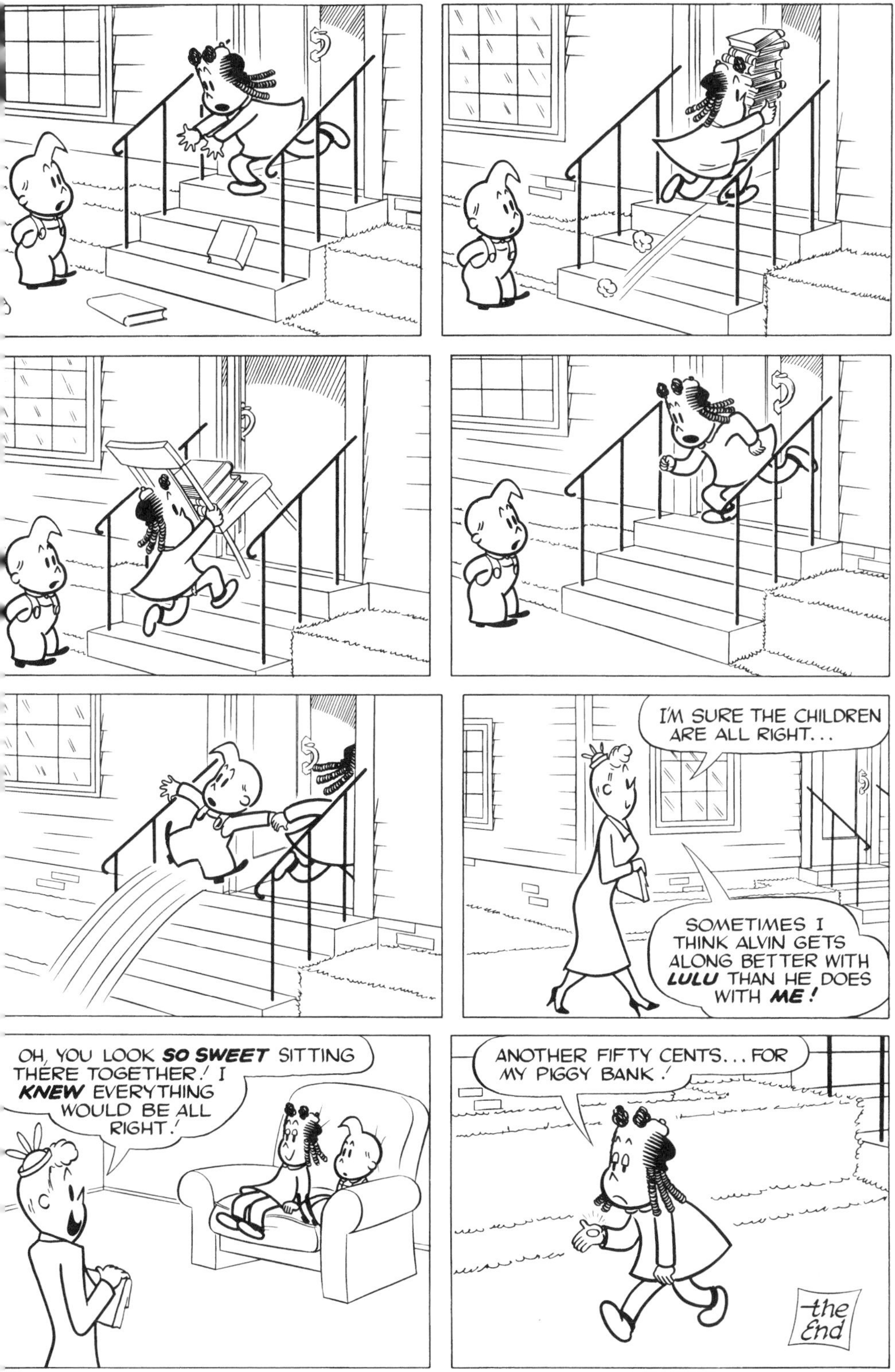
I'M SURE THE CHILDREN ARE ALL RIGHT...
SOMETIMES I THINK ALVIN GETS ALONG BETTER WITH LULU THAN HE DOES WITH ME!
OH, YOU LOOK SO SWEET SITTING THERE TOGETHER! I KNEW EVERYTHING WOULD BE ALL RIGHT!
ANOTHER FIFTY CENTS... FOR MY PIGGY BANK!
the End

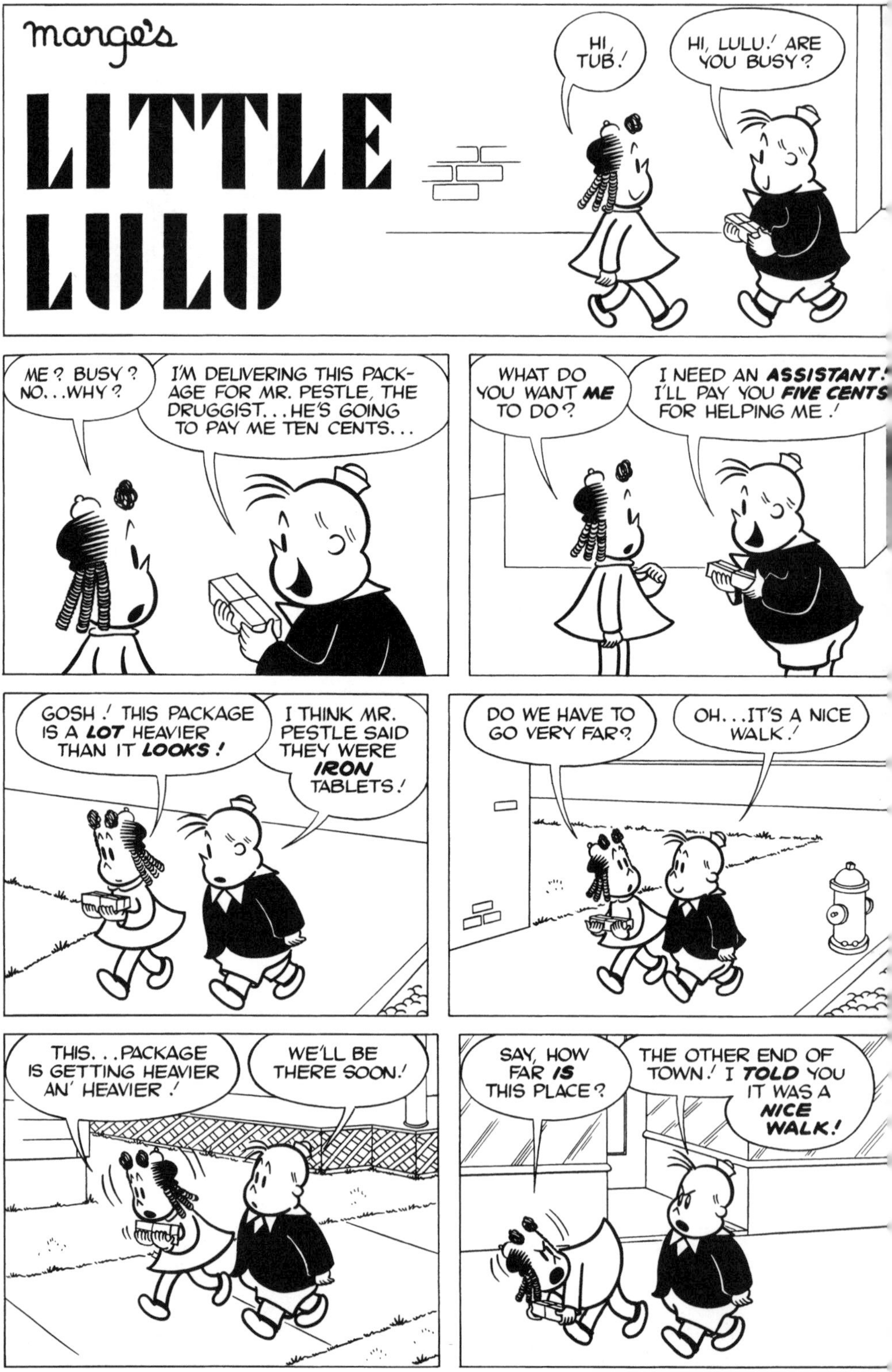
marge's
LITTLE LULU
HI, TUB!
HI, LULU! ARE YOU BUSY?
ME? BUSY? NO...WHY?
I'M DELIVERING THIS PACKAGE FOR MR. PESTLE, THE DRUGGIST...HE'S GOING TO PAY ME TEN CENTS...
WHAT DO YOU WANT ME TO DO?
I NEED AN ASSISTANT! I'LL PAY YOU FIVE CENTS FOR HELPING ME!
GOSH! THIS PACKAGE IS A LOT HEAVIER THAN IT LOOKS!
I THINK MR. PESTLE SAID THEY WERE IRON TABLETS!
DO WE HAVE TO GO VERY FAR?
OH...IT'S A NICE WALK!
THIS...PACKAGE IS GETTING HEAVIER AN' HEAVIER!
WE'LL BE THERE SOON!
SAY, HOW FAR IS THIS PLACE?
THE OTHER END OF TOWN! I TOLD YOU IT WAS A NICE WALK!

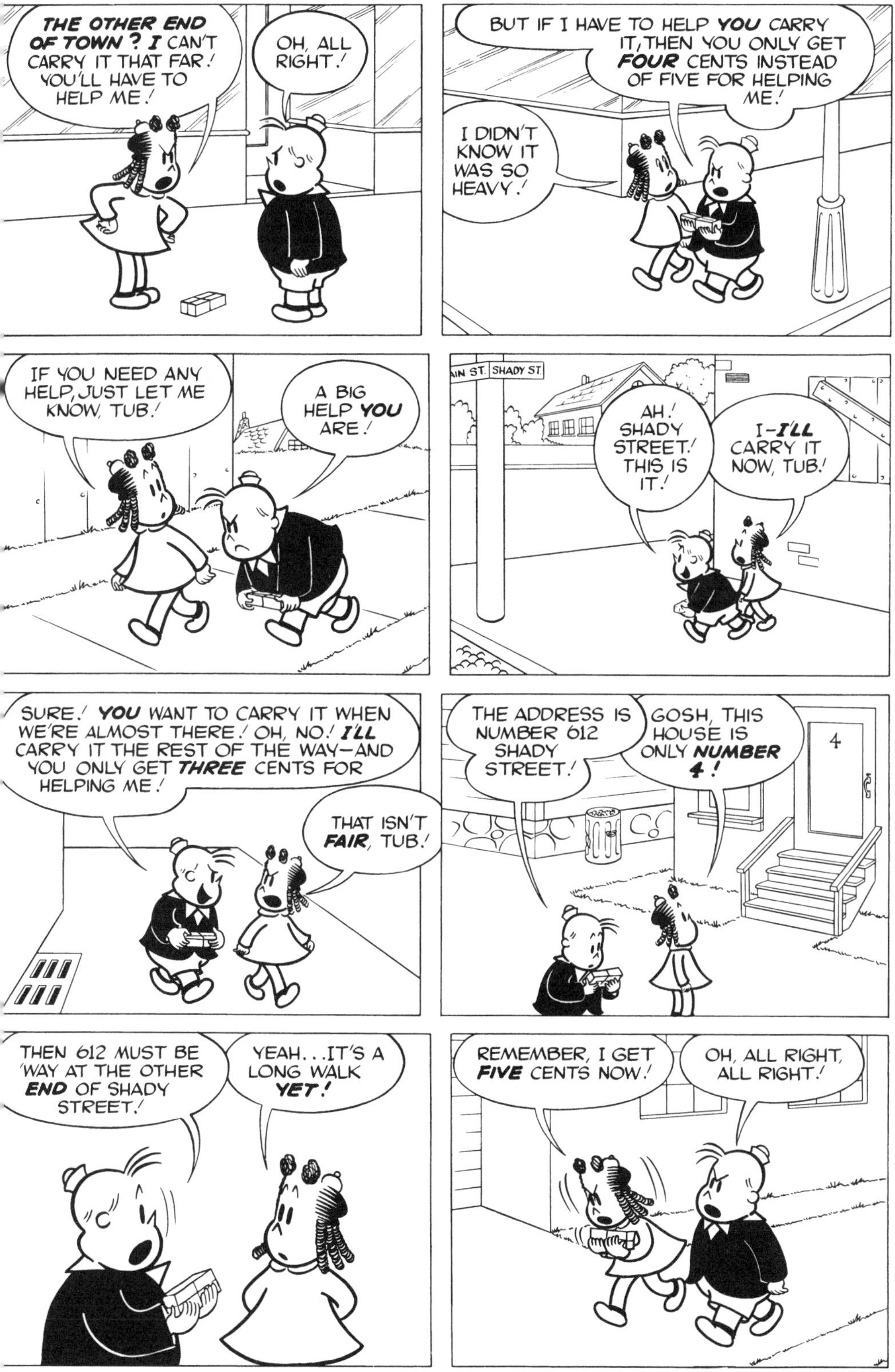
THE OTHER END OF TOWN? I CAN'T CARRY IT THAT FAR! YOU'LL HAVE TO HELP ME!
OH, ALL RIGHT!
BUT IF I HAVE TO HELP YOU CARRY IT, THEN YOU ONLY GET FOUR CENTS INSTEAD OF FIVE FOR HELPING ME!
I DIDN'T KNOW IT WAS SO HEAVY!
IF YOU NEED ANY HELP, JUST LET ME KNOW, TUB!
A BIG HELP YOU ARE!
AIN ST.
SHADY ST.
AH! SHADY STREET! THIS IS IT!
I-I'LL CARRY IT NOW, TUB!
SURE! YOU WANT TO CARRY IT WHEN WE'RE ALMOST THERE! OH, NO! I'LL CARRY IT THE REST OF THE WAY—AND YOU ONLY GET THREE CENTS FOR HELPING ME!
THAT ISN'T FAIR, TUB!
THE ADDRESS IS NUMBER 612 SHADY STREET!
GOSH, THIS HOUSE IS ONLY NUMBER 4!
4
THEN 612 MUST BE 'WAY AT THE OTHER END OF SHADY STREET!
YEAH...IT'S A LONG WALK YET!
REMEMBER, I GET FIVE CENTS NOW!
OH, ALL RIGHT, ALL RIGHT!

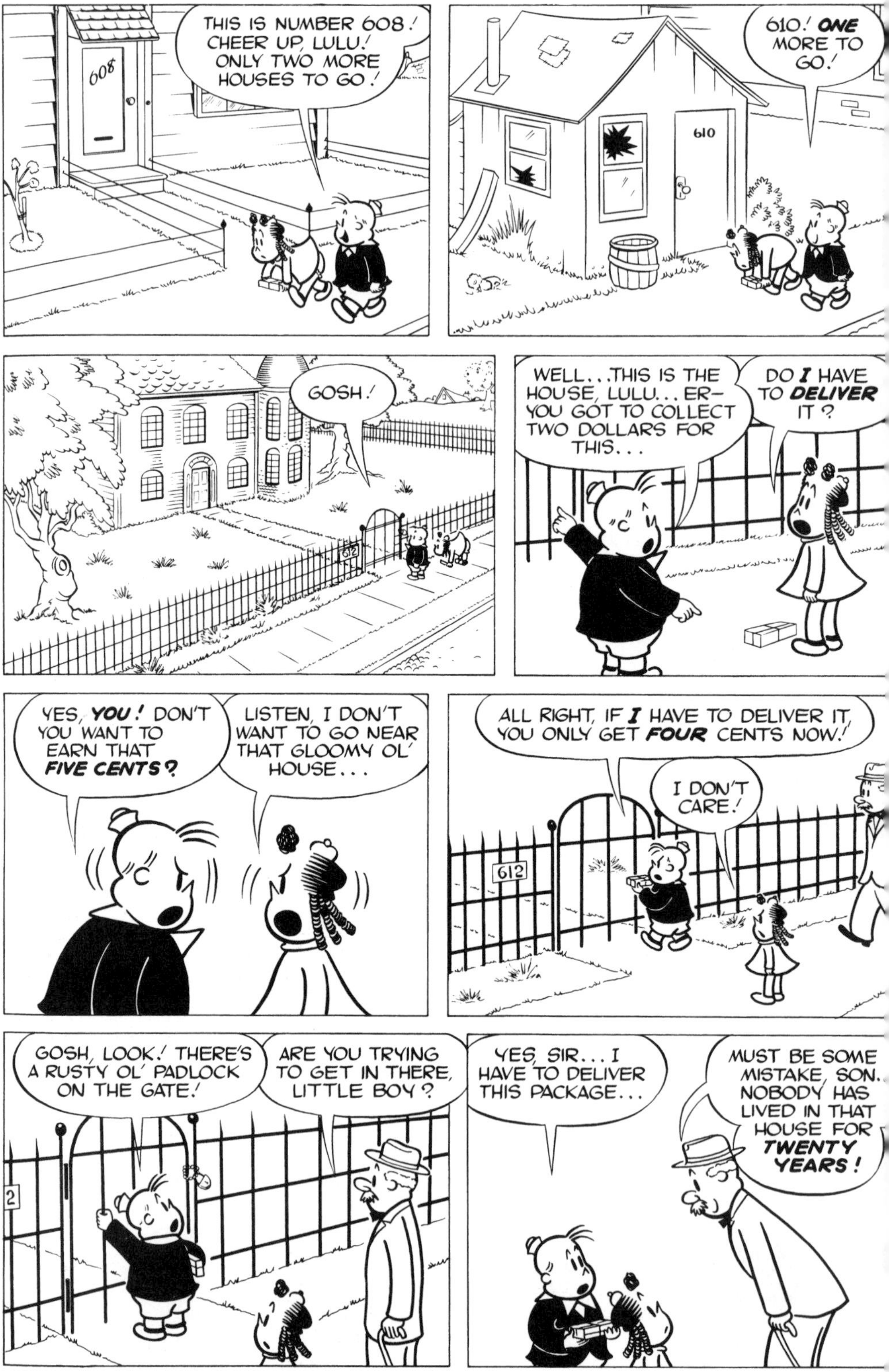
THIS IS NUMBER 608! CHEER UP, LULU! ONLY TWO MORE HOUSES TO GO!
608
610! ONE MORE TO GO!
610
GOSH!
612
WELL...THIS IS THE HOUSE, LULU... ER- YOU GOT TO COLLECT TWO DOLLARS FOR THIS...
DO I HAVE TO DELIVER IT?
YES, YOU! DON'T YOU WANT TO EARN THAT FIVE CENTS?
LISTEN, I DON'T WANT TO GO NEAR THAT GLOOMY OL' HOUSE...
ALL RIGHT, IF I HAVE TO DELIVER IT, YOU ONLY GET FOUR CENTS NOW!
I DON'T CARE!
612
GOSH, LOOK! THERE'S A RUSTY OL' PADLOCK ON THE GATE!
ARE YOU TRYING TO GET IN THERE, LITTLE BOY?
YES, SIR... I HAVE TO DELIVER THIS PACKAGE...
MUST BE SOME MISTAKE, SON. NOBODY HAS LIVED IN THAT HOUSE FOR TWENTY YEARS!

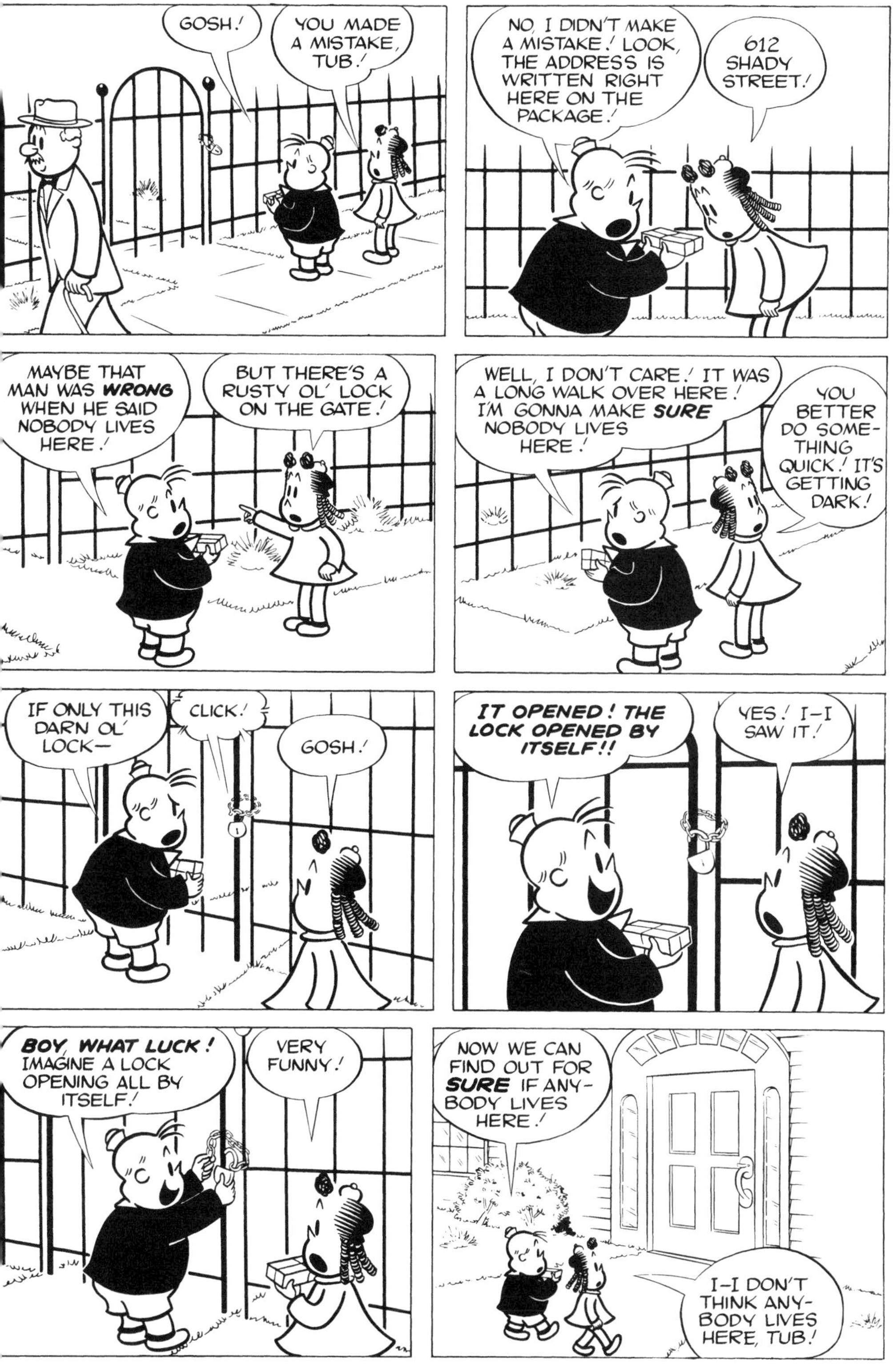
GOSH.!
YOU MADE A MISTAKE, TUB.!
NO, I DIDN'T MAKE A MISTAKE.! LOOK, THE ADDRESS IS WRITTEN RIGHT HERE ON THE PACKAGE.!
612 SHADY STREET.!
MAYBE THAT MAN WAS **WRONG** WHEN HE SAID NOBODY LIVES HERE.!
BUT THERE'S A RUSTY OL' LOCK ON THE GATE.!
WELL, I DON'T CARE.! IT WAS A LONG WALK OVER HERE.! I'M GONNA MAKE **SURE** NOBODY LIVES HERE.!
YOU BETTER DO SOME-THING QUICK.! IT'S GETTING DARK.!
IF ONLY THIS DARN OL' LOCK—
CLICK.!
GOSH.!
IT OPENED! THE LOCK OPENED BY ITSELF!!
YES.! I—I SAW IT.!
BOY, WHAT LUCK! IMAGINE A LOCK OPENING ALL BY ITSELF.!
VERY FUNNY.!
NOW WE CAN FIND OUT FOR **SURE** IF ANY-BODY LIVES HERE.!
I—I DON'T THINK ANY-BODY LIVES HERE, TUB.!

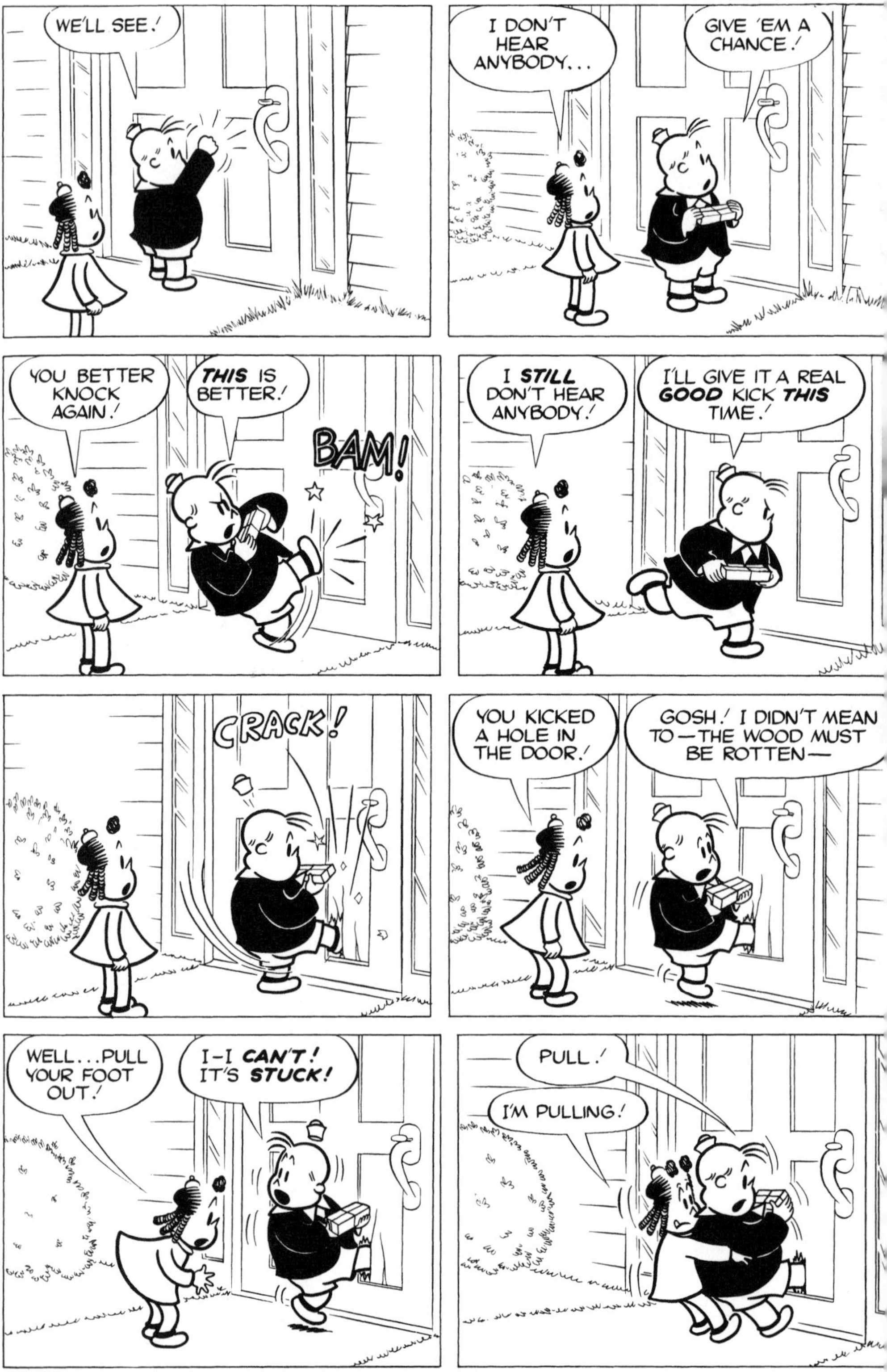
WE'LL SEE.!
I DON'T HEAR ANYBODY...
GIVE 'EM A CHANCE.!
YOU BETTER KNOCK AGAIN.!
THIS IS BETTER.!
BAM!
I STILL DON'T HEAR ANYBODY.!
I'LL GIVE IT A REAL GOOD KICK THIS TIME.!
CRACK!
YOU KICKED A HOLE IN THE DOOR.!
GOSH.! I DIDN'T MEAN TO—THE WOOD MUST BE ROTTEN—
WELL...PULL YOUR FOOT OUT.!
I-I CAN'T! IT'S STUCK!
PULL.!
I'M PULLING.!

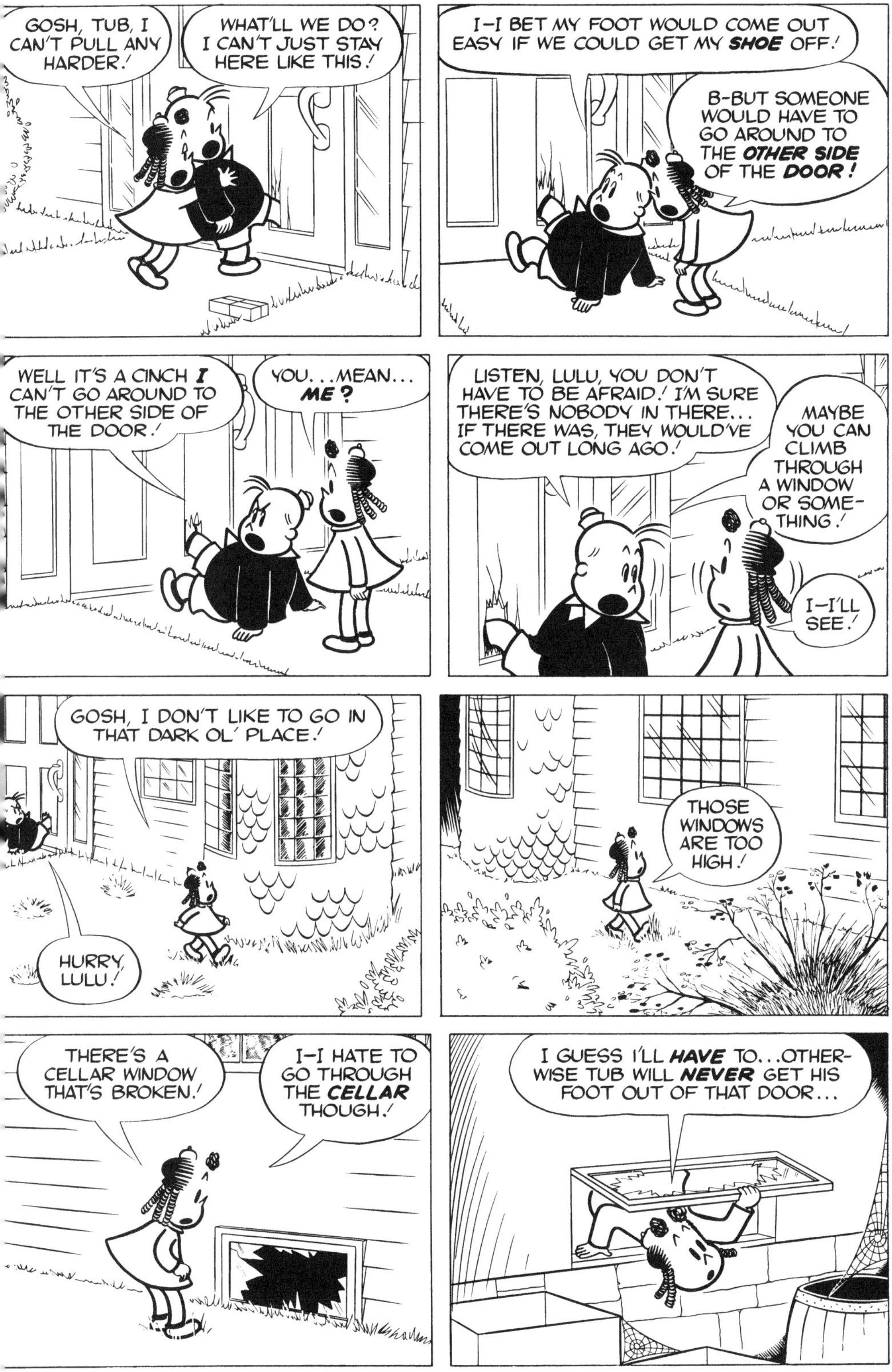
GOSH, TUB, I CAN'T PULL ANY HARDER!
WHAT'LL WE DO? I CAN'T JUST STAY HERE LIKE THIS!
I-I BET MY FOOT WOULD COME OUT EASY IF WE COULD GET MY SHOE OFF!
B-BUT SOMEONE WOULD HAVE TO GO AROUND TO THE OTHER SIDE OF THE DOOR!
WELL IT'S A CINCH I CAN'T GO AROUND TO THE OTHER SIDE OF THE DOOR!
YOU...MEAN... ME?
LISTEN, LULU, YOU DON'T HAVE TO BE AFRAID! I'M SURE THERE'S NOBODY IN THERE... IF THERE WAS, THEY WOULD'VE COME OUT LONG AGO!
MAYBE YOU CAN CLIMB THROUGH A WINDOW OR SOME-THING!
I-I'LL SEE!
GOSH, I DON'T LIKE TO GO IN THAT DARK OL' PLACE!
HURRY, LULU!
THOSE WINDOWS ARE TOO HIGH!
THERE'S A CELLAR WINDOW THAT'S BROKEN!
I-I HATE TO GO THROUGH THE CELLAR THOUGH!
I GUESS I'LL HAVE TO...OTHER-WISE TUB WILL NEVER GET HIS FOOT OUT OF THAT DOOR...

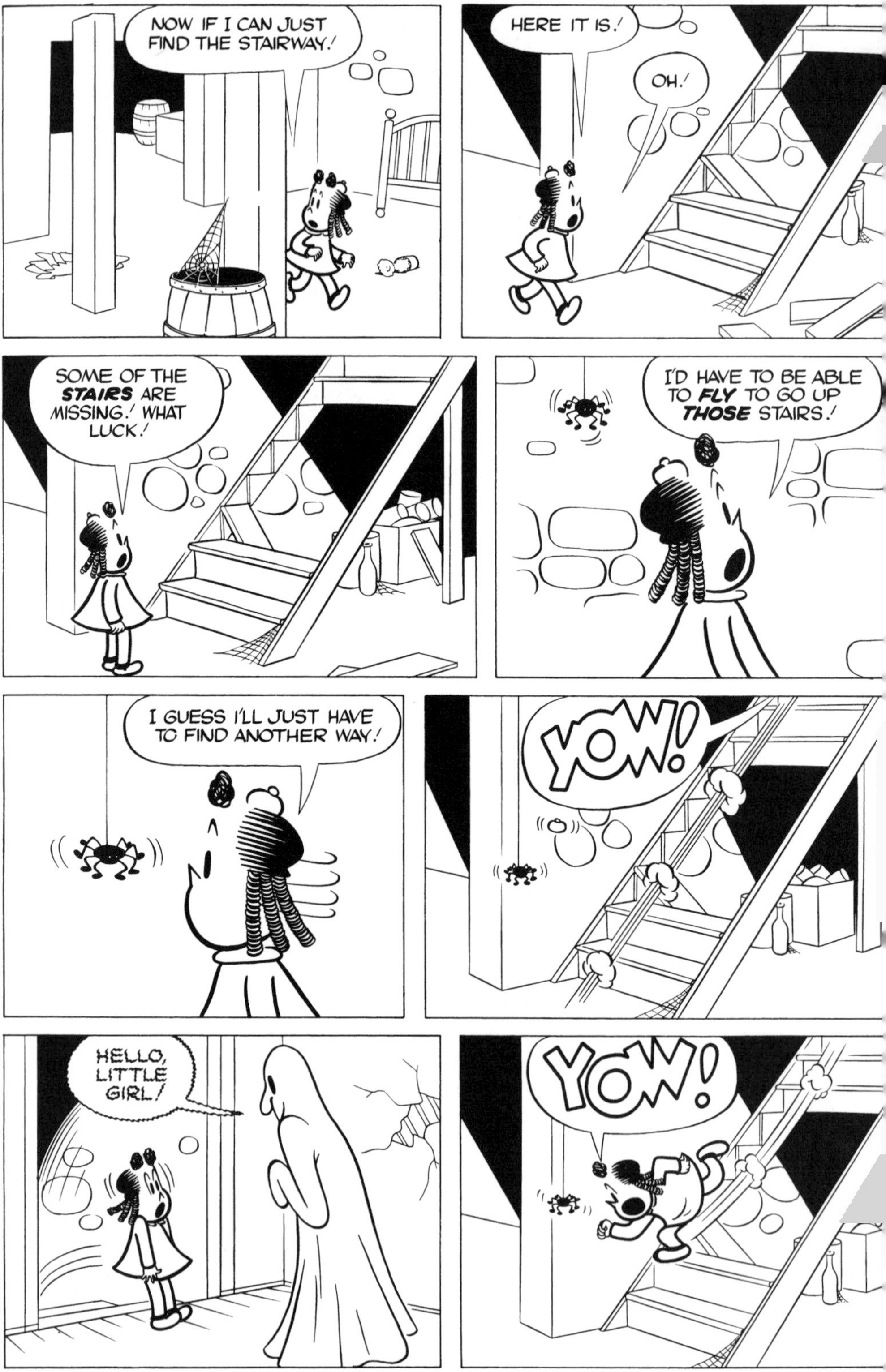
NOW IF I CAN JUST FIND THE STAIRWAY!
HERE IT IS!
OH!
SOME OF THE STAIRS ARE MISSING! WHAT LUCK!
I'D HAVE TO BE ABLE TO FLY TO GO UP THOSE STAIRS!
I GUESS I'LL JUST HAVE TO FIND ANOTHER WAY!
YOW!
HELLO, LITTLE GIRL!
YOW!

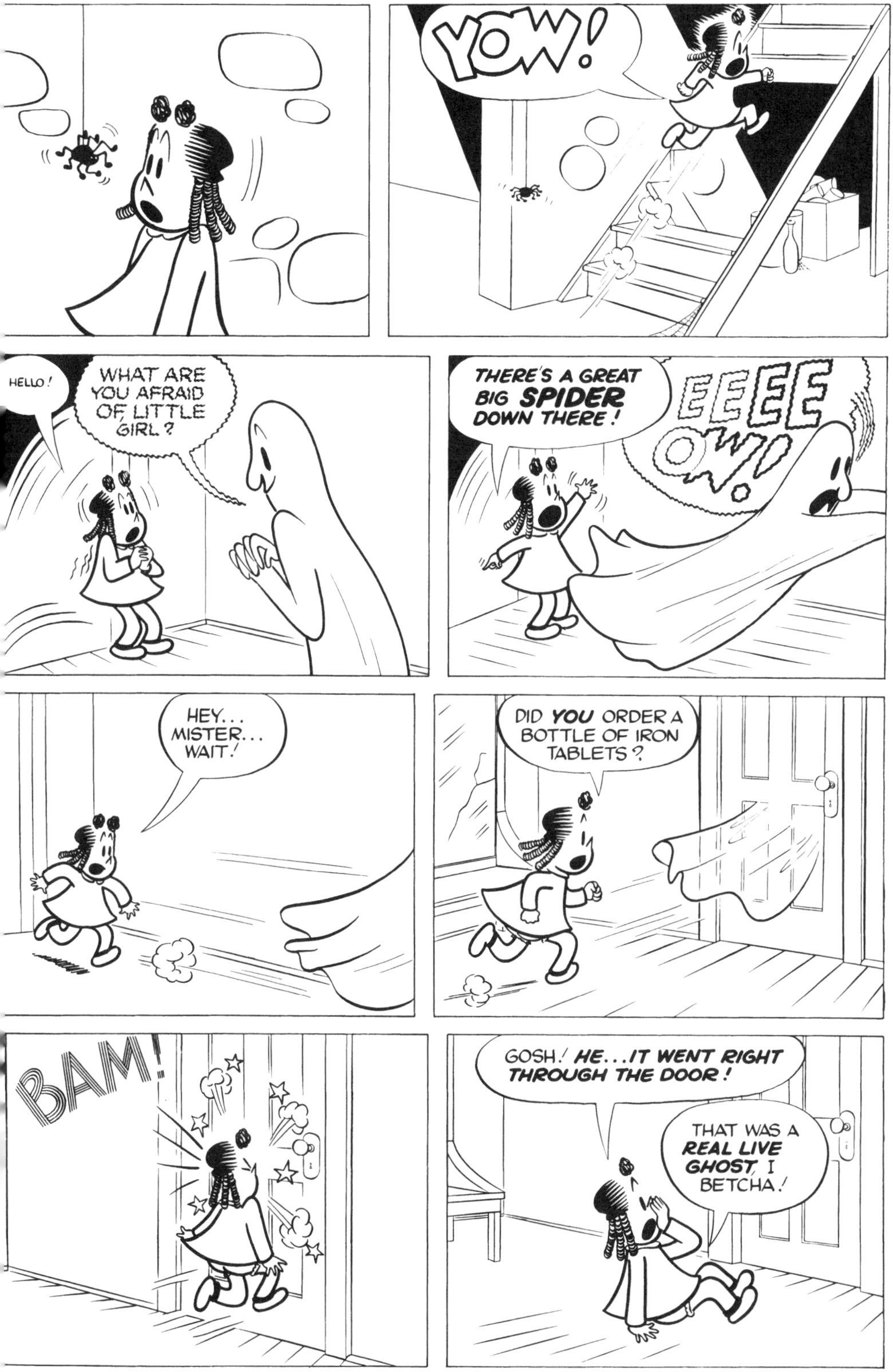
YOW!
HELLO!
WHAT ARE YOU AFRAID OF, LITTLE GIRL?
THERE'S A GREAT BIG SPIDER DOWN THERE!
EEEEE OW!
HEY... MISTER... WAIT!
DID YOU ORDER A BOTTLE OF IRON TABLETS?
BAM!
GOSH! HE...IT WENT RIGHT THROUGH THE DOOR!
THAT WAS A REAL LIVE GHOST, I BETCHA!

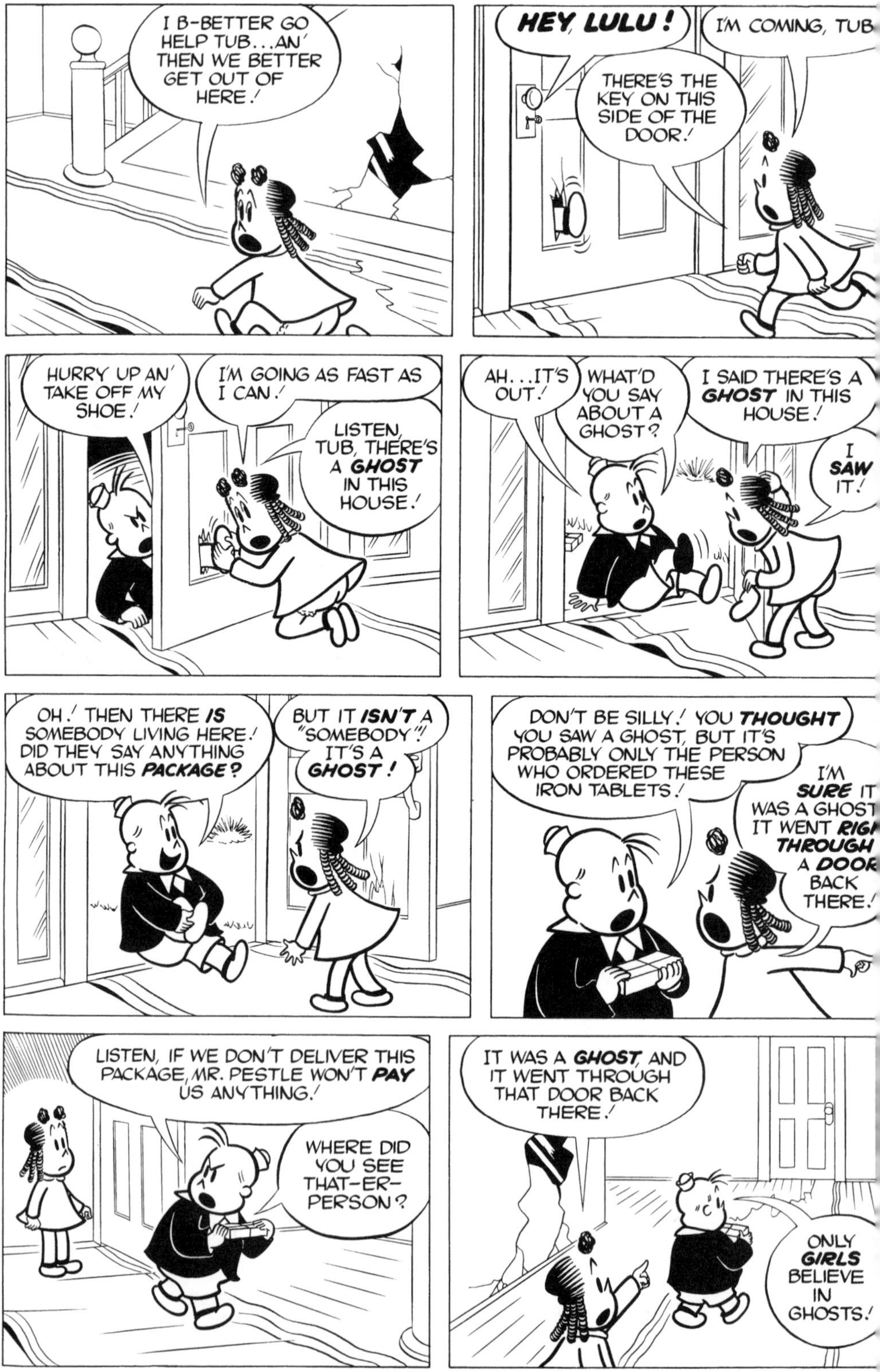

I B-BETTER GO HELP TUB...AN' THEN WE BETTER GET OUT OF HERE!
HEY, LULU!
I'M COMING, TUB
THERE'S THE KEY ON THIS SIDE OF THE DOOR!
HURRY UP AN' TAKE OFF MY SHOE!
I'M GOING AS FAST AS I CAN!
LISTEN, TUB, THERE'S A GHOST IN THIS HOUSE!
AH...IT'S OUT!
WHAT'D YOU SAY ABOUT A GHOST?
I SAID THERE'S A GHOST IN THIS HOUSE!
I SAW IT!
OH! THEN THERE IS SOMEBODY LIVING HERE! DID THEY SAY ANYTHING ABOUT THIS PACKAGE?
BUT IT ISN'T A "SOMEBODY"! IT'S A GHOST!
DON'T BE SILLY! YOU THOUGHT YOU SAW A GHOST, BUT IT'S PROBABLY ONLY THE PERSON WHO ORDERED THESE IRON TABLETS!
I'M SURE IT WAS A GHOST IT WENT RIG THROUGH A DOOR BACK THERE!
LISTEN, IF WE DON'T DELIVER THIS PACKAGE, MR. PESTLE WON'T PAY US ANYTHING!
WHERE DID YOU SEE THAT-ER-PERSON?
IT WAS A GHOST, AND IT WENT THROUGH THAT DOOR BACK THERE!
ONLY GIRLS BELIEVE IN GHOSTS!

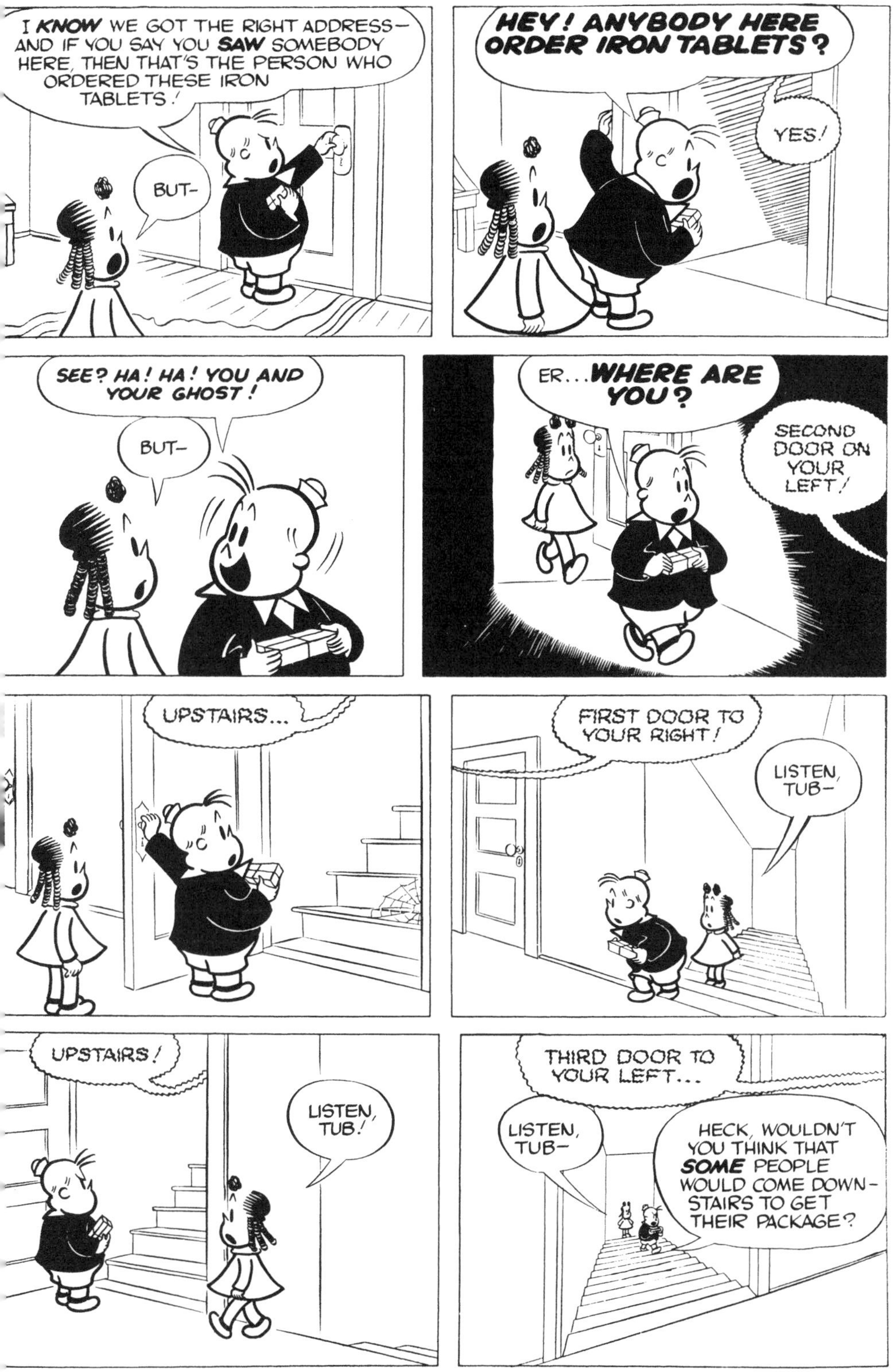

I KNOW WE GOT THE RIGHT ADDRESS— AND IF YOU SAY YOU SAW SOMEBODY HERE, THEN THAT'S THE PERSON WHO ORDERED THESE IRON TABLETS!
BUT-
HEY! ANYBODY HERE ORDER IRON TABLETS?
YES!
SEE? HA! HA! YOU AND YOUR GHOST!
BUT-
ER...WHERE ARE YOU?
SECOND DOOR ON YOUR LEFT!
UPSTAIRS...
FIRST DOOR TO YOUR RIGHT!
LISTEN, TUB-
UPSTAIRS!
LISTEN, TUB!
THIRD DOOR TO YOUR LEFT...
LISTEN, TUB-
HECK, WOULDN'T YOU THINK THAT SOME PEOPLE WOULD COME DOWN-STAIRS TO GET THEIR PACKAGE?

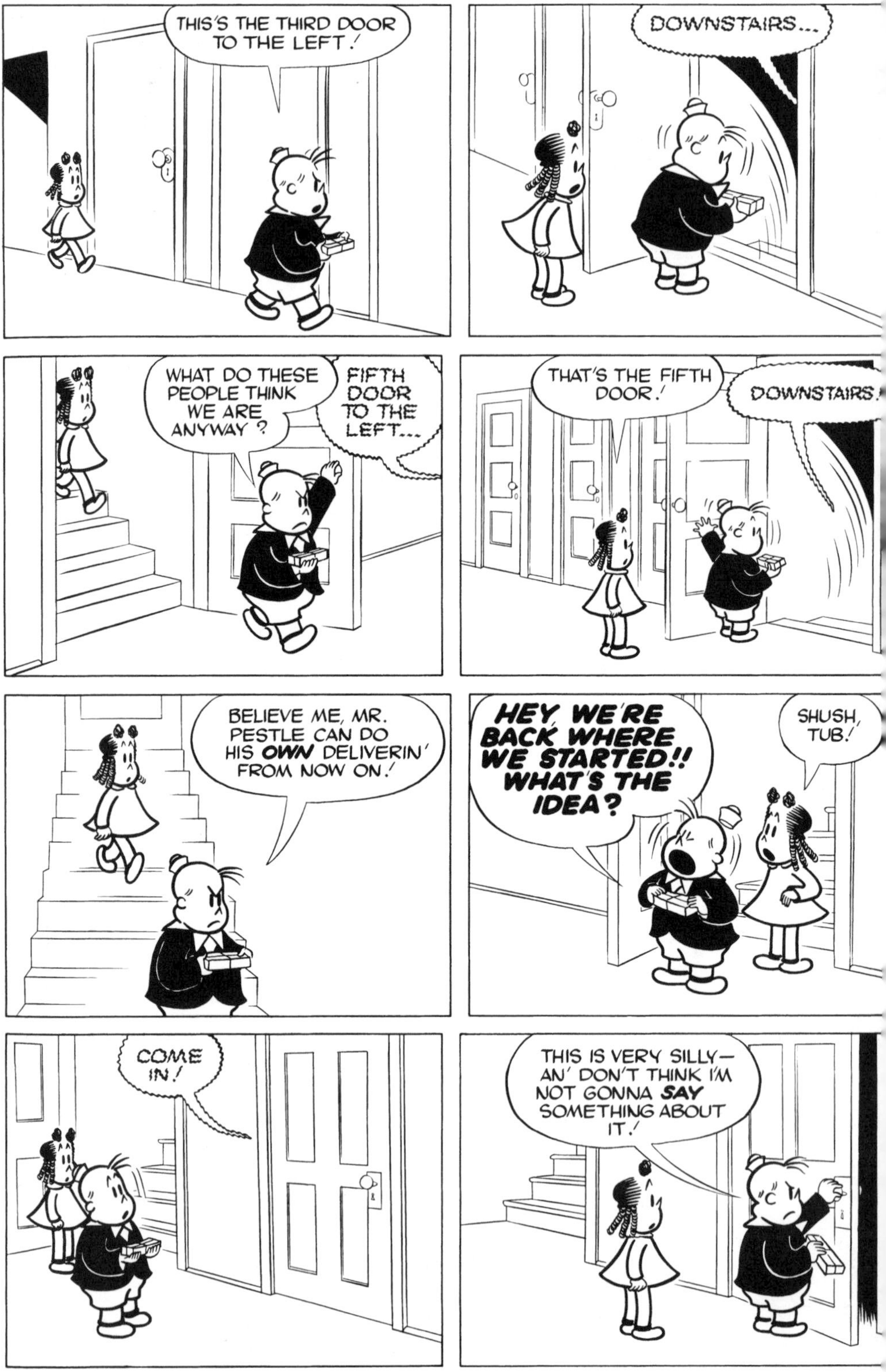
THIS'S THE THIRD DOOR TO THE LEFT.!
DOWNSTAIRS...
WHAT DO THESE PEOPLE THINK WE ARE ANYWAY ?
FIFTH DOOR TO THE LEFT...
THAT'S THE FIFTH DOOR.!
DOWNSTAIRS!
BELIEVE ME, MR. PESTLE CAN DO HIS **OWN** DELIVERIN' FROM NOW ON.!
HEY, WE'RE BACK WHERE WE STARTED!! WHAT'S THE IDEA?
SHUSH, TUB.!
COME IN.!
THIS IS VERY SILLY— AN' DON'T THINK I'M NOT GONNA **SAY** SOMETHING ABOUT IT.!

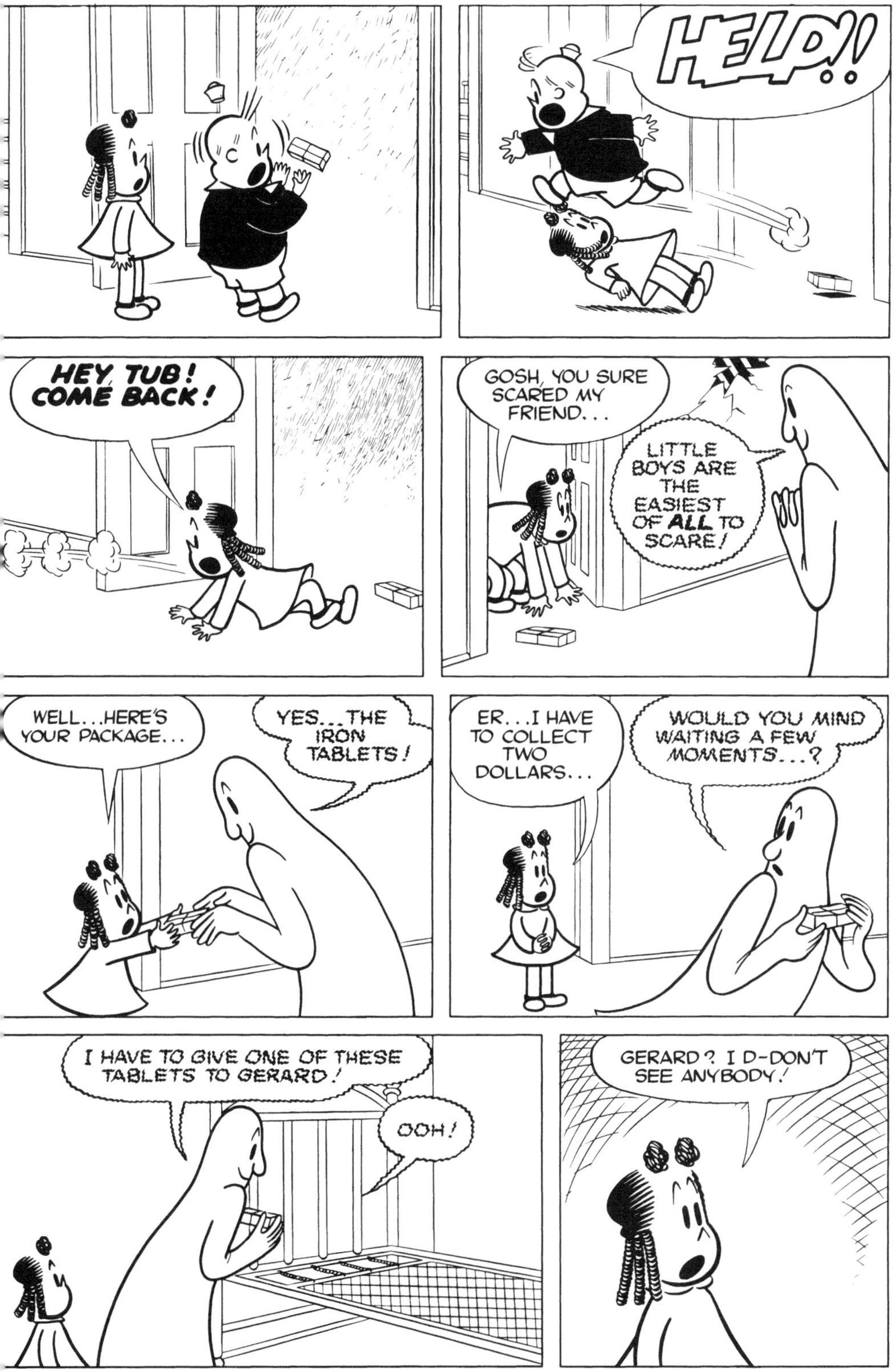
HELP!!
HEY, TUB! COME BACK!
GOSH, YOU SURE SCARED MY FRIEND...
LITTLE BOYS ARE THE EASIEST OF ALL TO SCARE!
WELL...HERE'S YOUR PACKAGE...
YES...THE IRON TABLETS!
ER...I HAVE TO COLLECT TWO DOLLARS...
WOULD YOU MIND WAITING A FEW MOMENTS...?
I HAVE TO GIVE ONE OF THESE TABLETS TO GERARD!
OOH!
GERARD? I D-DON'T SEE ANYBODY!

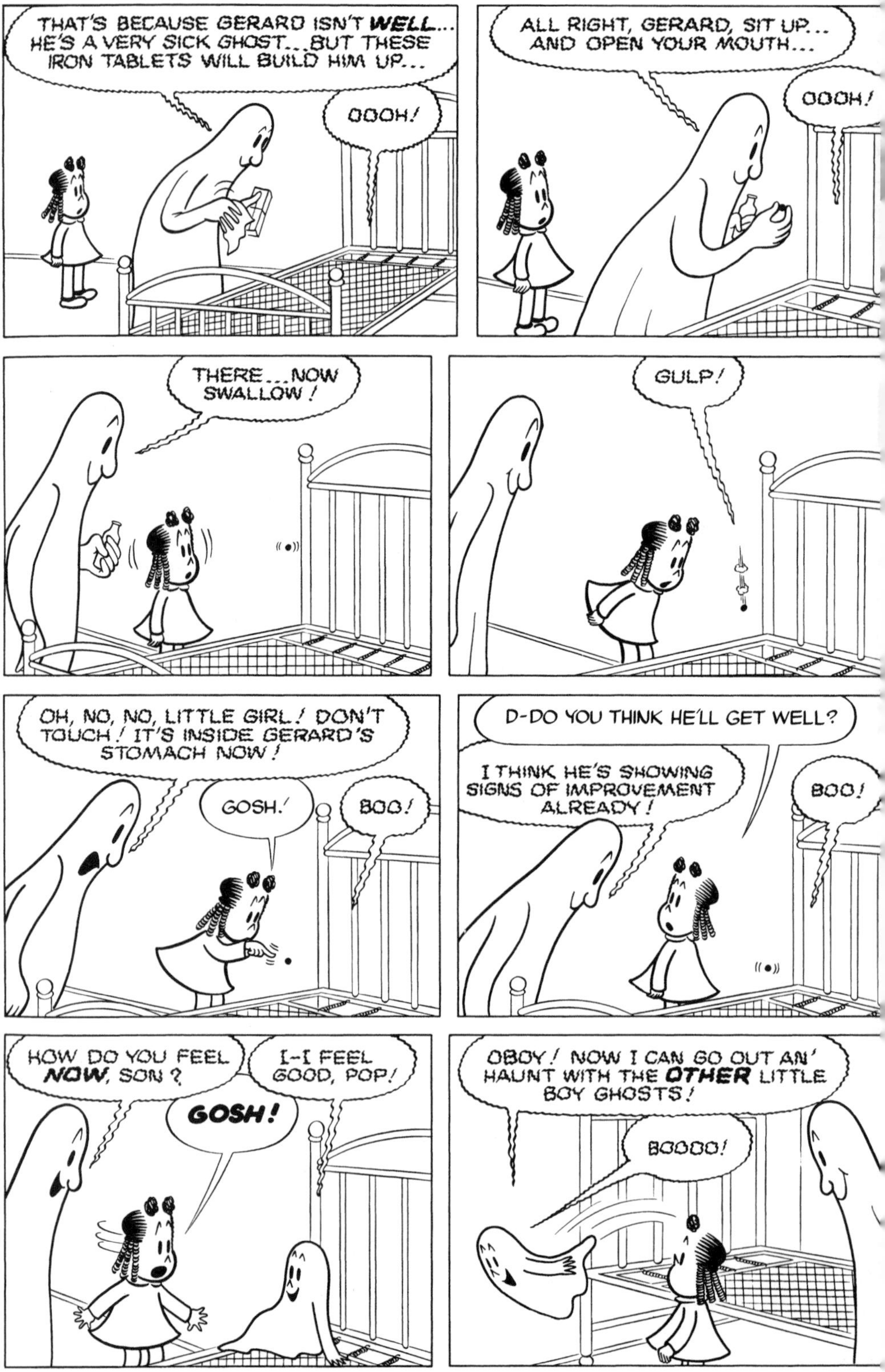
THAT'S BECAUSE GERARD ISN'T WELL... HE'S A VERY SICK GHOST... BUT THESE IRON TABLETS WILL BUILD HIM UP...
OOOH!
ALL RIGHT, GERARD, SIT UP... AND OPEN YOUR MOUTH...
OOOH!
THERE... NOW SWALLOW!
GULP!
OH, NO, NO, LITTLE GIRL! DON'T TOUCH! IT'S INSIDE GERARD'S STOMACH NOW!
GOSH!
BOO!
D-DO YOU THINK HE'LL GET WELL?
I THINK HE'S SHOWING SIGNS OF IMPROVEMENT ALREADY!
BOO!
HOW DO YOU FEEL NOW, SON?
I-I FEEL GOOD, POP!
GOSH!
OBOY! NOW I CAN GO OUT AN' HAUNT WITH THE OTHER LITTLE BOY GHOSTS!
BOOOO!

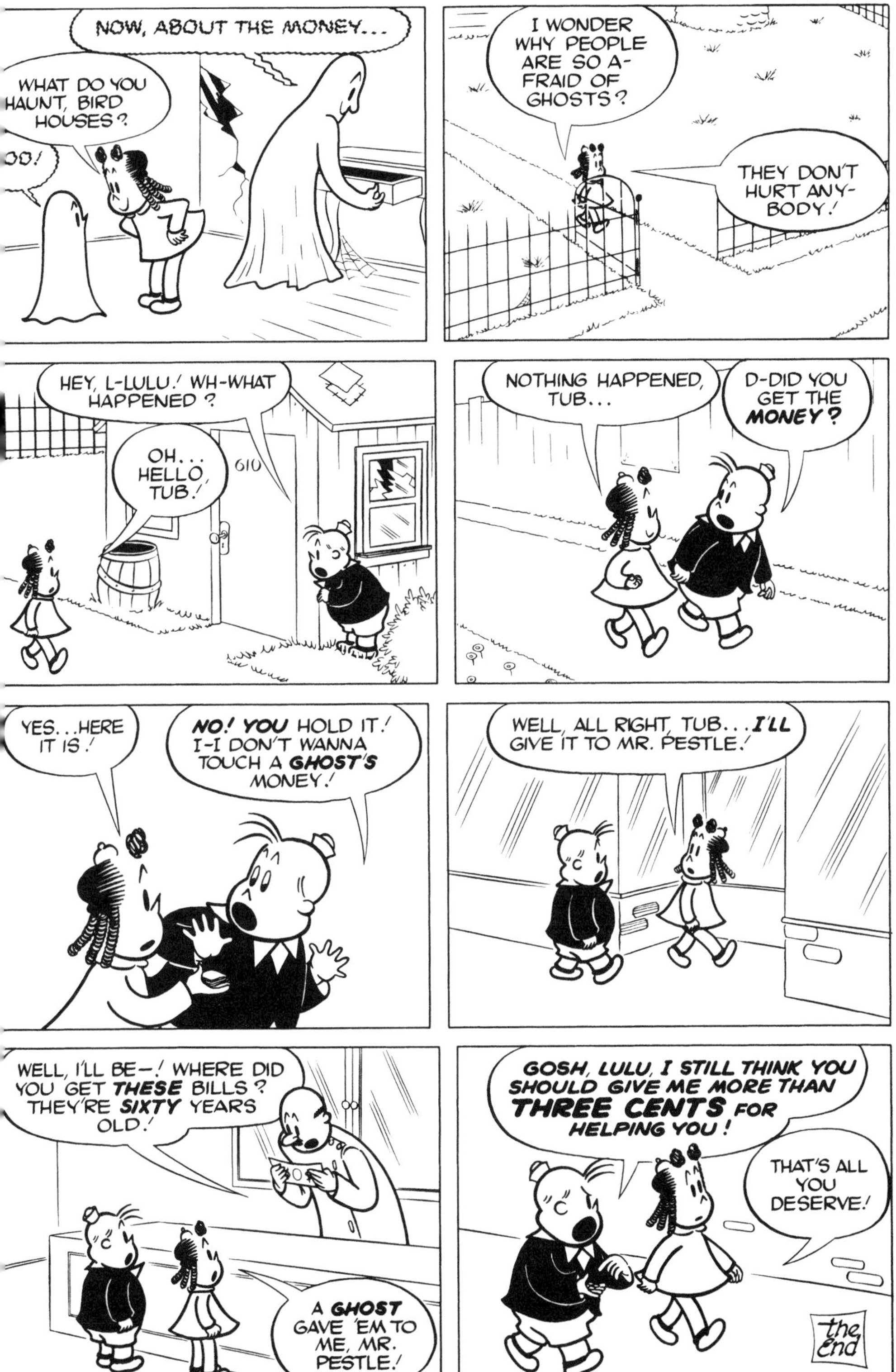
NOW, ABOUT THE MONEY...
WHAT DO YOU HAUNT, BIRD HOUSES?
OO!
I WONDER WHY PEOPLE ARE SO A-FRAID OF GHOSTS?
THEY DON'T HURT ANY-BODY!
HEY, L-LULU! WH-WHAT HAPPENED?
OH... HELLO, TUB!
610
NOTHING HAPPENED, TUB...
D-DID YOU GET THE MONEY?
YES...HERE IT IS!
NO! YOU HOLD IT! I-I DON'T WANNA TOUCH A GHOST'S MONEY!
WELL, ALL RIGHT, TUB...I'LL GIVE IT TO MR. PESTLE!
WELL, I'LL BE—! WHERE DID YOU GET THESE BILLS? THEY'RE SIXTY YEARS OLD!
A GHOST GAVE 'EM TO ME, MR. PESTLE!
GOSH, LULU, I STILL THINK YOU SHOULD GIVE ME MORE THAN THREE CENTS FOR HELPING YOU!
THAT'S ALL YOU DESERVE!
the End

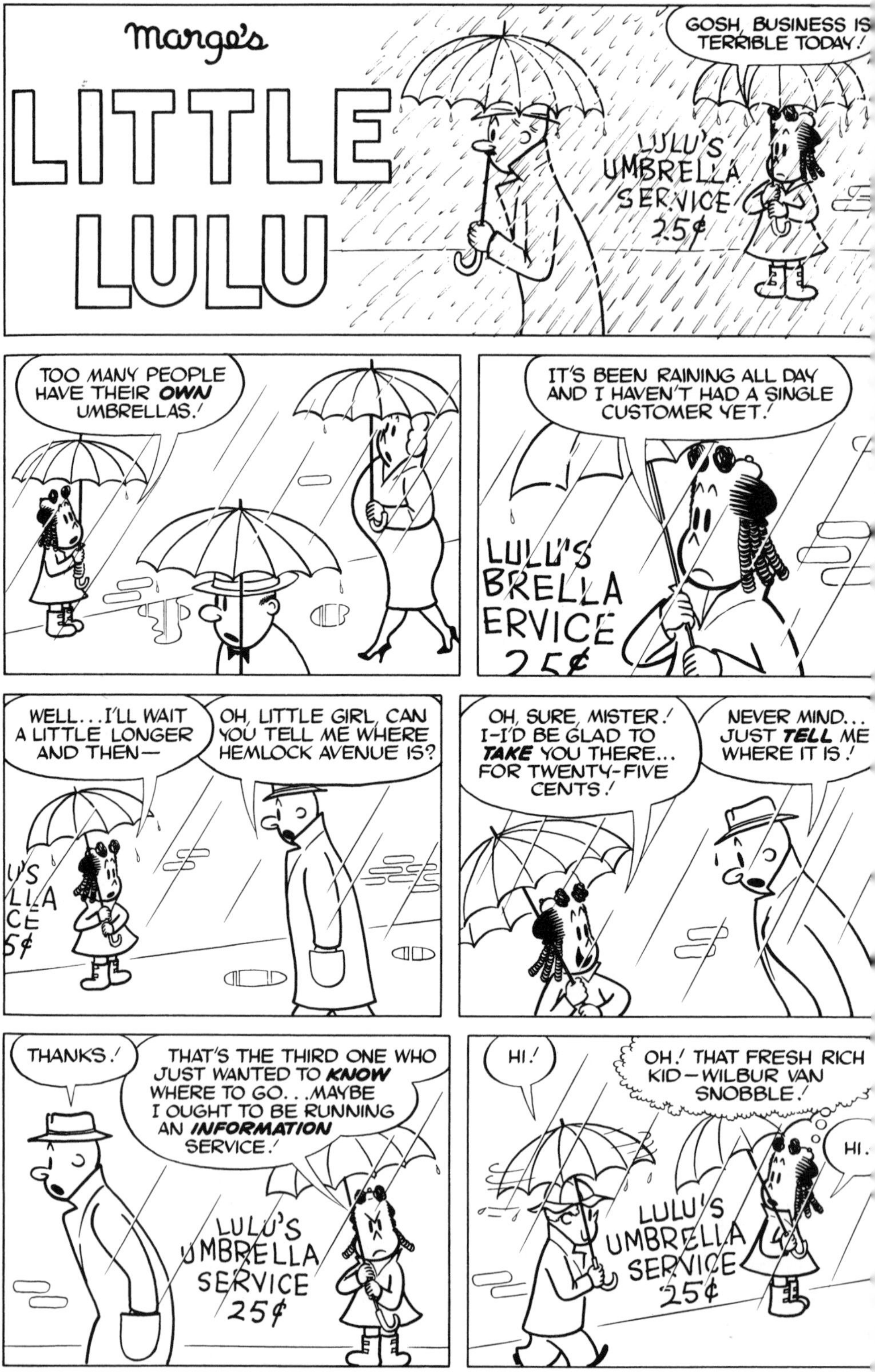
marge's
LITTLE LULU
GOSH, BUSINESS IS TERRIBLE TODAY!
LULU'S UMBRELLA SERVICE 25¢
TOO MANY PEOPLE HAVE THEIR OWN UMBRELLAS!
IT'S BEEN RAINING ALL DAY AND I HAVEN'T HAD A SINGLE CUSTOMER YET!
WELL...I'LL WAIT A LITTLE LONGER AND THEN—
OH, LITTLE GIRL, CAN YOU TELL ME WHERE HEMLOCK AVENUE IS?
OH, SURE, MISTER! I-I'D BE GLAD TO TAKE YOU THERE... FOR TWENTY-FIVE CENTS!
NEVER MIND... JUST TELL ME WHERE IT IS!
THANKS!
THAT'S THE THIRD ONE WHO JUST WANTED TO KNOW WHERE TO GO...MAYBE I OUGHT TO BE RUNNING AN INFORMATION SERVICE!
LULU'S UMBRELLA SERVICE 25¢
HI!
OH! THAT FRESH RICH KID—WILBUR VAN SNOBBLE!
HI.
LULU'S UMBRELLA SERVICE 25¢

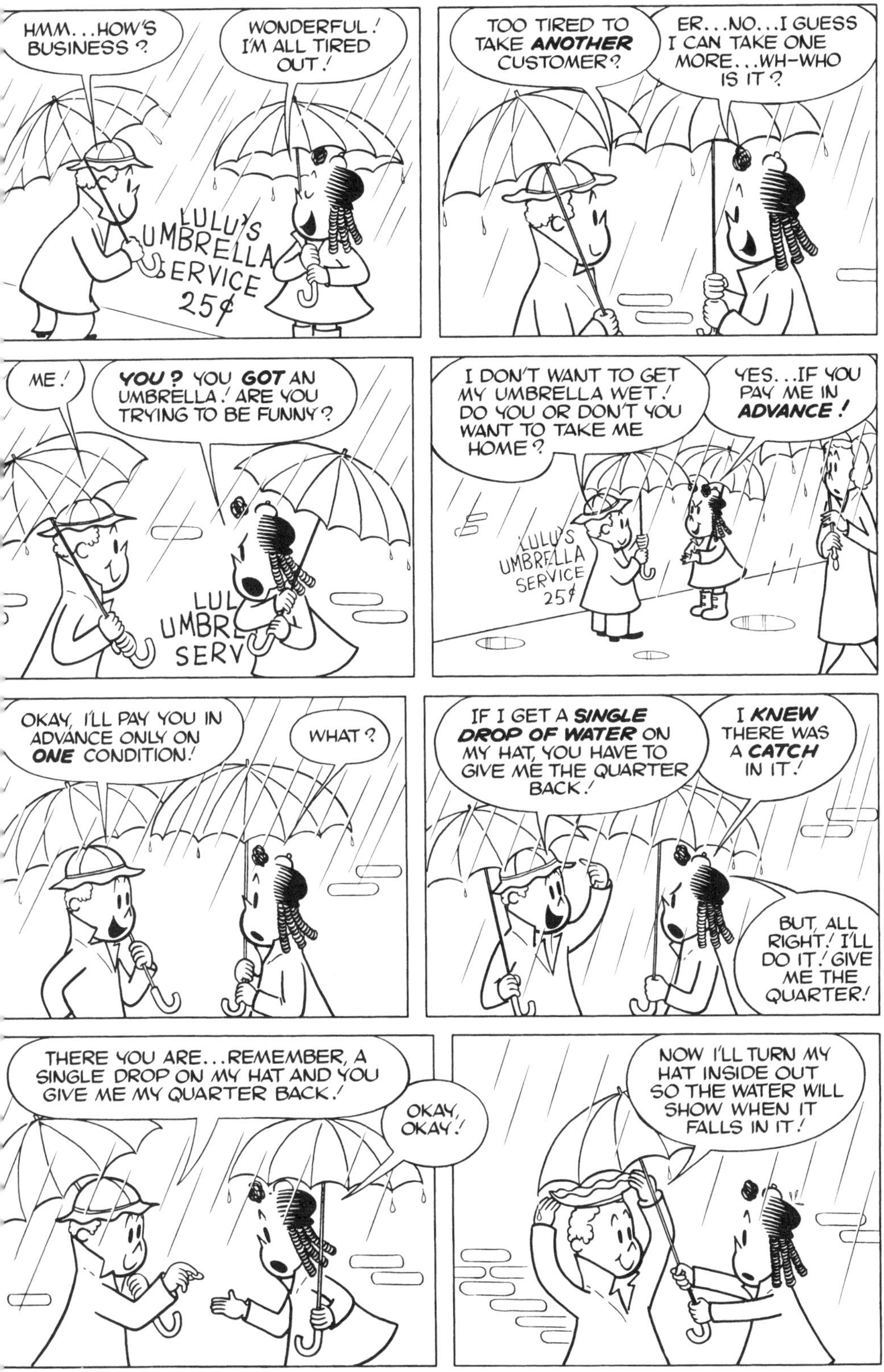
HMM...HOW'S BUSINESS?
WONDERFUL! I'M ALL TIRED OUT!
LULU'S UMBRELLA SERVICE 25¢
TOO TIRED TO TAKE **ANOTHER** CUSTOMER?
ER...NO...I GUESS I CAN TAKE ONE MORE...WH-WHO IS IT?
ME!
YOU? YOU **GOT** AN UMBRELLA! ARE YOU TRYING TO BE FUNNY?
I DON'T WANT TO GET MY UMBRELLA WET! DO YOU OR DON'T YOU WANT TO TAKE ME HOME?
YES...IF YOU PAY ME IN **ADVANCE!**
LULU'S UMBRELLA SERVICE 25¢
OKAY, I'LL PAY YOU IN ADVANCE ONLY ON **ONE** CONDITION!
WHAT?
IF I GET A **SINGLE DROP OF WATER** ON MY HAT, YOU HAVE TO GIVE ME THE QUARTER BACK!
I **KNEW** THERE WAS A **CATCH** IN IT!
BUT, ALL RIGHT! I'LL DO IT! GIVE ME THE QUARTER!
THERE YOU ARE...REMEMBER, A SINGLE DROP ON MY HAT AND YOU GIVE ME MY QUARTER BACK!
OKAY, OKAY!
NOW I'LL TURN MY HAT INSIDE OUT SO THE WATER WILL SHOW WHEN IT FALLS IN IT!

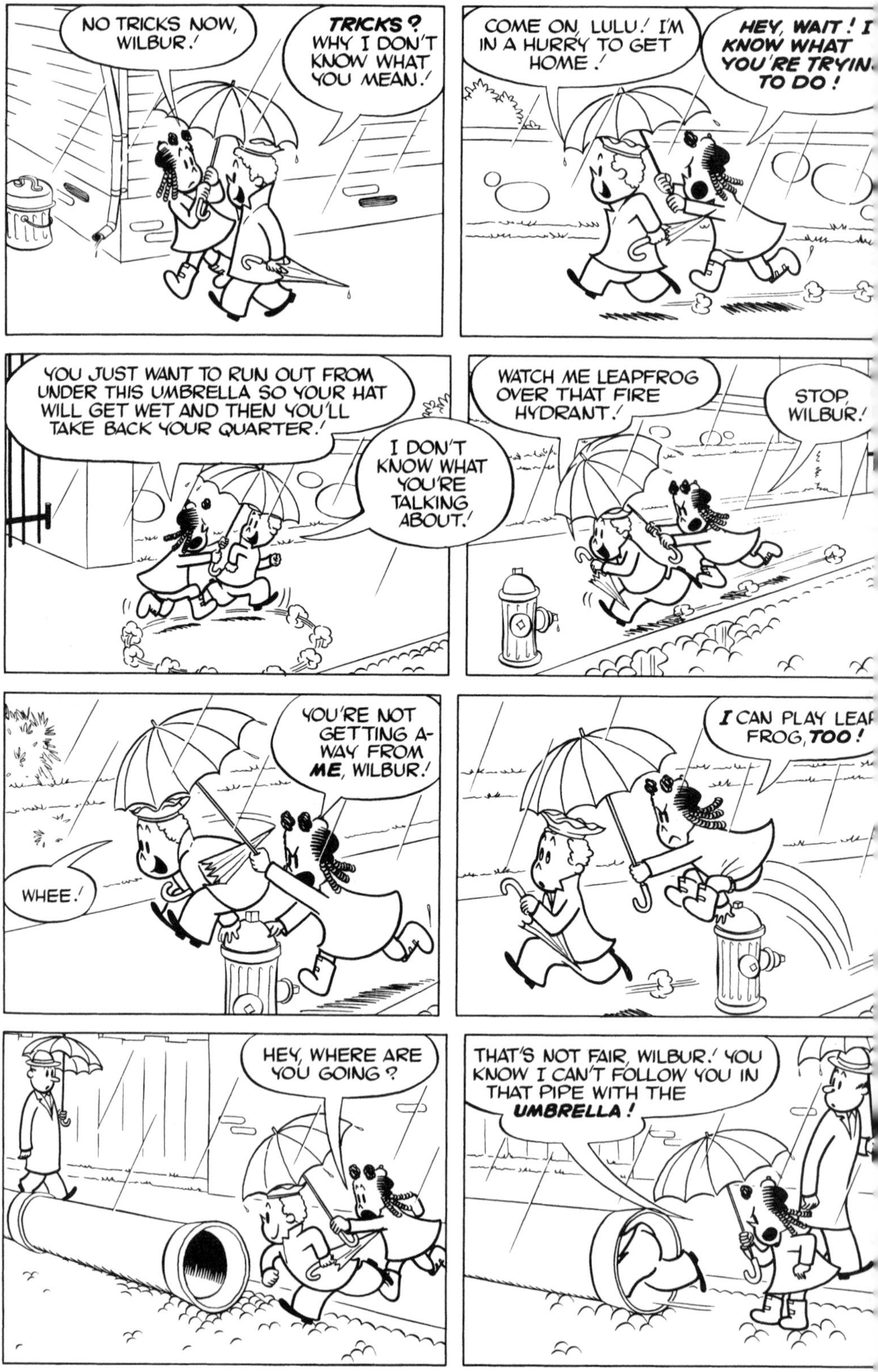
NO TRICKS NOW, WILBUR!
TRICKS? WHY I DON'T KNOW WHAT YOU MEAN!
COME ON, LULU! I'M IN A HURRY TO GET HOME!
HEY, WAIT! I KNOW WHAT YOU'RE TRYIN TO DO!
YOU JUST WANT TO RUN OUT FROM UNDER THIS UMBRELLA SO YOUR HAT WILL GET WET AND THEN YOU'LL TAKE BACK YOUR QUARTER!
I DON'T KNOW WHAT YOU'RE TALKING ABOUT!
WATCH ME LEAPFROG OVER THAT FIRE HYDRANT!
STOP, WILBUR!
YOU'RE NOT GETTING A-WAY FROM ME, WILBUR!
WHEE!
I CAN PLAY LEAP FROG, TOO!
HEY, WHERE ARE YOU GOING?
THAT'S NOT FAIR, WILBUR! YOU KNOW I CAN'T FOLLOW YOU IN THAT PIPE WITH THE UMBRELLA!

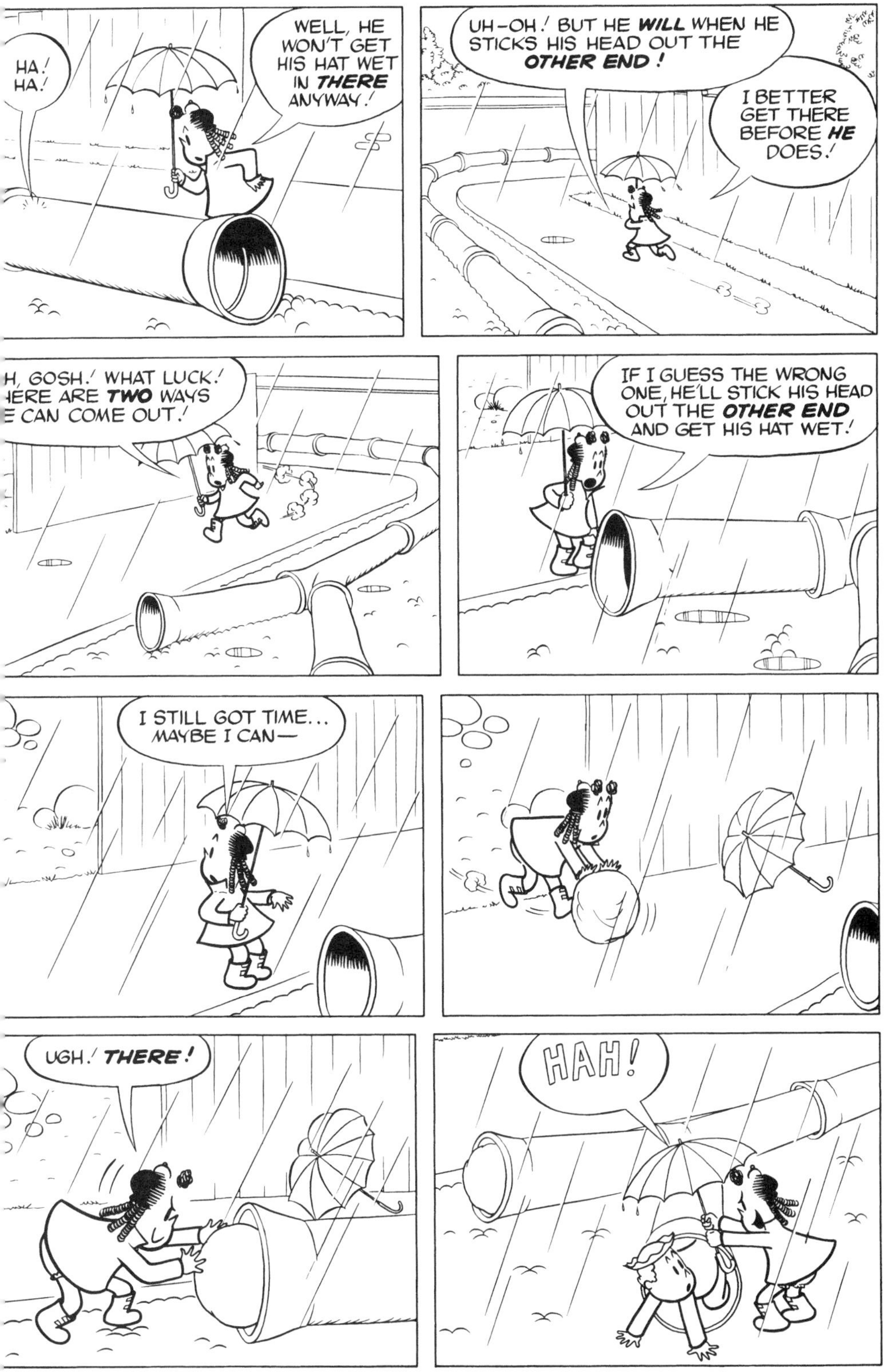
HA! HA!
WELL, HE WON'T GET HIS HAT WET IN THERE ANYWAY!
UH-OH! BUT HE WILL WHEN HE STICKS HIS HEAD OUT THE OTHER END!
I BETTER GET THERE BEFORE HE DOES!
H, GOSH! WHAT LUCK! HERE ARE TWO WAYS E CAN COME OUT!
IF I GUESS THE WRONG ONE, HE'LL STICK HIS HEAD OUT THE OTHER END AND GET HIS HAT WET!
I STILL GOT TIME... MAYBE I CAN—
UGH! THERE!
HAH!

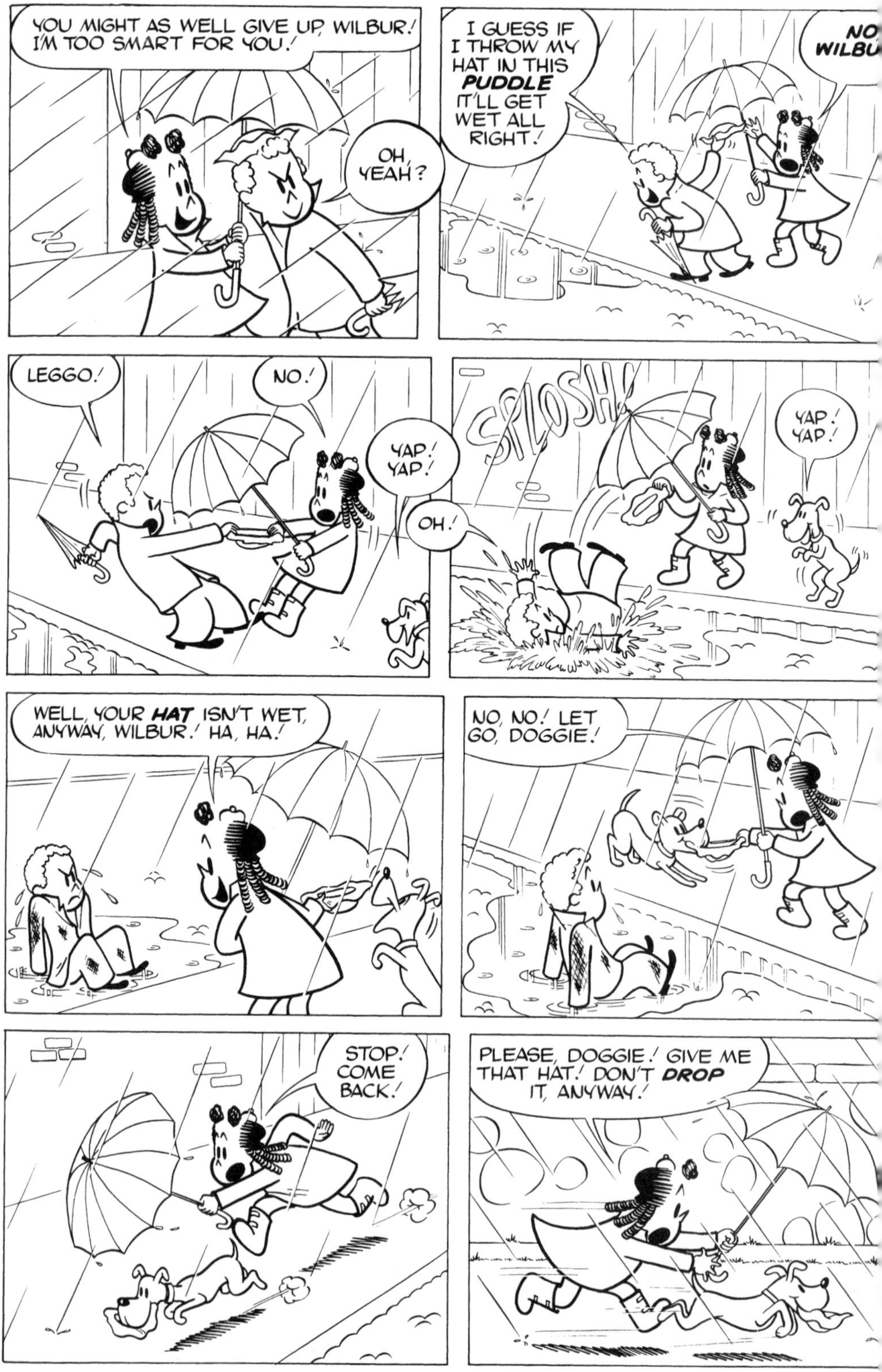
YOU MIGHT AS WELL GIVE UP, WILBUR! I'M TOO SMART FOR YOU!
OH, YEAH?
I GUESS IF I THROW MY HAT IN THIS PUDDLE IT'LL GET WET ALL RIGHT!
LEGGO!
NO!
YAP! YAP!
OH!
SPLOSH!
YAP! YAP!
WELL, YOUR HAT ISN'T WET, ANYWAY, WILBUR! HA, HA!
NO, NO! LET GO, DOGGIE!
STOP! COME BACK!
PLEASE, DOGGIE! GIVE ME THAT HAT! DON'T DROP IT, ANYWAY!

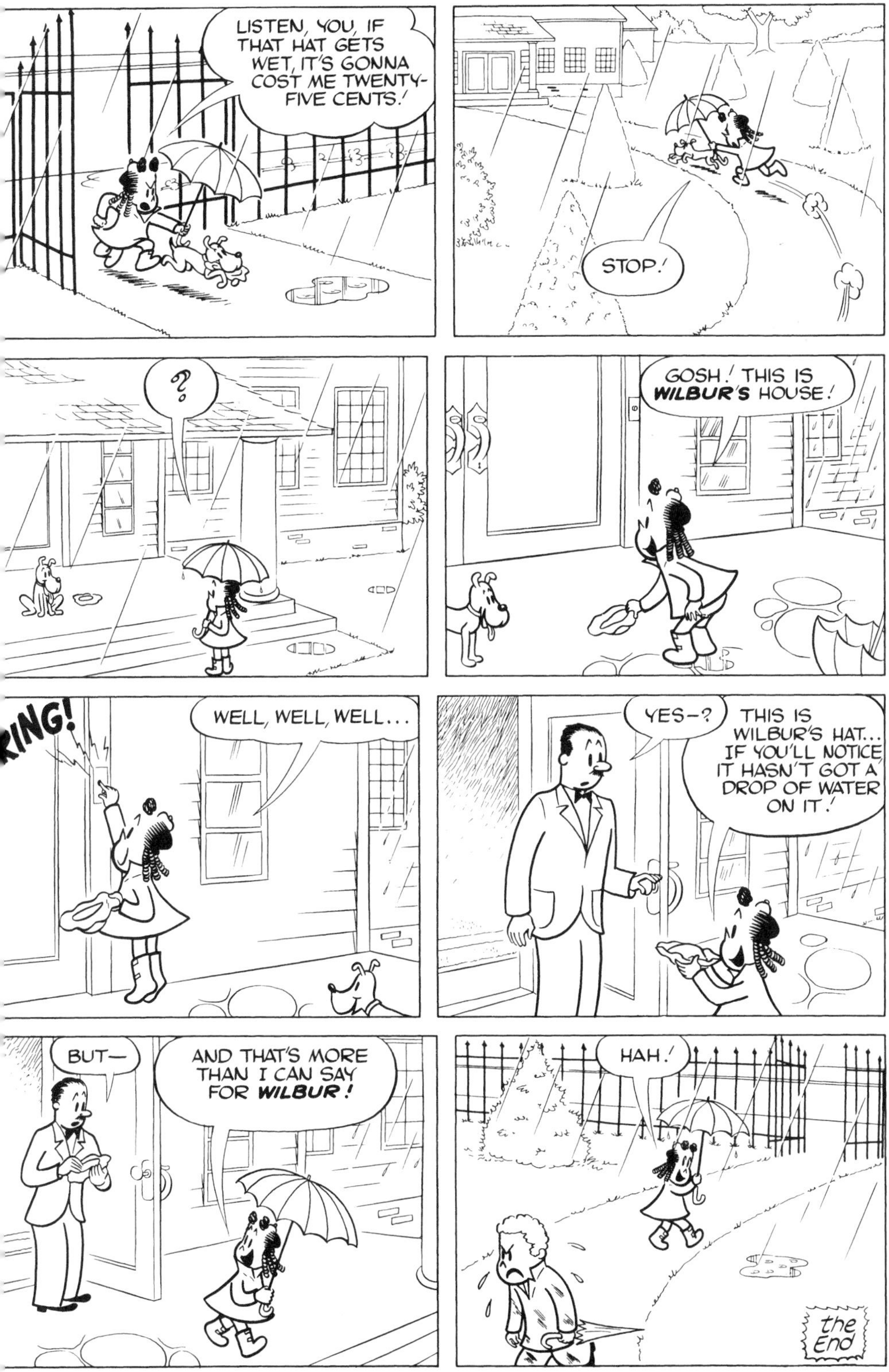
LISTEN, YOU, IF THAT HAT GETS WET, IT'S GONNA COST ME TWENTY-FIVE CENTS!
STOP!
?
GOSH! THIS IS WILBUR'S HOUSE!
RING!
WELL, WELL, WELL...
YES-?
THIS IS WILBUR'S HAT... IF YOU'LL NOTICE IT HASN'T GOT A DROP OF WATER ON IT!
BUT—
AND THAT'S MORE THAN I CAN SAY FOR WILBUR!
HAH!
the End

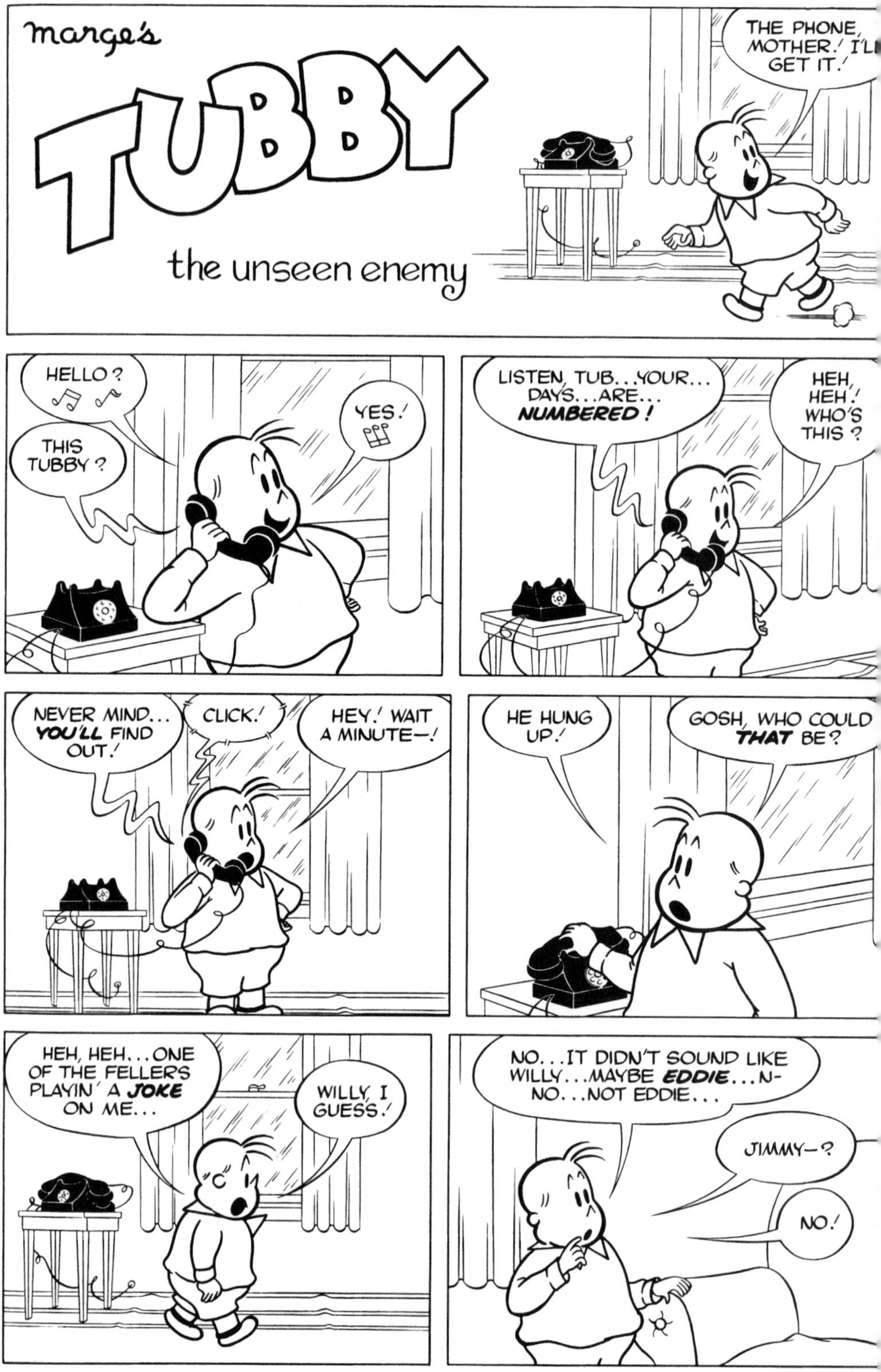
marge's
TUBBY
the unseen enemy
THE PHONE, MOTHER! I'LL GET IT!
HELLO?
THIS TUBBY?
YES!
LISTEN, TUB...YOUR... DAYS...ARE... NUMBERED!
HEH, HEH! WHO'S THIS?
NEVER MIND... YOU'LL FIND OUT!
CLICK!
HEY! WAIT A MINUTE—!
HE HUNG UP!
GOSH, WHO COULD THAT BE?
HEH, HEH...ONE OF THE FELLERS PLAYIN' A JOKE ON ME...
WILLY, I GUESS!
NO...IT DIDN'T SOUND LIKE WILLY...MAYBE EDDIE...N-NO...NOT EDDIE...
JIMMY—?
NO!

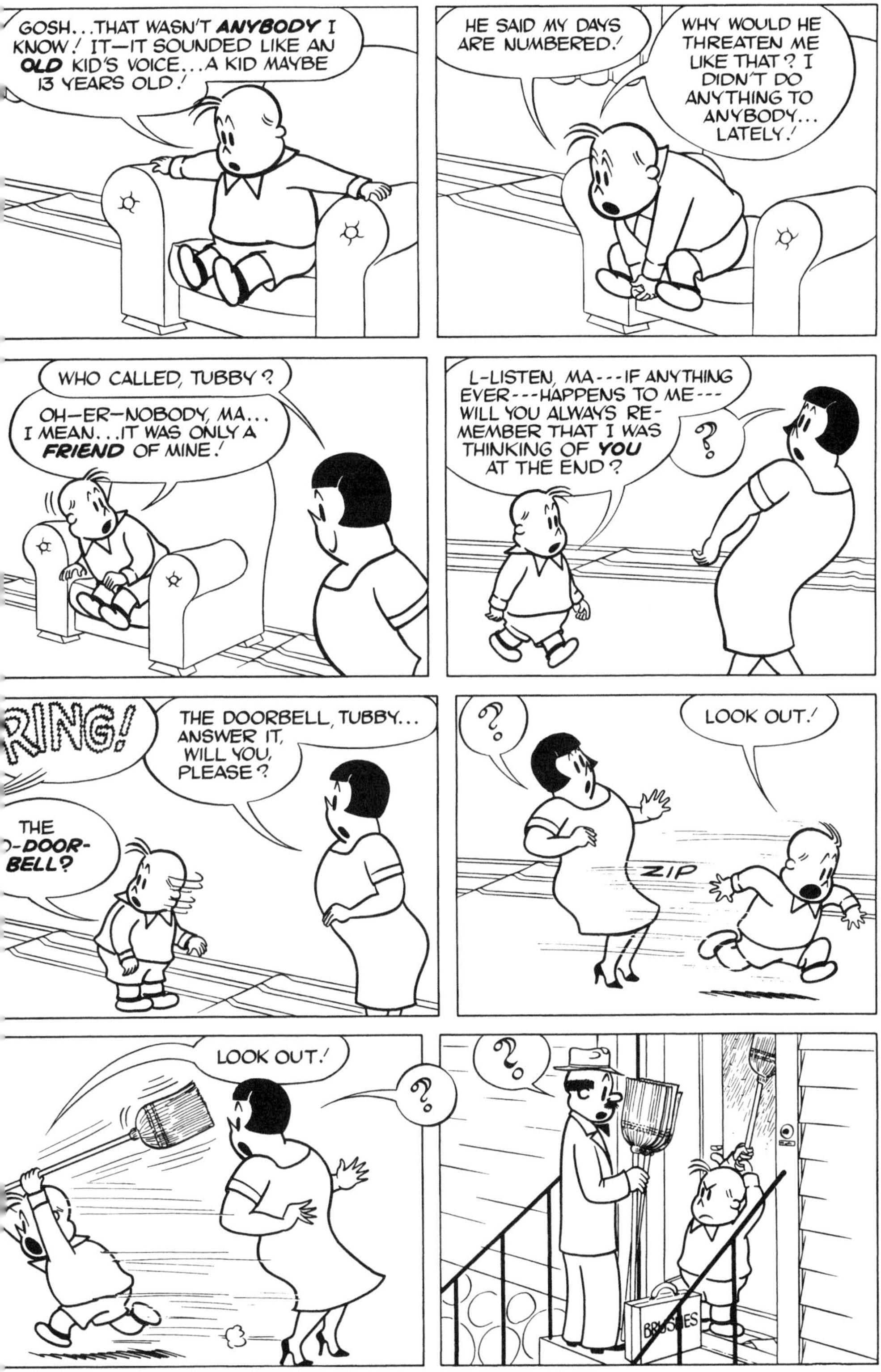
GOSH...THAT WASN'T ANYBODY I KNOW! IT—IT SOUNDED LIKE AN OLD KID'S VOICE...A KID MAYBE 13 YEARS OLD!
HE SAID MY DAYS ARE NUMBERED!
WHY WOULD HE THREATEN ME LIKE THAT? I DIDN'T DO ANYTHING TO ANYBODY... LATELY!
WHO CALLED, TUBBY?
OH—ER—NOBODY, MA... I MEAN...IT WAS ONLY A FRIEND OF MINE!
L-LISTEN, MA---IF ANYTHING EVER---HAPPENS TO ME--- WILL YOU ALWAYS RE-MEMBER THAT I WAS THINKING OF YOU AT THE END?
?
RING!
THE DOORBELL, TUBBY... ANSWER IT, WILL YOU, PLEASE?
THE -DOOR-BELL?
?
LOOK OUT!
ZIP
LOOK OUT!
?
?
BRUSHES

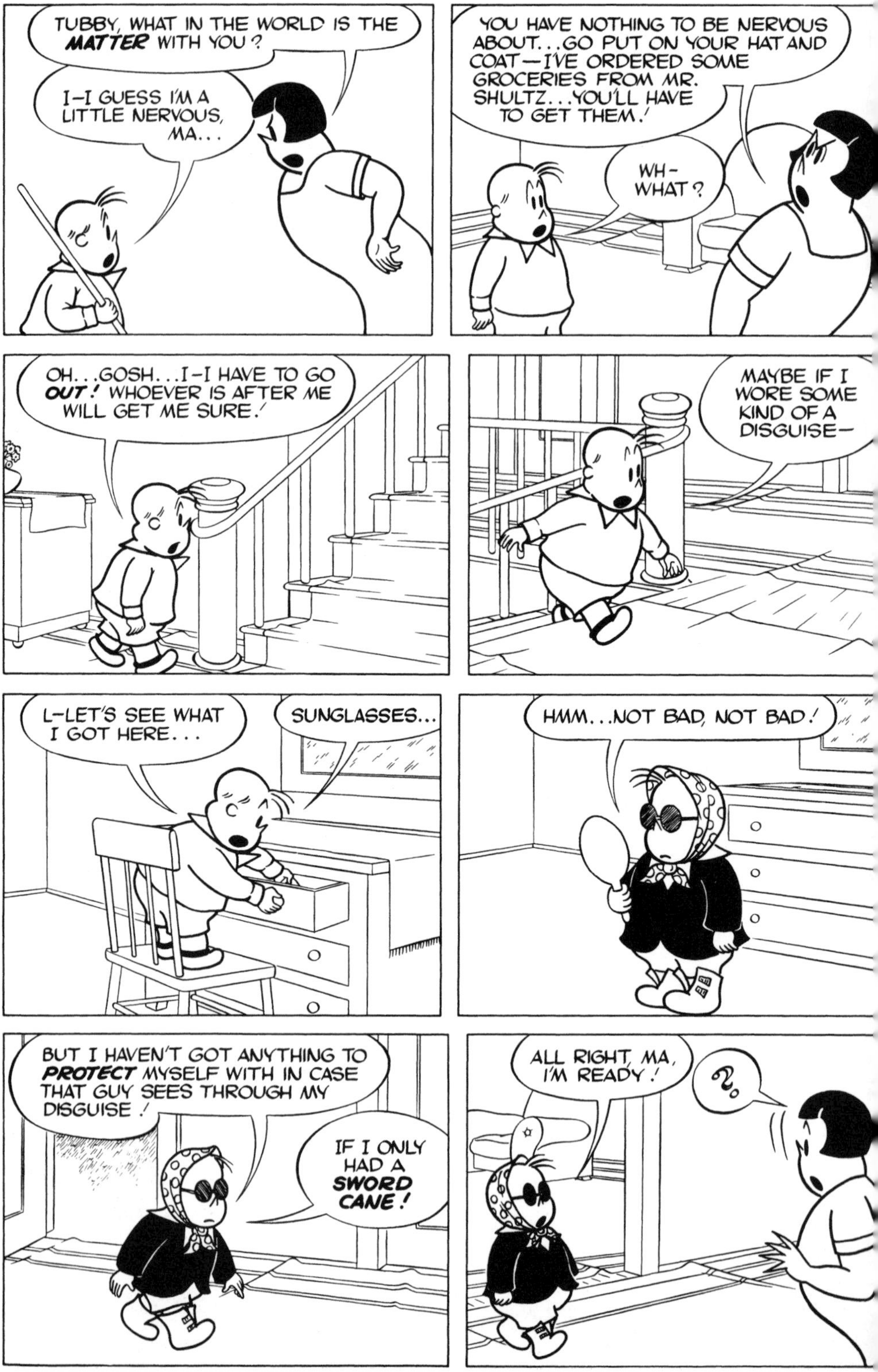
TUBBY, WHAT IN THE WORLD IS THE MATTER WITH YOU?
I-I GUESS I'M A LITTLE NERVOUS, MA...
YOU HAVE NOTHING TO BE NERVOUS ABOUT...GO PUT ON YOUR HAT AND COAT—I'VE ORDERED SOME GROCERIES FROM MR. SHULTZ...YOU'LL HAVE TO GET THEM!
WH-WHAT?
OH...GOSH...I-I HAVE TO GO OUT! WHOEVER IS AFTER ME WILL GET ME SURE!
MAYBE IF I WORE SOME KIND OF A DISGUISE—
L-LET'S SEE WHAT I GOT HERE...
SUNGLASSES...
HMM...NOT BAD, NOT BAD!
BUT I HAVEN'T GOT ANYTHING TO PROTECT MYSELF WITH IN CASE THAT GUY SEES THROUGH MY DISGUISE!
IF I ONLY HAD A SWORD CANE!
ALL RIGHT, MA, I'M READY!
?

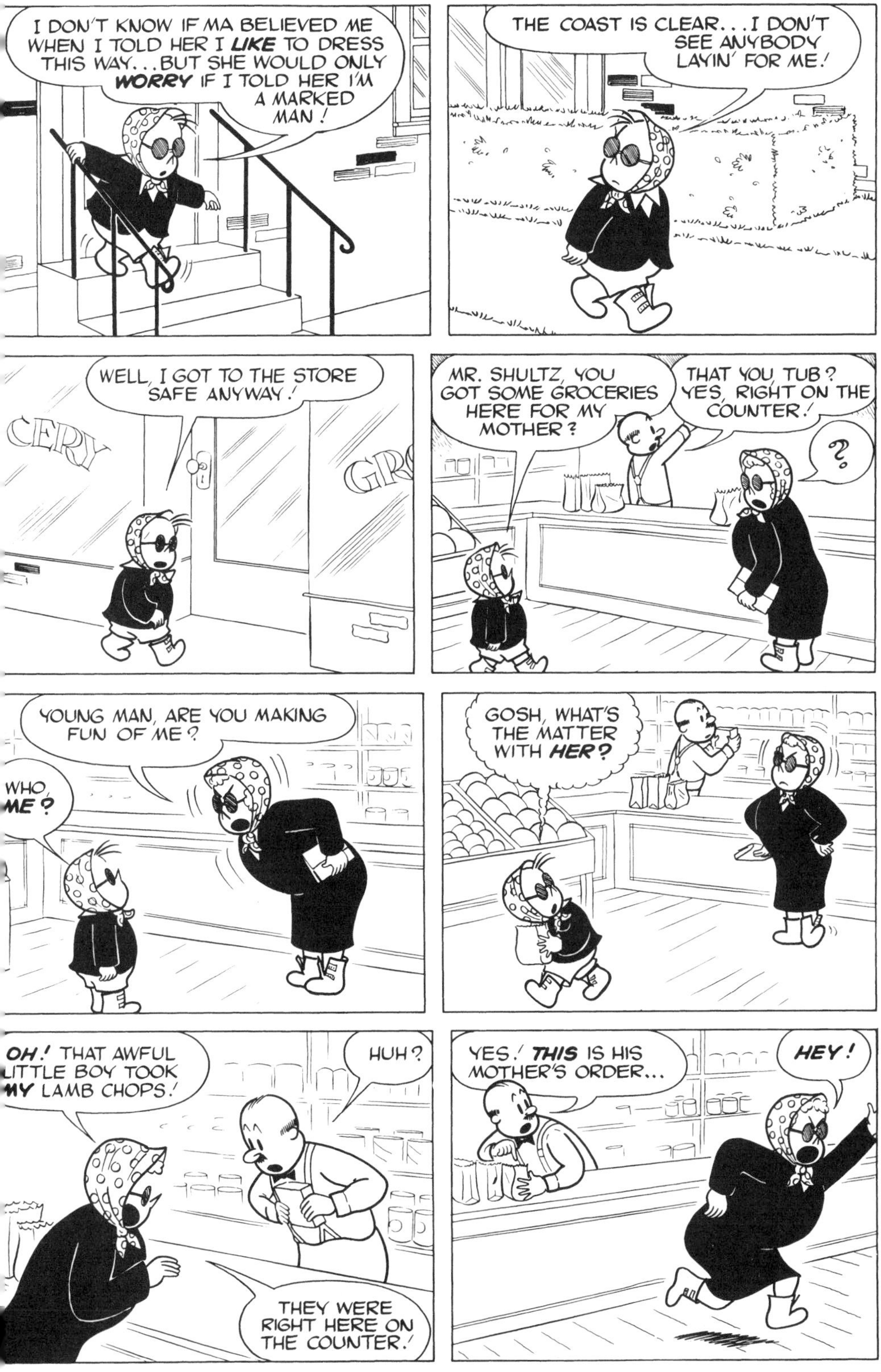
I DON'T KNOW IF MA BELIEVED ME WHEN I TOLD HER I **LIKE** TO DRESS THIS WAY...BUT SHE WOULD ONLY **WORRY** IF I TOLD HER I'M A MARKED MAN!
THE COAST IS CLEAR...I DON'T SEE ANYBODY LAYIN' FOR ME!
WELL, I GOT TO THE STORE SAFE ANYWAY!
CERY
GR
MR. SHULTZ, YOU GOT SOME GROCERIES HERE FOR MY MOTHER?
THAT YOU, TUB? YES, RIGHT ON THE COUNTER!
?
YOUNG MAN, ARE YOU MAKING FUN OF ME?
WHO, **ME?**
GOSH, WHAT'S THE MATTER WITH **HER?**
OH! THAT AWFUL LITTLE BOY TOOK **MY** LAMB CHOPS!
HUH?
THEY WERE RIGHT HERE ON THE COUNTER!
YES! **THIS** IS HIS MOTHER'S ORDER...
HEY!

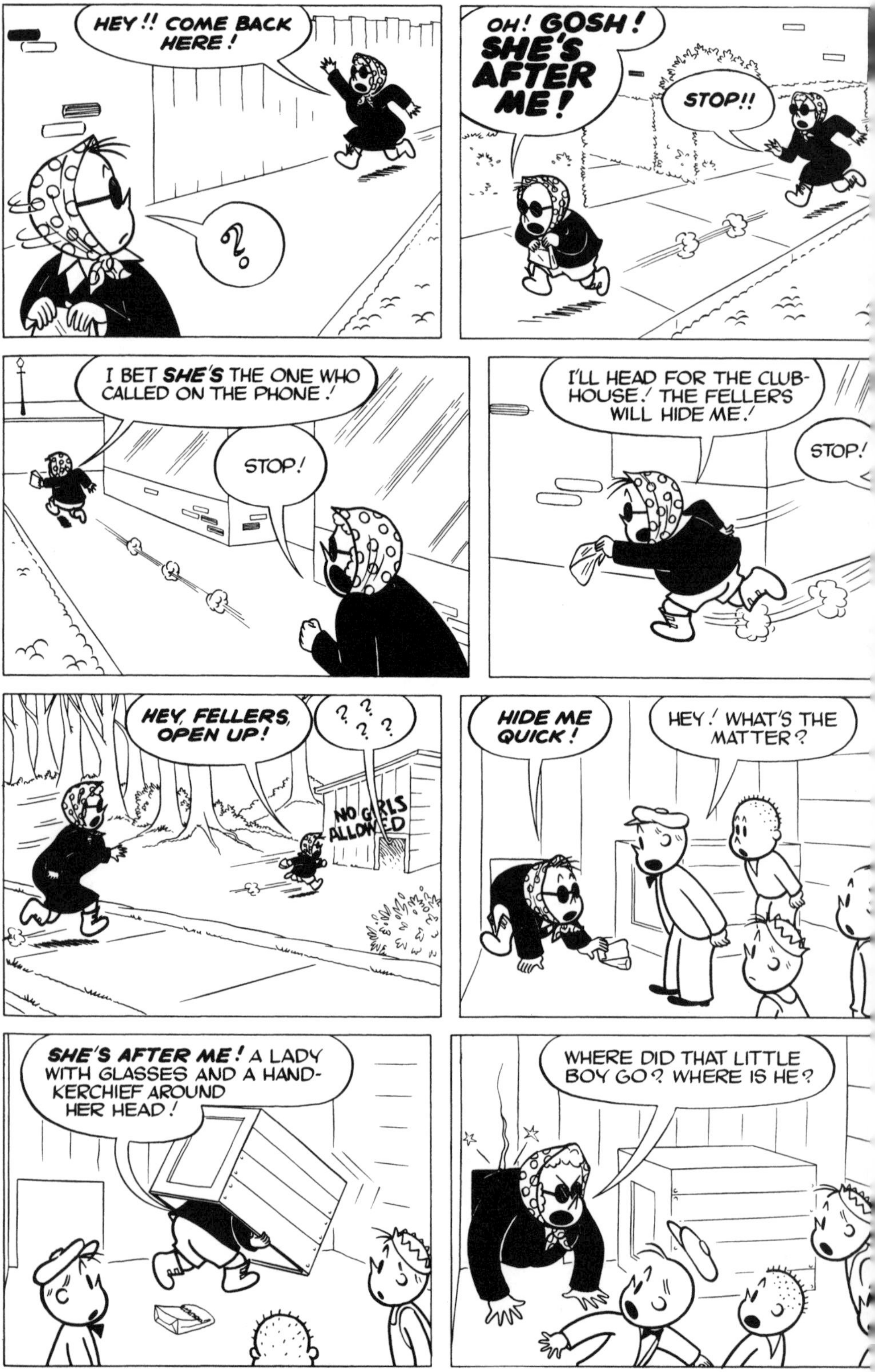
HEY !! COME BACK HERE !
?
OH! GOSH ! SHE'S AFTER ME !
STOP!!
I BET SHE'S THE ONE WHO CALLED ON THE PHONE !
STOP!
I'LL HEAD FOR THE CLUB-HOUSE! THE FELLERS WILL HIDE ME !
STOP!
HEY, FELLERS, OPEN UP!
? ? ? ?
NO GIRLS ALLOWED
HIDE ME QUICK !
HEY ! WHAT'S THE MATTER?
SHE'S AFTER ME ! A LADY WITH GLASSES AND A HAND-KERCHIEF AROUND HER HEAD !
WHERE DID THAT LITTLE BOY GO? WHERE IS HE?

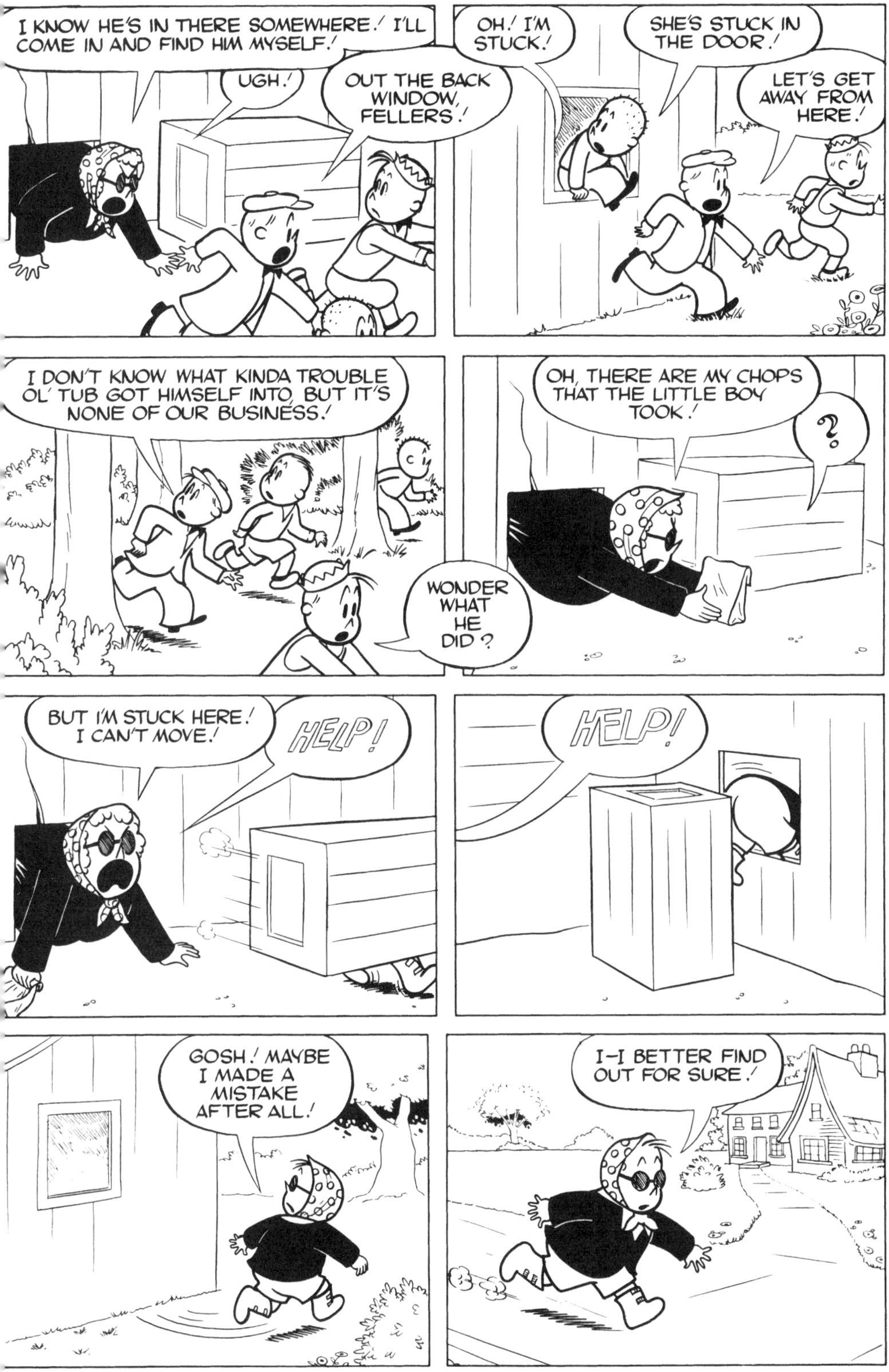
I KNOW HE'S IN THERE SOMEWHERE! I'LL COME IN AND FIND HIM MYSELF!
UGH!
OUT THE BACK WINDOW, FELLERS!
OH! I'M STUCK!
SHE'S STUCK IN THE DOOR!
LET'S GET AWAY FROM HERE!
I DON'T KNOW WHAT KINDA TROUBLE OL' TUB GOT HIMSELF INTO, BUT IT'S NONE OF OUR BUSINESS!
WONDER WHAT HE DID?
OH, THERE ARE MY CHOPS THAT THE LITTLE BOY TOOK!
?
BUT I'M STUCK HERE! I CAN'T MOVE!
HELP!
HELP!
GOSH! MAYBE I MADE A MISTAKE AFTER ALL!
I-I BETTER FIND OUT FOR SURE!

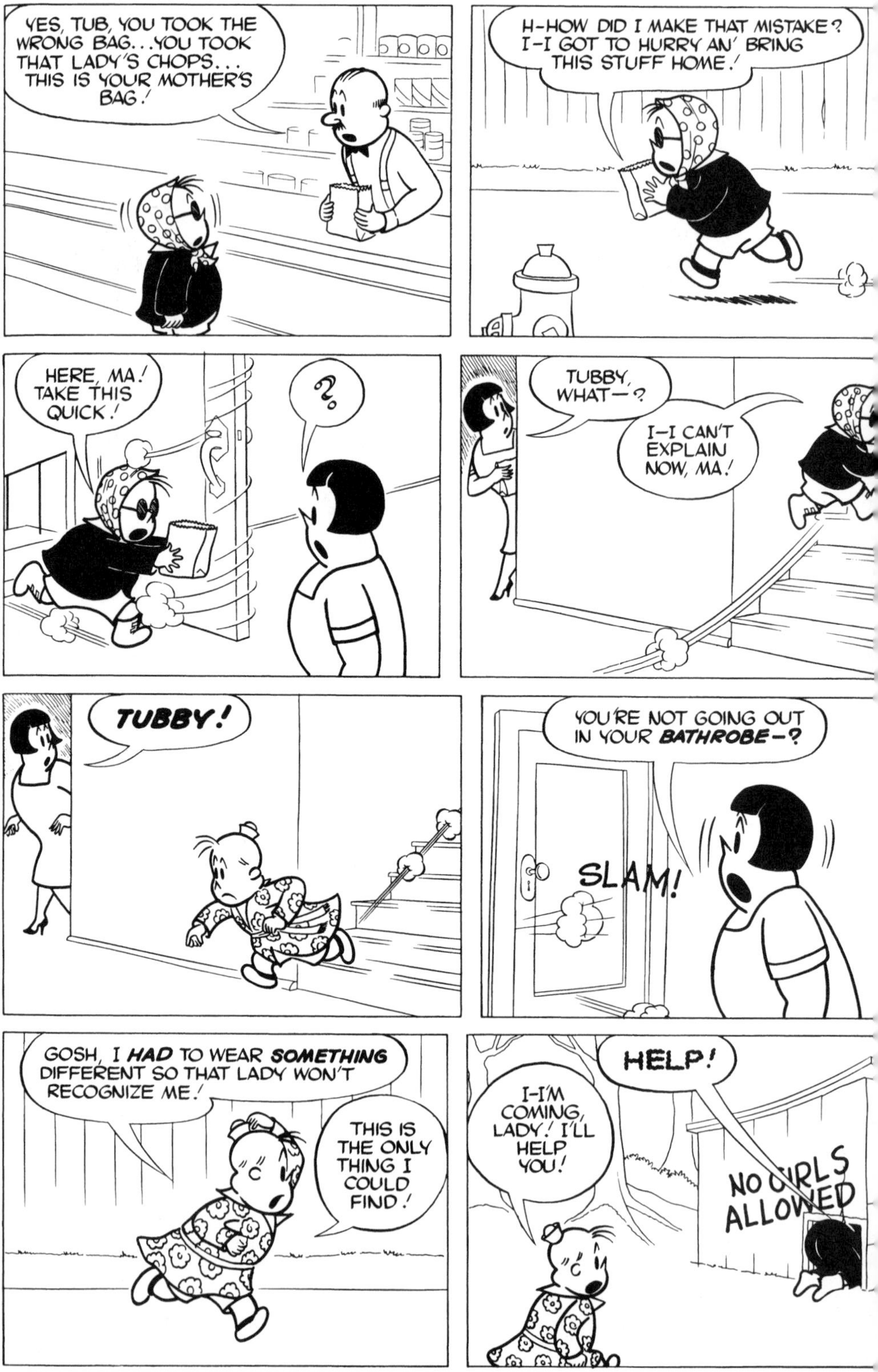
YES, TUB, YOU TOOK THE WRONG BAG...YOU TOOK THAT LADY'S CHOPS... THIS IS YOUR MOTHER'S BAG!
H-HOW DID I MAKE THAT MISTAKE? I-I GOT TO HURRY AN' BRING THIS STUFF HOME!
HERE, MA! TAKE THIS QUICK!
?
TUBBY, WHAT—?
I-I CAN'T EXPLAIN NOW, MA!
TUBBY!
YOU'RE NOT GOING OUT IN YOUR BATHROBE—?
SLAM!
GOSH, I HAD TO WEAR SOMETHING DIFFERENT SO THAT LADY WON'T RECOGNIZE ME!
THIS IS THE ONLY THING I COULD FIND!
HELP!
I-I'M COMING, LADY! I'LL HELP YOU!
NO GIRLS ALLOWED

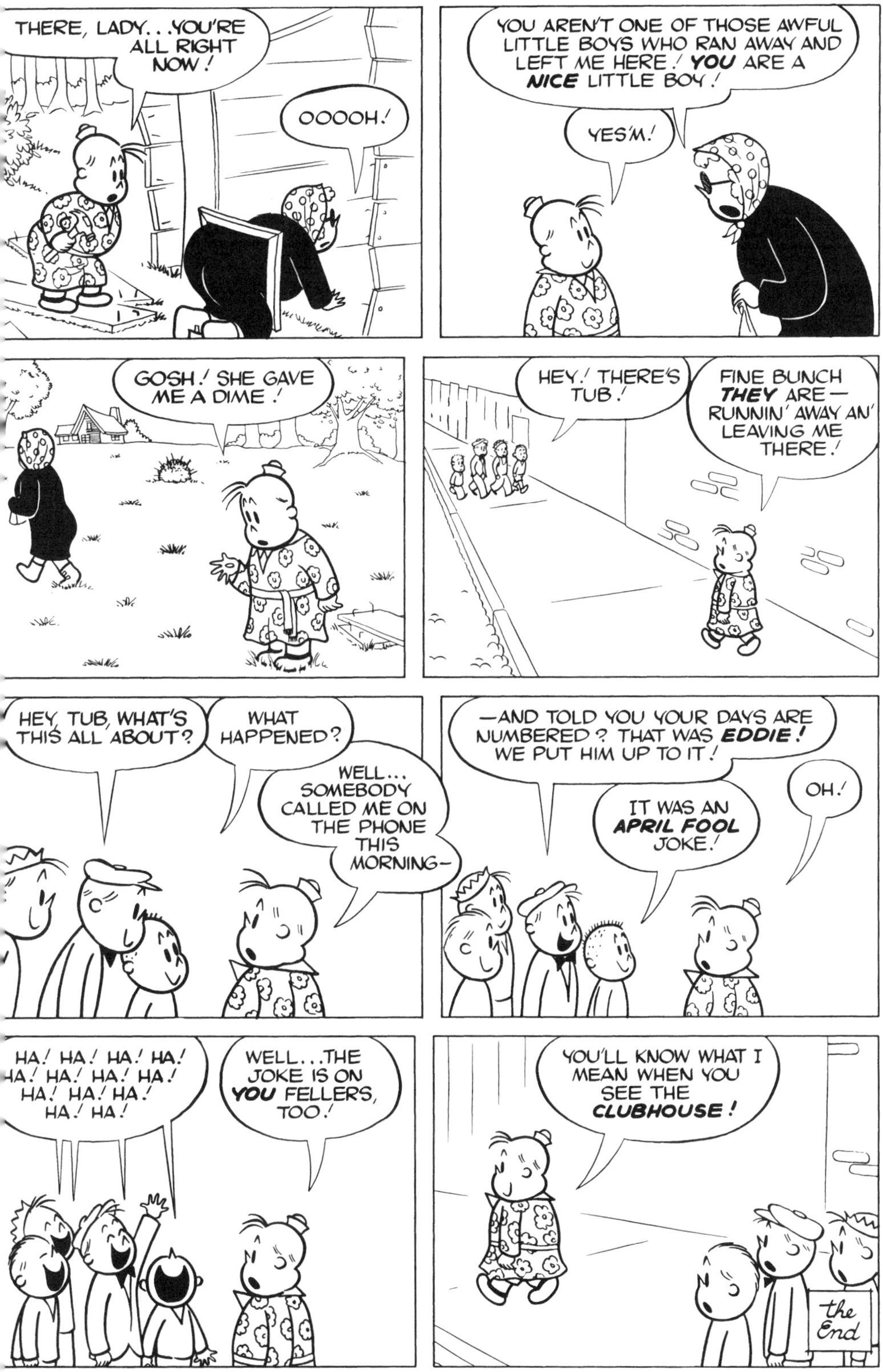
THERE, LADY...YOU'RE ALL RIGHT NOW!
OOOOH!
YOU AREN'T ONE OF THOSE AWFUL LITTLE BOYS WHO RAN AWAY AND LEFT ME HERE! YOU ARE A NICE LITTLE BOY!
YES'M!
GOSH! SHE GAVE ME A DIME!
HEY! THERE'S TUB!
FINE BUNCH THEY ARE— RUNNIN' AWAY AN' LEAVING ME THERE!
HEY, TUB, WHAT'S THIS ALL ABOUT?
WHAT HAPPENED?
WELL... SOMEBODY CALLED ME ON THE PHONE THIS MORNING—
—AND TOLD YOU YOUR DAYS ARE NUMBERED? THAT WAS EDDIE! WE PUT HIM UP TO IT!
IT WAS AN APRIL FOOL JOKE!
OH!
HA! HA! HA! HA! HA! HA! HA! HA! HA! HA! HA! HA! HA!
WELL...THE JOKE IS ON YOU FELLERS, TOO!
YOU'LL KNOW WHAT I MEAN WHEN YOU SEE THE CLUBHOUSE!
the End

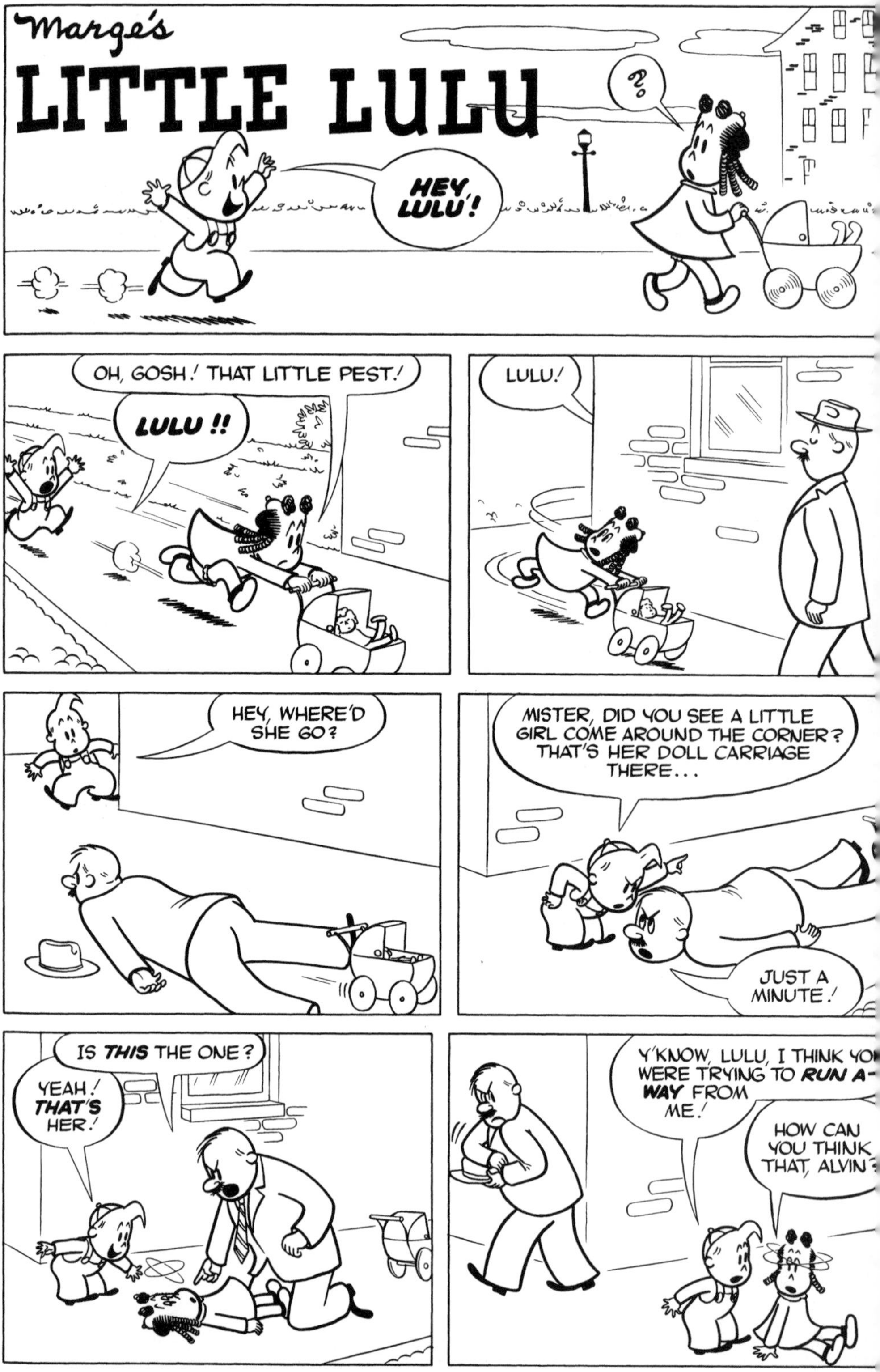
Marge's
LITTLE LULU
?
HEY, LULU!
OH, GOSH! THAT LITTLE PEST!
LULU !!
LULU!
HEY, WHERE'D SHE GO?
MISTER, DID YOU SEE A LITTLE GIRL COME AROUND THE CORNER? THAT'S HER DOLL CARRIAGE THERE...
JUST A MINUTE!
IS THIS THE ONE?
YEAH! THAT'S HER!
Y'KNOW, LULU, I THINK YO WERE TRYING TO RUN A-WAY FROM ME!
HOW CAN YOU THINK THAT, ALVIN?

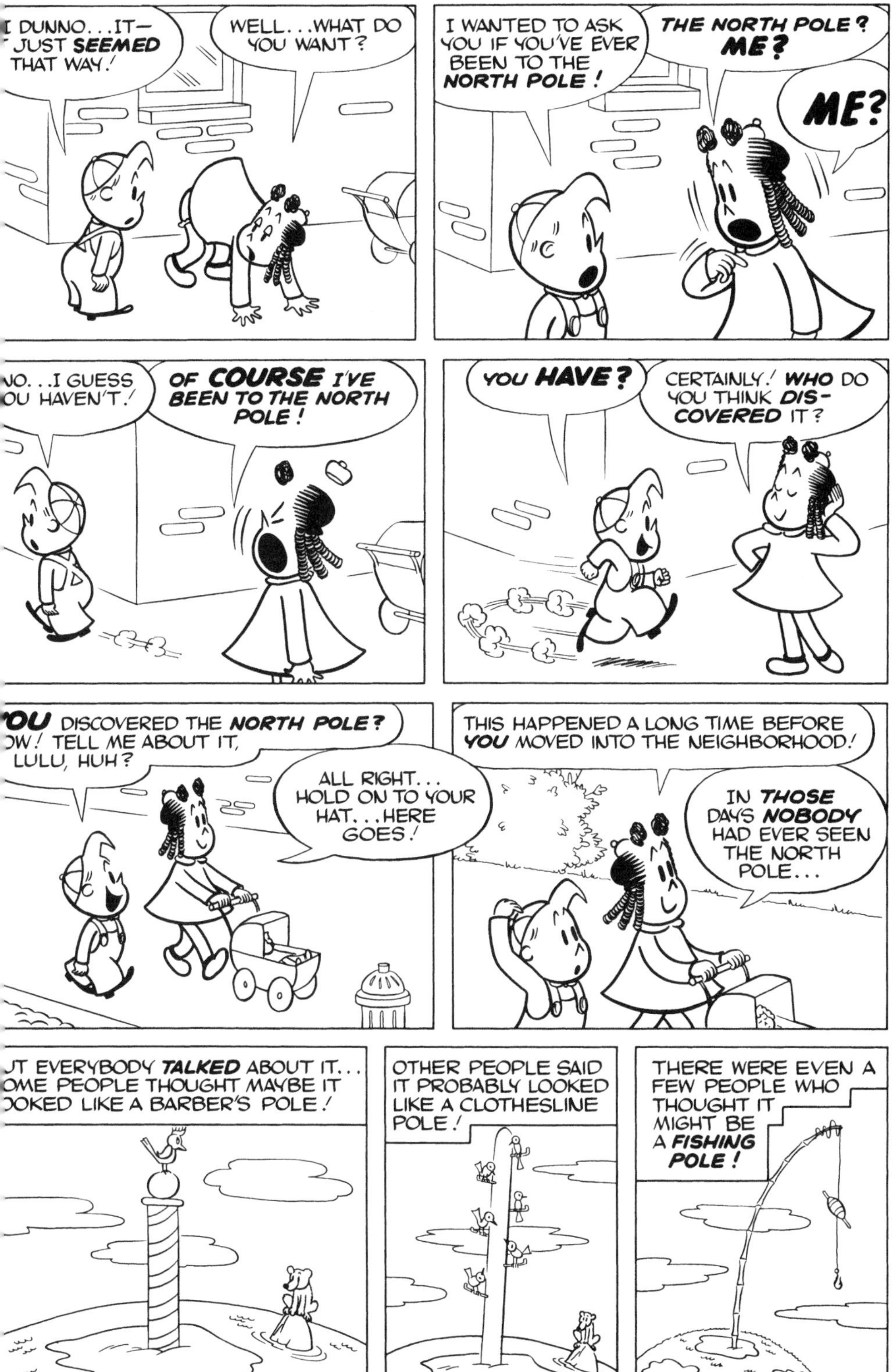

I DUNNO... IT— JUST SEEMED THAT WAY!
WELL... WHAT DO YOU WANT?
I WANTED TO ASK YOU IF YOU'VE EVER BEEN TO THE NORTH POLE!
THE NORTH POLE? ME?
ME?
NO... I GUESS YOU HAVEN'T!
OF COURSE I'VE BEEN TO THE NORTH POLE!
YOU HAVE?
CERTAINLY! WHO DO YOU THINK DISCOVERED IT?
YOU DISCOVERED THE NORTH POLE? OW! TELL ME ABOUT IT, LULU, HUH?
ALL RIGHT... HOLD ON TO YOUR HAT... HERE GOES!
THIS HAPPENED A LONG TIME BEFORE YOU MOVED INTO THE NEIGHBORHOOD!
IN THOSE DAYS NOBODY HAD EVER SEEN THE NORTH POLE...
UT EVERYBODY TALKED ABOUT IT... OME PEOPLE THOUGHT MAYBE IT OOKED LIKE A BARBER'S POLE!
OTHER PEOPLE SAID IT PROBABLY LOOKED LIKE A CLOTHESLINE POLE!
THERE WERE EVEN A FEW PEOPLE WHO THOUGHT IT MIGHT BE A FISHING POLE!

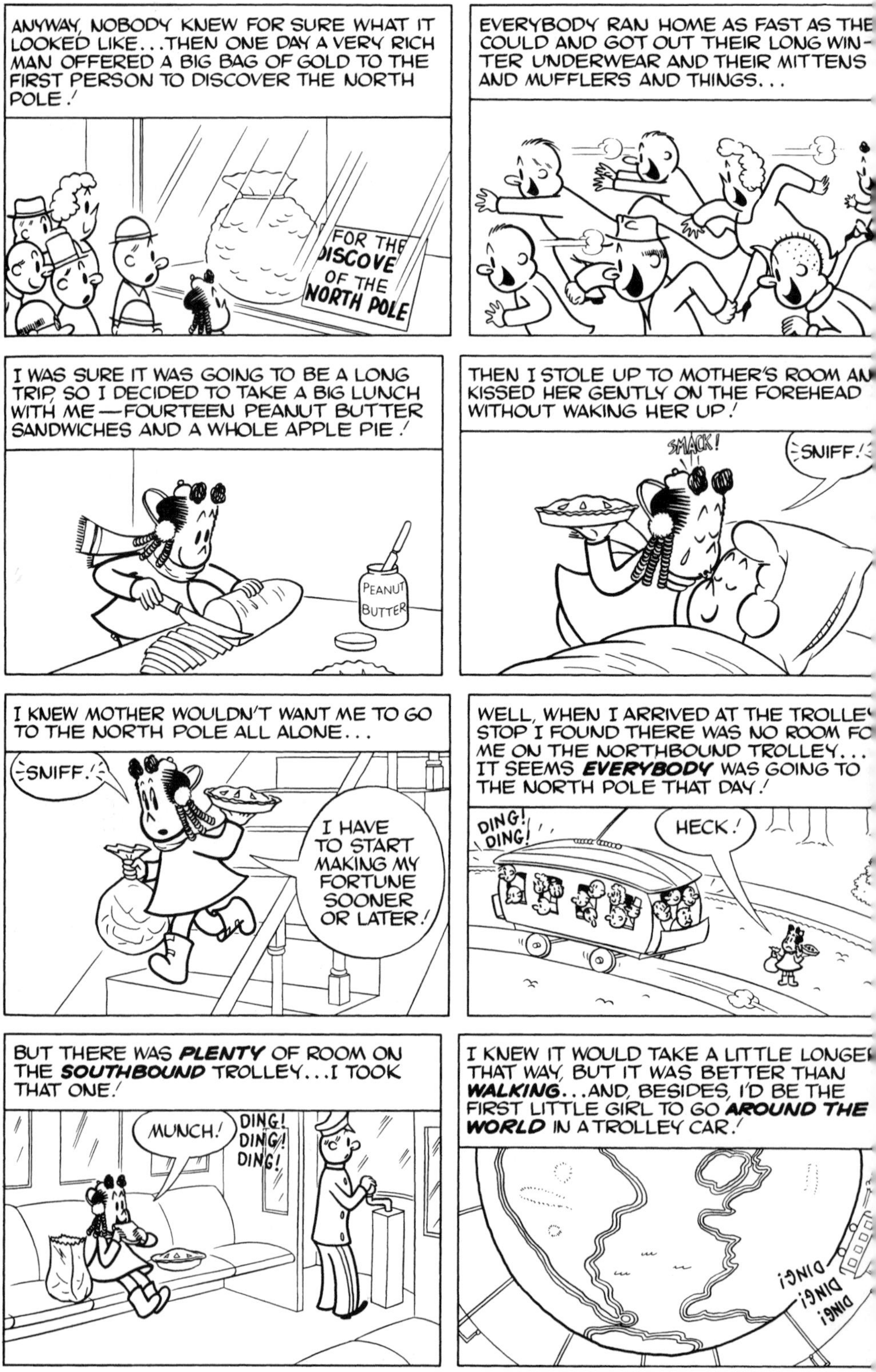
ANYWAY, NOBODY KNEW FOR SURE WHAT IT LOOKED LIKE...THEN ONE DAY A VERY RICH MAN OFFERED A BIG BAG OF GOLD TO THE FIRST PERSON TO DISCOVER THE NORTH POLE!
FOR THE DISCOVE OF THE NORTH POLE
EVERYBODY RAN HOME AS FAST AS THE COULD AND GOT OUT THEIR LONG WINTER UNDERWEAR AND THEIR MITTENS AND MUFFLERS AND THINGS...
I WAS SURE IT WAS GOING TO BE A LONG TRIP, SO I DECIDED TO TAKE A BIG LUNCH WITH ME—FOURTEEN PEANUT BUTTER SANDWICHES AND A WHOLE APPLE PIE!
PEANUT BUTTER
THEN I STOLE UP TO MOTHER'S ROOM AN KISSED HER GENTLY ON THE FOREHEAD WITHOUT WAKING HER UP!
SMACK!
SNIFF!
I KNEW MOTHER WOULDN'T WANT ME TO GO TO THE NORTH POLE ALL ALONE...
SNIFF!
I HAVE TO START MAKING MY FORTUNE SOONER OR LATER!
WELL, WHEN I ARRIVED AT THE TROLLE STOP I FOUND THERE WAS NO ROOM FO ME ON THE NORTHBOUND TROLLEY... IT SEEMS **EVERYBODY** WAS GOING TO THE NORTH POLE THAT DAY!
DING! DING!
HECK!
BUT THERE WAS **PLENTY** OF ROOM ON THE **SOUTHBOUND** TROLLEY...I TOOK THAT ONE!
MUNCH!
DING! DING! DING!
I KNEW IT WOULD TAKE A LITTLE LONGE THAT WAY, BUT IT WAS BETTER THAN **WALKING**...AND, BESIDES, I'D BE THE FIRST LITTLE GIRL TO GO **AROUND THE WORLD** IN A TROLLEY CAR!
DING! DING! DING!

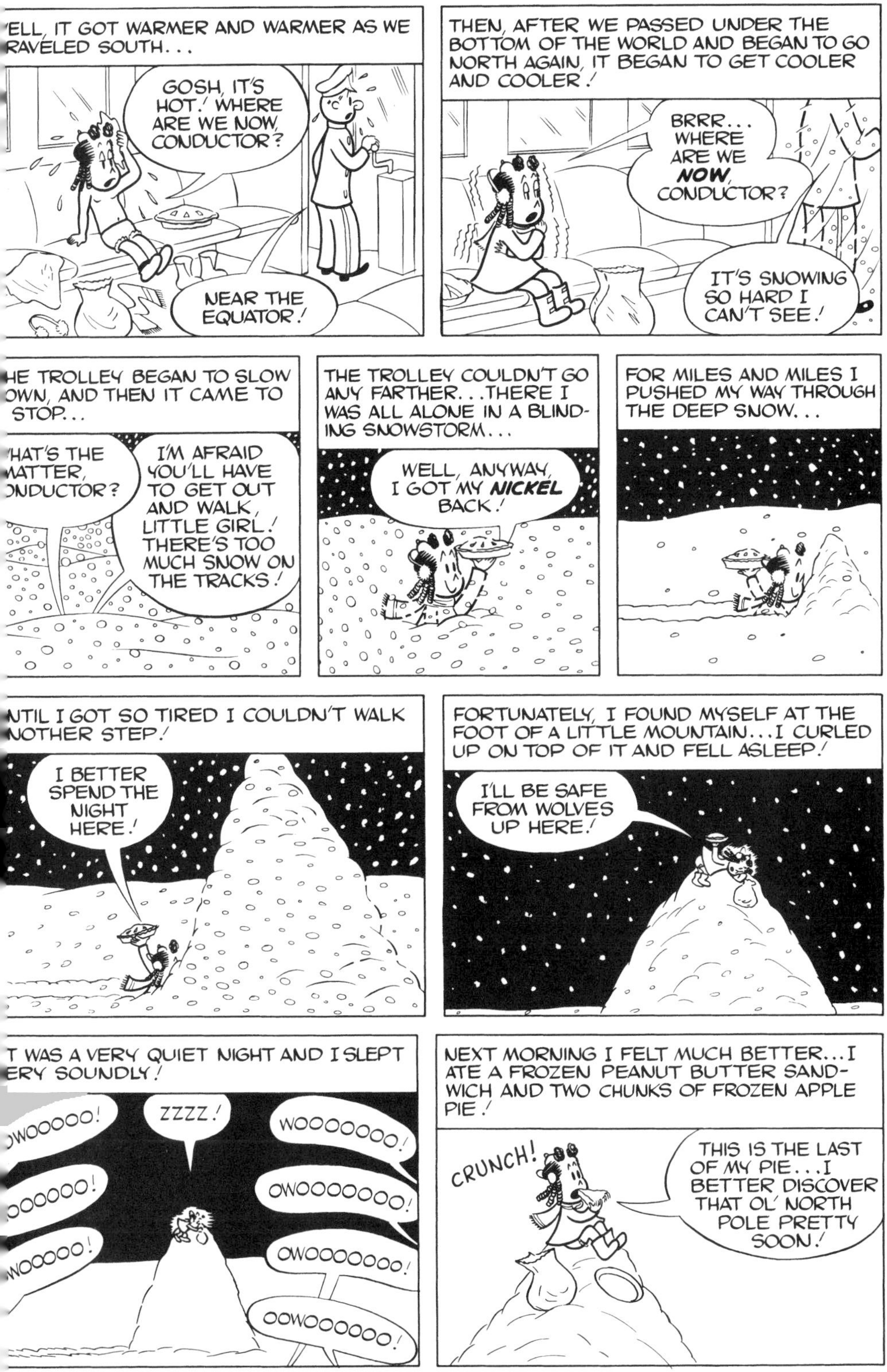

'ELL, IT GOT WARMER AND WARMER AS WE RAVELED SOUTH...
GOSH, IT'S HOT! WHERE ARE WE NOW, CONDUCTOR?
NEAR THE EQUATOR!
THEN, AFTER WE PASSED UNDER THE BOTTOM OF THE WORLD AND BEGAN TO GO NORTH AGAIN, IT BEGAN TO GET COOLER AND COOLER!
BRRR... WHERE ARE WE NOW, CONDUCTOR?
IT'S SNOWING SO HARD I CAN'T SEE!
HE TROLLEY BEGAN TO SLOW OWN, AND THEN IT CAME TO STOP...
'HAT'S THE MATTER, ONDUCTOR?
I'M AFRAID YOU'LL HAVE TO GET OUT AND WALK, LITTLE GIRL! THERE'S TOO MUCH SNOW ON THE TRACKS!
THE TROLLEY COULDN'T GO ANY FARTHER... THERE I WAS ALL ALONE IN A BLINDING SNOWSTORM...
WELL, ANYWAY, I GOT MY NICKEL BACK!
FOR MILES AND MILES I PUSHED MY WAY THROUGH THE DEEP SNOW...
NTIL I GOT SO TIRED I COULDN'T WALK NOTHER STEP!
I BETTER SPEND THE NIGHT HERE!
FORTUNATELY, I FOUND MYSELF AT THE FOOT OF A LITTLE MOUNTAIN... I CURLED UP ON TOP OF IT AND FELL ASLEEP!
I'LL BE SAFE FROM WOLVES UP HERE!
T WAS A VERY QUIET NIGHT AND I SLEPT ERY SOUNDLY!
ZZZZ!
WOOOOOOO!
OWOOOOOOOO!
OWOOOOOOOO!
OOWOOOOOOOO!
WOOOOOO!
OOOOOO!
WOOOOO!
NEXT MORNING I FELT MUCH BETTER... I ATE A FROZEN PEANUT BUTTER SANDWICH AND TWO CHUNKS OF FROZEN APPLE PIE!
CRUNCH!
THIS IS THE LAST OF MY PIE... I BETTER DISCOVER THAT OL' NORTH POLE PRETTY SOON!

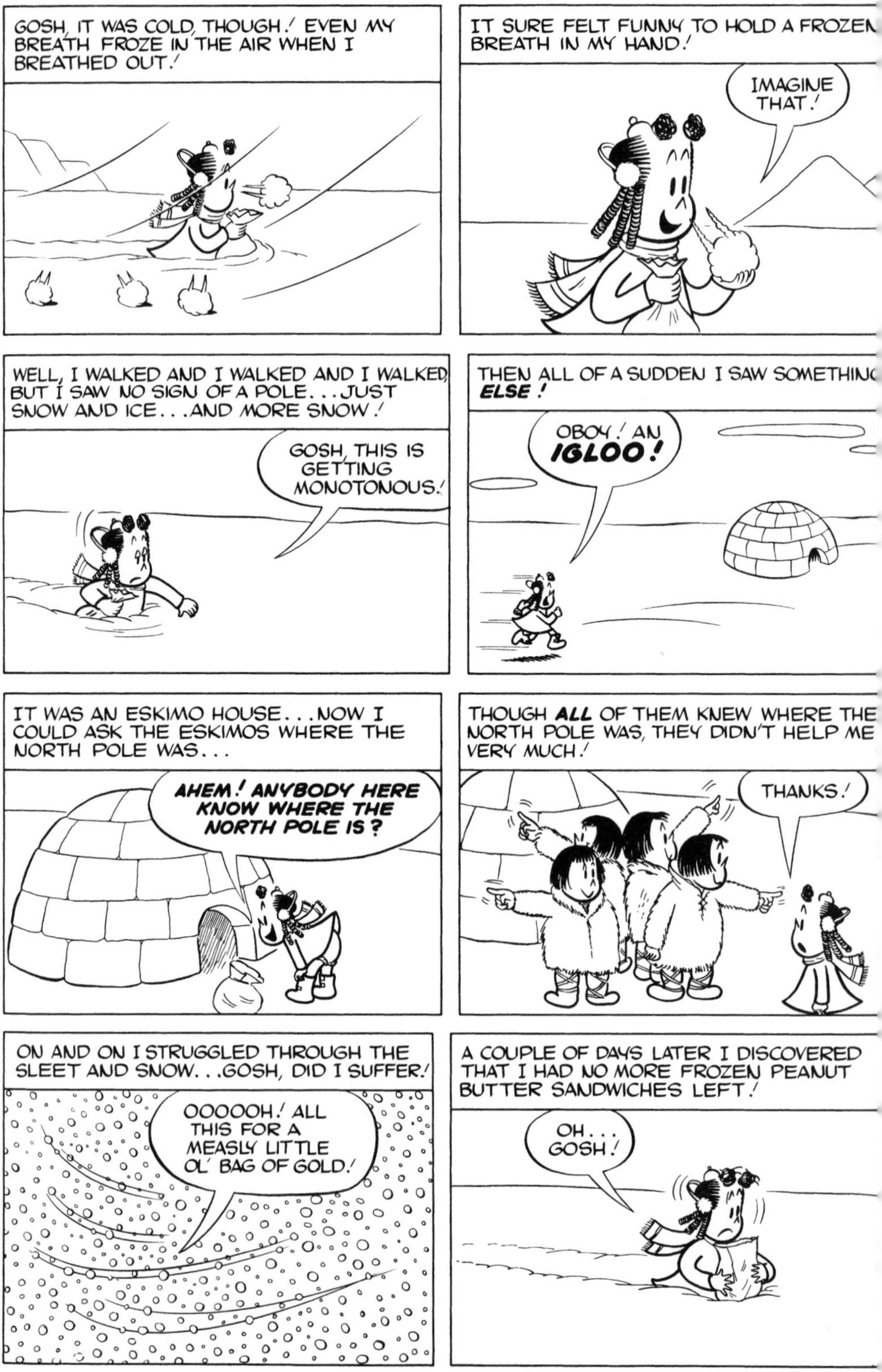
GOSH, IT WAS COLD, THOUGH.! EVEN MY BREATH FROZE IN THE AIR WHEN I BREATHED OUT.!
IT SURE FELT FUNNY TO HOLD A FROZEN BREATH IN MY HAND.!
IMAGINE THAT.!
WELL, I WALKED AND I WALKED AND I WALKED, BUT I SAW NO SIGN OF A POLE...JUST SNOW AND ICE...AND MORE SNOW.!
GOSH, THIS IS GETTING MONOTONOUS.!
THEN ALL OF A SUDDEN I SAW SOMETHING ELSE!
OBOY.! AN IGLOO!
IT WAS AN ESKIMO HOUSE...NOW I COULD ASK THE ESKIMOS WHERE THE NORTH POLE WAS...
AHEM.! ANYBODY HERE KNOW WHERE THE NORTH POLE IS?
THOUGH ALL OF THEM KNEW WHERE THE NORTH POLE WAS, THEY DIDN'T HELP ME VERY MUCH.!
THANKS.!
ON AND ON I STRUGGLED THROUGH THE SLEET AND SNOW...GOSH, DID I SUFFER.!
OOOOOH.! ALL THIS FOR A MEASLY LITTLE OL' BAG OF GOLD.!
A COUPLE OF DAYS LATER I DISCOVERED THAT I HAD NO MORE FROZEN PEANUT BUTTER SANDWICHES LEFT.!
OH... GOSH.!

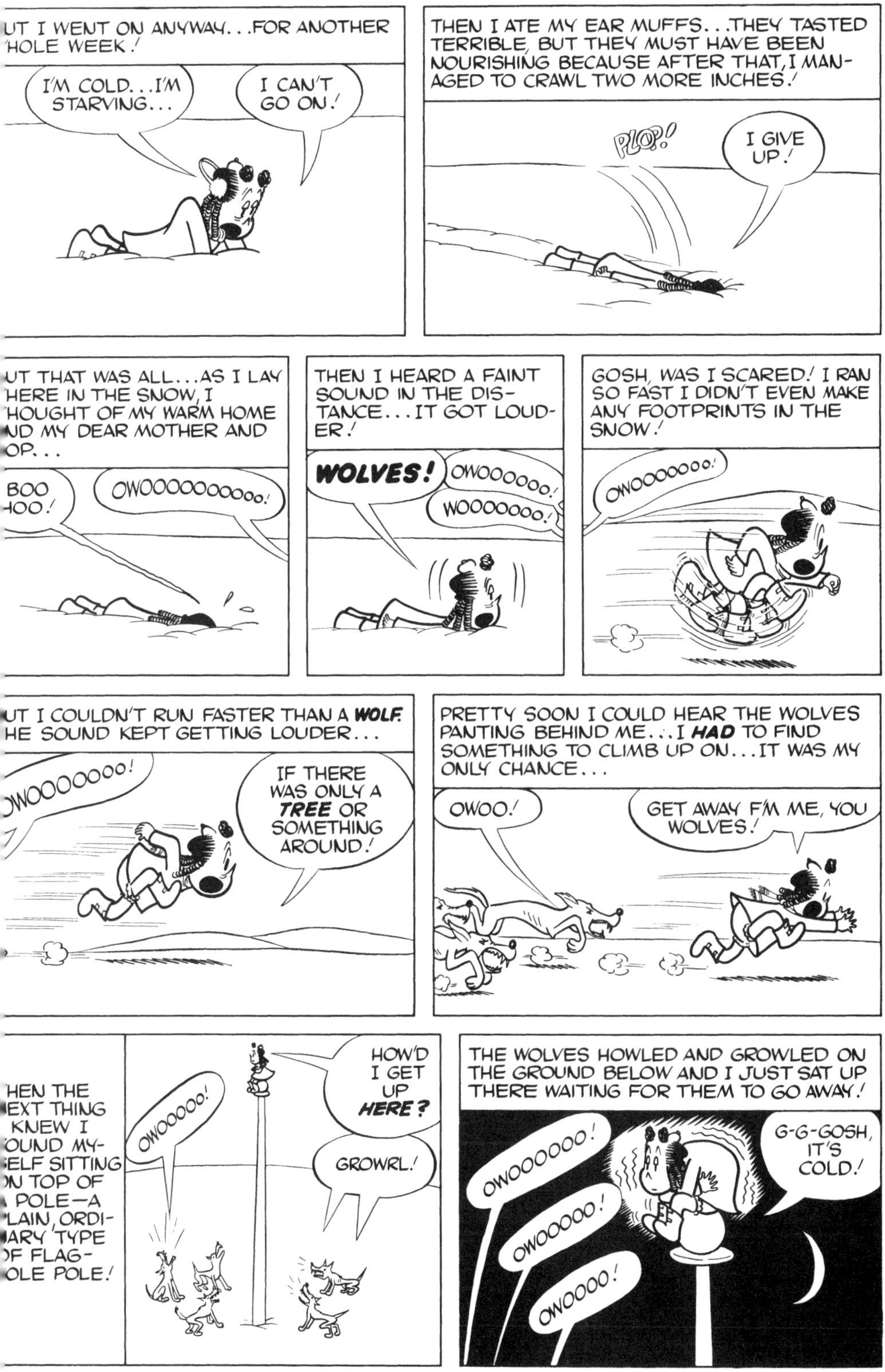
UT I WENT ON ANYWAY...FOR ANOTHER 'HOLE WEEK!
I'M COLD...I'M STARVING...
I CAN'T GO ON!
THEN I ATE MY EAR MUFFS...THEY TASTED TERRIBLE, BUT THEY MUST HAVE BEEN NOURISHING BECAUSE AFTER THAT, I MANAGED TO CRAWL TWO MORE INCHES!
PLOP!
I GIVE UP!
UT THAT WAS ALL...AS I LAY HERE IN THE SNOW, I 'HOUGHT OF MY WARM HOME ND MY DEAR MOTHER AND OP...
BOO HOO!
OWOOOOOOOOOOoo!
THEN I HEARD A FAINT SOUND IN THE DISTANCE...IT GOT LOUDER!
WOLVES!
OWOOOOOOO!
WOOOOOOO!
GOSH, WAS I SCARED! I RAN SO FAST I DIDN'T EVEN MAKE ANY FOOTPRINTS IN THE SNOW!
OWOOOOOOOO!
UT I COULDN'T RUN FASTER THAN A WOLF. HE SOUND KEPT GETTING LOUDER...
OWOOOOOOOO!
IF THERE WAS ONLY A TREE OR SOMETHING AROUND!
PRETTY SOON I COULD HEAR THE WOLVES PANTING BEHIND ME...I HAD TO FIND SOMETHING TO CLIMB UP ON...IT WAS MY ONLY CHANCE...
OWOO!
GET AWAY F'M ME, YOU WOLVES!
HEN THE EXT THING KNEW I OUND MYSELF SITTING N TOP OF POLE—A 'LAIN, ORDINARY TYPE OF FLAG-OLE POLE!
OWOOOOO!
HOW'D I GET UP HERE?
GROWRL!
THE WOLVES HOWLED AND GROWLED ON THE GROUND BELOW AND I JUST SAT UP THERE WAITING FOR THEM TO GO AWAY!
OWOOOOOOO!
G-G-GOSH, IT'S COLD!
OWOOOOOO!
OWOOOO!

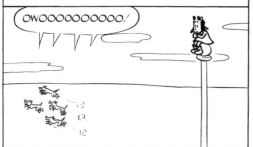

THEY STAYED THERE FOR TWO WHOLE DAYS, BUT FINALLY THEY JUST GAVE UP AND WENT AWAY!

OWOOOOOOOOOO!

BUT BY *THAT* TIME I WAS FROZEN SO STI I COULDN'T EVEN WINK!

GOSH

NOW I KNO HOW A POP SICLE FEEL

ONE DAY A WEEK OR SO LATER, WHEN I HAD JUST ABOUT DECIDED I WAS GOING TO STAY THERE FOREVER, I THOUGHT I HEARD THE SOUND OF VOICES IN THE DISTANCE!

I WISH I COULD TURN AROUND TO LOOK!

BABBLE, BABBLE, BABBLE, BABBLE, BABBLE, BABBLE!

SURE ENOUGH, IT WAS PEOPLE! ALL THOS PEOPLE WHO STARTED OUT A LONG TIM AGO ON THE NORTHBOUND TROLLEY!

YAY!

THE NORTH POLE!

YAY!

YAY!

THEN I LEARNED I WAS SITTING ON THE NORTH POLE!

CONGRATULATIONS!

YOU DISCOVERED THE NORTH POLE!

BUT I COULDN'T SAY ANYTHING...I COULDN'T MOVE...I WAS FROZEN AS STIFF AS A BOARD!

FOR SHE'S A JOLLY GOOD FELLER—

WELL, WHEN I GOT HOME THEY HAD A GREAT BIG PARADE FOR ME, CONFETTI AND EVERYTHING!

YAY!

WHEEE!

MY MOTHER, OF COURSE, WAS *VERY* GLAD TO SEE ME—EVEN IF I *WAS* FROZEN STIFF!

YOU'LL THAW OUT AFTER A WHILE, DEAR!

SUR SHE WILL

238

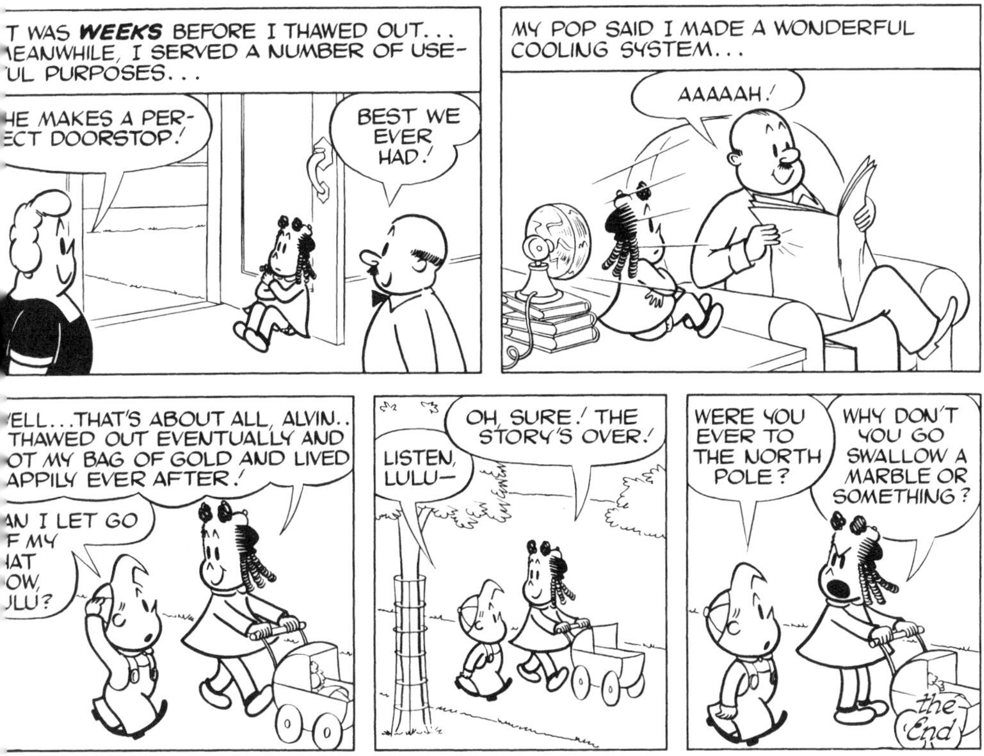
T WAS WEEKS BEFORE I THAWED OUT... IEANWHILE, I SERVED A NUMBER OF USE-'UL PURPOSES...
HE MAKES A PER-ECT DOORSTOP!
BEST WE EVER HAD!
MY POP SAID I MADE A WONDERFUL COOLING SYSTEM...
AAAAAH!
'ELL...THAT'S ABOUT ALL, ALVIN.. THAWED OUT EVENTUALLY AND OT MY BAG OF GOLD AND LIVED APPILY EVER AFTER!
AN I LET GO F MY IAT OW, LULU?
LISTEN, LULU—
OH, SURE! THE STORY'S OVER!
WERE YOU EVER TO THE NORTH POLE?
WHY DON'T YOU GO SWALLOW A MARBLE OR SOMETHING?
the End

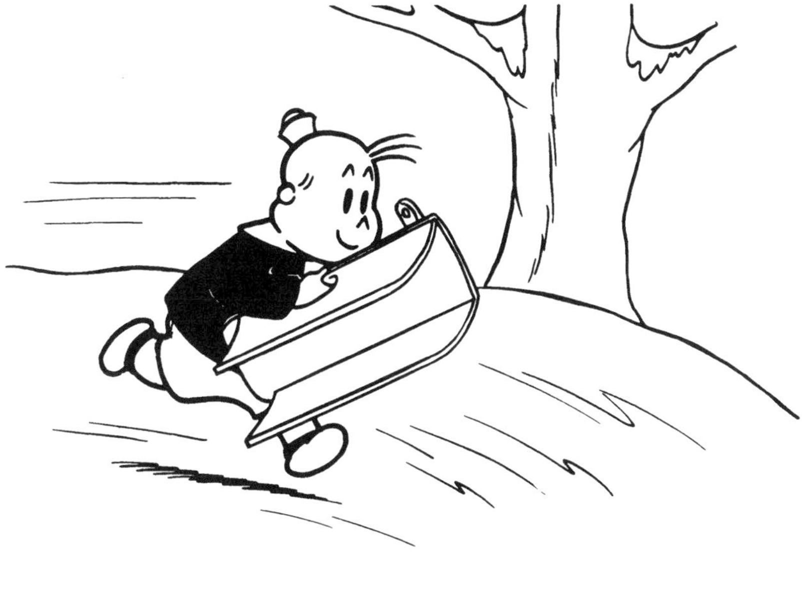

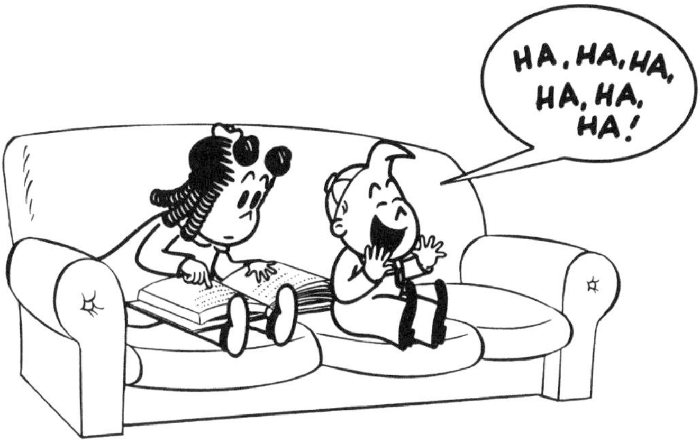
HA, HA, HA, HA, HA, HA!

Little Lulu ®

Lulu Goes Shopping
ISBN: 1-59307-270-8 / $9.95

Lulu Takes a Trip
ISBN: 1-59307-317-8 / $9.95

My Dinner with Lulu
ISBN: 1-59307-318-6 / $9.95

Sunday Afternoon
ISBN: 1-59307-345-3 / $9.95

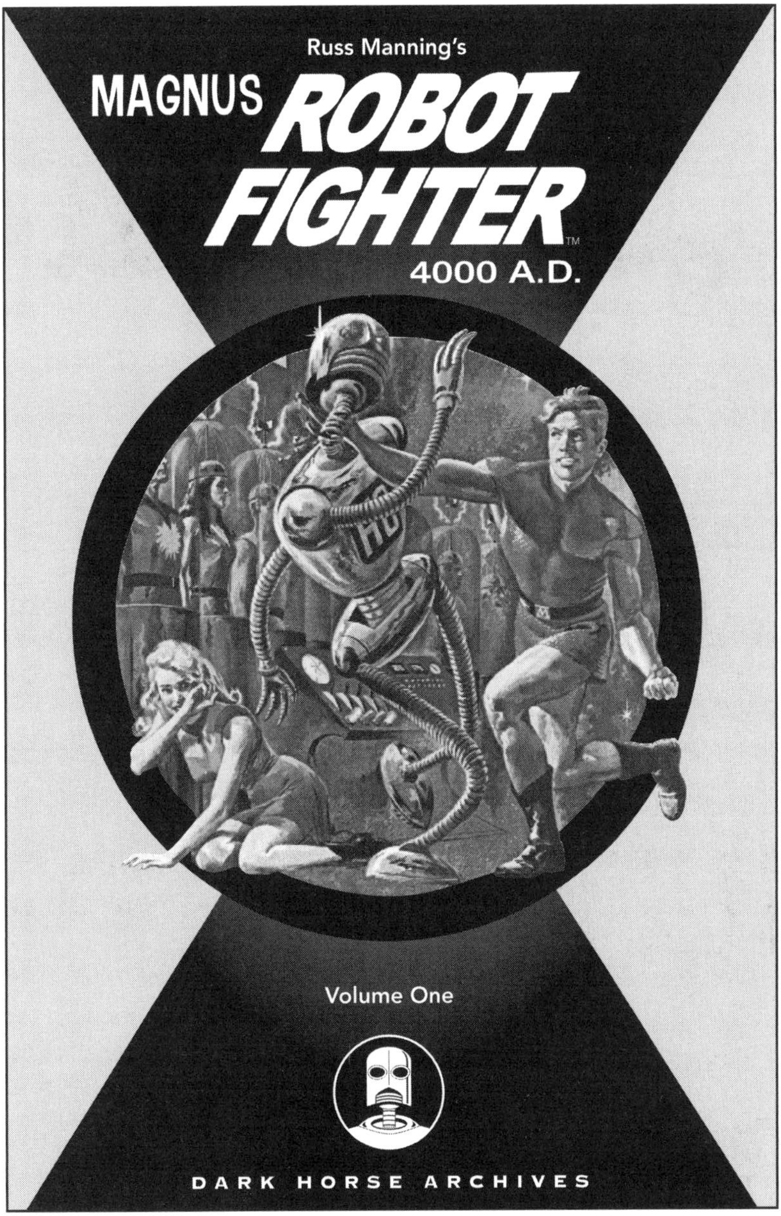
Russ Manning's
MAGNUS ROBOT FIGHTER TM
4000 A.D.
Volume One
DARK HORSE ARCHIVES

Sergio Aragonés GROO

The Groo Houndbook
ISBN: 1-56971-385-5 / $9.95

The Groo Inferno
ISBN: 1-56971-430-4 / $9.95

The Groo Jamboree
ISBN: 1-56971-462-2 / $9.95

The Groo Kingdom
ISBN: 1-56971-478-9 / $9.95

The Groo Library
ISBN: 1-56971-571-8 / $12.95

The Groo Maiden
ISBN: 1-56971-756-7 / $12.95

The Groo Nursery
ISBN: 156971-794-X / $11.95

The Groo Odyssey
ISBN: 1-56971-858-X / $12.95

The Most Intelligent Man in the World
ISBN: 1-56971-294-8 / $9.95

Groo and Rufferto
ISBN: 1-56971-447-9 / $9.95

Mightier than the Sword
ISBN: 1-56971-612-9 / $13.95

Death and Taxes
ISBN: 1-56971-797-4 / $12.95

BOOKS

The Adventures of Tony Millionaire's Sock Monkey
1-56971-490-8 $9.95

Tony Millionaire's Sock Monkey A Children's Book
1-56971-549-1 $9.95

The Collected Works of Tony Millionaire's Sock Monkey Volumes 3 and 4
1-59307-098-5 $12.95

Tony Millionaire's Sock Monkey The Glass Doorknob
1-56971-782-6 $14.95

Tony Millionaire's Sock Monkey Uncle Gabby
1-59307-026-8 $14.95

Tony Millionaire's Sock Monkey That Darn Yarn
1-59582-009-4 $7.95

MERCHANDISE

Tony Millionaire's Sock Monkey Journal
1-56971-856-3 $9.99

Tony Millionaire's Sock Monkey Stationery
1-56971-875-X $4.99

Sock Monkey Bendy Toy
1-56971-705-2 $9.99

Sock Monkey Plush
1-56971-708-7 $19.99

Sock Monkey Statue
statue stands 8" tall
item #10-279 $75.00

Sock Monkey Lunch Box (& Postcard)
1-56971-706-0 $14.99

Sock Monkey Zippo® Lighter
item #10-149 $29.99

Sock Monkey Magnet Set
1-56971-707-9 $9.99

Sock Monkey Shot Glass
item #10-134 $6.99

Mr. Crow Shot Glass
item #10-137 $6.99

Sock Monkey T-Shirt
youth tee, white

Small	item #11-191
Medium	item #11-196
Large	item #11-200
X-Large	item #11-203
S-XL	**$17.99**

Sock Monkey T-Shirt
adult tee, white

Medium	item #11-207
Large	item #11-212
X-Large	item #11-216
XX-Large	item #11-220
M-XL	**$17.99**
XXL	**$19.99**

Mr. Crow T-Shirt
youth tee, white

Small	item #11-224
Medium	item #11-228
Large	item #11-231
X-Large	Item #11-234
S-XL	**$17.99**

Mr. Crow T-Shirt
adult tee, white

Medium	item #11-236
Large	item #11-239
X-Large	item #11-242
XX-Large	Item #11-244
M-XL	**$17.99**
XXL	**$19.99**

Sock Monkey Stickers

Sticker #1	item #11-360
Sticker #2	item #11-363
Sticker #3	item #11-366
Sticker #4	item #11-368
all stickers are each	**$1.99**

Tony Millionaire's Maakies: Drinky Crow
comes with interchangeable eyes and a bottle of booze!
1-56971-809-1 $19.99

Uncle Gabby
comes with removable hat and brain!
1-59307-041-1 $24.99

Drinky Crow Coaster Set
item #12-240 $9.99

Tony Millionaire's Sock Monkey™ & © 2005 Tony Millionaire

ook For

What's Michael?

At Your Bookstore Today!

e One: Michael's Album TPB
1-56971-247-6
$5.95

e Two: Living Together TPB
1-56971-248-4
$5.95

e Three: Off the Deep End TPB
1-56971-249-2
$5.95

e Four: Michael's Mambo TPB
1-56971-250-6
$5.95

e Five: Michael's Favorite Spot TPB
1-56971-557-2
: $8.95

e Six: A Hard Day's Life TPB
: 1-56971-744-3
: $8.95

e Seven: Fat Cat in the City TPB
: 1-56971-914-4
: $8.95

e Eight: Show Time TPB
: 1-56971-972-1
: $8.95

e Nine: The Ideal Cat TPB
: 1-59307-120-5
: $8.95

What's Michael? Michael is a cat. A cat that is inexplicably attracted to the smell of raw fish, yet horribly repulsed by the smell of toothpaste. In short, Michael is a cat like any other cat. *What's Michael?* is an amusing look at the lives of cats, written and illustrated by manga master Makoto Kobayashi. In these books you'll find answers to some of the burning "cat" questions that you've been dying to have answered, such as: Do cats always land on their feet? Do cats make good detectives? Are cats better pets than dogs? And the often-asked but seldom-answered, why do cats dance? Of course, there are more than just cats in *What's Michael?* The stories show us how people interact (and often make idiots of themselves) in the presence of felines. These tales allow us to look in on the lives of cats and the people who love (and hate) them.

e at your local comics shop or bookstore
a comics shop in your area, call **1-888-266-4226**

re information or to order direct:
web: www.darkhorse.com
mailorder@darkhorse.com
1-800-862-0052 or (503) 652-9701 Mon.-Sat. 9 AM to 5 PM Pacific Time

PAUL CHADWICK'S Concrete

®

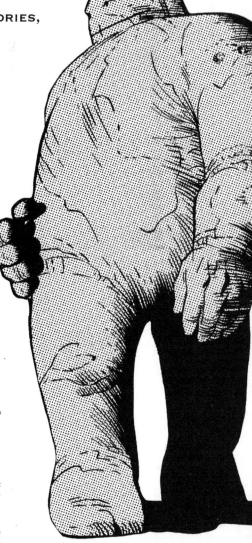

THE COMPLETE SHORT STORIES, 1986-1989
ISBN: 1-56971-114-3
$15.95

FRAGILE CREATURE
ISBN: 1-56971-022-8
$15.95

THE COMPLETE CONCRETE
ISBN: 1-56971-037-6
$24.95

KILLER SMILE
ISBN: 1-56971-080-5
$16.95

THINK LIKE A MOUNTAIN
ISBN: 1-56971-176-3
$17.95

STRANGE ARMOR
ISBN: 1-56971-335-9
$16.95

Available at your local comics shop or bookstore!

To find a comics shop in your area, call 1-888-266-4226.

For more information or to order direct visit darkhorse.com or call 1-800-862-0052 Mon.-Sat. 9 A.M. to 5 P.M. Pacific Time.

Prices and availability subject to change without notice.

DARK HORSE BOOKS